LAW AND ADMINISTRATION

LAW IN CONTEXT

Editors: Robert Stevens (Haverford College, Pennsylvania),
William Twining (University College, London) and
Christopher McCrudden (Lincoln College, Oxford)

Law and Administration

CAROL HARLOW
Lecturer in Law at the London School of Economics

RICHARD RAWLINGS
Lecturer in Law at the London School of Economics

WEIDENFELD AND NICOLSON
London

George Weidenfeld and Nicolson Ltd
91 Clapham High Street London SW4 7TA

ISBN 0 297 78239 8 cased
ISBN 0 297 78240 1 paperback

Typeset by Deltatype, Ellesmere Port
Printed by Butler & Tanner Limited,
Frome and London

M. Barthelemy, the Dean of the Faculty of Law in the University of Paris, relates that thirty years ago he was spending a week-end with the late Professor Dicey. In the course of conversation M. Barthelemy asked a question about administrative law in this country. 'In England', replied Dicey, 'we know nothing of administrative law; and we wish to know nothing.'

W. A. Robson, 'The Report of the Committee on Ministers' Powers', (1932) 3 *Political Quarterly*, p. 346

CONTENTS

CASES

Page numbers in **bold** type indicate extracts.

STATUTES

PREFACE

Administrative law raises fundamental questions about our constitutional and political arrangements to which the standard texts pay little attention. It is often argued that legal treatises should not devote space to such issues since law is mechanistic and the uses to which machinery is put are not the concern of the mechanic. In the case of student texts, the argument runs that students must learn the law before they can criticize it. We believe the reverse to be true. Questions about the proper ambit of judicial review, its legitimacy, or the relationship of law to political and economic theory, are not incidental matters to be swept to one side but crucial to the understanding of our subject. Administrative law theory is thus our natural starting point. We do not attempt in our first two chapters to propound our own theory of administrative law, but allow theorists to advance a variety of views in their own words. We have tried not to take sides in a debate which, as you will see, is often acrimonious. Our concern has been to show the width of opinion in the literature of English public law, too often devalued.

The themes of this book could be summarized in three currently fashionable terms: 'process', 'legitimacy' and 'competency'. The first theme finds a place particularly in the last six chapters, which contain microstudies of three important areas of administration: planning, immigration and social assistance. Here we ask how law actually operates in an administrative and political framework. We examine the uses to which it is put and identify those who participate in administrative decision-taking or play the administrative law game.

Although in the first section we draw on decision-taking theory to deal generally with the administrative process, we do not intend to convey a monolithic vision of a 'state' serviced by faceless Weberian bureaucrats. It is right to stress at the outset that administrative agencies differ in size, importance and function. Our book contains no description of governmental institutions such as you will find in David Foulkes's *Administrative Law* (5th edn, 1982). We have tried throughout to allow administrators and politicians to speak with their own voices – in evidence to select committees, speeches in Parliament, occasional lectures and so forth. Nor do we assume an inevitable antithesis between 'citizen' and 'state'. State workers are clients of the welfare services while citizens participate in decision-taking – a theme explored particularly in the context of planning. Like judges, ombudsmen reveal themselves as individuals, with their own opinions and style. Permanent secretaries and local authority executives are 'state officials' but they may hold very different views of their respective functions. Administrative agencies also possess their own distinctive ethos.

English administrative law has always been concerned with procedure and it is natural for the textbooks to follow the two major reviews, Donoughmore and Franks, in their concern with the topic. Ours is no exception, though our emphasis is somewhat different. Adjudication is an expensive form of decision-taking whose competency ought not lightly to be assumed. In Chapter 3 we explore the situations for which adjudication might be appropriate. In Chapter 5 we make a parallel study of rule-making procedure. A lawyer might protest that efficiency is immaterial; justice demands judicial procedures and ultimately access to the ordinary courts. English, as opposed to American, literature glides softly over a number of questionable assumptions about the place of judicial review in the constitution. Our view is that the allocation of functions is a central problem for administrative law, and in Chapter 11 we try to face the concept of justiciability squarely.

It is not our purpose, however, to provide intractable problems with simple answers, an attitude reflected in the questions inserted into the text. Some are merely to guide students through difficult case law. Others invite reflection on subjects of interest and importance.

Times change. What is good administration today may seem wasteful, inefficient or unjust tomorrow. Dramatic changes in the political climate in the last few years have brought to the fore different political theories and alterations in administrative practice. Already this is reflected in reports from ombudsmen and select committees, and attitudes to planning or participation. Some of the questions asked and answers propounded in the affluent 1970s seem unobtainable, outdated or even naive. Of course, the fashionable nostrums of the 1980s may prove equally transient. Administrative law is a tangled web of political, social, economic and legal strands. Some of the threads have proved durable. Whether they will continue to hold, time alone will tell.

January 1984

CAROL HARLOW
RICHARD RAWLINGS

ACKNOWLEDGEMENTS

We would like to thank all those who have helped us in writing this book. Without Alison Real, our research assistant, the work would never have been completed in time. Patricia Selley compiled much of the statistical information and drew up the tables and diagrams. Susan Hunt and Jane Heginbotham typed innumerable drafts. Our friends Charles Blake, John Griffith, Martin Loughlin, Victor Moore, Andrew Nicol, Martin Partington, made comments at various stages. We also received help and advice from Christopher McCrudden and William Twining, the academic editors. The indexes were compiled by Felicity Wright and Elizabeth Ingham.

The authors and publishers thank the following for their permission to reproduce copyright material: J. Alder (*Modern Law Review*, 'Time Limit Clauses and Conceptualism – A Reply'); R. Austin (Stevens, 'Judicial Review of Subjective Discretion – At the Rubicon; Whither Now?'); K. Banting (Macmillan, *Poverty, Politics and Policy: Britain in the 1960s*); Commission for Local Administration in England (annual and investigation reports); Controller of Her Majesty's Stationery Office (Hansard, Parliamentary papers and government publications); S. de Smith and J. Evans (Sweet and Maxwell, *Judicial Review of Administrative Action*); W. Friedmann (Stevens, *Law in a Changing Society*); J. Friend, M. Laffkin and M. Norris (Public Administration, 'Competition in Public Policy: The Structure Plan as Arena'); G. Ganz (Sweet and Maxwell, 'Allocation of Decision-Making Functions'); N. Gravells (*Modern Law Review*, 'Time Limit Clauses and Judicial Review – The Relevance of Context'); M. Hill (Martin Robertson, *The State, Administration and the Individual*); H. Hodge (Frances Pinter, 'Test Case Strategy' (in M. Partington and J. Jowell, *Welfare Law and Policy*)); M. Holdsworth (*Local Government Chronicle*, 'The Other Side of the Ombudsman'); the Incorporated Council for Law Reporting and Butterworth & Co. (extracts from cases); J. Jowell (Sweet and Maxwell, 'The Legal Control of Administrative Discretion'); *Justice*/All Souls (*Review of Administrative Law in the United Kingdom: A Discussion Paper*); R. Lister (Child Poverty Action Group, *Council Inaction*); P. McAuslan (Pergamon Press, *The*

Ideologies of Planning Law); P. Payne (Royal Town Planning Institute, 'Planning Appeals'); T. Prosser (Basil Blackwell, 'Poverty, Ideology and Legality: Supplementary Benefit Appeal Tribunals and their Predecessors'); C. Reich (Random House, *The Greening of America*); Royal Town Planning Institute ('The Public and Planning'); A. Shonfield (Oxford University Press, *Modern Capitalism*); R. Stewart (Harvard Law Review Association, 'The Reformation of American Administrative Law'); H. Street (Sweet and Maxwell, *Justice in the Welfare State*); M. Vile (Oxford University Press, *Constitutionalism and the Separation of Powers*); H. Wade (Oxford University Press, *Administrative Law*); R. Wraith and P. Hutchesson (George Allen and Unwin, *Administrative Tribunals*).

Note on References
The references in brackets in the text are to the authors and publication dates of books and articles listed in the Bibliography.

I
Red light theories

1 Politics, government and the state

Behind every theory of administrative law there lies a theory of the state. Laski once said that constitutional law was unintelligible except as the expression of an economic system of which it was designed to serve as a rampart.[1] By this he meant that the machinery of government is necessarily an expression of the society in which it operates and that it is impossible to understand the one except in the context of the other. Both constitutional and administrative law are concerned with the machine of government.[2] Laski's aphorism is applicable to the one just as it is to the other.

To an American or continental reader, this statement would seem unexceptional. English lawyers, on the other hand, might find it unpalatable. Modern textbooks of administrative law do not stress the relationship between law and political science; indeed, it is fair to say that they do their utmost to separate law from its political context. Earlier writers, however, were alive to the relationship between constitutional law and political theory and were themselves well grounded in the latter.[3] In 1941, Sir Cecil Carr gave a series of lectures at Harvard University on the subject of administrative law, in the course of which he said:

We nod approvingly today when someone tells us that, whereas the State used to be merely policeman, judge and protector, it has now become schoolmaster, doctor, housebuilder, road-maker, town-planner, public utility supplier and all the rest of it. The contrast is no recent discovery. De Tocqueville observed in 1866 that the State 'everywhere interferes more than it did; it regulates more undertakings, and undertakings of a lesser kind; and it gains a firmer footing every day, about, around and above all private persons, to assist, to advise, and to coerce them' (*Oeuvres*, III, 501). Nassau William Senior, a Benthamite ten years older than Chadwick, a colleague of his on the original Poor Law Commission, had justified this tendency. A government, he thinks, must do whatever conduces to the welfare of the governed (the utilitarian theory); it will make mistakes, but non-interference may be an error too; one can be passively wrong as well as actively wrong. One might go back much earlier still to Aristotle, who said that the city-state or partnership-community comes into existence to protect life and remains in existence to protect a proper way of living. What is the proper standard? That is an age-long issue which is still a burning question of political controversy. The problems of administrative law are approached in the light of that fire. Those who dislike the statutory delegation of legislative power or the statutory creation of a non-judicial tribunal will often be those who dislike the policy behind the statute and seek to fight it at every stage. On the one side are those who want to step on the accelerator, on the other those who want to apply the brake. [Carr 1941, pp. 10–11.]

Here Carr accepts that administrative law is customarily judged by subjective rather than objective standards, everything being dependent on the political viewpoint of the observer. We would do well to bear this in mind when reading arguments about whether the English possess 'a developed system' of administrative law or, indeed, any administrative law at all.[4] What exactly *is* a developed system? Is it an elegant intellectual structure, like that of France, where the spirit of Descartes reigns supreme? Is it like that of America, in which we are told that the administration has been brought to heel?[5] Each observer has his preference which is, more often than not, a political preference. In Chapters 1 and 2 it will be seen that writers advocate very different objectives for administrative law. These we have loosely grouped under two headings: 'green light' and 'red light' theories.

By including in *A Grammar of Politics* a chapter about the judicial process, Laski (1925, Ch. 10) was affirming his belief that the legal system forms part of the wider political scene; Carr made the same point in a different fashion. However, in modern times, the dominant view has been that law is *not* a branch of political science, a view unthinkingly accepted by lawyers and political scientists alike:[6]

Judicial theory has not constituted a major part of the body of political ideas in Britain. The law has been considered to be a world neutrally detached from the contests of political ideas and argument. Particular laws and particular legal judgments may have had recognized political consequences which have been applauded or resisted, but the general character of the judicial system and the general assumptions of law have been little considered in debates about the political character and goals of the nation. Dicey had of course given an account of the basis of rights and of the rule of law which was allied to his preferences for limited and general government, and the discussions of administrative law and of delegated legislation continued to be carried on with reference to such preferences. The phrase 'the rule of law' was later in the present century employed by Hayek to express and legitimize his own political ideas and beliefs. But in general, legal ideas were invisible in the elaboration of political argument. [Barker 1978, p. 95.]

This vision of the world of law as apolitical, neutral and independent of the world of government, politics and administration, has its roots deep in legal theory. It is enough here to stress the link between legal theory and the development of constitutional and administrative law and to summarise the position by saying that two legal traditions have been particularly influential. In the early stages of the development of Anglo-American constitutional law, natural law was very important.[7] Let us take two illustrations at random. Fundamental to modern administrative law is the idea of 'legality', i.e. that the administration must act 'legally' and observe the law. This idea can be traced back to Aristotle's government of 'laws not men' and is developed in modern philosophy as the ideal of the rule of law. An important feature of Anglo-American constitutional law is the right assumed by the judiciary to 'review' the acts of government and to declare them lawful (in legal terminology, intra vires) or unlawful and in excess of power (ultra vires). Natural law doctrines provide the basis for this common law power which, even in the written constitution of the United States, does not find statutory expression.

Administrative law started to emerge as an independent subject of study during the nineteenth century as a natural consequence of the growth of the modern state. At the same time, the views of thinkers like Jeremy Bentham (1748–1832) and John Austin (1790–1859) were becoming influential throughout the English-speaking world. These men were 'rationalists', concerned to expel mysticism from the philosophy of law. They believed that law was capable of reduction to rational, scientific principles. Later, this method was introduced to the field of public law by Dicey, who was:

the first to apply the juridical method to English public law. Blackstone's incursions into this field were jejeune. Austin was essentially a civilian. Pollock and Salmond have made a science out of English private law. Maitland's scattered contributions were of the greatest possible value, but his main work was done in the historical field. [Dicey's] style, too, though somewhat verbose and repetitive, was eminently readable. His influence upon the development of public law in England has been immense. His authority to-day is greater than that of any other public lawyer; it is probably true to say that in no country have the views of a public lawyer of a past generation the same weight as Dicey's possess in England. [Jennings 1935, p. 133.]

In the field of legal history, simplification is particularly dangerous. In the first place, legal thought frequently wanders across the boundaries we try to establish. Bentham, for example, to whom modern Anglo-American legal theory owes a particular debt, called himself a rationalist. Yet Lloyd (1972, p. 76) observes 'in some ways, his principle of utility was a canon of value not susceptible of proof but only justifiable if at all by a metaphysical argument, and therefore idealist in character'. Secondly, modern jurisprudence is much concerned with linguistic analysis. Disputes over definition and classification assume great importance. How, for example, is 'positivism' to be defined or 'formalism' pinned down? Is Dworkin a positivist or not? Who were the realists and was Holmes, as some insist, only a precursor?[8] For our purposes, it is enough to differentiate two legal traditions. We shall describe legal positivism loosely as those theories which focus on law as a system of rules and downplay the link between law and morality. Realists, on the other hand, are primarily interested in law in action or law as it functions in society. We would then summarize the prevailing tradition of English administrative law as positivist, a point made by several American observers (below, Chapter 11).[9] The prevailing tradition of American administrative law is much less clearly positivist (below, Chapter 2).[10] This must be borne in mind when reading American authors. Equally, American writing must be situated in the framework of a written and federal constitution whose machinery of government is by no means identical to that of England.

Not everyone would agree that the positivist tradition of 'law-without-politics' is well suited to public law. Predictably, Laski did not. He attributed the inability of public law to deal with the problems posed by modern society to a lack of originality in English legal theory. Griffith has suggested that legal training induces an inflexible cast of mind which cuts lawyers off from other social scientists:

A lawyer is *bound* by certain types and habits of belief . . . A man who has had a legal training . . . is never able to look at institutions or administrative practices or even social or political policies, free from his legal habits of belief. It is not easy for a lawyer to become a political scientist. It is very difficult for him to become a sociologist or a historian . . . he will fight to the death to defend legal rights against persuasive arguments based on expediency or the public interest or the social good . . . he believes, as part of his mental habits, that they are dangerous and too easily used as cloaks for arbitrary action. [Griffith 1959a, pp. 117–19.]

Shklar draws on this passage to describe the consequences of 'lawyerly' habits of mind for the legal system:

The urge to draw a clear line between law and non-law has led to the constructing of ever more refined and rigid systems of formal definitions. This procedure has served to isolate law completely from the social context within which it exists. Law is endowed with its own discrete, integral history, its own 'science', and its own values, which are all treated as a single block sealed off from general social history, from politics, and from morality. The habits of mind appropriate, within narrow limits, to the procedures of law courts in the most stable legal systems have been expanded to provide legal theory and ideology with an entire system of thought and values. This procedure has served its own ends very well: it aims at preserving law from irrelevant considerations, but it has ended by fencing legal thinking off from all contact with the rest of historical thought and experience. [Shklar 1964, pp. 2–3.]

Throughout administrative law examples may be found of the approach described by Shklar. To anticipate subsequent discussion, de Smith's classic work, *Judicial Review of Administrative Action*, first published in 1959, is devoted to a study of case law, divorced from its administrative context. Yet de Smith himself (1959, p. 3) describes judicial review as 'sporadic and peripheral'. Is this what administrative law should be about? Shklar sees as typical the construction of 'refined and rigid systems of formal definitions'. Consider the case law concerning ouster of judicial review in Chapter 4. Has conceptual analysis been allowed to run riot? The rules of natural justice certainly define justice and fairness in terms of 'procedures appropriate to law courts'. Are lawyers guilty of imposing their own procedural model indiscriminately? And, finally, did administrative lawyers of the 1970s believe that they could define all relationships between the governors and the governed in terms of rules (below, Chapter 5)?

The positivist ideal is often called the model of 'autonomous law'. It relates closely to the constitutional principle which we know as the rule of law:

A cardinal feature of the rule-of-law model, and a bulwark of institutional autonomy, is the disjunction of political will and legal judgment. Law is elevated 'above' politics; that is, the positive law is held to embody standards that public consent, authenticated by tradition or by constitutional process, has removed from political controversy. The authority to interpret this legal heritage must therefore be kept insulated from the struggle for power and uncontaminated by political influence. In interpreting and applying the law, jurists are to be objective spokesmen for historically established principles, passive dispensers of a received, impersonal justice. They have a claim to the last word because their judgments are thought to obey an external will and not their own. [Nonet and Selznick 1978, p. 57.]

While some lawyers urge the apolitical and objective nature of law, most sociologists and political scientists disagree. Legal systems necessarily incorporate the ethical and political values of the society which surrounds them. Failure to face up to this fact allows lawyers unthinkingly to perpetuate traditional values. The exclusion of politics and sociology from legal training means that lawyers are less likely to be sensitive to changes in society. Marxists, but not only Marxists, believe that the idea of apolitical law is itself political. It developed in conjunction with the nineteenth-century laissez-faire, or market, economy in which economic activity was not regulated but left to individual enterprise.[11] Administrative law, we have said, deals with the activities of government. It follows that ideas concerning the legitimacy of state or government activity must affect administrative law.

2 A growing state

In 1981, an unofficial Committee under the auspices of *Justice* and All Souls College, Oxford, considered the current state of English administrative law. This is their description of the state in which we find ourselves:

In 1900 government interfered hardly at all in the way people ran their daily lives; and it provided virtually no personal social services. Today quite the reverse is true. The state has assumed an ever increasing range of responsibilities. Through nationalisation it controls most of the basic industries and the goods and services they supply. It runs a comprehensive system of social services providing benefits from just before the cradle (by way of pre-natal services and a maternity grant) to the grave (with a death grant) and in between it provides education, a health service, sickness benefits, unemployment benefits and old age pensions.

The state also seeks to control much of the environment in which we live . . .

This enormous growth in the nature and ambit of state power can be illustrated in a number of ways. First, there has been a vast increase in public expenditure. In 1870 it was £100 million, 9% of the gross national product and £3 per head of the population. A hundred years later it was £20,000 million, 43% of the gross national product and £400 per head of the population. Today it is over £52,000 million, 42% of the gross domestic product and about £1,000 per head of the population.

Secondly, there has also been a massive increase in the number of those employed to administer our affairs. In 1900 there were 50,000 civil servants employed by central government; in 1980 there were 548,600 non-industrial civil servants. If to that is added about 600,000 officials in local government and about 100,000 who administer the health service, there are some 1.25 million officials without including administrators in such bodies as the water and sewerage authorities and the nationalised industries.

Thirdly, there has been a spate of increasingly complex Acts of Parliament and regulations flowing from the government machine. Thus in 1900 Acts of Parliament covered 198 pages of the Statute Book; in 1935, 1,515 pages, in 1975 2,800 pages. As for regulations, there were comparatively few before the First World War; in 1947 statutory instruments covered 2,678 pages; in 1975, 8,442 pages. All this legislation is subject to the process of amendment; and some outlives its useful life. Nobody knows how many statutes and regulations/statutory instruments have a real impact today. [*Justice*/All Souls Review 1981, paras. 18–22.]

In this context they saw their main concern as being to ascertain whether the rights and liberties of the individual are adequately protected today against the vast increase that has taken place this century in the power of the state and in the range of its activities.

Where did the Committee get the idea that, before 1900, the state hardly interfered with the way people ran their lives? The state has always proscribed certain behaviour as criminal, described other behaviour as immoral and often prescribed people's religious or political beliefs. If you read the passage carefully, however, you can see that the Committee's concern is with the state as an entrepreneur controlling industry, and as a provider of services and benefits. This is what we call the 'interventionist' or 'collectivist' state. Contrary to the Committee's belief, the bones of the interventionist state existed well before the end of the nineteenth century. Dicey and Maitland both realized this[12] and modern historians confirm it:[13]

Britain, in the nineteenth century, saw a remarkable series of extensions of State intervention in society. Not only were many Acts of Parliament passed which were intended to have a major impact upon the behaviour of individual citizens, but means were devised to enforce these Acts much more effectively than had ever been the case before. The basis of the modern civil service was laid, local government was reformed and a variety of effective ad hoc bodies were created.

Many of the key reforms of this period involved compromises with the older system of decentralized government. To enforce new laws without radically altering the administrative machinery, agencies were set up to inspect and supervise the activities of local organizations. The Poor Law Act of 1834, for example, set up a Poor Law Commission to supervise the activities of the local Guardians of the Poor and to organise them into Unions of parishes. Then, gradually through the century, the extent of central intervention increased. The Commission was transformed into the Poor Law Board and then, in 1871, into the Local Government Board, with a Cabinet Minister as Chairman. The relationship between citizen and administration, as far as the recipients of poor relief were concerned, remained a local one. But even at this level it was increasingly the case that the administrators were full-time officials, while the lay Guardians faded into the background. The lash of State control was felt by the more prosperous, who were forced to contribute to increasing levels of 'poor rates' as the Guardians were forced by the Government to raise standards.

A similarly indirect pattern of relationships between the State and citizens developed in the public health field. Here the initial legislation was largely permissive. Then, as this was seen to be ineffective, local agencies were required to take prescribed steps to curb dangers to public health . . . In this area too, a corps of professionals began to be built up, operating at both local and national level to deal with, and draw attention to, public health problems: the medical officers.

Public health legislation was one of the most significant nineteenth-century contributions to the extension of the coercive power of the State; its key characteristic was the prevention of actions that might harm others. Factory legislation had similar characteristics. To be effective, such legislation had to bring in its wake a most significant extension of State bureaucracy. A new kind of policing role had to be played by officials appointed to ensure that legislation of this kind was carried out. An important Victorian addition to the apparatus of the State was, therefore, the government inspector. Capitalists were to be free to pursue profits. They were to be involved in decentralized government through the local authorities and the various ad hoc bodies, but were to operate in both these spheres within a framework of rules and restrictions laid down by central government and enforced by a cadre of inspectors. [Hill 1976, pp. 23–4.]

Some writers have suggested that the apparatus of the state insinuated itself, a 'trojan horse' into our unsuspecting society:

The first stage was the discovery of some 'intolerable' evil, such as the exploitation of child labour. Legislation was passed to prevent this. In the second stage, however, it was discovered that the legislation was ineffective. New legislation was passed with stronger provisions and inspectors were employed to ensure enforcement. Third, many of the new groups of professionals recruited to enforce legislation themselves became lobbyists for increases in the powers of their agencies. Fourth, this growing corps of professional experts made legislators aware 'that the problems could not be swept away by some magnificent all embracing gesture but would require continuous slow regulation and re-regulation' [Fraser 1973, p. 106]. Finally, therefore, a quite elaborate framework of law was developed with a complex bureaucratic machine to enforce it. The professionals helped to transform the administrative system into a major organization with extensive powers, almost without Parliament realizing it. [Hill 1976, p. 27.]

The trojan-horse theory could be used to explain the unsystematic development of English administrative law. For example, Robson's description of the development of administrative tribunals (see below, p. 21) exactly parallels Hill's explanation. An identical argument could be made about the practice of delegating rule-making powers to government departments, i.e. that Parliament simply did not notice what was happening. Ask yourselves as you read on, whether lawyers like Hewart subscribe to the theory.

Hill himself is not entirely convinced that these modern developments were fortuitous. He discusses two further ideas. First, the same phenomenon can be explained as a deliberate process of 'social engineering', that is, state intervention may be used consciously to remodel society. For example, society does not stop short at prohibiting child labour but goes on to make positive provision for education, welfare, health and nutrition of children. Ultimately, if parents do not carry out their responsibilities, children may be removed into the care of the state. This might be described as a socialistic and idealistic view of society; for example, the idea formed the basis of Beveridge's key report on the social services after the Second World War with its attack on the five giant evils of Want, Disease, Ignorance, Squalor and Idleness.

But many writers are cynical about the process of social engineering and would prefer to substitute the term 'social control', which appropriately conveys their sense of paternalism or authoritarianism. The term has no fixed definition. One argument runs that the aim of those who govern is to preserve their own position, using welfare benefits like carrots to 'buy off' the working classes and undermine the solidarity of the socialist movement by making conditions just sufficiently tolerable to avoid outbreaks of public disorder. But cynicism is not confined to one end of the political spectrum and the term may equally imply socialist infringement of the classic liberal principle of freedom of choice.[14]

The growth of modern government entailed a radical change of outlook. Until the Industrial Revolution, the functions of the state had been assumed to be limited and largely negative in character. Its role was to act as a 'policeman', providing the framework in which citizens could go about their business. According to Locke, the state's functions are limited to the preservation of the rights of its members against infringement by others. Each individual has a right to security of his person and property and to liberty of action in so far as he does not use this liberty to infringe the rights of others. The task of the state is to repress any violation of these rights by the use of force, to deter any man from injuring another in respect of his person, property or freedom and, where it is not successful in deterring, to punish. It is this and nothing more; a state exceeds its legitimate function if it endeavours to go beyond these limits. And this idea has never been abandoned. It finds support in a body of modern writing, notably Hayek, *The Road to Serfdom* (1947) and *Law Legislation and Liberty* (1969) or Nozick, *Anarchy, State and Utopia* (1974).[15]

Barker argues that, by the end of the nineteenth century, all the major political parties had, for practical purposes, abandoned the ideal of limited, and accepted the necessity of interventionist, government:

Whereas the old conception of government had been static the new was, if not dynamic, then at least ambulatory. The old conception had viewed government as administering laws, keeping the peace and defending the frontiers. But it was not a part of government's function to act upon society, nor was it expected that legislation would do much more than sustain clear and established customs. In contrast the new conception was of government as the instigator of movement. This conception of movement was not restricted to the parties of progress or reform; the Conservative and Unionist Party at the beginning of the twentieth century was increasingly character-ized, despite opposition, by a commitment to tariff reform, a programme of discriminatory trade duties designed to . . . provide funds for new military and social expenditure at home. Government was not merely to regulate society, it was to improve it. [Barker 1978, p. 11.]

Modern societies, in other words, do not conform to Locke's model, but are more like those portrayed by Hill. In Friedmann's description we begin to see the machinery of what today is known as 'corpor-atism':

The growth of the administrative process has been a universal phenomenon of contemporary society, although both speed and manner of its development have varied greatly from country to country. A minimum of administration is, of course, inherent in the very notion of government. The most ardent advocates of *laissez faire* policy concede to government the minimum functions of defence, administration of justice and police. But, regardless of political philosophy, the needs of an increasingly complex society have forced upon one country after another a multiplicity of additional functions: to the protection of elementary standards of health and safety, both for the public in general and employees – which accounted for the first major growth of public services in nineteenth-century England – were rapidly added a vast number of additional social services, from elementary measures of public assistance to the highly diversified social-security systems of the mid-twentieth century;

the supervision of public utilities, labour relations, and many other economic and social processes intimately affecting the public interest . . .

The mixed economies which today characterize the political and economic systems of many States . . . have a combination of managerial and regulatory administrative functions. Certain industries and public utilities are operated by the State itself – either through government departments or with increasing frequency through semi-autonomous public corporations, responsible to government but equipped with more or less far-reaching managerial autonomy.

At the same time, the bulk of industry and business, which remains in private ownership, is subject to varying degrees of public supervision and regulation, while another set of public authorities administers the various social services. [Friedmann 1964, pp. 273–4.]

To meet these increased obligations, the state needs more administrators. Bureaucracy develops, with its own ideology. Weber (1864–1920) describes the goals of modern bureaucracy.[16] (Weber is careful to associate bureaucracy with industry as well as with public administration. Later writers are not so scrupulous in this regard.)

Bureaucratization offers above all the optimum possibility for carrying through the principle of specializing administrative functions according to purely objective considerations. Individual performances are allocated to functionaries who have specialized training and who by constant practice learn more and more. The 'objective' discharge of business primarily means a discharge of business according to *calculable rules* and 'without regard for persons' . . .

The second element mentioned, 'calculable rules', also is of paramount importance for modern bureaucracy. The peculiarity of modern culture, and specifically of its technical and economic basis, demands this very 'calculability' of results . . . [The] specific nature [of bureaucracy], which is welcomed by capitalism, develops the more perfectly the more the bureaucracy is 'dehumanized', the more completely it succeeds in eliminating from official business love, hatred, and all purely personal, irrational, and emotional elements which escape calculation. This is the specific nature of bureaucracy and it is appraised as its special virtue. [Weber 1948, p. 215.]

There are common elements here and in Shklar's description of lawyerly habits of thought. The conduct of this bureaucracy, based closely on rules to which the actors are careful to conform, might be described as 'legalistic'.

3 The Diceyan inheritance

We could briefly summarize the argument at this stage by saying that while there has been a continuous and sustained growth in state activity, many writers have largely ignored, or lost sight of, the inevitable link between administrative law and political theory. The two phenomena can be linked together, because behind the tradition that law is apolitical one may discern a certain hostility to the idea of state intervention or interference, except in the traditional fields of defence, security, criminal law and public order. We have called this notion that administrative law should aim at *curbing* or *controlling* the state 'red light theory'.

Administrative law deals with one aspect of the problem of power. During the last hundred years the conception of the proper sphere of governmental activity has been completely transformed. Instead of confining itself to defence, public order, the criminal law, and a few other general matters, the modern state also provides elaborate social services and undertakes the regulation of much of the daily business of mankind. The state has seized the initiative, and has put upon itself all kinds of new duties. Hand in hand with these new duties must go new powers. In order to carry out so many schemes of social service and control, powerful engines of authority have to be set in motion. To prevent them running amok there must be constant control, both political and legal. Ultimately the political control rests with Parliament, though in reality much power is in the hands of ministers and officials. The legal control is the task of the courts of law. This legal control . . . provides the principal subject-matter of administrative law.

Any attempt to define the subject scientifically leads to a number of arguable questions. The easiest, though perhaps the least satisfactory, of the possible definitions is to be found by appropriating one of the three sectors of the traditional separation of powers. If the powers and authorities of the state are classified as legislative, administrative, and judicial, then administrative law might be said to be the law which concerns administrative authorities as opposed to the others. But then our territory would include the whole of constitutional law, except the parts of it which concern the legislature and the judiciary . . .

A more useful approximation is to say that administrative law is concerned with the operation and control of the powers of administrative authorities, with emphasis on function rather than on structure. This leads directly to the root of the matter: the question is, what has the law to do with the way in which administrative powers are exercised? But it is better to mark out the field by reference to administrative authorities than by reference to administrative powers as such. For the authorities can easily be recognised: the Crown, ministers, local authorities, police, and so forth. It is harder to define administrative powers, since there is the above-mentioned overlap with legislative powers. When the Minister of Transport makes regulations controlling traffic, there is no doubt that he is an administrative authority, but the nature of his power is legislative as well as administrative . . .

Since it deals with the exercise of governmental power, administrative law is itself part of constitutional law. Nor is there any other department of constitutional law which displays such an active conflict of forces. We are here on the most lively sector of the front in the constant warfare between government and governed. Whole new empires of executive power have been created. For the citizen it is vital that all power should be used in a way conformable to his ideas of liberty, fair dealing, and good administration. This is a matter of great consequence and of some difficulty, for social needs and ancient liberties are frequently hard to reconcile. It is in order to concentrate on this great question, the *manner* of the exercise of power, that our definition of administrative law is somewhat narrow. In many other countries the corresponding subject is treated more widely. But definitions exist for convenience, and there can be no doubt where the need lies. Until certain fundamentals are more generally understood than they are at present, attention must be focused on the core of the subject. [Wade 1st edn 1961, pp. 1–3.]

Some of the themes of this passage are already familiar. The suspicion of the growing power of the administration, emphasis on 'control' and 'ancient liberties' which are being eroded and the fear that government will 'run amok'. Behind the narrow definition which Wade has chosen, lies a long tradition which we can study in the writings of its greatest exponent, Dicey (1835–1922).

(a) 'The English have no administrative law'

In many continental countries, and notably in France, there exists a scheme of administrative law – known to Frenchmen as *droit administratif* – which rests on ideas foreign to the fundamental assumptions of our English common law, and especially to what we have termed the rule of law. This opposition is specially apparent in the protection given in foreign countries to servants of the State, or, as we say in England, of the Crown, who, whilst acting in pursuance of official orders, or in the *bona fide* attempt to discharge official duties, are guilty of acts which in themselves are wrongful or unlawful . . . [This] forms only one portion of the whole system of *droit administratif*, but it is the part of French law to which I wish to direct particularly the attention of students. I must, however, impress upon them that the whole body of *droit administratif* is well worth their study. It has been imitated in most of the countries of continental Europe. It illustrates by way of contrast, the full meaning of that absolute supremacy of the ordinary law of the land – a foreign critic might say of that intense legalism – which we have found to be a salient feature of English institutions . . .

For the term *droit administratif* English legal phraseology supplies no proper equivalent. The words 'administrative law', which are its most natural rendering, are unknown to English judges and counsel, and are in themselves hardly intelligible without further explanation.

This absence from our language of any satisfactory equivalent for the expression *droit administratif* is significant; the want of a name arises at bottom from our non-recognition of the thing itself. In England, and in countries which, like the United States, derive their civilisation from English sources, the system of administrative law and the very principles on which it rests are in truth unknown . . .

Anyone who considers with care the nature of the *droit administratif* of France, or the topics to which it applies, will soon discover that it rests, and always has rested, at bottom on two leading ideas alien to the conceptions of modern Englishmen.

The first of these ideas is that the government, and every servant of the government, possesses as representative of the nation, a whole body of special rights, privileges, or prerogatives as against private citizens, and that the extent of these rights, privileges, or prerogatives is to be determined on principles different from the considerations which fix the legal rights and duties of one citizen towards another. An individual in his dealings with the State does not, according to French ideas, stand on anything like the same footing as that on which he stands in dealings with his neighbour.

The second of these general ideas is the necessity of maintaining the so-called 'separation of powers' (*séparation des pouvoirs*), or, in other words, of preventing the government, the legislature, and the courts from encroaching upon one another's province. The expression, however, separation of powers, as applied by Frenchmen to the relations of the executive and the courts, with which alone we are here concerned, may easily mislead. It means, in the mouth of a French statesman or lawyer, something different from what we mean in England by the 'independence of the judges', or the like expressions. As interpreted by French history, by French legislation, and by the decisions of French tribunals, it means neither more nor less than the maintenance of the principle that while the ordinary judges ought to be irremovable and thus independent of the executive, the government and its officials ought (whilst acting officially) to be independent of and to a great extent free from the jurisdiction of the ordinary courts . . . [Dicey 1885, pp. 328, 388.]

Aucoc, a distinguished French contemporary of Dicey, defined administrative law as determining: '(1) the constitution and the relations of those organs of society which are charged with the care of those collective interests which are the object of public administration, by which term is meant the different representatives of society among which the State is the most important, and (2) the relations of the administrative authorities with the citizens of the State.'[17] Can it be said that, in this sense, the English have and had no administrative law? Of course not. Dicey gave the term a very limited meaning. He meant that in England (1) public servants possess no professional privileges which (2) protect them from the jurisdiction of the ordinary courts of the land and (3) that the state does not possess special powers in its own name. Dicey, in short, favoured the view that the relationships between citizens and public officials are not radically different from the relations of citizens with each other. In the Diceyan model of administrative law, *individual* citizens assert their rights and protect their interests against named *individuals* who represent the public service. The 'state' does not feature in this equation.

Let us take a simple example. Y, a police officer, arrests and prosecutes X without good reason. If the state is a corporate entity with rights and duties, then X might sue 'the state' or the police authority arguing that the organization of its police service was at fault. In England, X would sue Y and, before the Police Act 1964, the police authority was not even vicariously liable. Dicey argued that this model was superior because individuals retained responsibility for their own actions.

Dicey showed no interest in Aucoc's idea that administrative law might regulate the relationships between public authorities, as today it is increasingly asked to do as, for example, in the *Bromley* or *Tameside* cases (see below, Chapter 11). What concerned Dicey was the control of arbitrary power, or, more correctly, of administrative power, which he assumed to be arbitrary in character. The centrepiece of his theory was his ideal of the rule of law in which (a) the state possessed no *exceptional* powers and (b) *individual* public servants were responsible to the ordinary courts of the land for their use of statutory powers.

(b) Dicey and the rule-of-law state

When we say that the supremacy of the rule of law is a characteristic of the English constitution we generally include under one expression at least three distinct though kindred conceptions.

[First] that no man is punishable or can be lawfully made to suffer in body or goods except for a distinct breach of law established in the ordinary legal manner before the ordinary courts of the land. In this sense the rule of law is contrasted with every system of government based on the exercise by persons in authority of wide, arbitrary or discretionary powers of constraint . . .

[Secondly], not only that with us no man is above the law, but (what is a different thing) that here every man, whatever be his rank or condition, is subject to the ordinary law of the realm and amenable to the jurisdiction of the ordinary tribunals.

In England the idea of legal equality, or of the universal subjection of all classes to one law administered by the ordinary courts, has been pushed to its utmost limit. With us every official, from the Prime Minister down to a constable, is under the same responsibility for every act done without legal justification as any other citizen . . .

[Thirdly] that the general principles of the constitution (as for example the right to personal liberty, or the right of public meeting) are with us the result of judicial decisions determining the rights of private persons in particular cases brought before the courts; whereas under many foreign constitutions the security (such as it is) given to the rights of individuals results, or appears to result, from the general principles of the constitution. [Dicey 1885, pp. 187–96.]

By 1885, when Dicey wrote, the expansion of state power was well under way, and in his later works he recognized this. But Dicey did not consider that his theory needed modification to meet this situation. In the seventh edition of his work in 1908, he wrote, 'The innovations, such as they are, have been suggested merely by considerations of practical convenience, and do not betray the least intention on the part of English statesmen to modify the essential principles of English law. There exists in England no true *droit administratif*.' (Dicey 1885, p. 391.)[18]

Let us digress for a moment to consider the source of such powers. The first, and most important, is statute. The extent to which government functions are today regulated by statute will become increasingly clear. But government has available to it other, less specific powers. Next in importance come the common law powers which we all possess; for example, the right to sue or to enter into contracts or sign leases. These powers may be of great importance to the government.[19] In Dicey's day, it is noteworthy that these powers were in practice often exempt from control by the courts because the Crown was immune from proceedings in contract and tort. It was left to his successors to fight for an end to this immunity.[20]

Last but not least are the prerogative powers of the Crown. Blackstone (Comm. i. 239) stated these powers to be over and above the common law, comprising 'those rights and capacities which the King enjoys alone, in contradiction to others, and not those which he enjoys with any of his subjects'. Dicey's definition was wide enough to include *all* governmental discretionary and common law powers because he said that 'Every act which the executive government can lawfully do without the authority of an Act of Parliament is done in virtue of [the] prerogative' (Dicey 1885, p. 425). Whichever is correct,[21] the two types of extra-statutory authority may lock together in practice to give the government exactly the 'body of special rights, prerogatives and immunities' which Dicey thought no longer existed. Take the case of *Malone* v. *Metropolitan Police Commissioner* [1979] 2 WLR 700. The plaintiff asked for a declaration that it was unlawful for the Commissioner, in the absence of statutory authority, to authorize the tapping of his telephone. After a careful examination of the authorities, Sir Robert Megarry VC refused to grant the declaration. In the course of his judgment he said that at common law every act is lawful unless it is specifically prohibited; the Commissioner was able to benefit from this presumption. He also said that he, as a judge, was unable to extend the law, as this would amount to usurpation of the legislative function. Somewhat ironically, the result of discounting the 'special' position of state officials was that the parliamentary authorization which, in the case of governmental powers of this type, would be considered proper, was not required.[22]

This case can be used to demonstrate why some authors feel that Dicey left English administrative law with a great mistrust of executive or administrative action but without any theoretical basis for its control. By refusing to accept the reality of state power and acknowledge 'the state' as a legal entity possessing inherent powers of government, his theory disguised a vital and inevitable inequality between the state and its citizens. This inequality is of such fundamental importance that the rules of private law are unable to cope with it:

The fallacy of Dicey's assumptions lies in his contention that the rule of law demands full equality in every respect between government and subjects or citizens. But it is inherent in the very notion of government that it cannot in all respects be equal to the governed, because it has to govern. In a multitude of ways, government must be left to interfere, without legal sanctions, in the lives and interests of citizens, where private persons could not be allowed to do so . . . The refusal of the courts to make planning or policy decisions of government the subject of legal action, also shows that the inequality of government and governed in certain respects is an indispensable fact of organized political life. Where the borderline between governmental freedom and legal responsibility has to be drawn, is, indeed, a very difficult problem. It may be described as the key problem of administrative law. But we can only begin to understand it after having accepted, unlike Dicey, that inequalities between government and citizens are inherent in the very nature of political society. [Friedmann 1964, pp. 276–7.]

Some of the writers who felt this dissatisfaction moved on from Dicey's rule-of-law ideal to investigate other legal techniques which they felt to be superior to control by the courts. Such an approach was adopted by Davis, for instance (see below, Chapter 5). Others turned for help to the continental systems which Dicey had disparaged, arguing that these, because they acknowledged the state as a legal entity whose powers distinguished it in character from all other persons or bodies, had developed systems of 'public law' which were appropriate to its special nature.[23] For example, in the *Malone* case, if one were to acknowledge that the state was using its power to tap individuals' telephones, one might go on to argue that the state ought not to benefit from the principle that everything which is not expressly prohibited is lawful, because the state controls the legislative power which ought to be used to clarify and, where necessary, to limit the rights of its citizens. This would be a 'public law' solution which took into account the difference between the Metropolitan Police Commissioner and a private citizen.

In his critique,[24] Jennings made the different point that Dicey's theory of administrative and constitutional law sprang from his belief in individualism and dislike of the collectivism which, by the end of the nineteenth century, was beginning to flourish around him. This led him to adopt a narrow view of the constitution as 'an instrument for protecting the fundamental rights of the citizen, and not an instrument for enabling the community to provide services for the benefit of its citizens'. This approach in turn led him to confuse 'discretionary' with arbitrary powers, which were 'unconstitutional'. For Dicey, 'the constitution excludes wide discretionary authority; therefore it forbids large administrative powers; and therefore . . . the collectivism of the twentieth century parties, and collectivism generally, are unconstitutional' (Jennings 1935, p. 132).

Jennings described Dicey's ideal as the individualist, laissez-faire, policeman state. Wide administrative powers, which Dicey feared because of their collectivist connotations were, in Dicey's model, restricted in two ways. On one side stood Parliament which, because it was still dominated by Whig ideas, would not tolerate administrative interference with individual rights; on the other stood the courts dominated by a similar ideology:

[Dicey's] propositions condemn wide administrative powers. Wide administrative powers mean the exercise by administrative authorities of some at least of the major functions of the State. In the individualist constitution, the police State, the State 'holds the ring'. It creates crimes, and it gives remedies for wrongs. The administrative powers of punishing crimes and granting remedies are exercised by and under the control of the Courts. Collectivism places the Courts in a relatively inferior position. The hegemony of the lawyer is broken. Moreover, the legal profession in England is, subject to its own 'trade union' regulations, highly competitive or individualistic. For these reasons the 'Rule of Law' is intensely popular among most lawyers. This popularity is increased by the current contempt for foreign constitutions which runs, half submerged, throughout the book. English law, it is assumed, better protects the individual because it does not give him worthless paper guarantees which can be torn up like any other scrap of paper, but provides him with substantive remedies enforced by the Courts. Moreover, these Courts are free, independent and unbiased. There are no 'administrative courts', whose function it is, if we are to believe Dicey, to decide cases in which the administration is concerned in favour of the administration and against the citizen. Thus Dicey's views were in accord with the strongly nationalistic sentiments which pervaded English society until 1919. Patriotism insisted that the British Constitution not only worked better than other constitutions, but was intrinsically better. Dicey showed where the superiority was to be found. [Jennings 1935, p. 132.]

So Dicey's account of the English constitution is not merely a description. It is an interpretation inspired by an ardent belief in individualism, in laissez-faire economic policy and in the rectitude of lawyerly values.

(c) Dicey and the allocation of functions

Although Dicey spoke disparagingly of the French theory of separation of powers, Vile reminds us that his dream of 'the balanced constitution', in which executive power is constantly subject to checks and balances from both Parliament and the law courts, is a variation on the theme of separation of powers. Vile calls it 'the theory of law' and notes its peculiar attraction for lawyers. (Jennings suggests where its attraction lies.) Vile points out that Dicey's theory becomes untenable once it is admitted that, in practice, the executive and legislature are one and the same. 'If the subordination of the executive to the law was the keynote of [Dicey's] work, it would be to reduce this principle to nonsense to assume that legislators and executive were identical, that the powers of government were "fused" . . .' (Vile 1967, p. 230).

Vile calls a second constitutional theory 'the theory of government'. Here executive and legislative powers are fused, both being at the disposal of the government. This he associates particularly with Bagehot's *The English Constitution* (1867). The theories were until the end of the last century capable of reconciliation:

The theory of parliamentary government, with its balance between government and parliament, the fusion of the legislative and executive powers, and the subordination of the executive to the law were all quite cheerfully accepted as principles of British government. They were in fact all capable of being reconciled to a considerable extent. The reconciliation between the theory of law and the theory of government was achieved through the principle of ministerial responsibility. This idea enabled the two theories to be knitted together, and the differing functional concepts they embodied to be brought into a working relationship. The 'executive' must act according to the law, the 'government' must exercise leadership in the development of policy; but if the government was subject to the control of parliament, and the executive to the control of the courts, then a harmony could be established between the two roles of the ministers of the Crown. Ministerial responsibility, legal and political, was thus the crux of the English system of government. Whilst it remained a reality the whole edifice of constitutionalism could be maintained; should it cease to be a workable concept the process of disintegration between the legal basis and the operation of the government would begin. [Vile 1967, p. 231.]

As Vile hints, the growth of the state gave predominance to the 'theory of government' as administrators gained powers to make regulations and to adjudicate upon matters affecting the state's subjects. Lawyers and administrators were pulling in opposite directions. Lawyers, trained in the Diceyan mode of thought, regarded these developments as threatening, respectively, Parliament and the courts. They were also conditioned to suspect administrative discretion. When Lord Chief Justice Hewart bemoaned the destruction of the balanced constitution,[25] and the substitution of a 'New Despotism', the analogy was with Stuart autocracy:

The paradox which is in course of being accomplished is, indeed, rather elaborate. Writers on the Constitution have for a long time taught that its two leading features are the Sovereignty of Parliament and the Rule of Law. To tamper with either of them was, it might be thought, a sufficiently serious undertaking. But how far more attractive to the ingenious and adventurous mind to employ the one to defeat the other, and to establish a despotism on the ruins of both! It is manifestly easy to point a superficial contrast between what was done or attempted in the days of our least wise kings, and what is being done or attempted today. In those days the method was to defy Parliament – and it failed. In these days the method is to cajole, to coerce, and to use Parliament – and it is strangely successful. The old despotism, which was defeated, offered Parliament a challenge. The new despotism, which is not yet defeated, gives Parliament an anaesthetic. The strategy is different, but the goal is the same. It is to subordinate Parliament, to evade the Courts, and to render the will, or the caprice of the Executive unfettered and supreme. [Hewart 1929, p. 17.]

The consequence for administrative law was the establishment of the Donoughmore Committee on Ministers' Powers.[26] Its terms of reference were 'to consider the powers exercised by or under the direction of (or by persons or bodies appointed specially by) Ministers of the Crown by way of (a) delegated legislation and (b) judicial or quasi-judicial decision, and to report what safeguards are desirable or necessary to secure the constitutional principles of the sovereignty of Parliament and the supremacy of the law' (Cmnd 4050 (1932)). Of these Robson (1951, p. 423) commented, 'the committee started life with the dead hand of Dicey lying frozen on its neck'. What do you think he meant?

What courses of action were open to Donoughmore? After all, the state, and with it administrative law, was moving fast in the opposite direction. This, in Robson's view, was inevitable. On the subject of administrative adjudication,[27] he said:

Parliament did not merely overlook the courts of law. But the possibility of setting up new organs of adjudication which would do the work more rapidly, more cheaply, more efficiently than the ordinary courts; which would possess greater technical knowledge and fewer prejudices against government; which would give greater heed to the social interests involved and show less solicitude for private property rights; which would decide the dispute with a conscious effort at furthering the social policy embodied in the legislation: this prospect offered solid advantages which no doubt induced Parliament to extend the administrative jurisdiction of government departments so as to include judicial functions affecting the social services. In doing so Parliament was only repeating a process which had happened again and again in the history not only of England but of many civilised countries.

The Committee thus came to be faced with a *fait accompli*. Broadly speaking, three courses were open to it. It could (in theory at least) have recommended a return to the eighteenth-century position. It could have accepted proposals . . . to rationalise and institutionalise the administrative jurisdiction in a boldly-conceived system of administrative courts separated to a large extent from the ordinary routine of departmental administration and free from indirect ministerial interference. Or thirdly, it could accept the patchwork quilt of ill-constructed tribunals which at present exists, and endeavour to remedy some of their more obvious defects. It is this last-named alternative which the Committee has adopted. [Robson 1932, p. 359.]

Robson's attack on the work of Donoughmore is also interesting because it contains a more general attack on the legal profession. Robson is not complaining that lawyers are wrong in seeking to protect individual rights, though he might query their limited definition. His real complaint is that the tools which they use are inadequate for the task. And he goes further, alleging that a profession which is incapable of reforming the judicial process ought not to be let loose on the administrative process. Given the record of the legal profession in reform, this criticism has still to be taken very seriously:

The disappointing feature of the Report is its failure to make any significant contribution to the structure of the system. Instead of endeavouring to increase the sense of responsibility and independence of the administrative tribunals, the Report relies on a hostile judiciary to provide 'checks and balances'. It recommends, accordingly, that the supervisory jurisdiction of the High Court to compel ministers and administrative tribunals to keep within their powers and to hear and determine according to law be maintained; and further, that anyone aggrieved by a decision should have an absolute right of appeal to the High Court on any question of law.

This is the means by which the rule of law is to be perpetuated and the liberty of the subject protected for all eternity. It sounds admirable. But when one looks a little deeper doubts begin to arise. In the first place, it is often extraordinarily difficult to discover any essential difference between a question of law and a question of fact. A question of fact in one generation sometimes becomes a question of law in the next; and a vast body of precedents is almost certain to arise on hair-splitting distinctions between questions of law and questions of fact in the field of public administration. When the courts want to interfere they will seek to find that a question of law is involved; and *vice versa*. Second, the procedure for getting a decision reviewed on a question of law by the courts is, to quote the Report, 'too expensive and in certain respects archaic, cumbrous and too inelastic'; and the Committee recommends a cheaper and more simple procedure. One must consider the implications of this criticism. Here are the judges and the lawyers complaining that they are not empowered in all cases to interfere with judicial decisions by administrative tribunals, and clamouring for more power. Yet in the large sphere where the right of judicial control over the executive *does* exist, the courts have done absolutely nothing to modernise, to cheapen or to bring into accord with modern needs a fantastic procedure which has been obsolete for at least a century . . . It is difficult to believe that the legal profession retains any considerable capacity for reforming either the law or the practice of the courts. [Robson 1932, pp. 360–1.]

Robson refers to 'hair-splitting distinctions'. In similar fashion he criticized the Donoughmore Committee's attempts to distinguish 'judicial', 'quasi-judicial' and 'administrative' decisions. Because this is the type of *conceptual* reasoning dear to the heart of many administrative lawyers and used traditionally by courts to solve administrative law problems, it merits a closer look.

4 The allocation of functions: 'terminological contortions'?

(a) Two opposing academic views

The meanings attributed by the courts to the terms 'judicial', 'quasi-judicial' 'administrative', 'legislative' and 'ministerial' for administrative law purposes have been inconsistent. This is doubtless unfortunate, for specific legal consequences may flow from the manner of characterising a particular function; and to use the same word to denote different things and different words to denote the same thing inevitably generates confusion. It is sometimes impossible to discern why a court has characterised a given function as judicial or administrative. Often, it is true, the method of characterisation can be seen as a contrivance to support a conclusion reached on non-conceptual grounds. But in many cases the terms seem to have been used loosely and without deliberation; and in some cases definitions propounded in earlier reported cases appear to have dominated the juristic analysis of the case in hand and indeed the conclusion reached by the court

... recent English caselaw has tended to blur rather than clarify the distinctions between the two most important classes of function, the judicial and the administrative. And . . . as distinctions have been blurred, so has their practical importance tended to dwindle. Seldom does the outcome of a case nowadays turn purely on the mode of classifying a function vested in the competent authority. The intrinsic difficulties of the topic under consideration have not diminished, but they are no longer as oppressive as they once were. [de Smith, 3rd edn 1973, pp. 58–9.]

Whilst doubt has been cast in recent years on both the pragmatic utility of and logical justifications for the drawing of abstract theoretical distinctions between different decision-making techniques, this writer is of the view that such distinctions cannot only be made, but are amply justified on grounds of logic, principle and pragmatic utility, in addition to the pedagogic benefits . . .

In administrative law, by far the most important consequence of classification of function has been the denial or granting of the benefits and protection of the rules of natural justice. Though the crucial significance of classification in this area has perhaps declined with the application to administrative acts of the duty to act fairly, the administrative/judicial distinction remains in some cases a highly influential factor. [R. C. Austin 1980, p. 298.]

(b) The Committee on Ministers' Powers

The Donoughmore Committee defined 'judicial', 'quasi-judicial' and 'purely administrative' decisions as follows:

A true judicial decision presupposes an existing dispute between two or more parties and then involves four requisites: (1) the presentation (not necessarily orally) of their case by the parties to the dispute; (2) if the dispute between them is a question of fact, the ascertainment of the fact by means of evidence adduced by the parties to the dispute and often with the assistance of argument by or on behalf of the parties on the evidence; (3) if the dispute between them is a question of law, the submission of legal argument by the parties; and (4) a decision which disposes of the whole matter by a finding upon the facts in dispute and an application of the law of the land to the facts so found, including where required a ruling upon any disputed question of law.

A quasi-judicial decision equally presupposes an existing dispute between two or more parties and involves (1) and (2), but does not necessarily involve (3), and never involves (4). The place of (4) is in fact taken by administrative action, the character of which is determined by the Minister's free choice.

Decisions which are purely administrative stand on a wholly different footing from quasi-judicial as well as from judicial decisions and must be distinguished accordingly. Indeed the very word 'decision' has a different meaning in the one sphere of activity and the other. When a person resolves to act in a particular way, the mental step may be described as a 'decision'. Again, when a judge determines an issue of fact upon conflicting evidence, or a question of law upon forensic argument, he gives a 'decision'. But the two mental acts differ. In the case of the administrative decision, there is no legal obligation upon the person charged with the duty of reaching the decision to consider and weigh submissions and arguments, or to collate any evidence, or to solve any issue. The grounds upon which he acts, and the means which he takes to inform himself before acting, are left entirely to his discretion.

But even a large number of administrative decisions may and do involve, in greater or less degree, at some stage in the procedure which eventuates in executive action, certain of the attributes of a judicial decision. Indeed generally speaking a quasi-judicial decision is only an administrative decision, some stage or some element of which possesses judicial character- istics. And it is doubtless because so many administrative acts have this character that our terms of reference have specially included quasi-judicial decisions. [Cmnd 4050, pp. 73–4.]

On judicial decisions, the Committee's reasoning follows this pattern: *Question*: Is X an administrative or judicial decision? *Answer*: It is judicial because it involves: (1) presentation of a case by parties; (2) ascertainment of facts by means of evidence; (3) submission of legal argument; and (4) a decision based on facts and law.

Jennings commented:

Is the analysis correct? Its essence, clearly, is in requisite (4), which in fact does nothing else than repeat the hoary fallacy that a judge is concerned with law and not with policy . . . Any case which gets into the law reports implies a new rule of law, and that new rule is made by the judge in the case. He is legislating: and he is necessarily legislating in accordance with a policy. He cannot apply law to make new law. The law is not in his breast ready to be pulled out. A judge is not a legal slot-machine . . . There is no essential distinction between an administrative decision in an individual case and a judicial decision. There are three possible elements in each, (a) the facts (b) the rules of law, and (c) the policy which the law is intended to further. Where the whole question is (a), it is commonly left to a court unless the subject is so technical that the elucidation of the facts is best left to an expert. Where the emphasis is upon (c), the question is commonly left to be settled by an administrator. Where there is a doubt as to (b) then either the court or the administrator will have also to consider (c). [Jennings 1932, pp. 345–6.]

Do you agree? The Committee used its definitions to answer two questions suggested by the reference in its brief to 'safeguards'. In the Committee's own words: 'The real questions for us to answer would seem to be: (a) To what extent should judicial functions be entrusted (i) to Ministers and (ii) to Ministerial Tribunals: (b) What are the right methods for the exercise of such functions? What are the proper safeguards?'

We will take these questions in reverse order: *Question*: What procedures ought to be imposed on the person who takes decision X?

Answer: X is a judicial decision, therefore judicial procedures are appropriate. *Question*: To what type of person should decision X be allocated, to a minister, to a tribunal or to a court? *Answer*: Tribunals and courts are judicial bodies using judicial procedures. In the case of the Minister, the procedures 'are left entirely to his discretion'. Decision X, being judicial, should be allocated to a judicial body.

If you think carefully about the totality of the Committee's reasoning, you will find it circular.

(c) The courts

As Austin notes, the judicial/administrative dichotomy has been used in the common law doctrine of natural justice. This doctrine, considered more fully in Chapter 3, contains two elements: first, that no man shall be condemned unheard and, second, that no man shall be judge in his own cause. Certain judges have used the dichotomy to determine whether the requirements of natural justice apply to a particular decision-making process. In the following cases, rigid classificatory distinctions are sometimes adopted and sometimes not. Austin's views can be tested against those of de Smith. Is the judicial/administrative distinction useful or not? And does it help the court towards a logical and/or sensible result?

Cooper v. Wandsworth Board of Works
(1863) 14 CB (NS) 180

The plaintiff brought an action for trespass against the defendant board, for ordering the demolition of his house, acting under powers granted by the Metropolis Management Act 1855. The Board argued that the plaintiff had not given the statutory notice of intention to build and that it was lawful to demolish the house. The plaintiff argued that he was entitled to notice and to a hearing.

ERLE CJ: It has been said that the principle that no man shall be deprived of his property without an opportunity of being heard, is limited to a judicial proceeding, and that a district board ordering a house to be pulled down cannot be said to be doing a judicial act. I do not quite agree with that; neither do I undertake to rest my judgment solely upon the ground that the district board is a court exercising judicial discretion upon the point: but the law, I think, has been applied to many exercises which in common understanding would not be at all more a judicial proceeding than would be the act of the district board in ordering a house to be pulled down . . . The district board must do the thing legally; there must be a resolution; and if there be a board, and a resolution of that board, I have not heard a word to shew that it would not be salutory that they should hear the man who is to suffer from their judgment before they proceed to make the order under which they attempt to justify their act.

BYLES J: It seems to me that the board are wrong whether they acted judicially or ministerially. I conceive they acted judicially, because they had to determine the offence, and they had to apportion the punishment as well as the remedy. That being so, a long course of decisions . . . establish that, although there are no positive words in a statute requiring that the party shall be heard, yet the justice of the common law will supply the omission of the legislature. The judgment of Mr Justice Fortescue, in *Dr Bentley's case* [(1723) 1 Str. 557] is somewhat quaint, but it is very applicable, and has been the law from that time to the present. He says,

> The objection for want of notice can never be got over. The laws of God and man both give the party an opportunity to make his defence, if he has any. I remember to have heard it observed by a very learned man, upon such an occasion, that even God himself did not pass sentence upon Adam before he was called upon to make his defence. 'Adam' (says God), 'where art thou? Hast thou not eaten of the tree whereof I commanded thee that thou shouldest not eat?' And the same question was put to Eve also.

If therefore, the board acted judicially, although there are no words in the statute to that effect, it is plain they acted wrongly. But suppose they acted ministerially – then it may be they were not bound to give the first sort of notice, viz, the notice of the hearing; but they were clearly bound, as it seems to me, by the words of the statute, to give notice of their order before they proceeded to execute it . . .

Local Gvt Board v. *Arlidge* [1915] AC 120

The respondent contested a closing order made by the Board in respect of his property under the provisions of the Housing, Town Planning etc Act 1909. The Board had set up a public inquiry as it was required to do and had followed the procedure laid down by the Act. The respondent argued that he had a right (a) to present his case orally to the decision-maker in person, (b) to know which of the Board's officers had actually taken the decision and (c) to see the report made by the Inspector at the public inquiry. Failure to observe these procedures was a breach of the rules of natural justice. The House of Lords disagreed.

VISCOUNT HALDANE LC: My Lords, when the duty of deciding an appeal is imposed, those whose duty it is to decide it must act judicially. They must deal with the question referred to them without bias, and they must give to each of the parties the opportunity of adequately presenting the case made. The decision must be come to in the spirit and with the sense of responsibility of a tribunal whose duty it is to mete out justice. But it does not follow that the procedure of every such tribunal must be the same. In the case of a Court of law tradition in this country has prescribed certain principles to which in the main the procedure must conform. But what that procedure is to be in detail must depend on the nature of the tribunal. In modern times it has become increasingly common for Parliament to give an appeal in matters which really pertain to administration, rather than to the exercise of the judicial functions of an ordinary Court, to authorities whose functions are administrative, and not in the ordinary sense judicial. Such a body as the Local Government Board has the duty of enforcing obligations on the individual which are imposed in the interests of the community. Its character is that of an organization with executive functions. In this it resembles other great departments of State. When, therefore, Parliament entrusts it with judicial duties, Parliament must be taken, in the absence of any declaration to the contrary, to have intended it to follow the procedure which is its own, and is necessary if it is to be capable of doing its work efficiently . . . In the case of the Local Government Board it is not doubtful what this procedure is. The Minister at the head of the Board is directly responsible to Parliament like other Ministers. He is responsible not only for what he himself does but for all that is done in his department. The volume of work entrusted to him is very great and he cannot do the great bulk of it himself. He is expected to obtain his materials vicariously through his officials, and he has discharged his duty if he sees that they obtain these materials for him properly. To try to extend his duty beyond this and to insist that he and other members of the Board should do everything personally would be to impair his efficiency. Unlike a judge in a Court he is not only at liberty but is compelled to rely on the assistance of his staff. When, therefore, the Board is directed to dispose of an appeal, that does not mean that any particular official of the Board is to dispose of it . . .

LORD MOULTON: I confess that I am unable to understand the meaning of the phrase 'contrary to natural justice' in connection with such a matter as is involved in the present case. The original closing order and the refusal to determine it were administrative acts which the local authority was authorized to do in the interests of public health. Their authority was purely statutory, and if the statute had authorized them to do these acts without giving any appeal, the legislation might be considered to be unwisely drastic, but it would have to be recognized and enforced by the Courts, and no such question as to whether or not it was 'contrary to natural justice' could possibly be considered by the Courts. Such a question would be unmeaning in such a connection. And although the Legislature has not followed such a course in connection with closing orders, it is easy to call to mind many matters in which prompt action is so necessary that provisions as drastic as those I have described might be necessary. Cases of quarantine regulations or the destruction of unwholesome food exposed for sale might under certain circumstances be well left to the decision of executive officers without any appeal being given.

In the present case, however, the Legislature has provided an appeal, but it is an appeal to an administrative department of State and not to a judicial body. It is said, truthfully, that on such an appeal the Local Government Board must act judicially, but this, in my opinion, only means that it must preserve a judicial temper and perform its duties conscientiously, with a proper feeling of responsibility, in view of the fact that its acts affect the property and rights of individuals. Parliament has wisely laid down certain rules to be observed in the performance of its functions in these matters, and those rules must be observed because they are imposed by statute, and for no other reason, and whether they give much or little opportunity for what I may call quasi-litigious procedure depends solely on what Parliament has thought right. These rules are beyond the criticism of the Courts, and it is not their business to add to or take away from them, or even to discuss whether in the opinion of the individual members of the Court they are adequate or not.

Why did Viscount Haldane think the Minister was acting in an 'administrative' capacity? Did Lord Moulton agree? Does Lord Moulton's definition of 'acting judicially' satisfy you? Why did he think that the rules of natural justice were irrelevant? Was the result 'fair' to the applicant?

In *Cooper* v. *Wilson* [1937] 2 K B 309, the Court of Appeal was asked to consider whether the rules of natural justice applied to the dismissal of a police sergeant by the Watch Committee after disciplinary charges had been preferred against him. Scott LJ, who had succeeded the Earl of Donoughmore as Chairman of the Committee on Ministers' Powers, tried to classify the proceedings by reference to the Committee's definitions of quasi-judicial and judicial. He was forced to the conclusion that, in such proceedings, 'quasi-judicial approaches in point of degree very near to the judicial. This does not of course mean that because the Watch Committee was then exercising nearly judicial functions, it was tied to ordinary judicial procedure . . .' The Court went on to hold, however, that the rules of natural justice were applicable to the proceedings of the Watch Committee.

Ridge v. *Baldwin* [1964] AC 40

The appellant was appointed Chief Constable of Brighton, subject to the provisions of the Police Act and regulations. Subsequently he was charged with conspiracy, suspended by the Watch Committee and then acquitted. No evidence was offered on a second, lesser, charge of corruption. After his acquittal, the appellant applied to be reinstated but the Watch Committee, acting under s. 191(4) of the Municipal Corporations Act 1882, dismissed him after listening to his solicitor. No specific charges were made, but the Committee considered the record of the criminal trial, including adverse comments by the trial judge concerning the appellant's lack of 'professional and moral leadership'. The appellant's appeal to the Home Secretary was dismissed; he therefore applied for a declaration that his dismissal was void for breach of natural justice. He sought financial compensation, not reinstatement. In the Court of Appeal, it was held that the Watch Committee was exercising an administrative function and that the principles of natural justice were not applicable. The House of Lords reversed this decision.

LORD REID: The appellant's case is that . . . before attempting to reach any decision [the Committee] were bound to inform him of the grounds on which they proposed to act and give him a fair opportunity of being heard in his own defence. The authorities on the applicability of the principles of natural justice are in some confusion . . . It appears to me that one reason why [this is so] is that insufficient attention has been paid to the great difference between various kinds of cases in which it has been sought to apply the principle. What a minister ought to do in considering objections to a scheme may be very different from what a watch committee ought to do in considering whether to dismiss a chief constable . . . [Lord Reid dealt with cases of dismissal which he classified into three types: (a) dismissal of a servant by a master (b) dismissal from an office held during pleasure and (c) dismissal from an office where there must be something to warrant dismissal. Holding this case to fall in the third category, he continued:]

The question [for] the watch committee . . . was not [simply] whether or not the appellant should be dismissed. There were three possible courses open to the watch committee – reinstating the appellant as chief constable, dismissing him, or requiring him to resign. The difference between the latter two is that dismissal involved forfeiture of pension rights, whereas requiring him to resign did not . . . The appellant's real interest in this appeal is to try to save his pension rights.

It may be convenient at this point to deal with an argument that, even if as a general rule a watch committee must hear a constable in his own defence before dismissing him, this case was so clear that nothing that the appellant could have said could have made any difference. It is at least very doubtful whether that could be accepted as an excuse. But, even if it could, the respondents would fail on the facts. It may well be that no reasonable body of men could have reinstated the appellant. But as between the other two courses open to the watch committee the case is not so clear . . . [Lord Reid considered the early case law beginning with *Cooper* v. *Wandsworth Board of Works* and concluded:]

If the present case had arisen thirty or forty years ago the courts would have had no difficulty in deciding this issue in favour of the appellant on the authorities which I have cited. So far as I am aware none of these authorities has ever been disapproved or even doubted. Yet the Court of Appeal have decided this issue against the appellant on more recent authorities which apparently justify that result. How has this come about?

At least three things . . . have contributed. [First] there have been many cases where it has been sought to apply the principles of natural justice to the wider duties imposed on Ministers and other organs of government by modern legislation. For reasons which I shall attempt to state in a moment, it has been held that those principles have a limited application in such cases and those limitations have tended to be reflected in other decisions on matters to which in principle they do not appear to me to apply. Secondly . . . those principles have been held to have a limited application in cases arising out of war-time legislation; and again such limitations have tended to be reflected in other cases. And, thirdly, there has . . . been a misunderstanding of the judgment of Atkin LJ in *Rex* v. *Electricity Commissioners, ex p. London Electricity Joint Committee Co.* [1924] 1 KB 171.

In cases of the kind I have been dealing with the Board of Works or the Governor or the club committee was dealing with a single isolated case. It was not deciding, like a judge in a lawsuit, what were the rights of the person before it. But it was deciding how he should be treated – something analogous to a judge's duty in imposing a penalty. No doubt policy would play some part in the decision – but so it might when a judge is imposing a sentence. So it was easy to say that such a body is performing a quasi-judicial task in considering and deciding such a matter, and to require it to observe the essentials of all proceedings of a judicial character – the principles of natural justice.

Sometimes the functions of a minister or department may also be of that character, and then the rules of natural justice can apply in much the same way. But more often their functions are of a very different character. If a minister is considering whether to make a scheme for, say, an important new road, his primary concern will not be with the damage which its construction will do to the rights of individual owners of land. He will have to consider all manner of questions of public interest and, it may be, a number of alternative schemes. He cannot be prevented from attaching more importance to the fulfilment of his policy than to the fate of individual objectors, and it would be quite wrong for the courts to say that the minister should or could act in the same kind of way as a board of works deciding whether a house should be pulled down. And there is another important difference. As explained in *Local Government Board* v. *Arlidge* a minister cannot do everything himself. His officers will have to gather and sift all the facts, including objections by individuals, and no individual can complain if the ordinary accepted methods of carrying on public business do not give him as good protection as would be given by the principles of natural justice in a different kind of case . . .

In [the *Electricity Commissioners* case] the commissioners had a statutory duty to make schemes with regard to electricity districts and to hold local inquiries before making them. They made a draft scheme which in effect allocated duties to one body which the Act required should be allocated to a different kind of body. This was held to be ultra vires, and the question was whether prohibition would lie. It was argued that the proceedings of the commissioners were purely executive and controllable by Parliament alone. Bankes LJ said [that] 'powers so far-reaching, affecting as they do individuals as well as property, are powers to be exercised judicially, and not ministerially or merely . . . as proceedings towards legislation.' So he inferred the judicial element from the nature of the power. And I think that Atkin LJ did the same . . . There is not a word in Atkin LJ's judgment to suggest disapproval of the earlier line of authority which I have cited. On the contrary, he goes further than those authorities. I have already stated my view that it is more difficult for the courts to control an exercise of power on a large scale where the treatment to be meted out to a particular individual is only one of many matters to be considered. This was a case of that kind, and, if Atkin LJ was prepared to infer a judicial element from the nature of the power in this case, he could hardly disapprove such an inference when the power related solely to the treatment of a particular individual . . . I would hold that the power of dismissal in the Act of 1882 could not then have been exercised and cannot now be exercised until the watch committee have informed the constable of the grounds on which they propose to proceed and have given him a proper opportunity to present his case in defence.

Did Lord Reid bypass the analytical classification used by the Donoughmore Committee and in *Cooper* v. *Wilson*? What factors were particularly influential in persuading him that the rules of natural justice should be applied?

> *R.* v. *Commission for Racial Equality ex p. Cottrell
> and Rothon* [1980] 1 WLR 1580

The applicants, a firm of estate agents, allegedly discriminated against coloured people in the course of their business. A complaint was made to the Commission by an ex-employee of the firm. The Commission conducted an investigation using the procedures set out in s.48 of the Race Relations Act 1976. The firm applied unsuccessfully for review on the ground that the rules of natural justice had not been applied and that trial-type procedures (e.g. cross-examination) had not been used.

LORD LANE CJ: Possibly the most important matter is the nature of the provisions of the Race Relations Act 1976 itself . . . there is no mention in any section of any right to cross-examine any of the witnesses. That perhaps is a surprising omission if it was the intention of Parliament to allow a person in the position of the firm in this case the full panoply of legal rights which would take place at a judicial hearing.

It seems to me that there are degrees of judicial hearing, and those degrees run from the borders of pure administration to the borders of the full hearing of a criminal cause or matter in the Crown Court. It does not profit one to try to pigeon-hole the particular set of circumstances either into the administrative pigeon-hole or into the judicial pigeon-hole. Each case will inevitably differ, and one must ask oneself what is the basic nature of the proceeding which was going on here. It seems to me that, basically, this was an investigation being carried out by the commission. It is true that in the course of the investigation the commission may form a view, but it does not seem to me that that is a proceeding which requires, in the name of fairness, any right in the firm in this case to be able to cross-examine witnesses whom the

Commission have seen and from whom they have taken statements. I [note] the wording of section 58(2) in emphasis of that point: 'If in the course of a formal investigation the commission become satisfied that a person is committing . . .' and so on. It seems to me that that is so near an administrative function as to make little difference and is the type of investigation or proceeding which does not require the formalities of cross-examination.

We are not here to substitute our view for the view of the commission. They undoubtedly went to very great lengths to investigate and examine all the voluminous evidence which was before them. There is now before us the report of the formal investigation which was carried out and a copy of which was sent to each member of the commission (60 pages in all). No one can complain that this matter was not thoroughly investigated . . . There was no breach of the rules of fairness in that cross-examination was not permitted and that the witnesses did not attend.

Does this decision support de Smith's view that the practical importance of the 'administrative/judicial' distinction is dwindling? What new terminology is introduced? Is it more helpful to the court?

5 Quangos and quangocide

Although we have talked about the growth of the 'state', we have not defined this term. Pressed for a definition, most people would associate the state with central government, many would include local authorities, some would go on to provide a catalogue:[28] nationalized industries and public enterprises like water authorities, public services like the N H S, boards, committees, commissions and inspectorates, the police, all the multifarious public authorities which make up the 'public sector' of our complicated society. Lawyers might mention 'the Crown' as symbolic of government or perhaps as 'a convenient cover for ignorance' (Maitland 1908, p. 418).

For some, this pragmatic treatment characterizes the Diceyan legacy, with its strong tradition of localism and jealousy of central-ized, autocratic powers. For others, the traditional treatment com-placently ignores the march of the modern state towards centralism and corporatism (see below, Chapter 2), concealed by the use of local government to operate services on behalf of central government and by the intermediate device of the autonomous or semi-autonomous government agency or quango.

If you return to Hill (see above, p. 8), you will see that independent boards, committees and commissions are not entirely new.[29] But their rapid growth does in some way typify modern

administration. In descending order, the three growth areas of
modern government have until reecently been local government, the
NHS and quangos. The rapid proliferation of the latter was partly a
response to the recommendations of the Fulton Committee (Cmnd
3638, 1968), which 'enthusiastically endorsed the pattern of
government growth by bureaucratic stasis at the centre and growth at
the fringes of Whitehall by its doctrine of "hiving off" units from civil
service departments to non-departmental bodies' (Hood 1980,
p. 247). There is no typical quango. Some exercise policy-making
functions and tender advice to the Minister, like the now defunct
SBC, whose diverse work is described more fully in Chapter 18.
Others, like the Health and Safety Executive, whose job is to promote
industrial safety, have statutory powers of supervision and control
including the power to issue 'stop' orders comparable to the
injunctive powers of courts. The Advisory, Conciliation and Arbitration Service (ACAS), which deals with trade unions and industry,
is empowered to negotiate agreements and codes of practice and to act
as an arbitrator. The Civil Aviation Authority (CAA) possesses
licensing powers which you will see described as 'quasi-judicial'.
Other organizations, like the CRE,[30] are empowered to conduct
investigations and provide support for court proceedings in the name
of individuals, much in the way the Attorney-General represents 'the
public interest' in litigation (see below, Chapter 10). The Council on
Tribunals (see below, Chapter 6) is more like an old-fashioned,
advisory committee.

For 'the balanced constitution' these proliferating administrative
agencies can seem threatening. Their functions cross classificatory
frontiers. Perhaps this is why in *ex p. Cottrell and Rothon*, the court felt
the need to expand the traditional terminology. Their 'semi-
autonomy' undermines the doctrine of ministerial responsibility,
although alternative methods of securing accountability have not
been provided.[31] And the informal, discretionary 'old-boy-network'
system of appointments allows the government powers of patronage
wholly incompatible with the Weberian model of bureaucracy. We
shall refer to this again in the context of the Council on Tribunals.

Green light theorists like Ganz (see below) and Farmer, who see the
development of new and flexible administrative procedures as an
important task for administrative law, are encouraged by these new
agencies with their mixed functions. 'If a complaint is to be made, it
must surely be that administrative agencies are not employing

are developing' (Farmer 1970, p. 119). But following the 1979 election, quangocide became a popular sport with a government committed to pruning bureaucracy and cutting back the public sector,[32] and a few quangos bit the dust. Yet recently two key White Papers, 'Public Transport in London' (Cmnd. 9004 (1983)) and 'Streamlining the Cities' (Cmnd. 9063 (1983)), have proposed the transfer of important public services from elected local authorities to non-elected administrative agencies. So whether the frontiers of the state are really being pushed back, or whether a move to more centralized decision-taking is under way, remains to be seen.

2
Green light theories

1 The foreign connection

In Chapter 1 we concentrated on one view of English administrative law as an instrument for the *control* of power and for the protection of individual liberty, the emphasis being on courts rather than on government and the state often being regarded in the light of an intruder. Here and there, however, we caught glimpses of an alternative tradition in which the use of executive power to provide services for the benefit of the community seemed entirely legitimate and the function of courts in checking executive action was a questionable activity. In this chapter, we look more closely at what we have called 'green light' theories.

In using this phrase, we do not wish to imply that green light theory favours unrestricted or arbitrary action by the state. While red light theory was indissolubly linked to the model of the balanced constitution, green light theory finds the 'model of government' more congenial. Red light theorists look first to the law courts for control of the executive; green light theorists are inclined to pin their hopes on the political process. Here Robson contrasts the 'model of law' and the 'model of government':

An opposition has for long existed in Britain between the idea of 'law' and the idea of 'government'. This is a heritage from the conflict in the seventeenth century between, on the one side, a sovereign claiming to rule by divine right and to exercise an undisputed prerogative in all matters of government, and, on the other side, a nation claiming a supreme law to which even the sovereign should be subject. That struggle between king and commons has become transformed in our own day into a conflict between the executive, on the one hand, and the judiciary and legal profession on the other. The lawyers still regard themselves as champions of the popular cause; but there can be little doubt that the great departments of state . . . are not only essential to the well being of the great mass of the people, but also the most significant expressions of democracy in our time. Considerations of this kind, however, could scarcely be expected to weigh with the predominantly upper middle-class conservative legal mind. [Robson 1951, p. 421.]

Writing at the London School of Economics in the inter-war period, Laski, Robson and Jennings (among others) attempted to redress the balance. Their new ideas were less insular and less hostile to socialist doctrine. Conscious of the close relationship between law, politics and social policy,[1] they were able to draw inspiration from the work of lawyers in other countries.

In the United States, where realist and sociological jurisprudence was influential, administrative law was more sophisticated and the gap between law and administration was narrower. Realists stressed that law could be studied only in its social context, indeed, in many cases they included in their definition of law elements which positivists would seek to exclude. Holmes admitted the role of the judge as law-maker, thus emphasizing his responsibility for the development of policy.[2] The effectiveness of the legal system became an object of study for sociologists of law. A method known as functionalism was born. We do not want to define functionalism narrowly nor to sever it artificially from realism; but, briefly, functionalists interest themselves in the way in which rules actually operate:

The functional method poses such questions as: How do rules of law work? Are certain rules of law, so-called, merely ritual observances which have no verifiable relation to the decisions of judges who recite them? To what extent are laws actually obeyed? What are the limits of effective law enforcement? What are the social mechanisms and institutions that make certain rules of law effective and leave others dead letters? When rules of law are obeyed or disobeyed, what consequences actually follow from such conduct? More generally, these questions may be compressed in the formula 'What is the human meaning of the law?' [Cohen 1937, p. 6.]

The functionalist method appeared particularly appropriate to administrative law, where the relationship between law and administration is often more complex than the pictures drawn in the theories of the balanced constitution might suggest. Functionalists found a new objective for research in administrative law: to describe the relationship between law and administration. This entailed a new definition. Administrative law became *all* the law relating to the administration and not merely that concerned with *control* of executive power. But not all functionalists were content merely to describe. Many went on to *prescribe* new remedies for old maladies. This involved the design of new administrative procedures suited to the modern administrative process. These procedures were to be assessed in their particular administrative context rather than measured against the *general* principles of, for example, natural justice. Take *Cottrell and Rothon* (see p. 31), for example. In what respect could this be called a 'functionalist' decision?

Realists and functionalists were reformers by temperament and in this they looked back to the example of Jeremy Bentham. Bentham long ago envisaged a more active role for government and legis-lature.[3] He believed it to be the duty of the sovereign to engage actively in legislation to ensure that the principle of utility prevailed through the legal system. Moreover, both Bentham and Austin discounted law courts as efficient vehicles for law reform – even for reform of their own archaic procedure. Many years later, Nonet, himself the author of an important functionalist study of the work of an American administrative organization, described the attitude of sociological and realist jurisprudence to state interventionism:

With the advent of the New Deal, the legal order suddenly turned from an obstacle and an enemy into a friend and a positive support . . . The active state was emerging and a new idea of law, already embodied in the flowering legal realism, was now presenting it as an active instrument of political and social change. [Nonet 1969, p. 83.]

Also influential in shaping new theories of administrative law was the work of a French jurist, Léon Duguit (1859–1928). Duguit developed his theory of public law under the influence of the great French sociologist Emile Durkheim (1858–1917). Durkheim's work on the *Division of Labour* (1893) started life as a dissertation on 'the relationship of individualism and socialism'; Duguit's theory was premised on a socialistic state in which strong government was a necessity.[4]

Like Bentham, Duguit accepted the need for a state whose activities stretch far beyond the traditional areas of law, order, justice and defence. He believed in a collective state whose function was to secure the provision of public services. These he defined as including 'any activity that has to be governmentally regulated and controlled because it is indispensable to the realisation and development of social solidarity . . . so long as it is of such a nature that it cannot be assured save by governmental intervention' (1921, p. 48). Duguit's theory lays the basis, therefore, for a corporatist state (defined below) in which planning and the control of private economic activity in the interests of the collectivity are legitimate state activities. Duguit foresaw that transport, mining and electricity would ultimately become public services.

Yet whether Duguit would have approved the evolution of modern society towards corporatism is extremely doubtful. He rejected the idea of the state as a corporate entity with a legal life and legal powers of its own. The state was merely a collection of individuals 'inter-dependent upon one another even for their daily and elementary needs'. Sovereignty itself was a misconception; the state had 'duties' rather than 'rights' or 'powers'. This view transformed the character of 'public law':

Public law is no longer a mass of rules which, applied by a sovereign person with the right to command, determine its relations between the individuals and groups on a given territory as a sovereign dealing with its subjects. The modern theory of the state envisages a mass of rules which govern the organization of public utilities and assure their regular and uninterrupted function . . . The one governmental rule is the governmental obligation to organize and control public services in such a fashion as to avoid all dislocation. The basis of public law is therefore no longer command but organization . . . government has . . . a social function to fulfil. [Duguit 1921, pp. 48–9.]

Duguit's theory had much in common with that of his great contemporary, Dicey. In his theory, 'two things are clear: the state is reduced to the level of a private citizen since the activities of each are brought within the scope of an objective law; and, further, there is no distinction between the nature of public and of private law, since each is subject to the criterion of social solidarity' (Laski 1933, p. 56). Duguit did not believe in absolute power, whether or not it was subject to control. Power was subject to inherent limitations and the rulers, defined as those who possessed the power of implementing decisions, had only a limited mandate to act in the public interest or in the interests of social solidarity:

Government and its officials are no longer the masters of men imposing the sovereign will on their subjects. They are no longer the organs of a corporate person issuing its commands. They are simply the managers of the nation's business. It should thus be clear, contrary to the usual notion, that the growth and extension of state activity does not necessarily increase the government's power. Their business increases, their duties expand; but their right of control is extinct because no one any longer believes in it . . .

In whatever manner the business of the state is managed its fundamental idea is thus clear: government must perform certain definite functions. As a consequence a public service is an institution of a rigorously objective order controlled by principles equally imposed on the government and its subjects. [Duguit 1921, pp. 51–4.]

Like Dicey's, Duguit's theory was individualistic, though the individualism differed in its character. It was:

... a doctrine which makes against authoritarianism. The only justification for any public act is that its result in public good should be commensurate with the force that is involved in its exercise. But that, after all, is ultimately a matter for the private judgement of each one of us; and a real impetus is thus given to the initiative of the private citizen. Room is left for that reservoir of individualism upon which, in the last resort, so much of the welfare of society depends. [Laski 1933, pp. 56–7.]

What was the function of public law in Duguit's state? First and foremost, to provide the framework inside which the efficient operation of the public services could at all times be assured. Regulation and rules, which set out the principles of operation, at once become more important than the adjudication of disputes. Duguit's theory did find a place for adjudication. Administrative law limited state action in two distinct ways: (a) through the notion that the state can act only in the public interest and for the public good and (b) through the principle that the state must observe the law. In case of doubt, administrative courts could pronounce on the legality of administrative action. They had a third function. Duguit believed that the state was fully responsible for its acts and that every citizen was entitled to equality of treatment. Where a citizen suffered abnormal loss in the interest of the collectivity, compensation was due; loss caused by a state enterprise must be repaired by the state. These two ideas formed a complete new theory of administrative liability (Duguit 1921, pp. 197–242). Disputes between citizen and state were to be referred to administrative courts.

2 A new beginning

New accounts of administrative law, showing the influence of these various ideas, appeared in England.[5] These accounts were *administration centred*. The role of administrative law was not to act as a counterweight to the interventionist state but to facilitate government action. The theories were permissive rather than negative:

The task of the lawyer as such is not to declare that modern interventionism is pernicious, but, seeing that all modern states have adopted the policy, to advise as to the technical devices which are necessary to make the policy efficient and to provide justice for individuals ... The problem to be discussed is the division of powers between administrators and judges and, given that judges must exercise some functions, the kind of courts and the judicial procedure necessary to make the exercise of the functions most efficient. [Jennings 1936, p. 430.]

The centre of gravity changed naturally from judge-made law to legislation and regulation. Compare the width of Jennings' definition with that proposed by Wade (see above, p. 12). Attitudes towards state intervention underlie their different descriptions:

Administrative law is the law relating to the Administration. It determines the organisation, powers and duties of administrative authorities. Where the political organisation of the country is highly developed, as it is in England, administrative law is a large and important branch of the law. It includes the law relating to public utility companies, and the legal powers which these authorities exercise. Or, looking at the subject from the functional instead of the institutional point of view, we may say that it includes the law relating to public health, the law of highways, the law of social insurance, the law of education, and the law relating to the provision of gas, water, and electricity. These are examples only, for a list of the powers of the administrative authorities would occupy a long catalogue. [Jennings 1938, p. 194.]

We can find in these two passages mention of every preoccupation characteristic of green light theory. In the first, we see tacit approval of the interventionist state. Only the apolitical role of technical adviser is allocated to the lawyer. The reference to 'efficiency' is significant. Procedural efficiency has become a major goal of many modern functionalist writers. This passage also opens for discussion the constitutional role of the courts and the proper ambit of judicial influence. The second passage defines administrative law widely, suggesting the priority of legislation and regulation. One senses, too, the functionalist concern with how things actually work; this leads Jennings towards a *descriptive* role for academic administrative law.

At this point it is convenient to distinguish three main areas of interest for green light theorists. Two can be shortly disposed of because they are developed at length in other chapters; the third needs fuller treatment at this stage.

A first task for administrative lawyers is to examine the system in operation. This can be done in two ways. Cohen's functionalist method can be applied to the traditional subject matter of administrative law. Robson, for example, produced a classic study of administrative adjudication, *Justice and Administrative Law* (1928), which ultimately persuaded him of the necessity for an administrative appeals tribunal. Later in this book, we shall try to apply the functionalist method to the subject of judicial review, asking how it really operates and whether its control of administration is really as effective as red light theory implies. Alternatively, administrative lawyers can be 'functionalist' in the sense in which Jennings uses the word. The author concentrates his attention on a specific area of government activity, the operation of which he describes. Jennings himself published studies of housing law.[6] Later authors added extended studies of new and developing areas of administrative activity: welfare, planning, housing etc. Short functionalist studies of this type may be found at the end of this book.

Perhaps because of their inter-disciplinary character, functionalist studies are often more innovative. In the study of welfare and immigration for example, the ideas of non-lawyers are helpful in interpreting concepts like 'discretion', crucial to administrative law. One unhappy consequence of their development was, however, that as the new subjects took root and blossomed in their own right, the parent stock of administrative law was left as an unreformed core subject, dominated by general principles and the tradition of legalism.

A second concern of many green light writers is to minimize the influence of courts. Courts, with their legalistic values, are seen as obstacles to progress and the control which they exercise as unrepresentative and undemocratic. Jennings introduces, but never comes to grips with, the issue of 'justiciability'. Griffith affirms his faith in the political and parliamentary process in 'The Political Constitution' (1979). Dismissing the fashionable constitutional device of a Bill of Rights, justiciable and enforceable in courts of law, to enshrine and protect individual 'rights', Griffith describes these rights as group interests which he designates 'claims'. These claims, enforced by one class of society against others through the political process, are inevitably divisive and contentious. In Chapter 11, we will see how Griffith develops the argument by prescribing a reduced role for the judiciary and a diminution in the amount of discretionary power at its disposal.

Discussing the allocation of functions in the English governmental and administrative system, Ganz advances a similar argument. First, she criticizes the way in which theories of the balanced constitution seek to distinguish 'legislative', 'judicial' and 'administrative' functions. Like Jennings, she sees decision-taking as a spectrum ranging from 'fixed rules at one end of the spectrum to a purely discretionary act at the other. No clear lines can be drawn where the one activity stops and the other begins as they shade off into one another imperceptibly'. Each involves value-judgements. 'Rules are themselves value-judgements whereas discretion is the power to make a value-judgement. In practice the difference may not be very great . . . where the rule contains words such as "reasonable" which amount to a delegation of discretion to make value-judgements.' Everything, therefore, *depends on the choice of decision-maker*:

When the problem arises of who should make decisions in a particular field the controversy should centre not on whether these involve the application of rules or discretion but on who should make the necessary value-judgements. Looking at this from the point of view of the legislature there is a wide area of choice.

Parliament may make the value-judgements itself and embody them in reasonably precise rules in statutes. This narrows the area of discretion to be exercised by whoever is charged with the application of the rules but does not eliminate it. The choice has to be made between the courts, administrative tribunals and sometimes even ministers or independent statutory bodies as interpreters of the rules laid down.

In many areas it is not, however, possible or even desirable to formulate value-judgements in the shape of detailed rules. Especially in a new field it may be necessary to make value-judgements on a case-to-case basis. This can be done by laying down rules embodying very broad standards or conferring wide discretionary powers. These powers may also be given to courts, administrative tribunals, Ministers or a specially created statutory body. [Ganz 1972, pp. 215–16.]

In the work of some green light theorists, the view is expressed that courts should not interfere with the allocation of functions as established by statute. For example, Griffith argues that the *Anisminic* case (below, p. 102) is wrongly decided because it arrogated to the House of Lords a decision which Parliament had allocated to the Foreign Compensation Commission. Where courts cross jurisdictional boundaries to impose 'judicial' procedures on the administration or to rule on 'political questions', it is argued that they are only substituting their own value-judgements for those of the rightful decision-maker. We will leave this point here to pick it up again in the *Laker* case.

3 Green light theory and control

Few administrative lawyers – or, indeed, citizens – would wish to set sail in a barque as frail as that of ministerial responsibility. If the model of law is to be abandoned, then many feel that something other than the traditional model of government must take its place.

Because it revealed the inadequacies of ministerial responsibility, Crichel Down is often described as the beginning of modern administrative law. Very briefly,[7] Crichel Down was acquired before the Second World War by the Air Ministry as a bombing range. Subsequently, when no longer required for these purposes, it was transferred to the Ministry of Agriculture. Later, a dispute arose when the Ministry, wishing to dispose of the land, instead of allowing its original owners to buy it back, tried to let it as a single unit to a new tenant. Fierce objections from the original owners forced a public inquiry which established the responsibility of civil servants both for the policy and also for its execution. Crichel Down exposed a world of administrative policy and decision-making apparently immune from political and parliamentary controls. In Griffith's phrase, 'the fundamental defect revealed was not a failure in the constitutional relations of those involved nor the policy decisions nor even the length of the struggle [the complainant] had to wage. It was in the method and therefore in the mental processes of the officials' (Griffith 1955, p. 569). But Griffith concluded that the civil service must be left to put its own house in order. He was content to rely on 'that personal integrity which is so much more than an absence of corruption'. Once again, we find the characteristic reliance on political and administrative institutions. For those who were less trusting, yet did not wish to tip the balance too far in the direction of judicial control, the challenge was to provide alternatives. In the aftermath of Crichel Down, this became a major preoccupation for administrative lawyers and a consensus probably existed that more effective controls were needed.

Discussing 'control' theories of administrative law, we did not stop to consider what was meant by the word. Control can be symbolic or real; it can mean to check, restrain or govern. Griffith and Street (1952, p. 24) clearly sense latent ambiguities. They say 'A great deal turns on the meaning which is attached to the word "controls". Banks control a river; a driver controls his car. The influence of a parent over a child may be greater than the power of a prison guard over a convict.' If you try applying these metaphors to the administrative process, you will see that these 'controls' are direct and internal rather than indirect and external. Dicey's controls were *external*; to extend our metaphors, a river bank may be inspected by an officer of the catchment board to see that it is in good repair; a policeman may stop the driver and caution him for speeding; a health visitor may advise the child's parents to exert a different kind of influence; and the prison guard may be questioned by the board of visitors. These are all controls, but they are external.

The idea of the balanced constitution emphasizes external control. Obviously, however, the first control of administrative activity is *internal* and supervisory. Consider the doctrine of individual ministerial responsibility. One function of the doctrine is to provide internal control because the minister must, as head of his department, supervise the activities of his subordinates by establishing policies and checking the way in which they are implemented. The doctrine also provides for external control through responsibility to Parliament, but this is envisaged as a last resort. And Griffith hints at the superiority of internal control when he prescribes as a remedy for Crichel Down 'more "red tape" not less'.

Because they see their own function as the resolution of disputes, and because they see the administrative function from outside, lawyers traditionally emphasize firefighting and adjudication. To the lawyer, law is the policeman; it operates as an external control, often retrospectively. The search for bureaucratic efficiency leads administrators to prefer firewatching to firefighting. As prevention is proverbially better than cure, so firewatching is more efficient than firefighting. Jennings' use of the adjective 'efficient' signified a shift of emphasis in modern administrative law and, indeed, a foretaste of the priorities in modern public administration.

A second distinction is between *prospective* and *retrospective* control. Judicial review of administrative action is primarily retrospective yet it does possess a prospective element if the administration accepts that judicial precedent establishes the limits of its future conduct. Legislation can also be described as a prospective control. Like the banks of the river, legislation controls administrative activity by prescribing its limits.

When an administrator asks 'May I do X?' the lawyer replies 'if the law permits'. He knows where to find the law: statute, regulations, precedent etc, and he knows how to rank it when it has been found. Lawyers like to assume that administrators approach law in the same way:

To the public administrator, law is something very positive and concrete. It is his authority. The term he customarily uses to describe it is 'my mandate'. It is 'his' law, something he feels a proprietary interest in. It does three things: tells him what the legislature expects him to accomplish, fixes limits to his authority, and sets forth the substantive and procedural rights of the individual and group. Having a positive view of his mandate, the administrator considers himself both an interpreter and a builder. He is a builder because every time he applies *old* law to new situations he builds the law. Therefore law, like administration, is government in action. It is operational, functional, sociological.

Like the judge, the administrator 'finds' the law . . . [He proceeds by asking] What is our statutory authority? What is the ruling case law as found in court cases that serve as precedents? What are our own sublegislative or policy interpretations of statutory authority by means of which we give effect to steps in the administrative unfolding of the law not specifically provided in the words of the statute? [Dimock 1980, p. 31.]

This passage contains clues to the fact that the author had a legal training. Generally speaking, administrators do not seek their mandate in law but in policy; they are, in other words, policy-orientated. Viewed positively, administrators see law as a set of pegs on which to hang policies; viewed negatively, the law may be a series of hurdles to be jumped before policy can be implemented. If law conflicts with policy, the administrator tries to change the law and, if this proves impossible, he may sometimes set it aside or ignore it. Again, consider Dimock's neat pyramid of legal norms; statute, case law, formal rules. There is much evidence that administrators do not always understand this hierarchy. They follow policy directives in preference to regulations, do not always know of the existence of case law or realize its significance. This partly represents divergent attitudes of the two professions, lawyer and administrator, which it is well to bear in mind. As we develop the argument in later chapters, however, an infinitely more complex pattern will emerge.

The trend of modern administrative law is towards controls which are internal and prospective. You will see in Chapter 5 how, under the influence of Davis, the focus has shifted from adjudication (external) to rule-making (internal) as a means of control. New administrative agencies, like the Council on Tribunals, have been set up to carry out firewatching functions. Such agencies, like the Parliamentary Commissioner (PCA) or the Supplementary Benefits Commission (SBC) are often only semi-autonomous. These developments are frequently misunderstood by administrative lawyers who, using the courts as their paradigm, doubt the independence and integrity of the new institutions. Again, because they rely on negotiation rather than command ('control'), they are often described as 'toothless watchdogs'. This controversy will recur in later chapters.

Green light theorists prefer political controls. We have mentioned Griffith's faith in control by Parliament. Throughout his writings, he also emphasizes the need for access to information, open government, a free and powerful press. Jennings and Robson each showed interest in the idea of an administrative court,[8] while Laski advocated citizen participation:

During most of his long career, Harold Laski was aware of the bureaucratic problem. In addition to proposing a system of parliamentary advisory committees to oversee the work of government departments, he advised attaching to each department an advisory committee of citizens affected by its operations and the creation of a small, clearly impartial committee to investigate fully serious charges against departments. [Gwyn 1971, p. 389.]

Participation in government is not a new idea, but it is blurred by our traditional theory of representation, according to which we all participate in government through our elected representative(s). When, in 1953, for example, the House of Commons discussed the effectiveness of the procedures for scrutinizing delegated legislation, a Member remarked 'It has been perhaps rather noticeable that all through this afternoon we have been discussing this merely from the point of view of Parliament and MPs. We have not let the public creep into the discussion at all.' He wanted to set up a procedure whereby members of the public could complain of, or ask for changes in, regulations, but the idea was dropped because 'aggrieved persons have their grievances brought to the attention of the House by Members' (HC 310 (1952/3), p. 141). But when, in 1966, the introduction of an ombudsman ('grievance man') was under discussion and Members used the same argument, it did not succeed. Concessions were made in the form of 'the MP filter', but their objections could not prevent the new institution entirely.

In the early years of this century, committees were seen as a useful, procedural device to ensure public participation:[9]

If bureaucracy is to be controlled, the future lies with increasing the opportunities of the public to temper the rule of the official. The system of administration by committee, the basis of modern local government, is one of the healthiest features of to-day. For it affords a means of imposing a more or less personal responsibility to its members on the officials of the particular service administered by the committee ... In short, any device to secure more directly government by the consent of the governed rather than by rule of the expert is to be commended to those who share Dicey's ideal of democracy and distrust and dislike of the expert. [E. C. S. Wade 1939, pp. 494–5.]

In recent years, an important goal for many administrative lawyers has been to secure control of the decision-taking process through participation at an early stage. To return to our metaphors, we might describe the aim as being to share in mapping the course of the administrative river. Complex and sophisticated machinery has been devised, especially in the area of land-use planning, to secure participation in the administrative process. But not only does participation theory cut across our dominant political traditions; it is also at cross-purposes with the individualistic model of our legal process. Characteristically, pressure groups, rather than individuals, are able to participate. This clash of objectives is discussed at length in Chapter 15. Here it is enough to notice that the problem exists.

4 Stop, go, amber?

If the arrangement of our chapters has suggested polarity, this is an over-simplification. The history of political ideas in Britain is peculiarly rich, the tradition of public law less so. It is nonetheless a plural tradition, even if this truth has sometimes been ignored. Few lawyers would today advocate a theory of the balanced constitution as extreme as that of Hewart; few people, on the other hand, would be content to leave control entirely to Parliament. Bradley (1981) deplored the polarization of public law and exhorted public lawyers to occupy the middle ground. In fact, the middle ground was already densely populated. There was, and had been for many years, a measure of consensus about the need for a sophisticated system of administrative law to monitor and discipline the powers of the state. Red light theorists were coming to accept that these powers were here to stay; green light theorists were sensitive to the needs of individuals.[10] Keeton (1949, p. 230), reflecting on the imminent demise of the common law, said of the Donoughmore Committee that in no important respect did it 'influence, much less delay, the onrush of administrative power, and the supersession of the ordinary forms of law which is today taking place'. He thought the day of peoples' courts was in sight, 'so far have we travelled in the past twenty years'. Yet Keeton himself warned the lawyers that their case was not infallible, 'it may well be that the administrator has as strong a case against [the lawyer] as he has against the administrator'. Twenty-five years later, peoples' courts had not arrived, the Franks Committee had tilted the balance of power sharply in favour of the 'ordinary' courts (see below, Chapter 4) and Scarman, reflecting on the still imminent demise of the common law, felt able to advise lawyers that the remedy lay entirely in their own hands. If lawyers were more imaginative in their approach to developing areas like welfare law, the power of the common law would be renewed.[11]

Yardley, like Wade, sees control by courts as the centrepiece of administrative law, but nonetheless defines its functions as 'the control of power, and the maintenance of a fair balance between the competing interests of the administration (central government, local government or specialised agencies) and the citizen' (Yardley 1981, p. viii). A humane administration which would combine efficiency with fairness became the goal for administrators and administrative lawyers alike.

Courts came under pressure to open their doors and widen their horizons. Charles Reich, in a classic article, argued that courts can, and should, extend their protection to a wider selection of 'property interests'. The courts should, in other words, take on the duty of securing individual interests against an increasingly powerful state:

One of the most important developments in the United States during the past decade has been the emergence of government as a major source of wealth. Government is a gigantic syphon. It draws in revenue and power, and pours forth wealth: money, benefits, services, contracts, franchises, and licenses. Government has always had this function. But while in early times it was minor, today's distribution of largesse is on a vast, imperial scale.

The valuables dispensed by government take many forms, but they all share one characteristic. They are steadily taking the place of traditional forms of wealth – forms which are held as private property. Social insurance substitutes for savings; a government contract replaces a businessman's customers and goodwill. The wealth of more and more Americans depends upon a relationship to government. Increasingly, Americans live on government largesse – allocated by government on its own terms, and held by recipients subject to conditions which express 'the public interest'.

Eventually those forms of largesse which are closely linked to status must be deemed to be held as of right. The presumption should be that the professional man will keep his license, and the welfare recipient his pension. These interests should be 'vested'. If revocation is necessary, not by reason of the fault of the individual holder, but by reason of overriding demands of public policy, perhaps payment of just compensation would be appropriate. The individual should not bear the entire loss for a remedy primarily intended to benefit the community.

The concept of right is most urgently needed with respect to benefits like unemployment compensation, public assistance, and old age insurance . . . Only by making such benefits into rights can the welfare state achieve its goal of providing a secure minimum basis for individual well-being and dignity in a society where each man cannot be wholly the master of his own destiny . . .

If the individual is to survive in a collective society, he must have protection against its ruthless pressures. There must be sanctuaries or enclaves where no majority can reach. To shelter the solitary human spirit, does not merely make possible the fulfilment of individuals; it also gives society the power to change, to grow, and to regenerate, and hence to endure. These were the objects which property sought to achieve, and can no longer achieve. The challenge of the future will be to construct, for the society that is coming, institutions and laws to carry on this work . . . We must create a new property. [Reich 1964, pp. 733, 785–7.]

Students of the power game were observing the rise of 'corporatism', whereby a centralized state combines with the giant enterprises of modern capitalism to channel power into the hands of a powerful elite.[12] In the passages which follow, the authors' definitions of corporatism vary as opinion varies concerning the source of danger. The political right fears the bureaucratic network of departments, nationalized industry and semi-autonomous boards and commissions. It aims to dismantle or 'privatize' the proliferating organisms of the state. The political left fears monopolist, multi-national corporations, against which it hopes to oppose the power of the state in combination with organized labour. But the essence of corporatism is centralization and a state in which public and private are inextricably tangled.[13] Notice how Reich poses individuals against giant corporations, an interesting variant on traditional administrative law:

The American Corporate State today can be thought of as a single vast corporation, with every person as an involuntary member and employee. It consists primarily of large industrial organizations, plus non-profit institutions such as foundations and the educational system, all related to the whole as divisions to a business corporation. Government is only a part of the state, but government coordinates it and provides a variety of needed services. The Corporate State is a complete reversal of the original American ideal and plan. The State, and not the market or the people or any abstract economic laws, determines what shall be produced, what shall be consumed, and how it shall be allocated. It determines, for example, that railroads shall decay while highways flourish; that coal miners shall be poor and advertising executives rich. Jobs and occupations in the society are rigidly defined and controlled, and arranged in a hierarchy of rewards, status, and authority. An individual can move from one position to another, but he gains little freedom thereby, for in each position he is subject to conditions imposed upon it; individuals have no protected area of liberty, privacy or individual sovereignty beyond the reach of the State. The State is subject neither to democratic controls, constitutional limits, or legal regulation. [Reich 1970, pp. 89–90.]

Observers predicted that traditional, democratic controls would be inadequate to tame the new Leviathan of economic planning. Shonfield, for example, claimed that corporatism and economic regulation are difficult to reconcile with:

> . . . the existing structure of Western democratic institutions. Who controls the planners? It is not just a matter of getting parliamentary approval for the broad outline of a scheme for raising the standard of living of a nation by a certain amount over a stated period of years. A plan is a living body of economic policy, adapting itself constantly to changing circumstances, sometimes undergoing drastic alteration in its component parts in order to secure particular objectives which come in time to acquire a new order of priority. The traditional Western parliament, a non-expert body, by instinct non-interventionist unless there is some manifest abuse or need for legislation, is hardly equipped for the job of supervising the systematic intervention which planning implies. That is perhaps the justification for the tacit consensus among the planners that it is, on the whole, best to bypass the parliamentary process. [Shonfield 1965, p. 230.]

But law, the other dimension of the balanced constitution, was no more effective. Two reasons were advanced. First, law had been subverted from a 'control' to an administrative technology. Is this the logical product of Jennings' definition?

> The Corporate State is a distinctively legalistic society. It utilizes law for every facet of its activity – there has probably never been a society with so much law, or where law is so important. Thus it might be expected that law would represent a significant control over the power of the Corporate State, and a source of guidelines for it. But law in the Corporate State is something very different from a codification of values. The State has transformed it.
> During the New Deal period the law was gradually changed from a medium which carried traditional values of its own to a value-free medium that could be adapted to serve 'public policy', which became the 'public interest' of the Corporate State. This produced law that fell into line with the requirements of organization and technology, and that supported the demands of administration rather than protecting the individual. Once law had assumed this role, there began a vast proliferation of laws, statutes, regulations, and decisions. For the law began to be employed to aid all of the work of the Corporate State by compelling obedience to the State's constantly increasing demands. [Reich 1970, pp. 117–18.]

And Shonfield describes how the procedural controls for which administrative law had so ardently been striving could be subverted in the same way:

> What is characteristic of a would-be 'nomocracy' like Britain is an overwhelming emphasis on legal procedure. Again, this has in the past helped to secure some large gains in individual liberty. It still gives an Englishman more protection against arbitrary imprisonment, for example, than a Frenchman has. But procedural guarantees, however elaborate, are a feeble

weapon against a determined official who knows how to stick to the formalities and to use them to get his own way. They then appear as a ceremonial hoax, the more obnoxious for the pretence of having something to do with human rights . . . [[14]]

The exclusive concern with judicial ritual is itself a reflection of the myth that the law, when properly made, is fixed, transparent and unequivocal. The only problem then is to provide a legal procedure which will ensure that the facts of any case are sufficiently established to attract the relevant bit of the law to its judgment. The procedural approach is of course a convenient one; it is politically attractive; above all, it saves fuss, involving as it does no more interference than that of a referee whom the players like to have about in order to ensure that they all stick to the rules of the game. [Shonfield 1965, pp. 419–20.]

Secondly, Winckler argues[15] that a characteristic of the corporate state is a 'retreat from legalism'. Although in the corporate state 'all distinction between law and policy disappears', government is still unwilling to submit to the procedural restraints and inhibitions of legalism:

A corporatist State will resist the use of law for both practical and ideological reasons. Practically, corporatism is a goal-oriented system in which success in the achievement of collective goals is one of the primary values. In pursuit of these goals, a corporatist State will have to adjust its policies, techniques and instruments in response to changing problems and circumstances and to changes in the goals themselves. Against that requirement, the law is in three senses a fetter. First, the law is a source of delay. The elaborate formal process of legislative enactment means that it is perpetually liable to be in arrears of current needs. Secondly and more important, the law is a constraint. So are judicial precedents. Indeed, all rules are constraints. This is obvious in the case of prohibitions. But prescriptive rules are likewise constraining because they enjoin some forms of behaviour rather than others. A goal-oriented State will seek to avoid constraints on its freedom of action. In theory, a corporatist State will only try to avoid the interdictive functions of law. But this is impossible, because the constraints of law are part of the very notion of a rule. Thus it will be inclined to avoid the use of law altogether. More exactly and also more broadly, it will be inclined to resist the codification of all its operating rules, in all forms – statutes, administrative regulations, department circulars, memoranda of guidance, advisory notes, white papers, policy guidelines, statements of intent, etc. Thirdly, the technicalities of due process may hinder the prompt restoration of productive activity, in the event of a dispute. The focus on goal-achievement inevitably inclines a corporatist state to resist codification. It is not just a narrow, positivist conception of law which is being rejected. There is no definition of 'law' however reconceptualised (administrative law, informal law, delegated legislation, living law, natural law, free law, will of the sovereign, *voluntas*, prerogative etc) which can encompass such a fundamental rejection of all rule codification. Corporatism is in principle antinomian. [Winckler 1975, pp. 117–18.]

5 **The Skytrain affair**

One celebrated modern decision, *Laker Airways* v. *Department of Trade* [1977] QB 643, epitomizes many of the problems with which modern administrative law is called upon to deal. We have been discussing 'corporatism'. The *Laker* case involves on one side the state, represented by successive governments of different political persuasions and the Civil Aviation Authority (CAA), a semi-autonomous institution with ill-defined functions; on the other side, the 'individual' is represented by Laker Airways. In the wings stand other international corporations, a state-owned enterprise (British Airways) and the United States Government. The case concerned the grant, followed by the withdrawal, of a licence to run a trans-Atlantic passenger service (Skytrain) in competition with other designated airlines. Is this valuable franchise an example of the 'new property' which Reich urges courts to protect?

Again, the case raises important questions concerning the allocation of functions. Ganz argued that courts should follow the intention of Parliament in this matter. But this case is very complex. The background to the disputed legislation, the Civil Aviation Act 1971, was one of continuous disagreement. Before 1971 licensing was carried out by the Air Transport Licensing Board (ATLB) with right of appeal to the Minister. The question of possible reform was originally referred to a Select Committee (the Edwards Committee) which recommended delegation of licensing to an *independent* body (see Cmnd 4018). This would have pleased the independent airlines, which felt that they did not get a fair deal from a government department. But the Board of Trade was convinced that the Minister must retain a firm grip on policy if international obligations were to be carried out and the national interest protected. His overall control must extend to licensing. So the 1971 Act represented the same uneasy compromise as its predecessor of 1960. The 1971 Act established the CAA which was responsible (inter alia) for licensing. S.3(1) set out statutory policy objectives for the CAA. S.3(2) allowed the Minister to issue 'guidance' to the CAA in the performance of its functions while s.4 allowed him to give express 'directions' in certain cases, specified by the section. Read the sections carefully. Why did the draftsman distinguish 'guidance' from 'directions'? Does the ministerial power to give guidance in s.3(2) prevail over the statutory criteria in s.3(1) or vice versa?

3(1) It shall be the duty of the Authority to perform the functions conferred on it otherwise than by this section in the manner which it considers is best calculated – (a) to secure that British airlines provide air transport services which satisfy all substantial categories of public demand (so far as British airlines may reasonably be expected to provide such services) at the lowest charges consistent with a high standard of safety in operating the services and an economic return to efficient operators on the sums invested in providing the services and with securing the sound development of the civil air transport industry of the United Kingdom; (b) to secure that at least one major British airline which is not controlled by the British Airways Board has opportunities to participate in providing, on charter and other terms, the air transport services mentioned in the preceding paragraph . . . (2) Subject to the following subsection, the Secretary of State may from time to time, after consultation with the Authority give guidance to the Authority in writing with respect to the performance of the functions conferred on it otherwise than by this subsection; and it shall be the duty of the Authority to perform those functions in such a manner as it considers is in accordance with the guidance for the time being given to it in pursuance of this subsection. (3) No guidance shall be given to the Authority in pursuance of the preceding subsection unless a draft of the document containing it has been approved by a resolution of each House of Parliament.

S.4: . . . (3) The Secretary of State may, after consultation with the Authority, give to the Authority directions to do a particular thing which it has power to do or refrain from doing a particular thing if the Secretary of State considers it appropriate to give such directions – (a) in the interests of national security; or (b) in connection with any matter appearing to the Secretary of State to affect the relations of the United Kingdom with a country or territory outside the United Kingdom; or (c) in order to discharge or facilitate the discharge of an obligation binding on the United Kingdom by virtue of its being a member of an international organisation or a party to an international agreement; . . . and in so far as any directions given in pursuance of this subsection conflict with the requirements of any provision of this Act except subsections (1) and (2) of this section those requirements shall be disregarded.

Early in 1972 the Minister issued his first guidance under the 1971 Act (Cmnd 4899). Later in the year Laker applied for a licence to run a Skytrain service to the United States, in competition with British Airways and British Caledonian. The first step was to acquire a licence. After a hearing at which all three parties were represented, a licence was granted and upheld on appeal by the Minister. Laker now needed 'designation' as a carrier on the Atlantic route. The British Government 'designated' Laker and requested ratification by the US Government. A hearing was held by an administrative judge after which the US Civil Aeronautics Board (CAB) recommended the issue of a 'foreign air carrier permit'. This recommendation was never ratified by the President. In January 1975, the CAA refused an application by British Airways to revoke the licence. But in Britain, the Government had changed. A Labour Minister told the House of Commons that the Skytrain service could not be allowed to start. The British Government now refused to 'designate' Laker as a permitted carrier. Consequently, the CAB withdrew its unratified US permit. In the litigation which followed, the Government claimed that the power to 'designate' was a prerogative power.

The Minister issued new guidance (Cmnd 6400), duly approved in terms of s.3(3). The relevant paragraphs read:

Para. 7: In the case of long-haul scheduled services . . . the Authority should not . . . license more than one British airline to serve the same route . . . The Authority should review existing licences and exemptions in the light of this paragraph and take appropriate action . . .

Para. 8: Nothing in paragraph 7 should, however, prevent the licensing of: . . . (b) . . . another British airline to provide a scheduled service within British Airways' sphere of interest . . . provided British Airways has given its consent . . .

The Court of Appeal granted declarations that the guidance was ultra vires:

LORD DENNING MR: In carrying out its functions (including granting of licences) the Authority has to do its best to satisfy [the] objectives in s.3.(1) . . . Those objectives are expressed in very general terms. In putting them into practice, Parliament thought that some guidance would be desirable for the Authority. So it provided for it in section 3(2) and (3) . . . One of the matters much discussed before us is the scope of the 'guidance' authorised by those provisions. In my opinion the Secretary of State can give guidance by way of explanation or amplification of, or supplement to, the general objectives: but not so as to reverse or contradict them . . .

Section 4 of the statute confers exceptional powers on the Secretary of State. It enables him to override the statutory requirements as to licences and also to by-pass the general objectives. But only in carefully defined circumstances . . . Section 4(3) confers large powers in respect of international relations. For instance, if the Secretary of State thought that one of our airlines was acting in such a way as to affect our relations with another country, he could direct the Authority to revoke its licence. Or if diplomatic pressure was brought for the purpose, he could direct the revocation of the licence. And he could do this without any inquiry or hearing at all. The Secretary of State would have to consult the Authority before issuing a direction, but that is all. Once he gave a direction, it could not be challenged in the courts. The only way would be by a question in the House . . .

The word 'direction' in section 4 is in stark contrast with the word 'guidance' in section 3 . . . It denotes an order or command which must be obeyed, even though it may be contrary to the general objectives and provisions of the statute. But the word 'guidance' in section 3 does not denote an order or command. It cannot be used so as to reverse or contradict the general objectives or provisions of the Statute. It can only be used so as to explain, amplify or supplement them. So long as the 'guidance' given by the Secretary of State keeps within the due bounds of guidance, the Authority is under a duty to follow his guidance. Even so, the Authority is allowed some degree of flexibility. It is to perform its function 'in such a manner as it considers is in accordance with the guidance'. So, while it is obliged to follow the guidance, the manner of doing so is for the Authority itself. But if the Secretary of State goes beyond the bounds of 'guidance' he exceeds his powers: and the Authority is under no obligation to obey him . . .

Ultra vires
. . . The new policy guidance of 1976 cuts right across [the] statutory objectives. It lays down a new policy altogether. Whereas the statutory objectives made it clear that the British Airways Board was not to have a monopoly, but that at least one other British airline should have an opportunity to participate, the new policy guidance says that the British Airways Board is to have a monopoly. No competition is to be allowed. And no other British airline is to be licensed unless British Airways had given its consent. This guidance was not a mere temporary measure. It was to last for a considerable period of years.

Those provisions disclose so complete a reversal of policy that to my mind the White Paper cannot be regarded as giving 'guidance' at all. In marching terms it does not say 'right incline' or 'left incline'. It says 'right about turn'. That is not guidance, but the reverse of it.

There is no doubt that the Secretary of State acted with the best of motives in formulating this new policy – and it may well have been the right policy – but I am afraid that he went about it in the wrong way. Seeing that the old policy had been laid down in an Act of Parliament, then, in order to reverse it, he should have introduced an amending bill and got Parliament to sanction it. He was advised, apparently, that it was not necessary, and that it could be done by 'guidance'. That, I think was a mistake . . . It was in this respect ultra vires and the judge was right so to declare.

Prerogative
The Attorney-General contended that the power of the Secretary of State 'to withdraw' the designation was a prerogative power which could not be examined in the courts. It was a power arising under a treaty which, he said, was outside the cognizance of the courts. The Attorney-General recognised that by withdrawing the designation, the Secretary of State would put a stop to Skytrain, but he said that he could do it all the same. No matter that Laker Airways had expended £6 million to £7 million on the faith of the designation, the Secretary of State could withdraw it without paying a penny compensation . . .

The prerogative is a discretionary power exercisable by the executive government for the public good, in certain spheres of governmental activity

56   LAW AND ADMINISTRATION

for which the law has made no provision, such as the war prerogative (of requisitioning property for the defence of the realm), or the treaty prerogative (of making treaties with foreign powers). The law does not interfere with the proper exercise of the discretion by the executive in those situations: but it can set limits by defining the bounds of the activity: and it can intervene if the discretion is exercised improperly or mistakenly. That is a fundamental principle of our constitution . . .

[Holding that the court could review the exercise of the prerogative powers, Lord Denning continued:]

It is necessary to see just how far Skytrain had got . . . The one thing that remained was for the President to sign the United States of America permit: but this was little more than a formality, seeing that the President was under a treaty obligation to sign it 'without undue delay' . . . The question is: Was it proper for the Secretary of State at that stage to stop it himself? Could he do it by withdrawing the designation . . . ?

In answering this question, it is important to notice that if there was a proper case for stopping Skytrain, there were available some perfectly good means of doing it. They were already provided by the Statute. One particular means was provided by section 4 of the Act. Under that section the Secretary of State could himself get the licence revoked. He could direct the Civil Aviation Authority to revoke it and they would have to obey . . . But in this case the Secretary of State did not give any direction under section 4. So, presumably, the circumstances did not exist to permit him to do so. Another means of stopping Skytrain would be for the British Airways Board to apply again to the Civil Aviation Authority asking for the licence to be revoked – for instance, on the ground that traffic would be diverted from them. But in that case there would have to be a fresh inquiry. There would have to be a hearing at which Laker Airways could state their case. An independent and expert body would make the decision.

Seeing then that those statutory means were available for stopping Skytrain if there was a proper case for it, the question is whether the Secretary of State can stop it by . . . withdrawing the designation? Can he do indirectly that which he cannot do directly? Can he displace the statute by invoking a prerogative? If he could do this, it would mean that, by a side wind, Laker Airways Ltd. would be deprived of the protection which the statute affords them. There would be no inquiry, no hearing, no safeguard against injustice. The Secretary of State could do it off his own head – by withdrawing the designation without a word to anyone. To my mind such a procedure was never contemplated by the statute. The Secretary of State was mistaken in thinking that he could do it . . . He misdirected himself as to his powers. And it is well established law that, if a discretionary power is exercised under the influence of a misdirection, it is not properly exercised, and the court can say so.

Arguably the Government made a tactical error in choosing to rely on prerogative powers. Lawton and Ormrod LJJ thought that the prerogative was superseded by statute (see *A-G* v. *De Keyser's Royal Hotel* (below, Chapter 12)). Lord Denning MR preferred the view that the court can review the use of prerogative powers (see the later judgment of the House of Lords in *Gouriet*'s case (below, Chapter 10)). Is it desirable for the Government to possess residual powers of this type, uncontrolled by courts, whose extent is unknown?[16] Does the Government's reliance on prerogative power show an inclination to avoid 'the use of law altogether'? Is it a 'retreat from legalism'? Here Baldwin argues that the power is essential:

The judges of the Court of Appeal strove to protect the CAA's discretion and to cut down the Minister's discretion. In doing so they conceived of the CAA as a traditional body with 'quasi-judicial' functions. They saw it as a court giving licences with rights to be protected by legal due process and as a judicial body deserving protection from executive interference. They failed to see the significance of the CAA as a new form of multi-faceted agency of government, attempting to combine judicial and executive methods in a delicately balanced legal framework whilst acting in a politically contentious area. In attempting to preserve for the CAA an independent judicial status the judges sought to achieve the impossible. No one expected the CAA to be fully independent of government, in the manner of a court. As was pointed out in the Court of Appeal, the Government could always control the agency in ways other than by using Guidance. The Court of Appeal decision damaged a system of balance based on compromise because the system of control fitted no neat jurisprudential category . . . It was considered that the existence of other powers of control under the Act implied that the Guidance should not be used to stop Skytrain. This argument failed to appreciate that the Guidance system was set up to supersede those very methods of control which had produced all the deficiencies of the [previous] system.

. . . the argument that the prerogative could not be used to withdraw designation because of the existence of the licensing system and the description of the use of the prerogative as a 'side wind' seems wrongly to have assumed that the CAA was set up to control a licensing system which included all matters relating to designation and traffic rights. Civil aviation licensing has always operated in parallel to designation but always separately. The Government has always controlled designation and the possession of a licence has never been seen as a guarantee of designation. The idea that Laker had a valuable commodity in their licence wrongly assumed both that licensing gave a right and that it was conclusive of that right. It failed to recognise that the gaining and allocation of traffic rights is a complex system of regulation in itself. The prerogative to designate allowed the Government to engage in international bargaining concerning traffic rights, it was not merely a device used to interfere with CAA's licensing decisions. The Government may well have had excellent reasons for thinking that designation of Laker would adversely affect the British position in any renegotiation of the Bermuda Agreement. [Baldwin 1978, pp. 79–80.]

The 'system of balance' was changed by the Civil Aviation Act 1980. 'Guidance' was abolished. The primary objective of the CAA is now that set out in s.3(1)(a) of the 1971 Act. A new section, 23(1)(a), provides that the Authority shall have regard

(a) to any advice received from the Secretary of State with respect to the likely outcome of negotiations with the government of any other country or territory for the purpose of securing any right required for the operation by a British airline of any transport services outside the United Kingdom.

The Minister described this as 'taking both hands off the wheel', yet he preserved the right of appeal from decisions of the CAA to the Minister. The Franks Committee recommended that appeal should not normally lie from a tribunal to a Minister. Is the CAA a 'tribunal'? It exercises judicial functions and is listed in the Tribunals and Inquiries Act (see below). Yet Farmer (1974, p. 183) says 'The new Civil Aviation Authority is even less like the conventional judicial-type tribunal than Franks typified and in many ways represents an important development in the gradual evolution of independent or partly independent agencies exercising wide functions and powers along the lines of the American Federal regulatory procedures'. Did Lord Denning classify it incorrectly, as Baldwin suggests, or are the appeals arrangements inconsistent with the CAA's status? Baldwin argues (1980, p. 298) that the new legislation allows the Minister to establish policy through piecemeal adjudication – an inefficient method. The Minister should make rules. 'The imposition of broad policy would be achieved more openly by guidance. This would make Parliament the forum for essentially political decisions instead of burying these beneath a guise of quasi-judiciality.'

Earlier, we saw Ganz argue that courts should not interfere with the allocation of functions intended by Parliament. Baldwin argues that the Minister was intended to control the licensing function directly or indirectly; Lord Denning believed that 'an independent and expert body' should make the decision.

Ganz also argues that the value-judgements made in given situations depend on the choice of decision-maker. This emerges clearly from the *Laker* case, where the procedural values of lawyers conflicted with the policy judgements of Ministers. In the course of these chapters, the procedural emphasis of lawyers has been described as old-fashioned, legalistic and inappropriate to modern administration. Here Vile reminds us that procedures, too, reflect value-patterns:

Procedure, the rules governing behaviour, reflect certain value-patterns. The way in which things are done makes a very great difference. Men could be condemned to death, and in some countries are, by an administrative procedure. Roads could be built by a collegium determining by vote, after discussion, where every stroke of the pick should be made. The judicial method involving open discussion and an adversary procedure before a jury could be used to determine important questions of foreign policy and diplomacy. The results of allocating these tasks of government to be decided in this way would undoubtedly be disastrous. The present-day procedures in Britain and the United States, and the matters decided by them, have not been evolved by chance; they represent the collective judgment of centuries concerning the way in which certain things should be decided. This is not an argument against all innovation, but it should lead us to enquire into, and to examine the values which these procedures embody, and to look very closely at new procedures, and at the allocation of tasks to them, in order to be sure what we are doing. [Vile 1967, p. 347.]

The clash of values which marked the Skytrain affair demonstrates that consensus in the sense of universal agreement can seldom be obtained. By and large, however, the years since Crichel Down have seen a measure of agreement over the need for 'justice in the welfare state'. Independence as a value has been tested in the growth of administrative agencies described in the last chapter. Significantly, this period of consensus corresponds with one of broad political consensus over the aims of the welfare state. The period ended abruptly in 1979 and it may be that Bradley was unknowingly writing the obituary of consensus in administrative law. Before you read on, consider the state and the society in which you live. Is it collectivist, centralist, corporatist? What are its political objectives, its priorities and its values? What sort of administrative law would you expect from such a society?

3
Adjudication and the allocation of functions

Deciding is universal and adjudication is not. [Dimock 1980, p. 126.]

We left Vile arguing that the choice of particular procedures reflected value-judgements. Let us pursue this by considering some ways in which governmental decisions can be taken. In Chapter 5 we consider the uses of rules and of Dicey's *bête-noire*, administrative discretion. In this chapter and the next we focus on adjudication, the form of decision-making most familiar to lawyers.

We must not lose sight of what has gone before. Throughout these chapters themes and issues previously introduced will recur. We begin this chapter by addressing the question raised by Vile, why particular decisions are taken by different procedures. When we consider practical examples, the theoretical debate emerges in terms of competing descriptions of what actually happens. Different theoretical perspectives seem to produce variously coloured pictures of the facts. In Chapter 4 we examine ouster clauses, designed to protect determinations by administrative tribunals from judicial intervention. The conflict is, at one level, between two types of adjudicative institution and, at another, between Parliament and the judges. Should courts or tribunals have the final say on matters of law? Should Parliament or the judiciary answer this question? Predictably, rival theorists hold different views about what ought to happen. Ouster clauses also illustrate the point made by Ganz that value-judgements may depend on the choice of decision-maker; our two questions are inter-related since the answer to the first may be dictated by the answer to the second. Courts are unlikely to

undermine their own dominance in making authoritative pro-
nouncements on law. And the same point arises with procedural
fairness, which we consider later in this chapter. When scrutinizing
the administrative process, how far should the courts go in imposing
the procedures with which they are most familiar? From their
different perspectives, lawyers and administrators may provide
divergent answers. We will meet here another set of issues touched on
in Chapters 1 and 2. What is the nature of legal reasoning and how
should judges arrive at their decisions? This prompts questions about
whether courts are well equipped to decide complex policy issues and,
more fundamental still, whether, in our unwritten constitution, the
judiciary should claim to determine them. We are back once again
with the allocation of decision-making functions.

1 Administrative procedure and participation

Fuller (1978, p. 364) identifies the distinguishing characteristic of
adjudication as being to confer 'on the affected person a peculiar kind
of participation in the decision, that of presenting proofs and reasoned
arguments for a decision in his favor'. Its hallmark is *procedural*; for a
decision to be adjudicatory, certain procedural restraints must be
placed on the decision-maker. Jowell, discussing 'judicialisation'
which he defines as 'the process of submitting official decisions to
adjudicative procedures', compiles a list:

> The proofs and arguments that are presented by the litigants ought to be
> presented to a decision-maker who is impartial, and has not reached his
> conclusion prior to the presentation of the case of either side. The decision-
> maker should not hold private conferences with either party, otherwise the
> party excluded from the conference may not know to what issue he should
> direct his proofs and arguments. Both parties should have the opportunity to
> cross-examine the other . . . It should be borne in mind that adjudication
> referred to here constitutes an 'ideal-typical' characterisation. Clearly some
> or all of the procedural requirements mentioned could be dispensed with, and
> the decision still be regarded as having been determined by means of a
> basically adjudicative technique . . . However . . . the 'integrity' of the
> process of adjudication becomes eroded or destroyed if the reality veers too far
> from the ideal. Adjudication [is] the technique of decision-making that
> guarantees participation to parties affected, through a number of procedural
> devices. The more procedural devices used, the more 'judicialised' the
> process will be. [Jowell 1973, pp. 195–6.]

The author's 'ideal-type' is instantly recognisable; it closely
resembles procedure in the ordinary courts. But adjudication is not

restricted to its 'ideal-type'; it can encompass other proceedings, like those in administrative tribunals, which share some of the same features. Consider the two strands of natural justice, 'no man a judge in his own cause' and 'no man to be condemned unheard'. How much have these in common with Jowell's prescriptions? They too reflect procedure as it has developed in courts of law. As Ganz points out, whenever the two 'rules' are imposed on the administration, the courts are asking for adjudication to be incorporated into the administrative process. Fuller's definition concedes that adjudication is but one form of participation in decision-making; Ganz invites us to question the 'ideal-type':

The greatest disservice that administrative lawyers can render administra-tive law is to mould the administrative process in their own image. The rules of natural justice have a great deal to answer for in this respect. They are modelled on the gladiatorial combat between two parties before an impartial judge. Recent developments in the realm of administrative procedure have shown a marked trend away from the adversarial process. These have taken different forms depending on the type of case concerned. In some areas conciliation procedures have been imposed on the ordinary procedures of which another illustration is the written representation procedure which has been adopted to save time in some cases.[1] But the most important development has been the recognition that an administrative decision is not a narrow contest between two parties but a determination of what ought to be done in the public interest in a particular case. This has led to the decision-maker taking a more active part than the courts in the gathering of material on which to reach a decision and also to wider participation before the decision by persons who are not the parties to the dispute . . . As participation cannot take place meaningfully without information, it is interrelated with the demand for open government at all levels. (Ganz 1974, pp. 1–2.]

In gladiatorial combat, a participant often dies; in adjudication, one side wins, the other loses. Adjudication, subject to the possibility of out-of-court settlements, lacks the capacity for accommodation and compromise present in other decision-making techniques, like negotiation and conciliation. One reason for the growth of regulatory agencies such as ACAS and the CRE is to permit deviation from the traditional model, thereby avoiding some of its deficiencies. Ganz suggests that, in modern society, no man is an island. An adjudi-cator's decision often affects parties other than the litigants yet he is not usually required to consult them. Participation is restricted.

Some writers suggest that certain problems, which they call 'polycentric',[2] are, by their very nature, unsuitable for resolution through adjudication. As defined by Jowell (1973, p. 213), polycentric problems 'involve a complex network of relationships, with interacting points of influence. Each decision made communicates itself to other centres of decision, changing the conditions so that a new basis must be found for the next decision'. Fuller provides a hypothetical example:

Suppose in a socialist regime it were decided to have all wages and prices set by courts which would proceed after the usual forms of adjudication. It is, I assume, obvious that here is a task that could not successfully be undertaken by the adjudicative method. The . . . point is that the forms of adjudication cannot encompass and take into account the complex repercussions that may result from any change in prices or wages. A rise in the price of aluminium may affect in varying degrees the demand for, and therefore the proper price of, thirty kinds of steel, twenty kinds of plastics, an infinitude of woods, other metals etc. Each of these separate effects may have its own complex repercussions in the economy. In such a case it is simply impossible to afford each affected party a meaningful participation through proofs and arguments. It is a matter of capital importance to note that it is not merely a question of the huge number of possibly affected parties, significant as that aspect of the thing may be. A more fundamental point is that each of the various forms that award might take (say, a three-cent increase per pound, a four-cent increase, a five-cent increase, etc) would have a different set of repercussions and might require in each instance a redefinition of the 'parties affected'. [Fuller 1978, pp. 394–5.]

Here the nature of adjudication is linked with that of polycentric problems. Since adjudication depends on the presentation of 'reasoned proofs and arguments' and this cannot be 'meaningful' if the problem is polycentric, it follows that polycentric problems are unsuitable for resolution by adjudication.[3] Other informal, fluid processes of consultation and collective interest representation may, by broadening the issues, provide better solutions. However Fuller concedes that polycentricity is a matter of degree, polycentric elements existing in many questions presently resolved through adjudication. It provides an uncertain guide by which to determine whether decisions should be taken by, or *allocated* to, adjudicatory processes. 'It is not . . . a question of distinguishing black from white. It is a question of knowing when the polycentric elements have become so significant and predominant that the proper limits of adjudication have been reached' (Fuller 1978, pp. 397–8). Suppose (a) a local education authority awards a place at its most sought-after secondary school, (b) a housing authority allocates a vacant council house to persons on its housing waiting list, (c) a local office of the DHSS makes an 'exceptional needs payment' to a supplementary benefits claimant. All these decisions possess the potential for changing the basis on which subsequent applications have to be decided. As every university admissions tutor knows, being too generous with offers in November leads to rejecting better qualified students later on. In the allocation of scarce resources, one decision may communicate itself to others. Individual SB claimants can appeal to a Supplementary Benefits Appeal Tribunal (SBAT) and, under the Education Act 1980, parents unhappy with their LEA's choice of secondary school may put a case to a special 'appeals committee'.[4] But council house allocation is governed, at most, by rudimentary informal procedures. Are the three hypothetical decisions suitable for determination through adjudication? Or does the degree of polycentricity differ between them? In other words, is the extent of 'communication' always the same?

We can go further, seeking to assess the strategic advantages and disadvantages of adjudication for both administrators and direct participants. For 'litigants', participation renders it less likely that their arguments will go by default and, with personal knowledge of the facts, they may be able to present the strongest case. Moreover

the decision-maker is normally under a duty to articulate a reasoned basis for his decision. [This] will provide a check against the use of criteria that are improper, arbitrary, legalistic or that fail to achieve congruence between the effect of the decision and official objectives . . . Thus adjudication will . . . provide an opportunity for scrutiny and thus for the accountability of the decision-makers to their clientele and to the public. [Again] the . . . judicial decision must be justified by a rule, standard or principle. The relevance of ascriptive or particularistic criteria will by implication be reduced. The litigants will make their claims as members of a legally defined class, as particular instances of a generalised category. In consequence, an appeal to power, private interests, or political expediency will be inappropriate. The adjudicator will in turn be bound to evaluate the relative merits of claims in the light of accepted techniques for determining their importance and weight, and by reference to authoritative guides, irrespective of his personal view of the result. [Jowell 1973, p. 197.]

Jowell, in stressing that judgments must be justified by rule, standard or principle (see Chapter 5), is no slot-machine theorist. He does not suggest that adjudicators lack discretion. Rather, as Nonet explains, adjudicatory processes may impose certain disciplines on the decision-maker, serving, in indirect fashion, to prevent arbitrary conclusions:

The difference between administration and adjudication is not that one involves discretion whereas the other does not. The judge may, indeed, have considerable leeway in choosing and interpreting the standards he applies; his distinctiveness lies . . . in the special burden of justification that is thrown upon him . . . Accountability to rules does not necessarily reduce discretion; rather it disciplines its exercise by imposing on the decider a duty to establish a reasoned relation between his judgment and recognised authoritative standards. [Nonet 1969, p. 236.]

Such themes infused the work of Reich whose ideas proved influential in the growing welfare rights movement of the late 1960s. The expansion of the 'new property' had facilitated interference in the lives of recipients; their independence from the governors had been reduced. What was needed was 'rights' to welfare benefits (not discretionary largesse), protected by procedural restraints. Similarly, many English welfare lawyers felt that SBATs, which had largely escaped the post-war trend towards formalization, should be judicialized (below, Chapter 19).

Yet from the litigant's viewpoint, adjudication does not solve all ills. Judicialization imposes procedural safeguards; it does not change the substantive law. That SB claimants can appeal to a SBAT does not mean that their entitlements are generous. And giving rights of appeal to immigrants refused entry has not made it easier for people from New Commonwealth countries to settle in Britain; tighter immigration controls have seen to that. Again, certain litigants are better equipped than others to participate and this inequality may be accentuated by increased judicialization. Some may be confused by legal jargon while others will find the delays and expense involved intolerable. Similarly, a number of potential participants may be frightened off if the proceedings are made too formal, a point central to traditional Labour Party thinking about tribunals (below).[5]

Adjudication also possesses advantages for the administration, not all to the taste of litigants. Jowell contends that it may serve to depoliticize disputes and render official determinations more palatable. He considers adjudication more flexible than decision-making by rules. His suggestion that rules may emerge slowly from individual decisions is familiar to common lawyers.

[First] the claimant's appeal to a rule, principle or standard reduces the possibility of litigants appealing to political or private interests. In this sense, therefore, the decision-maker will be insulated from such pressures. [Secondly] a reasoned decision [will be] made and . . . openly arrived at with equal participation. The process of adjudication, irrespective of the substance of a decision, might therefore itself provide administrative action with the gloss of legitimacy. [Thirdly] adjudication . . . allows incremental elaboration of laws on the basis of a case-by-case treatment of issues. Although an organisation might feel itself bound by its own decisions, adjudication deals with a specific fact-situation, and later cases can be 'distinguished' from earlier ones on the basis of the facts. Thus, despite pressures for consistency and the gradual reduction of discretion . . . adjudication tends to allow an administrative body to deal with specific classes of case as they arise, to change its mind, and to build its commitments gradually. [Jowell 1973, pp. 197–8.]

Yet decision-making through adjudication is no administrator's panacea. Leaving aside polycentric problems, the 'impartiality' of adjudicators implies a loss of governmental control, although in practice it may be maintained by indirect methods like appointments, procedures and staffing. The growth of adjudication may also over a period of time alter the attitudes and objectives of the administrators concerned. This is one theme of *Administrative Justice* (1969), Nonet's study of the Californian Industrial Accidents Commission, a regulatory agency responsible for administering workmen's compensation laws. As more lawyers became involved and the agency's procedures formalized, the I AC gravitated from initiating new policies and carrying out surveillance and education in the workplace to determining individual claims. Adjudication represented a 'flight from policy':

When an agency becomes primarily oriented to the *recognition of claims*, when it develops this dominant concern with the impact of public policy on individual interests, it begins taking on the attributes of a court. Administration gives precedence to the accomplishment of the social objectives defined in public policy; in this perspective, individual claims appear as incidental to this pursuit. They may provide opportunities for the furtherance of public objectives, or conversely they may raise obstacles to it; they are treated accordingly. In adjudication the perspective is reversed; in a court, public policy is tested in view of the interests of the persons affected. [Nonet 1969, pp. 234–5.]

Adjudication is a more expensive and time-consuming form of administration than rule-making and rule-application. So it may be invoked by those seeking to frustrate or postpone the implementation of official policies. Dimock sees the post-war trend towards judicializing the American administration as part of a conservative reaction to the New Deal. 'To fully judicialize administration is to kill it' (Dimock 1980, p. 18). In England today, things are not so simple. The welfare rights movement has fought for certain procedural restraints, the present Conservative Government has been concerned to abandon others. For example, it has stressed the need to cut 'red-tape' in planning, allowing developers to get on with developing.

Similarly, it has put the case for withdrawing some rights of appeal in immigration matters, contending that these slow down the decision-making process and absorb scarce financial resources.

Jowell's checklist of the strategic advantages and disadvantages of adjudication is complex. It is also theoretical. To add to the complexity we find governments of competing political persuasions 'weighing' the considerations in different ways. The choice of a particular type of administrative process may be an important policy decision. Because policy development tends to be shrouded in official secrecy, it is difficult to identify the exact reasons for the allocation of decision-making functions to one body rather than another. We can, however, provide a few practical illustrations which show how complex the issues may be. Turn back to the *Laker* case study (Chapter 2). Why were licensing functions entrusted to the CAA and why did appeal lie to the Minister? In the next section we develop the point by examining some general explanations for the emergence of administrative tribunals and then looking in greater detail at why particular institutions were established.

2 'They just growed like Topsy'[6]

Throughout this century 'administrative tribunals' have proliferated,[7] taking widely differing forms as they have become established in different spheres of government activity. We might say that their chief characteristic is variation.[8] As Robson (1951, p. 314), commenting on his own classic survey, put it: 'Whatever else may be said of our inquiry, it is scarcely one which is remarkable either for the simplicity of the phenomena under observation, or the homogenous nature of the legal institutions with which it is concerned.'

Although Table 1 presents only a small selection of tribunals, the diversity of subject matter is obvious. Questions concerning individual welfare benefits arise before SBATs and the national insurance tribunals, while personal liberties are in issue before the Mental Health Review Tribunals and the Immigration Appeal Tribunal (IAT). The transport tribunals, on the other hand, are concerned with the regulation of the economy, and the interest of the state in raising revenue is in issue before the Commissioners of Income Tax and the VAT Tribunals. Not all tribunals deal directly with disputes between the citizen and the administration. For instance, the rent tribunals resolve landlord/tenant disputes,

Table 1 Selected Tribunals 1961–81

Tribunal	1961	1966	1971	1976	1977	1978	1979	1980	1981
Supplementary Benefits Appeal Tribunals	14,922	12,335	29,648	54,407	63,943	62,308	46,403	44,518	43,232
National Insurance Local Tribunals	39,731	36,409	29,334	37,425	34,825	39,798	34,786	25,258	32,048
National Insurance Commissioners (later Social Security Commissioners)	1,624	2,500	2,212	1,803	1,540	1,555	2,146	2,934	2,739
Mental Health Review Tribunals	830[3]	1,195	1,021	764	805	707	790	709	708
Immigration Adjudicators	*	*	1,944	10,282	9,135	8,443	9,153	11,020	11,637
Immigration Appeal Tribunal	*	*	118	434	352	446	374	324	434
Traffic Commissioners[1]	14,408	19,080	17,212	21,187	19,281	21,286	22,438	20,528	10,566
Goods Vehicle Licensing Authority[2]	8,706	3,357	5,770	2,449	3,639	2,310	3,079	2,782	2,592
Transport Tribunal	72	69	17	27	16	10	21	23	29
Civil Aviation Authority[1]	2,104[4]	2,026	4,284	1,271	1,174	1,186	1,092	1,002	1,232
General Commissioners of Income Tax	***	***	910,629	966,017	905,995	874,280	approximately 1 million Source(2)	***	***
Value Added Tax Tribunals	*	*	*	440	636	669	631	***	***
Local Valuation Courts	**	41,368	82,620	383,872	331,222	217,943	189,268	155,806	134,636
Lands Tribunal	467	568	1,108	1,426	1,555	1,673	1,653	1,237	1,145
Rent Tribunals/Assessment Committees	8,181	13,744	19,701	18,741	19,118	15,121	13,730	14,820	16,521
Industrial Tribunals	*	3,846	8,736	39,706	39,678	39,118	37,518	31,736	41,031

Sources: (1) Council on Tribunals Annual Reports; (2) Board of Inland Revenue 123rd and 124th Reports 1980–1, Cmnd 8160 and 8514. Statistics are for all cases disposed of.
* Tribunal not in existence. ** Tribunal not under Council jurisdiction. *** Statistics not available for Report.
[1] Year ending March. [2] Year ending September. [3] 1.12.1960–31.12.1961. [4] 1.10.1960–31.3.1962.

although the issues are settled within the statutory framework of rent control.

Table 1 illustrates the important role played by certain tribunals in dispute resolution. Some of the broad statistical fluctuations indicate how these bodies, once in being, are often expanded into new areas. Development has been piecemeal, not systematic. For example, Industrial Tribunals, created by the Industry Training Act 1964, were chosen to hear claims arising under the Redundancy Payments Act 1965. In 1970 they were given jurisdiction to hear disputes concerning the Equal Pay Act and, by the Industrial Relations Act 1971, complaints of unfair dismissal. Subsequently, the Sex Discrimination Act 1975 and the Race Relations Act 1976 gave them power to deal with discrimination occurring in employment.

Procedures are also variable. Tribunals have stretched from the informal to the judicialized, the trend, since the report of the Franks Committee (Committee on Administrative Tribunals and Enquiries (1957) Cmnd 218), being towards the latter. Today some, like the Lands Tribunal, are close to Jowell's ideal-type: its procedural rules provide for affidavit evidence, discovery of documents and the hearing of preliminary points of law. The Tribunal so closely resembles the judicial model that in *Attorney-General* v. *British Broadcasting Corporation* [1980] 3 W L R 109 some of the law lords considered it a 'court'.

Tribunals occupy different positions in decision-making chains. Only some, like Immigration Adjudicators and SBATs, directly check administrative determinations. Others, for example the CAA, take the initial decision, while bodies like the IAT hear appeals from other inferior tribunals. Even this classification is over-simple. What constitutes an 'administrative determination' varies, and listing institutional structures tells us little about practical relationships. Departmental influence over tribunals may be secured by various means, for example the manipulation of membership and training. Agencies like the CAA may, to a greater or lesser extent, be hemmed in by policy guidance issued by ministers. To return to the Skytrain affair (Chapter 2), the way in which the Civil Aviation Act 1980 altered the previous balance is evident.

The picture is one of *pluralism*. And if we ask why some issues have been allocated to tribunals and others not, we find that no clear pattern emerges in the allocation of decision-making functions as between courts, tribunals, ministers and other statutory bodies.

One of the criteria put forward for allocating decisions to a Minister is that the decision is largely determined by policy based on a consideration of what is desirable in the future in the public interest rather than on a finding as to past fact or an interpretation of a statute or accepted principle of common law or equity. But this is by no means a decisive factor in practice. Decisions of this nature have been conferred on independent bodies such as the Traffic Commissioners, the Independent Broadcasting Authority and the Civil Aviation Authority even if one excludes the Restrictive Practices Court which gave rise to considerable controversy on this point. On the other hand the interpretation of the Housing Act 1957, s. 4 (unfitness for human habitation) and the Industrial Development Act 1966 (investment grants) was entrusted to a Minister rather than a court or tribunal.

Similarly the lack of 'fixed or measurable criteria' has not been the determining factor in allocating decisions to Ministers. It has been the justification for Ministerial decisions in the case of office and industrial development certificates and appeals against refusal of planning permission but there were no fixed criteria for the allocation of television contracts or for licensing private airlines or for some of the decisions which the immigration tribunals will have to take.

The scale of a decision is also not decisive. In the case of schemes under the Highlands and Islands Development Act 1965 and to some extent in the case of slum clearance this has been the justification for reserving decisions to Ministers but the Minister also retained control over investment grants.

Questions of national security are always reserved for the Government but in other areas it is impossible to generalise. The decisions which are regarded as non-delegable will vary with the Government in power. Whether an area should be taken out of politics and given to an independent body may be a matter of acute political controversy as in the case of the Restrictive Practices Court and immigration appeals. On the other hand there may be all-party agreement as in the case of the allocation of television contracts. In this area ... governments both Labour and Conservative have felt that political considerations should be eliminated. [Ganz 1972, pp. 307–8.]

Why is the distribution of decision-making powers byzantine? One partial explanation is that the two major reports on non-judicial adjudication failed to develop workable guidelines by which governments might determine which issues should be allocated to which agencies. Donoughmore attempted the task, distinguishing 'judicial', 'quasi-judicial' and 'administrative' decisions, but the Committee's circular reasoning provided no pointer for the future. Indeed, Donoughmore adopted a more traditional division of responsibility, aiming to give 'judicial' decisions to the judiciary and 'administrative' and 'quasi-judicial' decisions to ministers. Only in exceptional circumstances would ministerial tribunals be required. Quangos like the CAA emerged in profusion later on. Twenty-five years of proliferation later, Franks accepted that tribunals were here to stay and that the judicial/administrative dichotomy did not yield a valid principle on which the allocation of decision-making functions might proceed. But the Committee failed to develop prescriptive criteria of its own, commenting only that, in the absence of 'special considerations', courts, not tribunals, should adjudicate and that, in turn, tribunals were preferable to ministerial adjudication, save where policy could not be articulated easily in regulations amenable to administration by tribunals. Instead, Franks concentrated on the existing system, suggesting that a new body, the Council on Tribunals, should tackle questions of allocation. In Chapter 6 we will see how successive governments have prevented the Council from fulfilling this role.

A second explanation concerns the reasons behind the development of tribunals. Wade (1982, pp. 777–9) gives a lawyer's account: 'Tribunals exist in order to provide simpler, speedier, cheaper and more accessible justice than do the ordinary courts ... An accompanying advantage is expertise.' This essentially technical explanation may be contrasted with Banting's description, based on the diaries of the responsible minister, Richard Crossman, of how Labour introduced Rent Assessment Committees (RACs) in 1965. Banting highlights the significance of political beliefs and of governmental infighting:

From the beginning Crossman and his group [of outside advisers] were agreed on the creation of tribunals, and little consideration was given to the use of the courts. The Labour Party had long regarded courts as intimidating and expensive institutions with an undue sensitivity to property rights. 'Appeal to the courts is no protection for the tenant', Bevan argued in 1953, since 'in a vast number of cases the tenant would rather pay the increase than expose himself to having to go to court.' Twelve years later another Labour MP echoed his thoughts: 'having to go into a court ... puts the fear of death' into working-class families. The party clearly preferred informal rent tribunals. Bevan had established them for the furnished sector during the post-war Labour Government, and their subsequent operations reinforced Labour's liking of them ...

Extensive debate centred on the qualifications of the three people who would sit on the [RACs] and who would set the precedents within which the rent officers would operate. Everyone accepted that there should be a professional valuer such as a chartered surveyor, but the role of lawyers provoked disagreement. To what extent should the committees be modelled on the judicial process with legally trained members, court procedures and parties represented by counsel? Crossman and most of his advisers wished to maximise the informality of the process, for fear of biasing it in favour of large landlords, but this preference ran counter to deeply entrenched administrative norms. The Franks Committee had emphasised the need for legally trained chairmen and judicial procedures in such regulatory bodies. Their report had been particularly critical of the informality of Bevan's tribunals and, when the Government accepted the basic Franks doctrine, the Ministry of Housing and Local Government had been forced to reform them. Thus, in drafting the new legislation Ministry officials accepted that, in the end, the same principles would have to be adopted. If Crossman did not accept some formalisation, there would be conflict with the Lord Chancellor and the Attorney-General in cabinet. 'In the post-Franks world, opinion was very firm on this', explained an official. 'The Lord Chancellor's Department had built up a position and we officials couldn't have shifted it. It would have required a very powerful Minister.'

Crossman's position was modified in the light of the opposition of his officials and his negotiations with the Lord Chancellor, Lord Gardiner [who] was given control over the people appointed as chairmen of the committees . . . His appointees were to be primarily lawyers and, in the absence of centrally established procedures, were to determine the degree of formality in the committee proceedings. Thus the [RACs] emerged as highly professional bodies with two professionals and only one layman. The procedures that resulted were not as formal as those of the courts, since the committees could not administer an oath and were not bound by formal rules of evidence. But in many cases the Minister was not pleased with the degree of formality that developed. [Banting 1979, pp. 51–4.]

Not only may a particular allocation of decision-making functions be a party-political issue, individual politicians and officials may hold differing views. The central departments of state are not a simple, homogenous whole. Again, administrators do not exist in a vacuum, they may be constrained in their choice by a variety of political and institutional pressures. For example, campaigning organizations or powerful business interests may become involved, as in the concession of an independent regulatory agency to the airlines. We might say that 'legalism' has infiltrated Wade's view of history. To quote Shklar (1964, p. 3) again: 'Law is endowed with its own discrete, integral history . . . sealed off from general social history, from politics, and from morality'. The constitution, which to competing theorists is intrinsically political, is thereby sanitized. Robson's account of the development of tribunals (see above, p. 21), is rather different.

Wade's description, confined to a choice between courts and tribunals, ignores a more fundamental question: why was adjudication, rather than decision-making by discretion or rules, adopted in the first place? His treatment of courts and tribunals together carries the implication, vigorously asserted by Franks, that tribunal decision-making should be viewed as an external control on administrators, not as one form of administration. Having listed as advantages of tribunals over courts 'cheapness, accessibility, freedom from technicality, expedition and expert knowledge of their particular subject', Franks continued:

> Tribunals are not ordinary courts, but neither are they appendages of Government Departments. Much of the official evidence . . . appeared to reflect the view that tribunals should be properly regarded as part of the machinery of administration, for which the Government must retain a close and continuing responsibility . . . We do not accept this view. We consider that tribunals should properly be regarded as machinery provided by Parliament for adjudication rather than as part of the machinery of administration. The essential point is that in all these cases Parliament has deliberately provided for a decision outside and independent of the Department concerned . . . The intention of Parliament to provide for the independence of tribunals is clear and unmistakable. [Cmnd 218, para. 40.]

The reasoning here is founded on three assumptions. The first is that Parliament, in setting up tribunals, necessarily intended to establish decision-making agencies *independent* of departments. Remember Baldwin's criticism of the *Laker* case (see above, p. 57). Is this first assumption too easily made by lawyers? Secondly, the reasoning suggests that parliamentary and governmental intentions are separate. The Committee chose to disregard the governmental view 'that tribunals should properly be regarded as part of the machinery for administration'. Is it realistic to suggest that machinery inserted in a statutory scheme by civil servants who think of it as 'administrative' is transmuted during its passage through Parliament into 'machinery for adjudication'? Thirdly, is it true that 'machinery for adjudication' can never be 'machinery for administration'? Griffith does not think so:

> The dichotomy is false. There is no reason why the machinery for adjudication should not be part of the machinery for administration. Indeed in one sense it must be precisely that, however independent the tribunals are. [Griffith 1959b, p. 129.]

Wade's conception of tribunals as mini-courts also occurs in Street's explanation:

> It is the extension of the Welfare State which leads to matters being taken away from the courts. When the State provides benefits for citizens it has to devise machinery for ascertaining who has a good claim. When the State imposes controls there has to be a procedure which ensures that the citizen's freedom is not interfered with in an arbitrary manner. [Street 1975, p. 2.]

But earlier, we remarked that some writers are distrustful of social engineering. In the opinion of one welfare lawyer: 'the welfare state does not perform merely a philanthropic function. If one views society in terms of political and economic conflict it can be seen as having a role in preserving political order, in acting as a "shock absorber" to prevent more serious attacks being made on the social order . . .' (Prosser 1977, p. 52). Compare this explanation with the arguments of the Wilson Committee on Immigration Appeals (Cmnd 3387 (1967)) why, during a period when the state was imposing tougher immigration controls, there should be introduced appeals to tribunals for intending immigrants excluded at ports of entry. At the time, decisions were taken by immigration officers exercising a statutory discretion regulated by Home Office instructions; the Committee's recommendations provided the framework for the appeals system set up by the Immigration Appeals Act 1969. How many different reasons can you find?

Almost without exception our witnesses advocated the establishment of some sort of appeal system . . . There were those who alleged that, under existing conditions, many decisions are made which result in the improper exclusion of intending immigrants . . . that the operation of the present method of control can be arbitrary and capricious, and that an applicant's case often does not receive the full attention which it deserves. We think that in all but a few cases these strictures are not supported by the facts . . . the great majority of cases which arise at the ports are fairly and properly decided, having regard to the sometimes very great difficulty of establishing the true facts or a person's real intentions. We nevertheless think that cases do from time to time occur in which the decision would have been different if it had been made by an appellate authority after a dispassionate review of the relevant evidence. That consideration alone would go far to justify the setting up of an appeal system.
    The other main argument in favour of an appeal system rests on a basic principle. Its advocates contend that, however well administered the present control may be, it is fundamentally wrong and inconsistent with the rule of law that power to take decisions affecting a man's whole future should be vested in officers of the executive, from whose findings there is no appeal. In our opinion these critics have reached the heart of the matter. Even if, generally speaking, justice is being done under the present system, it is not apparent that this is the case. It is one thing for us, after a protracted inquiry, to express our confidence that the power of final decision entrusted to officers of the Immigration Service is being exercised fairly; it is another thing to expect a newly arrived immigrant, and his relatives and friends at the other side of the barrier, to feel the same confidence. They are not aware of the safeguards provided by the immigration officer's responsibility through his superiors to the Home Secretary, and the Home Secretary's responsibility to

Parliament: all that seems evident to them is that an immediate and summary power to refuse admission rests with one or two officials at the port. In this situation it is understandable that an immigrant and his relatives or friends should feel themselves from the outset to be under a disadvantage, and so should be less willing than they might otherwise be to accept the eventual decision. If a Commonwealth citizen or alien claims afterwards that 'they didn't give me any reason for the decision' or 'they wouldn't listen to what I said', he may only be trying to save face, but we believe that such complaints quite often express the feeling that the person concerned never had a chance to confront his interrogators on equal terms. Allegations of this kind are hard to counter when the whole process has taken place in private. They reflect unfairly on the officials concerned, and cumulatively they give rise to a general disquiet in the public mind. The evidence we have received strongly suggests that among the communities of Commonwealth immigrants in this country, and among people specially concerned with their welfare, there is a widespread belief that the Immigration Service deals with the claims of Commonwealth citizens seeking admission in an arbitrary and prejudiced way. We doubt whether it will be possible to dispel this belief so long as there is no ready way of having decisions in such cases subjected to an impartial review.

In many other fields of public law [there are procedures] requiring a clear statement of the administration's case, an opportunity for the person affected to put his case in opposition and support it with evidence, and a decision by an authority independent of the Department interested in the matter. The safeguards provided by such a procedure serve not only to check any possible abuse of executive power but also to give a private individual a sense of protection against oppression and injustice, and of confidence in his dealings with the administration, which are in themselves of great value. We believe that immigrants and their relatives and friends need the same kind of reassurance against their fears of arbitrary action on the part of the Immigration Service. [Cmnd 3387, paras. 83–5.]

Did the Committee share Street's belief in tribunals as a protection against arbitrary action? Blake and Gillespie suggest that it was concerned with 'symbolic reassurance', i.e. with producing an appearance of fairness which legitimates, but does not correspond with, reality:

The prime aim of those who designed and set up the immigration appeals system was to provide a means of demonstrating the assumed and un-questioned fairness and impartiality of decision-making in immigration control. This was necessary in order to make the growing strictness of immigration policy more acceptable both to those directly affected and to the resident immigrant community. [Blake and Gillespie 1979, p. 9.]

Their point is not that judicialization would fail to counterbalance the Government's policy of tighter restrictions on entry, but that it *positively abetted* administrators in achieving their goals. For Bridges

(1975, p. 224): 'immigration appeals were a perfect legal buffer, enabling the State to maintain a liberal image while pursuing essentially illiberal policies'. After watching the present appeals system at work, Blake and Gillespie ascribe to it a related function, which they term 'legal ritual'. Jowell also identifies this function; it represents the government's gain in depoliticizing disputes:

The state . . . presiding over a strict control of immigration, has every interest in presenting the issue of immigration control to those affected adversely in a de-politicised, neutral form: this is an ideal method of deflecting political opposition and challenge to the assumptions on which immigration control is founded. The review of decisions within the immigration appeals process serves to promote this image of immigration policy [as] a politically neutral issue in several ways. First, the . . . emphasis on procedural fairness directs attention away from possible substantive injustice.

Second, within the appeals process the conflict between the appellant and the state is treated as capable of resolution by entirely formal rational means, without the intrusion of value-judgements. The problem is seen as being of finding facts, interpreting the relevant rule and applying the rule to those facts . . .

[Third] the appeals process . . . contributes to the deflection of political opposition [because] it is inherent in the adjudication process that each appellant's case is dealt with as an isolated individual instance. The focus of attention is on the complex facts of each individual case. Accordingly, there is no challenge to the underlying ideology of immigration control such as would be presented by collective political protest. [Blake and Gillespie 1979, pp. 12–14.]

Some historical evidence derived from pre-war government documents, now made available, allows us to make a similar point about the Aliens' Deportation Advisory Committee, a non-statutory body appointed by the Home Secretary and chaired by a King's Counsel, which used to review proposed deportation orders. One civil servant wrote, 'The advantages are mainly [of] what I may call the window dressing character'. When the Committee was disbanded, the chairman was thanked for 'protecting successive Home Secretaries against criticisms of arbitrary and unfair action'.[9]

Here is Prosser drawing upon Lynes' research into the introduction by the Unemployment Assistance Act 1934 of an appeals system for non-contributory relief. These tribunals formed the basis of the present system of SBATs and you will be better able to assess the argument when we have followed their development into modern times. Prosser sees the machinery as providing a legal buffer against political action and ties the creation and functioning of the tribunals explicitly to their social context:

It was decided to introduce [appeals machinery] for two main reasons: firstly to help avoid any possibility of ministerial responsibility for individual cases; secondly, and crucially, it was clear that the cuts in benefit were foreseen, as was mass opposition to them. The unemployed had shown themselves quite prepared to use violence against the less generous Public Assistance Committee (e.g. in 1932 a demonstration in Birkenhead had resulted in four days of battles between police and the unemployed). The introduction of appeals machinery provided a means of defusing the opposition by directing it into channels where it could be controlled and have a minimal effect . . .

This function of the tribunals implied a conflict between their symbolic role and their actual operation. They had to appear independent and prepared to protect recipients of assistance to ensure that they would be used in preference to other forms of protest. It was necessary also that they be carefully controlled to prevent them from undermining the [Unemployment Assistance] Board's policy. This was accomplished by appointing one member specifically to represent the Board and by ensuring that each of these members sat frequently enough to acquire expertise in handling appeals whilst the balancing workpeople's members were appointed from large panels so that each sat only occasionally. Secondly, the clerk to each tribunal (whose duties included advising the tribunal on its powers, the law, etc.) was invariably a senior officer of the Board, and it held conferences for the chairmen of the tribunals and issued to them the instructions given to its officers and unpublished memoranda . . . Finally in the highly politically contentious area of the household means test the Board was prepared to press its policies onto the tribunals by direct means, either through the clerk or by sending its officers to talk to tribunal members before appeals were to be heard . . .

The introduction of the tribunals . . . is shown as being an expression of forces very different from the gradual development of procedural protection to meet new needs generally put forward to account for the development of rights of appeal. The tribunals were not established to make up for defects in the judicial system. The choice was never between appeal to tribunals and appeal to the courts but between appeal to tribunals and no appeal. Their introduction did not represent an incorporation of the idea of legality into new areas of society for its own sake. The provision of a formal right of appeal was not a recognition of the rights of those receiving assistance or an attempt to provide an element of 'fairness' in the relationship between the State and the individual. Instead it was introduced as a counter-measure to political protest and as a means of making oppressive changes in the relief of poverty more palatable by giving a symbolic appearance of legality whilst ensuring that this had no real effect. It can be seen as a particular example of . . . the conformative role of the state: that of providing institutions which incorporate and moderate conflict and keep it within the bounds of order . . . the procedural protection of a right of appeal need not arise to protect the interests of those to whom it is given. [Prosser 1977, pp. 42–4.]

How different this description is from the explanations of Franks, Wade or Street. No legalism here! Is it surprising that Ganz could establish no simple distribution of decision-making functions? In a political constitution, the influences and motivations are infinitely complex.

3 Informal adjudication and procedural fairness

Established under statute with procedures governed by statutory instruments, the tribunals listed in Table I are the products of formal rule-making. They are also relatively *formalized*; we have as yet not strayed very far from Jowell's ideal-type. If we turn our attention to the bottom end of his sliding-scale, we find that adjudication blends imperceptibly into decision-making by rules and/or discretion. The point at which participation by 'proofs and reasoned arguments' becomes so restricted that a given process can no longer be characterized as adjudicatory is difficult to judge.

We have already met examples of the multiplicity of informal adjudicatory mechanisms, statutory and otherwise, which form part of our administrative arrangements. For instance, there was the Aliens' Deportation Advisory Committee and the statutory right of appeal from determinations of the CAA to the Minister. Further illustrations can be found in natural justice cases. Consider, for example, the non-statutory procedure at issue in *Hosenball*'s case (below). Under the Immigration Act 1971 the Secretary of State is empowered to deport an alien if he 'deems his deportation to be conducive to the public good'. Where such a decision is made as being 'in the interests of national security or of the relations between the U K and any other country or for other reasons of a political nature' no right of appeal exists, but representations can be made to a non-statutory panel advising the Home Secretary.[10] After the Minister's initial decision to deport, the person concerned is told such particulars of the allegations against him as will not necessitate disclosure of sources of evidence. Mr Maudling has explained to Parliament (HC Deb. vol. 819, cols. 376–7) what happens next:

The advisers will then take account of any representations made by the person concerned. They will allow him to appear before them, if he wishes. He will not be entitled to legal representation, but he may be assisted by a friend to such extent as the advisers sanction. As well as speaking for himself, he may arrange for a third party to testify on his behalf. Neither the sources of evidence nor evidence that might lead to disclosure of sources can be revealed to the person concerned but the advisers will ensure that the person is able to make his points effectively and the procedure will give him the best possible opportunity to make the points he wishes to bring to their notice . . . Since the evidence against a person necessarily has to be received in his absence, the advisers in assessing the case will bear in mind that it has not been tested by cross-examination and that the person has not had the opportunity to rebut it . . . On receiving [their] advice . . . the Secretary of State will reconsider his original decision, but the advice given to him will not be revealed.

How close is this procedure to the ideal-type of adjudication?

So far, we have concentrated on choices made by politicians and administrators. Reference to *Hosenball*'s case reminds us that judges may also take a hand in the matter. In the guise of natural justice and of its youthful offshoot procedural fairness, courts can impose adjudicatory procedures where previously none existed or hold that others are not sufficiently judicialized. In short, judges can influence the final shape of the administrative process.

Some writers believe that the procedures associated with adjudication are essential to decision-making, and that to see them observed is a key objective of administrative law. Ganz, on the other hand, suggested that by insisting on their retention, lawyers are seeking to mould administration in their own image; the identity of the decision-maker dictates the procedural choice. Farmer saw the intervention of lawyers as inhibitory, dragging administrators inexorably back to outmoded procedures, discouraging experiment and innovation. Red light theories push the courts towards control of administrative procedures, while green light theorists urge them to hold back. This tension was evident in the *Laker* case.

In Chapter 1 we saw how judges attempted to distinguish the 'judicial', 'quasi-judicial' and 'administrative' functions of government in order to determine whether natural justice applied. This 'analytical theory' came to be criticized in two ways: first, it was difficult, if not impossible, to separate different types of functions; secondly, with the growth of the state, increasing numbers of (administrative) decisions were rendered devoid of procedural protections. In *Nakkuda Ali* v. *Jayaratne* [1951] AC 66, for example, a Ceylonese textile trader, alleged to have acted fraudulently, was deprived of his trading licence by the Controller of Textiles. The Privy Council held that this exercise of statutory discretion did not require any kind of hearing; the Controller was acting neither 'judicially' nor 'quasi-judicially', but merely withdrawing a 'privilege'. This is the type of decision which inspired Reich's 'The New Property'.

In recent years, the courts have moved some way towards developing a doctrine of 'procedural fairness' consisting of a *variable* duty to act fairly not tied to the older classification of governmental functions. The seeds of this can be found in Lord Reid's speech in *Ridge* v. *Baldwin* (see above, p. 28); it emerged more fully in *Re H.K. (an infant)* [1967] 2 QB 617. An immigration officer refused to admit a boy travelling from Pakistan on the ground that he appeared to be well over 16, under which age he would have possessed a statutory right to enter. Lord Parker CJ doubted whether the officer had acted in a 'judicial' or 'quasi-judicial' capacity, but thought that in any event:

> ... he must ... give the immigrant an opportunity of satisfying him [that he was under 16] and for that purpose let the immigrant know what his immediate impression is so that the immigrant can disabuse him. That is not ... a question of acting or being required to act judicially, but of being required to act fairly. Good administration and an honest or bona fide decision must ... require not merely impartiality, not merely bringing one's mind to bear on the problem, but acting fairly; and to the limited extent that the circumstances of any particular case allow, and within the legislative framework under which the administrator is working, only to that limited extent do the so-called rules of natural justice apply.

The notion of variant procedural protections is antithetical to the general solutions implicit in the exposition of the two strands of natural justice, no man to be condemned unheard and no man a judge in his own cause, as 'fundamental rules' (Wade 1977, p. 394). Functionalist writers who favour *contextual*, not conceptual, judicial review argue that judges should become more pragmatic or result-orientated, tailoring decisions to the particular subject-matter in issue. The desire for general principles, part of the Diceyan inheritance, should be suppressed; diversity should become the order of the day.

Hartley and Griffith suggest that many of the procedural fairness cases are explicable in terms of an 'interest theory'.

According to this theory the applicability of natural justice depends on the impact of the decision on the interests of the individual affected. The more seriously his interests are affected the more likely it is that natural justice will apply. The questions to be considered are: first, does the decision directly affect an individual person's interests; secondly, is the interest affected one which the courts are prepared to protect; and thirdly, how seriously is the interest affected? The interests of the individual, however, are not the only interests to be considered. There is also the public interest. This requires, for example, that the administrative process should not be unduly hampered by unreasonable procedural requirements. The interests of the individual concerned must be balanced against the public interest and the extent to which natural justice will apply (if it applies at all) will depend on the way the balance is struck. [Hartley and Griffith 1981, p. 334.]

The authors refer to the 'applicability of natural justice' and 'the extent to which natural justice will apply'; the interest theory deals with both the scope and content of procedural restraints. This may be contrasted with the 'analytical theory' which is concerned primarily with applicability: if the governmental function is held to be judicial or quasi-judicial, the court may be faced with a separate question as to what natural justice actually requires.

The interest theory is not the only theory of variability. Here is Mullan's 'spectrum theory' of procedural fairness represented diagramatically, with the author's explanation underneath.

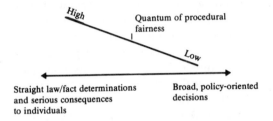

Why not deal with problems of fairness and natural justice simply on the basis that, the nearer one is to the type of function requiring straight law/fact determinations and resulting in serious consequences to individuals, the greater is the legitimacy of the demand for procedural protection but as one moves through the spectrum of decision-making functions to the broad, policy-oriented decisions exercised typically by a minister of the crown, the content of procedural fairness gradually disappears into nothingness, the emphasis being on a gradual disappearance not one punctuated by the unrealistic impression of clear cut divisions presented by the classification process? [Mullan 1975, p. 300.]

How do the interest and spectrum theories differ? Try applying Mullan's proposal to the *Laker* case (see above, p. 52). Where on his sliding scale should the judicially imposed procedural restraints be?

Mullan claims two advantages for his model. First, it avoids the pitfalls of classification: the difficulties entailed in drawing lines made apparent by cases like *Racal* (see below, p. 115); the arbitrary divisions between decision-making processes which may ensue; and the unrealistic results produced when two marginally different cases fall on opposite sides of a dividing line. Secondly, the theory permits the courts to tailor procedural restraints to the particular decision-making process:

> The development of the doctrine of procedural fairness is . . . desirable primarily because it allows the courts to ask what kind of procedural protections are necessary for a particular decision-making process unburdened by the traditional classification process . . . It recognizes that there is a very broad spectrum of decision-making functions for which varying procedural requirements are necessary and rejects the notion that such functions can be categorized satisfactorily into either one of two categories. The classification process was essentially accepted at a time when the administrative process was far less sophisticated. Its deceptive simplicity was perhaps adequate initially but it rapidly ceased to be realistic . . . If individual decision-making functions have different characteristics then they deserve different procedural requirements. [Mullan 1975, pp. 300–1.]

Although Mullan's analysis may appear beguiling, it raises a series of difficult questions which we introduce here, to develop in subsequent chapters. So often in administrative law, an apparently simple comment or proposal rests upon unexpressed assumptions or beliefs about the nature and aims of the subject and its institutions. First, we cannot assume the existence of a simple command theory of law: that judges dictate and administrators obey. Their relationship is far more complex. A drift towards tailoring judicial review to particular contexts may cause the 'gap' between court decisions and administrative behaviour to widen. And those who favour general principles of administrative law may contend that procedural fairness purchases flexibility at the expense of predictability and certainty. Let us follow this a little further.

Atiyah (1978) distinguishes two facets of the judicial function. The first is the 'hortatory'. Here the court orientates its decision towards encouraging society to adopt particular kinds of behaviour. Atiyah suggests that the primacy of this function leads courts to enunciate general principles. By laying down and consistently applying simple notions such as 'promises must be kept', the courts aim to educate members of society into keeping them. Atiyah argues that this teaching function, which he considers valuable, may be diminished if the judges over-emphasize their second role of dispute resolution which leads courts to strive for the most sensible solution in the particular case. Atiyah contends that this second, 'pragmatic' approach has increasingly found favour among the judges.[11]

We might describe the rise of procedural fairness as a manifestation of pragmatism in the public law field. Some may go on to suggest that courts, by focusing upon specific factual contexts, fail to educate administrators in proper procedural restraints. Clark makes this argument in criticizing *Glynn* v. *Keele University* (see below, p. 285), where the judge exercised his discretion not to grant a remedy although a breach of natural justice had occurred:

Natural justice is more than a means to an end (a right decision in individual cases) . . . The goal of administrative justice can never be attained by necessarily sporadic and *ex post facto* judicial review. The essential mission of the law in this field is to win acceptance by administrators of the principle that to hear a man before he is penalised is an integral part of the decision-making process. A measure of the importance of resisting the incipient abnegation by the courts of the firm rule that breach of *audi alteram partem* [no man to be condemned unheard] invalidates, is that if it gains ground the mission of the law is doomed to fail to the detriment of all. [Clark 1975, pp. 58, 60.]

Secondly, what does 'tailoring' decisions involve? Mullan's proposal is reminiscent of the search by K. C. Davis for the individualised 'optimum' on a line between discretion and rules (see Chapter 5). But is the 'optimum' an *absolute* standard or is it *relative*? In other words, does it depend upon one's personal viewpoint? Both the interest and spectrum theories involve the weighing of competing considerations and require the courts to assess the interests of, or serious consequences to, individuals. Does there exist a community consensus about the proper results? Will we all define 'interests' in the same way? And will we all ascribe the same 'weight' to different types of 'interest'? For example what weight should be ascribed to the right to remain in a university or the right to remain in a trade union? Again, what is the 'public interest'? Can it, as Hartley and Griffith imply, be equated with administrative convenience? Or might it also encompass upholding the 'rule of law' or securing 'fair' or 'good' administration? In short, is there really a simple antithesis between the 'public' and the 'private' interest? (See below, Chapter 12.)

A third issue is raised. If the 'optimum' is not instantly recognizable, the judiciary will have to make choices or exercise discretion. Procedural fairness, by releasing judges from the constraints of legal concepts, may enlarge their freedom of manoeuvre. Since pragmatism implies discretion, it may alarm the green light theorists who believe that the courts already choose to favour particular social groups and prompt some of them to seek (like red light theorists) firm principles of judicial review. Griffith compares the natural justice cases concerning disciplinary sanctions imposed on trade union members with those involving students:

The contrast ... is very great. In the [student cases] the courts seek assiduously to find some ground on which to disregard breach of the rules of natural justice. In the trade union cases they very rarely allow any such breach to be overlooked. Both groups of cases concern the right to work. Frequently both concern expulsions. The consequences of expulsion in both may be most serious to the livelihood of the individual ... It is right that the courts should protect the individual against a trade union which fails to proceed fairly against him. But why should the protection be denied to a student? [Griffith 1977, pp. 169–70.][12]

Models of procedural fairness like the spectrum theory invite consideration of the judicial function. They also invite consideration of the courts' own procedures. Could the courts cope with such variability? Should they even try? Loughlin ponders some of the consequences for the legal system of adopting Mullan's proposal, in particular the incorporation into judicial decision-making of notions like 'efficiency'. It might, for example, be necessary to admit, as American courts do, a wider range of evidence. Turning Ganz's aphorism around, judges would have to mould the judicial process in the administrators' image:

Mullan argues that 'if individual decision-making functions have different characteristics then they deserve different procedural requirements.' How-ever, bearing in mind the multifarious situations involving sensitive policy issues into which administration enters, such a role will result in a tremendous expansion of the number of factors which the court must consider in looking at administrative decision-making in the context of procedural fairness ... The result would be, in effect, to vest in the judiciary supreme authority to determine which decisions will be made by what process. As the court's role would be to deal almost solely with policy issues, a mode of argumentation similar to the Brandeis brief technique,[13] (which would include socio-economic data to demonstrate potential or actual effects of alternative procedures for the goals of a particular administrative system), would become the dominant form of legal discourse ...

Procedural fairness ... undermines the concept of the rule of law. The notion of generality of the legal order, achieved primarily by the use of general rules, is undermined by abandoning the formal rules of natural justice in favour of a flexible principle which cannot be individuated as its operation is governed by such notions as the most efficient way of attaining the presumed goals of a system. Also, autonomy of the legal order as an ideal is undermined as flexible standards like procedural fairness invite the court 'to make use of the technician's conception of efficiency or the layman's view of justice.' This destroys the distinctiveness of the methods and functions of administration and adjudication. [Loughlin 1978, pp. 236–7, 240.]

Before we examine a selection of cases, it is worth emphasizing that although procedural fairness has gained ground at the expense of the analytical theory, the process of replacement is by no means complete. *Cottrell and Rothon* (see above, p. 31) illustrates how some of the key vocabulary from the older theory lingers on. Further, the judges have disagreed about the relationship between natural justice and 'the duty to act fairly'. Sometimes the latter appears as a watered-down version of the former, a formulation which fits the spectrum theory. On other occasions a more analytical division is adopted; we are informed that natural justice and the duty to act fairly apply to judicial and administrative proceedings respectively.

Schmidt v. *Secretary of State for Home Affairs*
[1969] 2 WLR 337

The plaintiff was an alien and a student at a college of scientology. The Home Secretary, in furtherance of government policy aimed at discouraging the growth of scientology, refused to extend his residence permit. At the time there was no statutory right of appeal in such cases and, although the plaintiff had not been afforded a hearing, the Court of Appeal considered there had been no breach of natural justice. The Minister was under no duty to listen to representations.

LORD DENNING MR: Where a public officer has power to deprive a person of his liberty or his property, the general principle is that it is not to be done without his being given an opportunity of being heard and of making representations on his own behalf. But in the case of aliens, it is rather different; for they have no right to be here except by licence of the Crown. And it has been held that the Home Secretary is not bound to hear representations on their behalf . . .

Some of the judgments in [earlier] cases were based on the fact that the Home Secretary was exercising an administrative power and not doing a judicial act. But that distinction is no longer valid. The speeches in *Ridge* v. *Baldwin* . . . show that an administrative body may, in a proper case, be bound to give a person who is affected by their decision an opportunity of making representations. It all depends on whether he has some right or interest, or, I would add, some legitimate expectation, of which it would not be fair to deprive him without hearing what he has to say. Thus in *In re H. K. (An Infant)* . . . a Commonwealth citizen had a right to be admitted to this country if he was (as he claimed to be) under the age of 16. The immigration officers were not satisfied that he was under 16 and refused him admission. Lord Parker C.J. held that, even if they were acting in an administrative capacity, they were under a duty to act fairly – and that meant that they should give the immigrant an opportunity of satisfying them that he was under 16 . . . [But an alien] has no right to enter this country except by leave: and, if he is given leave to come for a limited period, he has no right to stay for a day longer than the permitted time. If this permit is revoked *before* the time limit expires, he ought, I think, to be given an opportunity of making

representations: for he would have a legitimate expectation of being allowed
to stay for the permitted time. Except in such a case, a foreign alien has no
right – and, I would add, no legitimate expectation – of being allowed to stay.
He can be refused without reasons given and without a hearing. Once his time
has expired, he has to go.

How does Lord Denning's analysis compare with Hartley and
Griffith's interest theory? Does Lord Denning claim to balance the
'public' and 'private' interest and, following his reasoning, would
Nakkuda Ali be decided differently?

> *R. v. Gaming Board for Great Britain ex p. Benaim*
> *and Khaida* [1970] 2 All E R 528

One of the purposes of the Gaming Act 1968 was to break the link
between gambling and organized crime. The statute laid down that
before a person could apply for his premises to be licensed he had to
obtain a certificate of consent from the Gaming Board. The Board
was to decide whether the applicant was a fit person, taking into
account his character, reputation and financial standing. The
applicants (on behalf of Crockford's gaming club) had a long meeting
with the Board where they answered questions on a series of issues,
such as their alleged underworld connections and past business
dealings. The questions were based on information obtained by the
Board, the source or sources of which were not disclosed. Subsequently, the Board refused to grant the certificate of consent,
declining to pinpoint which issues were still troubling it and to give
reasons for the decision. The Court of Appeal held that the Board had
not acted contrary to natural justice.

LORD DENNING MR: [Counsel] spoke as if Crockford's were being deprived
of a right of property or of a right to make a living. He [told us] that
Crockford's has been established for over a century and is a gaming club with
a world-wide reputation for integrity and respectability [whose] assets and
goodwill . . . were valued at about £185,000. [He] said that they ought not to
be deprived of this business without knowing the case they had to meet . . .

[He] put his case, I think, too high. It is an error to regard Crockford's as
having any right of which they are being deprived. They have not had in the
past, and they do not have now, any right to play these games of chance . . .
for their own profit. What they are really seeking is a privilege – almost, I
might say, a franchise – to carry on gambling for profit, a thing never hitherto
allowed in this country. It is for them to show they are fit to be trusted with
it . . .

It is not possible to lay down rigid rules as to when the principles of natural
justice are to apply; nor as to their scope and extent. Everything depends on
the subject-matter . . .

So let us . . . consider the task of the Gaming Board and what they should do . . . The Board have a duty to act fairly. They must give the applicant an opportunity of satisfying them of the matters specified . . . They must let him know what their impressions are so that he can disabuse them. But I do not think that they need quote chapter and verse against him as if they were dismissing him from an office, as in *Ridge* v. *Baldwin,* or depriving him of his property, as in *Cooper* v. *Wandsworth Board of Works.* After all, they are not charging him with doing anything wrong. They are simply inquiring as to his capability and diligence and are having regard to his character, reputation and financial standing. They are there to protect the public interest, to see that persons running the gaming clubs are fit to be trusted . . .

I do not think they need tell the applicant the source of their information, if that would put their informant in peril or otherwise be contrary to the public interest . . . The Board was set up by Parliament to cope with disreputable gaming clubs and to bring them under control. By bitter experience it was learned that these clubs had a close connection with organised crime, often violent crime, with protection rackets and with strong-arm methods. If the Board were bound to disclose their sources of information, no one would 'tell' on those clubs, for fear of reprisals. Likewise with the details of the information. If the Board were bound to disclose every detail, that might itself give the informer away and put him in peril. But, without disclosing every detail, I should have thought that the Board ought in every case to be able to give to the applicant sufficient indication of the objections raised against him such as to enable him to answer them. That is only fair . . .

I think that the Board acted with complete fairness. They put before the applicants all the information which led them to doubt their suitability. They kept the sources secret, but disclosed all the information . . . The Board gave the applicants full opportunity to deal with the information. And they came to their decision . . .

Why does Lord Denning think that Crockford's have no 'right' to run a gaming club? Do you agree? Are *Ridge* v. *Baldwin* (see above, p. 28) and *Cooper* v. *Wandsworth* (see above, p. 25) distinguished satisfactorily (compare Megarry V C's treatment of *Benaim and Khaida* in *McInnes* v. *Onslow-Fane* (below))?

R. v. *Secretary of State for Home Affairs*
ex p. Hosenball [1977] 1 W L R 766

H, a United States citizen, was an investigative journalist resident in England. He was informed that the Minister, acting on information that H had sought and obtained material prejudicial to national security, had decided to deport him. The Home Secretary, again pleading national security, also refused to disclose the particulars of the case against H, including the dates on which the breaches of security allegedly occurred. Following a hearing before the advisory panel (above) at which H made representations and called witnesses, the Minister made the deportation order. H argued unsuccessfully that there had been a breach of natural justice because he was not told the case he had to answer.

LORD DENNING MR: The information supplied to the Home Secretary by the Security Service is, and must be, highly confidential. The public interest in the security of the realm is so great that the sources of information must not be disclosed – nor should the nature of the information itself be disclosed – if there is any risk that it would lead to the sources being discovered. The reason is because, in this very secretive field, our enemies might try to eliminate the sources of information. So the sources must not be disclosed. Not even to the House of Commons. Nor to any tribunal or court of inquiry or body of advisers, statutory or non-statutory. Save to the extent that the Home Secretary thinks safe. Great as is the public interest in the freedom of the individual and the doing of justice to him, nevertheless in the last resort it must take second place to the security of the country itself . . .

There is a conflict here between the interests of national security on the one hand and the freedom of the individual on the other. The balance between these two is not for a court of law. It is for the Home Secretary. He is the person entrusted by Parliament with the task. In some parts of the world national security has on occasions been used as an excuse for all sorts of infringements of individual liberty. But not in England. Both during the wars and after them, successive ministers have discharged their duties to the complete satisfaction of the people at large. They have set up advisory committees to help them, usually with a chairman who has done everything he can to ensure that justice is done. They have never interfered with the liberty or the freedom of movement of any individual except where it is absolutely necessary for the safety of the state. In this case we are assured that the Home Secretary himself gave it his personal consideration, and I have no reason whatever to doubt the care with which he considered the whole matter. He is answerable to Parliament as to the way in which he did it and not to the courts here.

Griffith (1977, p. 81) commented: 'Lord Denning M.R. seemed to accept that the courts had no part to play because the Government never erred.'[14] Do you agree? How can Lord Denning know that ministers 'have never interfered with the liberty . . . of any individual except where it is absolutely necessary for the safety of the state'? How effective a safeguard is ministerial responsibility to Parliament likely to be in this type of case? Lord Denning's judgment provides a clue; for the answer, see HC Deb. vol. 931, cols. 367–411. Might the outcome of this case have been different if Mullan's model had been applied?

McInnes v. *Onslow-Fane* [1978] 3 All ER 211

The plaintiff, who had been licensed as a boxing promoter, trainer and master of ceremonies, had been repeatedly refused a manager's licence by the British Boxing Board of Control. He applied once again, asking for an oral hearing and for prior information of anything which might be held against him. The Board, in refusing the plaintiff's application, also denied his other requests. The plaintiff failed in his claim that this was contrary to natural justice.

MEGARRY VC: I think it must be considered what type of decision is in question. I do not suggest that there is any clear or exhaustive classification; but I think that at least three categories may be discerned. First, there are what may be called the forfeiture cases. In these there is a decision which takes away some existing right or position, as where a member of an organisation is expelled or a licence is revoked. Second, at the other extreme there are what may be called the application cases. These are cases where the decision merely refuses to grant the applicant the right or position that he seeks, such as membership of the organisation, or a licence to do certain acts. Third, there is an intermediate category, which may be called the expectation cases, which differ from the application cases only in that the applicant has some legitimate expectation from what has already happened that his application will be granted. This head includes cases where an existing licence-holder applies for a renewal of his licence, or a person already elected or appointed to some position seeks confirmation from some confirming authority . . .

It seems plain that there is a substantial distinction between the forfeiture cases and the application cases. In the forfeiture cases, there is a threat to take something away for some reason: and in such cases, the right to an unbiased tribunal, the right to notice of the charges and the right to be heard in answer to the charges . . . are plainly apt. In the application cases, on the other hand, nothing is being taken away, and in all normal circumstances there are no charges, and so no requirement of an opportunity of being heard in answer to the charges. Instead, there is the far wider and less defined question of the general suitability of the applicant for membership or a licence. The distinction is well-recognised, for in general it is clear that the courts will require natural justice to be observed for expulsion from a social club, but not on an application for admission to it. The intermediate category, that of the expectation cases, may at least in some respects be regarded as being more akin to the forfeiture cases than the application cases; for although in form there is no forfeiture but merely an attempt at acquisition that fails, the legitimate expectation of a renewal of the licence or confirmation of the membership is one which raises the question of what it is that has happened to make the applicant unsuitable for the membership or licence for which he was previously thought suitable. [Megarry VC characterized the case as one of 'application' not 'expectation' because the plaintiff had only held different types of licence. He then dealt with the argument, founded upon *ex p. Benaim and Khaida* and *Re H.K. (an infant)*, that the Board had to provide the plaintiff with some information about the case against him:]

These cases seem to me to be very different from the case before me. In each there was a statute which conferred the power and the duty to decide on some defined issue. Here there is no statute and no defined issue but merely a general discretion. In the *Gaming Board* case the character, reputation and financial standing of the applicants were in issue, so that the refusal of the certificate of fitness would be a slur on the applicants. In *In re H.K. (An Infant)* the question was whether or not the immigrant had a statutory right of entry . . . The refusal of the plaintiff's application by no means necessarily puts any slur on his character, nor does it deprive him of any statutory right. There is no mere narrow issue as to his character, but the wide and general issue whether it is right to grant this licence to this applicant. In such circumstances . . . the board are fully entitled to give no reasons for their decision, and to decide the application without any preliminary indication to the plaintiff of those reasons . . .

There is a more general consideration. I think that the courts must be slow to allow any implied obligation to be fair to be used as a means of bringing before the courts for review honest decisions of bodies exercising jurisdiction over sporting and other activities which those bodies are far better fitted to judge than the courts. This is so even where those bodies are concerned with the means of livelihood of those who take part in those activities . . . Bodies such as the board which promote a public interest by seeking to maintain high standards in a field of activity which otherwise might easily become degraded and corrupt ought not to be hampered in their work without good cause. Such bodies should not be tempted or coerced into granting licences that otherwise they would refuse by reason of the courts having imposed on them a procedure for refusal which facilitates litigation against them.

Why should it matter whether the duty to decide is conferred statutorily? Is the argument that the imposition of procedural restraints will cause the Board to change policy convincing?

Calvin v. *Carr* [1979] 2 WLR 755

The plaintiff's racehorse had shown good form in New Zealand but disappointed on its first appearance in Australia. After an inquiry, the stewards charged the plaintiff with failing to run the horse on its merits, contrary to the Australian Jockey Club rules. Subsequently they disqualified him from running horses for one year. He appealed to the Committee of the Jockey Club which upheld the stewards' decision. The plaintiff claimed that the stewards had acted in breach of natural justice but conceded that the subsequent hearing before the Committee was unimpeachable. The crucial issue was the extent to which a breach of natural justice could be cured by a subsequent (fair) rehearing or appeal. The Privy Council, faced with a series of conflicting Commonwealth decisions on the point, assumed, for the purposes of argument, that the stewards had committed a breach of natural justice.

LORD WILBERFORCE: No clear and absolute rule can be laid down on the question whether defects in natural justice appearing at an original hearing, whether administrative or quasi-judicial, can be 'cured' through appeal proceedings. The situations in which this issue arises are too diverse, and the rules by which they are governed so various, that this must be so. There are, however, a number of typical situations as to which some general principle can be stated. First there are cases where the rules provide for a rehearing by the original body, or some fuller or enlarged form of it. This situation may be found in relation to social clubs. It is not difficult in such cases to reach the conclusion that the first hearing is superseded by the second . . . At the other extreme are cases, where, after examination of the whole hearing structure, in the context of the particular activity to which it relates (trade union membership, planning, employment, etc) the conclusion is reached that a complainant has the right to nothing less than a fair hearing both at the original and at the appeal stage . . . These may very well include trade union cases where movement solidarity and dislike of the rebel, or renegade, may make it difficult for appeals to be conducted in an atmosphere of detached impartiality and so make a fair trial at the first – probably branch – level an essential condition of justice. But to seek to apply it generally overlooks . . . both the existence of the first category, and the possibility that, inter-mediately, the conclusion to be reached, on the rules and on the contractual context, is that those who have joined in an organisation, or contract, should be taken to have agreed to accept what in the end is a fair decision, notwithstanding some initial defect.

In . . . [intermediate cases] it is for the court, in the light of the agreements made, and in addition having regard to the course of proceedings, to decide whether, at the end of the day, there has been a fair result, reached by fair methods, such as the parties should fairly be taken to have accepted when they joined the association. Naturally there may be instances when the defect is so flagrant, the consequences so severe, that the most perfect of appeals or re-hearings will not be sufficient to produce a just result . . . There may also be cases when the appeal process is itself less than perfect [for example] there may be doubts whether the appeal body embarked on its task without predisposition . . . In such cases it would no doubt be right to quash the original decision . . .

It is undesirable in many cases of domestic disputes, particularly in which an inquiry and appeal process has been established, to introduce too great a measure of formal judicialisation. While flagrant cases of injustice, including corruption or bias, must always be firmly dealt with by the courts, the tendency . . . in matters of domestic disputes should be to leave these to be settled by the agreed methods without requiring the formalities of judicial processes to be introduced . . .

It remains to apply the principles . . . to the facts of the present case . . . Races are run at intervals; bets must be disposed of according to the result. Stewards are there in order to take rapid decisions as to such matters as the running of horses, being entitled to use the evidence of their eyes and their experience. As well as acting inquisitorially at the stage of deciding the result of a race, they may have to consider disciplinary action: at this point rules of natural justice become relevant. These require, at the least, that persons should be formally charged, heard in their own defence, and know the evidence against them. These essentials must always be observed but it is inevitable, and must be taken to be accepted, that there may not be time for procedural refinements. It is in order to enable decisions reached in this way to be reviewed at leisure that the appeal procedure exists. Those concerned know that they are entitled to a full hearing with opportunities to bring evidence and have it heard. But they know also that this appeal hearing is governed by the Rules of Racing, and that it remains an essentially domestic proceeding, in which experience and opinions as to what is in the interest of racing as a whole play a large part, and in which the standards are those which have come to be accepted over the history of this sporting activity. All those who partake in it have accepted the rules of Racing, and the standards which lie behind them: they must also have accepted to be bound by the decisions of the bodies set up under those rules so long as they can be said, by an objective observer, to have had fair treatment and consideration of their case on its merits.

In their Lordships' opinion precisely this can, indeed must, be said of the present case. The plaintiff's case has received, overall, full and fair consideration, and a decision, possibly a hard one, reached against him. There is no basis on which the court ought to interfere.

Do you agree that a decision of the Jockey Club is distinguishable from that of a trade union's disciplinary committee? What about a university's decision to send down a student? Suppose you were asked by an organization falling within Lord Wilberforce's 'intermediate category' to devise procedural rules for a two-tiered system of appeal in disciplinary proceedings. How helpful would you find his Lordship's speech as a practical guide?

Elliott (1980a, pp. 67–8) suggests that in *Calvin* v. *Carr*: 'the Privy Council . . . stated that, in natural justice, transaction-typing and a contextual policy analysis has ousted abstract principles . . . In different circumstances "natural justice" *means different things*'. By 'transaction-typing' Elliott means the consistent application of rules in 'particular subject-areas' such as 'the case of sport'. He sees the beginnings of consistency in *Calvin* and *McInnes*, pointing out that in both cases the court stressed that the resolution of sporting disputes should be left, wherever possible, in the hands of those with expertise. Refer back to *McInnes*. Did Megarry VC base his judgment on 'transaction-typing'? Might we characterize 'transaction-typing' as simply a more sophisticated species of conceptualism than the 'judicial', 'quasi-judicial', 'administrative' classification?

Cinnamond v. *British Airports Authority* [1980] 2 All ER 368

The plaintiffs were minicab drivers who touted for fares at Heathrow Airport, so bypassing the lines of waiting taxicab drivers. The BAA, which owned and managed Heathrow, had tried for some years to stop the practice, but repeated convictions under the Airport byelaws failed to produce results because the plaintiffs left the fines unpaid. Eventually the BAA wrote to the plaintiffs informing them that forthwith and until further notice they were prohibited from entering the airport save as *bona fide* passengers. The plaintiffs argued unsuccessfully that there had been a breach of natural justice because the BAA had not afforded them an opportunity to be heard.

LORD DENNING MR: In cases where there is no legitimate expectation, there is no call for a hearing . . . Suppose that these car-hire drivers were of good character and had for years been coming into the airport under an implied licence to do so. If in that case there was suddenly a prohibition order preventing them from entering, then it would seem only fair that they should be given a hearing and a chance to put their case. But that is not this case. These men have a long record of convictions. They have large fines outstanding. They are continuing to engage in conduct which they must know is unlawful and contrary to the byelaws . . . Now when the patience of the authority is exhausted, it seems to me that the authority can properly suspend them until further notice . . . In the circumstances they had no legitimate expectation of being heard. It is not a necessary preliminary that they should have a hearing or be given a further chance to explain . . . The simple duty of the airport authority was to act fairly and reasonably. It seems to me that it has acted fairly and reasonably.

Would you characterize this judgement as contextual? Should a person's prior conduct be taken into account in determining what is fair procedure? Drawing on our necessarily limited sample,[15] do you consider that in practice procedural fairness possesses the flexibility of Mullan's spectrum theory?

Elliott contends that judicial implementation of natural justice is impaled upon the horns of a dilemma: general principles and contextualism are both, for different reasons, doomed to fail.

Many of the modern cases on natural justice . . . assert that the rules are not immutable but change according to the context in which they operate; a moment's thought on the multifarious subject matters of administrative law cases surely indicates that any other position would be unworkable if a balance between administrative justice and efficiency is to be maintained . . .

Nonetheless, there are disadvantages with [the] self-consciously pragmatic analysis of procedure. An administrative law adversarial action before judges with necessarily limited knowledge may not be the best place to assess the procedures that particular situations require, given in particular the tension between public and private benefits so often latent in administrative law cases, and also the well-known problem of polycentricity of administrative disputes. But these difficulties should not be allowed to drive administrative lawyers back into a land where immutable rules are asserted in the abstract, only to vaporise when confronted with reality. Rather, administrative lawyers should be looking for new fora for administrative disputes, new rights, new methods of protecting them and new principles upon which administrative behaviour should be based. For the time being, as *Calvin* v. *Carr* eloquently testifies, the only available principle is pragmatism. [Elliott 1980a, pp. 68–9.]

Elliott is saying that the traditional demarcation between adjudication and administration has proved unworkable. The courts have jettisoned their rigid framework but have found nothing to replace it. A new framework must be developed but, until this is achieved, the pragmatism of procedural fairness is the only answer. Elliott reiterates Ganz's invitation to question the ideal-type of adjudication, asking administrative lawyers to turn their attention to other methods of administration. Yet Elliott does not suggest jettisoning the courts' role in shaping the administrative process nor does he advocate restricting judicial intervention. Instead Elliott proposes that the courts should intervene on a pragmatic (discretionary) case-by-case basis. Is this the optimum solution, or might we conclude that haphazard cross-the-border raids by a judiciary wedded to the court-ideal represent the worst of all worlds? Try to form a view, and remember to try again after reading more about justiciability Chapters 10–12.

4
Judicialization from within and without

1 **Franks revisited**

In Chapter 3, we remarked that administrative tribunals have become markedly more judicialized since the Franks Report in 1957. The Committee's formation can be seen, like Donoughmore, as a governmental response to a crisis of public confidence. If Donoughmore was prompted by Hewart's outburst, Franks arose from the disquiet engendered by Crichel Down. But with hindsight, Franks also appears as part of a general reaction to war-time and post-war controls. Robson's description of the contemporary political scene indicates how the conditions were right for the Report to prove an important catalyst for change. His analysis warns against the trite assumption that red and green light theories dovetail neatly with party allegiance. There was an emerging political consensus on the need to protect the individual:

Politicians have at last become aware of the need to safeguard more effectively the individual citizen in his dealings with the state. Conservative opinion, which in the past had shown blind and unfailing confidence in the ability of the courts to establish and maintain a genuine system of administration according to law, has recently shown signs of distinct uneasiness at the difficulties which for various reasons often make it impossible to secure judicial review of executive action in the ordinary courts . . .

The posture of the Labour Party has also changed. The party's commitment to central economic planning and regulation, the nationalisation of industry, a vast development of the social services, and the general policies of the Welfare State and Socialism, have predisposed Labour supporters to regard a strong executive armed with extensive discretionary powers as necessary for the realisation of their objectives. Neither the leaders nor the rank and file of the party had appreciated that the greater the powers which are given to public authorities, the more essential does it become to safeguard the citizen against their harsh or improper exercise. Most Labour politicians have assumed until recently that the elected representatives of the people in Parliament or on local councils would suffice to protect the citizen in his unequal contest with great public authorities . . . The first glimmering sign of uneasiness at this attitude was Mr R. H. S. Crossman's Fabian pamphlet bearing the title 'Socialism and the New Despotism' published in 1956. In it he declared that 'the growth of a vast, centralised State bureaucracy constitutes a grave potential threat to social democracy. The idea that we are being disloyal to our socialist principles if we attack its excesses or defend the individual against its incipient despotism is a fallacy.' A great deal of what Mr Crossman wrote would have been acceptable to the late Lord Hewart. [Robson 1958, pp. 12–13.]

Its terms of reference required the Franks Committee to examine statutory tribunals and administrative processes involving inquiry procedures (a brief which Franks interpreted strictly, determining that non-statutory inquiries of the type conducted in Crichel Down were excluded). Asked to consider only further decisions (i.e. decisions to confirm, cancel or vary original ones), the Committee was unable to scrutinize far wider areas of departmental decision-taking. Griffith commented:

The main weakness of the whole inquiry, not that the Committee was remotely responsible for this, was that it was directed in exactly the wrong direction. The Committee was told, in short, to look at procedures which were predominantly open, fair and impartial and asked to see if they could be made any more so . . . But into the closed, dark and windowless procedures the Committee was not asked to let air and light. [Griffith 1959b, p. 127.]

The Franks Committee, having concluded that Parliament intended tribunals to be machinery for 'adjudication' not 'administration', asserted (Cmnd 218, para. 41): 'Parliament in deciding that certain decisions should be reached only after a special procedure must have intended that they should manifest three basic characteristics: openness, fairness and impartiality.' The Committee then described its task:

The choice of a tribunal rather than a Minister as the deciding authority is itself a considerable step towards the realisation of these objectives, particularly [impartiality]. But in some cases the statutory provisions and the regulations thereunder fall short of what is required to secure [them]. Our main task . . . will be to assess the extent to which the three objectives are capable of attainment in the field of tribunals and to suggest appropriate measures. [Cmnd 218, para. 41.]

So Franks considered that Parliament intended tribunals to possess certain attributes, determined that these had not always been secured and set out to make good the legislature's omissions. How convincing is this line of reasoning?

The Committee translated its view of tribunals as 'machinery for adjudication' into two sets of recommendations. First, tribunals were to be reformed from within or remade in the image of the ordinary courts. Franks recommended that chairmen be legally qualified; that more 'orderly' procedures be followed; that hearings be generally in public; that the right to legal representation be observed and the provision of legal aid extended; that full reasons be given; that systems of precedent be developed; and so on. In short, the Committee aimed to push tribunals closer to the ideal-type of adjudication. Although not all of its recommendations have been implemented, a large measure of judicialization has occurred, in part through the stimulus provided by the Council on Tribunals. Some changes, such as the duty to give reasons on request, were incorporated in the Tribunals and Inquiries Act 1958, while others, for example, the opening-up of hearings to the public, have come about either through delegated legislation or administrative action.

Tribunals were also to be captured by the lawyers from without; Franks proposed to put them under the control of the ordinary courts. The Committee argued that in general an appeal from tribunal decisions should be provided. Its first reason, that the right of appeal 'is salutary and makes for right adjudication', involves notions of firewatching; the very existence of a check may improve the quality of initial decision-taking. A second, that with an appeal 'the system of adjudication can hardly fail to appear fair to the applicant', was criticized by Griffith. Compare his comment, which reminds us that Franks' concept of 'fairness' extended only to procedural and not substantive fairness, with the notion that adjudication can legitimate decisions:

Life and human nature are, I think fortunately, not like that. A man wants what he considers to be his 'rights'. And if he feels deeply enough and is determined enough, he will fight every way to get them. But if finally he loses, he will condemn the law and, deprived of his substance, will not rejoice overlong at the fairness of the procedure. Indeed, he would regard the distinction as sophistry. [Griffith 1959b, p. 140.]

Although Franks did not recommend appeal to the courts on issues of fact, conceding that this would pass decisions from bodies expert in their particular subject-areas to generalists, it was 'firmly of the opinion that all decisions of tribunals should be subject to review by the courts on points of law' (Cmnd 218, para. 107). Yet the Committee gave no reasoned explanation: this proposal to secure the dominance of the ordinary courts rested on nothing more than an expression of 'firm opinion' that it was the right thing to do. The 'dead hand' of Dicey had not yet lost its grip!

Once again, Franks built enthusiastically on unsure theoretical foundations. The Committee recommended a statutory right of appeal on a point of law from most tribunals. Ouster clauses were to be cut back: the prerogative remedies of certiorari, mandamus and prohibition (see below, p. 258) ought always to be available. And by requiring tribunals to give reasoned decisions, Franks believed it would be giving the courts an effective 'record' on which review for 'error of law on the face of the record' could be based. The significance of these recommendations may be understood by considering the judicial reaction to ouster clauses in the post-Franks era.

2 Ouster, jurisdiction and error of law

Acting through Parliament, administrators have at different times deployed a variety of devices designed to restrict or exclude judicial review of administrative action.[1] We focus on two direct[2] types of ouster. The total ouster or 'preclusive' clause attempts to render administrative decisions unchallengeable in the courts. Examples are the so-called finality clause ('any decision of X shall be final') and the no certiorari clause ('the decision of X shall not be removed by certiorari'). Secondly, there is the 'time-limit clause' which attempts to limit recourse to the courts to actions commenced within a specified time from the date of the impugned decision.[3] The best-known example is the six weeks clause frequently used in planning and compulsory purchase statutes.

Judges have traditionally been hostile to such clauses, developing a common-law presumption that access to the courts is not to be denied save by clear statutory words (see Viscount Simonds in *Pyx Granite Co. Ltd* v. *Minister of Housing and Local Government* [1960] AC 260). So, for example, in *R.* v. *Medical Appeal Tribunal ex p. Gilmore* [1957] 1 QB 574, Lord Denning, following precedents stretching back to the seventeenth century, said that a finality clause did not prevent judicial review by certiorari either for an excess of jurisdiction or for error of law on the face of the record. In short, the finality clause only took away any right of appeal. Similarly, even when faced with a no certiorari clause, the courts have been prepared to grant certiorari in respect of an excess of jurisdiction (*R.* v. *Wood* (1855) 5 El & Bl 49). This enmity is hardly surprising because ousters raise directly the allocation of decision-making functions within the constitution. In what circumstances should the executive, acting through Parliament, be able to exempt governmental activities from judicial intervention? Should non-judicial bodies be able to decide questions of law free from control by the ordinary courts? Or, turning the issues around, what is the proper scope of judicial activity? Should the ordinary courts enjoy a monopoly of determining issues of law? While ousters may be favoured for reasons ranging from distrust of a conservative judiciary to the administrator's desire for finality and expertise, supporters of 'the balanced constitution' would urge that the courts must retain overall control. As regards tribunals, it is this view which has been dominant in the post-Franks era. Not only have the courts emphasized their opposition to ousters, government has largely conceded the issue. The key provision was s.11 of the Tribunals and Inquiries Act 1958:

11.(1) . . . any provision in an Act passed before the commencement of this Act that any order or determination shall not be called into question in any court, or any provision in such an Act which by similar words excludes any of the powers of the High Court, shall not have effect so as to prevent the removal of the proceedings into the High Court by order of certiorari or to prejudice the powers of the High Court to make orders of mandamus . . .

(3) Nothing in this section shall affect section twenty-six of the British Nationality Act, 1948, or apply to any order or determination of a court of law or the Foreign Compensation Commission or where an Act makes special provision for application to the High Court . . . within a time limited by the Act.[4]

The saving proviso partially explains the subsequent case law. As will be seen, the courts have had to deal with time-limit clauses (*Ostler's* case), preclusive clauses protecting orders or determinations of courts of law (the *Pearlman* and *Racal* cases) and determinations of the Foreign Compensation Commission (the *Anisminic* case).

The kernel of judicial review in England is the ultra vires doctrine. If a public authority steps outside its statutory powers, it acts ultra vires or in excess of jurisdiction and the courts may intervene. In *R.* v. *Nat Bell Liquors* [1922] 2 AC 128, Lord Sumner summarized judicial review of inferior tribunals as going 'to two points: one is the area of the inferior judgment and the qualifications and conditions of its exercise; the other is the observance of the law in the course of its exercise'. An example may make the first situation, lack or want of jurisdiction, clear. Suppose a tribunal is empowered 'to grant licences within the environs of Cardiff'; one way of interpreting this phrase is to distinguish between the jurisdiction of the tribunal, i.e. its power to grant licences, and the preliminary issue of fact (whether the relevant premises are within the environs of Cardiff). Adopting this type of distinction, the courts have stressed that the jurisdiction of tribunals is limited and depends on the existence of these preliminary or 'jurisdictional' facts. So where a tribunal has made a mistake concerning a jurisdictional fact, the courts have been prepared to quash, as a nullity, any purported exercise of jurisdiction. In *White & Collins* v. *Minister of Health* [1939) 2 K B 838 a local authority was statutorily empowered to acquire compulsorily any land which did not form part of a private park. An order made and confirmed by the Minister was successfully challenged on the basis that the land made the subject of the order was in fact part of a park. Luxmoore LJ commented:

> The jurisdiction to make the order is dependent on a finding of fact; for, unless the land can be held not to be part of a park . . . there is no jurisdiction in the borough council to make, or in the Minister to confirm, the order. In such a case it seems almost self-evident that the Court which has to consider whether there is jurisdiction to make or confirm the order must be entitled to review the vital finding on which the existence of the jurisdiction relied upon depends. If this were not so, the right to apply to the Court would be illusory.

How do we distinguish jurisdictional facts from other facts which are within the jurisdiction of the tribunal to decide? This is an important question since the courts, in exercising their supervisory powers, will not normally review an erroneous finding of fact. The answer lies in statutory interpretation and the judicial freedom of manoeuvre which that implies.

Lord Sumner's second point is complicated by the coexistence of two heads of judicial review: jurisdictional error and error of law on the face of the record. Traditionally, not all errors of law have been regarded as automatically going to jurisdiction, but non-jurisdictional errors of law might be corrected by means of certiorari provided they appeared on the record of the inferior court's decision.[5] In *R.* v. *Northumberland Compensation Appeal Tribunal ex p. Shaw* [1952] 1 K B 338 this doctrine was applied to a statutory tribunal whose decision was quashed because it had misinterpreted the relevant regulations. However, the immediate consequences were limited. Since many tribunals were under no statutory obligation to provide reasons, their records might be singularly uninformative, rendering it unlikely that an error of law would be disclosed.

Following the Franks Committee's recommendations, s.12 of the 1958 Act attempted to deal with the problem by requiring tribunals within the jurisdiction of the Council on Tribunals to provide reasons for their decisions.[6] Even so the significance of error of law on the face of the record has remained limited. Since Parliament adopted Franks' recommendation of a right of appeal on law from most tribunals to the High Court, the doctrine has been partially superseded because appeal on law is wider in scope. And in cases like *Anisminic* (below) the courts have characterized more errors as errors going to jurisdiction. As this process develops (and the chances of obtaining certiorari for ultra vires increase), so the importance of error of law declines. The point is significant because in cases involving ouster clauses the courts sometimes consider that certiorari is only available for jurisdictional error.

A word of warning is in order prior to examining the leading cases. It should not be assumed from our presentation of preclusive and time-limit clauses together that the courts either do or should deal with them in similar fashion. Much of the recent controversy surrounding ousters concerns this very issue.

Smith v. East Elloe Rural District Council [1956] AC 736
The Council compulsorily purchased the plaintiff's house under the Acquisition of Land (Authorisation Procedure) Act 1946. Para. 15 of the First Schedule to this Act laid down that a compulsory purchase order (CPO) could be challenged on specified grounds within six weeks. Para. 16 contained the time-limit clause: 'Subject to the provisions of the last foregoing paragraph, a compulsory purchase order ... shall not ... be questioned in any legal proceedings whatsoever'. The plaintiff subsequently discovered facts which indicated that the town clerk and Council had acted fraudulently and in bad faith. Six years after the CPO was made, she brought an action claiming damages for trespass, an injunction to restrain the Council's employees from trespassing on her land and a declaration that the order had been wrongfully made and in bad faith. The law lords (by a 3–2 majority) rejected her argument that the statutory time-limit only applied to prerogative orders.

VISCOUNT SIMONDS: It was [argued] that, as the compulsory purchase order was challenged on the ground that it had been made and confirmed 'wrongfully' and in 'bad faith' paragraph 16 had no application. It was said that that paragraph, however general its language, must be construed so as not to oust the jurisdiction of the court where the good faith of the local authority or the Ministry was impugned and put in issue . . . My Lords, I think that anyone bred in the tradition of the law is likely to regard with little sympathy legislative provisions for ousting the jurisdiction of the court, whether in order that the subject may be deprived altogether of remedy or in order that his grievance may be remitted to some other tribunal. But it is our plain duty to give the words of an Act their proper meaning and, for my part, I find it quite impossible to qualify the words of the paragraph in the manner suggested . . . words are used which are wide enough to cover any kind of challenge which any aggrieved person may think fit to make. I cannot think of any wider words. Any addition would be mere tautology. But, it is said, let those general words be given their full scope and effect, yet they are not applicable to an order made in bad faith. But, my Lords, no one can suppose that an order bears upon its face the evidence of bad faith. It cannot be predicated of any order that it has been made in bad faith until it has been tested in legal proceedings, and it is just that test which paragraph 16 bars. How, then, can it be said that any qualification can be introduced to limit the meaning of the words? What else can 'compulsory purchase order' mean but an act apparently valid in the law, formally authorized, made, and confirmed? . . .

If the validity of such an order is open to challenge at any time within the period allowed by the ordinary Statute of Limitations with the consequence that it and all that has been done under it over a period of many years may be set aside, it is not perhaps unreasonable that Parliament should have thought fit to impose an absolute bar to proceedings even at the risk of some injustice to individuals . . . The injustice may not be so great as might appear. For the bad faith or fraud upon which an aggrieved person relies is that of individuals, and this very case shows that, even if the validity of the order cannot be questioned and he cannot recover the land that has been taken from him, yet he may have a remedy in damages against those individuals.

Anisminic Ltd v. *Foreign Compensation Commission*
[1969] 2 WLR 163

Egypt had agreed with the UK that it would provide limited compensation in respect of British property nationalized after the Suez crisis in 1956. The British Government handed over responsibility for administering the share-out to the Foreign Compensation Commission, a statutory body established by the Foreign Compensation Act 1950. The FCC was required to act according to an Order in Council which included provisions concerning the nationality of claimants for compensation. These were intended to ensure that only British nationals, be they the original owners of the relevant property or their 'successors in title,' obtained compensation. The property of Anisminic, a British company, had been nationalized but was then sold by the Egyptian Government to an Egyptian concern. The FCC interpreted the Order as excluding the company from the compensation scheme because of the Egyptian nationality of its successor in title. This determination was protected by a preclusive clause (expressly preserved by s.11(3) of the 1958 Act): 'The determination by the commission of any application made to them under this Act shall not be called in question in any court of law'. The House of Lords held by a majority (Lord Pearson dissenting) that the FCC had misconstrued the Order. The issues then became two. Had the FCC, in making its determination, fallen into an error which went to jurisdiction? If not, the preclusive clause would deny Anisminic relief. Second, if there had been jurisdictional error, what effect did this have on the preclusive clause? By a majority (Lord Morris dissenting), the House decided that the FCC had committed a jurisdictional error against which, it was held unanimously, the preclusive clause offered no protection.

LORD REID: The respondent [the FCC] maintains that [the words of the preclusive clause] are plain words only capable of having one meaning. Here is a determination which is apparently valid; there is nothing on the face of the document to cast any doubt on its validity. If it is a nullity, that could only be established by raising some kind of proceedings in court. But that would be calling the determination in question, and that is expressly prohibited by the statute. The appellants maintain that this is not the meaning of the words of this provision. They say that 'determination' means a real determination and does not include an apparent or purported determination which in the eyes of the law has no existence because it is a nullity. Or, putting it in another way, if you seek to show that a determination is a nullity you are not questioning the purported determination – you are maintaining that it does not exist as a determination. It is one thing to question a determination which does exist: it is quite another thing to say that there is nothing to be questioned. It is a well established principle that a provision ousting the ordinary jurisdiction of the court must be construed strictly – meaning, I think, that, if such a provision is reasonably capable of having two meanings, that meaning shall be taken which preserves the ordinary jurisdiction of the court . . .

If the draftsman or Parliament had intended to . . . prevent any inquiry even as to whether the document relied on was a forgery, I would have expected to find something much more specific than the bald statement that a determination shall not be called in question in any court of law. Undoubtedly such a provision protects every determination which is not a nullity. But I do not think that it is necessary or even reasonable to construe the word 'determination' as including everything which purports to be a determination but which is in fact no determination at all. And there are no degrees of nullity. There are a number of reasons why the law will hold a purported decision to be a nullity. I do not see how it could be said that such a provision protects some kinds of nullity but not others; if that were intended it would be easy to say so . . .

The case which gives most difficulty is [*East Elloe*] where the form of ouster clause was similar to that in the present case. But I cannot regard it as a very satisfactory case . . . As [it] never reached the stage of a statement of claim[7] we do not know whether her case was that the clerk of the council had fraudulently misled the council and the Ministry, or whether it was that the council and the Ministry were parties to the fraud. The result would be quite different, in my view, for it is only if the authority which made the order had itself acted in mala fide that the order would be a nullity. I think that [her] case . . . must have been that the fraud was only the fraud of the clerk because almost the whole of the argument was on the question whether a time-limit in the Act applied where fraud was alleged; there was no citation of the authorities on the question whether a clause ousting the jurisdiction of the court applied when nullity was in question, and there was little about this matter in the speeches. I do not therefore regard this case as a binding authority on this question. I have come without hesitation to the conclusion that in this case we are not prevented from inquiring whether the order of the commission was a nullity . . .

There are many cases where, although the tribunal had jurisdiction to enter on the inquiry, it has done or failed to do something in the course of the inquiry which is of such a nature that its decision is a nullity. It may have given its decision in bad faith. It may have made a decision which it had no power to make. It may have failed in the course of the inquiry to comply with the requirements of natural justice. It may in perfect good faith have misconstrued the provisions giving it power to act so that it failed to deal with the question remitted to it. It may have refused to take into account something which it was required to take into account. Or it may have based its decision on some matter which, under the provisions setting it up, it had no right to take into account. I do not intend this list to be exhaustive. But . . . if it is entitled to enter on the inquiry and does not do any of those things which I have mentioned in the course of the proceedings, then its decision is equally valid whether it is right or wrong subject only to the power of the court in certain circumstances to correct an error of law . . .

It appears from the commission's reasons that they construed [the] provision as requiring them to inquire, when the applicant is himself the original owner, whether he had a successor in title. So they made that inquiry in this case and held that [the Egyptian concern] was the applicant's successor in title. As [that concern] was not a British national they rejected the appellants' claim. But if, on a true construction of the Order, a claimant who is an original owner does not have to prove anything about successors in title, then the commission made an inquiry which the Order did not empower them to make, and they based their decision on a matter which they had no right to take into account . . . It was argued that the whole matter of construing the Order was something remitted to the commission for their decision. I cannot accept that argument. I find nothing in the Order to support it. The Order requires the commission to consider whether they are satisfied with regard to the prescribed matters. That is all they have to do. It cannot be for the commission to determine the limits of its powers. Of course if one party submits to a tribunal that its powers are wider than in fact they are, then the tribunal must deal with that submission. But if they reach a wrong conclusion as to the width of their powers, the court must be able to correct that – not because the tribunal has made an error of law, but because as a result of making an error of law they have dealt with and based their decision on a matter with which, on a true construction of their powers, they had no right to deal. If they base their decision on some matter which is not prescribed for their adjudication, they are doing something which they have no right to do and their decision is a nullity.

Here is one view of *Anisminic*:

The net result was that [the law lords] had disobeyed the Act, although nominally they were merely construing it in a peculiar but traditional way . . . The judges appreciate, much more than does Parliament, that to exempt any public authority from judicial control is to give it dictatorial power, and that this is so fundamentally objectionable that Parliament cannot really intend it . . . There can be abuse of legislative power, not indeed in the legal sense, but in a distinct constitutional sense, for example if Parliament were to legislate to establish one-party government, or a dictatorship, or in some other way were to attack the fundamentals of democracy. To exempt a public authority from the jurisdiction of the courts of law is, to that extent, to grant dictatorial power. It is no exaggeration, therefore, to describe this as an abuse of the power of Parliament, speaking constitutionally. This is the justification . . . for the strong, it might even be said rebellious, stand which the courts have made against allowing Acts of Parliament to create pockets of uncontrollable power in violation of the rule of law. Parliament is unduly addicted to this practice giving too much weight to temporary convenience and too little to constitutional principle. The law's delay, together with its uncertainty and expense, tempts governments to take short cuts by elimination of the courts. But if the courts are prevented from enforcing the law, the remedy becomes worse than the disease. [Wade 1980, pp. 65–6.]

Wade's approach to administrative law is clear; to upset the 'balanced constitution' is dangerous and justifies the courts in taking extraordinary preventive measures. What might Wade mean by his appeal to 'constitutional principle'?[8] Would you equate access to the courts with the 'rule of law'? If the courts are excluded, does power become 'uncontrollable'?

It should not be assumed that all judges agree with Wade; in *East Elloe*, for example, Viscount Simonds stressed his duty to obey Parliament and recognized a need for finality so that administrators could get on with implementing government policy. We will meet a similar division of opinion in the *Burmah Oil* case (Chapter 12). In the unwritten British constitution, the allocation of decision-making functions is a matter of continuing dispute. Here is Griffith's view:

Where Parliament enacts positively that certain questions should be decided finally by a public authority, whether a Minister or a specialized tribunal or commission (as in *Anisminic*), the courts should respect this decision and should not assume that judges, however eminent, are the better deciders of complex issues. The whole history of administrative tribunals shows the need for specialist bodies in certain areas of administration and adjudication. Certainly, if such bodies deal with questions which they were not set up to deal with, and . . . so act outside their jurisdiction, they should be reviewable by the courts. Otherwise they should not be interfered with by the judges who are more likely than not to introduce inconsistency and injustice into complex areas of administration. [Griffith 1983, pp. 56–7.]

So Griffith does not advocate abolishing judicial review but rather curtailing it. Like Lord Morris in *Anisminic*, he favours a limited notion of jurisdictional error (and see below, p. 345):

If an Act of Parliament says that A [a public authority] shall be the person to settle certain specified questions and that there shall be neither appeal to nor review by . . . the courts, then A's decisions are unchallengeable so long as (a) it is A, not another, who decides, (b) A decides those specified questions and not others and (c) A does not act in bad faith or with similar impropriety. The *Anisminic* decision goes much further than this and says in effect that A's decision can be set aside by the courts if they disagree with his interpretation of the rules which he is required to apply. [Griffith 1977, pp. 123–4.]

Whatever Parliament had 'really' intended, the Government reacted swiftly to *Anisminic*. It tacked on to a Foreign Compensation Bill, coincidentally before the House of Commons, an amendment designed to nullify the decision prospectively by enabling an Order in Council to be made establishing the finality of a purported deter- mination by the FCC. Lord Chalfont, the Minister of State at the Foreign and Commonwealth Office, argued (HL Deb. vol. 299, col. 17) that the nature of the FCC's task rendered judicial review inappropriate. Was this because the problem was polycentric?

[The] Commission cannot avoid interpreting the Orders under which it carries out the distributions entrusted to it. [The *Anisminic*] judgment would therefore make it possible . . . for the Commission's determinations, made in perfectly good faith and after the most careful deliberation, to be challenged in a wide range of cases. The consequences of this . . . would be most unfortunate. The task of the Commission, which is of a special character, is to determine claims and to arrange for distribution on a rateable basis to successful claimants, of what are nearly always finite 'lump sums' either received in the form of cash from foreign Governments, or . . . raised by the disposal of foreign assets in this country . . . Until all obligations, or at any rate all those of any substance or magnitude, have been disposed of, it is impossible for the Commission to judge with any degree of certainty what will be the share attributable to each successful application and so to pay anything like a final dividend at all to them. If there is to be a risk that their determinations may be challenged in the courts . . . the claimants, who have usually already been waiting for a very long time . . . may well have to wait a further substantial period before they can touch their awards or at any rate the greater part of them.

Faced by some angry letters from eminent lawyers to *The Times*[9] and by a hostile amendment, supported by the law lords and carried in the Upper House (HL Deb. vol. 299, cols. 640-54), the Government backtracked. Does the resulting provision, s.3 of the Foreign Compensation Act 1969, strike the right balance? It provides for direct appeal to the Court of Appeal on a question of law concerning the construction of an Order in Council. No further appeal lies to the House of Lords. Otherwise, save in cases of natural justice, a determination (including a purported determination) is not to be called in question in any court of law.

There was much academic speculation about the impact of *Anisminic* on the previous case law. Was Diplock (1974, p. 243), writing extra-judicially, correct to claim that the decision 'renders obsolete the technical distinction between errors of law which go to "jurisdiction" and errors of law which do not'? Gould hailed a new millenium:

The effect of the actual decision on the facts in *Anisminic* and of the wide-ranging dicta . . . is to reduce the difference between jurisdictional error and error of law within the jurisdiction almost to vanishing point. This, despite the Lords' explicit denial that they were tampering in any way with the separate category of error within the jurisdiction . . . Any error can be accurately described as arising from a failure to take into account a relevant factor or a taking into account of an extraneous consideration. The mere fact that an error occurred is evidence that one of these two things happened . . .

If the practical outcome of *Anisminic* is to be the virtual end of error of law on the face of the record and its replacement by an all-embracing category of jurisdictional error, can this be supported in principle? It is submitted that it is not only supported, but actually required by principle. There is after all something rather odd about a doctrine which allows that bodies are set up, and their powers defined, by law, but which allows such bodies to break the law and yet remain within their jurisdiction. [Gould 1970, pp. 360–1.]

What was the effect, if any, of *Anisminic* on *East Elloe*? The latter had been heavily criticized but not explicitly overruled. Did it survive? If so, how were the two decisions to be reconciled? Alder (1975, pp. 284–5) claimed that they might be distinguished through a literal interpretation of time-limit clauses. He noted that the statutory formula often associates a time-limit clause with a statutory remedy by reference to words like 'decisions' or 'orders' and also provides that these are unreviewable 'except as provided by the Act'. (*East Elloe* illustrates the point.) Alder then argued that since in cases like *Ridge* v. *Baldwin* the courts have established that an ultra vires decision is a nullity and because one of the statutory grounds for review is that the 'decision' or 'order' is ultra vires, it follows that the term 'decision' has to be construed as to include a nullity. He could thus distinguish the reasoning in *Anisminic* since that was predicated on being able to construe the term 'determination' in the preclusive clause as excluding a purported determination which was in fact a nullity. Alder's is a difficult if logical argument: a rereading of Lord Reid's judgment may help to make it clear.

More fundamental is the question whether judicial review should depend on this type of analytical reasoning. Should the courts be more concerned with the practical consequences of their decisions? This question has been posed in the wake of our next case, the first to consider directly the relationship of *Anisminic* and *East Elloe*.

R. v. *Secretary of State for the Environment ex p. Ostler*
[1977] QB 122

O did not go to a local inquiry into a proposed by-pass, having no objection to the planned route. The scheme was approved and the stopping-up and compulsory purchase orders made in May 1974. O subsequently attended a second inquiry into the provision of access roads, since his business premises would be affected by the widening of one of these, Craythorn Lane. He failed in his objection and the supplementary order dealing with the access roads was confirmed in July 1975. A few months later O discovered that, prior to the first inquiry, an objector had withdrawn an objection after a secret undertaking by a DOE official that access to his business would be ensured by the widening of Craythorn Lane. Claiming that had he known of the undertaking and thus the potential consequences for him, he would have objected at the initial inquiry, O sought certiorari to quash the original orders, 19 months after their confirmation. He argued that the DOE had acted in bad faith and contrary to natural justice. The Court of Appeal, proceeding on the assumption that this was so, held that challenge to the confirmed orders was barred by a time-limit clause identical to that in *East Elloe*.

LORD DENNING MR: Is . . . *East Elloe* . . . a good authority or has it been overruled by *Anisminic* . . .? I think that . . . *East Elloe* . . . must still be regarded as good and binding on this court. It is readily to be distinguished from the *Anisminic* case . . . The points of difference are these:

First, in the *Anisminic* case the Act ousted the jurisdiction of the court altogether. It precluded the court from entertaining any complaint at any time about the determination. Whereas in the *East Elloe* case the statutory provision has given the court jurisdiction to inquire into complaints so long as the applicant comes within six weeks. The provision is more in the nature of a limitation period than of a complete ouster . . .

Second, in the *Anisminic* case, the House was considering a determination by a truly judicial body, the [FCC] whereas in the *East Elloe* case the House was considering an order which was very much in the nature of an administrative decision. That is a distinction which Lord Reid himself drew in *Ridge* v. *Baldwin* . . . There is a great difference between the two. In making a judicial decision, the tribunal considers the rights of the parties without regard to the public interest. But in an administrative decision (such as a compulsory purchase order) the public interest plays an important part. The question is, to what extent are private interests to be subordinated to the public interest.

Third, in the *Anisminic* case the House had to consider the actual determination of the tribunal, whereas in the . . . *East Elloe* case the House had to consider the validity of the process by which the decision was reached.

So . . . *East Elloe* . . . must still be regarded as the law in regard to this provision we have to consider here. I would add this: if this order were to be upset for want of good faith or for lack of natural justice, it would not to my mind be a nullity or void from the beginning. It would only be voidable. And as such . . . it should be challenged promptly before much has been done under it . . .

Looking at it broadly . . . the policy underlying the statute is that when a compulsory purchase order has been made, then if it has been wrongly obtained or made, a person aggrieved should have a remedy. But he must come promptly. He must come within six weeks. If he does so, the court can and will entertain his complaint. But if the six weeks expire without any application being made, the court cannot entertain it afterwards. The reason is because, as soon as that time has elapsed, the authority will take steps to acquire property, demolish it and so forth. The public interest demands that they should be safe in doing so. Take this very case. The inquiry was held in 1973. The orders made early in 1974. Much work has already been done under them. It would be contrary to the public interest that the demolition should be held up or delayed by further evidence or inquiries.

GOFF LJ: The *Anisminic* case is distinguishable on two grounds. First . . . *Anisminic* dealt with a judicial decision . . . It is true that the Minister has been said to be acting [here] in a quasi-judicial capacity, but he is nevertheless conducting an administrative or executive matter, where questions of policy enter into and must influence his decision . . .

Where one is dealing with a matter of that character and . . . the order is one which must be acted upon promptly, it is, I think, easier for the courts to construe Parliament as meaning exactly what it said – that the matter cannot be questioned in any court . . . than where, as in *Anisminic*, one is dealing with a statute setting up a judicial tribunal and defining its powers and the question is whether it has acted within them . . .

[Second] the ratio in the *Anisminic* case was that the House was dealing simply with a question of jurisdiction, and not a case where the order is made within jurisdiction, but it is attacked on the ground of fraud or mala fides . . . [The] determination was a purported determination only, because the tribunal, however eminent, having misconceived the effect of the statute, acted outside its jurisdiction, and indeed without any jurisdiction at all, whereas here one is dealing with an actual decision made within jurisdiction though sought to be challenged.

In these judgments four different antitheses are used to distinguish *Anisminic* from *East Elloe*: judicial/administrative decisions; juris-dictional/non-jurisdictional errors; void/voidable decisions (see below, p. 288) and total/limited ousters. There are several possible criticisms of this conceptual analysis. Lord Denning, by refusing to apply Lord Reid's statement in *Anisminic* that bad faith renders a decision a nullity, places the victim of administrative fraud in a worse position than other aggrieved persons. Does Griffith favour judicial intervention in such circumstances? Remember the scorn with which Jennings greeted Donoughmore's suggestion that 'judicial' and 'administrative' decisions could be distinguished because the former involved no element of policy; in *Ostler*, Goff LJ makes this very argument. And Lord Denning informs us that in 'judicial' decisions the 'public interest' is not regarded. Compare the final paragraph of his own judgment.

Another line of attack, characteristic of American realism, stresses the policy issues involved in deciding cases and suggests that conceptual analysis is nothing more than window-dressing. Judges do not use concepts in order to reason towards particular conclusions, but deploy them as ex post facto rationalizations or shrouds for policy decisions which have already been taken. If this were so, then the judiciary could be criticized for a lack of openness but, in the vast majority of cases, it is incapable of proof.

It is also contended that the results produced by the antitheses are unsubtle; that, for example, to treat all time-limit clauses, whatever the circumstances, as different from all preclusive clauses, is arbit-rary. 'Finality may be equally desirable in either case; rights may need protection in either case; the public may suffer in either case' (Leigh 1980, p. 51). As with procedural fairness, some functionalists advocate replacing conceptualism in judicial review with context-ualism:

> There seems . . . to be no compelling reason why the decision in . . . *East Elloe* should have been affected by the *Anisminic* case. The respective subject-matter of the two cases was completely different – a compulsory purchase order and a determination of the [FCC]. Yet the interrelation of the two decisions has continued to provoke extensive academic debate (in the form of successive attempts to reconcile the decisions on a conceptual basis) because each involved a statutory provision which sought to exclude or restrict judicial review of administrative action. It is [my] thesis that the disparity of the subject-matter renders the protracted debate and attempts at conceptual reconciliation meaningless since, in terms of the redress of grievances, considerations relevant to awards of compensation for the expropriation of property overseas have no relevance to planning decisions. The implication is that the conflict between the operation of the *Anisminic* principle on the one hand and the effective restriction of a time-limit clause on the other hand cannot be resolved in the abstract, divorced from the factual context of the dispute . . .
>
> It is arguable that [this] is a fundamental issue underlying much of modern administrative law . . . Ultimately every challenge to administrative action can be seen to represent a conflict between, on the one hand, the constitutional priorities of fairness and the rule of law, and, on the other hand, the administrators' priorities of expedience and finality. Since, however, there is in reality no typical administrative process nor typical administrator, it follows that the resolution of these conflicting priorities will tend to vary with the particular process in question; different considerations will apply in different contexts and the relevance of the same considerations will vary according to the circumstances. In other words, there can be no such thing as a general solution: rather there must be a series of particular solutions. [Gravells 1978, pp. 383–4.]

Gravells does not think *Ostler* wrongly decided; rather the Court of Appeal should have reached the same conclusion by different means. This is how he would balance the competing considerations:

> If the *Anisminic* principle were held to be applicable to the instant case, it would follow that at any time after the order was confirmed, it could be challenged and declared a nullity. Where the public authority concerned and individuals have relied on the impugned decision for some considerable time, it is obviously unreasonable and contrary to the public interest to permit any challenge to a compulsory purchase order, for example, to be made years afterwards when the land may already have been developed at a vast cost to public funds; and no less important, if public authorities are unable to rely on planning orders as being conclusive and exempt from further challenge, there is a danger that major construction work and the development of land for the benefit of the community at large will be postponed, with consequent escalation of costs when finally completed, if not abandoned altogether . . .
>
> Even where the . . . context of land development warrants a limited period

for challenge, if the particular circumstances of the actual case in dispute do not support the rationale of the imposition of a limitation period then no such limitation period should be strictly applied. In other words the justification for the time-limit clauses should be a rebuttable presumption . . . Where . . . only minor development has been implemented, little expenditure has been incurred and no third party rights have accrued, there can be no justification for failing to examine the substance of a complaint against a public authority; and so much the more where the public interest in good administration as well as individual interests is at stake. On the facts of . . . *Ostler* it is clear that . . . expediency must prevail. All the relevant factors which together form the rationale of the expediency argument are present: the completion of ninety per cent of the demolition work, the acquisition of eighty per cent of the necessary property and the expenditure of large sums of money. Conflicting considerations as to the maintenance of good administration may certainly be said to weigh more heavily in the circumstances of the present case than in most situations, but it must be remembered that the Court of Appeal *assumed* that bad faith and breach of natural justice had been established: those factual issues had not been resolved by the court. [Gravells 1978, pp. 394–8.]

This form of contextualism is different from Elliott's 'transaction-typing'. Not only should cases involving cpos be irrelevant to those concerning determinations by bodies like the FCC, the courts should tailor their decisions to individual fact situations arising *within* administrative activities such as 'land development'. The application of time-limit clauses should be a rebuttable presumption. We can see from this how difficult contextual judicial review might actually prove. Not only might it change the mode of adjudication, leading judges openly to articulate criteria and strike balances which might prove highly controversial.[10] The judges must also specify the relevant 'context' within which each judgment is to proceed.[11] Should it, for example, be the particular fact situation or the relevant 'transaction type'? If the latter, should the subject-area (to adopt Gravells' examples) be defined as 'compulsory purchase orders', 'land development' or 'planning decisions'? What approach, respectively, did Mullan and Lord Parker CJ in *Re H.K. (An Infant)* intend? (See above, pp. 80–2).

Responding to Gravells, Alder defended conceptual analysis, arguing that a highly individuated form of contextualism grants the courts too broad a discretion to deal with issues properly determined by Parliament. It represents a shift in the allocation of decision-making functions to the judges.

[Gravells] postulates some kind of dispensing power in the judges not to apply the time limit in a case where on the particular facts the injustice to the applicant outweighs the public interest in administrative finality and against a general background of respect for the rule of law . . . [In] the particular context of land development . . . the proposal is undesirable. First, it gives the judiciary an unacceptably wide discretion to assess matters of public interest which are better determined by the legislature. Secondly it creates the very mischief which the time limit clause was introduced to eradicate, that is uncertainty. A developer would not know even after the expiry of the time limit whether he could safely go ahead until a court had adjudicated . . . It is better to tolerate the exceptional case like *Ostler* . . . bearing in mind that he is not left entirely without remedy. It is for the legislature to decide what classes of decision should be immune from review not for the judiciary . . .

Concepts are general principles and one objective of legal reasoning is to translate policies and values into concepts which are then used as tools of analysis. They provide a point of reference against which judgments of the courts can be evaluated . . .

This is well illustrated by the distinction . . . between [the] judicial and administrative. [It reflects a] basic constitutional idea and although [it is] not necessarily applied to [its] logical extent [it does] provide a touchstone against which deviations from principle have to be justified. Law need not be logical but logic is valuable if only to make the law comprehensible so that if logic is outweighed in a particular case by other values, the competing considerations can be openly presented . . .

Gravell's . . . thesis that the methodology of administrative law should avoid general principles in favour of a series of particular policy based solutions is to be resisted. It is true that in the last analysis everything depends upon the particular legislation under which the decision is made. But a rational and comprehensible legal system depends upon the application of general principles even if they only rank as presumptions against which to construe the legislation. If review of governmental activity is to depend upon balancing policy considerations then . . . this is not a task which should be undertaken by the ordinary English courts as now constituted. [Alder 1980, pp. 672–4, 679–80.]

Commenting on *Ostler* in his book *The Discipline of Law*, Lord Denning criticized his own reasoning. Repudiating the void/voidable distinction, he conceded that although 'the Minister's decision was an administrative decision . . . that gives no exemption from judicial review. If the decision was reached contrary to natural justice or in bad faith, it was beyond the power of the Minister . . . So it would be a nullity and void' (Denning 1979, pp. 108–9). Instead the decision, which Lord Denning still thought correct, should have been based on the final paragraph of his judgment (above). This passage is functionalist in tone. Does Lord Denning assert a dispensing power or adopt a more generalized contextual approach? How does the analysis compare with Gravells' balancing act? Are the courts equipped to weigh policy considerations in the manner suggested? And can Loughlin's critique of procedural fairness also be directed at Gravells' thesis? (See above, p. 84).

Pearlman v. *Keepers and Governors of Harrow School*
[1979] QB 56

P sought certiorari to quash a determination made by a county court under the Housing Act 1974. Contrary to a prior county court decision, the judge had decided that P was not entitled to a reduction in the rateable value of his tenanted property because the installation of a central heating system did not constitute the 'structural alteration' required by the Act. Without the reduction P could not purchase the freehold of the property under the Leasehold Reform Act 1967. Unanimously, the Court of Appeal held that the judge had made an error of law in interpreting the phrase 'structural alteration' and that P's installation of central heating fell within that category. The issue then became whether the error was jurisdictional because the Court (Lord Denning dissenting) accepted that s.107 of the County Courts Act 1959[12] precluded certiorari for error of law on the face of the record where county courts were concerned. A majority[13] (Geoffrey Lane LJ dissenting) considered the error went to jurisdiction.

LORD DENNING MR: The distinction between an error which entails absence of jurisdiction – and an error made within jurisdiction – is very fine. So fine . . . that in truth the High Court has a choice before it whether to interfere with an inferior court on a point of law. If it chooses to interfere, it can formulate its decision in the words: 'The court below had no jurisdiction to decide this point wrongly as it did'. If it does not choose to interfere, it can say: 'The court had jurisdiction to decide it wrongly, and did so' . . .

This distinction should now be discarded. The High Court has, and should have, jurisdiction to control the proceedings of inferior courts and tribunals by way of judicial review. When they go wrong in law, the High Court should have power to put them right. Not only in the instant case to do justice to the complainant. But also so as to secure that all courts and tribunals, when faced with the same point of law, should decide it in the same way . . . The way to get things right is to hold thus: no court or tribunal has any jurisdiction to make an error of law on which the decision of the case depends. If it makes such an error, it goes outside its jurisdiction and certiorari will lie to correct it.

Lord Denning appears to demolish another antithesis used in *Ostler*.[14] His judgment exemplifies pragmatism; the need for legal consistency justifies intervention here. Although in ushering in Gould's millenium he transgresses established authority, including the dicta in *Anisminic* itself, the result produced has the virtue of simplicity.[15] Since error of law on the face of the record would be rendered otiose (because all errors of law would be jurisdictional), a unitary head of judicial review, ultra vires, would be established. No longer, for example, would it be necessary to define the scope of the 'record' or to distinguish jurisdictional from non-jurisdictional error. Lord Denning characterizes that particular line-drawing exercise as nothing more than an ex post facto rationalization of what has gone before, a confession which provides ammunition for an American realist critique of conceptual analysis. Compare Jowell's suggestion that the obligation to justify a judicial decision by means of 'rule, standard or principle' imposes discipline. Judges, it transpires, may play games with rules.

By extending the courts' supervisory jurisdiction beyond the already expansionist decision in *Anisminic*, Lord Denning brings into sharp focus the constitutional dimension of ousters. Even Wade (1979, p. 166) warns against maintaining the 'balanced constitution' in this manner: 'If every error is now to be jurisdictional, ouster clauses will have no sphere of operation at all, and the judicial attitude will be exposed as one of naked disobedience to Parliament. This may prove a misfortune.' This is how the House of Lords has recently tried to solve the problem.

Re Racal Communications Ltd [1981] AC 374

Under s.441 of the Companies Act 1948 a High Court judge may authorize the inspection of a company's books provided there is reasonable cause to believe that an officer of the company has committed an offence 'in connection with the management of the company's affairs'. The DPP, who suspected that there had been fraudulent overcharging of Racal's customers, applied for authorization but Vinelott J held that the alleged offence fell outside the ambit of the statute. However, on being told that other judges had taken a different view, he volunteered leave to appeal. Yet s.441(3) laid down that 'the decision of a judge of the High Court . . . in an application under this section shall not be appealable'. The Court of Appeal, Lord Denning presiding, considered that Vinelott J had misconstrued the scope of the statute, that this was an error of law going to jurisdiction and that therefore s.441(3) did not prevent it hearing the case. The House of Lords overturned this decision.

LORD DIPLOCK: In *Anisminic* . . . this House was concerned only with decisions of administrative tribunals . . . It is a legal landmark; it has made possible the rapid development in England of a rational and comprehensive system of administrative law on the foundation of the concept of ultra vires. It proceeds on the presumption that where Parliament confers on an administrative tribunal or authority, as distinct from a court of law, power to decide particular questions defined by the Act conferring the power, Parliament intends to confine that power to answering the question as it has been so defined: and if there has been any doubt as to what that question is, this is a matter for courts of law to resolve in fulfilment of their constitutional role as interpreters of the written law and expounders of the common law and rules of equity. So if the administrative tribunal or authority have asked themselves the wrong question and answered that, they have done something that the Act does not empower them to do and their decision is a nullity. Parliament can, of course, if it so desires, confer upon administrative tribunals or authorities power to decide questions of law as well as questions of fact or of administrative policy; but this requires clear words, for the presumption is that where a decision-making power is conferred on a tribunal or authority that is not a court of law, Parliament did not intend to do so. The break-through made by *Anisminic* was that, as respects administrative tribunals and authorities, the old distinction between errors of law that went to jurisdiction and errors of law that did not, was for practical purposes abolished. Any error of law that could be shown to have been made by them in the course of reaching their decision on matters of fact or of administrative policy would result in their having asked themselves the wrong question with the result that the decision they reached would be a nullity . . .

But there is no similar presumption that where a decision-making power is conferred by statute upon a court of law, Parliament did not intend to confer upon it power to decide questions of law as well as questions of fact. Whether it did or did not and, in the case of inferior courts, what limits are imposed on the kinds of questions of law they are empowered to decide, depends upon the construction of the statute unencumbered by any such presumption. In the case of inferior courts where the decision of the court is made final and conclusive by the statute, this may involve the survival of those subtle distinctions formerly drawn between errors of law which go to jurisdiction and errors of law which do not that did so much to confuse English administrative law before *Anisminic* . . . But upon any application for judicial review of a decision of an inferior court in a matter which involves, as so many do, interrelated questions of law, fact and degree the superior court conducting the review should not be astute to hold that Parliament did not intend the inferior court to have jurisdiction to decide for itself the meaning of ordinary words used in the statute to define the question which it has to decide. This, in my view, is the error into which the majority of the Court of Appeal fell in *Pearlman* . . .

There is . . . however, also an obvious distinction between jurisdiction conferred by a statute on a court of law of limited jurisdiction to decide a defined question finally and conclusively or unappealably, and a similar jurisdiction conferred on the High Court or a judge of the High Court acting in his judicial capacity. The High Court is not a court of limited jurisdiction and its constitutional role includes the interpretation of written laws. There is thus no room for the inference that Parliament did not intend the High Court or the judge of the High Court acting in his judicial capacity to be entitled and, indeed, required to construe the words of the statute by which the question submitted to his decision was defined. There is simply no room for error going to his jurisdiction, nor . . . is there any room for judicial review. Judicial review is available as a remedy for mistakes of law made by inferior courts and tribunals only. Mistakes of law made by judges of the High Court acting in their capacity as such can be corrected only by means of appeal to an appellate court; and if, as in the instant case, the statute provides that the judge's decision shall not be appealable, they cannot be corrected at all.[16]

By confining the scope of *Anisminic*, Lord Diplock creates a hierarchy of decision-making agencies in which, to varying degrees, confidence may be reposed. High Court judges (acting in their 'judicial capacity') can be trusted with all questions of law; inferior courts with some and administrative tribunals and authorities with none. Lord Diplock preserves at least the illusion of parliamentary sovereignty, so avoiding the charge of 'naked disobedience'. He states that *Anisminic* is based on a presumption concerning parliamentary intention, suggesting that, where there are 'clear words', the presumption may be rebutted. What words do you think would satisfy Lord Diplock (or Lord Denning)?

To functionalists, Lord Diplock's three-fold classification may appear over-simple. It means, for example, subject to the absence of 'clear words' to the contrary, that all 'administrative tribunals and authorities' should be treated in one way, whatever the consequences for a particular administrative process, and all 'inferior courts', whatever functions they are carrying out, in another. Bearing in mind that there exists no clear pattern in the allocation of decision-making functions, is this any less arbitrary than a strict division between time-limit and preclusive clauses? Lord Diplock involves the courts in a series of line-drawing exercises of the type denigrated by Lord Denning. In respect of inferior courts, the judges must engage in what Lord Diplock (1974, p. 238) has elsewhere called a 'barren' and 'esoteric' controversy, the distinction between jurisdictional and non-jurisdictional errors of law. Nor is the position of administrative tribunals or authorities as simple as may first appear. Since only certain facts are jurisdictional, the courts retain the freedom of manoeuvre implicit in the need to distinguish 'fact' from 'law'. And Lord Diplock requires the drawing of a new dividing line between 'inferior courts' and 'administrative tribunals and authorities'. This distinction is different from the judicial/administrative dichotomy although it bears obvious similarities to it. Alder, supporting the old classification, is dismayed:

Since there is no conceptual distinction between an inferior court and some administrative tribunals this is less satisfactory. There is no clear definition of a court and use of the term seems to indicate only a certain formality of procedure so that there may be no important difference between a body called a court and one styled tribunal . . . [Alder 1980, p. 678.]

5
Getting things taped

1 Above the Plimsoll line: formal rule-making

Earlier we found some writers describing a dichotomy between 'law' and 'government'. The law model was based on *rules*, described as systematic and calculable, and possessed its own characteristic (judicial) procedures. The model of government implied *discretionary power* which, because it was not governed by rules, seemed uncertain, incalculable and tainted by caprice and arbitrariness. The contrast is caught admirably in a passage from Hewart describing how departments seem to him to take decisions:

The exercise of arbitrary power is neither law nor justice, administrative or at all. The very conception of 'law' is a conception of something involving the application of known rules and principles . . . There are no rules or principles which can be said to be rules or principles of this astonishing variety of administrative 'law', nor is there any regular course of procedure for its application. It is possible, no doubt, that the public official who decides questions in pursuance of the powers given to his department does act, or persuades himself that he acts, on some general rules or principles. But, if so, they are entirely unknown to anybody outside the department, and of what value is a so-called 'law' of which nobody has any knowledge? [Hewart 1929, p. 44.]

Implicit in this passage is the familiar, Diceyan, idea that administrative decision-taking is somehow 'arbitrary'. The administrator decides each case on its facts without reference to any system of principles or precedents which the lawyer could call 'law'. Further examination will show that this is a total misconception; administrators prefer to operate by the rulebook. But the principles and precedents which administrators devise for themselves do not always fall within the lawyer's definition of 'rules'. They might instead be described dismissively as 'policies', 'advice' or 'guidance'. Just as lawyers approach tribunals on the assumption that they are court-substitutes, so they approach administrative rule-making on the basis that it is a legislation-substitute and suspicion of executive legislation, like suspicion of discretionary executive power, is an inescapable feature of our constitutional heritage:

Suspicion of governmental powers was a characteristic of the constitution from the opening of the seventeenth century until the close of the nineteenth; and even with a Government which owes its authority only to a majority in Parliament, based on a free demonstration of public opinion, it has not wholly disappeared. If the King could legislate and tax otherwise than in Parliament he could govern without Parliament, and it was therefore a cardinal doctrine of the Parliamentary party that the King had no such powers. [Jennings 1957, p. 473.]

The lawyer's concern with an administrative rule is to discover whether it is a rule in the sense that it is 'binding' or creates 'rights'. Thus the hierarchy inevitably starts at the top with legislation. Usually the lawyer's interest ends where the authorization of Parliament can no longer be spelled out either explicitly or by implication:

There is no power to issue regulations 'in execution of the laws' as there is in democratic countries which follow the French tradition. Such a power is necessarily restricted, since there must first be laws before regulations can be issued for their execution; with us there must be not only laws but also specific power to issue regulations. Numerous powers of this kind have been conferred; but express authority for their exercise must always be shown; and so powerful is the tradition that powers of law-making (except by courts) are inherently dangerous that protests are often raised even against the narrowly defined powers which are frequently conferred upon Ministers . . . [Jennings 1957, p. 474.]

The administration in 'legislating' wears borrowed feathers, always with the fictional consent of the legislature. So Griffith and Street (1973, p. 32) refer to the miscellaneous rules, regulations, orders, schemes, byelaws, licences, directives, warrants, instruments of approval or minutes which made up the ragbag of delegated legislation, as the 'children' and 'grandchildren' of statute.

Why, then, does Parliament wish to delegate the legislative power? The traditional answer is that the practice is necessitated by pressure on parliamentary time and accordingly that a division of functions should be devised in which Parliament assumes control of policy and the administration is left to finalize matters of detail. C. K. Allen, in his classic exposition, *Law and Orders*, cites Lord Thring, an experienced parliamentary draftsman of the nineteenth century:

The adoption of the system of confining the attention of Parliament to material provisions only, and leaving details to be settled departmentally, is probably the only mode in which Parliamentary government can, as respects its legislative functions, be satisfactorily carried on. The province of Parliament is to decide material questions affecting the public interest, and the more procedure and subordinate matters can be withdrawn from their cognisance, the greater will be the time afforded for the consideration of the more serious questions involved in legislation. [Allen 1965, p. 35.]

The growing power of the state combines with the complex pattern of governmental institutions – central and local authorities, boards, commissions and nationalized industry – to create a need for administrative rule-making. Griffith and Street (1973, p. 71) only hint at the need for such a power:

If an Administration wishes to change part of the structure of society, it must use the device of delegated legislation . . . the details of extensive changes cannot be so accurately foreseen that they can be provided for in the principal statutes. Statutory provisions must be adaptable; discretionary powers must be entrusted to the Administration.

Jennings goes rather further:

It is clear that powers to make delegated legislation must grow in number as the scope of governmental power increases . . . Though . . . they were not . . . uncommon early in the nineteenth century, they have grown in number and importance with the development of the 'period of collectivism' which is usually said to begin about 1870. For the most part, the earlier developments were in the cognate fields of local government and public utilities . . . Since 1906 however, the Central Government has been given many direct administrative functions, and there has consequently been an increase in the statutory instruments issued by departments to supplement the legislation applying to their own centrally administered services. [Jennings 1957, p. 477.]

So, once more, the Donoughmore Committee was faced with a *fait accompli*. Delegated legislation, like administrative adjudication, existed because it had to exist, and, as with the allocation of decision-making functions, the constitution provided no logical framework:

With the haphazard habit characteristic of English political life the constitutional practice has grown up gradually, as and when the need arose in Parliament, without any logical system. The power has been delegated by Parliament for various reasons, because, for instance, the topic involved much detail, or because it was technical, or because the pressure of other demands upon Parliamentary time did not allow the necessary time to be devoted by the House of Commons to the particular Bill. The limits of delegated power, the methods of ministerial procedure, and the safeguards for the protection of the public or the preservation of Parliamentary control thus appear often to have been dictated by opportunist considerations, peculiar to the occasion. [Cmnd 4060, (1932), p. 16.]

The Committee's proposed 'safeguards' were designed to strengthen traditional controls (see Cmnd 4060, pp. 64–70). Parliament was to devise better machinery for scrutiny; and certain policy matters (e.g. powers to amend legislation or impose taxes) were characterized as unsuitable for delegation. To strengthen control by the judiciary, draftsmen were exhorted to eschew ouster clauses and to include, whenever possible, statutory guidelines defining the limits of the powers supposed to be delegated. There were recommendations concerning publicity, today contained in the Statutory Instruments Act 1946, which, in time, replaced the Rules Publication Act 1893. These recommendations were influential. From the limited angle of an administrative lawyer, they were likely to prove generally acceptable. For red light theorists, they go some way to restore the balance of the constitution; for green light theorists, they strengthen political control over government. Here, for example, is Robson:

These recommendations appear to combine practical common sense with theoretical wisdom. They avoid the danger of attempting to lay down inflexible dogmas to guide the orthodox for all eternity, while at the same time they are based on recognisable principles. They distinguish between the normal and the abnormal; they embody the indispensable feature of perpetual scrutiny by members of the legislature; they observe the need for expert assistance to aid the Parliamentary Committees in their task; they emphasise the importance of good drafting, publicity, uniformity of procedure and rationalisation of method. They endeavour to make Parliament more conscious of what it is doing or about to do than to persuade it to accept self-denying penances in the future. Inevitably, there are obvious doubts which arise in connection with some of the recommendations. One wonders, for instance, how a single Committee of each House will manage to cover the whole vast field of delegated legislation without missing the significance of many of the statutory rules and orders. One questions the ability of the Committees to report on form while avoiding judgment on the substance. But these and similar criticisms are purely hypothetical. Taken as a whole, the recommendations of the Committee on delegated legislation seem to be exceedingly good. [Robson 1932, pp. 354–5.]

So these recommendations confirmed the link between administrative rule-making and the legislative function. Regulations were legislation for which Parliament could not quite find time and whether it would find time properly to *scrutinize*, was 'hypothetical'.

It is fair to summarize developments since 1932 by saying that, although delegated legislation has steadily increased in volume, the arrangements for publication and for parliamentary control have also improved, with added momentum in the last decade. Not surprisingly, the impetus for reform has more often than not come from Parliament itself. The first Commons Committee on Statutory Instruments was established in 1944. In 1953, it was the subject of a report by a select committee (HC 310 (1952–3)). Since then the subject has been considered by a series of select committees. A survey of the arrangements in 1971 led to a measure of rationalization. The Special Orders Committee of the House of Lords merged with its Commons equivalent as a joint 'Scrutiny Committee'. A Commons committee was left to deal with those instruments which need be laid only before the House of Commons. To relieve pressure on parliamentary time, a procedure was instituted by which certain statutory instruments are not dealt with on the floor of the House of Commons, but are taken in Standing Committee.[1]

But experts agree that the reforms to date are still inadequate and that parliamentary 'control' is unreal. The difficulties are more often than not procedural. There is, for example, inadequate machinery for voting out defective regulations by means of 'prayers'.[2] Again, regulations may be affirmed by the House before the Scrutiny Committee has reported on them. Also, no amending procedure exists. Unless the Scrutiny Committee can negotiate amendments before the instrument reaches the House, it must either stand or fall. It has been argued that no government can afford to concede to the House of Commons the power of control it is asking for, notably in a report from the Select Committee on Procedure (HC 588 (1977–8)), because to do so might mean losing control of the legislative process. In other words, to strengthen the Scrutiny Committee until it could function properly, would mean creating a select committee of the type now established to monitor the operation of departments.[3] These committees are known to develop a critical personality which frequently cuts across party lines. This might defeat the whole purpose of delegating legislative powers to the executive. At least one MP discounts this argument:

If these very necessary reforms were to make ministers a little more reluctant to use statutory instruments instead of putting detail in Bills, that is no cause for alarm. It is far more alarming that ministers should find it so convenient to write the law long after Parliament thinks it has done so itself, and that they should have so little difficulty in ensuring a smooth passage through Parliament for what is in effect legislation by the executive . . . [Beith 1981, p. 173.]

Would greater control over regulation really lead to more legislation? The more likely effect would be that departments would by-pass Parliament altogether. Thus, in its first special report, the Joint Committee deplored

> . . . the recurring tendency of Departments to seek to by-pass Parliament by omitting necessary detail from instruments (or alternatively by qualifying detailed provisions) and thus confer wide discretion on the Minister to vary the provisions without making a further instrument . . . The Committee fully appreciate that the justification for the granting of delegated legislative powers is to remove subsidiary or procedural details from the Statute Book and to afford to the Executive flexibility and the ability to alter detailed provisions to fit changing circumstances, without the need to enact a new Statute. The corollary of this, however, must be that the delegated legislation itself should be detailed, specific and self-explanatory and should not depend on the exercise of ministerial or departmental discretion unless provision to that effect is expressly contained in the enabling Statute. Circulars explaining or amplifying the contents of either primary or delegated legislation can be very useful to the general public and to the administrators. But the Committee hope that Parliament will condemn subordinate legislation by Departmental Circular when Parliament has itself passed a parent Act which requires such legislation to be by statutory instrument. [HL 51, HC 169 (1977/8), paras. 9–12.]

Even where Parliament authorizes the making of circulars and other informal rule-making, members may remain dissatisfied. This can be seen from debates during the passage of the Employment Act 1980. S.3 of the Act empowers the Employment Secretary to issue 'codes of practice containing such practical guidance as he thinks fit for the purpose of promoting the improvement of industrial relations'. The section also provides for the codes to be laid in draft and approved by each House of Parliament before being brought into operation by statutory instrument. The first two codes received additional parliamentary scrutiny because they were the subject of a report by the Select Committee on Employment. So they were relatively formal, provision being made for parliamentary control. Yet during the passage of the Bill, one member called the codes 'unconstitutional'. He was concerned about their status as 'law'. By s. 3(8) the codes are admissible as evidence and can be used to assist in the determination of questions in the course of legal proceedings; on the other hand, breach of the codes does not, in itself, give rise to legal liability. Mr Gorst argued:

> They constitute the first step down a slippery slope. If we have semi-judicial edicts that are quasi-binding on the courts and that have been produced by

Ministers who haven't had the courage to enshrine them in the law, worse developments will follow. The codes will bring the spirit of the law into industrial relations but not the certainty and precision of the letter of the law. [HC Deb. vol. 992, cols. 675–6.]

This concern for certainty and precision was echoed by Baroness Sear in the House of Lords:

What is happening is that when we have a really controversial piece of legislation we tend to say . . . 'We will not have this in the Act. We will put it into a code of practice.' When you put it into a code of practice you do not have to be so clear about what 'it' really is, because it does not have the force of law . . . this is a thoroughly muddle headed way of dealing with new developments . . . an escape route from difficult matters which we don't wish to thrash out in legislation . . . [HL Deb. vol. 44, col. 1522.]

Informal, unsupervised, semi-contractual arrangements have always prevailed in the field of industrial relations. 'British industrial relations have always been regulated by "codes" in the sense of voluntarily agreed rules which may have a legal effect: the collective agreement, the union rule book, the TUC's inter-union "Bridlington" procedure, and the more recent TUC "Guides". Statutory Codes have also proliferated. Safety representatives function within a framework of regulations, codes and guidance notes' (R. Lewis 1981, p. 198). In one sense, then, the new arrangements increased formality and represented a tightening of parliamentary control. (Though, if you consider them carefully, you can see why the new codes required supervision when the old did not.)

The legislative function is reserved for Parliament because in constitutional theory, if not always in practice, Parliament represents the nation. Parliament is rightly jealous of its powers of scrutiny and the preoccupation with the formalities of executive law-making represents a concern for the fundamental constitutional norm of representative government. From this perspective, any attempt to by-pass control of the legislative and regulatory process can be read as an example of Winckler's retreat from law. It is not surprising, then, to find examples of draconian powers in the field of economic planning. Korah (1976), for example, described the Minister's powers under the Counter-Inflation Act 1972 and the regulations made thereunder – to define the limits of his own jurisdiction; to amend earlier legislation and to define conclusively the meaning of terms used in the statute – as 'a threat to Parliamentary Sovereignty'. On the other hand, the executive would no doubt argue that exceptional powers were dictated by the need to act quickly in the public interest. And administrators have their own, different, reasons for avoiding the parliamentary process whenever possible. The procedures are cumbersome and lead to delay, while the 'certain, precise' language of statute is not particularly helpful. Streatfield J once said of a ministerial circular:

> Whereas ordinary legislation, by passing through both Houses of Parliament, or, at least lying on the table of both Houses, is thus twice blessed, this type of so-called legislation is at least four times cursed. First, it has seen neither House of Parliament; secondly, it is unpublished and is inaccessible even to those whose valuable right of property may be affected; thirdly it is a jungle of provisions, legislative, administrative or directive in character, and sometimes difficult to disentangle one from the other; and fourthly, it is expressed not in the precise language of an Act of Parliament or an Order in Council, but in the more colloquial language of correspondence, which is not always susceptible of the ordinary canons of construction. [*Patchett* v. *Leathem* (1949) 65 T L R 69.]

The precise language of statute is more easily construed by judges than by the common man, though even law lords, groping their way through the convoluted phrases, may find themselves at a loss. One eminent judge has said that statutory interpretation 'vexes us daily . . . Even the simplest words give rise to acute differences between us. Half the judges think the interpretation is clear one way. The other half think it clear the other way . . . It shows what a gamble it is. Change the constitution of the Court by one and you have a different result'.[4]

Although the Renton Report[5] pointed out that legislative draftsmanship is designed to please the legislator rather than the public, pleas for reform have fallen on deaf ears.[6] Little or nothing has changed since Allen complained (1965, pp. 176–7) of the Control of Tins, Cans, Kegs, Drums, and Packaging Pails (No. 10) Order, 1943, a statutory instrument of 169 words whose sole effect, we learn from the explanatory note, was to enable tin plate to be used 'for tobacco and snuff tins other than cutter lid tobacco tins'.

Legal language is itself an important factor in driving the administrator towards informal rule-making. Expressed in terms of statute and regulation, he can no longer understand his own policies. Memoranda are not legislation; they are necessary guides to explain the meaning of the law to the public servants who have to administer it. You will understand this criticism more clearly after looking at the regulations made under the Social Security Act 1980 (below, Chapter 19) which reorganized the supplementary benefits scheme. Informal 'guidance' on their interpretation had to be issued to officers, together with a handbook explaining their rights to members of the public.

Something of the puzzlement felt by public servants brought into contact with legislative drafting is conveyed by a senior civil servant in the Customs and Excise Department, describing the introduction in the Finance Act 1972 of the new Value Added Tax. Johnstone (1975, pp. 50–3) tells us that meetings with parliamentary counsel were always 'chaperoned by lawyers from the staff of the departmental solicitor', convention decreeing that 'a lawyer should usually speak first on behalf of the department'. The first drafts by parliamentary counsel produced 'a mental effect somewhat analogous to the physical sensation of touching a block of dry ice . . . and for a time, our own intellectual capacities were fully extended in trying to identify the pattern of his thinking and accommodate our own to it'. Yet the administrators had themselves been working with their own draft. This actually formed part of the instructions to parliamentary counsel who 'with great good nature – and I fear considerably against his better judgment' consented to read it as a starting-point. The whole cumbersome drafting process absorbed four months.[7]

Once again, we can see a difference of perspective. Administrators hope to get things done; in other words, their interest lies in the efficient implementation of policy. Delays and technicality of language drive them away from the law-making process. They prefer to proceed by administrative methods: circulars, guidance, codes, instructions, directives. Lawyers, on the other hand, are interested in 'law'. They show no interest in the paper which circulates in government offices unless intentionally or otherwise it seems to have legal effects:

Not long ago, practitioners could live with reasonable comfort and safety in a world bounded by Acts of Parliament, Statutory Rules and Orders and judicial decisions. One of the tendencies of recent years is for this world to become an expanding universe. Decisions of administrative tribunals are comparatively well-known additions to the lawyer's burden. A more interesting and perhaps less well-known accretion consists of what may be called administrative quasi-legislation. This falls into two categories. First, there is the State-and-subject type, consisting of announcements by administrative bodies of the course which it is proposed to take in the administration of particular statutes. Thus . . . from time to time the Inland Revenue Authorities announce concessions which will be made to the taxpayer . . .

It is true that arrangements such as these, operating in favour of the individuals concerned at the expense of taxpayers as a whole, are technically not law, but although no Court would enforce them, no official body would fail to honour them, and as they are not merely concessions in individual cases but are intended to apply generally to all who fall within their scope, the description of 'quasi-legislation' is perhaps not inept. Announcements operating against the individuals concerned, on the other hand, will normally be open to challenge in the Courts and so can be said to have the practical effect of legislation only to the extent that the expense, delays and uncertainties of litigation in general, and of opposing the unlimited resources of the Administration in particular, make those affected prefer to be submissive rather than stiff-necked.

The second category of administrative quasi-legislation is the subject-and-subject type, consisting of arrangements made by administrative bodies which affect the operation of the law between one subject and another . . . [The author gives the example of an arrangement negotiated by the Home Office between insurers that they would not press the defence to a common law action in damages of acceptance of compensation under the Workmen's Compensation Acts: see *Deane* v. *Edwards* [1941] 3 All E R 331. He continues:]

It is hard to believe that there would have been serious opposition to the passage of the short remedial legislation required to carry out this reform. Yet without any change being made in the law, a substantial change has been made in the advice a solicitor should give his client . . . Administrative quasi-legislation is thus somewhat of a curate's egg. On the one hand, announcements by official bodies on points of procedure and the way in which it is proposed to deal with doubtful points of interpretation have much in their favour, while on the other hand there are substantial objections to administrative quasi-legislation which overrides clear law or seeks to deal with matters between subject and subject . . . It is clear that no lawyer will view with pleasure a process whereby . . . the unrepealed words of the statute book may be emasculated, not by the legislature or the judiciary but by mere administrative process . . .

Perhaps the main objection to administrative quasi-legislation is its haphazard mode of promulgation. . . Before it is too late, some uniform official method of publication should be adopted, to include under some title such as 'Administrative Notifications and Decisions' all the matters mentioned above. It might be convenient to divide the publication into various series according to the subject matters, and to frame some test for inclusion, such as whether the effect or interpretation of some statute or case-law was affected. [Megarry 1944, pp. 126–9.]

Taken alone, Megarry's short statute may be a political possibility; multiplied, it certainly is not. And is it feasible to expect public servants to publish all circulars, practice statements and directives? What practicable test could be devised? Megarry's own concern is for his client's 'rights'. Judged by this standard, can his second example really be 'legislative' in character or is it simply a voluntary agreement negotiated by the Home Office, comparable to the codes of practice operating before 1980 in the industrial relations field?

The Donoughmore Committee found it 'difficult in theory and impossible in practice to draw a precise dividing line between the legislative on the one hand and the purely administrative on the other; administrative action so often partakes of both legislative and executive characteristics' (Cmnd 4060 (1932), p. 17). The case-law is hardly more precise. Allen (1965, p. 187) describes the early cases as 'prompted by expediency', by which he means that the classification merely provides a means to an end.[8] The classification is actually immaterial. If a court wishes to cut down an administrative circular as effecting too great an interference with private rights, it can take one of two courses. It can describe the document as 'legislative' and hold it not to be empowered by the enabling Act; this was the reaction to standing orders of the Prisons Department which prevented free correspondence between prisoners and their solicitors in *Raymond* v. *Honey* [1982] 2 WLR 465. Alternatively, the document may be classified as 'administrative', in which case it is purely advisory and its legality falls to be determined by the court (see the *British Oxygen* case, below). Was this the approach to 'guidelines' and 'directives' used in *Laker*'s case?

In practice, courts often shy away from this difficult point. The status of the Immigration Rules has never been conclusively determined. Two cases which concern the Attorney General's 'Guidelines on Jury Vetting' are also inconclusive. In some police areas, the records of every member of a jury panel are checked against the Criminal Records to facilitate challenge by the prosecution. There is no direct statutory authority for the practice. By 1974, the Attorney General and Home Secretary were sufficiently concerned to issue informal guidelines to all prosecuting authorities. When this was made public, the practice was challenged. In *R.* v. *Sheffield Crown Court ex p. Brownlow* [1980] 2 WLR 892, the challenge failed on the ground that the Court of Appeal had no jurisdiction in the matter. Lord Denning was prepared to assume that the guidelines were 'legitimate' though he thought jury-vetting 'unconstitutional'. In *R.* v. *Mason* [1980] 3 WLR 617, Lawton LJ thought jury-vetting 'legitimate' and 'reasonable', though, 'Both the circular and the statement [guidelines] contained advice: they were not directions having the force of law'.[9]

Harman and Griffith were less easily satisfied. They once more advanced the constitutional argument against this type of 'quasi-law':

> The Attorney-General explained that while he did not see fit to issue the guidelines to M Ps or publish them . . . he circulated them to all chief officers of police, to the Director of Public Prosecutions and his staff, and to prosecuting counsel in every case where vetting has taken place. What the Attorney-General did not explain, however, was why, in view of the obvious concern of M Ps over the years, he had not allowed jury-vetting to be debated in the House. He had had an ideal opportunity because the very year, 1974, that he . . . [was] drawing up guidelines, the Juries Act was passing through Parliament . . . Looking at the Juries Act, M Ps and lawyers get an incomplete picture. The Attorney-General, the Home Secretary and the DPP had legislated by stealth in drawing up vague guidelines which went far beyond the provisions of the Act . . . But asked about this in a parliamentary question [the AG replied] 'The Guidelines are a means of controlling an administrative practice which is inappropriate for legislation. The government has no intention of enacting the guidelines' . . . [Harman and Griffith 1979, pp. 24–5.]

2 The administrative doughnut: discretion and rules

It is becoming apparent that there may be rules and rules. Administrative rule-making is not always legislation; rule-making is part of the process of administration.

Modern political scientists[10] have taken their analyses much further. They describe political structures as fulfilling one of two main functions: input and output. 'Input' structures are those designed to secure, for example, political communication, political solidarity or the articulation of interests (interest-representation). The 'output' structures of government are rule-making, rule-application, rule-determination (adjudication) and, last but not least, discretion. In this analysis, rule-making is not the monopoly of the legislature; administrative rule-making is a valid source of law in a modern, bureaucratic society where all groups may participate in a fluid and dynamic law-making process:

> One of the main shortcomings of jurists who try to reduce management to a hierarchy of rules is that they overlook the stimulus/response nature of law. Like everything in nature, law grows. It is spelled out when courts speak, and it is equally spelled out when the legislature or the administrative agency speaks. Law is not the monopoly of a profession or even of one branch of the government. It is something that grows and responds to society itself and all three branches take part in that response. [Dimock 1980, p. 98.]

Not only is the administrative process one dimension of the political process, it is also a political world in miniature. All four 'output' structures are necessary for its healthy operation. The administration cannot operate without rule-making powers but equally it cannot operate without discretion. Circulars, directives, guidelines etc., permit administrative organizations to communicate internally and with one another. This is necessary because most bureaucracies are hierarchical; that is to say, important decisions are made at the top while routine decisions are delegated. The policies are formulated by managers to be applied by subordinates to individual cases. Where functions are split, for example, between central and local government, the hierarchy is not always clear. The question may then arise whether one body can direct or issue orders to the other. This is the problem of allocation of functions which was illustrated in the *Laker* case, when the court decided that ministerial 'guidance' was advisory rather than binding.

Decision-making needs to be delegated if only to prevent over-loading managers. Subordinates need instructions and guidance. But managers know that the absence of any discretionary element in the workload of their subordinates leads to frustration and apathy. To balance the elements of discretion and rules nicely is a difficult task:

Attempts have been made to decentralize decision-making, without sacrificing central control and direction, by limiting the top echelons to the determination of broad strategies which set guidelines for more specific decisions lower down. They tend to become impaled on the dilemma that if the policies are too specific they become too restrictive and lead to inappropriate action, while if they are too general they tend to lack impact. [Brown and Steel 1971, p. 193.]

A concrete example may help. Suppose that powers are delegated to welfare officers to make payments 'in case of exceptional need'. The officers are exercising discretion. A large number of claims produces inconsistent decisions; complaints are heard of discrimination and unfairness. What are the managers to do? They can (a) introduce an appeal system which would, in time, through the doctrine of precedent, rationalize the pattern of decision-making or (b) they can fetter the discretion of the officials through a system of rules, formal or informal. This is a skeleton structure for our supplementary benefits scheme. It also summarizes the argument of Nonet's study of the use of adjudication and rule-making to formalize the pattern of decision-taking in the Californian Industrial Accident Commission.

Before we can follow this further, we need to go back to the stage where rules were characterized as certain, predictable and binding, while discretion was the area of uncontrolled freedom in which rules did not operate. Dworkin added depth to this simple model by pointing out that discretion was not necessarily *uncontrolled*. Discretion did imply choice, but the choice was seldom unlimited. 'Discretion like the hole in the doughnut does not exist except as an area left open by a surrounding belt of restriction. It is therefore a relative concept. It always makes sense to ask "Discretion under which standards?" or "Discretion as to which authority?" ' (Dworkin 1977, p. 31.)

In his celebrated book, *Discretionary Justice*, first published in 1969, Davis used the idea of relative discretion in the context of administrative decision-making. Davis (1971, p. 4) said that 'a public officer has discretion whenever the effective limits of his power leave him free to make a choice among possible courses of action and inaction'. He did not believe that discretion could or should be eliminated:

Even when rules can be written, discretion is often better. Rules without discretion cannot fully take into account the need for tailoring results to unique facts and circumstances of particular cases. The justification for discretion is often the need for individualized justice. This is so in the judicial process as well as in the administrative process.

Every governmental and legal system in world history has involved both rules and discretion. No government has ever been a government of laws and not of men in the sense of eliminating all discretionary power. [Davis 1971, p. 17.]

In the 'rule-of-law' ideal, the controls or limits on discretion are external. Davis was more interested in internal control through the hierarchical structures of the bureaucracy itself, believing that the administration should be encouraged to 'structure' its discretion by formulating its policies as rules. Davis was not thinking primarily of rules as 'legislation' or 'quasi-legislation'. He therefore turned to Dworkin's division between 'rules', 'principles' and 'standards', here reformulated by Jowell in administrative terms:

Principles
Principles arise mainly in the context of judicial decision-making. They involve normative moral standards by which rules might be evaluated. They are frequently expressed in maxims, such as 'No man shall profit by his own wrong,' 'He who comes to court shall come with clean hands.' They have developed in the judicial context over time, and are less suited to administrative decision making because they do not address themselves to economic, social or political criteria, but to justice and fairness largely in the judicial situation. A principle that may arise in the administrative context would be

the maxim: 'Like cases shall receive like treatment.'

Rules

Roscoe Pound defined a rule (Jurisprudence (1959) vol. 2, p. 124) as a 'legal precept attaching a definite detailed legal consequence to a definite detailed state of fact.' . . . The process of legalisation involves the transformation of policies into rules. Policies are broad statements of general objectives, such as 'To provide decent, safe and sanitary housing,' 'To prevent unsafe driving.' The policy is legalised as the various elements of housing and driving are specified, providing, for example, for hot and cold running water, indoor toilets, maximum speed limits and one-way streets. A rule thus is the most precise form of general direction, since it requires for its application nothing more or less than the happening or non-happening of a physical event. For the application of the maximum speed rule, all we need do is determine factually whether or not the driver was exceeding thirty miles per hour . . .

Standards

The feature of standards that distinguishes them from rules is their flexibility and susceptibility to change over time. In 1955, for example, 'average' and 'prudent' university administrators probably had little difficulty in determining a standard requiring 'neat' dress in university lecture halls. Obviously skirts for women, and collar and ties for men, were essential criteria of 'neatness'. Some years later, however, the standard could alter, allowing trousers for ladies, open collars for men, or indeed anything if not nothing at all . . . [Jowell 1973, pp. 201, 204.]

Jowell describes discretion as a scale on which the decision-maker may have wide powers of choice (strong discretion) or limited powers (weak discretion):

Discretion is rarely absolute, and rarely absent. It is a matter of degree, and ranges along a continuum between high and low. Where he has a high degree of discretion, the decision-maker will normally be guided by reference to such vague standards as 'public interest' and 'fair and reasonable'. Where his discretion is low, the decision-maker will be limited by rules that do not allow much scope for interpretation. For example, a police officer's discretion is high when he has the power to regulate traffic at crossroads 'as he thinks fit.' If he were required to allow traffic to pass from East to West for three minutes and then from North to South for two minutes, subject to exceptional circumstances, then his discretion would be greatly reduced. A traffic light possesses no discretion at all. [Jowell 1973, pp. 179–80.]

Rules still need to be divided into the legislative (which have binding force) and the non-legislative (which do not). But they can also be divided into types according to their generality. 'Rules' are precise and specific; 'principles' and 'standards' are less specific and more flexible. The rule-maker's objectives influence his choice. If he wants strong discretion he will probably turn to standards; weak discretion means rules. The factors which influence the administrator are something like those which push him towards or away from the formal rule-making procedures:

> Most agencies making decisions do so in a manner which can be located on a continuum somewhere between discretion at one end and rules at the other. Competing values push the character of the decision between these two ends of the continuum. Thus accountability, efficiency, rationality and entitlement push the agency towards rules, and generosity, relevance, individuality, sensitivity and choice push it towards discretion. [Bradshaw 1981, p. 139.]

3 Structuring discretion

Davis had three main priorities. He was concerned that administrative lawyers were studying only areas of administrative activity which were relatively open and controlled:

> If we stay within the comfortable areas where jurisprudence scholars work and concern ourselves mostly with statutory and judge-made law, we can at best accomplish no more than to refine what is already tolerably good. To do more than that we have to open our eyes to the reality that justice to individual parties is administered more outside courts than in them, and we have to penetrate the unpleasant areas of discretionary determinations by police and prosecutors and other administrators, where huge concentrations of injustice invite drastic reforms. [Davis 1971, p. 215.]

His work was influential in stimulating a body of 'functionalist' research into neglected areas of discretionary power and in developing techniques for their control.[11] Secondly, he was concerned to achieve a balance between rules and discretion:

> The problem is not merely to choose between rule and discretion but is to find the optimum point on the rule-to-discretion scale. A standard, principle, or rule can be so vague as to be meaningless, it can have a slight meaning or considerable meaning, it can have some degree of controlling effect, or it can be so clear and compelling as to leave little or no room for discretion. The degree of discretion depends not only on grants of authority to administrators but also on what they do to enlarge their power. In general, [the] thesis is that the degree of administrative discretion should often be more restricted; some of the restricting can be done by legislators but most of this task must be performed by administrators. [Davis 1971, p. 215.]

Thirdly, Davis hoped that the rule-making process would bring policies into the open and allow citizens to participate in 'a miniature democratic process'.

Davis himself showed particular interest in the 'unpleasant area' of pre-trial procedures, many of which seemed to him to involve arbitrariness rather than discretion. His work showed the relevance of administrative law techniques to the proper administration of the criminal justice and penal systems.[12] In this account of remodelling the Oregon parole system, you can see how Davis hoped his theory of rule-making would work.

Remodelling the Oregon parole scheme

When in 1975 Ira Blalock was appointed to the Parole Board, the parole provisions, contained in the Oregon Revised Statutes (ORS 144.75) and modelled on the American Model Penal Code, provided:

Whenever the State Board of Parole considers the release of a prisoner who, by its rules or orders, is eligible for release on parole, it shall be the policy of the Board to order his release unless the Board is of the opinion that the release should be deferred or denied because: (1) There is a reasonable probability that the inmate will not, after parole, remain outside the institution without violating the law and that his release is incompatible with the welfare of society; (2) There is a substantial risk that he will not conform to the conditions of parole; (3) His release at that time would depreciate the seriousness of his crime or promote disrespect for the law; (4) His release would have a substantial adverse affect on institutional discipline; or (5) His continued correctional treatment, medical care, or vocational or other training in the institution will substantially enhance his capacity to lead a law-abiding life when released at a later date.

[The statutes also required the Board, in making a determination about release:] . . . to look at the prisoner's personality, e.g. his maturity, stability, sense of responsibility, and any other personality attributes which would help him conform to the law. The adequacy of his parole plan was also a factor. Other considerations to be considered were: his willingness to undertake responsibilities; his past employment record; the type of residence; his use of narcotics and dangerous drugs; whether or not he made excessive use of alcohol; his mental and physical makeup; and his attitude toward the law and record of conduct in the institution as well as any previous experience on probation or parole. [Blalock 1981, p. 102.]

The Board did not hold formal hearings nor did it give its reasons at length, though it did sometimes make informal comments. This is how Blalock describes the discretionary and haphazard decision-taking process:

It was the practice of the Parole Board at that time to meet in panels of three. The panel would review each prisoner's case material prior to the hearing. This material, gleaned from the prisoner's file, included such items as a report from the institution, after-sentence reports from the judge and the district attorney, and psychiatric reports. The panel would review twenty or so cases every day; each prisoner would be brought before the panel and the panel members would take turns leading the interview.

[At one of my first hearings] the interviewer suggested a reset of the parole hearing of twelve months. He said something like, 'I'd set him to July of '76.' The other panel member said, somewhat more harshly, 'That isn't nearly enough, I'd set him to July of '77.' They then looked to me who was apparently expected to resolve this dispute by coming down on one side or the other, or offering yet a third alternative, perhaps a compromise. I indicated that I really wasn't sure how to resolve the issue and appealed to them for suggestions.

One said, 'Well, you just have to assess it on an individual basis.' 'I know,' was my response, 'But how long do you normally give a burglar in the first degree? This prisoner has committed a first degree burglary; what is an appropriate term for him?'

The other Board member replied, 'It all depends.' I persisted and said, 'Yes, but isn't there a customary range? Do you keep a burglar ten years or two?' 'It all depends,' said one Board member, 'on the individual case . . . We have to listen to and talk with the offender. You can't make up your mind until you actually have the prisoner sitting in front of you. Some offenders are ready for release early in their term. In fact, some are ready as soon as they are sentenced. Others don't get the message until they have served substantial portions of their sentence. You just can't tell in advance; each case is unique.' [Blalock 1981, pp. 100–10.]

In the United States, administrative actions are normally subject to procedural constraints set out in a model code of the Federal administration, the Administrative Procedure Act, discussed in greater detail below. Briefly, the legislation imposes a duty to afford a hearing to individuals affected by an administrative decision. In the case of general rule-making, there are parallel procedures, designed to provide for consultation (see below, p. 155).

Prior to restructuring, these procedures did not apply to the Parole Board. A major step was to get the Oregon legislature to amend the law removing this immunity:

The first guidelines for the Oregon Parole Board were developed and implemented early in 1976 and followed the lead of the U.S. Parole Commission. The Board worked with an interim committee of the Oregon legislature to draft legislation . . . First, it delegated to the Parole Board the authority to fix sentences through parole decision making, regulating the length of prison terms. The Board was required to establish presumptive ranges to be given to an offender for each crime in the penal code. Second, the legislation removed the Parole Board's exemption under the State's Administrative Procedure Act and required the Board to follow the rule-making procedures of that act. Those rule-making procedures required the Board to give notice, hold public hearings, allow interested parties to propose rules on their own initiative, and required that the rules be published . . . These two procedures were directed toward reducing the disparity in prison terms that offenders actually served and making the rules explicit and public, and knowable. Offenders with similar criminal backgrounds and crimes were more likely to serve prison terms which were similar. [Blalock 1981, p. 106.]

What sort of person or body might wish to participate in the rule-making process? The Oregon Administrative Rules provide that notice must be given (inter alia) to the following bodies: the state bar and the press, the administration's own corrections division, the criminal defense attorneys' association, every public defender's office in the state, the law schools of several universities, the prisoners' legal service, and the American Civil Liberties Union. In Chapter 18 we will be looking at the making of social security regulations. You will see how limited the input from interested parties or pressure groups can be in the United Kingdom.

The administrative guidelines to which Blalock refers were rather special. Just as actuaries use statistical tables to calculate life assurance premiums, so penologists have increasingly turned to statistical models in the sentencing field. Statistical data fed into computers allows tables to be developed which allow decisions to be made with the help of a simple 'points' system. A scheme of this kind has been introduced in the United Kingdom by s.19 and Sched. 7 of the Transport Act 1981 to regulate sentencing disparities between magistrates' courts in 'totting up' road traffic offences and endorsing licences. More sensitive models can be developed which, for example, help to predict the chances of recidivism.

These two models are rather different and this fact has some bearing on Davis' argument. Davis talks of an optimum between rules and discretion. Blalock realized that the optimum would inevitably be dictated by the policy goal. For many years, rehabilitation had been the orthodox policy goal of US sentencers; now the tide had turned towards equality of treatment ('justice as fairness'). For the following reason, Oregon chose the latter:

Presumably, the indeterminant sentence was designed to keep the inmate as long as rehabilitation required. The problem was that experience and research indicated that it was difficult, if not impossible, to determine when the 'optimal' time for release had arrived. Consequently, prisoners have been incarcerated for disproportionately long periods of time for the sake of rehabilitation treatment. Yet . . . imprisonment is, no matter what else it may be called, punishment. [Blalock 1981, p. 103.]

The new goal of 'justice as fairness' suggested a move from discretion towards rules.

Tables 2–5 represent our own *simplified* version of the tables lying at

138

Table 2 Oregon Parole Board – Criminal History/Risk Assessment Score

DATA		SCORE
A Previous convictions:	None	3
	1	2
	2–3	1
	4 and over	0
B Previous custodial sentences:	None	2
	1–2	1
	3 and over	0
C Age at first custodial sentence:	26+	2
	19–25	1
	18 or less	0
D Escapes, violations, probation or parole:	None	2
	1 incident	1
	2 or more	0
E No drug or alcohol addiction problems:		1
One or more of the above		0
F 4 years conviction-free in community:		
Before instant crime		1
Otherwise		0
Total Criminal History/Risk Assessment score	Max.	11
	Min.	0

Table 3 Oregon Parole Board – Presumptive Ranges of Time to be Served

Severity of offence	Examples of offences in category	Total score from Criminal History/Risk Assessment			
		Excellent 11–9	Good 8–6	Fair 5–3	Poor 2–0
		← Increasing score →			
Category 1	Welfare fraud	6*	6	6–12	12–22
Category 2	Burglary II	6	6–10	10–18	18–28
Category 3	Theft over $5,000 value	6–10	10–16	16–24	24–36
Category 4	Burglary of non-residential property	10–16	16–22	22–30	30–48
Category 5	Minor robbery or rape	18–24	24–30	30–48	48–72
Category 6	Serious robbery, rape and arson	36–48	48–60	60–86	86–133
Category 7	Murder 2	8–10 yrs	10–13 yrs	13–16 yrs	16–20
	Murder 1	10–14 yrs	14–19 yrs	19–24 yrs	24–Life

(Decreasing severity ↑ applies to Categories 1–7)

* Ranges for categories 1–6 shown in months.

Table 4. Oregon Parole Board.– Factors in Aggravation/Mitigation

Aggravation	Mitigation
Production/use of weapon during offence	Substantial provocation/ misconduct by victim
Threat or violence toward witness(es) or victim(s)	Cooperation with criminal justice agencies in resolving other criminal activity
The prisoner knew/had reason to know the victims were particularly vulnerable (i.e. aged, handicapped, very young)	Effort to make restitution or reparation, particularly before required to do so by sentencing
Ability to make restitution/ reparation and failure to do so	The degree of property loss/ personal injury was substantially less than is characteristic for the crime
Violation of position of public trust or of recognized professional ethics	Special efforts by perpetrator to minimize the harm/risk in the crime
The degree of property loss/ personal injury was substantially greater than is characteristic for the crime	Peripheral involvement in the criminal episode (e.g. passive accessory)
There is a single conviction for a crime involving multiple victims	Evidence of duress, necessity, or diminished mental capacity indicative of reduced culpability
More than one concurrently imposed conviction, not arising out of the same criminal episode	Sentence to pay restitution after imprisonment
Verified instances of repetitive assaultive conduct	

Table 5 Oregon Parole Board – Maximum Variations Permitted from Presumptive Ranges by Reason of Aggravation/Mitigation

Severity of offence	Discretion of Panel/Board	Total score from Criminal History/ Risk Assessment			
		Excellent 11–9	Good 8–6	Fair 5–3	Poor 2–0
		← Increasing score →			
Category 1	Panel	+2*	+2	+3	+4
	Full Board	±4	±4	±6	±8
Category 2	Panel	+2	±3	±4	±6
	Full Board	±4	±6	±8	±12
Category 3	Panel	±3	±4	±6	±8
	Full Board	±6	±8	±12	±16
Category 4	Panel	±4	±6	±8	±10
	Full Board	±8	±12	±16	±20
Category 5	Panel	±6	±8	±10	±14
	Full Board	±12	±16	±20	±26
Category 6	Panel	±12	±14	±18	±24
	Full Board	±24	±26	±30	±36
Category 7	Full Board	±3 yrs	±3 yrs	±3 yrs	±3 yrs/NA

(Decreasing severity — indicated along the Severity of offence column, Categories 1–7)

* Ranges for categories 1–6 shown in months.

the heart of the Oregon guidelines or 'matrix'. Under the new scheme, decisions about release are usually made by a two-man panel, although in some cases, for example those involving life sentences, the full five-man Board decides. Theoretically, to make their determination, panel members must use each table in turn. First, they have to calculate the criminal history/risk assessment score in accordance with Table 2. For example, if the prisoner has three previous convictions and was 28 at the time of his first custodial sentence, he would be given 1 point and 2 points respectively. Having scored each category, the members add the results together to provide the total. They then move to Table 3, feeding in the total derived from Table 2 along the top axis and the nature of the offence for which the prisoner is presently incarcerated along the other:

The two dimensions, seriousness of offense and prior criminal history, are plotted in a manner not unlike the mileage charts appearing on highway maps. One reads across one dimension to determine the criminal history in one of four categories and then turns to the other dimension which lists offense severity. At the intersection, two numbers appear, and the numbers refer to the range of time to be served in months. [Blalock 1981, p. 109.]

So if the prisoner has a Risk Assessment total of 10 points and the instant conviction is for minor robbery, the range to be served would be 18–24 months. However, this range is not conclusive; the Administrative Rules state: 'A parole release date will normally be set within the applicable guidance range. The Board may only vary from the ranges if it finds the presence of aggravation or mitigation.' So the panel must look to Table 4 which lists the usual factors in aggravation or mitigation; for instance, the members might use a prisoner's intimidation of a witness to justify setting a term in excess of the presumptive range. But these factors are not exclusive; the Rules empower the Board to consider other matters in aggravation or mitigation not listed in Table 4. On the other hand, the Rules require written reasons for moving outside the guideline range and curtail the extent of departure. If the panel members find aggravation or mitigation, they must consult Table 5 which shows a panel's maximum permitted upward or downward variation from a range. For instance, if a prisoner is serving time for a Category 4 offence and possesses a total Risk Assessment score of 7 points, the maximum variation allowed to the panel is 6 months. Since, according to Table 3, the relevant presumptive range is 16–22 months, the members could set a term of between 10–28 months. If they think that the aggravation or mitigation factors are so substantial that a greater departure is required, they have to refer the case to the full Board. In such circumstances, the Board is permitted by Table 5 a wider band of variation than is the panel; in our example + or − 12 months. Moreover, the Board is not bound by these wider bands if, for example, the offence involved particularly violent conduct or if there is a psychiatric diagnosis of severe emotional disturbance. Here if four out of the five members agree and written reasons are given, the Board can either step outside the bands or refuse parole.

You may obtain a better understanding of the scheme if, using the guidelines, you take a decision about the release of the hypothetical X. Born in 1947, X is a heroin addict. He was first imprisoned (for theft) in 1968, being subsequently convicted twice for assault and (in 1979) imprisoned again for burglary II. Both his prison governors report that X was a model prisoner. In 1981, having admitted to burning down a toy factory valued at $7 million, he was tried for arson. He pleaded not guilty, claiming that he had not intended the conflagration; while sleeping rough, he had lit a bonfire to keep warm and this had spread. The prosecution accepted that X had summoned the fire brigade. The jury found him guilty. In prison, X volunteered information about drug-trafficking in Portland; as a result three men were tried but all were acquitted.

Rules are supposed to make the administrator's task simpler; is it easy to apply the scheme? In making your determination, how much discretion did you possess? When did you feel it necessary to 'interpret' the guidelines?

If guidelines like these are to operate fairly, the Board must possess accurate information. The primary technique adopted is documentary, panel members being presented with a parole analysis report by the prison authorities, together with other information made available by the police, lawyers, and others with 'a special interest in the case'. (Who might they be?) It is the administrators in the prisons service, not the panel members, who carry out many of the calculations previously described. The analysis report sets out the risk assessment score, offence severity, application of the Table 3 matrix, and factors in aggravation and mitigation. It also includes recommendations about release which panel members are at liberty to follow.

The scheme substantially strengthened the procedural protections associated with adjudication, and introduced an appeals system.

Compare Blalock's description of the previous practice when 'due process was essentially limited to an appearance before the Board at a hearing'. In the remodelled scheme:

The Board was required to disclose the material it was going to consider and give the inmate an opportunity to present evidence to rebut information the Board was utilizing. The law required written and particularised reasons for all actions, that is, boiler-plate reasons were not sufficient to justify deferral of parole . . . [Blalock 1981, p. 107.]

An administrative advantage of the scheme is that it can be constantly monitored to assess its efficiency. Parole decisions are now subject to two forms of review: first, an administrative review by the Chairman of the Board or, if he participated in the decision, another member; secondly, review by the Oregon courts on the grounds that the guidelines have not been properly applied. In *Eggsman* v. *State Board of Parole* 60 Or App. 381 (1982), an application for review on the ground that an offence had been classified as a Category 7 offence in consideration of factors relevant to the risk assessment score, partially succeeded. The Board was ordered to make a new determination.

This is not the place to evaluate the experience of parole and sentencing models.[12a] But you can check the Oregon model against the values of its protagonists. Does it provide Blalock's procedural fairness and equality of treatment? Is it a miniature democratic process (Davis)?

Are there administrative gains? The prisoner might say that rules have (a) clarified his position, (b) brought policy into the open where he and his supporters can challenge it, and (c) reduced the possibility of discrimination against him. There may be gains for the Board. The guidelines may have (a) encouraged consistency, (b) reduced the time taken for routine decisions, allowing more time for hard cases, and (c) allowed general policy to develop.

Perhaps you would like to check the Oregon model of rules against English parole procedures. The starting point is ss. 59–62 of the Criminal Justice Act 1967. The parole system is in the hands of the Home Secretary and the Parole Board. The Board operates partly through Local Review Committees (LRCs) whose practice is governed by the Local Review Committee Rules 1967. In *Payne* v. *Lord Harris* [1981] 1 WLR 754, Lord Denning summarized the procedure:

The prisoner (if he is willing) is interviewed by a member of the local review committee. At that interview 'he shall be given a reasonable opportunity to make any representations he wishes to be considered by the Committee': rule

3(2). The member writes a report of the interview. He includes in it any representations made by the prisoner. The local review committee considers the report of their member. They then make a report to the Secretary of State of the suitability of the prisoner for release on licence. The Secretary of State then refers the case to the Parole Board. The Parole Board advises the Secretary of State.

A unanimous report from the LRC allows the Home Secretary to parole the prisoner or dismiss his application without referring the case to the Parole Board in a majority of cases (see s.35 of the Criminal Justice Act 1972). Although he rarely does so, he may reject the Board's recommendation for parole, but he may not parole someone whom the Board has not recommended.[13] How does this procedure compare with the non-statutory panel which advises the Home Secretary in some deportation cases (above, p. 78)?

In 1975, the Home Secretary (Mr Jenkins) insisted that the criteria on which the Board based its decisions should be published (HC Deb. vol. 897, col. 25). Since then, they have been annexed to each annual report of the Parole Board. Amongst the questions considered are: the home background, the current offence, circumstances of the offence, behaviour in prison, health, future prospects and circumstances on release. The Board will also consider public opinion and other miscellaneous factors. In addition to these rather general criteria, the Home Secretary uses prediction models, similar to those now used in Oregon. The difference is that these have never been made public although specimen tables, together with an assessment, are published by the Home Office in *Parole in England and Wales*. Discussing the possibility of moving towards a rule-based scheme, the Home Office, in an internal review, concluded:

Inevitably the individual prisoner who is trying to weigh up his chances will find . . . [the] material insufficiently precise to enable him to foresee with any certainty what the outcome of his case will be. There can be no such precision or certainty in a system of discretionary release . . . A bureaucratic system would work differently, comparing one case with another and building up continuously on precedent. This system would have its own disadvantages which are common to bureaucratic methods, such as inflexibility, substantial resource needs and delay. The Parole Board . . . [believes] it to be better to consider each prisoner's case as separate and individual. This system is more responsive to varying circumstances and more humane in the sense that each prisoner is considered as a person rather than as a 'case' . . . [*Review of Parole in England and Wales*, 1981, para. 6.]

Do you agree with this assessment? Should individuals participate in important decisions concerning them? The English system does not provide for a hearing; the prisoner is limited to 'making representations' to the LRC. In practice, this amounts to an interview. Compare this with Oregon. Are the objectives of parole in England and Oregon similar?

In *Payne* v. *Lord Harris*, a prisoner who had been turned down for parole and wanted to know how to prepare a second application, applied to the court for a declaration that he should know the reasons for the refusal (compare *Eggsman*'s case, above). The Court of Appeal held that the legislation and rules constituted a complete code which should not be modified by grafting on 'a duty to act fairly' (compare *Furnell*'s case, below). Shaw LJ said:

It is not easy, even if it were desirable, to give expression to or to define the subjective reasons in the minds of the members of the board; it is often virtually impossible to communicate them in exact terms via a third party. Not only is there no statutory requirement to disclose to a prisoner the reasons for an adverse recommendation ... but I doubt whether there is any statutory authority to make such a disclosure.

By statute, reasons have to be given for *revocation* of a parole licence, but not for refusal to grant parole. The Home Office gives this explanation of the difference: 'The issue was not raised during the passage of the legislation; at that time the concept of parole was seen quite clearly as a privilege'.

The Home Office has come to realize, however, that there is 'much to be said from the point of view of humane administration for giving reasons'. So an experiment has been conducted. The Parole Board circulated a standard list of 'reasons' to LRCs, many of which 'experienced difficulty in selecting appropriate reasons' from the list. Finally, the Parole Board wrote to the Home Secretary recommending against the giving of reasons which, they thought, would 'invite disclosure of the reports' on which the Board's decision was based. This in turn would invite applications for judicial review in which discovery of the dossier might be ordered. Ultimately all this 'would substitute for a system under which parole is a privilege to be earned a system under which it would be a right to be claimed' (*Review*, paras. 72–81 and App. M). Do you find these arguments against the giving of reasons persuasive? Is parole a form of 'new property' which courts should protect?[14]

4 Rules, generality and individuation

Just as adjudication has its advantages and disadvantages, so rules have a negative side for both citizens and administrators. Rules cannot cater easily for hard cases:

> The relative certainty of rules may, at times, prove a hindrance both to the administrator and the client. The administrator who wishes to avoid committing himself to a course of action might regard a rule as a fetter upon his future options ... Interference with interests who have built a reliance upon the rule may be considered unfair, and resistance or procedural technicalities may make change difficult. Announcing policy through case-by-case determinations (or through flexible advisory circulars) may be seen as a strategy better suited to its gradual elaboration ...
>
> [Rules] may easily catch within their ambit technical violators whose actions could not be said to have contravened the objectives of the enforcing administration. For example, a parking meter will not show understanding or mercy to the person who was one minute too late to place his coin in the slot, because he was helping a blind man cross the street. Rules thus permit legalism, which, because of its close affinity to arbitrariness (namely, lack of rational relation to official ends), may cause dissatisfaction ...
>
> However, techniques to temper strict rule enforcement do exist ... An administrative technique is selective enforcement or non-enforcement of rules allowing, for example, a police officer to refrain from charging a doctor speeding to the scene of an accident, or a driver narrowly exceeding the speed limit in the early hours of the morning. But selective enforcement may create as many problems as it solves and, furthermore, is only possible in the situation where the administrator has the opportunity to refrain from setting legal enforcement in motion. [Jowell 1973, pp. 191–3.]

From the administrator's viewpoint, there is a further disadvantage. Routinization encourages administrative apathy. Without the power of choice, officials lose interest in their work and with it, their sense of responsibility:[15]

> Bureaucracy is not a dynamic institution committed to solving problems and attaining objectives. Rather, it is a relatively passive and conservative system preoccupied with the detailed implementation of received policies ...
>
> Like autonomous law, bureaucracy is mainly a way of over-coming the arbitrary decision-making of an earlier era ... The chief bureaucratic device for ensuring official integrity is the narrowing of administrative discretion: policies are codified; decision-making is routinized; delegation is limited; authority is concentrated at the top. As in autonomous law rules are the chief vehicles of administrative regularity. They protect institutional autonomy – the civil service – while promising those who govern a more reliable execution of policy. [Nonet and Selznick 1978, pp. 64–5.]

Thus rules are introduced to eliminate arbitrariness. But the *generality* of rules can prove counter-productive. Rules create the mechanistic arbitrariness of the traffic light. In order to cater for the needs of the individual, a margin of *discretion* is necessary.

The distinction between rules and discretion is a matter of degree.

The Donoughmore Committee said that the rule-making function blended into the administrative function; the same is true of rule-making and adjudication.

Rule-making is the process by which the administrator lays down new prescriptions to govern the future conduct of those subject to his authority; adjudication is the process by which the administrator applies either law or policy or both to the facts of a particular case. Rule-making is *general* and looks only to the *future*; adjudication is *particular* and looks also to the *past*. But no test can draw anything like a mathematical line between rule-making and adjudication. [Schwarz and Wade 1972, p. 93.]

Our skeleton SB scheme shows why this is so. Rationalizing decisions through an appeals system means that principles may evolve from adjudication which will be disseminated by a system of precedent. This is why the common law can be described as a system of rules. Nonet's study showed how important adjudication could be as a source of administrative policy and principle.

The traditional model with which this chapter opened equated 'law' with rules and judicial procedure (adjudication). It relegated discretion to the other side of the line. Dworkin's great contribution to legal theory was to find room for discretion as an essential element in adjudication.[16]

Now we can see that these methods of decision-taking are not separate; they blend into each other. The pattern is complex. Not only do rules tail off into discretion according to the way in which they are drafted, but rules can emerge from adjudication. Adjudication contains an element of discretion. Formal adjudication, permitting participation through proofs and reasoned argument, diminishes gradually into decision-taking without these constraints. Discretion may be necessary to fit rules to individual cases (individuation). Judicial methods may also seem appropriate to the consideration of individual cases, though not invariably so. The complexity of this pattern makes it harder than Davis suggests to choose the optimum point on the scale between rules and discretion. What we are seeing is not a one-dimensional scale but a number of intersecting scales.

Administrators, who see large numbers of cases, are inclined to give preference to the value of equal treatment.[17] To single out individual cases for special treatment (individuation) means, if like cases are still to be treated alike, reconsidering every other decision which has been made. We know that this is considered to be a principle of good administration because, after a High Court decision had changed the law affecting the pension rights of one successful litigant, the PCA insisted that the department should take out and reconsider every file which might be affected by the decision.[18] It must be remembered, however, that policies are often devised with the aim of rationing scarce funds. Exceptions may have devastating effects on departmental budgets.

The DHSS, for example, has a strictly limited budget for invalid aids and, using discretionary powers granted by the Health Services and Public Health Act 1968, schemes have been devised for their allocation. One such scheme governs the allocation of cars or invalid carriages (tricycles) to severely disabled people. Cash grants towards the upkeep of a private car can also be made. Invalid carriages are, partly for safety reasons, being phased out (see HC 529 (1974–5), pp. 162–81) and replaced by cash mobility allowances. The scheme has therefore been amended from time to time to reflect departmental policy changes. Here is an obvious advantage of informal rule-making: flexibility. A PCA report in 1975 listed some of the departmental guidelines defining the 'severely disabled':

Category 1 – those who have both legs amputated, one or both being above or through the knee:
Category 2 – those who suffer from a defect of the locomotor system or a severe chronic heart or lung condition so that they are to all intents and purposes unable to walk:
Category 3 – those who are slightly less severely disabled with a very limited walking ability, and, because of their disability, need a vehicle to get to and from full-time paid employment or to undertake the full range of duties of a household, including shopping. Those who would need to use a vehicle in the course of their employment, irrespective of their disablement, are not eligible for help under this category. [HC 496 (1975–6), p. 132.]

Complaints have been received by the PCA that the guidelines are interpreted rather legalistically by the DHSS.[19] In case A (HC 490 (1971–2), p. 99), for example, a pensioner argued for a car rather than a tricycle on the ground that without a car he would be unable to travel to work. The DHSS replied that nine medical examinations had shown that he did not meet the Category 2 test of 'inability to walk'. But, when the Department discovered that he was in hospital, they arranged a new test which showed him now to be eligible. The PCA found this to be satisfactory. In case B (HC 49 (1974/5), p. 77) a disabled person, who fell outside the categories, had been given a discretionary payment of £100 annually towards maintenance of his own car. The car became unroadworthy and the DHSS refused to provide a new one despite representations made by his MP, by his social worker and by a charity. The PCA reported that there had been no maladministration. He also declined to review the categories.

I am satisfied that all the various representations made on behalf of the complainant have been considered carefully; and that in deciding that a four-wheeled car cannot be provided to him the Department are acting in conformity with the rules they have laid down for the provision of such cars, which are strictly applied. Those who do not qualify are understandably deeply disappointed, and it would be open to me, as recommended by the Select Committee . . . [in] 1967–68 to enquire whether the Department have taken any action to review their rules, but I know that the whole subject is already being reviewed . . .

While I realise that my conclusion will bring no comfort to the complainant, I can only report that I do not find any maladministration by the Department . . . in handling his case.

In case C (HC 496 (1975/6), p. 132) the complainant had been receiving a private car allowance on the ground that he needed a car to get 'to and from full-time paid employment'. He was made redundant and negotiated new employment in which he collected the work from the factory in his car, completed it at home and returned the finished work by car. His allowance was terminated on the ground that he no longer met the departmental criteria. The PCA reported:

The distinction which the Department have drawn between these two sets of circumstances must seem to the complainant to be a fine one, as it does to me. But I know from other cases that it is the Department's policy to apply the conditions for payment of private car allowances quite strictly, and not to depart from those conditions, however sensible it may seem to do so in individual cases. That being so I do not consider I have sufficient grounds for criticising the Department's actions in this case.

Case D (HC 496 (1975/6), p. 149) is similar. A severely disabled widow had been loaned a small car by the Department on the ground that she was 'for a substantial part of the day in sole charge of a child under 14' (another guideline). She complained because her car had been withdrawn and replaced by a tricycle when her daughter reached the age of 14. Despite representations made by an MP and a voluntary organization, the DHSS refused to bend the rules. The PCA reported himself satisfied:

It is clear to me that under the Department's administrative rules, the complainant was no longer entitled to the loan of a Mini after the daughter reached the age of 14. The complainant and those acting on her behalf argue that she should have been treated exceptionally because of her daughter's backwardness. The Department acknowledge that there is force in this argument and they are aware that the strict application of their rules may have caused hardship in individual cases. But whenever they consider the question whether the age limit could be replaced by a judgment about the degree of care needed by a child, they concluded that even greater problems would be encountered in trying to decide who should, and who should not, be entitled to a car, and more indefensible anomalies would be created. They therefore applied the age limit strictly and consistently.

By substituting a test based on degree of care for a strict age-limit, the DHSS would be moving towards a discretionary system and a simple adjudicatory function. The PCA was unwilling to support this shift. But opening a critical evaluation of the relation of policy-making to discretionary power, Galligan suggests that courts may take a different view.[20]

There is an idea buried deep in the hearts of various constitutional theorists and judges that 'to discipline administrative discretion by rule and rote is somehow to denature it'. According to this idea, there is something about the nature of discretionary power which requires each decision to be made according to the circumstances of the particular situation, free from the constraints of preconceived policies as to the ends and goals to be achieved by such power. The circumstances of the situation will indicate the proper decision and policy choices must remain in the background . . . [Galligan 1976, p. 332.]

Here is a leading case in which the House of Lords considered the structuring of discretionary power by rules. Does it support Galligan?

British Oxygen Co. Ltd v. Board of Trade
[1970] 3 WLR 488

The Industrial Development Act 1966 empowered the Board of Trade to award discretionary investment grants in respect of new 'plant'. The Board had a rule of practice not to approve grants on items valued individually at less than £25. BOC asked for £4 million in respect of gas cylinders each valued at £20, but was refused. BOC sought declarations that the equipment was eligible for a grant.

LORD REID: I cannot find that these provisions give any right to any person to get a grant. It was argued that the object of the Act is to promote the modernisation of machinery and plant and that the board were bound to pay grants to all who are eligible unless, in their view, particular eligible expenditure would not promote that object. That might be good advice for an advisory committee to give but I find nothing in the Act to require the Board to act in that way. If the Minister who now administers the Act, acting on behalf of the Government, should decide not to give grants in respect of certain kinds of expenditure, I can find nothing to prevent him. There are two general grounds on which the exercise of an unqualified discretion can be attacked. It must not be exercised in bad faith, and it must not be so unreasonably exercised as to show that there cannot have been any real or genuine exercise of the discretion. But, apart from that, if the Minister thinks that policy or good administration requires the operation of some limiting rule, I find nothing to stop him.

It was argued on the authority of *Rex* v. *Port of London Authority, Ex parte Kynoch Ltd* [1919] 1 K B 176 that the Minister is not entitled to make a rule for himself as to how he will in future exercise his discretion. In that case Kynoch owned land adjoining the Thames and wished to construct a deep water wharf. For this they had to get the permission of the authority. Permission was refused on the ground that Parliament had charged the authority with the duty of providing such facilities. It appeared that before reaching their decision the authority had fully considered the case on its merits and in relation to the public interest. So their decision was upheld.

Bankes LJ said: 'There are on the one hand cases where a tribunal in the honest exercise of its discretion has adopted a policy, and, without refusing to hear an applicant, intimates to him what its policy is, and that after hearing him it will in accordance with its policy decide against him, unless there is something exceptional in his case. I think . . . that, if the policy has been adopted for reasons which the tribunal may legitimately entertain, no objection could be taken to such a course. On the other hand there are cases where a tribunal has passed a rule, or come to a determination, not to hear any application of a particular character by whomsoever made. There is a wide distinction to be drawn between these two classes.'

I see nothing wrong with that. But the circumstances in which discretions are exercised vary enormously and that passage cannot be applied literally in every case. The general rule is that anyone who has to exercise a statutory discretion must not 'shut his ears to an application' . . . I do not think there is any great difference between a policy and a rule. There may be cases where an officer or authority ought to listen to a substantial argument reasonably presented arguing a change of policy. What the authority must not do is to refuse to listen at all. But a Ministry or large authority may have had to deal already with a multitude of similar applications and then they will almost certainly have evolved a policy so precise that it could well be called a rule. There can be no objection to that, provided the authority is always willing to listen to anyone with something new to say – of course I do not mean to say that there need be an oral hearing. In the present case the respondent's officers have carefully considered all the appellants have had to say and I have no doubt that they will continue to do so . . .[21]

There is a clash here between the lawyer's attitude to discretion as an area of total freedom and the administrator's need for rules. Galligan suggests a compromise position. Judges should recognize the nature of the administrative hierarchy in which policy decisions taken at the top level are transmitted to subordinates. In other words,

. . . discretion entails a power in the decision-maker to make policy choices, not just to deal with the individual case, but to develop a coherent and consistent set of guidelines which seek to achieve ends and goals within the scope of powers . . . [Galligan 1976, p. 332.]

In short, 'discretion' includes the discretion to make rules.

5 **Individuation and procedural fairness**

If the BOC principle were applied to the invalid tricycle cases, would the result be different in any of the cases? If the PCA had investigated the BOC complaint would he have found maladministration? The two external monitors tell us that administrative rule-making is permissible and even laudable provided that the administrator is always prepared 'to listen to a case'. The invalid tricycle cases suggest that he need not listen very hard. We might ask two questions. Suppose a department will not entertain some types of represent-ation, e.g. it will not answer telephone applications or listen to pressure groups, what then? And what is the position if the department (as perhaps in case C) stands intransigently behind an unreasonable policy? In the Oregon parole scheme you will find adjudicatory restraints are incorporated in the shape of an oral hearing and a reasoned decision to provide a basis for review. Galligan argues that principles or rules are valueless without procedural reinforcements. Compare his approach to that of the cases on procedural fairness in Chapter 3.

The question is . . . whether a full oral hearing should be granted or not. Between these two extremes there is a great variety of possibilities including various types of hearings, oral submissions, written submissions and arguments and so on. The important point in regard to applying adminis-trative policies is that their evolutionary nature, which entails some consideration of the merits of each case, should guarantee some minimum level of participation by interested parties. It is essential that this guarantee should not become a unilateral formality. This minimum would seem to require at least the following: first, that the policies and their principles of individuation * upon which authorities act should be publicised in a manner readily accessible to interested parties; secondly, that there should be a greater effort by administrative bodies to develop principles of individuation in respect of discretionary power; thirdly, that where possible, the policy-making functions of authorities should be conducted through more formal-ised and public channels; fourthly, that an interested party should have some

---

* Notice that Galligan uses 'individuation' and 'principles of individuation' in an unusual sense to mean policy-making through rules and rulemaking (Galligan 1976, p. 334, notes 7 and 8). Elsewhere in this chapter we use the term to mean application of rules to individual cases.

opportunity of making representations in favour of an exception being made for him or the policy being modified; fifthly, that reasons be given by the decision-maker showing how the policy has been related to the particular situation. None of these proposals is intended to reduce the flexibility so important to administrative bodies; rather they are intended to develop more open and fair administrative procedures. [Galligan 1976, pp. 356–7.]

A similar idea was expressed in a *Justice* report, 'Administration under Law' (1971). *Justice* proposed a statutory code for the guidance of administrators:

Principles of Good Administration
1. Before making any decision, an authority shall take all reasonable steps to ensure that all persons who will be particularly and materially affected by such decision have been informed in sufficient time of its intention to make the decision and shall afford to all such persons a reasonable opportunity of making representations to the authority with respect thereto . . .

3. It shall be the duty of an authority in proceeding to a decision to take all reasonable steps to ascertain the facts which are material to the decision . . .

9. An authority shall take all reasonable steps to ensure that its decisions are made known to those persons likely to be affected by them . . .

Note: 'all reasonable steps' means measures by way of inquiry, verification, deliberation or otherwise as are in all the circumstances of the case necessary according to good administrative practice.

What sort of 'principles' are these? They are certainly not 'rules'. The first thought of a good manager would be to reformulate them as concrete instructions which subordinates could apply. Are they 'standards', which can be expected to vary with the departmental budget from year to year? Do these 'principles' merely embody what Holmes once called 'a benevolent yearning'? If so, they will fluctuate according to the prejudices of individual administrators and judges. But *Justice* do not object because they prefer rule-making by adjudication to administrative rule-making:

It would be for the courts to develop a body of caselaw to guide authorities as to the adequacy or inadequacy of the different techniques available: written representations, for example or individual private consultation, or public inquiry, committee 'hearings' (with or without legal representation), or reference to an independent person or body. In any particular case, the court would be required to 'have regard to' any special pre-decision rules already laid down by Parliament for that case. In this way, there would gradually emerge a body of case-law on the subject. [*Justice* 1971, pp. 15–16.]

The difficulties which might arise in practice are well illustrated by *Furnell* v. *Whangarei Schools Board* [1973] 2 WLR 92. Acting in conjunction with the appropriate unions, the New Zealand

Government prepared an elaborate disciplinary code which became the New Zealand Education Act 1964. In 1969, further disciplinary regulations were made, once more after consultation with the unions. The two procedures were not identical nor did they apply in the same situations.

Furnell was suspected of serious disciplinary offences. In accordance with the regulations, which applied to his case, a committee was set up to investigate. If the committee decided that the matter ought to go further, it had to arrange a hearing by the school board. The committee took this step without interviewing Furnell and he was suspended to await the hearing. Instead, he brought an action for a declaration alleging a breach of natural justice in that no opportunity to explain his case had been afforded before suspension. The Privy Council was divided. The majority held the disciplinary code to be all-embracing; Lord Reid, for the dissenting minority, held that natural justice had been breached.

LORD MORRIS: The rules of natural justice were invoked. It becomes necessary therefore to consider whether the detailed and elaborate code which prescribes the procedure to be followed when there is a suggestion of an offence ... is a code which gives scope for unfairness and whether in its operation the court in the interests of fairness must supplement the written provisions. In the present case do the well-known words of Byles J in *Cooper* v. *Wandsworth* [see above, Chapter 1] apply: 'although there are no positive words in a statute requiring that the party shall be heard, yet the justice of the common law will supply the omission of the legislature'? Or is the code one that has been carefully and deliberately drafted so as to prescribe procedure which is fair and appropriate? The appellant as a teacher ... agreed to serve under the conditions laid down in the regulations and unless some provisions are to be read into them ... it is clear that they were faithfully followed. It is not lightly to be affirmed that a regulation that has the force of law is unfair when it has been made on the advice of the responsible Minister and on the joint recommendation of organisations representing teachers employed and those employing. Nor is it the function of the court to redraft the code ...

The whole scheme of the regulations and of the provisions of the Education Act point to the conclusion that the task of the ... sub-committee is to give consideration to a complaint with a view to presenting a report to the board (i.e the governing body of the school in question). Their finding may be that the complaint could be ignored as being mischievous or irresponsible. Their finding on the other hand may be that the complaint might have substance and could not be ignored. The absence of any provision relating to making a communication to the teacher concerned must have been deliberate since the regulations proceed with great particularity to specify when and how communication shall be made to him and when and how he should make response. The procedure for the preliminary investigation of a complaint before ever there is a charge is a procedure which must have been devised as an additional safeguard for teachers. If those investigating a complaint thought in any particular circumstances that it would be desirable for them to ask a teacher to see them with a view to seeking his explanation of some matter it would be open to them to take that course . . . But if they thought that a complaint (as for example a complaint of sustained and continuing inefficiency) could not be so simply disposed of and could really only be dealt with under the subsequent procedure as laid down there would be nothing unfair in their reporting to such effect without communicating with the teacher concerned. Certainly in the present case there are no grounds for holding that the sub-committee acted unfairly. When the nature of the detailed and formulated charges in this case and of the lengthy and detailed comments of the appellant are considered it seems reasonably clear that matters could not possibly have been disposed of without some kind of inquiry extending very much beyond any form of a preliminary investigation of complaints.

LORD REID (dissenting): Mr Furnell was not dealt with under [the Education Act]. He was proceeded against under the disciplinary regulations . . . as he was a teacher to whom they applied. The language of those regulations is clearly modelled on the provisions of the Act and if, as I think, the investigation by a committee appointed in accordance with the Act necessarily involves hearing both sides it is unlikely that investigation by a committee under the regulations was intended to have a different meaning . . .

It must have been thought that the regulations improved the position of the teachers to whom they applied. If, however, the contention of the Solicitor-General is right, their position was worse than it was under the Education Act 1964 for they can be reprimanded and censured by the board without having had an opportunity of putting forward their defence and of calling witnesses. That result cannot have been intended. That the disciplinary regulations contain a detailed disciplinary code is not disputable. That it is a complete code is . . . Regulation 8 does not give an accused teacher the right to cross-examine. There is no provision for repayment to him of salary he has lost while suspended if the board decide to take no further action though there is if he is acquitted by a teachers' disciplinary board.

Merely to have an opportunity of making a statement or giving an explanation after he has been criticised or condemned by the sub-committee, criticism that may lead to his immediate suspension and to his being censured by the board without any further inquiry, is no substitute for an opportunity to put forward his defence and to call witnesses. The opportunity to make a statement and to give an explanation after condemnation by a sub-committee is . . . analogous to a prisoner being asked whether he has anything to say before he is sentenced.

In my opinion the sub-committee failed to discharge [their] duty . . . by not giving Mr Furnell an opportunity of being heard by them.

Why does Lord Reid feel able to infer (a) that the regulations were intended to improve the situation of teachers; (b) that the code is not a complete code and (c) that the situation is analogous to a prisoner before sentence? Do you agree with him?

In the *Furnell* case, principles clashed with rules. If rules have to be abandoned when they come into conflict with a principle as general as that 'no man should be condemned unheard' then the model of rules has been destroyed. As can be seen from *Furnell's* case, the application of such a principle is difficult to predict. The good administrator must now have one eye on the rulebook and the other on the unpredictable reactions of the judge. Is this the optimum point on the spectrum? Many would think it the worst of both worlds. The existence of rules encourages legalism. But the adjudicatory model which has been grafted on via natural justice inhibits innovatory decision-taking techniques.

6 Rule-making procedures

The principles of natural justice belong to the adjudicatory process but the disciplinary regulations in *Furnell's* case had been the subject of group consultation and negotiation. If Lord Reid had had his way, adjudicatory procedures, which favour individuals, would have prevailed over the collective rule-making procedure. Is this what Galligan advocates?

The rule-making procedures with which Davis was familiar were those of the American Administrative Procedure Act 1946. These procedures may be formal and judicialized, as you saw in the Oregon study. More generally the Act provides that administrative agencies shall afford 'interested persons the opportunity to participate in the rulemaking through submission of written data, views or arguments with or without opportunity to present the same orally in any manner.' This is known as 'notice-and-comment' procedure. The Act also provides an informal right 'to petition for the issuance, amendment, or repeal of a rule'. Judicial review has been extensively used.[22]

Davis (1971, pp. 65–8) thinks the procedure a success. 'Anyone and everyone is allowed to express himself and to call attention to the impact of various possible policies on his business, activity or interest. The agency's staff sifts and summarizes the presentations and prepares its own studies. The procedure is both fair and efficient. Much experience proves that it usually works beautifully.'

But American administrators apparently find the APA procedures frustrating:[23]

> The actual agency experience with these procedural requirements raises doubts about their desirability. At best, some agencies have learned to live with them, even though preferable procedures are probably available. At worst, these procedures have warped regulatory programs or resulted in virtual abandonment of them . . . The primary impact of these procedural requirements is often not . . . the testing of agency assumptions . . . Rather these procedures either cause the abandonment of the program . . . the development of techniques to reach the same regulatory goal but without a hearing . . . or the promulgation of non-controversial regulations by a process of negotiation and compromise . . . In practice, therefore, the principal effect of imposing rulemaking on a record has often been the dilution of the regulatory process rather than the protection of persons from arbitrary action . . . Ultimately . . . the goal should be the complete elimination of mandatory trial-type procedures in rulemaking . . . [Hamilton 1972, pp. 1312–13.]

Compare this attitude with that of English administrators to formal legislative procedures. Again the rule-making procedures have become inflexible to the point at which they hinder dynamic administration. Dimock links legalism with weak administration, saying:

> Lawyers as a class are powerful in the United States; so are business executives. But public administrators, who do substantially the same kind of work, are, in terms of clout, a faint imitation of these other two groups . . . The conservative reaction to the New Deal had something to do with the subsequent decline of the government's administrative effectiveness. This campaign climaxed in 1946 with the passage of the Administrative Procedure Act. First, federal administration, and following that, a large percentage of state administrations, began to judicialize, which made them progressively tentative, formalistic and bureaucratic. [Dimock 1980, p. 3.]

In England, there is no general right to be consulted or participate in the rule-making process. Sometimes statutes provide that specified bodies or 'interested persons' are to be consulted before rules are made. For example, consultation procedures are built into planning legislation, though we shall see in Chapter 14 how uncertain their legal effect is. Similarly, the Education Acts provide for the wishes of parents to be taken into account when policy is being formulated. S.13 of the Education Act 1944 provided, for example, that whenever the local education authority intended to establish a new school or cease to maintain an existing school it 'shall forthwith give public notice' of the proposals which it has made to the Minister. This allowed 'the managers or governors of any voluntary school affected by the proposals or any ten or more local government electors' to submit objections to the Minister. Since education policy is controversial and often hotly contested, these provisions were often invoked.

When judges are asked to grant injunctions or other remedies to enforce procedural requirements they are faced with a dilemma. If they enforce the procedures too rigidly, then everything will have to be done again, causing delay and expense. The experience will encourage administrators to stick legalistically to the letter of the law in future cases. On the other hand, if procedural formality is waived, the values which underlie those procedures may be imperilled.

When in 1967 Enfield LBC wished to reorganize secondary education on a comprehensive basis, abandoning selective entry to grammar schools, its proposals were submitted to teachers, consultative bodies and public meetings at which parents spoke. After consultation with the Minister, it followed the provisions of s.13 in respect of most schools, but in relation to eight schools, which were to be combined or to become coeducational, it was advised that the procedures were not applicable. This decision was challenged. The Court of Appeal held that the section was applicable because the changes involved a fundamental alteration to the identity and character of the schools concerned (*Bradbury* v. *Enfield LBC* [1967] 1 WLR 1311). The judgment left Enfield with insufficient time to comply with statutory procedures before the school year started. It therefore fell back on a modified scheme involving a non-selective intake into Enfield Grammar School. A majority of the governors applied to the Minister to vary the articles to make this possible. Section 17 (5) of the Education Act required the Minister to 'afford . . . to . . . persons concerned with the . . . government of the School an opportunity of making representations.' The Minister wrote on 14 September, allowing four days, including a weekend, for such representations to be made. In *Lee* v. *Department of Education and Science* (1967) 66 LGR 211, Donaldson J granted a declaration that this time was wholly inadequate. The section was intended to give 'a real and not an illusory opportunity to make representations'. He dealt sharply with the argument that the matter was urgent. 'The urgency arises from two attempts to put into effect unlawful schemes which would have affected the school and their failure to admit boys to the school in accordance with the existing articles of government.' He concluded:

Bearing in mind the fact that the scheme for a three-form entry was first mentioned [16 days ago], the fact that what is proposed goes to the whole character of the grammar school as it has been known for 400 years, the fact that the governors or groups of governors may wish to consult together and formulate a collective view as to what is best for the school, and, lastly, the fact that this is the holiday period . . . I consider that the period of 4 weeks from [the date of the Minister's letter] would be reasonable but that a shorter period, or at any rate any substantially shorter period, would not be reasonable and would not comply with section 17.[24]

Contrast the case of *Coney* v. *Choyce* [1975] 1 W L R 422, where plans for reorganization of schools in Nottinghamshire were well publicized by meetings, newsletters and in churches. The authority failed to comply with s. 13 of the Education Act 1944 in that the requisite notice was not posted at or near a 'main entrance' of two schools in Worksop. Templeman J refused to intervene:

The objects of section 13(3), are to ensure that the public are aware of the proposals and of their rights to object to the Secretary of State: that is a preliminary to ensuring that objections reach the Secretary of State for consideration before he decides the facts of the proposals. The Minister cannot decide to approve the proposals unless he has in front of him the objections which can fairly be raised against them. The objects of section 13(3) were in my judgment achieved. The notices were well publicised . . .

The regulations are not designed to see that everybody knows. If they were, they would provide for different publicity. Suppose, for example, a notice is put up at the town hall, that it is published in the local paper, and that it is posted at the school, thus complying with the regulations. There must in the area of Worksop be a large number of citizens who go more frequently to the football ground and the public house than the town hall, who have children, none of whom are over the age of five, and who read the 'Daily Mirror', and nothing but the 'Daily Mirror'. Those persons probably never go near the particular places where the regulations have been fulfilled and the notices have been put up. The regulations are not designed to bring the matter home to everybody. If that was required there would have to be the town crier, or perhaps on the local radio announcements every quarter of an hour.

What the regulations require is that notices should be published in a manner designed to show a representative number of people what their rights are, and leave to them the organisation of others. In fact that is obviously what happened in this case. Some people, I think a great number, saw the notice. They organised the parents' association. No doubt they went around and said, 'Have you heard this monstrous proposal which has been going on for years; now it is coming to a head and if we are going to do anything about it we have got to write to the Minister. Will you sign a petition?'

If there had been more notices, even if the number of objectors had been doubled, it does not seem to me that that would be sufficient to make any real difference to the problem which troubled the Minister who sat down with the proposals on the one hand and the objections on the other.

Where consultation is not a statutory requirement, courts have not been anxious to supply the deficiency (compare their attitude to adjudicatory procedures). But in one special case, *R. v. Liverpool Corporation ex p. Liverpool Taxi Fleet Operators' Association* [1972] 2 WLR 1262, the Court of Appeal did make a foray into the area.

The case concerned the licensing of taxi-cabs in Liverpool. The corporation had for many years limited the number of cab licences to 300. The owners wanted the limit retained, the drivers wanted it increased. Liverpool Corporation tried to regulate matters by introducing a private Bill into Parliament to limit private hire cars. This was to be coupled with a corporation resolution to increase the number of taxi cabs. The corporation had earlier assured the owners that they would not proceed without listening to their representations. When the owners found that the matter had been determined by the corporation, they sought and obtained an order of prohibition to enforce the informal undertaking by prohibiting the corporation from acting on the resolutions without hearing representations.

LORD DENNING MR: First I would say this: when the corporation consider applications for licences under the Town Police Clauses Act 1847, they are under a duty to act fairly. This means that they should be ready to hear not only the particular applicant but also any other persons or bodies whose interests are affected . . .

It is perhaps putting it a little high to say they are exercising judicial functions. They may be said to be exercising an administrative function. But even so, in our modern approach, they must act fairly: and the court will see that they do so.

To apply that principle here: suppose the corporation proposed to reduce the number of taxicabs from 300 to 200, it would be their duty to hear the taxicab owners' association: because their members would be greatly affected. They would certainly be persons aggrieved. Likewise suppose the corporation propose to increase the number of taxicabs from 300 to 350 or 400 or more: it is the duty of the corporation to hear those affected before coming to a decision adverse to their interests . . .

The other thing I would say is that the corporation were not at liberty to disregard their undertaking. They were bound by it so long as it was not in conflict with their statutory duty.

It is said that a corporation cannot contract itself out of its statutory duties.[25] But that principle does not mean that a corporation can give an undertaking and break it as they please. So long as the performance of the undertaking is compatible with their public duty, they must honour it. And I should have thought that this undertaking was so compatible. At any rate they ought not to depart from it except after the most serious consideration and hearing what the other party has to say: and then only if they are satisfied that the overriding public interest requires it. The public interest may be better served by honouring their undertaking than by breaking it. This is just such a case. It is better to hold the corporation to their undertaking than to allow them to break it . . .

Applying these principles, it seems to me that the corporation acted wrongly . . . In the first place, they took decisions without giving the owners' association an opportunity of being heard. In the second place, they broke their undertaking without any sufficient cause or excuse.

Evans believes that this case is capable of generalization into a principle under which courts require that interested groups and individuals should be afforded prior notice and the right to present oral or written arguments before decisions of a legislative nature are made.[26] 'Participation at this level would significantly increase the opportunities for the examination and debate of governmental measures beyond those available through the traditional political process' (de Smith 1980, p. 181).

Wade, on the other hand, prefers to leave the matter to the good sense of administrators:

It may be that consultation which is not subject to statutory procedure is more effective than formal hearings which may produce legalism and artificiality . . . Consultation before rule-making, even when not required by law, is in fact one of the major industries of government. It is doubtful whether anything would be gained by imposing general legal obligations and formal procedures. At least, there appears to be no demand for any such reform. [Wade 1982, pp. 767–8.]

The *Liverpool* case shows how difficult it might prove to administer a general duty to consult. After the decision, the corporation invited representations, but unhappily, as it later conceded, the invitation was not sufficiently all-embracing. In a second application for prohibition, the Taxi Fleet Operators' Association succeeded in preventing the corporation from acting on its second resolution to increase the number of licences. The corporation then began a third attempt to deal with the problem. This time the invitation to submit representations was very widely phrased and widely publicized, and so many people turned up at the committee meeting that the majority could not be accommodated. The committee decided to exclude the public, except the press, because it thought it fairer that no-one should attend rather than an arbitrarily chosen few, and because it thought it best, in view of the high feelings involved and the notoriety of the matter, that those making representations should do so without the presence of those making conflicting representations. The operators, who had decided not to make representations but to listen to those made by others, were thus unable to attend the meeting. The committee recommended an increase in the number of licences and the corporation subsequently passed a resolution to this effect. The operators sought to have this resolution set aside on the grounds that the public had been improperly excluded from the meeting. This time they lost; the court held that the resolution to exclude the public was quite valid. Lord Widgery CJ commented, 'the local authority has perhaps at long last produced a resolution on this subject which is not subject to attack in this court' (*R.* v. *Liverpool City Council ex p. Liverpool Taxi Fleet Operators' Association* [1975] 1 WLR 701). This and the education cases show how the courts, in enforcing procedural requirements, may gradually be sucked into the administrative process.

It can be seen from these cases that interest representation in the rule-making process is typically *collective*: trade associations, trade unions, parents' associations and other pressure groups are involved. Discussing the experience of the VAT legislation, Johnstone suggests that this is inevitable:

Another problem in consultative technique, which [the Customs and Excise Department] did not fully solve and which may be incapable of full solution, is that of finding an appropriate place in the consultations for the 'small man' (or woman), whether firm or individual, who characteristically does not belong to any trade or professional association and takes little interest in the activities of the local chamber of commerce. In a sense this overlaps with the problem of keeping MPs in touch with the consultations, since every small man or woman has an MP; but it is also a separate problem, for one cannot realistically envisage a tripartite consultation with MPs specifically representing the small men and leaving it to the associations to speak for everyone else . . . One way of looking at it, no doubt, is that people who want to be consulted when the government are planning new measures affecting their business or professional activities ought to join a trade or professional association . . . But that would only transfer the onus of consulting them from the Civil Service bureaucracy to the association bureaucracy . . . [and] one cannot feel confident that it would necessarily be much easier for the association bureaucracy to do it. [Johnstone 1975, p. 36.]

By giving priority to individuation it could be argued that courts are unbalancing the political process and that the individuated procedures envisaged by Galligan with the fall-back of enforcement by litigation are, like the trial-type hearings of the Administrative Procedure Act, essentially unsuited to general administrative decision-taking and policy formulation.[27] Policy decisions of this type involve the balancing of disparate interests and require negotiation and conciliation. This argument is developed in Chapter 14.

7 Retreat from rules?

Reviewing *Discretionary Justice*, a sociologist thought Davis unduly optimistic about the power of rules to counter misuse of discretion. Davis had closed his eyes to how people really behave:

Davis relies on rule making as the principal means for confining discretion, on openness of discretionary processes as the major means for structuring discretion, and on supervision and review as the major means for checking discretion. These are, of course, the classic means and processes operating in modern bureaucracies. What is absent from his treatment, however – a deficiency that may puzzle behavioral scientists – is both a consideration of the relative importance of these factors and a consideration of how bureaucracies can turn these means to ends of justice or can find ways to circumvent them so that decisions go against the interests of individual parties . . .

Indeed, examination of the structure and nature of bureaucracies seems crucial for determining the quality of administrative justice. While it is a cardinal principle in the Weberian theory of bureaucracy that rules are a way of ensuring consistent treatment of all individual parties, it also is a principle that bureaucracies neutralize civic power. Paradoxically, then, protection exists only so long as bureaucratic officials behave properly. When they do not, the capacity for citizens to affect official actions is very limited. How can one ignore the fact that the power to litigate is the power to neutralize much administration, and that for every formal procedure there is an informal one of circumvention? [Reiss 1970, pp. 794–5.]

There is a great deal of evidence to suggest that people regulate their behaviour by reference to group ethos and the approval of their fellows rather than by 'the law'. In services which, like the police, are hierarchically organized, these pressures are particularly intense. For this reason, the Bennett Report into Police Interrogation Procedures in Northern Ireland recognized that new policies or rules concerning the conduct of police interrogation would be valueless unless they were supervised and reinforced by senior officers.[28] Although less well-documented, similar considerations may affect civil servants – one reason why, for example, benefit officers may follow policy directives in preference to statute (Chapter 18).

Welfare lawyers are particularly frightened of discretion because of its potency as a weapon for social control. They feel that social workers and benefit officers use discretionary power to manipulate their clients.[29] It is important to realize, however, that rules as well as discretion can be used to manipulate people and that administrators well understand how to play games with rules. 'Bad' clients find that officials stand on the letter of the law or lodge unnecessary appeals designed to postpone payment; 'good' clients may receive the benefit of loopholes and ambiguities. Both sides can play the game. Some seek to 'neutralize administration' by tying it in its own rules; e.g. by lodging unnecessary appeals, which use up resources and time and may even be designed to overload the system to provoke concessions. Schwarz and Wade mention a drive by US welfare groups which produced 7,503 requests for hearings after a single test case. They comment, 'Insistence upon an inexorable right to full judicialized trials in all welfare decisions can lead to virtual administrative breakdown . . . [and] would inevitably diminish the chances of fairness for any and all' (Schwarz and Wade 1972, p. 124). Similar considerations apply to consultation procedures. Planning decisions may be contested at every stage in the hope that the plan can be postponed indefinitely. Did something like this occur in the *Liverpool* case?

Earlier, Jowell mentioned the technique of 'selective enforcement' as an alternative way of mitigating the severity of rules. He gave the example of infringement of parking regulations in helping a blind man across the road. This example suggests that selective enforcement is reserved for individual hard cases – the severely disabled mother whose car is withdrawn when her daughter reaches the age of 14, for example. Selective enforcement of rules is actually quite common; think of the police discretion whether or not to prosecute. There is even evidence to show that discretionary powers of selective enforcement are sometimes, like statutory discretions, structured by rules.

In Megarry's description of 'quasi-legislation', you will find it stated that the Inland Revenue 'announce concessions which will be made to the taxpayer'. The official hierarchy of rules is being qualified by a discretion not to enforce the rules. In turn, the discretionary power has been structured by informal rules. Davis would, no doubt, be glad to find these concessions openly published and accessible to the public. We should pause for a minute to ask whether this is really so. Is there perhaps a further hierarchy of internal circulars and memoranda qualifying the *published* concessions? Earlier we saw Griffith and Harman attack the impropriety of legislating by administrative circular when opportunities existed to present the matter to Parliament. We all know that the passage of the annual Finance Act is an important ritual which provides the Inland Revenue with just such an opportunity. Why do they choose concessions instead? The behaviour is not atypical. You will find a further example in the *Home Loss* study (Chapter 8) which may provide some answers.

Megarry tells us firmly that the extra-statutory concessions are not 'law' because no court would enforce them. Are they then 'illegal'? Some cases do show courts looking on these Revenue practices with disfavour. For example, in *R. v. Commissioners of Customs and Excise ex p. Cook* [1970] 1 WLR 450 the Inland Revenue had agreed as a concession to accept excise duty in instalments rather than by a single, immediate payment. The Lord Chief Justice remarked: 'One approaches this case on the basis, and I confess for my part an alarming basis, that the word of the Minister is outweighing the law of the land.'[30] Yet the court did not actually halt the 'illegal' practice because it thought that the applicants had no locus standi. And, in the *Federation* case (see below, p. 300), you will see the House of Lords treating a similar, discretionary concession as reasonable and sensible.

Parliament itself has condoned similar practices. Indeed, in the *Home Loss* affair, the ombudsmen, the Select Committee and members on the floor of the House, all urged the administrators to depart from the letter of the law. The Select Committee on the PCA has encouraged the Inland Revenue to make concessions without express statutory authority. The Public Accounts Committee has accepted a need for extra-statutory concessions, yet the Inland Revenue itself, its bound volumes of extra-statutory concessions speaking against its own argument, has been heard to say that, without government authority, interest on over-payments of tax cannot be made.[31] Is selective enforcement 'illegal' or is it not? As usual, there is no conclusive answer.

It may be disappointing to discover that rules are not a panacea for all administrative evils, but it is hardly surprising. Rules and discretion are, after all, only machinery for the implementation of policy. And where the optimum lies on an imaginary scale between equality of treatment and individuation is, at the end of the day, a value-judgement on which there is unlikely to be consensus.

6
Firefighting to firewatching: the Council on Tribunals

In earlier chapters, we discussed the development of administrative tribunals. The work of Donoughmore and Franks was outlined, together with the failure of these Committees to consider a rational allocation of functions to tribunals.

In this context, we mentioned the interest shown by Robson in an administrative appeals tribunal to regulate the quality of administrative justice. Robson presented his case in evidence to Donoughmore, but his proposals were rejected. In evidence to Franks, Robson pursued a slightly different line. His concern now was with the proliferation of tribunals, the 'irregular and unsystematic development of administrative adjudication'. He thought a permanent supervisory body was needed to provide a 'focal point from which knowledgeable advice and guidance could be maintained'. This body should be concerned with *structure*.

In Chapter 5, we turned our attention to rule-making, noting the growing influence of this internal and prospective form of control in modern administrative law. Our main concern was the use of rules in policy development and to confine the boundaries of administrative discretion. In the course of the chapter, however, the importance of procedural rules became apparent. Procedural formalities protected the right to participate, whether individually or as a group, in decision-making. We looked at the standard procedures of the American Administrative Procedure Act and their operation in the Oregon parole scheme, contrasting the absence of standardization and formalization in England.

Tribunals, like courts, have rules of procedure and the evidence of

Wade to Franks recognized their importance. However informal a tribunal is intended to be, its proceedings must be orderly. Wade felt that it would be possible to identify 'generally acceptable' procedural standards. He recommended the creation of a standing body which would be able to enforce procedural standards through a rule-making power. Accepting the ideas of Robson and Wade, Franks proposed the creation of the Council on Tribunals.

Some writers might argue that the work of the Council is peripheral to the real subject of administrative law – the control of governmental power – others have called the Council a 'toothless watchdog'. But the work of the Council draws together the themes of rule-making, adjudication and procedural fairness, all matters of concern to administrative lawyers. The Council's development seems to reflect the movement in administrative law from firefighting to firewatching. Finally, the way in which this new administrative agency has been absorbed into the traditional constitutional pattern is, to some observers, characteristically British.

1 Origins

Franks (para. 43) considered 'its most important recommendation' to be that 'two standing councils, one for England and Wales and one for Scotland, should be set up to keep the constitution and workings of tribunals under continuous review'.[1] Franks envisaged a significant role for these bodies which, by the Tribunals and Inquiries Act 1958, subsequently became the Council on Tribunals and its Scottish Committee. While accepting that its creations would be advisory in character, Franks hoped the ambit of their advice would be considerable:

[Their] main function . . . should be to suggest how the general principles of constitution, organisation and procedure enunciated in the Report should be applied in detail to the various tribunals. In discharging this function they should first decide the application of these principles to all existing tribunals; thereafter they should keep tribunals under review and advise on the constitution, organisation and procedure of any proposed new type of tribunal. We recommend that any proposal to establish a new tribunal should be referred to the Councils for their advice before steps are taken to establish the tribunal. The Councils should have power to take evidence from witnesses both inside and outside the public service, and their reports should be published. All their functions should be statutory. [para. 133.]

At this point, a divergence of view surfaced which may have

ultimately affected the Council's usefulness. The Joint Permanent Secretary to the Treasury submitted that the Council should report to the Prime Minister (para. 130). Tribunals were 'part of the machinery of administration' for which the Prime Minister was generally responsible. Franks had insisted that tribunals were 'machinery for adjudication', so should report to the Lord Chancellor.[2] Franks argued:

If such a body were responsible to the head of the Government, its reports would acquire additional prestige, and it may therefore seem surprising that we have not been able to accept this suggestion. Our reason for recommending otherwise is that . . . we cannot accept the view that tribunals are part and parcel of the ordinary machinery of administration. We consider that they are properly to be thought of as independent organs of adjudication. Therefore we think that it would be more appropriate for the . . . body . . . to be appointed by and report to the Lord Chancellor. It should be named the Lord Chancellor's Council on Tribunals. [para. 30.]

Was this a mistake? The Prime Minister and the Treasury are powerful and possess great influence in other departments. The functions envisaged for the Council were supervisory and depended on negotiation. The Council on Tribunals was to possess a watching brief over the tribunals system as a whole and a responsibility for general, procedural standards. The support of a powerful Ministry could have been helpful.

The 'job description', set out in para. 133, charged the councils with the dissemination of the Franks ethos. In other words, it was to be through the councils that tribunals, after the initial reforms anticipated by Franks, were to be moved towards Jowell's ideal-type of adjudication. Note in particular that the standing bodies[3] were not to be restricted to scrutinizing existing tribunals: they were to have a hand in the creation of future tribunals. On the other hand, this role was perceived as being essentially reactive: the councils were to report upon particular proposals, not to initiate their own suggestions. Franks also envisaged that the councils would have important executive powers; e.g., the appointment of tribunal members (as distinct from chairmen), the formulation of procedural rules and the review of remuneration for tribunal appointees. Now consider the suggestions made for their staffing and constitution:

We think that in each case there will be advantage in a fairly small body, of nine or ten persons composed partly of lay members and partly of members with legal experience and qualifications, the lay members being in a majority. We think that the chairmen should be persons who have attained distinction in public life, but we do not think that they need be lawyers. They will doubtless be called upon to devote more of their time to the work than will the members of the Councils, and we therefore think that it would be right to offer them a salary. [para. 134.]

The standing bodies, despite the significant functions accorded them, were to consist of part-timers.[4] Nor was anything said about the funding and research capability of these bodies. The subsequent history of the Council on Tribunals demonstrates how this has worked out in practice. Garner found:

The staff of the Council is surprisingly small. The Secretary is a barrister and a civil servant of considerable experience; indeed, the fact that he has himself had a career in Whitehall and is well known to many civil servants in the various Ministries has clearly been of great assistance in getting the Council accepted in Government circles . . . In addition to the Secretary the Council employs two lawyer assistants (both members of the Bar), an experienced executive officer, two secretarial assistants and a messenger. The vote in the current annual Estimate for salaries and national insurance, etc. is £19,000 and there is a supplementary sum of £1,000 to cover travelling and other expenses; accommodation and office expenses are not separately assessed on the Council. The most determined critic of Government expenditure can therefore scarcely accuse the Council of extravagance in either man-power or finance. Indeed, one might almost describe the office as being conducted on a 'shoestring' . . . The Chairman [of the Council] is paid a salary (on a part-time basis) and the Chairman of the Scottish Committee also; the other members are entitled to claim fees and expenses . . . The Council is not a professional or legal body; all the members were before their appointment well-known persons in other walks of life, and clearly they are chosen from as broad a section of the community as possible. [Garner 1965, pp. 321–5.]

In 1980, during the course of an internal review into its own functions, the Council said:

In making appointments the practice has been to strike a balance between legal and other skills and experience . . . There is a preponderance of non-lawyers. One member is an academic with special experience of research in the field of social administration. Other members have a background of trade unionism, social work, consumer protection, public administration, business and agriculture . . . Our secretariat is very small. In addition to the Secretary, the staff of the Council consists of one Principal, two Senior Legal Assistants, one Higher Executive Officer, three Executive Officers and clerical staff. For operational purposes our organisation is regarded as part of the Lord Chancellor's Department; we rely on that department to authorise our expenditure and we have no independent budget. [Cmnd 7805, paras. 3.4, 3.10.]

The functions which were to be entrusted to the Council were primarily legal in character although some, particularly statutory drafting, are also highly technical. Yet a minority of members (22 out of the first 63) has been legally qualified and not all of these have had practical experience. And is it possible to choose 'from a broad section of the community' members who are to be 'well-known' prior to their appointment? In fact, the membership of the Council has been predominantly male (12 of the first 63 were women), white, and elderly. One student of the Council tells us that 'in general the majority of members were appointed only after they had established themselves successfully in their chosen careers, or had retired, and in the case of legal practitioners relatively soon before their elevations to the Bench'.[5] Again, with a few exceptions like Wade or Bell, both academics with a special interest in tribunals, the period of service is short (average three years). The members are necessarily dependent on the secretariat.

Look again at the 'shoestring' nature of the operation. By March 1982, the Council's budget had increased to £202,628. Staff salaries accounted for £130,549 and the chairman received £12,470, less than an under-secretary in the civil service earns. The four secretaries have been legally qualified, usually with previous public service experience, but they have had only two legal assistants. Compare the career of parliamentary counsel, a prestigious and well-paid, specialized job. Notice the absence of a careers structure. In the PCA's office, this difficulty is met by seconding staff from government departments. The job is popular and it is today accepted that return to the civil service is normally on promotion. There is no comparable 'tribunals service' from which staff could be seconded and inside which they could find promotion.[6] The Franks recommendations contained a latent defect. The Council was never adequately staffed for the tasks which Franks wished to entrust to it.

2 Experience and evolution

Successive governments, however, have accorded the Council a lesser role than that envisaged by Franks. The Tribunals and Inquiries Act 1958 which set up the Council granted it no executive powers; the Council was to be consultative and advisory:

The main powers . . . conferred on us . . . may be paraphrased as follows:
    (a) to keep under review the constitution and working of the tribunals specified in Schedule 1 to the Act;
    (b) to consider and report on particular matters referred to the Council by

the Lord Chancellor and the Lord Advocate with respect to any tribunal other than an ordinary court of law, whether or not specified in Schedule 1; and

(c) to consider and report on such matters as may be so referred, or as the Council may consider to be of special importance, with respect to administrative procedures which may involve . . . a statutory inquiry.[7]

However, we must also be consulted by the appropriate rule-making authority before procedural rules are made for any tribunal specified in Schedule 1 . . . and on procedural rules made by the Lord Chancellor in connection with statutory inquiries. We must be consulted before any scheduled tribunal can be exempted from the requirement under Section 12 of the Act to give reasons for its decisions upon request. The same situation applies to Ministerial decisions taken after a statutory inquiry. We may make general recommendations to appropriate Ministers about tribunal membership. We are required to make an Annual Report to the Lord Chancellor and the Lord Advocate, which must be laid by them before Parliament with such comments, if any, as they think fit. [Cmnd 7805, paras. 2.6, 2.8.]

The Council has not acquired the mandate, for which Robson argued, to deal with structure. It was given no *statutory* power to be consulted about the creation of new tribunals as opposed to those which already exist. (Later we shall see that it has persuaded some government departments to consult it on some occasions over draft primary legislation.) Street suggests that the Council has not interpreted its mandate to review the *working* of tribunals boldly.[8]

The Council has obviously been in difficulty with the word 'working'. Very occasionally it has recognised . . . that an investigation which confined itself to the procedural elements would be tackling the comparatively unimportant, the simple and straightforward aspects of a tribunal. That is why no doubt the Council has investigated the legal principles which rent tribunals apply in assessing a reasonable rent. If those legal principles are part of the 'working' it would seem to follow that all the law which all tribunals within its scope apply must be within the Council's jurisdiction. But that is not the way the Council has operated. Almost all the time it has contented itself with the simple issues of procedure . . . I do not criticise the Council. My main point is how relatively unimportant that aspect of a tribunal's work is. The boundary between procedure and substance is indistinct, but what really matters is whether a tribunal is performing efficiently in its area of activity. Then far and away the most important questions are the kinds of decisions which it is making and whether it has the appropriate powers and scope. This is not the Council's business, and it is nobody else's. Here there is a most serious gap in our control of administrative tribunals. [Street 1975, p. 64]

Yet it should not be thought that the watering down of the Council's functions has removed the difficulties inherent in the Council's part-time and shoestring character. Its role may not be that originally suggested but you can see how broad its mandate is by looking at Sched. 1 of the Tribunals and Inquiries Act 1971, which lists those tribunals falling within its jurisdiction. Today the Council oversees some 2,000 tribunals, divided into approximately 60 different types. Some of these, such as SBATs and Industrial Tribunals, have a massive workload (see Table 1 above, p. 68).

How does the Council go about its tasks? It is very difficult to know. This is partly because of the bland nature of the annual reports. And its special report, 'The Functions of the Council on Tribunals' (Cmnd 7805, 1980), gives little away. We learn, for example, that in 1975–6 the Council met 11 times and made 56 visits to 19 different types of tribunals, was consulted on eight listed bills and 'monitored' many more containing 'proposals affecting their jurisdiction or the working of the tribunals and inquiries under their supervision'. We sense that this is primarily a desk job. The committees of the Council 'conducted most of their business by correspondence'. The Council studied 110 'detailed internal papers (produced in the office) on the subjects covered by this summary and on other topics'. Its members:

... gave detailed consideration to 27 sets of draft rules of procedure for tribunals and inquiries. Most of the points raised ... were dealt with by correspondence with the rule-making authorities, but in some cases discussion with officials of Government departments took place. [Cmnd 7805, App. I para. 8.]

There is one significant omission. We are told:

No formal research project could be undertaken, but the staff carried out some 'desk-research' in relation to current business. Parliamentary papers, technical and other journals and the general Press were scrutinised for items which might necessitate action by the Council and for material suitable for the reference library. Information about overseas organisations with functions similar to those of the Council was also collected for study and reference. The Council took note of the results of such external research projects as came to their knowledge. [Cmnd 7805, App. I para. 10.]

A rather more illuminating description in the annual report for that year shows the Council performing three major functions: first, a supervisory role through its statutory power to 'keep under review the constitution and working' of Sched. 1 tribunals, together with a similar role in overseeing inquiries; secondly, a consultative role, laid down by statute, concerning proposed rules of procedure; thirdly, an informal consultative role in relation to draft legislation. We will take these functions one at a time.

(a) **The Council's supervisory role**

Constituted as we are of part-time Members, with a small supporting staff, we cannot do more than exercise a broad oversight over the working of tribunals, the detailed arrangements for which must remain the responsibility of Departments (shared with Presidents, Regional Chairmen or other similar authorities, where these exist). Our knowledge of the performance and problems of the tribunals under our supervision is obtained from such visits as individual Members can make (and we have done our best to increase the range and frequency of these), from complaints addressed to us, and perhaps most of all, from the initiative of those in close contact with the work of the tribunals (Departments, Presidents, etc.) in bringing to our notice difficulties or weaknesses and in discussing with us how these might be remedied. We are not an inspectorial body. Our visits to tribunals are for the purposes of familiarising ourselves with the work that they do, so that we have a better understanding of their procedural and other needs; of satisfying ourselves that the conditions and arrangements under which they work are reasonable both for the tribunals and the persons appearing before them; and of noting, with a view to remedial action, any apparent procedural defects or other problems affecting their work . . .

We are not an appellate body with powers to overturn or alter a tribunal's decision or a decision of a Minister reached after an inquiry or hearing; and we cannot concern ourselves with the merits of these decisions. It is true that where we are satisfied that an omission or defect of a procedural or administrative nature may have prejudiced a complainant, we may in certain limited circumstances advise that the matter should be reopened. But such instances of intervention in individual cases are perforce rare, and our main function must be to ensure that so far as possible any administrative or procedural weaknesses revealed by complaints are remedied, so that the cause of complaint will not recur.

Our success in achieving changes and improvements in the tribunal and inquiry systems – whether in structure and organisation or in procedure – depends on our ability to persuade the Government of the day to follow our advice, and in the main our influence must rest on quiet and unobtrusive work in co-operation with Departments and must depend largely on their being ready to consult us in good time and to take us into their confidence about their plans. [HC 236 (1976/7), paras. 14–17.]

Significantly, the Council sees visits and complaints as conduits for information and complaints are not so much grievances to be rectified as catalysts for more general administrative improvement.

Can we deduce that the Council is more concerned with fire-watching than with firefighting? Certainly the passage suggests that we cannot assess the Council's effectiveness by considering the number of complaints received and the remedies obtained. From the Council's viewpoint this is probably fortunate, if only because the number of complaints received (see Table 6), compared to the

Table 6. The Council on Tribunals 1959–82

	Visits		Conferences	Complaints received†	Sets of procedural rules considered	Draft legislation considered
	Tribunals	Inquiries*				
1959	97	NA	—	24	15	—
1960	75	18	—	52	7	1
1961	7 categories	NA	—	81	7	NA
1962	8 categories	NA	—	62	8	NA
1963	10 categories	NA	—	42	10	3
1964	'some'	'some'	—	60	7	3
1965	18	—	—	29	15	3
1966	9	—	—	42	23	8
1967	22	2	—	66	11	5
1968	55	3	—	82	15	7
1969/70	11 categories	3	—	88	28	5
1970/71	37	2	3	NA	24	3
1971/72	41	3	6	NA	19	8
1972/73	26	1	8	NA	9	7
1973/74	29	4	5	NA	22	8
1974/75	47	3	8	NA	19	9
1975/76	56	—	4	'nearly 100'	27	8
1976/77	78	11	6	'comparatively low'	29	8
1977/78	121	10	10	'slightly less'	26	5
1978/79	103	3	4	48	18	11
1979/80	85	7	15	25	31	9
1980/81	120	16	9	42	32	9
1981/82	136	27	21	25	31	9

Source: Annual Reports of the Council.
*The Council now also visits Examinations in Public into Structure Plans (below, pp. 473–8. In 1980–1, for example, 5 such visits were made.
†Figures for 1980–1 and 1981–2 relate to completed investigations into complaints.

workload of the tribunals under the Council's jurisdiction, is infini-tesimal. Wraith and Hutchesson suggest that the Council's attitude to complaints has changed over the years:

The Council was born and lived its early years very much under the influence of the 'Ombudsman idea'. The Council made it clear that they would welcome complaints from members of the public, and it was accepted as a matter of principle that complaints should not be used merely as 'pointers' to defects in the machinery but should be pursued with the responsible departments to the fullest possible extent in case . . . some redress could be provided . . . [This policy] may have encouraged a tendency to look to the Council as a 'court of appeal' against the decisions of tribunals and to feelings of disappointment among complainants when it had to be made clear that the Council had no power to function in this way . . . [Wraith and Hutchesson 1973, pp. 207–8.]

Lister's pamphlet for the Child Poverty Action Group (CPAG), a pressure group representing the interests of welfare claimants and families in need, concerning the Council's handling of complaints about the conduct of cases in SBATs during 1972–4 makes this point. The first case involved a complaint that DHSS observers had remained present while the tribunal considered its decision, a clear breach of procedure. Three and a half years later, it seemed that no adequate reply had been received by CPAG despite the intervention of Lord Chancellor Gardiner. However, the Council had replied to the Lord Chancellor, explaining that after the complaint, the DHSS had instructed its officers to make a written application to the tribunal for permission to be present as observers under rule 11(6) of the Supplementary Benefit (Appeal Tribunal) Rules 1971 which, in practice, would mean that officials would not be allowed to remain present during deliberations.

Lister commented:

As rule 11(6) does not mention who should be present at the actual deliberations, this arrangement was hardly satisfactory. The Council did admit that it was still not altogether satisfied and that the question would be taken up further with the DHSS. Now, in its 1973–74 report published this year, the issue has finally emerged publicly. The DHSS, it appears, has now issued instructions that its officials should withdraw at the end of the hearing together with the appellant and the presenting officer.

Thus, three years later, action has been taken following the complaint. But no comment has been made about the actual case which was the subject of the complaint, nor about the Group's recommendation that the tribunal regulations should be tightened up. Nothing has been written to us nor to [the complainant] . . . Indeed, had we not been avid readers of the Council's reports we would not even have known that the issue had been dealt with. It is hardly a satisfactory outcome . . . [Lister 1975, p. 2.]

Summarizing experience of ten complaints made to the Council, Lister reported little confidence in the Council's ability to handle complaints, though the Council, she thought, was not entirely to blame:

Invariably, lengthy delays have occurred in replying to complaints. In some instances they appear to have been ignored altogether. Replies, when they have finally arrived, have tended to be bland and unhelpful. In only two instances does positive action appear to have been taken by the Council . . .

If CPAG's experience is typical of the treatment of complaints by the Council it can only be concluded that it is a pretty ineffectual watchdog lacking both bark and bite. But although its failure to reply to complaints is inexcusable, the main blame for this state of affairs should not be placed on the Council itself.

If the Council is to fulfil its duties properly it must be given greater power and resources. As at present constituted it cannot act as an effective watchdog. However, even if the role of the Council on Tribunals were strengthened, it is doubtful whether this in itself would provide a satisfactory solution. With 58 types of tribunal under its supervision plus all statutory inquiries, the breadth of its responsibility is too wide for it to provide the kind of overview required for the SBAT system. [Lister 1975, pp. 12–13.]

How does Lister see the Council's role? Notice that she stresses the difficulties facing the Council in terms of power, resources and functions. We are back with the unequal equation of Franks. Street makes the same point in relation to the number of visits, the statistics for which are included in Table 6. Random visits are not even efficient as a method of securing information:

[A] member of the Council will occasionally give notice to a tribunal that he intends to be a spectator at a specific hearing; after attending, he will fill in a printed form reporting on the tribunal to the Council . . . Members simply have not the time to make frequent visits to particular local tribunals. It would be interesting to know how often, if at all, a lawyer-member of the Council has inspected a tribunal in the north west in the last ten years. It would be safe to assume that he has not inspected one hearing in a thousand in the area. I think it fair to say that the Council is playing no effective part in ensuring that the personnel are discharging their duties competently. Unannounced and frequent visits would be necessary. In order to assess the quality of the chairman's paper work random examination of decision files would have to be made. In fact not only does the Council not do this, it has not even the power. I am not criticising the Council; I repeat that it has not the resources to do more than it is doing already. I am emphasising that its supervision of tribunals is so slight as to be ineffective. It is unlikely to discover the existence of incompetent tribunal members. [Street 1975, p. 63.]

In another example, drawn from an annual report, allegations had been made that aged patients had been maltreated in public hospitals. The Minister told Parliament that he would have independent inquiries made, but instead of instituting his own inquiry under s.70 of the National Health Service Act 1946, he asked regional hospital boards to act independently. As a result, there was no common procedure at the inquiries and a pressure group, A E G I S (Aid for the Elderly in Government Institutions), complained. But an incidental and probably unintended effect of the procedure used was to remove the Council's jurisdiction, which is limited to statutory inquiries held by or on behalf of a Minister. The Council asked the Minister why he had taken this course and received the reply that he had not expected the Council to be concerned with that question, though he did go on to justify his course of action. The Council responded:

The division of responsibility between the Minister and the Regional Hospital Boards clearly made it difficult in some cases for him to decide whether or not to hold a statutory inquiry . . . But the nature of some of the complaints . . . made it, in our view, unfortunate that we had not the right to consider them. We therefore told the [Minister] . . . that for this reason we felt that a procedure which fell within our jurisdiction would have been more satisfactory, both in the interests of the complainants and of the hospital service. [HC 272 (1968/9), para. 52.]

From the firefighting angle, this complaint was wholly unsuccessful as it fell outside the Council's jurisdiction, but concern for its own standing led the Council to express its views and to attempt to establish a principle for the future. The Ministry agreed informally to follow the Council's recommendations in future cases, modifying its procedures accordingly.

Something comparable is recorded in 1966. The father of a Broadmoor patient complained of the procedure at a Mental Health Review Tribunal after a reference by the Home Secretary under s.66(6) of the Mental Health Act 1959. The complaint was that the Tribunal had given no reasons for its decision. The Tribunal's reply was that there was no duty to do so in the particular case. The Council accepted that to give reasons would be inappropriate because 'the Home Secretary must be free to disagree . . . and we do not think that anything is to be gained by the disclosure of a disagreement between the Home Secretary and the Tribunal' (AR 1966, pp. 12–13). But the Council discussed the matter further with the Home Office and obtained 'a very helpful response'. It was agreed that the Home Office would be willing to talk to interested relatives about the Minister's decisions. Tribunals would be authorized to inform the parties of this 'right' and a circular letter was sent to the clerks of Mental Health Review Tribunals instructing them on the new procedure. Can this administrative concession be considered satisfactory? What for Franks were the purposes of reasoned decisions? Compare the attitude of the Home Office to reasoned decisions concerning parole.

We must remember, however, that there are severe limitations on the Council's ability to process complaints. Compare this account of Council procedures with those of the PCA (see below, p. 203).

We lack specific statutory powers to conduct thorough investigations by delving beyond the material which may be voluntarily furnished or by taking statements from or interviewing those persons who may be involved. Moreover, our small staff cannot be expected to have the detailed and experienced knowledge to deal with the whole of the wide range of complex matters raised in complaints. Accordingly, for a proper appraisal of a complaint we are often largely dependent on Departments providing us with a full and complete account of the circumstances surrounding it and drawing to our attention relevant considerations (particularly of a detailed procedural nature) which we may not have taken into account. Where the authority accept that something has gone wrong, it is of course not difficult to deal with the complaint quickly and, where a change in administration or procedure would prevent a recurrence, to suggest a satisfactory solution. But in other cases the fact that the complaint must be pursued by correspondence inevitably leads to delay, and there are occasions when we are left with the feeling that our available powers have not enabled us to probe the matter sufficiently. Furthermore . . . it is rarely open to us to intervene to secure any redress for the individual complainant – unless perhaps a tribunal is able and willing to review a decision already taken or, in the case of an inquiry, the Minister has not given his decision and is prepared to reopen the inquiry. [HC 236 (1976/7), para. 25.]

A year after this was written, the flow of complaints had, according to the Council, diminished (see Table 6). But the Council was still worried by the inadequacy of its powers: 'We have no means of checking the truth of statements made to us . . . and neither the complainants nor those who are subjected to investigation can be satisfied with our all too frequent finding that we cannot reconcile different versions of the same event' (HC 74 (1978/9), para. 2.5).

One practical solution open to the Council is to act as a filter, passing complaints to those who *can* process them. We have seen the Council negotiating with the departments which operate tribunals or inquiries. The PCA is also an important link in the chain. He is an ex-officio member of the Council and also of the Commission for Local Administration (CLA). Any complaint concerning a department's procedures before and after a tribunal hearing can be referred to him. He can also investigate the way in which public local inquiries are conducted. A second general arrangement obtains with the Lord Chancellor's office. Recently the Council reported:

> The number of complaints which we deal with has been reduced in fairly recent times by an arrangement that complaints against chairmen and members of tribunals will be referred to the Lord Chancellor or to other Ministers who appoint such chairmen or members. [Cmnd 7805, para. 7.8.]

Let us consider the fate of one more complaint concerning SBATs, referred by CPAG, bearing in mind that at the time the arrangement was probably not in operation:

> The complaint referred to four occasions when advocates . . . came away from the hearing lacking that conviction that should follow the deliberations of any judicial or quasi-judicial body – namely, that the claimant's case had been considered carefully and seriously in the light of the relevant legislation. The whole tenor of these tribunals was such as to make representation extremely difficult, and to make it unlikely that claimants feel that they had been given a fair hearing. The letter pointed out that these were experienced advocates with a good idea of the normal conduct and standards of tribunal hearings, and therefore asked the Council to take the complaints seriously. Just how seriously the Council did take them can be gleaned from the fact that, apart from an acknowledgement of the letter, it has never bothered to reply. [Lister 1975, p. 5.]

This sounds unsatisfactory. But one obvious result of classifying tribunals as 'machinery for adjudication' is to bring into play the constitutional doctrine of 'judicial independence'. This means that 'judicial' decisions must be protected from interference by Ministers and their departments. Faulty decisions can be corrected only through the judicial machinery of appeal or judicial review. This is precisely the reason why neither the ombudsman nor the Council have jurisdiction in such matters.

The Lord Chancellor's department is included in the list of departments amenable to the jurisdiction of the PCA who has occasionally conducted investigations. In 1979, for example, he investigated a complaint that county court officials had recorded and subsequently failed to amend an address on a record of debt with the result that the complainant had unjustifiably been denied credit facilities. The department refused to accept any responsibility, blaming the solicitors and the credit reference agency for what had occurred; nor would they accept responsibility for the court officials. The PCA expressed dissatisfaction with this attitude:

The Department have told me that, in their view, once the complainant had drawn his trouble to their attention they acted promptly and effectively to correct the error which had occurred, and that their reply to him could not properly and prudently have been more apologetic than it was, given that the errors complained of had not been of their making. I think it a pity nevertheless that in the terms of their reply . . . they were not somewhat less defensive, selective, and unapologetic. Even if it is technically correct that the Department's employees in the county court were not directly engaged in exercising the Department's administrative functions, it is scarcely surprising that the citizen should look for explanations and apologies, when a public service fails, to the Department which provides it. I do not think it would have derogated from the Department's strict view of its legal liability for administrative error to have given the complainant an apology for what had been done under their apparent aegis. Merely to say that they were sorry that he should have been refused credit and put to some embarrassment and inconvenience, but that the real blame lay elsewhere, seems to me not enough to meet the case. Had they been a little more forthcoming, I do not believe any more would have been heard of this matter. But in all the circumstances I think that the vindication of the complaints and my criticism of the way they were handled by the Department will be a sufficient satisfaction for the complainant. [HC 351 (1979/80), pp. 64–5.]

In his next annual report, the PCA, evidently still dissatisfied, returned to the incident, insisting on his right to investigate in a proper case:

The Lord Chancellor combines in a constitutionally unique way a judicial and an executive function, and the organisation of his Department reflects this duality. His Department are naturally concerned to preserve the traditional separation of the judiciary from the executive. The distinction here can on occasion be a cause of difficulty. The Lord Chancellor's Department are rightly anxious to see that I do not step over the boundary of departmental administrative action into the area of judicial function. I hope that I never shall. But it is not every action taken by court officials in the course of court business which can sensibly be regarded as touching the judicial function and still less as cognizable and remediable by the judge if badly done. Yet such actions may seem to be excluded from the broad ambit of administration of *all* the courts which is the primary function of the Lord Chancellor's Department. There is a danger that unless common sense is permitted to temper legal nicety, many justifiable grievances could fall into a trap quite unintended by Parliament, wherein the unlucky complainant is caught without hope of a hearing or redress – or at best with a possibility of [legal] recourse which in my judgment it would be quite unreasonable to expect him to pursue . . .

My report did not reflect any wish to attempt to trespass on judicial matters. It would be quite wrong for me to do so. But in my view the essential point, in the interests of fairness, was to differentiate between on the one hand actions which are clearly the responsibility of judicial bodies, and for which any remedy desired can and should be sought in the courts themselves; and on the other hand actions for which it would be absurd to suggest that a remedy lies with the courts, even though they may have occurred in connection with court proceedings. [HC 402 (1980/1), paras. 107–9.]

Again, we might compare the experience of the Legal Action Group (LAG), a pressure group which devotes its energies to reform of the legal system, when it complained to Lord Chancellor Hailsham about the conduct of Barnet magistrates in a series of criminal trials which followed the Southall riots. Lord Hailsham refused to establish a formal inquiry and, in a letter, he urged the defendants to pursue their remedies by way of appeal or application for prerogative order. The letter continued, 'The fact that you appear willing to bring political pressure on me as Executive Minister only underlines the danger to judicial independence were this position interfered with'.[9] We should not look at the Council on Tribunals in isolation. Certain types of complaint are peculiarly recalcitrant and may provide problems for other, more powerful, monitors. Parliament has not shown itself particularly successful in redressing grievances which concern the judicial system.[10] It is perhaps a little naïve to blame the Council for faring no better.

The Council on Tribunals is aware that the existing arrangements for handling complaints are unsatisfactory. The 1980 review considered the possibility of a new 'tribunals ombudsman', an idea immediately rejected on the ground that it would 'add yet another to the existing variety of ombudsman-like offices, which is already confusing to the public' (Cmnd 7805, para. 7.15). It suggested instead an extension of the Council's jurisdiction. Complaints which did not raise a substantial point of principle would continue to be referred to departments. Where a complaint did raise 'a substantial point of principle *relating to procedure*', the Council's jurisdiction would 'extend to events which took place within the doors of the tribunal or inquiry'. It would be given ombudsman-type powers to send for papers and to ask questions. It would make reports to 'the complainant, the department, and at our discretion to anyone else'. This was 'not perhaps the best arrangement that could have been devised if Parliament had been starting with a clean sheet, [but it] is the best practical solution in the existing circumstances' (Cmnd 7805, paras. 7.17–7.21).

Administrative remedies have tended to proliferate and overlap. Committees and reviews like Franks or Donoughmore tend to accept the status quo and fail to tackle fundamental questions of principle. Could the Council tackle its increased workload? Would it be preferable to 'start with a clean sheet'? Are there other, preferable, solutions? The Council's description of its supervisory role admits to being largely dependent on the co-operation of those working *inside* the system. In Chapter 19, which deals with the restructuring of SBATs, you will see how senior chairmen, appointed with supervisory and training functions, have taken on the job of internal 'complaints-man'. It is worth asking whether such internal procedures could be formalized. In 1980, the Council expressed a fear that a substantial increase in its complaints' workload might affect its present relationship with government departments. Chairmen, members, and inspectors at statutory inquiries might become less helpful. 'In the long run, the balance of our work might be significantly changed, with the focus shifting to our role as ombudsman for tribunals and inquiries, in priority over our existing statutory functions. This in our view would be undesirable' (Cmnd 7805, para. 7.17). Does this conclusion undercut the Council's own proposal? We know that the Council wants to retain its complaints function as an aid to firewatching. It has said:

> We attach great importance to complaints since they help us in discharging our function of supervision, by enabling us to monitor the performance of the tribunal and inquiry systems, to identify weaknesses and shortcomings which might lead to unfairness, and to advise Departments on remedial action . . . We must therefore continue to receive complaints, and no bar to their receipt should be contemplated. [HC 236 (1976/7), para. 26.]

Has this wish influenced the Council? Are its recommendations entirely logical and does its previous record support its claims? It could be argued that its firewatching and firefighting functions are incompatible. For an agency to push too hard when it requires a high degree of official co-operation to secure compliance with its recommendations is to risk securing less.[11]

(b) **Rules of procedure**

We saw that Franks accepted Wade's case for procedural standards and envisaged the Council as the instrument for implementing its philosophy. The drafting of rules is desk-work, and, since it is carried on mainly behind the scenes through negotiation with departments, it is difficult to know exactly how the Council operates. From Table 6, however, it can be seen that procedural rules form the Council's staple diet. And, significantly, the Council feels that the greatest progress has been made in this area:

Ministers are under a statutory duty to consult us before making rules of procedure for tribunals under our general supervision. The Lord Chancellor is under a similar duty when he makes procedural rules or regulations for statutory hearings or inquiries . . . Other Ministers who make such rules are under no obligation to consult us even though the procedures in question may fall within our jurisdiction, but the practice of doing so has grown and now extends to most Departments.

Accordingly, a steady stream of rules of procedure both for tribunals and for statutory hearings or inquiries come to us for examination and comment. Many of them require careful and detailed scrutiny and together they occupy nearly all the time of a legally qualified member of the staff. Most of the detailed work on rules is now carried out by our Legal Committee, only issues of principle being considered by the Council (although a full report of the outcome is always made by the Committee).

Our advice is usually accepted by Departments or a satisfactory alternative solution is found. If a Department should fail to meet us on a matter which in our view raised an important issue of principle, we would not hesitate to bring it to public notice in whatever way might seem appropriate at the time.

There has been a growing tendency to consult us at an early stage, often before the rules are in draft. We have encouraged this and it has had the advantage that our staff have been able to steer departmental draftsmen towards procedures which it is known will meet with our approval. Indeed in some cases our staff have furnished the Department with a preliminary draft of suitable provisions. The extent to which we can enlarge our role in this way is strictly limited by our staff resources. But it has enabled us to achieve some success in standardising certain procedures . . . [HC 236 (1976/7), paras. 18–21.]

From our description of tribunals you will appreciate that procedural standardization has not gone very far. Franks, in fact, rejected the idea of a standard code or codes from which Parliament should choose when establishing a new tribunal:

We agree that procedure is of the greatest importance and that it should be clearly laid down in a statute or statutory instrument. Because of the great variety of the purposes for which tribunals are established, however, we do not think it would be appropriate to rely upon either a single code or a small number of codes. We think that there is a case for greater procedural differentiation and prefer that the detailed procedure for each type of tribunal should be designed to meet its particular circumstances. [para. 63.]

However, the Committee reported general agreement on the broad essentials which included: notice of a right to apply to a tribunal; notice of the case which the applicant has to meet; a reasoned decision; and notice of any right to appeal further. They stressed the need for 'the combination of a formal procedure with an informal atmosphere' and left the Council to spell out the details. Wraith and Hutchesson sum up the Council's attitude:

The Council's approach to [procedural] rules has been based on the general principles enunciated in the Franks Report that before the hearing the applicant or appellant should be aware of and fully understand, his right to apply to the tribunal and should know in good time the case he would have to meet; that the hearing itself should take place in public except in special circumstances; that there should normally be a right to legal representation; that after the hearing the decision of the tribunal and the reasons for it should be stated as fully as possible; and that the parties should be adequately and promptly notified of the decision, the findings of fact, the reasons for the decision and any right of appeal. But the approach has not been solely dictated by the Franks Committee's recommendations and the Council have developed their own jurisprudence in these matters. Generally, they have avoided any detailed prescription of the procedure to be followed at the actual hearing (since experience has shown that it is important to allow for considerable flexibility, particularly where the parties are unrepresented) and have left scope for innovation. Among the points over which they have developed new lines of policy are the hearing of proceedings in private, the giving of reasons for decisions and the right of representation and appearance. On this last point, they have on many occasions questioned draft rules restricting the right of representation to counsel or solicitor and have usually succeeded in getting the draft altered. The Council prefer to leave the door open to applicants and appellants to be represented by a person of their own choice unless there happen to be strong reasons for restricting the right of representation in some way . . . [Wraith and Hutchesson 1973, pp. 209–10.]

Let us follow two of these 'new lines of policy'. Remember the Franks formula of openness. When the Council was consulted by the DHSS over the Occupational Pensions Board (Determinations and Review Procedure) Regulations 1973, it was concerned about the Board's power to hold private hearings 'for special reasons'. It suggested restricting this power to cases 'involving financial or commercial considerations of an exceptional nature'. The DHSS did not agree; although private hearings 'should be rarely held, there might be considerations other than those of a financial or commercial nature which could be held to justify a private hearing'; and they felt that the Board 'could be trusted to exercise the discretion properly'. The Council was dissatisfied but agreed to accept the provision on condition that 'it would be subject to review after an initial period of working by the Board and that the Board would report to the Council all occasions on which private hearings had been held, indicating in each case the circumstances which had been held to justify a private hearing'. The Board duly agreed to report (HC 289 (1974/5), paras. 47–9). So here the Council took a comparatively tough line. When consulted in 1978 over the procedural rules for operating the Vaccine Damage Payments Scheme (see below, page 398) it showed itself more flexible:

We considered that neither too much nor too little emphasis should be placed on the holding of oral hearings before the tribunal makes decisions. On the one hand, bearing in mind that most cases will involve children suffering from considerable disablement, it may often be more appropriate and desirable that the tribunal reach their conclusions on the basis of the documents, provided that these are adequate, and without the parties having to attend before them. On the other hand, we expect many claimants to wish to attend . . . [HC 359 (1979/80), para. 4.14.]

It accepted provisions, now the Vaccine Damage Payments Regulations (SI No 432/79) which read:

8(3) Every hearing held by a tribunal shall be in public except in so far as the chairman may for special reasons otherwise direct and . . . the procedure shall be such as the tribunal shall determine . . .

8(5) The Secretary of State and the claimant shall have the right to be heard at a hearing of a tribunal.

8(6) If a claimant, to whom notice of hearing has been duly given should fail to appear at the hearing the tribunal may proceed to determine the case notwithstanding his absence, or may give such directions with a view to the determination of the case as they may think proper having regard to all the circumstances including any explanation offered for the absence.

The provision of legal representation in tribunals is an issue on which opinion continues to differ.[12] Some people believe that lawyers inevitably lead to legalism; consider, for example, Robson's attitude to the legal profession. Lawyers push tribunal hearings to formality and the absence of legal aid may prejudice the poor. Franks thought, however, that a ban on legal representation was, in principle, undesirable:

Although . . . the ban may often not work harshly in practice, it is difficult to justify the proposition that in certain types of legal proceeding a citizen shall not be able to call upon the services of a legal representative. We have no hesitation in recommending that this right should be curtailed only in the most exceptional circumstances, where it is clear that the interests of applicants generally would be better served by a restriction . . . [but] it would be wrong if the removal of the ban in the general interests of applicants were to have the result that Departments were legally represented whereas many applicants were unable to afford such representation . . . Government Departments should not be permitted legal representation before a tribunal unless the citizen for his part employs a lawyer. [para. 87.]

Quite logically, the Committee saw a strong argument 'for extending the legal aid scheme at once to those tribunals which are formal and expensive and to final appellate tribunals ... any extension of the scheme to cover a wider range of proceedings in courts should be accompanied by an extension of the scheme to other tribunals' (para. 89).

How has the Council interpreted these recommendations? In its first report the Council welcomed 'any steps that can be taken to make legal advice more available to applicants before tribunals', but was also considering a different approach:

There may be scope for the development of some form of lay assistance for applicants who do not belong to any organisation which might represent them at tribunal hearings. This is a matter which we hope to discuss with interested organisations in the social service field. We feel that this type of moral support by people accustomed to the atmosphere of tribunals, even though they could take no active part in the proceedings, would be welcomed by many people who are quite unused to finding themselves in such surroundings. [AR 1959, para. 77.]

A year later, the Council was considering the National Health Service (Service Committees and Tribunal) Regulations 1956, which dealt with the investigation by a lay tribunal (or service committee) of complaints against doctors and dentists. The Committee reported its findings of fact and recommendations to the Executive Committee from which, in most cases, appeal lay to the Minister. Regulation 5(1) contained a ban on legal representation. A complaint from a practitioner brought the matter before the Council. In a sense, this question was left over from Franks, which had considered the matter at length, finally coming down against legal representation in service committees. On the other hand, Franks had recommended that complainants (i.e. patients) should be entitled to apply for the services of a departmental or Executive Council official to assist them in presenting a case. The Council on Tribunals made 18 visits and heard oral evidence from the Ministry and several professional bodies before it came to its conclusions:

We were satisfied that the general procedure has so far worked well and that in practice no injustice has resulted from the ban on legal representation. It is clearly desirable, particularly in the interests of complainants, that the proceedings should be as informal as possible. There was a strong likelihood that if legal representation were permitted it would be the practitioners who would avail themselves of it, so that complainants would be deterred from coming forward. It seemed to us that practitioners were already sufficiently

safeguarded by their right of appeal . . . since the case is then re-heard and
legal representation is permitted . . . [AR 1960, para. 42.]

The Council felt that the intention of the regulations was to exclude
even friends and relatives of complainants who chanced to possess
legal qualifications. Although it was not able to give a definitive
interpretation of the meaning of Reg. 5(1), it asked the departments
concerned to take its view into account and issue guidance on the
meaning of the regulation. This was duly done.

The Council's recommendations may be related to the courts'
doctrine of procedural fairness. Could a complainant or a practitioner
argue that legal representation was required by natural justice?
Consider the judgments in *Furnell*'s case. Then look at the views of
Lord Denning in *Pett* v. *Greyhound Racing Association* [1969] 1 QB 125.
See also *Enderby Town Football Club* v. *Football Association* [1971] Ch
591, *McInnes* v. *Onslow Fane* (above, p. 88), *Calvin* v. *Carr* (above,
p. 90), *R.* v. *Board of Visitors of Wormwood Scrubs ex p. Anderson*, Chapter
15, n. 14.

In 1961, the Council was considering the other side of the case,
objecting to the Independent Schools Tribunals (Scotland) Regulations which had been submitted by the Lord President of the Court
of Session under s.111 of the Education (Scotland) Act 1946. These
tribunals dealt with complaints by the Ministry of Education that a
schoolmaster's performance was unsatisfactory. The regulations
restricted the right of representation to the applicant 'in person or by
counsel or solicitor'. The Council objected that it should 'be open to
parties to be represented by someone other than a lawyer, for example
by a partner or a friend' (AR 1961, para. 33). Its objection was
over-ruled and the Council had to content itself with an assurance
that this particular set of rules would not be regarded as a precedent.

A decade later, when the provision of legal aid for tribunals seemed
a possibility, the Council on Tribunals was asked to contribute to the
report of the Lord Chancellor's Advisory Committee on legal aid. The
Council 'welcomed and supported the principal recommendations (i)
that legal aid should be extended to all statutory tribunals under our
supervision in which legal representation is permitted and (ii) that
the machinery for administering such aid should be provided by an
extension of the green form advice and assistance scheme' (HC 679
(1975/6), para. 84).[13] But some members had reservations about the
extension of legal aid in tribunals:

We believe that . . . there is a substantial number of applicants for whom
non-legal advice or representation is required and is indeed the more

appropriate form of aid. There is a danger, in our view, that if there can be no assurance of non-legal advice and representation being available on an aided basis in appropriate cases there will be unnecessary recourse to legal aid . . . while we support the need for both legal and non-legal aid for certain applicants, we wish to make it clear that in our view it is the essence of the tribunal system that many if not most applicants should be able to present their cases satisfactorily without recourse to either form of assistance. The availability of such assistance should not lead to any slackening of the efforts of Departments to simplify the processes of appeal to tribunals and of tribunals to regulate their proceedings in such a way as to help the unrepresented applicant . . . [HC 679 (1975/6), paras. 85–6.]

The Council recommended a detailed study of the possibility of non-legal aid and representation by a specially appointed committee with 'special knowledge of the work being done by voluntary organisations' and expressed its willingness to cooperate. The Lord Chancellor refused, though he gave an assurance that the advantages of non-legal representation would be considered in the departmental study of unmet need for legal services. The Council's views are interesting. They suggest a move away from Franks' attempts to judicialize, though significant extensions of legal or non-legal aid are probably an academic question in the economic climate of the 1980s.[14]

What has been the Council's impact on procedure? In the only outside, full-scale survey, Wraith and Hutchesson conclude:

Given the limitations of its consultative role the Council has made numerous suggestions for the improvement of particular rules, many of which have been accepted by the departments concerned, but the fact remains that the Council is often consulted too late and must perforce confine itself to commenting within the framework proposed by the department. [Wraith and Hutchesson 1973, p. 156.]

They discuss two solutions, the first of which is a 'central drafting body' (we will return to this point at the end of the chapter). The second idea is the standardized code or codes, discussed by Franks. This they dismiss out of hand as 'no more practicable now than it was in 1956'. Their assessment is reinforced by Farmer's textual analysis of the standard procedural requirements, first of the American Administrative Procedure Act and secondly, of the Norwegian Administration Act 1967.

Farmer (1970) is opposed to both. Like Dimock, he thinks the American procedures too rigid: 'if all administration were conducted in this way, government would soon grind to a halt.' They encourage the development of informal, administrative bargaining which operates largely outside the Act. We have made this point before.[15] The Norwegian text, on the other hand, is too general and contains too many exceptions.

S.15: Except as otherwise necessitated by the nature of the proceedings . . . the person whom the proceedings concern shall have the right to have a witness present and shall be notified of this right.

S.17: . . . Advance notification can be omitted if such notification is not practicably possible or might prevent the execution of the decision . . . Advance notification can also be omitted . . . if such notification is evidently unnecessary for any other reason.

S.21: . . . To the extent permitted by the proper performance of the service, a party can on justifiable grounds be allowed to appear orally . . .

S.23: An individual decision shall be in writing except when this would be, for practical reasons, particularly onerous for the administrative agency.

S.27: . . . If it would be particularly onerous for the administrative agency to give written notification . . . the notification can be made verbally or by other means. Notification of the decision may be omitted insofar as it is obviously unnecessary and the decision does not harm or inconvenience the party in question.

What do you think s.23 is intended to mean? Is it a 'rule', a 'principle' or a 'standard'? How much discretion is left to the administrative agency? Davis insisted that rules should be checked and controlled by outside agencies such as courts. How much judgement or discretion would be left to the controlling agency? Compare the *Justice* 'Principles of Good Administration' (see above, p. 152). Are these provisions more or less rigorous? Farmer (1970, p. 116) concludes that a need exists for 'continuous examination of each administrative tribunal separately . . . so that the particular requirements of the tribunal, on the one hand, and the individual party, on the other, can be ascertained and assessed exactly'. Is this a 'functionalist' approach? Can you relate it to 'transaction-typing' (above, p. 92)?

We could argue that, even here, in its central area of activity, the Council has not been particularly innovative. We have described tribunals as closely modelled on the adjudicatory ideal-type. In Jowell's description it is clear that 'adversarial' proceedings, in which an impartial judge listens to a case presented by each party, are implied. Normally a 'hearing' is involved at which the parties can question each other. One party wins and the other loses. But in tribunals, where the department is often represented by a permanent presenting officer while the applicant is either absent or appears in person, this may be extremely unsatisfactory. The chairman must intervene to redress the balance, distorting the model. Jowell's description suggests that this is the only 'model of adjudication', but of course this is not so. Ombudsman investigations for example are 'inquisitorial'. They are also 'documentary'; hearings are exceptional. Continental legal systems are also inquisitorial. In such systems the judge controls the proceedings, asking for evidence and asking the questions. His function is to discover the truth. In French administrative law, the state's presenting officer (advocate general or government commissioner) has a duty to present the case impartially. These variant procedures rather than English courts' procedures might be better fitted to tribunals. Yet no report of the Council has devoted serious attention to the idea.[16]

(c) Legislation: structure of the system

The Council has no statutory right to be consulted over primary legislation which restructures existing tribunals and inquiries or establishes new ones. In practice, however, it is consulted increasingly often:

Early in our history, the Government agreed (with certain reservations) to consult us in advance on legislation establishing new tribunals, and although no similar undertaking exists in respect of legislation introducing ministerial hearing and inquiry procedures, of which there has been a steady flow in recent years, Departments have on the whole increasingly consulted us also about these. We have from time to time had reason to complain about lack of prior consultation or late consultation: a recent example occurred in relation to the Rent Act 1974. But for the most part Departments have in recent years brought to our attention in reasonably good time draft legislation or legislative proposals affecting tribunals and hearings or inquiries. This work has greatly increased the burden falling on our staff, who have often had to follow the relevant aspects of some legislation right through the stages of consultation document, drafting instructions, etc., to the introduction of the Bill and its passage through Parliament. But in our view it has been as important as any of our other activities. [HC 236 (1977/8), para. 28.]

The Rent Acts are a sore subject with the Council. In Chapter 3, we saw how, in 1965, the Labour Government established Rent Assessment Committees (RACs), in preference to courts, to hear disputes arising under their legislation. An alternative would have been to extend the jurisdiction of Rent Tribunals, but the Minister (Mr Crossman) objected on the ground that these seemed too rigid. He suggested to the Council that Rent Tribunals might be reconstituted on a wider regional basis in which case the two jurisdictions could be combined. The Council reported strongly in favour of a unitary system:

It seemed to us that it would be in many respects unsatisfactory to have two different systems of rent adjudication operating side by side. There would be problems of deciding which tribunals had jurisdiction and there would be competition between the tribunals for staff. The Bill appeared to present a golden opportunity to make a fresh start with one properly constituted system for the adjudication of residential rents which would have jurisdiction over furnished and unfurnished properties alike. We put forward this view very strongly to the Ministry of Housing and Local Government and the Scottish Development Department and suggested that, even if amalgamation could not be effected immediately, power should at least be taken in the Bill to carry out amalgamation . . . (as had been done in the case of Industrial Tribunals in the Redundancy Payments Bill) at an appropriate time. [AR 1965, para. 20.]

But the Minister was by now deeply committed to the dual system and the Ministry argued that the parliamentary timetable made it impossible to meet the Council's views. An amendment to ensure that Rent Tribunals and RACs could have the same membership was introduced at report stage. The Council thought the concession 'fell far short of what was really needed', namely a full amalgamation of the existing Rent Tribunals with the new RACs.

The weakness of the Council's position is underlined by what followed. In standing committee, the Minister suddenly conceded that new legislation would ultimately be needed to 'fully integrate the law on furnished and unfurnished dwellings, not making them identical, but at least bringing them under the same system of tribunal control'. Neither the Council nor the House of Commons was in a position to insist that this should be done immediately.[17]

Although the dual system satisfied no-one, and was criticized in 1971 by the Francis Committee on the Rent Acts, which expressed concern at the confusion and waste of time caused by applications made to the wrong tribunal, and reinforced the Council's demand for unification (Cmnd 4609 (1971), Ch. 32), the system survived. In 1977 the Council reiterated its 'frequently expressed view that the jurisdiction of the Rent Tribunals and [RACs] should be amalgamated. The review of the Rent Acts provides an opportunity to carry out this long-overdue reform' (HC 108 (1977/8), para. 3.15). In 1979, the Council reminded the DOE that the Housing Bill, under preparation for the new Conservative Government, would provide a new opportunity to effect 'this desirable reform'. The DOE mentioned possible amendments 'which would bring the two tribunals closer together' (HC 246 (1980/1), paras. 3.09–3.10). Seventeen years after the initial decision, s.72 of the Housing Act 1982 abolished Rent Tribunals and transferred their functions to RACs which, when exercising these functions, are to be henceforth known as Rent Tribunals!

The Council might prefer not to be judged by this episode but to set against it the review of SBATs prior to the Social Security Act 1980. (A detailed account of the restructuring is given in Chapter 19.) Called a case study, the Council's account (Cmnd 7805, App.3(a)) is intended to give 'more detailed information about the range and complexity of their work' than is available in the annual reports. The case study actually illustrates the point made earlier that the style of Council reports renders assessment of its contribution extremely difficult.

We learn, for example, that the Council was informed about research conducted by Bell for the DHSS into the operation of the SBAT system. This is hardly surprising as Bell was a long-standing member and later chaired its Functions Committee. The Council was consulted before publication of the review; later, it was represented on the consultative committee set up to implement the review's recommendations; its advice was, in the main, acceptable. But the DHSS consulted many other bodies, whose representations may have been equally or even more effective, about its proposed reforms. This is what happened when the procedural guide which the DHSS was issuing to all tribunal chairmen and members was under preparation. Remember that procedure is the Council's special expertise:

The advisory group set up by the DHSS to oversee the preparation of the procedural guide and the training of chairmen had its first meeting on 31 March 1977. It comprised representatives of various bodies with a knowledge of SBATs, including the DHSS, the Lord Chancellor's Office, the TUC, and one member of the Council. The Council made it clear that they wished to approve the guide before its publication. The DHSS were under pressure to have it in print by the end of the year, but the Council were concerned that it fell short of what Professor Bell had recommended, and they made various suggestions for its improvement, as did the consultative group. Some, but not all, of these suggestions were accepted by the Department.

The guide was published in December 1977. It included appendices which reproduced statements previously made or approved by the Council on the duties of clerks to SBATs, the naming of tribunal chairmen and members, the tape-recording of tribunal proceedings, and the provision of adequate reasons for decisions. [Cmnd 7805, App. 3(a) paras. 13–14.]

Yardley (1980, p. 266) suggests that this case study shows 'a high level of cooperation by the appropriate government department with the Council, resulting in considerable improvements in the [system]'. His comment echoes the Council's own evaluation of its performance:

Looking back, it would seem that our most important contribution lies in the influence we have steadily – one might say relentlessly – brought to bear on Government departments, as a result of which the general ideals of the Franks Committee have been translated into a workable and accepted code of principles and practice. Much of the work is conducted through written and verbal exchanges with Government Departments about particular issues as they arise, but, of course, through time, this has had a cumulative effect. Exchanges have taken place at one time or another with every major department and this work comes on all the time. By now most departments appear to recognise our contribution, value our advice and disregard it only after serious consideration. But disagreements occur and we reserve the right to make criticism both in our Annual Reports and, if necessary, in the production of Special Reports. [Council on Tribunals (Functions of the Council Committee), Position Paper (1978), p. 3.]

Does not the evidence point to the opposite conclusion? Government departments are happy to make minor changes but, on points of substance, they refuse to give way. The Council's 'right of criticism' then proves wholly irrelevant. Bearing in mind the diverse reasons which lead to the establishment of tribunals, you may think that the present pattern of decision-taking is inevitable:

The fundamental difficulty is that each government department frames its own proposals for tribunals, usually as part of a scheme of important legislation in which the tribunal machinery attracts little public and parliamentary attention. There is usually a tight time-table and a strong reluctance to disturb existing arrangements. In the result, legislation about tribunals tends to be shaped by the short term exigencies of political and administrative convenience rather than by any coherent long term policy. In particular, it may tend to produce relatively weak tribunals with awkward divisions of jurisdiction between them. [HC 72 (1970/1), para. 45.]

And the Council already felt that strictures in its annual report were not enough. It continued:

We consider that in the framing of legislation too little attention is paid to the system of tribunals as a whole, and we are inviting the Lord Chancellor to consider various remedies. One important matter is that departments should consult us on proposals concerning tribunals at the earliest possible stage, before decisions have become virtually irrevocable. Final decisions ought not to be taken on matters on which we are at issue with a department until we have had an opportunity of putting our case fully to the Lord Chancellor. In addition we think that there ought probably to be some machinery for making our views publicly known when Bills are before Parliament, since otherwise important provisions about tribunals may be enacted without any knowledge that we have studied them and made recommendations. [HC 72 (1970/1), para. 48.]

At least one critic feels that the Council is largely to blame. Rose is concerned about its failure to articulate principles which could guide departments in considering whether to establish new tribunals. In turn the Council is left in a weak negotiating position. 'Without some developed and agreed policy, consideration of each case can only be made against first principles with the Council having little to put forward in argument against political expediency which as a guide inevitably leads to proliferation and a lack of coherent structure.'

In 1979, reviewing its own functions, the Council returned to the theme. Tribunals were still proliferating. They operated in increasingly 'difficult and sensitive areas', e.g. immigration. Judicialization and formality had increased, making it difficult for the ordinary citizen to cope. Simplification was desirable 'wherever this is compatible with justice' and the need for a permanent advisory body to take 'a bird's eye view' had, if anything, increased. The Council asked for the power to draw the attention of Parliament to its differences with departments. It asked, too, for the Lord Chancellor to agree a code of practice with government departments. Was the Council about to enunciate standards for the rationalization of the ramshackle tribunals system? It was, in fact, asking departments: (a) to provide adequate time to formulate advice in each case; (b) to provide information and background material necessary for full consideration of the issues; (c) to give proper consideration to the advice given; (d) to discuss points of difference with the Council; and (e) to make public any points of substance not finally agreed in relation to draft legislation or regulations brought before Parliament.

Even this anodyne recommendation was unacceptably formal. Lord Hailsham replied to a parliamentary question from Lord Tweedsmuir, then Chairman of the Council:

The Government have given detailed consideration to the Special Report . . . [and] concluded that . . . the case has not been made out for any substantial widening of [the Council's] powers or functions on the lines proposed in the report's principal recommendations, particularly as this would create additional demands on resources. However, the Government do accept that, as proposed in the report, it would be desirable for the council's entitlement to be consulted about procedural rules for tribunals and inquiries to be restated in clearer and more general terms. The Government also accept that it may often be helpful and appropriate for departments to consult the council about draft primary legislation affecting matters within their field. Although there is no need for a formal code governing consultation between the council and departments, the possibility of introducing informal guidelines should be examined. It is understood that the council are already engaged on preliminary work in connection with such guidelines. [HL Deb. vol. 419, cols. 1118–19.]

The product of these labours can be found in Appendix C of the Council's Report for 1981/2 (HC 64 (1982/3)). The 'Code for Consultation with the Council' amplifies the provision of adequate time by asking departments to allow two months for routine proposals and four months for proposals raising major issues of principle. Even these are only *optimum* times. The next paragraph specifies four to six weeks as a minimum and continues: 'If, in cases of emergency, these minima cannot be adhered to and an explanation is made to the Council, the Council will certainly use their best endeavours to complete the consultation process in such shorter time as may be necessary.'

If the Council actually needs provisions of this nature, serious doubts concerning the efficacy of its work must arise.

3 Diagnosis to prescription?

Yardley, reviewing the Council's own review, gave the patient a 'clean bill of health'. Reform was unnecessary; the author found the Council's amateurish style endearing:

It is important for the Council to retain the confidence of the whole spectrum of the citizenry, and to this aim it is submitted that it should remain overtly part-time, that its staff should remain small, and that its funds should continue to be scant. This writer has always been an ardent admirer of the Council and hopes to remain so. Its reports are useful, but they are especially valuable because there are not too many of them, and they are not too long. Let the Council continue to engage upon special duties, but only where the need is clear, and not for the sake of building up work . . .

The main message coming from this report is nowhere directly expressed. But it is implicit from the comparatively minor nature of the recommendations that the Council is in fact working well, and that its achievements in the field of tribunals and inquiries have been substantial. It is a paradox that a body with a statutory constitution, but with no powers actually to achieve anything directly, should be so valuable. But it is submitted that this paradox is nonetheless true. [Yardley 1980, pp. 271–2.]

Other observers are less complacent. Rose believes that the Council has done nothing that a government department could not do and suggests that it has been sucked into the patronage system so characteristic of British government.[18]

Does this part-time collection of 'the not so good and great'[19] really retain the confidence of 'the whole spectrum of the citizenry'? Everything points to the fact that they have never heard of the Council or its chairmen. Indeed, in 1981, the Council admitted that, 'On very many occasions they had spoken to chairmen and tribunal members who still had no prior knowledge of our functions or indeed of our existence' (HC 89 (1981/2), para. 2.11). This is partly due to the fact that the Council lacks a power base. Without the help of a parliamentary select committee, it is in a much weaker position than the PCA. It is also partly due to the nature of its work. The scrutinizing and negotiatory functions which make its performance so difficult to assess also make its work difficult to publicize. The publicity which surrounded the Chalkpit affair or the Packington Estate scandal (below, Chapter 15) prove the greater publicity value of firefighting. Yet the Council has deliberately curtailed its fire-fighting role.

The Council's weakness is demonstrated by its inability to achieve even the limited reforms for which it has asked. The gaps in its jurisdiction are greater than it admits. In 1961 *Justice*, in the Whyatt Report, observed that the Council had been excluded from the crucial area of discretionary decision-taking where no formal procedures and no formalized method of challenge exist. Like its begetter, the Franks Committee, the Council was restricted to the open area of government. *Justice* recommended that the Council be empowered 'to survey those areas of discretion where decisions are made which are not at present subject to appeal and to make proposals for bringing such areas within the tribunal system whenever it is appropriate to do so' (*Justice* 1961, paras. 9, 15). The Conservative Government responded immediately:

The Government consider that there are serious objections in principle to [these] proposals and that it would not be possible to reconcile them with the principle of Ministerial responsibility to Parliament. They believe that any substantial extension of the system of reference to tribunals would lead to inflexibility and delay in administration . . . the Government have themselves undertaken a detailed review of the extent to which persons aggrieved can appeal against discretionary decisions. This review has disclosed a few instances in which provision for appeal might with advantage be introduced as an additional safeguard to the person affected by the decision, and these are being examined in greater detail. [HL Deb. vol. 244, cols. 384–5, Viscount Dilhorne.]

The conclusion to this affair proved the strength of the *Justice* case. The Council reported that the chairman had:

... informed the Lord Chancellor that we had noted with considerable interest [that the detailed review] was being carried out by the Government and expressed the hope that in the course of it there would be the earliest possible consultation with the Council, particularly as regards any proposals which might lead to the setting up of new tribunals. The Lord Chancellor replied that the Council would be consulted ... 'in accordance with the arrangements which were made some time ago as regards any proposals which may lead to the setting up of new tribunals', but he did not offer any opportunity to the Council to see the results of the survey ... or to express a view as to the cases in which appeal to a tribunal should be allowed. [AR 1962, para. 17.]

Assessing the English system of administrative law, Shonfield (1965, pp. 420–2) observed that the Council was kept 'at arm's length from the substance of any act of administrative discretion'. He went on to say that 'anyone coming unprepared on the work of the Council ... would be driven to the conclusion that it had been deliberately under equipped for a mock contest with the administration'. Any success achieved was due 'in part to the personal quality and determination of the people involved in the work – and more generally to the remarkable responsiveness of the British to even the feeblest kind of machinery for producing more fair play'.

The will to make the best of a botched job can, of course, have a negative side. Arguably, the Council mainly serves the important negative function of 'legitimation'. It suggests that the ramshackle tribunal system is monitored, supervised and controlled when nothing could be further from the truth. The Council is itself concerned about the absence of methodical research and study though, as we have seen, it has done little to put matters right:

The essential point is that our activity in relation to tribunals and inquiries must be founded on detailed knowledge. At present there is no other statutory body to collect information, on a methodical basis, about the operation of the tribunal and inquiry system. Departments do, of course, provide us with some statistics on tribunals and inquiries with which they are concerned, but the overall coverage is incomplete, uncoordinated and rather superficial. We ourselves do not have the resources to produce what is needed ... We believe that the advisory and consultative work of the Council cannot be as effective as it should be unless we can draw on a repository of knowledge and experience. [Cmnd 7805, para. 8.]

And, looking back on a lifetime's experience of administrative tribunals, Robson was pessimistic:[20]

No attempt has been made in any quarter, official or unofficial or even academic to define the kinds of issues which tribunals rather than the courts should hear and determine. The proliferation of tribunals has been growing at an ever increasing pace despite occasional protests by the Council on Tribunals. This should be a matter for public concern. [Robson 1979, p. 107.]

So in each area of the Council's work – (a) supervision of the system, (b) procedural rule-making and (c) restructuring the system – there are doubts about its achievements. In addition, it has failed to initiate or sponsor adequate research. Perhaps we should consider axing the Council to allow Parliament to make a fresh start? The Pliatsky Report on Non-Departmental Public Bodies (Cmnd 7797 (1980), p. 98) passed it by with the non-committal remark that there was no further scope for rationalization in the Lord Chancellor's department; but at the time the Council's budget was only £144,000 and the inquiry was not aiming to increase expenditure.

Without imposing this restriction on ourselves, let us do the Committee's work again. First, in discussing complaints, we made reference to complainants' inevitable disappointment when they learned that the Council could not investigate the merits of a tribunal decision or order a rehearing. We suggested that there might be a parallel here with courts. The Lord Chancellor implied that judicial errors would be corrected through the process of appeal and review. But anyone familiar with the operation of the criminal justice system knows that this is not the case (below, Chapter 13). And, for cases in which the complaint rests on a *course* of conduct by a particular tribunal or court, appeal is quite inadequate. We surmise that there is a large number of complaints concerning the administration of justice but we do not know what happens to them. No doubt some go to the Law Society, others to the Lord Chancellor's office and some are taken up by MPs or pressure groups like *Justice* and LAG. A 'Justice Ombudsman' could handle complaints throughout the courts and tribunals system.[21] No doubt his existence, like that of the other ombudsmen, would soon become known and in any case, one ombudsman can pass incorrectly referred complaints to another.

Secondly, let us look at Wraith and Hutchesson's argument for a centralized drafting agency. Reread the Council's remarks on p. 192; is such an agency a practical proposition? If procedural regulations are ancillary to substantive policies, then arguably they must be left with the department responsible for the tribunal. Compare the attitude of departments to the Council with the reverence shown to Parliamentary Counsel (Johnstone, above, p. 127). If this comparison suggests to you that a specialist agency is needed, then the responsibility should rest with the Lord Chancellor's department. The case for strengthening the Council would be transformed into a case for a strong Ministry of Justice.

Alternatively, we might link scrutiny of procedural rules to the wider question of scrutiny of delegated legislation. We have already noted the difficulties experienced in this field by the parliamentary scrutiny committees. In France, scrutiny of executive legislation is an important part of the work of the Conseil d'Etat, a unique French institution which combines the functions of administrative court and adviser to government and administration.[22] A body modelled on the Council on Tribunals, sufficiently professional, adequately financed and staffed, could perform a similar function in Britain. Alternatively, a large and well-qualified staff could be placed at the disposal of the Joint Scrutiny Committee. Procedural rules would form part of the general work of these experts. Of course, each of these options would require more than a 'shoestring' budget. In return, we could expect more than a 'shoestring' performance.

7
Ombudsman techniques

I am, in fact, a middle of the road man. Nye Bevan used to say that 'the man who walks in the middle of the road is the man who gets run over'. So perhaps I am in danger. [Sir Edmund Compton 1970, p. 10.]

I Means and objectives

In the last chapter we saw how firewatching through persuasion has evolved as the key function of the Council on Tribunals. By contrast the courts are primarily firefighters. Judges react to pre-existing disputes, although, in resolving these, they establish precedents which may help to prevent future outbreaks. Ombudsmen combine elements of both functions. Although they are 'grievance men', they take a more direct interest than courts in stimulating administrative improvement and may pursue their goals not only by 'judgments' but by less formal negotiations or consultations. During the last twenty years, many countries have established ombudsmen[1] but since the original Swedish concept has been adapted to local conditions, the institutions vary in constitutional position, operating methods and objectives. In Britain, there is disagreement about all these basic issues.

(a) Redressing grievances
The notion that ombudsmen are primarily firefighters infused the influential report 'The Citizen and the Administration' (1961) which recommended that an impartial officer called a 'parliamentary commissioner' should investigate and report on complaints of 'maladministration'. A lawyerly emphasis was not surprising. The report (Director of Research, Sir John Whyatt) was drawn up by *Justice*, a pressure group of lawyers dedicated, according to its

constitution, to the 'preservation of the fundamental liberties of the individual'.

In the Introduction, Lord Shawcross argued that the extension of administrative discretion necessitated greater protection for the citizen. Stressing that with the growth of the state, 'large areas of discretion are created in regard to all sorts of matters affecting the lives and rights of ordinary people', he considered that 'the man of substance can deal with these situations. He is near to the establishment [and] can afford to pursue legal remedies'. But the 'little man' could not: 'the little farmer with four acres and a cow would never have attempted to force the battlements of Crichel Down'. Whyatt pursued this theme, contending that the traditional controls left a gap into which an ombudsman should be inserted.[2] While judicial review, three years before *Ridge* v. *Baldwin*, was too limited and too expensive, parliamentary techniques were ineffective. Adjournment debates and parliamentary questions[3] were 'uneven contests' because only the executive possessed all the relevant information, and ad hoc inquiries were a little-used Rolls-Royce machinery unsuited to everyday matters. The report, directed to the redress of grievances did not examine a second objective of complaints machinery, the identification of administrative inefficiency with a view to its eradication. It identified as the key administrative benefit that individual civil servants, falsely accused, would be able to clear their names.

In advocating informal investigatory techniques designed to minimize administrative disruption, *Justice* recognized that departments expend resources meeting investigations. But there was no analysis of the consequences for decision-making generally. It was left to others to point to the *defensive* administrative techniques which may develop:

The danger . . . is that the activities of an external critic, far from improving the quality of public administration, may instead serve to drive civil servants further into those very bureaucratic vices that so often give rise to complaints in the first place. Junior officials, with little discretionary leeway, might make a point of sticking .even more rigidly and inflexibly to departmental regulations, resolving never to deviate one iota from them – whatever the circumstances – for fear of being publicly criticised should their well-intentioned efforts to avoid inconveniencing the public somehow go wrong. More senior civil servants – at levels where discretionary decisions that frequently and inevitably upset individual members of the public are taken – might become excessively cautious, spending far longer on each decision than is really necessary. Or, apprehensive about the possibility of being investigated and criticised they may become increasingly reluctant to exercise the authority delegated to them, preferring instead to push the responsibility for decisions that ought to be taken at their own level up to superiors in the administrative hierarchy. What is more, in order to be able to justify to the hilt action which they know might afterwards be investigated, officials might take to recording and explaining in elaborate detail what they are doing while they are doing it, thereby adding considerably to the time spent on every transaction. [Gregory and Hutchesson 1975, pp. 369–70.]

In response to *Justice*, the Conservative Lord Chancellor (Lord Dilhorne) emphasized this aspect of the ombudsman idea (HL Deb. vol. 244, cols. 384–5). He argued that a 'Parliamentary Commissioner would seriously interfere with the prompt and efficient despatch of public business'. Once more any simple characterization of the political parties' attitudes towards controlling bureaucracy breaks down; it was left to the incoming Labour Government to establish the Parliamentary Commissioner for Administration or PCA. The Parliamentary Commissioner Act 1967 envisaged fire-fighting in a restricted form. First, following pressure from MPs concerned for their traditional constituency role of handling complaints[4] and concern that, in a country as highly populated as Britain, the new machinery might be swamped, Labour's proposals (Cmnd 2767) represented a further extension of parliamentary control and not an autonomous institution like the Swedish office.[5] The PCA was to aid and supplement, not replace, Parliament's function of ventilating grievances. As a consequence, he cannot investigate those bodies, like local authorities, for which ministers are not responsible. And he can intervene only after receiving a complaint from an MP; an individual cannot complain direct. Secondly, parliamentary attachment to ministerial responsibility dictated that the PCA probe only the administrative activities of government and not the exercise of its policy-making or political powers. Adopting the terminology conveniently provided by Whyatt, the PCA was only to investigate complaints of injustice caused by 'maladministration' which the Government spokesman, Mr Crossman (HC Deb. vol. 734, col. 51), described as including 'bias, neglect, inattention, delay, incompetence, ineptitude, perversity, turpitude, arbitrariness and so on'. To make doubly sure, Lord Chancellor Gardiner drafted s.12(3):

It is hereby declared that nothing in this Act authorises or requires the Commissioner to question the merits of a decision taken without maladministration . . . in the exercise of a discretion vested in [a] department.

As an appointed official,[6] the PCA was not to possess enforcement powers; ultimately ministers should justify their decisions to Parliament. Suppose, then, he upholds a complaint and recommends a remedy. In practice this varies from an apology to ex gratia compensation or reversal of the original decision, coupled with a change in departmental procedure or policy. Legally, the department may refute his criticism and/or decline to provide redress. For example, in *Court Line* (HC 498 (1974/5)) the PCA strayed into high politics by criticizing ministerial statements for implying that the troubled holiday firm would not collapse. Labour promptly rejected the finding,[7] Mr Heffer (HC Deb. vol. 897, cols. 566–7) considering it 'a political judgment', a reproach not unknown to the courts. But such outright refusals are rare; as a firefighter, the PCA can look to the media and public opinion. And here his parliamentary links come into play. He lays his various reports as parliamentary papers and dispatches individual findings to the referring MP. If, after criticizing a department, he considers it will not provide adequate redress, he can issue a special report to Parliament. Most important, unlike the Council on Tribunals, he possesses within Parliament a specific constituency. The Select Committee on the PCA[8] follows his investigations, summons witnesses and issues its own reports on matters arising. Thus recalcitrant departments may encounter severe parliamentary pressure to give way, receiving written representations from members, facing parliamentary questions, and finding their highest officials cross-examined by the Select Committee.

The PCA's capacity to redress grievances was hedged around with further limitations. Sched. 3 exempted from investigation some key governmental concerns like commercial transactions, civil service personnel matters and, originally, official action taken abroad. Similarly, s.6(4) initially required that the complainant be resident in, or that the complaint relate to action taken while he was in, or relate to rights and obligations accruing in, the UK. Other provisions, like the one year time-limit for complaints and the locus standi test that the complainant be the 'person aggrieved', may be waived by the PCA in certain circumstances. S.5(2) represents a modest attempt to avoid overlapping remedies. The Labour Party did not intend the PCA to supplant the pre-existing adjudicatory methods of obtaining redress. On the other hand, Mr Crossman (HC Deb. vol. 734, col. 52) voiced its traditional view that the expense and popular awe of the courts might frighten people away, an argument extended by MPs, against the Government's advice, to tribunals. So s.5(2) provides that where a complaint relates to a matter giving rise to a right of appeal to a tribunal or to a court remedy, the PCA shall not investigate unless 'satisfied that in the particular circumstances it is not reasonable to expect [the complainant] to resort or have resorted to it'. Lastly, in addition to this unstructured discretion, the PCA possesses an overarching power because s.5(5) lays down that in determining whether to initiate, continue and discontinue an investigation, he shall 'act in accordance with his own discretion'. Thus the PCA possesses considerable freedom of manoeuvre. And so far the courts have declined to intervene (see *Re Fletcher's Application* [1970] 2 All ER 527 and (on the CLA) *R.* v. *Local Commissioner for Administration for the North and East Area of England, ex p. Bradford MBC* [1979] QB 287.)

Sir Idwal Pugh describes the different steps involved in handling a complaint. In contrast to the courts' adversarial techniques, the PCA's are inquisitorial:

Before any investigation can begin, the complaint must be screened to determine whether it has been properly referred and whether it is within my jurisdiction . . . In 1976, as a result of the screening process, 505 complaints out of a total of 815 submitted through [MPs] had to be rejected. [If] accepted investigation begins. I am required by the Act to afford the principal officer of the department concerned . . . the opportunity to comment on the complaint. For this purpose I prepare a statement of complaint setting out the material facts of the case. I send this to the permanent secretary concerned together with a letter requesting his comments. If a complaint names a particular member of the department, a second copy of the statement of complaint will be sent so that he can have it . . .

When I receive the principal officer's reply, it is open to me to accept it and issue a report on the basis of that reply. In some cases I do so but usually only if the department fully accepts the validity of the complaint and makes full restitution. In other cases the principal officer's reply is only the starting point of the real investigation. This normally begins with a detailed enquiry into the statements or remissions which appear from an examination of the department's reply. It will consist of examining departmental papers, discussion with officers of the department concerned or further correspondence with the department. In about half the investigations members of my staff go on to take oral or further written evidence from the complainant. When all this has been done, a draft 'results report' on the case is prepared and is submitted to me and is often the subject of a case conference. This sets out all the facts of the case, the course of the investigation and the conclusion and findings on the complaint. If the complaint is upheld, it will also specify the remedy which is called for. I then send the draft report to the permanent secretary of the department concerned. I do this for the following reasons. First, so that he can check, as far as the department's records are concerned, that I have correctly reported facts. Secondly, so that he can confirm that the department will or will not agree to a remedy where one is included in the report. Thirdly, so that he may also decide whether or not in the very rare case to ask the minister in charge of the department to use the right which he has under the statute to prevent disclosure of information [when it] 'would be prejudicial to the safety of the State or otherwise contrary to the public interest'. I have never been called upon to comply with this part of the statute . . . This description of my investigations will reveal two things. Firstly, that they are extremely independent and secondly that they are extremely thorough. [Pugh 1978, pp. 134–6.]

Figure 1. The Parliamentary Commissioner for Administration 1967–82

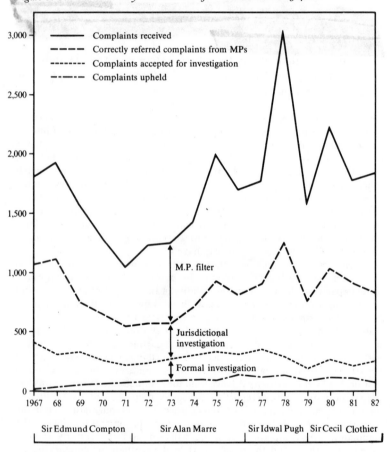

Source: Annual Reports of the PCA.
Note. The figures for 'complaints accepted for investigation' for 1967–74 and 1981–2 are calculated by difference; the 1975–80 figures appear in the Annual Reports.

Figure 1 translates this account into statistical terms. It illustrates
how the various restrictions reduce the original number of complaints
to the comparatively few (67 in 1982) investigation reports establishing maladministration causing injustice. Pugh (1978, p. 138) tells
us that between 1967 and 1977 the reasons for not accepting
complaints referred by MPs through the jurisdictional screen broke
down, in percentage terms, as follows:

Authorities (like nationalized industries) outside scope	33
Complaints not properly referred, not about administrative action	17
Public service personnel matters	15
Right of appeal to tribunal	11.5
PCA's overarching discretion	10.5
Time bar	6
Court remedy	1.5
Commercial transactions	1.5
Locus standi	0.5
Official action abroad	0.5
Residence requirement	0.15

One response to Figure 1 is to press for change, to urge that the
restrictions be relaxed, so permitting the PCA to redress more
grievances. There has already been some expansion. The first two
PCAs considered that direct complaints failed; Sir Idwal, however,
developed the practice of sending these complaints, with the complainant's consent, to the constituency MP, requesting that he decide
whether or not to refer the complaint back formally. In 1980 this
loosening of the MP filter[9] generated a small number (29) of
additional properly referred complaints. Secondly, maladministration, like the grounds of judicial review, is elastic.[10] Sir Edmund
Compton, for example, initially took a narrow view. Citing s.12(3), he
would only investigate maladministration in the process leading to a
discretionary decision, not the quality of the decision itself. But
pushed by his Select Committee (HC 350 (1967/8), p. 383), he
accepted that where a decision was 'thoroughly bad in quality' he
could infer that there must have been maladministration in its taking.
Again, Sir Edmund quickly encountered 'legalism', finding cases
where the correct application of a rule produced 'manifest hardship'.
Early on he characterized such decisions as 'injustice without
maladministration', but subsequently circumvented s.12(3), which
he considered prevented him from criticizing the content of rules, in
tortuous fashion. He would check whether officials, aware of the
hardship produced, had taken proper steps to review the rule. If not,
he could make an adverse finding.

Thirdly, successive PCAs have taken a liberal approach to some of the discretionary jurisdictional limitations,[11] in particular, the availability of court remedies. For the present incumbent, Sir Cecil Clothier:

... where there appears on the face of things to have been a substantial legal wrong for which, if proved, there is a substantial legal remedy, I expect the citizen to seek it in the courts and I tell him so. But where there is doubt about the availability of a legal remedy or where the process of law seems too cumbersome, slow and expensive for the objective to be gained, I exercise my discretion to investigate the complaint myself. [HC 148 (1980/1), p. 1.]

Some matters (such as rudeness) would not found a legal remedy, but others, like the department's misleading assurances in the *Green Honey* case (HC 261 (1970/1), p.16) that denatured sugar would not turn the complainant's bees and honey green, might. The overlap is particularly marked in discretionary decision-taking. Just as courts intervene by judicial review, so ombudsmen criticize administrators for omitting to take relevant considerations into account, proceeding upon insufficient evidence, considering irrelevant factors, and failing to provide complainants with an opportunity to present their case. The external monitors partially duplicate each other's work.

Statistically, however, few gains have been made and the invalid tricycles cases (Chapter 5) illustrate how Sir Edmund's indirect ways of attacking 'bad' decisions and rules have not greatly increased the chances of a PCA finding maladministration. *Justice*, in its report 'Our Fettered Ombudsman' (1977), concluded that although the new institution had worked well, it had done so within a very restricted frame of reference. By comparison with foreign ombudsmen, who handled a proportionately greater number of investigations per head of population, the PCA was 'considerably under-utilized'. Better publicity was needed and direct access should be an alternative to the MP filter. While Sir Idwal's elaborate investigations were appropriate for difficult cases, informal methods (e.g. telephone inquiries) would produce immediate redress in routine cases. 'Maladministration' should be replaced with the supposedly wider formulation 'unreasonable, unjust or oppressive action' and most of Sched. 3 abandoned, in particular, two statistically significant exclusions – personnel matters and commercial transactions. Behind all this lay a conception of the ombudsman function reminiscent of Whyatt:

The continuous growth of the administration ... calls for a parallel development of effective checks and balances if the citizen is not to be submerged by bureaucracy. The [PCA] has the possibility . . . of becoming one of the most important of the safeguards for the citizen against the administration, and to that end should be developed to its full . . . The most important consideration is that as many as possible of bona fide grievances against government departments should be investigated by [him]. [*Justice* 1977, pp. 6, 18.]

(b) **Or improving administration?**

Harlow criticized the *Justice* view. Stressing the second objective of scrutinizing the administrative process, she was more concerned with quality than quantity. From this perspective, Figure 1 is not overly significant. Not only does it fail to measure the potential 'ripple' effect of individual investigations, for example in the *War Pensions* affair (HC 312 (1977/8)) where, in consequence of a single adverse report, 24 similar cases were administratively reviewed and restitution made. More important, it focuses only on redressing grievances:

The advocates of reform direct their attention to those barriers which seem to hinder the PCA from processing the maximum number of 'small claims' . . . These are fallacious arguments because PCA procedure is not really appropriate to handle a large number of [cases] . . . [His] investigatory procedure is thorough but costly: a PCA investigation may cost as much as £2000. It is [also] time-consuming . . . Obviously the PCA cannot abandon the investigation of individual complaints if only because, without complaints, grave administrative deficiencies would rarely come to light. But the arguments for removal of the ' MP filter' should be rigorously examined. The new compromise [above] . . . allows the MP to settle the trivial administrative muddles, resubmitting only the hard nuts. Even then the PCA probably needs to develop a subsidiary procedure for very small cases to run alongside his 'Rolls Royce method' . . .

When we turn to the second Ombudsman function . . . we find the PCA is uniquely well placed to undertake the task and that his procedures are entirely appropriate . . . Parliamentary questions are a blunt instrument. The classic doctrine of Ministerial Responsibility may actually shelter more administrative blunders than it exposes. The efficacy of court orders is limited by the absence of supervisory powers. The PCA, on the other hand, has available to him all the information on which the disputed decision was based. He has behind him the considerable authority of a Parliamentary Select Committee. [So] his *primary* role should be that of an independent and unattached investigator, with a mandate to identify maladministration, recommend improved procedures and negotiate their implementation. Changes in his jurisdiction and procedures should be made only if they facilitate the execution of this task.

If this is right, the individual complaint is primarily a mechanism which draws attention to more general administrative deficiencies. [And] the essential question with regard to access is whether the PCA should be given power to intervene of his own initiative. It is submitted that he should. [Harlow 1978, pp. 450–3.]

Using complaints to promote change in the bureaucratic process has its drawbacks. Because certain complaints will not be justified, considerable investigative effort may promote no administrative improvements. Since, for whatever reason, many citizens do not complain, the discovery of departmental error may remain patchy. Despite Lord Shawcross's concern for the 'little man', some men remain littler than others. *Justice*, in its report, 'The Local Ombudsmen: a Review of the First Five Years' (1980), found that 'complainants to the Local Ombudsman are older, more likely to be in non-manual (and especially professional and managerial) occupations and better educated than the population as a whole'. So Harlow goes further, seeking to detach the PCA from his dependence upon complaints. The analysis is avowedly functionalist. She tries to identify the policy-goal which the PCA is best equipped to secure and then suggests he devote his resources accordingly. Here the author does not compartmentalize: the office should be evaluated not as a discrete institution but as one of a variety of complaints' procedures. Different agencies have different strengths and we should play to them. Lawyers may view the PCA, like tribunals, as a cheap method of providing redress. If we compare the MP's letter which produces a departmental change of heart, our perception will differ. It matters not that the PCA conducts fewer investigations than foreign ombudsmen; what is important is that individual complaints are channelled towards agencies adept at handling them. MPs, and not the PCA, should pick up the telephone in routine cases.

In the event, the Select Committee in its detailed *Review of Access and Jurisdiction* (HC 615 (1977/8)) took a middle way. Recommending better publicity and the investigation of commercial transactions and certain civil service personnel matters, it also accepted that Sir Idwal's interpretation of maladministration already approximated to *Justice*'s proposed reformulation and advocated retaining the MP filter. Discovering that the ombudsman's case load was dwarfed by the 100,000-plus constituents' complaints which are dealt with annually by MPs, the Select Committee reasserted Labour's original view that the prime responsibility for protecting the citizen against the administration rested, and ought to rest, with MPs. It also took faltering steps towards a firewatching function. The Swedish ombudsman can act without complaints, either by initiating his own investigations, for example after adverse press reports, or by inspecting institutions within his jurisdiction. The Committee considered the former irreconcilable with the PCA's constitutional position but recommended that, if on the basis of previous complaints, he believed that a particular office was working inefficiently, he should be able, subject to the Committee's approval, to mount a systematic investigation with a view to making recommendations for putting things right.

The Government's response (Cmnd 7449) was perhaps revealing. Its refusal to countenance major jurisdictional extensions[12] had little to do with arguments about the PCA's functions. It contended that monitoring externally departmental commercial activities would be unfair, because contractees – in the modern state, companies not private individuals – would be exempt from investigation. The personnel exclusion was justified by the demands of 'consistency'. Since the means of redress available to civil servants in employment matters were not inferior to those in the private sector, 'it would be unacceptable for this group to have the right, not available to others, to invoke the intervention of the PCA'. The rejection of an inspecting power as 'unnecessary and undesirable' discloses, however, what those subject to investigation consider the PCA's function ought to be.[13] While Sir Idwal, a former senior civil servant, thought this the most important of the Committee's recommendations (HC 205 (1978/9), p. 5), the Government contended (Cmnd 7449, pp. 5–6):

It would place a heavy burden on the Commissioner if he were required in effect to 'audit' the administrative competence of government departments and would distract him and his staff from *their central purpose of investigating* complaints . . . Where the Commissioner investigates a series of complaints relating to a particular area of administration he is . . . able to form a clear view of the procedures in force there and to make recommendations . . . Any lessons to be drawn from investigations by the Commissioner are already studied by departments and acted upon . . . It should be for Ministers and their departments to decide what action is necessary to prevent further maladministration by a particular branch or establishment, and to be answerable to Parliament for the adequacy of the action . . . taken.

Like Harlow, Sir Cecil Clothier, a lawyer, believes that the PCA should concentrate his efforts. But his objective (HC 258 (1981/2), p. 2) is quite different:

Since the complaints fully investigated by me are a small fraction of the total investigated by departments in direct communication with [MPs], it seems right that I should give them the most thorough and careful treatment of which my Office is capable. And the justification is to be found in the fact that in almost every second case investigated, there is a change in the department's previous stance. My concern is . . . to see that this careful process and my valuable resources are not wasted on trivial or unworthy causes.

(c) Tending the roots

The Commission for Local Administration in England,[14] which investigates the doings of local government, sees its 'main objective' as 'securing both satisfactory redress and better administration' (AR 1982/3, p. 64).[15] Action required by these two aims does not entirely overlap. For example, devoting resources to publicizing the lessons learnt from individual investigations does not directly secure speedy redress in referred cases. Recently the CLA, under pressure from its paymasters, local authorities themselves subject to financial restraint, has had to contemplate a period of retrenchment. This can force painful choices whether to restrict all activities or to emphasize some at the expense of others. For instance, during 1977/8 (AR p. 24) the CLA recommended that it should investigate parish councils. But in 1980/1 (AR p. 41), while reasserting that no local authority should be outside its jurisdiction (which presently includes metropolitan and district councils and police and water authorities), it conceded 'there are important resource implications for [the Commission] and for the councils and . . . implementation of the recommendation may have to be delayed in the present national economic climate.' Again, the CLA initially considered whether or not to investigate solely on the basis of written submissions. But when a pilot study disclosed that interviewing complainants caused it to accept cases which on the papers would have been refused, the CLA adopted oral procedures for up to 20 per cent of complaints. During 1980/1 (AR p. 44) it indicated that further extension of the practice would be difficult because 'the costs of such interviews have to be borne in mind at a time of pressure on resources.'

The CLA describes as 'supporting objectives' 'to encourage authorities to develop and publicize their own procedures for the fair local settlement of complaints, and to settle as many as possible' and 'to encourage the local settlement of complaints' made to the Commission. We should not assume that the CLA and PCA always pursue the same policy goals; the CLA has placed greater emphasis on this facet of its work.[16] Local settlements can avoid the time and expense involved in the CLA's comparatively elaborate investigations.[17] Baroness Serota, the Commission's first chairman, gave as another reason the constitutional argument that authorities should be primarily responsible to their electorates:

I knew when I was first invited . . . to establish and develop an independent Ombudsman system for local authorities . . . that this would be no easy task. Local authorities are fiercely independent elected bodies . . . directly accountable to the citizens they serve – and they do not take kindly to any outside criticism, from however impartial and independent a source. The system . . . depended for success on cooperation and consent from local authorities and complainants alike and that is why I wrote in my first annual report 'I have always personally hoped that it will prove possible for many complaints to be settled without formal investigation and [the Commission's] procedures . . . are designed to support, not to inhibit, the traditional process of remedying grievances whenever possible within the democratic local government framework'. [AR 1981/2, foreword.]

In presenting its scheme, the CLA has stressed *voluntarism*. In Mr Cook's words (AR 1977/8, p. 125), 'the success of the service will rest ultimately on acceptance and consent, not on narrow legalism.' What arguments, if any, can be made against the CLA pursuing local settlements?

We might take this further. At first sight the outline of the two ombudsman schemes is similar. For instance both offices possess access filters, though the CLA's is weaker. A complaint must normally be referred through a councillor but the CLA can waive the requirement if satisfied that the member has declined to forward it. Both PCA and CLA search for 'maladministration causing injustice'. The CLA cannot scrutinize actions which, like rate increases, affect all or most local inhabitants nor, like the PCA, investigate commercial transactions and (subject to discretion) matters given over to adjudication. There is, however, a key distinction between the two schemes. Denied the PCA's parliamentary links, the CLA starts from a weaker position. It reports to the 'Representative Body' which consists of local authority members. This usually opposes CLA proposals for expansion and does not supply the pressure which the PCA's Select Committee can provide. Sir Cecil Clothier believes that his institution's strength enables him to behave like a judge. The investigatory process differs, but in the end:

I must adjudicate impartially upon the facts disclosed . . . and here I make no presumption in favour of either citizen or department. Rarely do I need to act the part of negotiator in securing an adequate remedy . . . This is because in almost every instance government departments are quick to put right anything I find to have been done wrong. [HC 148 (1980/1), p. 2.]

In contrast, the CLA invokes less formal methods. If a commissioner issues an adverse report, the relevant authority is statutorily required to consider it, inform the commissioner of any remedial action it proposes to take and arrange for local publicity. If the commissioner is not satisfied with the council's suggestions, he may issue a second report indicating appropriate action. To avoid second reports, the CLA has developed an extra-statutory procedure. If it believes that the authority will not take appropriate action, it seeks meetings with top councillors and officials and tries to persuade them of the rightness of providing redress. The extent to which this involves bargaining and compromise remains speculative because, like most activities of the Council on Tribunals, these meetings are private.

The CLA expresses general content with the cooperation received, although it concedes considerable delay (AR 1982/3, p. 6). It describes as 'satisfactory' the settlements obtained in 1,075 cases involving adverse investigation reports during 1974–83, as against 78 'unsatisfactory' outcomes. *Justice*, however, is more circumspect because it is the CLA which defines what is 'satisfactory'. Finding in surveys a marked discrepancy between the number of cases which the CLA (5 per cent) and complainants (20 per cent) described as producing 'unsatisfactory' results, *Justice* (1980, p. 44) concluded that 'a major cause of complainant dissatisfaction lies with the redress which the local Ombudsman has obtained'. In proposing that, at the complainant's suit, the courts should be able to quantify the loss and make orders accordingly, *Justice* was not only concerned to guarantee individuals redress. Like administrators, the new external monitor needed monitoring:

In deciding whether or not to be satisfied with the action taken by the authority, the Local Ombudsman is taking a discretionary decision . . . for which he is not accountable to any other person or body. Furthermore, there is no body in local government comparable to the [PCA] Select Committee to counsel or advise [him] or say whether it agrees with the way in which that discretion is being exercised . . . In [its] absence . . . the institution best able to influence the exercise of [his discretion is] the court. [*Justice* 1980, p. 46.]

The CLA's policy of encouraging local settlements is everywhere apparent in its handling of complaints. The small number of adverse investigation reports significantly understates the Commission's work. At the filter stage the CLA advises those complaining direct about the proper procedure, apparently with considerable success. Table 7 reveals that about half the direct complaints return properly referred. In addition it often asks the authority concerned to consider the possibility of settling locally; in 1981, a record 110 cases were concluded in this matter. The CLA sometimes acts more positively during the investigatory process. Here the position is complicated because the CLA has changed operating procedures. Initially it distinguished between preliminary screening and formal investigations, although in many cases (53 per cent in 1979) the screening process ranged well beyond scrutinizing the complaint. In addition to interviewing some complainants, the CLA took the extra-statutory step of asking many authorities for their preliminary comments and occasionally examined their files. So when *Justice* (1980, p. 142) found that in 1975–9 the failure to indicate 'maladministration causing injustice' as distinct from dislike of the authority's decision was the reason in 70 per cent of cases for rejection at the screening stage, it also discovered that the CLA had made 'informal inquiries' in 28 per cent of these. This stage also involved the CLA in another extra-statutory activity, conciliation. Some disputes are resolved simply by encouraging the parties to agree. As Table 7 reveals, the number of local settlements at this stage has risen significantly. In Baroness Serota's words (AR 1977/8, pp. 112–13):

A number of authorities have been willing for me to act as an independent mediator in an endeavour to settle a complaint without the time and cost inevitably involved in a formal investigation . . . I am always glad to assist in settling complaints in this way with the agreement of both sides.

In 1980, recognizing that any clear-cut distinction between screening and investigating had been blurred, the CLA reclassified all dealings with complaints inside its jurisdiction as 'investigations'. There are now four parts of what amounts to a rolling procedure. In some cases the complaint is promptly rejected as disclosing no element of maladministration. More often, the authority is asked for comments and if, after consideration, the commissioner decides not to proceed, the complainant is informed accordingly. In cases where he decides to continue, the files are examined and interviews conducted. But, with the twin aims of speeding-up investigations and saving work for authority and scrutineer, the commissioner keeps open the option of discontinuance if it emerges that the complaint is unjustified or there has been maladministration causing injustice which the authority is prepared to remedy. Only in the remaining cases does investigation continue to a formal report. In 1981/2 (AR, pp. 3–4) CLA 'investigations' broke down as follows (the bracketed figure

Table 7. The Commission for Local Administration (England) 1976–83

	1976*	1977	1978	1979	1980	1981	1982	1983
Complaints:								
Received direct	813†	1202†	780	1063	911	938	976	1023
Direct and then referred	88	247	629	836	810	827	977	1022‡
Correctly referred	1348	828	1055	1280	1371	1607	1729	1741
Total	2249	2277	2464	3179	3092	3372	3682	3786
Complaints rejected: (can include some carried forward)								
Outside jurisdiction	563†	518†	308	456	646	} 658	} 607	} 772
Directed to merits not manner	783	895	377	510	371	}	}	}
Decision after informal inquiries	403	258	488	605	501	1031	1226	1618
Withdrawn	} 65	} 62	57	37	N/A	N/A	N/A	N/A
Settled informally/locally	}	}		97	175	299	389	(388)
Total	1814	1733	1230	1705	1693	1988	2222	2390
Accepted for investigation during current year: (including those carried forward to next year)	528	907	732	844	935	446	484	373
Investigation findings:								
Discontinued	3	8	12	11	19	N/A	N/A	57
No maladministration found	47	74	95	124	166	132	106	129
Maladministration only	3	8	13	9	14	17	15	17
Maladministration and injustice	49	107	169	182	213	166	158	170
Total	102	197	289	326	412	315	279	373

Source: CLA Annual Reports.

* In line with the CLA's reporting period, the statistics are for the year ending in March of that year.

† In 1976 and 1977 the CLA Annual Reports included complaints sent direct in the category of complaints rejected. From 1978 onwards only those complaints correctly referred are placed in this category.

‡ Approximate.

( ) no longer shown as a separate category for rejection analysis.

discloses the number of cases settled locally at each stage):

660 (53)   examined but not pursued
1,458 (288) investigation terminated after consideration of
             authority's comments
104 (48)   investigation discontinued at a later stage
279   investigation continued to formal report

Like the PCA, the number of complaints handled by the CLA is negligible when compared with the number of decisions taken daily by administrators within its jurisdiction. The CLA has attempted a pre-emptive strike, seeking to stimulate improvements in local authorities' *own* grievance mechanisms. Lewis and Birkinshaw (1979a, 1979b) emphasize how little research has been done into this area of public administration. Predictably, they found that the statutory provisions requiring local authorities to provide minimum procedural protections like the individual's right to receive information, to put his case and to obtain a reasoned decision, were extremely haphazard. Echoing Robson and Ganz in other contexts, they concluded (1979a, p. 132) that existing procedures owed 'as much to chance and political pressure as to any analytic design'. Their examination of non-statutory complaints procedures revealed a similar story of variation and omission. Some subject-areas like school allocation and personnel matters were well provided for, others not. And there were considerable differences between the 304 local authorities surveyed. Almost half claimed to have no recognizable procedures while only 22 afforded complainants an interview. Forty-three had developed informal methods, for example, complaints to the chief executive would be referred to the head of department concerned. Ninety-one authorities claimed more formal procedures, the majority (77) using their committees or subcommittees to resolve resistant disputes. The remaining 14 had established some kind of centralized system for handling complaints against the various departments or had appointed an 'executive ombudsman', an internal monitor of their activities.

Lewis and Birkinshaw (1979b, p. 11) suggested a correlation between the number of complaints referred to external monitors and the provision of internal grievance procedures. This one executive ombudsman 'had considerably reduced the potential for constituents' complaints being referred to outside agencies, whether the Commission, the courts or elsewhere'. Recognition that complaints machinery ought to be assessed in the light of other grievance mechanisms underlies the joint promulgation by the CLA and the local authorities associations of a voluntary code of practice ('Complaints Procedures' (1978)) for authorities dealing with complaints. The code's authors believe 'that there is more chance that [these] will be settled [locally] if there are clear and simple procedures for raising complaints and dealing with them'. One part of the code, dealing with those cases where complaints are sent to the CLA, is designed to further the process of achieving local settlements in referred cases. Here the CLA seeks to prepare the administrative terrain for its activities. The code indicates those items which should be included in any internal procedure established for dealing with the ombudsman. An outline procedure is attached, showing one possible approach. For example, to improve the prospects for local settlement via discontinuation just prior to formal report, the code reminds councils that:

Complaints do not become sub judice because an investigation is being made by a Local Commissioner. Provision needs therefore to be made within the Authority for considering whether action could be taken to resolve the complaint in the light of facts which are established during the Local Commissioner's investigation. This could well lead to the investigation being discontinued.

So the outline procedure informs authorities that on receipt by the chief executive of the CLA's draft factual section of the investigation report, they should take the following action: (1) Circulate draft for comment and verification to members and officers involved in the investigation. (2) Consider whether facts reveal action which might properly be taken to settle the complaint without awaiting Local Commissioner's recommendations. (3) Return comments to Local Commissioner.

The code also concerns authorities' handling of complaints without the CLA being involved. The term 'complaint' is here broadly defined, denoting not only 'the small minority of matters which are clearly complaints and may end as allegations . . . referred to a Local Commissioner', but also 'queries', defined as 'those approaches to Authorities, whether for advice, information or to raise an issue, which, if not handled properly, could turn into complaints'. The code sets out guidelines and provides a checklist against which authorities can measure the adequacy of their existing procedures for dealing with the public. But it proceeds with caution. Our initial discussion of the interplay between rules and discretion, being posed largely in terms of the state's dealings with individuals, presupposed that the administrative rule-maker was free to choose between 'weak' and 'strong' discretion. Here, however, the situation is far more complex. The Representative Body and the CLA are proposing a set of procedural rules which 'fiercely independent' local authorities can decide whether or not to accept. So the tendency towards flexible standards rather than specific and rigid rules is explained in the code as a recognition of pluralism and local autonomy. (In Chapter 14, we shall find a similar situation obtaining in the planning field.)

The detail of [complaints] procedures may well vary between Departments, especially in big Authorities, but the principle of having procedures – as opposed to relying on ad hoc arrangements or none at all – has been accepted by many Authorities. Circumstances clearly differ not only within authorities but also between authorities. For example, the complaints procedure required by the GLC will differ from that needed by a [small] District Council . . . This Code therefore does not attempt to set out a detailed Model Complaints Procedure. Instead it provides guidelines only. In commending [these] it is recognised that many authorities will already have adopted their own procedures and that . . . it is for each authority to decide how it wishes to handle complaints or indeed if formal procedures are required. [The guidelines] have been prepared . . . with the aim of assisting authorities in ensuring that their own methods of handling complaints are fully effective. Accordingly, no attempt has been made to suggest a rigid procedure to be followed in all circumstances.

Here are some of the guidelines. Compare the language used in the Oregon parole scheme and *Justice*'s 'Principles of Good Administration'.

Authorities can reduce the risk of complaints by ensuring that the public are told if, for financial or other reasons, services are to be reduced or desirable improvements postponed.

Authorities should ensure that effective and continuing information is available to the public about channels through which queries can be raised or complaints made. This can be done, for example, by notices in public places, and simple, well-designed and readily available information leaflets . . .

There should be easy access by the public to those responsible for dealing with queries and complaints whether officers or Members operating, for instance, through 'surgeries'. Contact points should be widely publicized, including the names and addresses of Members and appropriate officers . . .

There need to be simple systems for recording complaints and queries, other than those which can be fully and successfully dealt with on the spot.

Clear instructions should be given to staff so that they know who is responsible for dealing with those queries or complaints which cannot be dealt with on the spot by the staff receiving them.

Responsibility for acknowledging queries and complaints, for keeping enquirers and complainants informed of progress and conveying decisions (with or without any report on them made to a Committee or sub-Committee) should be clearly established . . .

There should be a willingness to see enquirers and complainants (by asking them to call to see a named person or, if necessary, by a personal visit) particularly when the issues are complicated or the facts need to be clarified . . .

Arrangements should be made to monitor queries and complaints to see if collectively they indicate trends which require changes of policy or procedure.

Lewis and Birkinshaw criticize these guidelines, seeing them as:

clearly directed to management efficiency – to ensuring that a local authority is not 'caught out' by making elementary mistakes. Publicity and consumerism do rate mention periodically, but . . . where information for the public [about complaints procedures] and public involvement [in them] are outlined . . . the provisions are on the tepid side. For example, 'there should be a willingness to see enquirers and complainants' . . . Compare this minimum standard with the practice of some authorities of allowing a complainant to be present at a committee accompanied by a legal representative. This is particularly true in the field of planning and hackney-cab licensing. [Similarly on] the need for publicity . . . there is a danger that the rather exiguous suggestions which [the code] contains may be construed as a maximum rather than a minimum. There is no emphasis upon actually informing the complainant at the time he makes his complaint of procedures available, let alone recommendations for the content of such procedures. [Lewis and Birkinshaw 1979b, pp. 11–12.]

The code's authors have conceded the particular difficulties of policy implementation via cooperation, finding (AR 1979/80, pp. 14–15) that 'whilst marked progress had been made by authorities in introducing or reviewing local complaints procedures, it was clear that some authorities did not propose to introduce them, that relatively few procedures were well-publicized, and that some were over-elaborate and complicated'. Lewis and Birkinshaw are not voluntarists. They demand legislation requiring the opening-up and publicizing of complaints procedures. Pointing to a local authority sub-committee which dispatched up to 35 'unusual or difficult' housing transfer and allocation cases per hour, they are particularly concerned by the lack of statutory minimum criteria for fairness and openness where authorities use this method of redressing grievances. The reply by Evans, a chief executive and chairman of the working party which produced the code, discloses a senior administrator's belief that management efficiency is no bad thing and that procedural protections advocated by lawyers like Lewis and Birkinshaw would overload the system and bring administration to a grinding halt （compare Dimock's views above, p. 156):

(compare Dimock's views above, p. 156):

[Lewis and Birkinshaw are not] wrong in seeing the need for essentially legal procedures and safeguards in dealing with some complaints. There clearly is a class of complaints (the Maria Colwell case[18] being one example) which raises such public concern and such important issues that they need to be investigated by a procedure closely following judicial procedure ... Few complaints however come into this category and one should not readily accept that [they] are of great analogical potential for dealing with the main body of complaints ... The adoption by local authorities of Complaints Procedures which satisfy the [code] would itself go a long way towards ensuring that complainants have their complaints dealt with efficiently and effectively. In that connection, the criticism which the authors make that 'its emphasis is so clearly directed to management efficiency' could be a very valuable safeguard for the interests of the complainant ... There are occasions when a personal appearance by a complainant before the decision-making body is highly desirable ... However, the approach needs to be selective. Local government in this country is a system based firmly on the fact that councillors are part-time councillors not able to devote the whole of their time to council work. Bearing in mind the volume of work which councillors must discharge, one questions whether it would be practical to give a personal hearing to anyone who wanted one ... how would the [authors'] sub-committee ... function if the 35 decisions they took 'within the hour' had each been the subject of a personal appearance by the person affected by it? Local government is a very practical operation and the arrangements by which it works must be practical as well. [Evans 1979, pp. 24–6.]

2 Monitors and monitored

The code is directed towards both firefighting and firewatching. One aim is to foster local settlement as a quick and cheap way of resolving disputes. Another is to reduce the number of complaints arising by encouraging authorities to improve procedures for dealing with 'queries'. The broader impact of ombudsmen on administrative decision-taking raises complex questions. On the positive side ombudsmen's reports sometimes induce administrators to review their policies: for an example, see below p. 409. There are also many instances where investigation provides a catalyst for improvement in administrative procedure. For example, in *Kensington and Chelsea* (Inv. 1308S of 15/3/76) the complainants had rented premises on the understanding that their planning application would be treated favourably. Baroness Serota found that there had been a long delay in processing the application, during which time the complainants were unable to use the premises. The Council resolved not only to refund the rent paid but to eradicate the possible causes of excessive delays. Staff were instructed to answer all letters within three days and, if this proved impossible, to send an acknowledgment. All relevant telephone calls were to be recorded and a new filing system introduced. Outstanding cases were to be monitored and liaison between the town clerk and the borough solicitor improved. To secure implementation, the managing services officer was given specific responsibility for ensuring compliance.

In such cases the ombudsmen, unlike the courts, are directly concerned with administrative change because making good administrative deficiencies constitutes one element in providing satisfactory redress. Sometimes they check up. Donning his Health Commissioner's hat, Sir Cecil Clothier investigated a complaint (HC 306 (1980/1), p. 140) that, because only one doctor had been on duty in a hospital's accident department, a boy had had to wait over four hours for two stitches. The PCA, 'disturbed to find that such a delay, while not commonplace, was not exceptional', considered it 'quite unacceptable'. After an interval he asked the Area Health Authority about the implementation of a long-standing proposal to allow nurses to perform such operations. The PCA was pleased to confirm its introduction, characterizing his intervention as a contributory factor.

Reports may also have substantial knock-on effects. Administrators may learn from the publicized mistakes of others. And Sir Edmund Compton contended (1968, p. 108) that the very existence of an external check stimulated administrative improvements; it gave administrators an added incentive to avoid maladministration. (Compare Franks' reasoning above, p. 97). Such effects cannot be quantified. Certainly the influence of external monitors depends on officials being made aware of their opinions. The way in which this information is disseminated varies. The judges can rely on commentators to synthesize their decisions into sets of 'rules' and 'exceptions' capable of guiding future conduct. By contrast little interest has been shown in synthesizing ombudsman findings. Since they have not produced a 'Code for Good Administration' like that proposed by *Justice*, the ombudsmen must look to their annual reports and also their investigation reports which, in the CLA's case, are unindexed and difficult to obtain and, in the case of the PCA, only selectively published. The ombudsmen place great emphasis on fostering contacts with both administrators and complaints conduits like Citizens Advice Bureaux (CABs) and trade unions. Visits, seminars and conferences are especially important for the CLA which faces particular difficulties in spreading the gospel. In a central department, all senior officials learn of an adverse PCA report; in local government, administrators in Blackpool may not know what happened in Bognor.

Ombudsmen reports do not always get a positive response. Administrators may choose to run the gauntlet of public opinion and, in the PCA's case, parliamentary pressure. One point to bear in mind is that a decision may affect other people. For example, in *Ashford* (Inv. 377S of 15/8/75) Baroness Serota upheld a complaint that, contrary to its own policy, the planning committee had failed to consult neighbours before granting an applicant planning permission to build a bungalow. In deciding subsequently not to revoke the permission, the authority had not only to consider the neighbours, but also the applicant's position. Similarly, there often exists a high degree of polycentricity in school and council-house allocation. In response to CLA investigations, some councils have rehoused complainants or sent their children to the schools of their choice. But since council housing is in short supply and some schools are considered more desirable than others, remedying particular griev-ances may prejudice other applicants. The Commission is not unaware of the problems which authorities face and sometimes tempers its approach accordingly. In *Haringey* (Inv. 45/S/78 of 1/2/79), for example, the complainant was allocated a council house but, before she could take possession, it was squatted by a family fleeing the troubles in Northern Ireland. The council's possession proceed-ings took six months, after which there was a further fortnight's delay while the squatters were found a house large enough for their seven children. The complainant, who in the meantime had to endure extremely poor housing, complained of the council's delay in moving the squatters. Baroness Serota concluded:

Although I have every sympathy with the complainant for [these] very trying circumstances ... I can also understand the dilemma which the Council faced. They had to weigh the discomfort of the complainant against the problem of what to do with a homeless family with seven children who had already suffered considerable hardship. I have seen nothing to suggest that they did not consider this difficult matter reasonably and properly and I therefore find no maladministration by the Council.

On other occasions, authorities consider that the CLA has gone too far. Courts and ombudsmen tend to focus on the individual case;

officials must take account of the wider implications. In *Wakefield* (Inv. 75C of 9/6/75) Mr Cook found unreasonable delay in council-house repairs. Faced with a second report, the Authority pointed to similar defects in other houses; the fact that the particular house had been the subject of a CLA investigation was no reason to single it out for special attention. Moreover, although it was prepared to complete the repairs to this and other houses, it could only do so when funds were available 'which was unlikely to be in the foreseeable future'. Similarly, accepting a CLA finding may set a precedent for compensation in other cases. In *Weymouth and Portland* (Inv. 261H of 8/9/75) Mr Harrison found delay in dealing with a complaint that an adjoining development had not taken place in accordance with approved plans. While he stressed the importance of remedying the individual's injustice, the Authority argued that to pay out might produce a rash of similar complaints. Again, local authorities' concern to conserve financial resources can produce clashes over policy. In *Cambridgeshire* (Inv. 3332C of 16/3/77) the Council, hoping to obtain a better social mix, moved some children to new schools. It undertook to provide free transport for any child who, in consequence, had to travel further. Seven years later, as a result of government demands for spending cuts, the Authority decided to terminate such transport. Upholding a parent's complaint, the Commissioner focused on the breach of an undertaking made to individuals. Rejecting the finding, the Council asserted a right to change its policy, especially in a period of financial retrenchment.[19]

But detailing administrative responses to particular investigations only takes us so far. It is possible for ombudsmen, by stimulating defensive practices, to have an adverse effect on bureaucratic decision-making generally. The PCA Select Committee, which early on (HC 385 (1968/9), p. 219) took evidence on this issue, was reassuring. Departmental Principal Officers did not consider the workload in meeting investigations to be unmanageable and the Committee concluded that Lord Chancellor Dilhorne's fears that decision-making would be slowed down were being dispelled. Gregory and Hutchesson (1975, pp. 362–70) conducted an impressionistic survey based on departmental comments and interviews with officials and reached a similar conclusion. The direct work produced which, though it varied, was often 4 to 5 man-days per complaint, did not, spread over the administration as a whole, constitute a significant extra burden. Again, there had been 'some –

but not much' growth in defensive administration. Slightly more concrete evidence is available concerning the CLA and local government. Stungo (1976, p. 728), researching the additional work which investigations produced for planning offices in London, found that officers' views varied sharply. While some downplayed the extra costs involved, another 'was deeply concerned at the strain such investigations are putting upon the resources of my department'. *Justice* (1980, pp. 97–8) also discovered a marked variation in the effect on authority workload and staff morale. It concluded that such impact would be greatest 'in small authorities which have been investigated rather more than usual and which have a local press which places considerable emphasis on maladministration findings'. Holdsworth, reporting the anxieties of local authority officers attending a seminar chaired by Baroness Serota, presents the most negative view. Compare the fears expressed here with the potential debits detailed by Gregory and Hutchesson (above) and with Jowell's similar assessment of rules (above, p. 145).

First, a growth in TCIC attitudes ('Thank Christ I'm in the clear!'). The primary objective of how best to deal with a difficult case becomes replaced by one of 'How can I handle this so that if something goes wrong it will not be my fault?' The easiest way of doing this, especially for lower-paid staff, is to push it up the ladder . . .

Second, if a local authority has a policy of doing more than the statutory minimum – as in planning application consultations – it will be guilty of maladministration if it does less in an individual case even if it nevertheless does more than the statute requires. This has happened, and the inevitable result is that the local authority will at least consider whether it would not be better to go back to doing nothing more than the statutory minimum.

Third, informality and flexibility, even unorthodoxy if the situation calls for it – which I believe to be good characteristics of good local authorities – are more risky in this context than formal rules and procedures. The result? More written rules, less discretion, less scope to adapt to an individual's needs. Short-cuts through red tape become hazardous.

Fourth, wasteful and counter-productive changes in working methods. This can take various forms such as noting on the file all telephone and personal conversations; even, I have heard, recording receipt and despatch of all mail in a postbook, a practice formerly thought to have died out in the late forties.

All this has been given added emphasis by the change in the economic climate. When the Commission was conceived, local government was in a major growth period, but staff are now anxious whether the Ombudsman's approach to complaints will take account of the retrenchment and economies, in staff and spending, currently being undertaken.

Authorities are having consciously to cease even to strive after 100 per cent perfection because of reduced budgets . . . The Ombudsman has said that she judges by high standards, because that is what the public is entitled to and that is what local government would wish to be judged on. Quite so, normally – but at present many are faced with having to make do with fewer staff and lower standards. [Holdsworth 1977, pp. 54–5.]

In Chapter 15 we consider evidence that Holdsworth's third point has been borne out. A series of adverse CLA and court decisions has apparently induced some local authorities to restrict oral advice about planning permission. His second prognostication has also come true. *Ashford* (above) is one case where a commissioner criticized an authority for not living up to its own policy, even though it was under no statutory duty to consult neighbours. The CLA (AR 1979/80, pp. 16–17) subsequently reported:

The Commission were disturbed to discover that the Association of District Councils had written . . . to all District Councils advising them:
(a) to avoid making formal resolutions committing the authority to undertake specified non-statutory neighbour or general public consultations in connection with planning applications in their area.
(b) formally to authorise their planning officers to undertake such informal consultations entirely at their own discretion . . .
(d) to suggest that their planning staff never make firm commitments to consult neighbours in respect of future possible applications not yet received.

The advice arose from consideration of cases where a Local Ombudsman has found maladministration because of a failure to consult neighbours on planning applications where the authority had a policy to consult but no statutory obligation to do so. The advice concluded:

District Councils who have already accepted the above suggestions have successfully avoided investigation and it is hoped that other member authorities will be able to benefit from the experience which they have gained.

The Commission expressed their regret to the Association of District Councils that this advice was given to Councils without consulting the Commission either directly or through the Representative Body. They pointed out that their experience strongly supported the need to give people an opportunity to make their views known about neighbouring developments if they wished . . . A meeting was held with representatives of the Association . . . who claimed that whilst the advice issued was aimed at reducing time-consuming investigations and findings of maladministration, it was likely to lead to more consultation about planning applications rather than less.

By trying too hard, the CLA may undercut its own policy. This is only part of the story. Holdsworth makes the point that with recent staff and spending cuts, the quality of administration may decline. There may be longer delays, more mistakes by hard-pressed officers and reductions in the level of advice proffered to citizens. Certain forms of decision-taking are more expensive than others. Rules are cheap, while interviews or hearings, traditionally valued by lawyers, are, as the C L A discovered, more costly than paper review. 'Good administration' is not a constant and the current fashion is to equate it with 'cost-effective' administration.[20] Caught between a Government committed to pruning public expenditure and a populace used to high standards in services and administration, Sir Edmund Compton's 'middle of the road man' may be in more danger than ever.

One response is to stand aside. In this more hostile climate, the ombudsmen, creatures of the affluent 1960s and early 1970s, may be tempted to lower their standards. In 1980 (HC 148 (1980/1), pp. 2–3), Sir Cecil Clothier could find no evidence to suggest hardship caused by economies in the public service, though he accepted that it might be too early to tell. He also sounded a warning:

As a people we have come to expect, and in general to get, a very high standard of civil administration giving prompt and accurate attention to our needs . . . It is right that we should try to maintain our standards. But it may be that for a time we shall need to learn to accept that standard of public service which we can afford as a nation, rather than that which we demand as individuals.

The PCA continued: '. . . if I find that a lapse in service has been caused either by uncontrollable difficulties in recruitment or by imposed restraints on resources, I will not necessarily feel justified in criticizing a department which is doing its best in difficulties; but I shall certainly want to be sure it is doing its best.' In 1981 he received cases where poor service could not, in his opinion, be ascribed to maladministration:

In two complaints . . . against the Land Registry . . . I found that . . . there had been unacceptable delay in dealing with applications due to a combination of a considerable increase of work with constraints on man-power and financial resources . . . The hard-pressed staff of the Land Registry had been doing all they could to minimise the inconvenience to the public, and satisfied me that the fundamental cause of the delay illustrated by these complaints could not reasonably be attributed to maladministration in the department . . . A somewhat similar situation was responsible for delay by the [DOE] in dealing with an application for a grant towards the cost of repairing a church . . . I [found] that the small number of inspectors and other staff available for this branch of the Department's work meant that they had been unable to keep pace with the steadily rising workload in the last few years and I could only conclude that the delay in this instance was largely caused by resource problems beyond the control of the Department. [HC 258 (1981/2), p. 14.]

Similar cases emerged in the NHS. Despite the Health Commissioner's follow-up into delays at a hospital accident department (above), the same department was again the subject of investigation in 1981. This time a 77-year-old woman had to wait four hours for treatment. Sir Cecil Clothier, who considered the delay 'far too long', discovered once again that 'such delays were not exceptional'. But in neither case was the delay due to maladministration:

In this and the earlier case . . . the delay arose primarily from the fact that only one [doctor] was on duty. No additional medical staff had been appointed in the year's interval between the events of the two cases, but I was satisfied that the need for additional staff continued to be recognised. I concluded that the unimproved position resulted not from maladministration by the [Area Health Authority] but essentially from financial constraints and the need to assess priorities between competing demands for additional posts. This was not a matter for me to resolve. [HC 419 (1981/2), p. 15.]

Compare this analysis with the 'Crossman Catalogue' (above) where, to use a single example, 'delay' is itself defined as maladministration. The catalogue suggests a notional standard of 'good administration' which dictates speedy decision-taking. For Sir Cecil Clothier, however, 'unacceptable delay' does not per se constitute maladministration. It must 'reasonably be attributed to maladministration' and not to 'resource problems beyond the control of the Department'. The elasticity of 'maladministration' allowed earlier ombudsmen to expand their jurisdiction. The same concept permits another, working in a changed economic climate, to apply the brakes. Like judicial review, ombudsman intervention can *contract*.

Are these external monitors of marginal significance? Certainly, in assessing the contribution of ombudsmen, more attention needs to be paid to their effects on the administrative process.[21] Given the present financial constraints, ombudsmen may seem luxuries, destined to play a less forceful role. Or perhaps they perform another function, of particular significance in the present climate? Like adjudicatory procedures, ombudsmen may provide 'symbolic reassurance'. One way of dealing with grievances is to persuade complainants that they lack justification.[22] Sir Cecil Clothier tells us:

As in previous years, slightly less than half of all the complaints submitted to a full investigation were upheld. But all complainants received a report containing a careful and exhaustive account of the facts and circumstances from which the complaint arose, written in the plainest language I could contrive. For most people this reassurance is as valuable as a favourable judgment. [HC 258 (1981/2), p. 1.]

8
Passing time, or how administrators apply the rules

The following case study, which traces a series of investigations into complaints about the handling of land compensation, illustrates the discussion in Chapter 7. We will encounter an extremely complex set of interactions taking place over a considerable time-period, involving central departments and local authorities, two sets of ombudsmen, and parliamentarians performing both their checking and legislative functions. The material provides another reason for studying our ombudsmen. They may not secure that long sought-after 'control', but they provide a window through which to view government. Despite the PCA's new practice of publishing only selected cases, ombudsmen's findings, unlike the Law Reports, contain a wealth of information about how public administration is carried on. Here, for instance, we will see how rules are actually administered, a governmental function or output structure which lawyers tend to ignore. Evidence will be found of bureaucratic attachment to Weber's model of administration through rules. This produces conflict with MPs who, pressing constituents' cases, sometimes demand individuation.

The Land Compensation Act 1973 introduced some new compensation schemes. S.29 as amended provided home loss payments (HLPs) for the personal upset and distress occasioned to people obliged by a public authority to move from their homes through compulsory acquisition, the making of a housing order, improvement or redevelopment. The Act required that the displacement be permanent, that the claimant had lived in the dwelling for five years and that he possess some interest or tenancy (including a council tenancy) in the property. The sum payable was calculated at 3 × rateable value without interest. Part I of the Act allowed depreciation payments (DPs) to the owners of property adversely affected by physical factors like noise and fumes emanating from 'public works', usually a highway, opened after October 1969. The amount of compensation payable by the relevant highway authority was negotiable, disputes being referred to the Lands Tribunal. In England, the highway authority for trunk roads and motorways was generally the Department of the Environment (DOE) while for local roads, the relevant council. This statutory division of responsibility meant that complaints to ombudsmen initially went in two different directions: to the PCA and to the CLA.

Both schemes imposed time-limits for making claims. HLP applications had to be submitted within six months of displacement; but people moving between October 1972 and May 1973 had until November 1973 to claim. For DPs the claim period commenced one year after the public works came into use and continued for two years thereafter. If the works had come into use between October 1969 and June 1973 the claim period was extended for two years until June 1975. In Standing Committee (HC SCA 1972/3, cols. 3–520) the Government justified the restrictions on the basis that public bodies should be able to achieve finality on items of expenditure. Neither scheme imposed a duty on local authorities or central government to notify possible claimants of their rights nor made the time-limits for claims conditional on a prescribed level of publicity. The original White Paper, 'Development and Compensation – Putting People First' (Cmnd 5124), stressed that 'People threatened by, or suffering from the effect of public works must be told, in an understandable way, their rights and the help which is available to them.' MPs generally agreed. The particular, foreseeable difficulty was that, because it would take some time for the public to become familiar with the novel types of compensation, some would claim out of time. Mr Eldon Griffiths (HC SCA 1972/3, col. 156), speaking for the Government, was reassuring:

I doubt very much that people will fail to make claims because they do not know . . . Even if one person has not noticed the Bill, it is extremely unlikely that none of his neighbours will have noticed and know about it . . . We shall do our utmost to see that the public is made fully aware of their rights in the matter.

The DOE issued a press notice and a series of booklets covering different aspects of the legislation was made available free from local authorities, CABs and the DOE's regional offices. The DOE also despatched a series of circulars to local authorities urging them to take additional measures. For example, circular No. 160/74 stated: 'local authorities are asked to take all necessary steps to ensure that those concerned are made aware of their rights in ample time to make their [HLP] claims.' So there was often extra publicity at the local level but this, as subsequent ombudsman investigations disclosed, was of variable quality.

By 1974, local authorities were receiving large numbers of HLP claims from people otherwise entitled but out of time. Some wished to meet these claims but lacked the statutory authority to do so. Members and officers who agreed to pay might be asked to refund the money if the district auditor decided to obtain a declaration that the payment was contrary to law (see *Roberts* v. *Hopwood* below, p. 321). A number of authorities therefore asked the Environment Minister to exercise his discretion under s.161(1) of the Local Government Act 1972 (now s. 19 (1) of the Local Government Finance Act 1982) to sanction the making of ex gratia payments. This sanction protected authorities from the district auditor.

By May 1975, the DOE had granted 685 of 1,039 sanction applications. Mrs Butler used an adjournment debate (HC Deb. vol. 892, cols. 1791–1802) to press the cases of two constituents where sanction had been refused. Both had been unaware of their HLP entitlement until after the claim-period had expired. Mrs Butler argued that such persons ought to be directly informed of their rights. She pressed the DOE to explain the criteria for determining sanction applications and to change its decision. Mr Oakes, for the Government, declined:

Some limit needed to be set on the claim period, for practical reasons . . . It would have been very difficult, and in some cases virtually impossible, to establish the validity of a claim made long after the facts of the original displacement had become obscure. Nor would it have been reasonable to impose a duty on authorities to inform claimants of their entitlements . . . Authorities do not, by any means, rehouse all potential claimants. Many move out of the area entirely and cannot be traced. Moreover, many potential claimants may be quite unknown to the authority – for example, private tenants . . . [The sanction powers] are used in only the most exceptional circumstances and only after the individual circumstances of each case have been thoroughly and carefully examined . . . If section 161 were . . .

extensively applied, the effect would be virtually a circumvention of statute – in short, legislation by administration. I am sure that no Hon. Member on either side of the House would willingly sanction that . . . Sanction has been given [in] nearly 70 per cent of the applications . . . These figures show that we have not been either unreasonable or ungenerous in our decisions. We have, however, taken the view that simple ignorance of the home loss provisions is not in itself a sufficient justification for sanctioning . . . The circumstances of the individual claimant must have been such that it would have been unreasonable to expect him to make a claim within the six months' period . . . One obvious example would be a case in which the claimant had been seriously ill . . . But it is difficult to generalise; every case has to be looked at on its merits.

This reply is based on the conventional hierarchy of legal norms; that is, administrative decisions cannot over-ride legislation. It discloses some of the internal criteria developed for the exercise of the discretionary power, although the final comment suggests that in this instance decision-taking was weighted more towards discretion than to rules. Meanwhile the PCA had received a similar case. The complainant had seen no press publicity nor received any information about HLPs. Initially unaware of his rights, he had claimed out of time. Sir Alan Marre's investigation (HC 496 (1975/6), p. 75) threw fresh light on the DOE's criteria but he declined to question the refusal to sanction:

The [minister] seeks to satisfy himself that [sanction] is justified in the particular circumstances of each case . . . This general approach is not unreasonable . . . the Department explained . . . that while they would think it appropriate to give sanction . . . where there was a strong presumption of maladministration on the part of the local authority, they did not see the complainant's case in that light . . . the 1973 Act imposed no duty on the local authority to inform claimants of their rights and an authority could not be said to have been in default if they had not done so. Even those authorities who had a policy of informing claimants, as far as possible, in accordance with the Department's recommendations in their circular might not all have adopted the method of individual notifications to claimants but might have used more general publicity locally. And other authorities might (in disregard of the Department's guidance) have taken no steps at all . . . In these circumstances they thought it would be likely to aggravate the problem of anomalies if they were to sanction [simply because a] claimant who was time-barred . . . had not been notified individually by his local authority whose general policy it had been to inform potential claimants of their rights.

The Department [emphasised] the need to ensure that decisions on all late claims were consistent . . . To that end . . . they had adopted criteria which . . . allowed payment to people who could not reasonably have been expected to make a claim within time; and the Department added that they would be prepared also to consider favourably a case where a claimant had been

misinformed or misled by the local authority into believing they had no right
to claim. In the light of these criteria they had reconsidered the complainant's
case but . . . they reaffirmed their view that it would be wrong to treat him
exceptionally and allow payment. They added that his case . . . was by no
means unique and told me they could not look at it in isolation. To allow it
simply because he had not been informed by the Council of his eligibility
would be . . . effectively to allow the express provisions of the [statute] to be
circumvented . . . I am satisfied that they have reached this conclusion after
full consideration of the arguments and without maladministration. It follows
that, under the terms of Section 12(3) of the Parliamentary Commissioner
Act, I am not entitled to question their decision. I can only report that
unfortunate and seemingly harsh outcome that the complainant has suffered
as a result of an acknowledged administrative failure by the Council to give
full effect to their intention to implement the Departmental guidance on
notifications, and that the Department's decision makes it impossible for
them to remedy this.

The DOE's response illustrates how consistency demands rules.
Does its description of the decision-making process differ from that of
Mr Oakes? We find that the introduction of discretion, in the guise of
'selective enforcement', is not the only administrative method of
mitigating the harsh effects of rules. A secondary system of rules can
be established for dealing with hard cases. Here the statutory
discretion to grant sanction is structured by administrative rules in
order to deal with claims falling outside the statutory rules contained
in the land compensation schemes. There are rules and more rules.

Sir Alan Marre also took a lenient view (HC 223 (1976/7), p. 33) of
DOE attempts to publicize DPs. The DOE was the highway
authority for a motorway opened in 1972. Because the complainant
had sold his house (moving some miles away) a special one-year
time-bar applied. He alleged that owing to defective publicity of this
particular provision, he had applied too late. Sir Alan found that the
original press notice had not dealt with the point and that the local
press, in reporting DPs, had, contrary to the terms of a subsequent
press notice, stated that residents 'could' (not 'should') apply at that
time. A third notice had omitted any reference to claims for works
opened between 1969 and 1972. The complainant's position was only
brought to public attention three months before his claim-period
elapsed, and then only briefly in one of the booklets. Sir Alan
criticized the terms of the first and third notices but argued that it was
not the DOE's fault that the local press had got the second notice
wrong. He declined to find maladministration causing injustice:

I accept the Department's view that it was reasonable to rely on general publicity to reach people who, like the complainant, had moved from the area . . . If [the complainant] had written to the Department . . . to find out when he would be able to claim, the Department should have been able to advise him about the limits on his entitlement to compensation . . . But he took no action . . . Although I consider the Department's measures to secure publicity about the [particular time-limit] to have been unsatisfactory, I find that the shortcomings in their publicity . . . were not sufficient to relieve the complainant of the responsibility for making his claim in time. I sympathise with him over the failure of his claim, and for their contribution to his loss of eligibility, the Department have asked me to apologise to him, which I am glad to do.

Another complainant (HC 223 (1976/7), p. 37) did take action. He had lived on a road which served as an access route to a newly opened motorway. Traffic increased and he decided to sell. He complained that the DOE's regional office gave him inadequate advice and information. When he informed the office of his intention to sell he was apparently assured that there was no need to worry because it could take years to settle claims. Shortly afterwards, he received a booklet which did not explain the impact of sale on entitlement to claim but did refer to the general time-limit. The complainant accepted that he should have noticed this. The DOE gave three reasons for refusing to meet his subsequent claim: (a) there was no provision for depreciation flowing from intensification of existing use; it had to be caused by physical factors arising on a stretch of new or altered road; (b) the complainant applied six weeks after the general time-period had expired; (c) in his particular case, he ought to have claimed before he sold his property. Was the DOE's original failure to make the complainant aware of this last fact maladministration causing injustice? The PCA concluded:

The Department take the view, with which I do not quarrel as a general principle, that the onus is on the individual to inform himself of what he may claim and how . . . There is uncertainty about what transpired when he telephoned them . . . [However] I see no grounds for doubting the complainant's assertion that [he indicated his intention to sell]. The Department had made inadequate arrangements for dealing with such inquiries and as a result the complainant was not sent the informative material about how, in his particular circumstances, he should proceed . . . the fact that he overlooked the [general] closing date . . . for claims and did not submit his own claim [in time] must obviously prompt the question whether he would have paid any more attention to a warning about an earlier date. But the Department were in my view clearly at fault in not sending him the material relevant to his own circumstances.

The Department should accept that they failed to provide all the relevant information that could be reasonably expected. This they have now done and they have asked me to express, on their behalf, their regret for this.

[I invited] the Department to examine the complainant's claim again in the light of that conclusion. The Department told me that even if they had been able to accept his claim at the time, any compensation payable by them might well have been an almost nominal sum because it appeared to them that much of the nuisance suffered would have been due . . . to increased traffic on the A road to and from the new works; and that would be a matter not for them but for the County Council, the highway authority for the A road. They also indicated that they had received many late claims which were equally deserving but that they had taken a firm line in not admitting them. Because of the justifiable uncertainty about what the complainant would have done if he had been sent [the correct information] and the degree of injustice he is likely to have suffered, I decided not to press [them] further.

In these cases the PCA uses notions familiar to lawyers. In the first case he emphasizes the complainant's fault; in the second he raises the issues of causation and quantification of loss. There is a common thread. The statute does not require the DOE to inform people of their rights. Who then ought to take the risk if people, unaware of their entitlement, fail to claim in time? The PCA adopts the departmental view and places the responsibility for securing information on the individuals concerned.

By this time, some people were trying another route. An adverse CLA report would not remove the need for sanction, but the DOE might be more sympathetic. In *Christchurch* (Inv. 2712H of 27/9/77) council tenants were rehoused in August 1974 but, not having been informed of their possible eligibility, only claimed HLPs in 1976. Officials explained that until a High Court decision in March 1975, it was unclear whether council tenants rehoused in other council accommodation qualified for HLPs. Mr Harrison gave two reasons for finding maladministration causing injustice. First, he noted that even after the judgment no action was taken by the officers to inform either the Housing Committee or any rehoused tenants of its consequences. This conclusion is surprising because the High Court decision was handed down more than six months after the complainants were displaced. How then could the subsequent omissions of the officers cause injustice to the complainants? Secondly, in contrast to the PCA, Mr Harrison stated that because the legislative scheme was complex and it was difficult for the ordinary citizen to understand his rights, the authority concerned had a clear responsibility correctly to inform those affected by its actions of any entitlement to compensation. Since, prior to the court decision, the complainants' entitlement to compensation was unclear, this amounted to a finding of maladministration without fault. A tough line was also taken by Baroness Serota. In *Elmbridge* (Inv. 2832S of 2/3/77) the authority misled the complainant into believing that she would be entitled to a HLP even if she was rehoused prior to a demolition order. The DOE refused sanction and Baroness Serota duly found maladministration causing injustice, rejecting Elmbridge's contention that it was unreasonable to expect the officers concerned to know the relevant legal provisions. In *Ealing* (Inv. 2385S of 14/7/76) the council's housing visitor had visited the complainant, Mr Farrar, a private tenant in a house which the council later purchased. His rehousing requirements were discussed but the officer did not mention compensation. Mr Farrar then received a letter offering him a council tenancy but, despite circulars like 160/74, it made no mention of HLPs. He moved and subsequently found himself 11 days out of time when, after hearing from another tenant that HLPs were available, he eventually claimed. Baroness Serota concluded:

The Council failed to inform the claimant and this amounted to maladministration causing the complainant injustice in that his claim for a home loss payment was out of time as a result . . . [It is] of paramount importance that persons whose homes are being affected by the actions of public bodies should be clearly told by those bodies what their rights are and what type of compensation if any is available.

Reactions to the reports varied. In *Christchurch* the council sought and obtained DOE sanction to compensate the complainants and other tenants in a similar position. In *Elmbridge* the authority risked the wrath of the District Auditor by making a payment without sanction. Ealing, armed with the Commissioner's report, sought sanction to pay the sum to which Mr Farrar would have been entitled. The DOE refused. Since this decision was outside the jurisdiction of the CLA, Mr Farrar went to his MP, Sir George Young. The DOE's response to Sir George's representations suggests that it considered that Baroness Serota had gone too far. Because there was no statutory duty to inform, an omission to do so could not warrant sanction (HC Deb. vol. 929, col. 1505):

To authorise an *ex gratia* payment simply because he had not been informed by the Council of his eligibility would be effectively to allow the express provision of the Land Compensation Act, 1973, to be circumvented, tantamount to legislation by administration. It would both conflict with the general intention of legislation under which sanction can be given and would give rise to other anomalies.

This reply, affirming the position as described by Mr Oakes and explained to Sir Alan Marre, is a reminder that a high regard for legality may operate against the citizen as well as in his favour. Harlow (1977, p. 304) commented, 'this particular case provides ammunition for those who argue that the place of administrative law in the administrative process should be strictly limited. It hints at the formalism and rigidity which may result from too close an attention to legality, and which may itself amount to maladministration'. In the ensuing adjournment debate (HC Deb. vol. 929, cols. 1502–12), Sir George Young argued:

[The reply] is . . . total nonsense. Basically, the Department is saying, first, that if it rectifies this injustice, it will suffer the administrative inconvenience of having to rectify other similar injustices as well, and secondly, that it would conflict with the general intention of the legislation. This is clearly untrue. The general intention of legislation was that Mr Farrar should have a payment for home loss, and that the local authorities should notify those involved of their rights to such payments. To imply that it is the will of the House that Mr Farrar should be denied his payment is quite obviously unrealistic since all hon. Members would react as I have done if a case like this was brought to them.

Sir George then played the card provided by Sir Alan Marre's earlier investigation. The DOE had told the PCA that it sanctioned payment in cases where there was a strong presumption of maladministration; yet here, in the face of a positive finding of maladministration, it had refused. Was this not a departure from departmental criteria? The Minister promised to investigate and subsequently the DOE granted sanction. Meanwhile, Sir George had directed Mr Farrar to a new PCA. Sir Idwal Pugh's investigation (HC 126 (1977/8), p. 40) disclosed more about the DOE's policy:

The [DOE] consider each case on its merits against a set of criteria approved by Ministers. These do not include simple ignorance of the time-limit as in itself a sufficient justification for sanctioning. I accept that this general approach is a reasonable one. [Sir Idwal referred to the DOE's previous admission to the PCA and continued:]

At the end of 1975 the Department had discussed this issue [with the CLA] but had not concluded that such a finding [of maladministration causing injustice] should lead automatically to sanction . . . In their view to do so would mean that a Local Commissioner could override the [minister's] discretionary powers . . . Against [the strong presumption] they had to weigh . . . the need to avoid abrogation of [his] powers in favour of the Local Commissioner, and the danger of granting sanction inconsistently and thus producing further and wider anomalies.

Two can play the legal game. Replying to Sir George, the DOE argued that to sanction payments because claimants were not told of their rights would, in effect, place on authorities a duty to inform when, statutorily, none exists. Here it points out that the Minister must not 'fetter his discretion' by delegating his powers (see Chapter 11). The contentions are connected. In *Ealing*, Baroness Serota considered that a failure to inform constituted maladministration causing injustice; to grant sanction automatically for an adverse CLA finding might undermine the DOE's position.

The DOE also disclosed to Sir Idwal that it had 'refined' the sanction criteria. Following the adjournment debate, ministers were apparently disturbed both about the particular case and that the established criteria could produce such a result. Previously the DOE had sanctioned where it considered that the claimant had been misinformed or misled. Ministers and officials had now agreed that where the CLA had found maladministration causing injustice and it was 'arguable' that the claimant had been misled, he should get the benefit of the doubt. So the criteria were altered but without conceding either that ignorance sufficed or that the CLA should have the final say. Applying the 'refinement', the DOE had granted Ealing sanction. Sir Idwal concluded inconclusively:

I recognise that the Department gave prolonged and careful consideration in this case. I have no doubt that they took into account the 'strong presumption' . . . The Department's decision in the end to sanction . . . is a satisfactory outcome and justifies [the] complaint to me. I am dismayed however that so much effort was necessary to achieve this result.

Meanwhile, the Select Committee on the PCA was discussing Sir Alan Marre's original investigation. Sir Robert Marshall (Second Permanent Secretary at the DOE) held the departmental line (HC 524 (1976/7), pp. 10–11):

We drew up criteria which we tried to make conform with the Act. Since the Act had not placed a duty on anybody to inform people who were eligible for this compensation payment obviously we could not make that one of the criteria. We did, however, think it right if a person has been very ill indeed and unable to read newspapers and keep himself informed, he could not be expected to make his claim in time. That was a fairly easy one. We also thought that if he had been in some way misinformed or misled by a public authority that this should be a criterion. If there had been misinterpretation of the statute in some way or other which had led to mis-information, we thought that that should be a criterion. We drew up fairly rigorous criteria of this kind which were explained in broad terms to the House. We have stood on that and, standing on that, we have scrutinised now something like 2,600 applications, so you can see the need for some consistency and the need for some guidelines for the staff dealing with these applications, and we have approved something like 2,000 and 500 or 600 have been disallowed and the complainant's case is one of those disallowed. He had been ill during the earlier part of the time. This was not pressed as an incapacitating illness, so it did not meet the criterion on that score. He had not been misinformed . . . If you just ignore the time limit and say that ignorance of the time limit makes no difference whatsoever to your entitlement then you are circumventing that aspect of the legislation.

Sir Robert promised to dispatch yet another circular urging authorities to inform people of their rights. But once again he pleaded the legal limitations on central government's powers:

[The DOE has already given] a number of quite clear but not very forceful pieces of advice, trying to keep on the right side of the law because local authorities might have some reason to complain if the Government, so to speak, makes an obligation of something which is not an obligation . . . I am not playing with words. I have to administer the statute and we are urging on local authorities that [informing people] is the right thing to do. We cannot enforce it. If they challenge us they will be right under the law . . . I do not think that we can make this retrospective. They have acted in full knowledge of the law and have kept within the law.

Sir Robert is arguing that administrators apply the rules but must not make them. He did concede that it would help to amend the law, placing the onus for informing on the authority so that if the information was not imparted, a payment could be made. The Committee duly recommended that 'urgent consideration should be given to introducing appropriate amending legislation to this effect'. This suggestion, if implemented, would have undercut the DOE's initial opposition to a statutory duty to inform and its subsequent attempts to head off outflanking movements. It soon made it clear that Sir Robert's concession was withdrawn. The promised circular (No. 75/77) reminded local authorities that the HLP scheme had generated a series of adverse CLA findings and urged them to action:

3. While the legislation does not place an obligation on authorities to notify claimants, nevertheless the Commissioners have found maladministration on the part of authorities not so much because people were not individually notified but rather because the authorities' handling was capricious in effect. It follows that, if findings of maladministration are to be avoided in the future, those authorities who have not so far adopted strict arrangements should now consider doing so. In any event all authorities are recommended to review their arrangements to make sure that they are working effectively and that a policy of individual notification is consistently maintained . . .

5. Where an authority adopts a new or adjusted policy on the basis of this

circular, it is recommended that not only should it be applied to those people displaced from that date but also to those displaced within the preceding six months who are still within the claim period.

6. Any extra work resulting from the adoption of new or improved procedures may well be compensated by a diminution of correspondence with 'late' claimants and the avoidance of complaints leading to investigation by the CLA.

The CLA welcomed the circular (AR 1977/8, p. 17), expressing the 'hope that it will lead to fewer complaints in the future'. But relate para. 3 to Baroness Serota's analysis in *Ealing*. Does it indicate misinformation, a form of negative administrative reaction to an inconvenient external monitor's decision?

In its observations on the Select Committee's report, the Government emphasized (Cmnd 7098, p. 4) that although a duty to notify potential claimants 'would plainly be helpful in general', it would cause 'practical difficulties':

In many cases the authority would not be in possession of sufficient information to judge whether the person displaced was entitled to a home loss payment; failure to notify might then involve the authority in a breach of statutory duty. There may be no way of completely guaranteeing that everyone is told in time; people may move house without waiting for the authority to require them to go. Nevertheless, so far as this can be done through administrative action, the Department . . .have by . . . circulars taken steps to achieve for the future largely what the Committee recommend. And within those practical considerations mentioned the Department are examining how best to give statutory force to the Committee's fundamental objective at the next legislative opportunity.

Throughout this period the CLA continued to receive complaints about the HLP scheme. Not all adverse investigation reports involved authorities in seeking sanction. Sometimes, for example, as in *Brent* (No. 1) (Inv. 4317S of 18/5/77), a council delayed beyond the statutory period of three months from the date of the claim prescribed for payment. Here the claimant possessed a statutory entitlement which the authority was legally empowered to meet without further ado. But, in other cases, the DOE's policy on sanction had important consequences for the CLA. Although the DOE had not conceded automatic sanction following an adverse investigation report, its concessions had drawn attention to the CLA as a mechanism for obtaining redress. The CLA began to receive cases where the authority seemed prepared to admit maladministration causing injustice but where the DOE had initially refused sanction. In

Lewisham (Inv. 3689S of 9/11/77) the complainant had not wished to move but said that he had been influenced to do so by officers' erroneous assurances (made in good faith) that he was entitled to a HLP. The DOE refused Lewisham's request for sanction. (Why did its own criteria (as disclosed to Sir Alan Marre) not dictate sanction? Did the complainant possess a legal remedy?) Baroness Serota felt compelled to investigate, an adverse finding duly emerged, and an ex gratia payment was made.

Mr Harrison tried to shortcut the investigatory procedure, but in *Reading* (Inv. 3914H of 27/9/77) and *S. Bedfordshire* (Inv. 4415H of 28/9/77) he failed to secure the DOE's cooperation. Of *Reading* he said:

> I suggested to the DOE that they should sanction the Council making an ex gratia payment in lieu of the Home Loss Payment to compensate the complainant for the consequences of the Council's failure and that if they did so, I would exercise my discretion not to investigate the complaint, thus saving time and public funds while securing redress for the complainant. [But] the Department indicated that it was helpful to them to have a Local Commissioner's finding available when a case is considered for sanction. In the interests of the complainant I therefore proceeded with my investigation . . . The Department [also] indicated that a Local Commissioner's investigation may well produce previously unknown facts in a case and against which a request for sanction previously rejected might be reconsidered.

Compelled to investigate, Mr Harrison's adverse conclusions were inevitable, but he avoided resting his findings on a failure to inform. Like judges, ombudsmen sometimes possess more than one string to their bow. The two cases were rather different. In *Reading* the council, because of a muddle, failed to operate its normal procedure of sending forms to all those who might be entitled. In *S. Bedfordshire*, a difference of opinion amongst council officers meant that some council tenants were notified of their rights, while others were not. Reading was criticized for not living up to its own policy. S. Bedfordshire, on the other hand, had fallen short of the bureaucratic ideal of consistency:

> They failed to secure that a uniform procedure for dealing with Home Loss Payments prevailed throughout their area [so] that, while payments were made in one part, [elsewhere] no action was taken . . . This capricious element in implementing the Act was inequitable and the Council should have treated equally all who were eligible.

Expressing disappointment that it was necessary to investigate cases where councils admitted fault, Mr Harrison (AR 1977/8,

p. 118) tried another, less direct, route. He acted as an information conduit to councils:

I have been advising . . . authorities who wish to make ex gratia payments without incurring the expense and trouble of an investigation about the criteria used by the Department when determining applications.

The CLA took on yet another new role. Hoping to reduce delays, it discussed sanction criteria with officials (AR 1977/8, p. 17). Again the DOE refused to budge: to grant sanction automatically following an adverse investigation report 'would fetter . . . discretion and be contrary to the law'.

At this point Harlow complained:

The departmental policy was bound to result in 'capriciousness', 'anomalies', in inequality and injustice. It was administratively expensive, in that it involved the staff of the DOE in making individual decisions in cases which could have otherwise been rapidly disposed of. Worse still, it led the DOE, totally misconceiving the role of the CLA, in effect to involve the CLA in the work of administration, by insisting that it should act as a 'filter' in assessing the complaints. An expensive 'judicial' decision was virtually made a prerequisite for payment . . . The DOE could easily have resolved these administrative anomalies if, when the excessive number of time-based complaints first came to light, they had immediately reconsidered their policy. An 'amnesty' could have been declared, and consideration given by local authorities to all applications on their merits. In this case, the economy argument is a weak one, because, if all the applications had been made in time, the funds to satisfy them would have been forthcoming, and a government given to lamenting the low level of 'take-up' of social service benefits ought to have realised this and been prepared to concede the point. Thus the failure to re-examine their policy in the face of widespread and informed criticism does seem to be attributable to stubbornness and does seem to amount to the sort of 'ineptitude' and 'incompetence' which Mr. Crossman included in his definition of maladministration. [Harlow 1977, p. 305.]

Do you agree? The saga was far from over. At least one local authority tried to make up time-barred HLPs by using alternative powers. In *Brent* (No. 2) (Inv. 125/S/77 of 7/11/77) council tenants moved because of a housing improvement scheme. They claimed to have been misled into believing that they would obtain a HLP when they decided not to return to their former home after the improvements had been completed. The problem was that Brent's housing manager and valuation officer had interpreted s.29(3A) of the 1973 Act in different ways. The subsection provides that 'a person shall not be treated as displaced from a dwelling in consequence of . . . the carrying out of any improvement . . . unless he is permanently

displaced from it in consequence of . . . the improvement in question.'
The manager's interpretation of the phrase 'permanently displaced'
was that it only required that the move be actually permanent; the
valuation officer believed that the tenants must not have been given
the option of returning. Brent's chief solicitor favoured the valuation
officer's view and so the tenants were refused H L Ps. Brent accepted
that the initial advice had been misleading. It turned to s.37(5) of the
Act, which permits discretionary 'disturbance' payments to cover the
reasonable moving expenses of tenants who move temporarily.
Members were advised that under s.38 these payments could not be
used to compensate for H L P ineligibility but must represent a
contribution towards reasonable expenses; any further payment
could be challenged on audit. Baroness Serota noted, 'in recognition
of the disappointment experienced by the complainants . . . [Brent]
applied the most generous interpretation possible to the disturbance
payments they have made'. But these totalled £83 whereas the
complainants, anticipating a H L P, had spent over £250 furnishing
their new home. The Commissioner concluded, 'I appreciate
[Brent's] action but the fact remains that the complainants are still
considerably out of pocket as a direct result of being misled by the
Council'. Brent duly paid the balance. What was the maladministration here? Do you agree with the valuation officer's interpretation?
(There has been no relevant reported case.) Should Baroness Serota
have advised on the point?

In mid-1977, with the Representative Body's support, the C L A
made an urgent recommendation to the Minister (A R 1977/8, p. 16).
Stressing the particular difficulties which had arisen over sanctioning
H L Ps, it proposed that, after an adverse C L A report, an authority,
if it wished to make a payment, should be empowered to do so without
the need to obtain sanction. This suggestion became the subject of a
private member's Bill introduced by Mr Clemitson, a member of the
P C A's Select Committee. The Government decided to adopt the Bill
which became the Local Government Act 1978. S.1 provides that
where a commissioner has issued a report finding maladministration
causing injustice, then, if

. . . on consideration of the report, it appears to the authority that a payment
should be made to, or some other benefit should be provided for, a person who
has suffered injustice in consequence of maladministration referred to in the
report, the authority may incur such expenditure as appears to them to be
appropriate in making such a payment or providing such a benefit.

Which of the cases so far discussed would be affected by this provision? And what legal difficulties might authorities face if they decided (see *S. Bucks* below) to pay a sum in excess of a time-barred HLP? It is important to note that the CLA's filtering role is not affected because an adverse investigation report is made the *condition precedent* to the exercise of the statutory power.

A number of cases emphasize this. First, *Islington* (Inv. 1004/S/77 of 6/11/78), where Baroness Serota elaborated the extent of an authority's obligation to seek out facts when determining entitlements. Islington decided to purchase the complainant's property but, while considering whether to rehouse him, enquiries were made, particularly of his tenant A, which led the Authority to believe that he was no longer living there. It refused to rehouse him. Subsequently the complainant claimed a HLP but the responsible official, the borough valuer, decided that he did not meet the residence qualification. Baroness Serota declined to find maladministration causing injustice, declaring that there was an adequate factual basis for the decision. (Compare Austin's formulation of a 'substantial evidence' rule for judicial review of discretionary power (see below, p. 332).)

[The Borough Valuer] told the Commission's officer that before he decided the complainant's application he made the following normal checks (a) checked with the Electoral Roll and the complainant's name was not shown at his house; (b) checked the Housing Department's correspondence which showed the Borough Housing Officer was not satisfied that the complainant lived at his house; and (c) checked Miss A's claim form for Home Loss Payment and the complainant's address was shown at Welwyn Garden City. This satisfied the Borough Valuer that the complainant was not entitled to payment and he made no other enquiries. The issue was a matter of fact, not a matter of law, so he did not refer it to the Borough Solicitor . . . I find . . . that the Council made reasonable enquiries and had sufficient information on which to make this decision. Accordingly, I find no maladministration . . .

Secondly, there are those cases where an authority concedes maladministration causing injustice, expresses its willingness to make an ex gratia payment, but feels compelled to wait for an investigation report containing what, in reality, is an inevitable finding. On the other hand, *S. Bucks* (Inv. 618/H/79 of 26/8/80) suggests that the 1978 Act has led to some complainants obtaining compensation where, previously, they would have failed. The Authority accepted that it had not met the complainant's valid HLP claim until 23 days after the three-month time-period for paying out had expired. It further conceded maladministration in that although the complainant had been informed verbally about the availability of HLPs, this was not confirmed to him in writing, so leading him to delay making his claim (although he had still submitted it in time). The Authority had apologized and had introduced a practice manual detailing the procedures to be followed in the future. It pointed out to Mr Harrison that the complainant had received no compensation for its delay, for his out-of-pocket expenses in pressing the matter, and for the worry and stress of the affair. The Authority informed the Commissioner that it wanted to make an additional payment of £75 but had no power to do so except under the 1978 Act. How does its second concession of maladministration compare with Baroness Serota's reasoning in *Ealing*? Prior to the 1978 Act, would the DOE have sanctioned payment (a) before the CLA issued an adverse report (b) after that event? Forced once more to play a filtering role, Mr Harrison did as little as he could. His investigation report did not probe the Authority's concessions but merely rubber-stamped them.

A storm was also brewing elsewhere. The PCA upheld a complaint (HC 598, 1977/8) that the DOE, the relevant highway authority, had failed to provide adequate publicity of DPs, so causing claims to be time-barred. The complainants lived on Rochester Way, Bexley, an old road which, after improvement, came back into use in 1971. Thus the retrospective provisions of the DP scheme applied, the time-period for claims expiring in June 1975. Sir Idwal Pugh came across a departmental circular to DOE local offices issued in November 1973:

Instructions were included about publicity for claims to the Department arising from future schemes and for those existing roads attracting the retrospective provisions. For the former, local offices were required to insert a Public Notice in the local press on two occasions, at the road's opening and a year later. For the Department's roads covered by the retrospective provisions and which were likely to give rise to claims they were required to publish one Notice in local newspapers. No indication was given when that Notice should be issued. The Circular carried, as annexes, draft Notices which Departmental offices were to use . . . [These] included the closing date for claims for new schemes but not for existing roads.

A model of obedience, the local office had inserted one such notice in the local press in July 1974. In 1973 the DOE had initiated a national publicity campaign about the retrospective provisions of the HLP scheme which expired in that year. The PCA discovered that a similar campaign had been intended for the retrospective provisions concerning D Ps and that provision had been made in the department's publicity estimates of 1975/6 for the insertion of paid advertisements in the national press during the two months prior to the closing date. However these were cancelled in March 1975 as a result of cuts in public expenditure. Instead the DOE decided to issue a press notice.

On 4 June the Department issued a Press Notice about the closing date for claims under the retrospective provisions and brief items appeared in two national daily newspapers . . . I know from other investigations that similar reports appeared in some local newspapers but none of these circulated in the vicinity of Rochester Way. There is no evidence of any consideration being given to additional measures in the event of the Press Notice attracting little publicity. And by selecting early June as the appropriate time for the issue of the Notice, the Department gave themselves no time to consider the position again before the closing date . . .

The Department have from the outset accepted an obligation to see that people entitled to claim compensation under Part 1 of the Act were aware of their rights. This was emphasised at all stages of the legislation and was given particular emphasis by Ministers in the Department.

There would have been considerable difficulty in getting in touch with all potential claimants and I am satisfied that Ministers were under no misapprehension that general notification through individual letter boxes was not contemplated. Effective publicity was to be the means of achieving the Department's goal.

There is no statutory obligation on the Department to issue any Public Notice. But their practice has been, in the case of retrospective schemes, to publish on one occasion only. I cannot conclude that this act thoroughly fulfilled the obligation that the Department had themselves accepted.

In the case of Rochester Way the only overt action taken by the Department was to publish one Notice in the local press in July 1974 and this at a time when it is said many people were away on holiday. The form of Notice was far less eye-catching than similar Notices in other parts of the country and it contained no reference to the date by which applications had to be made. I have no evidence that the omission misled anyone but I do not think it was logical to omit the date when it is indicated in notices about current schemes.

The Department themselves clearly recognised that more was needed, because they decided to put paid advertisements in the press to warn people of the terminal date for the submission of claims. Had these been inserted the Department's general publicity would have been beyond criticism, but they were cancelled as part of a cut in information expenditure. I think it is regrettable that the cut should have fallen on a form of expenditure intended to inform people of their rights under statute.

When the Department acquiesced in this reduction they then had to consider alternative action and . . . they again decided on a Press Notice. This would have been satisfactory if it had been carried by the relevant press. In fact it was not and, because this was always a possibility, I think the Department should have monitored results and then have taken alternative action.

I conclude in this case that there was a degree of defective administration on the part of the Department. It was not of major proportions in itself: it amounted in effect to a failure to take all the steps which in my view they should have taken to ensure that all members of the public affected by this particular road were given equal opportunity to be aware of their possible rights to compensation and what they had to do to claim those rights. But, relatively small though that defect may have been, it had the major effect of frustrating the intention of the Act and of Ministers in implementing the Act that people like the complainant should be entitled to claim compensation. That he did not do so is an injustice and was due at least in part to a failure of the Department's administration.

How does Sir Idwal's analysis of the DOE's self-imposed 'obligation' compare with Baroness Serota's view of the HLP scheme in *Ealing*? In what ways might divergent PCA and CLA approaches be justified? Consider Sir Idwal's argument that the DOE should have monitored the results of its press notice. Refer back to Sir Alan Marre's investigations into publicity and DPs. Do the cases suggest that parliamentary commissioners, like judges, sometimes differ in approach? Also compare *Rochester* with *Reading* where the Council had decided to distribute HLP claim forms to all potential claimants. In neither case were the authorities legally required to do so much but in both instances ombudsmen castigated the failure to meet declared policy objectives. *Rochester* illustrates how ombudsmen may become deeply involved in matters of resource allocation. Harlow (above) criticized the DOE's sanction policy for being 'administratively expensive'; choosing a particular method of administration involves decisions about the amounts of time and money to be expended. In *Rochester*, Sir Idwal does not attack the DOE for the sums allocated to compensation payments; he criticizes it for not directing sufficient resources towards the effective implementation of the scheme. But the PCA is also enmeshed in the substantive allocation of resources. The amount of expenditure provided (a) for payments and (b) for administration are interlinked because by saving on the latter, public authorities effectively reduce the number of claims made.

Sir Idwal felt that in the circumstances 'it would be reasonable for the Department to invite the complainant and others similarly placed to submit a claim . . . and consider such claims on an extra-statutory basis . . . This would be fair and humane administration.' However the Department of Transport (DTp), which had assumed responsibility for administering the scheme in 1976, thought otherwise. This time central government was paymaster not supervisor. And while the earlier PCA investigations involving refusal to sanction concerned the exercise of a statutory power under s.161, here no statutory power existed. Would central government exercise its common law power to make payment?[1]

The Department told me that after taking legal advice and that of the Treasury they had concluded that, as the Act clearly laid down a time limit for claims, they could allow claims submitted beyond then only in cases that were clearly exceptional. They argued that to admit claims on a wider basis would be to override by administrative action the expressed will of Parliament which had not made the time limit conditional on any prescribed level of publicity. The publicity given in this case was not in the Department's view significantly different from that given in most other similar cases at the period in question and the case could not, therefore, be distinguished from the generality of late claims on that basis. They maintained that to allow a payment in this and other similar cases would in their view require legislative authority.

For the first time, the PCA invoked s.10(3) of the 1967 Act which provides that if it appears to him that injustice has been caused as a result of maladministration and the injustice has not been or will not be remedied, he may lay before Parliament a special report. Prior to the Select Committee hearing, the DTp produced a local press cutting which had warned residents of the relevant time-limit. The PCA stopped pressing for a remedy in the *Rochester* case itself but, having ascertained that in two further cases, involving the Frimley–Popham and Frimley–Lightwater sections of the M3, the press notice had not been carried by the local press, he argued that his original findings in respect of *Rochester* were still applicable in those cases. Reiterating its position in a memorandum to the Committee (HC 91 (1978/9)), the DTp distinguished as 'exceptional' those cases where ex gratia payments had been made. It gave as an example a case where the department's notice omitted to mention one section of road, a failure which 'could have positively misled people who lived near that section of road into supposing that they had no right to claim'. The Permanent Secretary at the DTp (Sir Peter Baldwin) was summoned to appear. He too refused to budge. He contended that the only special feature in the disputed cases was the lack of interest shown by the local press, a matter over which the department had no control. The department had carried out its obligations by issuing the press notice and the degree of attention it received was a matter for the editors concerned. Sir Peter then made a new argument:

These cases are not exceptional in accordance with the policy which was being consistently pursued on publicity at the time when these matters were administered . . . There have been cases where there were exceptional features, where wrong information was given to the claimant, which has enabled me to say that I think that it clearly was an exceptional case in which it would be right to settle the claim even though the time limit had expired. The contrast between those cases which are exceptional because wrong information is given and these cases which followed exactly the policy of the day and no wrong information was given means that where those were exceptional, these were not and by the rules of Government accounting I do not therefore have the freedom as an official to call upon the use of public funds to make a payment . . . There is a limit to which an accounting officer can go in authorising an ex gratia payment.

The chairman pressed Sir Peter on the content of these internal accounting rules and also inquired whether his position was consistent with other cases of error and misleading advice. He was told that it was:

It is exactly in line with the rules laid down in Government accounting, as interpreted and expressed by the Treasury, and endorsed by repeated expressions of view over the years by the Public Accounts Committee [PAC]. The doctrine is that an ex gratia payment can be made if the circumstances are genuinely exceptional . . . If there is a class of cases which I chose to try to treat as suitable for ex gratia payments, then I could start a line of expenditure not envisaged in the Act and not endorsed by Parliament, and expressed in Government accounting as to close that option off.

Sir Peter stressed that, if he were to concede ex gratia payments, he would expect to be rapped over the knuckles by the Comptroller and Auditor General and the PAC. Legislation was therefore the only answer. The Committee was unimpressed. It was 'concerned that effect should be given to the will of Parliament' and accused the DTp of ignoring 'Parliament's main intention [which] was that people should be enabled to claim compensation from funds set aside for that purpose'. The Committee continued:

The Department had a duty to ensure that, after the planned paid advertisements were cancelled, adequate publicity was given by some other method to the retrospective provisions of the Act, and they are not satisfied that the degree of publicity which the Department's press notice received in the local newspapers circulating in the Rochester Way area was sufficient to discharge that obligation; still less so in the Frimley–Popham and Frimley – Lightwater cases, where the press notice received no local publicity. A press notice which is not carried by the papers concerned is no substitute for a paid advertisement, and yet the Department apparently failed to monitor whether or not the notice was carried, and Ministers do not appear to have been alerted to the consequences of the cancellation of the advertising campaign. Your Committee consider that the complainants have suffered injustice for which they should be compensated, either by an extra-statutory payment or, if the Department remains of the view that such payments would be improper, by amending the Land Compensation Act so as to enable these claims to be considered.

The latter recommendation bore fruit in October 1979 when the Minister of Transport told MPs (HC Deb. vol. 972 WA, cols. 80–1) that he had accepted the Committee's findings concerning inadequate publicity. Reasserting that 'it would not be right to override by administrative action [i.e. by ex gratia payment] the time-limits laid down by Parliament', he proposed legislation (a) to remove, prospectively, the time-limit on making DP claims and (b) to compensate time-barred claimants 'in cases where, in his view, the publicity was inadequate'.

This announcement received a warm welcome from the Select Committee, emphasis being put on the sums involved. The explanatory memorandum to the ensuing Local Government, Planning and Land (No. 2) Bill estimated the cost of meeting late claims at £4.5 million with an additional £3.4 million in interest payments. Approximately 9,000 late claims were received and accepted in anticipation of the change. Furthermore, the scheme would be improved for the future. Mr Lambie, however, wanted to know whether the PCA had made recommendations to the Government about future publicity. The reply illustrates how Sir Cecil Clothier sees his function:

I do not think we purported to tell them how to advertise or the media which they should use to advertise to the public the rights which Parliament has granted to them. What we did was to say that in this particular case these efforts were not sufficient . . . The characteristics of these roads vary enormously . . . It would be very difficult to lay down a positive set of rules or codes for how to [publicise] and in the end, I do not think probably it would be within my remit to do so. I think one can criticise what has been done when one sees the whole scene, but not lay down guidelines for the future as to how to run the Department. [HC 406/261 (1979/80), p. 4.]

Ss. 112–14 of the Local Government, Planning and Land Act 1980 contain the subsequent amendments to the 1973 Act. Ss. 112 and 114 remove prospectively the time-limits for DPs and HLPs, leaving the general six-year limitation period in their place. S. 113 provides a measure of retrospection for DPs only by laying down that claims which were already time-barred when the Act came into force and which had not previously been met by ex gratia payments may be considered validly made. But s.113(1)c limits the provision to those cases where:

> ... the Minister *is satisfied* that the publicity given to the right to claim compensation in respect of those works and to the period within which and the events before which claims should be made was not such as to make potential claimants sufficiently aware of those matters.

The italicized phrase suggests why s.113 may be a pyrrhic victory for the PCA. Suppose that X, alleging that he claimed late owing to inadequate information, invokes s.113. The Minister decides that there was sufficient publicity. What impact would his determination have on the PCA's capacity to investigate? What other remedies might the complainant have? Might we describe s.113 as an ouster clause?

S.113 applies only if a minister was the relevant highway authority. Where, as in *West Yorkshire* (Inv. 312/C/79 of 11/3/80), a local authority was responsible, complaints about publicity must be directed to the council and then to the CLA. This may confuse claimants; Mr Cook found evidence that some residents had applied to the DOE by mistake. S.113 imposes no duty to inform potential claimants of its provisions. In Standing Committee (HC SCD 1979/80, cols. 523–4, 528–9), Mr Oakes pondered how they would learn of its existence:

> The first [class of claimants] will be those who went to a solicitor or to a surveyor and put in their claim to the local authority and were then told that they had no claim; or, worse, went to court and were told that they had no claim. They are relatively easily traceable, and so do not present any great difficulty ... The other far more difficult and intractable cases will be those who did not put in their claim ... In those instances the local authority would have no record of the claim ... The primary people who can give assistance are the local authorities. They know what has been done, not only with regard to specific cases coming to them, but also where the development took place [and] whose home and whose land was affected by it ... I plead [with] local authorities to exercise good will and superb public relations by going out and seeking the people in the areas which they know.

Opposition and government shared these sentiments and the Committee was told that the DTp was considering the problem of publicity. But an ensuing DOE circular (No. 8/81) stated tamely: 'Authorities are requested to refer any would-be claimants who may approach them ... to the appropriate office of the Department of Transport.'

Meanwhile, the CLA continued to receive complaints about the HLP scheme. Only the time-limits had been removed and then prospectively. Some cases demonstrate how the CLA plays a part in securing control by elected representatives. Maladministration may be found not only in direct dealings with complainants but also in the handling of issues as between the parts of local government. In order to reach proper decisions, councillors depend on sound reports being presented by officers. If, as in *Blackburn* (Inv. 673/C/80 of 22/7/81), officials fail to place the complainant's case and the possible courses of action before the relevant committee or, as in *Tower Hamlets* (Inv. 551/S/79 of 29/12/80), produce a report which gives no reasons for their recommendation, an adverse investigation report may ensue.

Two cases shed further light on how the scheme is being operated. In *Portsmouth* (Inv. 340/H/78 of 24/1/80) the Council resolved to improve 'Red House', a block of council flats, thereby reducing the size of W's accommodation from three bedrooms to two. W was asked whether he would like to move temporarily or permanently and he chose the latter, moving into a two-bedroomed flat. Contrary to the advice contained in previous DOE circulars, Portsmouth did not inform tenants of their possible rights to HLPs. Nor, in response to circular 75/77 (above), did the Council follow the recommendation contained in para. 5. It decided to inform tenants in the future but not those who, like W, were still within the time-limit when 75/77 arrived. Even after Sir Robert Marshall's assurances to the Select Committee, a gap remained between policy formulation in the DOE and its implementation on the ground. When W subsequently found out about HLPs, Portsmouth rejected his claim as being out of time. He complained to council officials but, in accordance with advice received from the authority's legal department, was told that in any case he had no entitlement because his move was not compulsory. Since W only required a two-bedroomed flat, he had been given the option to return, which he had declined to exercise (compare the valuation officer's reasoning in *Brent* (No. 2)).

Persistent, W approached Mr Harrison, whereupon Portsmouth set in motion its own grievance procedure, a review sub-committee. The Council, concerned about the legal position, wrote to the DOE for clarification. In its reply, the DOE emphasized that the Secretary of State could not give a determination on any point of law, but commented:

Subject to any ruling of the courts . . . where a person chooses not to return to his home after improvements have been carried out, having been given the option to do so, it could hardly be maintained that he had been compelled to leave his home as a result of the Council's action.

Do you agree? The sub-committee duly accepted that W was not entitled to a HLP but found maladministration because the tenants of 'Red House' had not been informed of their potential rights. W's disturbance payment should be increased by £40 and an ex gratia payment of £50 made, compensating him for the inconvenience and upheaval caused. Like Baroness Serota in *Brent (No. 2)*, Mr Harrison did not question the administrators' legal interpretation. However, he continued his investigation in order to determine whether Portsmouth's remedy was adequate. Although he decided it was, his intervention stimulated administrative improvements via the Authority's 'thorough review' of its system for making HLPs. Mr Harrison's inquiries also had a marked 'ripple' effect, prompting Portsmouth to identify 13 further cases of lost HLP entitlement. The Council obtained DOE sanction to compensate in ten. Mr Harrison noted 'payments will be made [in the other three cases] under the Local Government Act 1978 after the issue of my report'. Bearing in mind that the tenants had not complained, did Portsmouth possess statutory power to make these three payments?

Sheffield (Inv. 301/C/80 of 17/12/81), where the council was criticized for not providing sufficient officers to process HLP claims, demonstrates, like *Rochester*, an ombudsman's involvement in the allocation of administrative resources. The Labour-controlled Authority was involved in large-scale slum clearance. In the twelve months commencing May 1980, 44 compulsory purchase order schemes became operative. The scheme involving the complainant, X, concerned 220 properties. She claimed her HLP but, within the three-month period that Sheffield had to meet her claim, complained to Mr Cook that the Council was not processing it. Sheffield explained that valuation officers in the estates surveyor's department, which dealt with HLPs, had been redirected to handle applications to buy council houses arising from the Conservative Government's Housing Act 1980. The Authority, opposed to that legislation, had initially taken no action to implement it, so a backlog of 4,000 'right to buy' applications had developed. After discussions with the Minister, who possessed enforcement powers, the council had agreed to process at least 100 applications per week, so involving its valuation officers in extra work. Mr Cook reported:

The Council said that this increased workload resulted in a dispute between the Council and the staff concerned; temporarily this affected the output of work from their Valuation Sections. They had to re-allocate manpower in the Estates Surveyor's Department in order to comply with the undertaking given to the Minister, to the detriment of other work. In practice four days each week had to be spent on valuing houses for sale and only one working day was left for other work, including valuations for slum clearance. The Council say that some additional work which would normally have been done by their own valuers was undertaken by the District Valuer on their behalf: and that strenuous efforts were being made to minimize the effect of this on persons affected by slum clearance. However, they accept that delays would have occurred until the backlog of work under the right-to-buy provisions had been overcome. Their intention has been to seek to comply with statutory time limits wherever possible . . . [They] point out that they are involved with many other CPOs. They say that from time to time Members have drawn their attention to cases of hardship and they have tried always to give priority to those . . . They have decided to employ four more temporary valuation assistants; they hope that this addition will relieve the pressure of work within the Estates Surveyor's Department and so serve to reduce delays.

The complainant obtained her HLP a few weeks after the three-month period had expired but pointed out that she had had to pay interest on a loan obtained to buy furniture and had suffered distress. Also she was the only person from the 220 properties to have been paid. Mr Cook took a tough line:

The Council have had to wrestle with great problems; the tasks with which they have been faced are formidable, particularly when seen against a background of general constraint in public expenditure. They decided to give priority to the work of selling their houses under the right-to-buy scheme, which led to delays in settling claims from people being moved from clearance areas, delays aggravated by industrial action. Those delays are not yet behind them . . . The Council can argue that in such circumstances the time taken to settle the X's claim was not unreasonable: and I am not out of sympathy with their position. However, I cannot avoid the conclusion that when there is a failure to meet a statutory requirement there is also a presumption of maladministration.[2] In my opinion the X's have suffered some injustice, even as a result of the relatively brief delay in settling their claims; I am glad to note that the interest on their loan may be admissible under the disturbance provisions – and hope that the Council will give sympathetic consideration to some such settlement. Their injustice can be redressed further by paying a sum equating the interest on the home loss payment from the end of the three months period (within which those payments should have been settled) to the date on which the payment was made.

Is *Sheffield*, which emphasizes that administration is not apolitical, a taste of things to come? Where the distribution of administrative resources becomes the stuff of party politics, ombudsmen can be drawn into the political arena. How realistic is Mr Cook's dismissal of arguments about the council's difficulties given the background of fiscal restraint on local authorities and the Minister's pressure on Sheffield to devote resources towards selling council houses? Compare Sir Cecil Clothier's interpretation of maladministration discussed in Chapter 7. Was Sheffield trapped in a Catch-22 situation? Look at the *Norwich* case[3] (below p. 296) for what might have happened had Sheffield not changed priorities. And comparing *Hendy*'s case (below p. 287), try to work out whether X possessed a legal remedy.

In 1980, *Justice* attacked the 1978 Act for not going far enough. It recommended that authorities be given statutory power to make payments 'where the Local Ombudsman certifies that he is satisfied that the payment is in respect of a complaint which would fall within his jurisdiction to investigate' (*Justice* 1980, p. 39). The CLA (AR 1980/1, pp. 45–6) noted that the statute does not empower councils to make payments if, after an internal investigation, maladministration causing injustice is found. In line with its emphasis on local settlements, it proposed that authorities 'should have power to make a payment to remedy an agreed injustice where the Local Commissioner certifies the authority's findings'. It is worth comparing the Representative Body's recommendation (AR 1980/1, p. 62):

... authorities [should have statutory power] in their own right to make compensatory payments when, after their own enquiry, they admit maladministration causing injustice. This would be cost-saving and allow restitution to the aggrieved to be made much quicker, but above all, would respect the right of local authorities to determine their own affairs.

The Government's provisional response[4] was that, given the availability of sanction, no specific power of the type envisaged by the CLA was required. Certainly the need to obtain an adverse investigation report would be diminished if sanction policy were relaxed. But two further investigations suggest that this has not happened. In *Walsall* (Inv. 90/H/80 of 16/6/81) Y took advantage of a vacancy in the larger terraced corner house next door. Eighteen months later, the Council discovered that the terrace foundations were unsafe and resolved on demolition. It rejected Y's HLP claim because, having moved, he had lost his previous five-year residence qualification. The DOE refused Walsall's request for sanction, arguing that 'it appears that [the Ys] were not displaced from their former [home] because of any of the actions by a local authority specified in s.29 . . . There would seem to be no basic entitlement to a [HLP]'. Since Mr Cook did not find maladministration causing injustice, the complainants lost out.

Meanwhile, the PCA (HC 132 (1981/2), p. 38) was still investigating such cases seven years after Sir Alan Marre's original inquiry. A council official determined that Z should be rehoused as quickly as possible for her own safety, owing to the dangerous condition of her roof. The Authority warned Z and offered her alternative accommodation. Alarmed, she promptly moved out. Unfortunately, the closing order had not been made so the Authority was compelled to refuse her HLP claim. Considering it unfair to deny Z compensation when she had been urged to leave a dangerous property, the Authority sought sanction and her MP made representations. The DOE's refusal discloses why in *Ealing* it was eventually prepared to sanction while in *Lewisham* and *Walsall* it was not:

Reasonableness does not in itself justify sanction, because sanctioning expenditure specifically beyond the scope authorised by Parliament could well represent amendment of the law at the discretion of Ministers or 'legislation by sanction'. It is therefore the practice to limit the use of sanction . . . to ex gratia payments where an authority has a clearly defined moral liability to make them . . . There was no suggestion in this case that the Council had a moral obligation to make a payment because their actions had in some way deprived the complainant of an entitlement she would otherwise have had . . . It would not be an appropriate use of the discretionary power of sanction simply to extend the availability of a home loss payment to circumstances beyond those provided for in the legislation.

Sir Cecil Clothier considered that Z should try again:

As I see it, the question of moral liability on the part of the Council rests on whether or not the complainant was compelled by them to leave when she did, and whether in so doing she thereby lost an entitlement which she would otherwise have had. Clearly she would have received a payment like the other residents if she had stayed until December. Nobody disputes that she could have been in grave danger had she chosen to stay in the flat. And it is equally clear that she would not have moved when she did if the Council had not told her of any danger . . . [But] the Department felt unable to sanction a payment . . . I do not criticise [them] for having taken that view. I can see that at the time it was a perfectly proper one from their standpoint. They took due account of all the information then available to them and I find no maladministration in the way they reached their decision not to sanction the proposed payment.

[However], only in the narrowest sense of the word could that move have been regarded as voluntary . . . It would have been quite unreasonable to expect an elderly woman like the complainant to risk serious injury when she

was being strongly advised to move . . . Furthermore . . . at the time she left
. . . the Council had already started action leading towards a closing order. I
therefore put it to the Department that they might like to reconsider their
decision . . . They responded by saying that, if the Council chose to make a
fresh application, they would be prepared to reconsider the matter. It will of
course be for the complainant to ask the Council if they will take such further
action on her behalf. Meanwhile, I regard the Department's willingness to
reconsider the matter as a very satisfactory outcome of my investigation.

To conclude this study, think carefully about the light shed on
rule-application and administrators' attitudes to 'law'. Try to link the
theoretical discussion of ombudsmen's means and objectives in
Chapter 7, e.g. on the comparative merits of firefighting and
firewatching. And look back at Harlow's assessment (above p. 240).
Five years on, how much had changed and how much had remained
the same?

9
Judicial review: the tip of the iceberg?

In Chapter 1 we stressed the diversity of opinion about the objectives of administrative law, suggesting that red light theories possessed special attractions for lawyers. Many public lawyers have made the courts their central concern and some, like Wade and de Smith, saw the primary academic role as the organization of case law into coherent groups of doctrine comprising 'rules' and their 'exceptions'. From their books emerge *general* principles of judicial review relevant to different types of government action. Their organizing categories are not 'immigration control' and 'land-use planning' or 'adjudication' and 'discretion' but 'natural justice' and 'review of discretionary powers'. This reinforces the idea that the courts (not the administration) are pivotal. In these works, especially Wade's, variability in judicial decision-making is presented as marginal, fostering the belief that administrative law (largely reconstituted as 'judicial review') comprises a body of coherent rules denying or at least minimizing judicial discretion. Yet, by concentrating so closely on doctrinal analysis, public lawyers have tended to assume two key elements in any effective control theory of judicial review: (a) that administrators take their lead from courts and not vice versa; and (b) that if proferred the bridle, administrators dutifully put it on. These classic texts pass lightly over a still more important question, namely the legitimacy of judicial 'control' of administrative power. Once again, this may have something to do with the prevailing tradition of positivism and the wish to sanitize the law by divorcing it from the political structure which underlies it.

We do not mean to imply opposites; for example, that courts are unimportant or their decisions ineffective, that administrators ignore case law, that administrative law is not a system of rules or that judicial review should be diminished. We think these difficult if not intractable problems. Our material on judicial review is divided into three chapters. In this chapter we examine the statistical information available and then explore the possible impact of judicial decision-taking, in part by a detailed study of the aftermath of one particular case. Chapters 10 and 11 are more theoretical in character, raising both the nature of justiciable issues and the constitutional position of the judiciary. The first focuses on doctrines used to limit access to courts, the second on the assumption that judicial review is a system of rules.

1 Quantifying judicial review

We begin with a surprising conclusion. Despite the major intellectual commitment of public lawyers to judicial review, significant gaps exist in the information available about judicial intervention in the administrative process. Doctrine and case-analysis we possess; research into *who* litigates, how *often*, and in respect of *which* governmental activities, has been singularly lacking. Yardley (1981, p. 229), for example, lists some ombudsman statistics and states that ombudsmen 'provide a useful adjunct to judicial review. The statistics of complaints registered and of findings of . . . maladministration bear out this view'. To demonstrate statistically that ombudsmen are an 'adjunct' to the courts also requires a statistical examination of judicial review. Yardley, prepared to assert (1981, p. 205) that 'the most central theme of administrative law is that of judicial control of power', fails to do this. Perhaps revealingly, the standard texts on judicial review take us little further. Wade ignores such questions. Evans, the current editor of de Smith, armed with an impressionistic comparison of the Law Reports for the years 1960–2 and 1976–8, assures us (1980, p. 31): '. . . over the past 15 years, and especially since 1967, there has been a striking increase both in the frequency with which judicial review has been invoked and in the readiness of the courts to intervene'.

Let us compare the statistical evidence. For many years the official Civil Judicial Statistics contained information about the four prerogative orders. These constitute the traditional common law method of reviewing the activities of administrative authorities and inferior courts. Mandamus lies where a public body fails to perform a public duty; prohibition, on the other hand, is essentially pre-emptive, ordering an authority not to do something which it has no legal power to do. This distinguishes it from certiorari which quashes a pre-existing determination for ultra vires or error of law on the face of the record. Habeas corpus orders the release of a person unlawfully detained. For all four remedies the court process is two-staged.[1] First, there is the 'sieve'; the applicant must, ex parte, seek leave to apply. The court, in determining whether or not to grant leave, considers whether the applicant possesses locus standi[2] or has unduly delayed. It also takes a preliminary view of the merits, discarding those claims thought frivolous. So, for example, one consequence of the *Bromley* case (below, p. 334), where the House of Lords held unlawful the GLC's supplementary rate levied to subsidize London Transport, was *R.* v. *House of Lords ex p. Brooks* (Application of 20 January, 1982). A law student, aggrieved because the resulting fare increases might make it more difficult for the unemployed to improve themselves by travelling to art galleries, etc., sought review of their Lordships' decision. Not surprisingly the judge refused leave, advising Brooks to ask one of his lecturers to explain that the High Court possesses no supervisory jurisdiction over courts superior to itself! If granted leave, an applicant may move to the second stage where the merits are tried. Figure 2 represents the number of applications for prerogative orders, leaves granted, and final orders obtained against public authorities. Table 8, containing also the number of leaves and final orders refused, breaks down the statistics for the individual remedies during 1980.

Table 8 Individual Prerogative Orders 1980

	Certiorari	Mandamus	Habeas Corpus	Prohibition
Applications	262	210	32	19
Leave refused	75	67	13	7
Leave granted	172	107	25	9
Order refused	64	24	15	3
Order obtained	84	30	3	7

The number of cases is infinitesimal compared with the millions of decisions taken daily by public authorities. (Compare the ombudsmen statistics (Chapter 7) and also the sample of tribunal determinations (Table 1)). Evans' 'striking increase' in prerogative order applications from 95 in 1968 to 364 in 1978 must be kept in perspective. The rise from 1978 onwards may be partially attribut-

Figure 2. Prerogative Orders 1959–80.

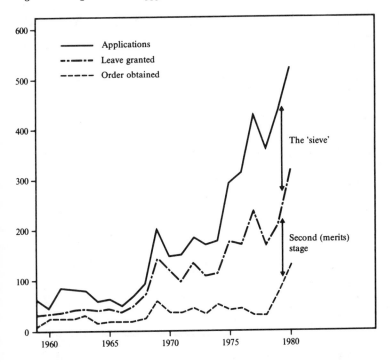

Note: The published statistics for 1970, 1971 are amended for clerical errors.

able to procedural factors. Prior to 1978, litigants had to choose between seeking prerogative orders and other forms of relief. The new Application for Judicial Review (below), which facilitates the combining of remedies, may have prompted the number of applications involving prerogative orders to rise.[3] The increase may also be linked to the lack of formality at the leave stage of the Application procedure. For £10 Mr Brooks could submit to the Crown Office an application form specifying the grounds of complaint and an affidavit verifying the facts relied upon. No legal advice or representation was involved and the judge, sitting alone, decided on the papers whether to grant leave.[4]

Evans' claim concerning judicial readiness to intervene seems more controversial. Despite the much heralded liberalization of the

Table 9 Applications for Judicial Review 1981

Respondent and/or subject matter	'Sieve' stage*		Second (merits) stage				Total
	Withdrawn or no order prior to leave	Leave refused	Awaiting disposal	Withdrawn or no order	Application dismissed	Relief granted	
Criminal proceedings (magistrates' and crown court)	7	45	11	16	42	44	165
Civil proceedings (magistrates' and crown court)	–	7	4	4	6	13	34
County courts and coroners	2	4	–	–	1	4	11
Immigration (Home Secretary and immigration tribunals)	4	69	6	21	64	21	185
Ministers and government departments	2	6	1	3	11	4	27
Local authorities (exc. H(HP) Act 1977)	2	7	3	14	12	7	45
Housing (Homeless Persons) Act 1977	–	1	–	2	4	2	9
Other†	10	18	4	16	23	13	84
Total	27	157	29	76	163	108	560

Source: Crown Office internal working paper. There are slight discrepancies with the Civil Judicial Statistics for 1981 (Cmnd 8770, Table A.6(a)). The official statistics provide no breakdown by category of litigation.
*The total number of leaves granted during 1981 was 376.
†This category encompasses a wide variety of subject matter; for example, applications concerning prison visitors, the police, district auditors and the Special Commissioners of Revenue.

grounds of judicial review from the mid-1960s onwards (see Chapter 11), there were only 11 more prerogative orders made against public authorities in 1978(31) than in 1967. The major leap occurred subsequently. Even so, during 1976–80 there were only 305 such orders made.

Although these figures may prompt us to question the intellectual focus of many public lawyers, we must beware over-hasty conclusions. Statistics only tell part of the story. They cannot measure the effect of one decision on, perhaps, thousands of similar cases. The mere existence of judicial review and the creation of precedent may influence future administrative behaviour (see below). And it would be naïve to argue, for example, that just because there are more tribunal cases, judicial review is less significant. The courts, with their high prestige and backed by a powerful profession and significant media interest, possess an influence disproportionate to their case load.

These statistics were not complete. First, a number of cases (see Table 9) are settled or withdrawn, sometimes to the applicant's satisfaction, sometimes not. Secondly, the statistics actually overstated the amount of relevant judicial review. The Crown Office[5] was double-counting certain composite applications: a joint application for two or more prerogative orders arising from the same complaint (for example, certiorari to quash a determination and mandamus requiring the authority to retake it) would be recorded in the statistics as two or more applications. The prerogative orders also concern the High Court's supervisory jurisdiction over inferior courts (e.g. magistrates' courts). These decide some matters (e.g. licensing) generally considered within the rubric 'administrative law', but also others, like traffic offences, which are not. Since the official statistics did (and do) not differentiate, they are for our purposes inflated, in particular by applications for mandamus requiring inferior courts to state a case and for certiorari to quash a decision in criminal proceedings. Sunkin's unpublished research into Applications for Judicial Review made during the first five months of 1979 showed the supervisory jurisdiction accounting for 43 per cent of Applications, nearly all relating to criminal law. A similar picture emerges from Table 9; 165 of the 560 Applications made in 1981 concerned the criminal jurisdiction of magistrates and crown courts.

In a different way, the statistics also understated judicial involvement with the administrative process because the prerogative orders are not the only means by which courts aim to control the administration. An applicant may seek an injunction, which prohibits authorities from doing something illegal, or a declaration, which states the law about the relevant issue. Although the latter is not coercive, administrators are unlikely openly to disobey it. The litigant may possess a statutory remedy: often the right of appeal on a point of law, available from most statutory tribunals; or, as is common in planning, the right to apply, usually within six weeks, to quash a decision for ultra vires or substantial prejudice resulting from non-compliance with prescribed procedure. Public authorities may be held liable in actions for damages in contract and tort (see e.g. *Cooper* v. *Wandsworth* above, p. 25). The courts may be seised of an administrative law matter in what are sometimes called 'collateral proceedings'. Suppose X is prosecuted for breaking a byelaw. If he contends that it is void as ultra vires, the court must determine its validity before deciding whether an offence has been committed. A similar situation arose in *Burnley B C* v. *England* (1979) 77 L G R 227. The council passed byelaws banning dogs from certain parks whereupon the seven defendant dog-owners, who subsequently helped form the Burnley Dog Owners' Action Committee, organized a protest march of 200–300 people and dogs in defiance of the ban. No prosecutions followed but when the authority refused to reverse its policy, the Committee announced its intention of repeating the protest. This time the council sought and obtained injunctions to restrain the defendants from breaking the byelaws or inciting others to do so. The defendants argued unsuccessfully that the byelaws were void as being wholly unreasonable (see *Kruse* v. *Johnson* [1898] 2 Q B 91).

Statistics relating to these alternative channels of redress have proved elusive. Claims for damages against public authorities, traditionally brought both in the High Court and county courts, have not been indexed separately. The incidence of collateral review has not been isolated, while only certain statistics concerning appeal on a point of law are published. The number of injunctions and declarations made against public bodies has been obscure. These, being also private law remedies, have traditionally been available by writ, originating summons or motion in the Chancery Division and county courts as well as in the Queen's Bench Division. Yet the official statistics have not even measured their incidence in Queen's Bench.

In 1978, following upon Law Commission recommendations

(Cmnd 6407), the new Order 53 (SI No. 1955/77) of the Rules of the Supreme Court came into operation, reforming the procedures for obtaining judicial review.[6] It allowed the combining of applications for one or more of the prerogative orders with a claim for an injunction, declaration or damages. Yet it was not till 1981 that the figures for the previously separate prerogative orders were replaced in the official statistics by a summary of action taken under the new umbrella procedure, the Application for Judicial Review made to the Queen's Bench Division. Table 9 adopts the changed format. Rule 1 of the new Order required that applications for prerogative orders, excepting habeas corpus, 'shall' be made via the Application procedure, which involves the two-staged court process previously described. However, by providing that declarations and injunctions 'may' be obtained via an Application, it seemed to reflect the Law Commission's view (Cmnd 6407, paras. 34, 58) that these remedies should remain available by ordinary action. To the extent that litigants could still seek these remedies and damages against public authorities in courts other than the Queen's Bench Division, Table 9 (which predates *O'Reilly* v. *Mackman* (below)) underestimates their incidence.[7]

2 **Rationalization or turning the screw?**

Underpinning the complexities of our account are two important features of English administrative law: the non-development of a strict jurisdictional dichotomy between 'public' and 'private' law and the related failure to establish a centralized system of judicial review within a specialist court. In the past, the Divisional Court of the Queen's Bench Division, which granted the prerogative orders, has been primus inter pares. But these characteristics are threatened by recent developments concentrating 'public law' work within Queen's Bench. As a sidewind we may gain a clearer statistical picture of judicial involvement with the administrative process.

Under the Application procedure, single judges preside at full hearings and the Lord Chief Justice has selected a group of judges considered specialists in some aspect of administrative law to take Order 53 cases.[8] Provision has been made (Practice Direction [1981] 1 WLR 1296) for transferring into the Crown Office list other High Court matters, for example Chancery Division cases or appeals on points of law from tribunals, considered to involve 'administrative law' issues. Clearly this requires a working definition of our subject. The courts have required some litigants against public authorities to proceed by Order 53 and not ordinary action. This facilitates centralization and specialization but, as will be seen, also raises some controversial issues.

Technically, there are differences between the two procedures. Although the costs of a full hearing will deter some litigants from using writs, invoking Order 53 grants certain protections to the respondent public authority. By ordinary action there is no preliminary 'sieve' to shield public bodies from frivolous and/or awkward claims; they must defend themselves at least by making an application to strike out. The time-limits for proceeding by writ, being the ordinary limitation periods, are more liberal than the discretionary provisions for Applications.[9] Subject to the general restrictions, there is by writ automatic cross-examination and discovery of documents (save against the Crown);[10] these lie within the court's discretion under Order 53.

Initially, in cases like *De Falco* v. *Crawley BC* [1980] QB 460, the courts accepted that the new Order 53 had established a permissive not a mandatory scheme for obtaining declarations, injunctions and damages against public authorities. The plaintiffs, who contended that the Council had failed to carry out its duties under the Housing (Homeless Persons) Act 1977, could still obtain these remedies by writ in the High Court and the cheaper, local county courts. But in other cases like *Heywood* v. *Board of Visitors of Hull Prison* [1980] 1 WLR 1386, judges expressed willingness to exercise their discretion to strike out such proceedings as an abuse of court process.[11] A prisoner had been disciplined by the Board for involvement in the Hull prison riots of 1976. Alleging breach of natural justice, he proceeded not by an application for certiorari but by writ in the Chancery Division for a declaration that the Board's determination was null and void. Goulding J struck out the claim saying it circumvented the 'safeguards' of Order 53 and hindered the rationalization of judicial review in one court.

Matters came to a head in *O'Reilly* v. *Mackman*. Like Heywood, the litigants claimed declarations by writ impugning Board of Visitors' determinations in the wake of the Hull prison riots. The Court of Appeal ([1982] 3 WLR 604), which considered that leave to make Applications would have been refused for delay, struck out the attempts to invoke the more generous time-limits for obtaining declarations. Noting the protections accorded public authorities by Order 53, Lord Denning commented:

None of these safeguards against abuse are available in an ordinary action . . . Some complainants . . . have seized upon this. They have brought actions at law instead of judicial review . . . Nearly all these people are legally aided. If they were allowed to proceed by ordinary action without leave . . . public authorities . . . would be harassed by all sorts of claims – long out of time – on the most flimsy of grounds . . .

[The] new procedure means that we have now an administrative court. It is a division of the High Court which might well be called the Administrative Division.

The House of Lords ([1982] 3 All E R 1124) dismissed the appeal:

LORD DIPLOCK: The public interest in good administration requires that public authorities and third parties should not be kept in suspense as to the legal validity of a decision . . . for any longer period than is absolutely necessary in fairness to the person affected by the decision . . .

Nevertheless I accept that having regard to the disadvantages, particularly . . . the absolute bar on compelling discovery of documents by the respondent public authority [in proceedings for] certiorari, and the almost invariable practice of refusing leave to allow cross-examination of deponents to affidavits lodged on its behalf, it could not be regarded as an abuse of . . . process, before the amendments made to Ord. 53 in 1977, to proceed by an action for a declaration of nullity . . . instead of applying for an order of certiorari; [although], by adopting this course, the plaintiff evaded the safeguards imposed in the public interest against groundless, unmeritorious or tardy attacks on the validity of decisions made by public authorities in the field of public law.

Those disadvantages, which formerly might have resulted in an applicant being unable to obtain justice . . . under Ord. 53, have all been removed by the new rules introduced in 1977. There is express provision for interlocutory applications for discovery of documents, the administration of interrogatories and . . . cross-examination. Discovery of documents . . . is not automatic as in an action begun by writ, but . . . discovery is obtainable on application whenever, and to the extent that, the justice of the case requires; similarly . . . applications for interrogatories [and] for cross-examination . . . It may well be that [following] *George* v. *Secretary of State for the Environment* (1979) 38 P. & C.R. 609 it will be only on rare occasions that the interests of justice will require that leave be given for cross-examination . . . in applications for judicial review. This is because of the nature of the issues that normally arise . . . The facts, except where the claim [is] that a . . . public authority . . . failed to comply with the procedure prescribed by the legislation . . . or failed to observe . . . natural justice or fairness, can seldom be a matter of relevant dispute on an application for judicial review since the . . . authority's findings of fact . . . are [generally] not open to review.[12] Nevertheless . . . the grant of leave to cross-examine deponents on applications for judicial review is [today] governed by the same principles as it is in actions begun by originating summons; it should be allowed whenever the justice of the particular case so requires . . .

Now that those disadvantages to applicants have been removed and all remedies for infringements of rights protected by public law can be obtained on an application for judicial review, as can also remedies for infringements of rights under private law if [these are] also . . . involved, it would . . . as a general rule be contrary to public policy, and as such an abuse of . . . process . . . to permit a person seeking to establish that . . . a public authority infringed rights to which he was entitled to protection under public law to proceed by . . . ordinary action and . . . evade the provisions of Ord. 53 for the protection of such authorities.

I have described this as a general rule for . . . there may be exceptions, particularly where the invalidity of the decision arises as a collateral issue in a claim for infringement of a right . . . arising under private law, or where none of the parties objects to [proceedings] by writ . . . Whether there should be other exceptions should . . . at this stage in the development of procedural public law, be left to be decided on a case to case basis . . . In the instant cases where the only relief sought is a declaration of nullity of the decisions of a statutory tribunal, the Board of Visitors . . . as in any other case in which a similar declaration of nullity in public law is the only relief claimed, I have no hesitation . . . in holding that to allow the actions to proceed would be an abuse of . . . process . . . They are blatant attempts to avoid the protections for the respondents . . . which Ord. 53 provides.

By requiring litigants to use a procedure which may diminish their chances of success, the courts may be tipping the balance towards public authorities. One man's 'abuse' is, after all, another's advantage; the 'protections' to which Lord Diplock refers are often the very reasons why litigants seek to avoid using Order 53. In short, why confine the 'public interest' to 'good administration'? Is there not a 'public interest' in individuals' access to justice? Lord Diplock circumvents the point by arguing that the past evils were cured in 1977. He does not mention the stricter time-limits on applications and the inevitable price of centralization, the loss of entitlement to sue local authorities etc. in the nearest county court. Lord Diplock brushes aside fears that discovery, interrogatories and cross-examination will be more restricted under Order 53, but cites the *George* case where Lord Denning said that the courts' discretion under Order 53 to allow detailed factual inquiries should not be exercised liberally. Of course only time will tell how the Queen's Bench judges approach these matters in practice. Lord Diplock's explanation is that litigants will not be prejudiced because in judicial review, with the exception of procedural complaints, the primary dispute is usually one of law not fact. This contrasts with Cane's view (see below, p. 306) that the grounds of ultra vires are so vague that the issue of whether a public authority has acted legally may itself be, at bottom, a question of fact to be determined from case to case.

O'Reilly v. *Mackman* raises issues about the boundaries of 'public' law, focused around the question of when Order 53 must be used and when it can be avoided. One issue is whether it is desirable to hive off 'public' from 'private' law in the modern state.[13] Another is how to draw the line. Lord Diplock creates no clear jurisdictional division. Litigants claiming that public authorities have infringed rights in 'public' law must generally use Order 53 but the courts are to proceed on a case by case basis. In *Cocks* v. *Thanet D C* [1982] 3 All E R 1135, the House of Lords applied *O'Reilly* v. *Mackman* expansively, requiring that Order 53 procedure be used in nearly all claims of damages for breach of statutory duty arising under the Housing (Homeless Persons) Act 1977. Yet in the later case of *Dary* v. *Spelthorne B C* [1983] 3 W L R 742 the law lords seemed to cut *O'Reilly* back, allowing indirect challenge of a planning decision by means of a negligence action. Similarly in *Law (subnom Tozer)* v. *National Greyhound Racing Club Ltd* [1983] 1 W L R 1302, the Court of Appeal upheld the decision of Walton J (*The Times*, 16 May 1983) dismissing applications by the club to strike out proceedings brought in the Chancery Division for declarations that it had acted contrary to natural justice when suspending trainers from racing. Order 53 procedure was not mandatory since there was no element of 'public' law in the decisions of this domestic body.[14] We might note that the case involved seven counsel, including three Q Cs, arguing not about whether the club had acted unlawfully, but in what court that question should be determined. 'Procedural public law' indeed!

Sunkin detects an extra dimension to *O'Reilly* v. *Mackman*. He sees the imposition of Order 53 as an assertion of judicial control over the legal process.

Unlike general civil proceedings where control is largely with the parties, in Order 53 control is always with the court. Thus the court decides whether to grant leave and determines the extent of the interlocutory facilities . . . This involvement . . . allows the higher judiciary to maximise its discretionary control over public law litigation and enables it to regulate its and the law's role within government . . . If Lord Diplock's lead is followed, judicial decision-making will become more overtly pragmatic, with the need to reason from legal principle and precedent declining. [Sunkin 1983, pp. 649, 653.]

We leave this point here to pick it up in Chapter 10.

3 Litigants and litigation

Before we leave the subject of statistics, we need to make a further, negative point. The published statistics provide no information about who litigates about what. Table 9, however, reveals that in 1981 62.5 per cent of Applications for Judicial Review concerned the supervisory jurisdiction over criminal proceedings and immigration matters. Immigration aside, only four final orders were made against central departments – the very category on which many public lawyers concentrate their efforts.

Of course the incidence of juridification can change. For instance, the present Conservative Government's tougher policies on immigration control have apparently stimulated a significant increase in the number of immigrants seeking judicial review, another reason for the upsurge in prerogative order applications visible in Figure 2. In Sunkin's survey of the 158 Applications made in the first five months of 1979, 21.5 per cent involved immigration matters. In 1982 the authors' follow-up study of 317 Applications produced a figure of 32.2 per cent.

The reasons why particular governmental functions do or do not attract litigation are complex. For example, informal conventions or trade practices about the utility of referring certain matters to the courts may exist amongst barristers or solicitors. In other words, lawyers feel that some matters are and others are not justiciable. A leading case like *Bromley* may draw the public's attention to the existence of a legal remedy, prompting other litigation (see below, Chapter 11). There may exist other, more convenient, channels of redress (compare the debate about the PCA's functions in Chapter 7). The relationship between the parties may militate against litigation. It may be one of mutual interdependence, e.g. between a department and a major government contractee. Here a party may lose more by disrupting the relationship through going to court than by compromising on the particular issue. At the other end of the scale, welfare recipients rarely possess the resources and know-how to invoke the aid of courts, although pressure groups may intervene on their behalf.

Dicey's model of administrative law stressed the personal nature of liability. Individual citizens sued individual public servants in protection of their interests. We saw, too, that Dicey showed little interest in the idea that administrative law could regulate relationships between public authorities. Later formulations which, like Wade's, adopted a model of citizen versus state often implied imbalance: that courts always control a 'strong' (and threatening) state for the benefit of 'weak' citizens. Today public law litigation is far more complex. The state is not homogenous. It is composed of a number of entities between which there may or may not be 'imbalance'. For example, the relationship between 'central' and 'local' authorities is not a simple one of principal and agent. Central control over the legislative process and (increasingly) finance means that the partnership is unequal, but each side requires the other in order to secure its respective policy goals.[15] Cases like *Bromley* (see below, p. 334) and *Tameside* (see below, p. 330) suggest that the allocation of functions between public authorities may often be the subject of dispute and that the resolution of differences between governmental agencies may increasingly become an important function for the courts.

We sense that 'individuals' are not identical. At one extreme, there are litigants in person like Mr Brooks; at the other, powerful trade unions and multinational companies, well able to afford the best legal advice. Disguised behind the names of individual applicants we often find interest groups of varying size and strength. Their 'interests' range from those of the Child Poverty Action Group (CPAG), which campaigns to improve the lot of poor families, to those of Burnley's dog-owners and of the right-wing National Association of Freedom which sponsored *Gouriet*'s case (see below, p. 291).

4 Test-case strategy

So the apparently simple notion of individual interest may conceal a wide variety of persons and corporate bodies. One way in which it has been stretched in recent years is by the adoption of 'test-case strategy', a technique born in the American civil rights movement and imported into the UK by groups like NCCL (National Council for Civil Liberties). During 1970–7, for example, CPAG was involved in 18 Divisional Court cases on behalf of SB claimants. This description by its legal director, Henry Hodge, also highlights a second litigation strategy, where the aim is to influence administrative decision-taking by flooding the process with large numbers of cases.

In 1969 . . . CPAG [established] a Citizens' Rights Office which was designed to be a Citizens' Advice Bureau 'with teeth' where families could come for advice, assistance and representation. [Our] legal department and the CRO were to work in tandem, with the CRO providing cases for the Group's lawyer to take to court or tribunal. These cases related to supplementary benefits, national insurance, other welfare benefits and some aspects of housing. This work was to be used to promote a test-case strategy where courts and tribunals would be asked to reach decisions on individual cases which favoured broad groups of claimants. It was also to be used to educate the public, advisers and lawyers about welfare rights and, combined with CPAG's campaigning activities, to show the need for changes in law, policies and attitudes which would favour poor families.

Case work has developed in two ways since 1970. First, attempts were made to establish precedents in courts and tribunals and secondly where no precedents were likely to be made, attempts were made to force changes in policy by promoting and publicising large numbers of similar cases. With no constitutional rights to pursue in Britain, precedent-making litigation has to concentrate on the interpretation of legislation. It was assumed that if cases were successful then the decision would be accepted and operated by administrators. Unsuccessful decisions, some of which could well be harmful to claimants, would generate publicity and reinforce arguments for the need for change. Thus, although losses could be expected, the strategy always assumed that success would come in the long run in the sense that favourable changes would occur for the poor. Legislators would be shamed into amending harsh legislation: administrative practices would alter; and families who had received no help might get such help as the knowledge gained from the cases spread. [Hodge 1979, pp. 241–2.]

Hodge emphasizes that test-case strategy is only one method by which pressure groups like CPAG may hope to secure their aims. The tactic is frequently a single element in a wider political campaign. Its goals are often complex and are not confined to winning individual cases and encouraging favourable legal settlements. Cases may be valuable as propaganda, 'to show the need for changes'. For Robertson,[16] an American proponent of the strategy, litigation 'in a civil rights context serves as a catalyst or focal point for community organisation. In many cases that organisation might not exist until the litigation is underway, networks of information and support will spring up once an agency is available and cases are taken on.'

Any statistically-oriented assessment of the 'impact' of review is frustrated by the broad goals of test-case strategy. To the extent that the aim is to win cases, the objective is to establish individual precedents which possess a marked 'ripple' effect, altering administrative practice in respect of large numbers of claimants. In the case of CPAG, the strategy was also an attempt to compensate for the under-representation of the under-privileged in the courts: between

1948 and 1970 there was no reported case involving judicial review of SB.

Hodge's description betrays the optimistic basis of the tactic: it was assumed that if cases were won they would be implemented and if they were lost legislators and bureaucrats would eventually see the error of their ways. Further, the strategy implied that courts would establish interpretations more favourable to claimants than pre-existing administrative practices. In Chapter 18 we will see that although some precedents of value to the poor were established, these assumptions have been badly dented. Sometimes it has seemed as if the more test-case strategy tries to achieve, the less likely it is to succeed (read *Metzger* v. *DHSS* [1977] 3 All ER 444). So we must consider the extent to which the strategy can constitute an effective means of stimulating social change.

Prosser (1979, p. 59) stresses that judicial review should not be seen in isolation, 'formal concepts of . . . review . . . form merely one factor in the many political influences shaping the outcome of conflict, and indeed may in practice be a factor of relatively small direct importance'. He points to a potential flaw at the very heart of test-case strategy when used by groups like CPAG. Efforts to compensate for the under-representation of the poor in the courts are likely to be undermined by a corresponding lack of political clout.

It has been asserted that 'legal advocacy offers a unique opportunity – it provides a forum that is in some degree independent of the power of participants'. [Nonet 1969, p. 8.] Yet . . . whether or not a successful legal challenge of administrative policy has effect depends on events in the traditional political area . . . It seems that the eventual outcome of legal challenge depends on the political status and resources of the group on whose behalf it is made. In the case of a group unable to mobilise considerable resources on its behalf, not only does it seem that the courts may not be prepared to extend public law norms for its protection, but legislative and administrative measures can remove the effects of any inconvenient decisions without real public debate and with a minimum of resistance. This does not mean that legal challenge of administrative action in such fields is necessarily futile, but does mean that the effect of administrative norms in bringing about real change is problematic and may be defeated by other political influences. The application of the norms of judicial review is just one part, indeed a subordinate part, of a wider political process. [Prosser 1979, pp. 82–3.]

This assessment may be contrasted with the optimism of Rogers in advocating court challenges to cuts in education imposed as a result of the present Conservative Government's concern to restrict public expenditure:

National surveys of the cuts in education . . . have revealed that many local authorities are in breach of their statutory duties under the 1944 Education Act . . . Local protesters are now consulting lawyers both about the predicament of individual schools and an authority's overall schools policy . . . Northamptonshire is next to bottom in the local authority league table of the amount spent on pupils for books and equipment. An acute textbook shortage, a worsening pupil/teacher ratio, a substantial cut in secondary science provision and the abolition of all remedial teaching in primary schools have galvanised the county's parent-teacher associations into taking legal advice. If their lawyers reckon the county is breaking the law, the PTAs are determined to take their case to court. In turn, the county has circularised headteachers ordering them not to discuss the effects of the cuts on their schools . . .

Earlier this year, the threat of court action was enough to make the London Borough of Ealing back down on its plan to abolish 'rising-fives' entry to its primary schools. Local protesters were aiming to use section 13 of the 1944 Education Act which forbids any significant change in the character of a school without the Secretary of State's approval. Cutting out the rising fives was considered to be doing just that.

Last year's attempt to use the law against Oxfordshire's decision to shut down all its nursery provision was foiled by the Education Secretary himself changing the law to get the county off the hook. For [DES] lawyers had earlier 'discovered' that local authorities were after all *legally* obliged to provide nursery schooling under section 8 of the 1944 Act. (They had known it for 35 years, but kept quiet). Mark Carlisle [then Education Secretary] added a new clause [now s.24] to his 1980 [Education] Act which turned that duty back to a discretionary one . . .

Until recently . . . campaigners [have been held] back from the courts [by] the lack of precision in the laws governing schooling (for example, no-one has yet defined what is 'sufficient provision'). [But] the cuts are now biting so deep that deciding what is sufficient is becoming easier as provision begins to disappear . . .

One test-case that goes the right way could stop the cuts in their tracks. [Rogers 1980, p. 16.]

Is Prosser's view justified by some of Rogers' own examples? Certainly, by illustrating the very different ways in which administrators may react, they indicate the complexity of the relationship between judicial review and administrative behaviour. As with ombudsmen, there can be *negative* responses, illustrated here by the resort to secrecy and valedictory legislation (whereby the administration uses its control of the law-making process to nullify, by legislation or regulations, inconvenient judicial decisions).[17] Red light theorists see the role of the courts as being to control administrators, to confine their discretion. But, in evaluating their views, we are entitled to ask whether control is actually achieved.

These negative responses point to an opposite conclusion.

In a country in which parliamentary sovereignty is the paramount constitutional norm, judges can never have the last word. Valedictory legislation does not deprive judicial review of all its 'impact'. One function of the judicial process may be to open up a particular policy to public debate, so allowing individuals to participate in the policy-making process. But this is not the same thing as 'control', which administrators may frequently circumvent. One technique is the process, after the court order, of taking the identical decision. The *Padfield* case (below, p. 327) provides a striking illustration, just because it was hailed as a significant step forward in the expansion of judicial control. The Minister was ordered to exercise his discretion in accordance with legislative policy and submit a complaint for investigation to the investigatory committee. So he did; but with what result? The Minister declined to follow the committee's advice. 'The remedy had proved illusory; the same decision could be reached with only nominal deference to the court, and the waste of time and money entailed is a deterrent to future complainants' (Harlow 1976, p. 120). A 'great' case in judicial review turns out, on closer inspection, to be something rather different.

Earlier we saw how Dicey initiated the formulation of general legal principles (which later writers have laboured mightily to complete). Dicey also stressed the 'deterrent' function of legal responsibility, by which he meant that public servants would be deterred from wrong-doing by the possibility of legal action against them. Atiyah (1978) talks of the 'hortatory' or educative function of law: the notion that a consistent judicial application of principle may influence members of society into adopting certain forms of action. Remember how Clark demanded 'firm rules' of natural justice in order to secure the 'acceptance by administrators' of fair procedures. Judicial review can have a firewatching as well as a firefighting role; both functions need to be assessed. In evaluating the impact of judicial review, we need to look at the extent to which its existence and the 'rules' which it establishes affect future administrative conduct. Of course, establishing causal connections between decisions and their alleged consequences is a notoriously difficult task, made even harder here by governmental secrecy. But 'law', to constitute an effective control by means of fire prevention, must have a significant role in the formulation of administrative policy. Officials are required to know the law and to decide to act in accordance with it. The following case study warns us that this is not always so. It also illustrates the two techniques of valedictory legislation and taking the same decision twice. Does the aftermath demonstrate the fragility of English public law, as Bradley (see below, p. 278) suggests?

5. If at first you don't succeed . . .

Prior to 1965, the recognized qualification for appointment to a teaching post in Scotland was that the teacher be 'certificated'. Mr Malloch (M) was employed by Aberdeen Education Authority in August 1965. He was one of a number of certificated teachers who, against the advice of their trade union, were unwilling to become registered teachers under a new scheme, based on the Teaching Council (Scotland) Act 1965, which established a General Teaching Council to regulate the teaching profession in Scotland. While M interpreted the scheme as permissive, the Scottish Education Department considered it mandatory. So, with effect from April 1968, regulation 4(2) of the pre-existing regulations, the Schools (Scotland) Code 1956, was amended by the Teachers (Education, Training and Registration) (Scotland) Regulations 1967 (S I No. 1162/67) in order to make registration compulsory: '. . . every teacher employed by an education authority shall be a registered teacher holding the qualifications' required by the Code.

The department interpreted the regulation to mean that every education authority must dismiss from employment any certificated teacher who did not register. Aberdeen Education Authority was advised that because M refused to register, his continued employment was unlawful. M's request to address the education committee was refused because Aberdeen considered his appearance pointless. When the committee met on March 18, 1969, M arrived and tried to speak, but the convener restored order by threatening to eject him. The committee duly passed a resolution for dismissal on the grounds that M and other teachers dismissed at the same time were unregistered and that their continued employment was no longer lawful by virtue of the Schools (Scotland) Code 1956 as amended.

The resolution had to be carried by a two-thirds' majority and there had in fact been an earlier meeting where this was not secured. During the interval between the two meetings, the committee received a strong letter from the Minister urging the dismissal of any teacher who refused to register. It also seems that committee members received some advice which might have been taken to mean that those who failed to vote for dismissal would incur personal liability.

Aberdeen gave M one month's notice. Some months later he raised an action against the Corporation asking for reduction[18] of the resolution and notice of dismissal. He was unsuccessful before the Scottish courts but in *Malloch* v. *Aberdeen Corpn* [1971] 1 WLR 1578 won by a bare majority in the House of Lords.

LORD WILBERFORCE: [M contends] that, before his dismissal became effective, he ought to have been given an opportunity of making written representations to or of being heard by the education authority. He had asked for this opportunity, and it is admitted that it was refused . . .

The appellant has first to show that his position was such that he had, in principle, a right to make representations before a decision against him was taken. But to show this is not necessarily enough, unless he can also show that if admitted to state his case he had a case of substance to make. A breach of procedure cannot give him a remedy in the courts, unless behind it there is something of substance which has been lost by the failure. The court does not act in vain . . . I now turn [to the first requirement].

[M's] appointment was held during pleasure, so that he could be dismissed without any reason being assigned . . . in *Ridge* v. *Baldwin* . . . Lord Reid said: 'It has always been held, I think rightly, that such an officer has no right to be heard before being dismissed'. As a general principle, I respectfully agree: and I think it important not to weaken a principle which, for reasons of public policy, applies, at least as a starting point, to so wide a range of the public service. The difficulty arises when, as here, there are other incidents of the employment laid down by statute, or regulation, or code of employment, or agreement. The rigour of the principle is often, in modern practice, mitigated for it has come to be perceived that the very possibility of dismissal without reason being given – action which may vitally affect a man's career or his pension – makes it all the more important for him, in suitable circumstances, to be able to state his case and, if denied the right to do so, to be able to have his dismissal declared void. So, while the courts will necessarily respect the right to dismiss without assigned reasons, this should not . . . prevent them from examining the framework and context of the employment to see whether elementary rights are conferred upon him expressly or by necessary implication, and how far these extend. The present case is . . . just such a case where there are strong indications that a right to be heard, in appropriate circumstances, should not be denied.

The significant section . . . is section 85(1) of the Education (Scotland) Act 1962 which reads:

No resolution of an education authority for the dismissal from their service of a certificated teacher . . . shall be valid unless – (a) written notice of the motion for his dismissal shall, not less than three weeks before the meeting at which the resolution is adopted, have been sent to the teacher and to each member of the education authority; and (b) not less than one half of the members of the education authority are present at the meeting; and (c) the resolution is agreed to by two thirds of the members so present.

I ask what purpose the imposition of these requirements could serve, if the teacher had no right in any circumstances to state his case? Why give him three weeks' notice of the motion, to be put to elected members, of which a two-thirds majority is required, if he can do nothing during the three weeks except wait for the announcement of his fate? How could any responsible body of men reach a fair decision without hearing him? I find the right to be heard in an appropriate situation clearly given by implication . . .

Then was there anything he could usefully have said, if a hearing had been given? The reason for his dismissal was . . . to say no more, controversial. At least on two points – the validity of the regulations and the construction of regulation 4 [as amended] – there were genuine contentions to be made. On the latter point I find it hard to believe that in a field of employment, based on the possession of qualifications historically accepted, it can really have been intended that men and women, validly qualified by certification before the regulation was amended, were ipso facto to be deprived of employment without any regard for vested rights. I would think there is much to be said for an interpretation of the amended regulation in such a manner as not to produce this result.

The case was then remitted to the Scottish courts with a direction to reduce the dismissal, which was done on the ground that M was entitled to a hearing before being dismissed. Soon afterwards, the education committee set down a motion to discuss M's position, informed him of its contents, and invited him to be heard upon it. The motion was for M's dismissal:

. . . on the ground that his failure to register with the [General Teaching Council] has made his continued employment a contravention of [regulation 4(2)] as amended, and therefore unlawful; and on the additional ground that, in any event, his continued employment as a teacher not registered as aforesaid is contrary to the policy of the said committee who are not prepared to employ in a school under their management any teacher who is entitled to be registered with the said council and is not so registered.

Five days before the proposed hearing, M raised a second action against the Corporation and the Secretary of State. Following the clues provided by Lord Wilberforce, M sought declarators (declarations) that the 1967 amendment was ultra vires and that, in any case, the amended regulation 4(2) did not, as a matter of construction, require that a teacher already in employment should become registered, but applied only to teachers entering employment after the amending regulation came into operation. He also sought a declarator that the Corporation could not dismiss him simply as a matter of policy.

At first instance (*Malloch* v. *Aberdeen Corpn* 1973 SLT 116) the Lord Ordinary, Lord Keith, held that the 1967 amendment made by the Secretary of State was ultra vires his enabling powers because it deprived M of a vested interest. But he refused to declare the dismissal bad, saying it was within the general discretion of the Corporation to formulate educational policy. M appealed unsuccessfully to the Court of Session (1974 SLT 253). The Court declined to determine whether the 1967 amendment was wholly outside the Minister's powers, confining its attention to the case of M, a teacher already certificated and in employment.

LORD MIGDALE: I cannot find in . . . any . . . of the so-called enabling provisions either express authority or material from which to draw any inference that Parliament intended to authorise the Secretary of State to make a regulation which would take away [M's] right to continue to teach in a local authority school.

Accordingly, I agree with the Lord Ordinary that . . . the Secretary of State [is not authorised] to amend the 1956 Code so as to take away any vested rights.

[The Minister] contended that all the amendment did was to require [M] to register . . . That was not taking away any right nor did it detract from the value of his certificate. It was still evidence of his qualification to teach. It is also his passport to registration . . . I do not agree. [M] was in employment and he was qualified to teach before the amendment by reason of his scholastic attainments and his certificate. After the amendment he was no longer eligible for employment as a teacher. Clearly this deprived him of a vested interest. To follow Malloch's analogy of the key and the door, his certificate no longer opened a door to employment but on to a register which imposed on him new conditions and new provisions about discipline. It will also cost him about £1 a year . . .

It follows that if the amended regulation is ultra vires . . . the first reason put forward by the Corporation for dismissal is bad. [M's] employment is not unlawful.

I now turn to the second issue raised before us. Is the Corporation entitled to dismiss Malloch by reason of their policy? Clearly he was employed at pleasure . . . It is well established law that if an employee is engaged 'at pleasure' his employer can dismiss him without giving reasons and cannot be compelled to state them, provided always that the power of dismissal is fairly and honestly exercised. The burden of showing that it has not been fairly and honestly exercised is on the employee. If, however, the employer chooses to give his reasons, a court may look at their sufficiency . . .

Two questions arise. The first is whether the second reason stated in the motion is independent of the first reason. The second question is, assuming it should be treated as an independent reason, whether it was arrived at in good faith or has been shown to be insufficient.

On the question of independence I am satisfied that the answer must be in the affirmative. The terms of the motion have clearly been framed with care and the two reasons are separated by the words 'and on the additional ground that in any event'. This is itself sufficient but the wording of the second reason also shows it has been reached independently of the view of their legal duties in the first reason. So even if the first reason is bad . . . the second reason falls to be considered on its own.

This second reason is that the education committee has decided as a matter of policy that it would not employ any teacher, qualified to do so, who had not registered. Malloch referred to pressure put on the committee from the outside to employ only registered teachers. There is no proof that this was done but even if there was canvassing of members by an outside body or person I do not think that would vitiate a decision on policy. The decision must have been reached by a majority. It may be that a minority took a different view, but the view of the majority would still rule. I find no evidence of bad faith, and divergence of opinion does not mean that the reason of the majority is insufficient . . .

It may well be that the education committee in this case thought that it was in the best interests of their schools that this dispute about registration should be settled by a decision to employ only registered teachers. I do not see how that can be said to be insufficient reason for dismissal.

The day after this decision, the Education (Scotland) Bill was presented to Parliament. The defence of judicial decision-making was initiated in the letters column of *The Times*:

The Bill now before Parliament . . . proposes retrospectively to validate the regulation judicially declared to be void. 'For the avoidance of doubt' it proposes to give retrospectively to the existing regulation an interpretation which had been questioned in the House of Lords . . . The Bill . . . seeks to give to the Secretary of State, with effect from November 1st, 1965, powers which two Scottish courts have declared he has never had.

Of course Parliament may well decide for the future that the registration of teachers in Scotland should be compulsory. I express no views on the merits of such a proposal. But if this Bill passes through Parliament with its retrospective effect unaltered, a serious inroad will have been made into the rule of law. The message for the citizen will be that it is worthless for him to seek a decision in the courts on the extent of the Government's powers since, if he wins in the courts, the Government will make use of its predominant position in Parliament to remove the victory from him . . .

This new Bill shows how fragile is our . . . system of public law. Why should the Executive ask Parliament to exercise its legislative omnipotence thus to cure defects and shortcomings in a matter of domestic administration? The present Bill makes neither for good law, nor for good government. [Bradley, *The Times*, 8 June 1973.]

Bradley added, 'documents produced before the Court of Session revealed that for a considerable period before the offending regulation was made, the Secretary of State had been advised that he had no power to introduce compulsory registration by regulation'.

In Committee (HC Scottish GC 1972/3, pp. 45–6), the Government announced an ex gratia compensation scheme for the certificated teachers dismissed by education authorities for failing to register. Authorities would receive a 100 per cent grant to make payments covering loss of earnings and entitlement under the teachers' superannuation scheme up until the date of the Bill's enactment. To secure uniformity of treatment, authorities would have to submit details of proposed payments to the Minister. The total sum involved was estimated as unlikely to exceed £50,000 and might be considerably less. The following extracts are from the House of Commons debate (HC Deb. vol. 859, cols. 1165–1218) on the successful third reading of the Bill.

MR MONRO [Under-Secretary of State for Health and Education, Scottish Office, moving the Bill]: It has been the policy of successive Governments since the passing of the Teaching Council (Scotland) Act 1965 that registration with the Teaching Council should be the mark of the qualified teacher . . . Until the recent Court of Session judgment, it was commonly accepted that the requirement [to register] was valid, and education authorities, the Council and the teachers as well as the Government proceeded on the basis that it was . . . This is a Bill aimed . . . at rectifying a recently discovered deficiency in the law. It makes no change whatever in what virtually everyone has thought the position to be since 1968 as was clearly indicated during the passage of the Bill in 1965.

MR BRUCE-GARDYNE: [Members] have argued that Parliament knew when it was passing the 1965 Act that compulsory registration for all teachers would automatically follow and that teachers who declined to register would be dismissed from their employment . . . That is a matter about which I must beg to differ . . .

Essentially, my case is that not only did Parliament not intend [to encroach on the vested rights of existing teachers] but the . . . then Secretary of State himself did not intend it . . . The substantive legislation was passed in 1965. In October 1966 the Scottish Education Department, presumably speaking on behalf of the [Minister], sent a memorandum to the General Teaching Council on the subject of the registration of teachers already in employment in the schools. It said:

If steps were taken . . . by the Secretary of State so to adjust various statutory regulations governing employment, salary and superannuation as to make the consequences of failure to register the deprivation of benefits under these regulations, such teachers might contest the propriety of such action on the ground that it infringed their existing 'rights' . . .

This evidently came as something of a shock to the General Teaching Council. It did not like it at all. It is recorded in the minutes . . . that several members emphasised that unless all or nearly all teachers registered, whether by compulsion or not, the council would have to depend for its income on disproportionately high fees from entrants or subventions from the Secretary of State . . .

The important fact is that . . . one year after the substantive legislation – in which we are told that this House knew were provisions for the automatic withdrawal of entrenched rights – the Secretary of State was saying that he could not do what the council wanted him to do because that would involve the infringement of those entrenched rights and would therefore be *ultra vires* . . .

The House must decide . . . whether we should go to the length of overriding the highest courts in Scotland and depriving individuals of a right which they have fought right through the courts to establish against the might of the Government machine in circumstances in which the [then Secretary of State] can be shown to have known that the legislation was faulty when he introduced it and whether we should do it retrospectively to save the [Minister's] bacon. That is not for me.

MR MACARTHUR: At the end of the day, 19 teachers lost their jobs. [They are] the only people who will suffer because of the Bill. The Government have accepted my proposals . . . that compensation should be paid to them, and those teachers who can show to the satisfaction of the local authorities which employ them that they have lost income or pension rights or in any other way will have that loss made up to them . . . Therefore, I believe that all grounds for opposition to the Bill have been removed.

MR MILLAN: I was the Under-Secretary of State responsible for handling matters affecting the General Teaching Council – responsible to [the Secretary of State] – during most of the period concerned. [Mr Bruce-Gardyne] said that not only were the regulations *ultra vires* but that the Secretary of State had been [previously so] advised . . . I say categorically that this is not the position . . . The Secretary of State never received that advice because it was never given to him.

MR PARDOE: Compensation. What a disgraceful offer to make! Those that have fought this case . . . have never stated any desire for compensation. All that they want is freedom to teach, and that is a freedom which the Bill will be taking away from them.

MR BRUCE-GARDYNE: The crucial point is far wider than the interests of the . . . people who were dismissed. It is in the interests of the community as a whole that the courts should not be overriden with retrospective legislation of this kind.

The Education (Scotland) Act 1973 (presently contained in s.90 of the Education (Scotland) Act 1980) had one operative section:

1.–(1) It is hereby declared that the power of the Secretary of State to make regulations under section 1(2) of the Education (Scotland) Act 1962 . . . includes power (and shall be deemed always to have included power on and after 1st November 1965) to prescribe in such regulations that only registered teachers shall be employed or continue to be employed as teachers by education authorities in the educational establishments to which the regulations apply, subject to such exceptions as may from time to time be so prescribed . . .

(3) For the avoidance of doubt, it is hereby declared that in the Schools (Scotland) Code 1956, as amended by the Teachers (Education, Training and Registration) (Scotland) Regulations 1967, regulation 4(2) shall be construed as having always applied to teachers in employment on 1st April 1968, as well as to teachers taken into employment after that date.

Three years later, the Court of Session had to consider this provision in *Scott* v. *Aberdeen Corpn.* 1976 SLT 141. S, a certificated teacher who declined to register, was dismissed at the same time and in the same manner as M. Following the example of *Malloch* v. *Aberdeen Corpn.*, S sought reduction of the resolution and notice dismissing him for breach of natural justice. The action was raised one month before the 1973 Act came into force and the statute was operative before the matter came to court. The Corporation contended that since after the 1973 Act his continued employment in 1969 was unlawful, S had to be treated as if originally he had had nothing to say. S argued that the case should be considered in the light of the situation existing in 1969 and that subsequent legislation could not alter the fact that at that date he had genuine contentions to make about the validity and construction of regulation 4(2). The 1973 Act was retrospective but such legislation should be construed strictly and it was not necessary to infer that a complaint of unfair procedure in a teacher's dismissal was affected.

LORD CAMERON: It was said that [natural justice] at least [involves] that one whose employment was in question should be given a hearing "in his defence" before the step of dismissal was taken. But if there is no possible "defence" to what end could a "hearing" be directed? . . . That such a situation could exist was plainly envisaged by . . . their Lordships in [*Malloch* v. *Aberdeen Corpn.*]. If . . . the law as it stood at 18 March 1969 required dismissal of an unregistered teacher then there was no good purpose to be served by inviting or permitting [S] to be heard. He had to go; there was no other way. It must be presumed that the [education] committee would act in accordance with the law . . .

I cannot accept the arguments pressed by [S] that his right to sue . . . in 1973 must be judged by the "factual" situation existing as at 18 March 1969 . . . The [1973] statute is plainly designed to have retrospective . . . effect. [S. 1] is declaratory of what shall be deemed to have been the law at the time of [S's] dismissal and therefore . . . that is the state of the law in the context of which the extent of [his] right to a hearing at the date – 18 March 1969 – must now be judged. Parliament is sovereign and has declared what the law should be held to have been at a given time, and that declaration . . .

must be accepted and . . . applied. If the necessary [consequence] is to deprive the subject of a right previously enjoyed . . . then deprivation must follow . . .

The factual situation in 1969 must now be judged in light of any changes which the later statute has brought about, and one of the facts which the [Corporation] had to take into account was the state of the law as it then existed, in the form as it is now declared to have been by the Act of the sovereign Parliament. The context of the whole proceedings has been changed by Parliament and, for [S], in a fatal way. It must now be assumed that on 18 March 1969 there was a valid amendment of regulation 4(2) and that that regulation expressly applied to [S] – he was one of a class of teachers singled out – those who were in employment on 1 April 1968. To do otherwise would in effect be to construe s. 1(3) as though it excepted from the operation of the regulation all certificated teachers who were dismissed without a hearing because of failure . . . to . . . obtain registration . . . and leave them free . . . to . . . succeed in proceedings to set aside that dismissal.

We must beware generalization. It may be objected that negative bureaucratic responses to judicial review are atypical and it does not follow that because some administrators disobey the law, that its firewatching function is irrelevant. Yet the *Malloch* saga suggests that models of administrative law, in which courts 'control' abuse of power, successfully defending the citizen's 'rights' against erosion by the state, demand some modification. It is not quite so easy to control the behaviour of administrators. In the next chapter we will see how the courts, conscious of this, may modify their own behaviour, further weakening control by declining jurisdiction in sensitive cases.

One response to any 'gap' between theory and practice, taken in conjunction with the statistical evidence of limited court involvement with the administrative process, is to query the traditional emphasis on judicial review. No longer should the courts be seen as the key control. Judicial review is external to the administrative process and is retrospective since it involves challenges to pre-existing or imminent bureaucratic decisions. The courts not only suffer from the inherent drawbacks of adjudication as a decision-making process, their limited capacity for control stems in part from the very nature of review.

Realization of a 'gap' has no doubt been one factor influencing public lawyers to search for superior control techniques. Davis's disenchantment with the rule of law ideal and involvement with rule-making stems from his belief in its greater efficiency. Other administrative lawyers seem to brush the point aside, hoping instead to expand court-oriented control by getting rid of restrictions like locus standi so that judges can sanction the administration more freely. This will be taken further in Chapter 10.

Rationing judicial review

1 Limiting devices

In Chapter 9 we saw that the jurisdictional distinction between 'private' law and 'public' law actions could be used to turn litigants away from the courts. The implication is that administrative illegality might then go unsanctioned and applicants with good cases might be turned down on a procedural technicality. The picture is not a novel one; precisely the same thing happened in *Ostler*'s case and *Smith* v. *East Elloe*. Limitation requirements and ouster clauses often defeat a good cause; indeed, the knowledge that this is so can tempt courts to temper the law to the shorn lamb as they did in the *Anisminic* case. Before the reform of Order 53, English administrative law was scornfully described as a law of remedies, 'over-technical, confusing and uncertain'.[1] Academics argued that the procedural technicalities distracted attention from the 'substance' of judicial review, by which they meant the grounds for review which to many seemed its core.

Locus standi or standing to sue is another limiting device. It cuts down the potential number of litigants by restricting access to courts to those able to demonstrate some particular 'interest', over and above that of the general public, in the matter in question. This requirement, developed at common law for judicial review and by Parliament in respect of statutory remedies, has traditionally been perceived as a separate issue or threshold requirement for the applicant, raising directly the right to apply for a remedy. A contrast can be drawn with the action in damages where 'right' and 'remedy' are treated as part of the same issue and the right to bring an action is indirectly restricted. To take a simple example, it is generally the rule that the witness of a street accident cannot bring an action in damages for nervous shock alone. The courts do not achieve this result by saying 'witnesses of an accident have no interest to sue'. They might say instead that the wrong-doer owed no duty of care to mere witnesses or that nervous shock is too remote a form of damage. (To see how this works in practice, turn to the *Dorset Yacht* or *Anns* cases in Chapter 12.)

Of particular relevance to the current debate surrounding standing, is the notion that remedies in judicial review are discretionary. It is not sufficient for the applicant to possess locus standi and to establish one of the grounds of review; he must also persuade the court to make an order. The cases suggest that this remedial discretion is operated in a discretionary fashion since the courts have not attempted to lay down firm guidelines for its exercise.

Some judges have focused on the conduct of the applicant.[2] In *Ex p. Fry* [1954] 1 WLR 730, for example, a fireman refused to clean a superior officer's uniform, claiming that the instruction to do so was unlawful. The Court of Appeal declined to quash the resulting disciplinary caution for breach of natural justice. Singleton LJ noted the existence of a complaints procedure and characterized Fry's disobedience as 'extraordinarily foolish conduct'. The fireman should have complied with the instruction and complained later. In *R. v. Aston University Senate ex p. Roffey* [1969] 2 QB 538 two students were required to withdraw from their course in December 1967 after failing certain examinations. In July 1968 they applied for certiorari to quash the decision and mandamus to compel the University to determine properly whether, in accordance with the course regulations, they should be allowed to resit or made to withdraw. The Divisional Court accepted that there had been a breach of natural justice but declined to grant the remedies. One student was said to have delayed too long; he should have applied prior to June 1968, the date of the next available examination. Blain J thought the 'court should not be used for the creation of a real life counterpart to Chekhov's perpetual student'. *Glynn* v. *Keele University* [1971] 2 All ER 89 is rather similar. A student who sunbathed naked on the campus was fined £10 and excluded from the University residence. Once again an established breach of natural justice went without remedy. Pennycuick VC refused to grant an injunction on the ground that, given the applicant's conduct, the end result was fair:

There is no doubt that the offence was one of a kind which merited a severe penalty according to any standards current even today. I have no doubt that the sentence of exclusion of residence in the campus was a proper penalty in respect of that offence. Nor has the plaintiff . . . put forward any specific justification for what he did. So the position would have been that if the [University] had accorded him a hearing before making [its] decision, all that he . . . could have done would have been to put forward some general plea by way of mitigation. I do not disregard the importance of such a plea in an appropriate case, but I do not think the mere fact that he was deprived of throwing himself on the mercy of the [University] in that particular way is sufficient to justify setting aside a decision which was intrinsically a perfectly proper one.

The case has been criticized for linking the issue of fair procedure to the merits of the decision. Wade (1982, pp. 476–7) argues fair procedure must come first since 'it is only after hearing both sides that the merits can be properly considered'. A judge should not deny natural justice on the ground that it would make no difference. But there is an opposite view, put by Donaldson LJ in *Roffey*, that 'prerogative writs are a discretionary remedy designed to remedy real and substantial injustice'. (Compare *Scott* v. *Aberdeen Corpn* (above, p. 281).) Is this too limited an objective for judicial review?

It is convenient, for the purposes of exposition, to depict judicial review as a three-stage process with locus standi, limitation and the doctrine that the courts will not review action taken under the royal prerogative on the threshold; the grounds of review in the middle; and remedial discretion at the end. Our illustrations suggest, however, that the *compartmentalization* of judicial review cannot be pushed too far. *Glynn*'s case, where the applicant's conduct is considered at the remedial stage, may be compared with *Cinnamond* (see above, p. 93), where Lord Denning uses it to reduce the content of procedural fairness. In *Calvin* v. *Carr* (see above, p. 90) the Privy Council, adopting a contextual approach to procedural fairness, refused to intervene in a sporting dispute. The court also approved *Reid* v. *Rowley* [1977] 2 NZLR 472, another sporting case, where the New Zealand Appeal Court emphasized judicial restraint through remedial discretion. Elliott (1980a, p. 69) commented, 'the flexibility of natural justice resolves itself into choosing the least painful way of skinning a cat: either by asserting binding 'rules' and derogating from them at the remedial stage, or by asserting different rules for different contexts.' Again, in *Ex p. Fry*, the Court of Appeal selected a second, substantive reason for refusal to quash: the proceedings were described as 'disciplinary' in character and the rules of natural justice were applicable only to 'judicial' proceedings. Further, we noted that locus standi is but one of a number of limiting devices, and later on we will see how the traditional dichotomy between standing and the grounds of review collapsed in the *Federation* case. Judicial review begins to emerge as a complex entity, its parts intricately interwoven, rather than as a series of discrete doctrines or 'obstacles' over which the applicant has to leap.

In Chapter 9, we learned not to assume that a court decision is necessarily the last word on a particular matter or that cases have a decisive and positive impact on the making of administrative policy. There is evidence in the remedial discretion cases of what may be termed *judicial reaction to administrative behaviour*: a recognition by the courts that to push too far in attempting to control the administration would be to invite governmental disobedience to their 'commands'. Some judges have restricted the grant of mandatory orders, refusing them where they may prove impossible, or even difficult, to execute. Not only is judicial review complex, the relationship between courts and administrators is itself a tangled web.

Both these points are illustrated by *R. v. Bristol Corpn. ex p. Hendy* [1974] 1 All ER 1047. Following a statutory closing order on H's flat, the authority offered him temporary accommodation until a council house became available. H sought mandamus to compel the authority to comply with its duty under s.39(1) of the Land Compensation Act 1973 'to secure that he will be provided with . . . other accommodation'. H argued that s.39 required the offer of permanent accommodation, so giving him priority over other persons on the housing list. However, the Court of Appeal interpreted the provision, in Lord Denning's words, as requiring only that the authority 'do their best, as soon as practicable, to get him other accommodation . . . His circumstances must be considered along with the others [on the housing list] and a fair decision made between them'. The willingness of Scarman LJ to safeguard the position of third parties through the exercise of remedial discretion shows, once again, how different paths can lead to the same result:

If, in a situation such as this, there is evidence that a local authority is doing all that it honestly and honourably can to meet the statutory obligation, and that its failure, if there be failure, to meet that obligation arises really out of circumstances over which it has no control, then I would think it would be improper for the court to make an order of mandamus compelling it to do that which either it cannot do or which it can only do at the expense of other persons not before the court who may have equal rights with the applicant and some of whom would certainly have equal moral claims.

In *R. v. Paddington Valuation Officer ex p. Peachey Property Co. Ltd* [1965] 2 All E R 836, an order was sought which would have entailed quashing the rating valuation lists for the Paddington area. It was argued that this should not be done as the valuation lists for the whole of London, possibly England, would be imperilled. The rating authorities would have to return to the previous lists and all the assessments and payments under the new lists would have to be unravelled. At first sight, the Court of Appeal took a robust view. Salmon LJ declared:

> Whatever inconvenience or chaos might be involved in [quashing the lists], the court would not be deterred from doing so if satisfied that the [Valuation Officer] had acted illegally. One of the principal functions of our courts is to protect the public from an abuse of power on the part of anyone, such as a valuation officer, entrusted with a public duty which affects the rights of ordinary citizens. If the valuation officer acted illegally and thereby produced an unjust and invalid list, this would be such an abuse of power and one which the courts would certainly redress. It could be no answer that to do so would produce inconvenience and chaos for the rating authority – otherwise the law could be flouted and injustice perpetrated with impunity.

The practice was rather different. The majority (Danckwerts LJ dissenting) held that, on the merits, the applicants had not made out their case. And Lord Denning, with Danckwerts LJ, found a novel way out. They asserted that the courts not only possess a discretion to grant or refuse a remedy but also to choose its timing. Applying *Smith v. East Elloe*, the list was 'voidable', not 'void',[3] and the court could send mandamus to order the preparation of a new list; when this was complete, the old one could be quashed:

> Everything done under the old list will remain good. The rates that have been demanded and paid cannot be recovered back. For it is a general rule that where a voidable transaction is avoided, it does not invalidate intermediate transactions which were made on the basis that it was good . . . By this solution, all chaos is avoided.

This judicial propensity to temper decisions according to the 'needs' of the administration was seen in *Smith v. East Elloe* itself. Of course, these 'needs' are those perceived by the courts; some observers may criticize the Court of Appeal in *Hendy* for assuming, as the framework for its decision, the inevitability of a housing waiting list. Again, in *Ostler*'s case, four different conceptual devices were deployed to justify the application of the time-limit clause, while Lord

Denning, who noted that much work had been done consequent to the planning orders, emphasized the practical difficulties of deciding otherwise. Harlow comments:

The longer the act has stood unchallenged and the wider the ambit of the act, the more difficult it is to declare that it is devoid of all legal consequences and has no legal existence. To declare the act null/void/invalid or non-existent is relatively simple; to unravel the factual consequences of the act is infinitely harder. The courts are naturally not blind to this, although they seldom discuss it openly. [Harlow 1976, p. 124.]

2 Locus standi

The notion of an 'interest', on which standing requirements depend, is complex. A wide variety of individuals and organizations may subjectively feel themselves 'affected' by an administrative decision. Suppose, for example, that a metropolitan county or conurbation decides to reduce its subsidy to local public transport. As a result, rates fall but fares rise. Who might be said to have an interest in this decision? The administrative lawyer might answer, 'local ratepayers and users of public transport', but they are not necessarily the only groups. Try to draw up a list and see if it corresponds with Lord Diplock's (see below, p. 337).

One person may be able to assert a variety of interests. An employer may be a ratepayer or a member of an environmental group; a ratepayer may oppose the decision because he lives in the inner city or because he is offended by urban deprivation. In short, there are different types of interest. Stewart (1975, p. 1734) distinguishes 'material interests', which concern an individual's 'economic or physical well-being', from 'ideological interests', which involve 'the affirmation of religious or moral principles' (e.g. that green areas should be protected or pornography controlled). If the classification is applied to our example, the open-ended nature of 'material interest' becomes apparent. A restrictive interpretation might confine decisions concerning an individual's 'well-being' to those which cause direct financial loss. If however, the notion encompasses non-pecuniary detriment, where is the line to be drawn? Might it, for example, include the anticipated loss of pleasure presently derived from walking along the leafy avenues of our hypothetical conurbation?

The significance of locus standi becomes apparent. The courts have used the doctrine to *select* from the variety of possible interests those which they will protect. Discussing procedural fairness, where the courts claim to balance 'private' and 'public' interests, we suggested that members of society might differ as to the significance of a particular asserted interest. Similarly, we are likely to disagree about which interests merit access to the courts and which do not, a point borne out by the case law, which developed as a mass of conflicting decisions sufficient to defeat even the most ardent rule synthesist. The conflict did not arise of its own accord, it occurred because different judges were prepared to protect different interests.

The applicant for a declaration or injunction, remedies derived from private law, traditionally had to demonstrate that unlawful administrative action had either infringed his 'private legal rights' (so giving a remedy in damages) or, less restrictively, had caused him 'special damage' over and above that suffered by members of the public. In *Gregory* v. *Camden LBC* [1966] 1 WLR 899, the plaintiff claimed that a grant of planning permission by the local planning authority for the building of a school at the rear of his property did not conform to the Greater London Development Plan. Although the authority was still empowered to grant permission, in the circumstances it was required by the Town and Country Planning (Development Plans) Direction 1954 to send copies and plans of the application to the Minister. The plaintiff sought a declaration that the permission was ultra vires since this had not been done. Paull J assumed the illegality of the decision but denied the plaintiff standing on the ground that the development on adjacent land did not infringe his legal rights as landowner. This decision seriously limited the interests enjoying court protection since 'private legal right' only encompassed 'material interests' of a certain kind. It was considered insufficient that the plaintiff would be inconvenienced (through noise etc.) by the proximity of the intended school, provided that the interference would not amount to a common law nuisance.

This stance was reasserted in *Gouriet* v. *Union of Post Office Workers* [1977] 3 WLR 300,[4] in the face of earlier attempts by Lord Denning to relax it. *Gouriet* also concerned the scope of the 'relator action' which provides an escape from the standing requirements for declarations and injunctions. (The term is explained in Lord Wilberforce's judgment (below)). The Attorney-General, who acts here in the name of the Crown, has discretion whether or not to consent to relator actions and also power, infrequently exercised, to control the conduct of the case. Two issues have divided the judges.

First, is the exercise of the Attorney-General's discretion reviewable by the courts? Secondly, can an individual sidestep a refusal to consent by bringing proceedings in his own name? Or is it only the Attorney-General, ministerially responsible to Parliament, who in these cases may represent the public interest? In *Attorney General ex rel. McWhirter* v. *Independent Broadcasting Authority* [1973] 2 WLR 344, M was upset by a decision to screen a television film which, from reading newspaper reports, he believed to be pornographic. He asked the Attorney-General to obtain an injunction ex officio, but, eight hours prior to the scheduled screening, the latter declined, saying that he would consider a proper request for relator proceedings. M decided, in view of the shortage of time, to proceed on his own, although the Attorney-General later assured the Court of Appeal that the formalities for instituting relators could be completed within an hour or so. Faced with this evidence, the Court held that since M had elected not to take the opportunity open to him of applying for relator proceedings, he should be denied standing. But Lord Denning declined to grant the Attorney-General the final word over access to the courts:

If the Attorney-General refused leave in a proper case, or improperly or unreasonably delays in giving leave, or his machinery works too slowly, then a member of the public, who has a sufficient interest, can himself apply to the court itself. He can ask for a declaration and, in a proper case, for an injunction . . . I regard it as a matter of high constitutional principle that if there is good ground for supposing that a government department or a public authority is transgressing the law, or is about to transgress it, in a way which offends or injures thousands of Her Majesty's subjects, then in the last resort any one of those offended or injured can draw it to the attention of the courts of law and seek to have the law enforced. But this, I would emphasise, is only in the last resort when there is no other remedy reasonably available to secure that the law is obeyed.

Gouriet v. *Union of Post Office Workers*, however, reached the House of Lords. The Union declared a one-day boycott of South African mail in protest against apartheid. The proposed action appeared contrary to the criminal law because s.58 of the Post Office Act 1953 made it an offence for anyone wilfully to detain or delay the mail. G, Secretary of the National Association of Freedom, an organization concerned to assert the 'freedom of the individual' against state and collectivist power, wished to challenge the legality of the Union's decision but disclosed no injury greater than that to the public at large. Here the position was complicated because trade unions enjoy wide immunity from actions in tort and the Post Office is similarly protected. If G had tried to show 'special damage', for example, that his business with South Africa would be affected, he might have been met by a plea of immunity from process. So he asked the Attorney General to institute relator proceedings for an injunction restraining the Union from soliciting persons wilfully to delay the mail. When this was refused, G brought proceedings in his own name. In the Court of Appeal, the majority repudiated Lord Denning's view that the Attorney-General's exercise of discretion to refuse consent could be cut down by a court if it was unreasonable and ultra vires. The majority also held that G had no locus standi to seek a permanent injunction. But, unanimously, the Court decided that he possessed standing to seek a declaration that the proposed boycott was illegal and also an interim injunction pending a final determination of the declaratory proceedings. The law lords supported the Court of Appeal majority against Lord Denning but rejected the unanimous decisions. The private individual was not to dodge the Attorney-General's refusal to consent by bringing his own action.

LORD WILBERFORCE: A relator action . . . is one in which the Attorney-General, on the relation of individuals (who may include local authorities or companies) brings an action to assert a public right. It [is] a fundamental principle of English law that private rights can be asserted by individuals, but that public rights can only be asserted by the Attorney-General as representing the public. In terms of constitutional law, the rights of the public are vested in the Crown, and the Attorney-General enforces them as an officer of the Crown. And just as the Attorney-General has in general no power to interfere with the assertion of private rights, so in general no private person has the right of representing the public in the assertion of public rights. If he tries to do so his action can be struck out . . .

[The] . . . relator action with which this appeal is concerned . . . is of a very special character, and it is one in which the predominant position of the Attorney-General is *a fortiori* the general case. This is a right, of comparatively modern use, of the Attorney-General to invoke the assistance of *civil courts* in aid of the *criminal law* . . . To apply to the court for an injunction at all against the threat of a criminal offence, may involve a decision of policy with which conflicting considerations may enter. Will the law best be served by preventive action? Will the grant of an injunction exacerbate the situation? (very relevant this in industrial disputes). Is the injunction likely to be effective or may it be futile? Will it be better to make it clear that the law will be enforced by prosecution and to appeal to the law-abiding instinct, negotiations, and moderate leadership, rather than provoke people along the road to martyrdom? All these matters . . . point the matter as one essentially for the Attorney-General's preliminary discretion . . . [His] right to seek, in the civil courts, anticipatory prevention of a breach of the law, is [part] of his general power to enforce, in the public interest, public rights . . . The decision to be taken before embarking on a claim for injunctive relief, involving as it does the interests of the public over a broad horizon, is a decision which the Attorney-General *alone* is suited to make . . .

[But] it is said, since the whole matter is discretionary it can be left to the court. The court can prevent vexatious or frivolous, or multiple actions: the court is not obliged to grant an injunction: leave it in the court's hands. I cannot accept this either. The decisions to be made as to the public interest are not such as courts are fitted or equipped to make. The very fact, that, as the present case very well shows, decisions are of the type to attract political criticism and controversy, shows that they are outside the range of discretionary problems which the courts can resolve. Judges are equipped to find legal rights and administer, on well-known principles, discretionary remedies. These matters are widely outside those areas . . .

Reliance was placed on [the] observations of Lord Denning in [the *McWhirter* case] that an individual member of the public can apply for an injunction 'if the Attorney-General refuses leave in a proper case, or improperly or unreasonably delays in giving leave, or his machinery works too slowly'. There is no authority for this proposition and in my opinion it is contrary to principle. In any event none of the stated hypotheses apply in the present case . . .

The majority of the Court of Appeal sought, in effect, to outflank the refusal of [consent] by allowing declaratory relief to be claimed and by permitting this to be used as a basis for granting an interim injunction. This produced the remarkable result that the plaintiff was more successful at the interim stage than he could possibly be at the final stage – for it was accepted that no final injunction could be claimed . . .[5] There is no support in authority for the proposition that declaratory relief can be granted unless the plaintiff . . . either asserts a legal right which is denied or threatened, or claims immunity from some claim of the defendant against him or claims that the defendant is infringing or threatens to infringe some public right so as to inflict special damage on the plaintiff. The present proceedings do not possess the required characteristic.

Turning to the prerogative orders, the dominant test used to be that the applicant be a 'person aggrieved'. This formula is also commonly used to denote the standing required for statutory quashing remedies, especially in planning.[6] However there was serious judicial conflict. First, the older cases and a few of the modern ones supported the test of 'private legal right' for mandamus. An example is *R. v. Hereford Corporation ex p. Harrower* [1970] 1 WLR 1424, which also indicates the distinction between this test and 'special damage'. The corporation was about to enter into a contract with the Midland Electricity Board for the provision of central heating in some council flats. The contract had not been put out for tender although the corporation's standing orders required that public notice should be given and that a reasonable number of firms on the corporation's list of approved contractors should be invited to tender. This list included the applicants. They challenged the procedures used, relying on s.266(2) of the Local Government Act 1933 which provided that contracts made by a local authority had to be made in accordance with its standing orders. They were held, as electrical contractors, to lack locus standi; because they had no right to contract with the corporation, they could show no infringement of a private legal right. The test of special damage might have produced a different result. Arguably, the applicants suffered more from the procedures used than did members of the public because, as contractors on the Corporation's list, they lost the chance of winning the contract. Is this an example of Reich's 'new property'?

Secondly, judges interpreted the open-ended phrase 'person aggrieved' in different ways. In other words, they disagreed as to which 'grievances' merited judicial protection. In *Buxton* v. *Minister of Housing and Local Government* [1961] 1 QB 278, for example, the formula was equated with the test of private legal right. So a landowner, as in *Gregory* v. *Camden LBC*, was denied standing to challenge development on adjacent land. But this restrictive interpretation stood in marked contrast to a liberalizing trend, initiated by Lord Denning, which significantly diluted, but did not abandon, standing requirements. In the *Paddington Valuation* case the applicants owned some purpose-built flats and felt aggrieved about the assessments contained in new valuation lists of their flats as compared with flats in converted houses. They sought mandamus requiring the valuation officer to prepare a list in accordance with his statutory duty or, alternatively, certiorari to quash the list. Lord Denning granted them standing as persons aggrieved:

[The respondents] contended that [the applicants] are not persons aggrieved because, even if they succeeded in increasing all the gross values of other people in the Paddington area, it would not make a pennyworth of difference to them . . . But I do not think grievances are to be measured in pounds, shillings and pence. If a ratepayer or other person finds his name included in a valuation list which is invalid, he is entitled to come to the court and apply to have it quashed. He is not to be put off by the plea that he has suffered no damage . . . The court would not listen, of course, to a mere busybody who was interfering in things which did not concern him. But it will listen to anyone whose interests are affected by what has been done.

The language is opaque. Will we all recognize a person 'whose interests are affected by what has been done' or might we think him a 'busybody'? Which was Gouriet? In *R.* v. *Greater London Council, ex p. Blackburn* [1976] 1 W L R 550 the applicant, a long-standing campaigner against pornography, sought prohibition against the G L C to prevent it from licensing films which he thought indecent. Lord Denning granted him standing:

> Blackburn is a citizen of London. His wife is a ratepayer. He has children who may be harmed by the exhibition of pornographic films. If he has no sufficient interest, no other citizen has. I think he comes within the principle which I stated in [*McWhirter*'s case], which I would recast today so as to [conclude]: 'then any one of those offended or injured can draw it to the attention of the courts of law and seek to have the law enforced, and the courts in their discretion can grant whatever remedy is appropriate' . . . One remedy which is always open, by leave of the court, is to apply for a prerogative writ . . . These provide a discretionary remedy and the discretion of the court extends to permitting an application to be made by any member of the public . . . though it will refuse it to a mere busybody who is interfering in things which do not concern him: see [the *Paddington Valuation* case].

Applying Stewart's classification, how would the interests which Lord Denning considers merit protection be characterized? What was McWhirter's interest? This liberal approach to locus standi is combined with a correlative belief in judicial discretion, which encompasses not only the manipulation of the standing test itself but also the discretionary nature of judicial remedies. So, although on Lord Denning's analysis more applicants may come before the courts, some of them are likely to leave empty-handed.

The cynic might describe judicial review as a series of exceptions to ill-defined rules and the escape routes around the doctrine of locus standi provide an example. Some judges have substituted for the examination of standing requirements in individual cases the concept of a class of persons nominally entitled to challenge. Thus ratepayers have been allowed to seek review of expenditure by local authorities.[7] *Harrower* is a useful example because it translates into legal form the idea that one individual may have a variety of interests to assert. The applicants, denied standing as electrical contractors, were granted it as ratepayers on the ground that these automatically possess an interest in the way in which the rate fund to which they must contribute is distributed.[8]

Public authorities often possess powers to invoke the law over and above those possessed by individuals. The relator action is one example but public bodies and local authorities may equally be authorized to bring their own proceedings; e.g. s.222 of the Local

Government Act 1972 provides that where an authority 'considers it expedient for the promotion or protection of the interests of the inhabitants in their area . . . they may prosecute or defend or appear in any legal proceedings and, in the case of civil proceedings, may institute them in their own name.' The realm of central-local government relations exhibits other techniques by which local authorities may be kept within the law. Ministers are often empowered, provided they are satisfied that an authority is not performing its statutory duties satisfactorily, to declare it in default and to transfer its functions, either to the centre or to another local authority. For example, the Housing Act 1980 gives local authority tenants the 'right to buy' their homes. S.23 provides that 'where it appears to the Secretary of State that tenants . . . have . . . difficulty in exercising their right to buy effectively and expeditiously, he may . . . do all such things as appear to him necessary or expedient' to enable tenants to exercise that right. Tenants complained that Norwich Council was delaying implementation of purchase procedures. The DOE took up the matter but the authority claimed that, given its other obligations, the steps it had taken represented a reasonable compliance with the Act. The Court of Appeal rejected the council's request to quash the Minister's subsequent decision to take sale of the council houses into central government hands (see *R.* v. *Secretary of State for the Environment ex p. Norwich City Council* [1982] 2 WLR 580). Similarly, where a district auditor believes that an item of expenditure is unlawful, he may seek a declaration from the courts that this is so. *Roberts* v. *Hopwood* (see below, p. 321) provides an illustration. If the declaration is granted, court orders against the persons responsible may ensue, barring them from public office and requiring repayment of the sums expended.

If government agencies refuse to act, standing to sue may prevent some issues from coming to court, either because nobody has the requisite interest or because the aggrieved person is unwilling or unable to act. The possible consequences are illustrated by the widespread practice of extra-statutory tax concessions. The taxpayers who benefit from the concessions are hardly likely to complain. If other, less fortunate, taxpayers are then denied standing to challenge concessions, a whole area of potentially illegal administrative action may be insulated from judicial review. Hodge highlights the practical difficulties caused by locus standi for campaigning organizations like CPAG:

It would be helpful if the administrative parties . . . could be challenged on behalf of the class of claimants who might be affected . . . Cases take a long time before they come for hearing. In homelessness cases this has been a key disadvantage, as people without a home cannot wait even a week until one is available. [Hodge 1979, pp. 261–2.]

So what interests *should* the courts allow 'individuals' to assert? Should we, for example, follow the lead of the United States? The basic test there is contained in s.10 of the Administrative Procedure Act: 'A person suffering legal wrong because of agency action, or adversely affected or aggrieved by [it] . . . is entitled to judicial review thereof.' Cases in the early 1970s drastically reduced the 'material interest' demanded, sometimes almost to vanishing point. In *US* v. *Students Challenging Regulatory Agency Procedures* 412 US 669 (1973), the applicants challenged a proposed surcharge on railroad freight charges as not fixing differential charges favourable to the transport-ation of recycled products. They alleged that their members' enjoyment of parks within the District of Columbia 'was directly disturbed by the adverse environmental impact caused by the non-use of recyclable goods brought about by the surcharge'. The Supreme Court granted them standing. On the other hand, in *Sierra Club* v. *Morton* 405 US 727 (1972), the Supreme Court refused to abandon altogether the need for some 'material interest'. The Club, a major conservation group, challenged a decision to grant permits for the commercial exploitation of a Californian game refuge. Although Club members actually used the threatened refuge for recreational purposes, counsel refrained from alleging the fact. Instead the Club relied on what Stewart would term its 'ideological interest': a 'special interest in the conservation and sound maintenance of the national parks, game refuges and forests of the country'. In effect, it sought carte blanche to challenge any environmental degradation. The Supreme Court denied standing.

MR JUSTICE STEWART: The trend of cases . . . has been toward recognising that injuries other than economic harm are sufficient to bring a person [within s.10] and towards discarding the notion that an injury that is widely shared is ipso facto not an injury sufficient to provide the basis for judicial review . . . [So] the interest alleged to have been injured 'may reflect aesthetic conservational, and recreational as well as economic values'. But broadening the categories of injury that may be alleged in support of standing is a different matter from abandoning the requirement that the party seeking review must himself have suffered an injury . . . A mere 'interest in a problem', no matter how longstanding the interest and no matter how qualified the organisation is in evaluating the problem, is not sufficient by itself to render the organisation 'adversely affected' or 'aggrieved' . . . The Sierra Club is a large and long established organisation . . . But if a 'special interest' in this subject were enough to entitle the Sierra Club to commence this litigation, there would appear to be no objective basis upon which to disallow a suit by any other bona fide 'special interest' organisation, however small or short-lived. And if any group with a bona fide 'special interest' could initiate such litigation, it is difficult to perceive why any individual citizen with the same bona fide special interest would not also be entitled to do so.[9]

How does this analysis compare with Lord Denning's approach in the *Blackburn* case? How convincing is the Supreme Court's reasoning? Do you think that ideological interests should ever be protected?

In *Sierra Club*, the Supreme Court also stopped short of protecting a third type of interest, identified by Stewart as the 'interest in enforcement of law'. According to Lord Wilberforce, this was asserted by Gouriet who 'at all times disclaimed having any interest in these matters apart from the interest which all members of the public have in seeing that the law is obeyed'. Stewart points out that this interest constitutes:

. . . a hybrid that is neither purely material nor purely ideological. Because the proper enforcement of law is important to the social security that underlies cooperative productivity and individual tranquillity, it is not fanciful to find a material interest in correcting instances of official lawlessness. It is, however, difficult to fix the importance of such an interest in all but the most egregious cases. On the other hand, the interest in law enforcement may be regarded as an ideological attachment to the principle that the law be obeyed for its own sake. [Stewart 1975, p. 1739.]

This particular interest is subversive of standing requirements because it implies that 'illegality', with which all members of society are said to be concerned, is the key criterion. Standing requirements should, logically, be abolished, permitting the *actio popularis* or citizen's action whereby any citizen (subject to issues of justiciability which are discussed below) may seek review of an illegal act. Feldman, who asserts a 'social interest that public authorities act according to the law', arrives at the same conclusion:

The idea that it is in the public interest that laws should be obeyed by governors as well as by governed is at the heart of the ideal of the rule of law . . . Public law in general, and judicial review in particular, is concerned with the control of excess or abuse of power by public bodies, and if a case of unlawful action is made out it would be a negation of public law principles if a remedy were denied solely because of the identity of the applicant or the nature of his interest. Public law is concerned less with righting individuals' grievances than with remedying public wrongs ... Arguments which concentrate on the position of the individual applicant, to the extent of excluding the social interest in maintaining the rule of law, are not properly admissible in a public law context. Others may benefit more than the applicant. In particular, society may benefit as a whole when courts impress on government agencies the need to act strictly within their legal powers. [Feldman 1981, pp. 1–3.]

3 Standing: rules to discretion?

Before embarking on our survey of the conflicting case law, we remarked that the conflict arose because different judges favoured the protection of different interests. This is scarcely acknowledged in the literature. The dominant response has been to call for clarification and simplification of the 'rules'. De Smith (1968, p. 574), commenting on locus standi for mandamus, 'hoped that an early opportunity will arise for a restatement of law on this confused topic'. The two Law Commission documents which preceded the recent reform of standing were devoid of any serious analysis of why particular interests do or do not deserve court protection. The initial working paper, 'Remedies in Administrative Law' (Law Comm. No. 40 (1971), paras. 125–7), envisaged a uniform and liberal standing test modelled along American lines: 'any person who is or will be adversely affected by administrative action'. In interpreting this formula, the courts were to be aided by guidelines; for instance, the graver the breach of law, the weaker the standing test. Here are the reasons proffered for this measure of liberalization:

First, it seems to us an elementary principle of justice that a person whose interests are affected adversely by illegal action should be entitled to challenge that action in the courts ... Secondly, this formulation of *locus standi* should be fairly easy to apply in the courts ... Thirdly, and perhaps most importantly, the existing law [on] certiorari has reached this liberal position.

Bearing in mind the interpretation placed on the American formula in *Sierra Club*, how cogent was the Commission's justification for *not* protecting non-material interests? 'We see no reason to complicate the position by giving the court power in its discretion to admit challenge by a complete stranger.'

Although the Law Commission backtracked significantly in its final report, the broader issues were again shunned. The preferred formula, that the applicant possess 'sufficient interest' in the matter to which the application relates, was chosen because it 'allows for

further development of the requirement of standing by the courts
having regard to the relief which is sought' (Cmnd 6407 (1976), para.
48). The last phrase suggests that, contrary to the working paper
proposal, standing is to vary as between the individual remedies. And
the Law Commission hands the issue of standing straight back to the
courts. Not surprisingly then, the imprecise formula 'sufficient
interest' provoked much debate when introduced by the new Order
53. Did it change the law?[10] If so, what did it mean and had it created
a uniform test? These and other issues provoked serious disagreement
in the leading case of *IRC* v. *National Federation of Self-Employed and
Small Businesses Ltd* [1980] 2 All ER 378 (DC, CA); [1981] 2 All ER
93 (HL).

Casual workers in the printing industry had, for some years,
evaded income tax by drawing their pay under false names. The
Inland Revenue made a 'special arrangement' with the employers,
employees and unions under which, in return for an end to this
practice, it undertook not to investigate back tax prior to 1977. The
50,000 strong Federation, whose name speaks for itself, challenged
the legality of the amnesty seeking, first, a declaration that the Board
of Inland Revenue had acted unlawfully in granting it and, second,
mandamus to compel the Board to assess and collect the lost tax.
Prior to the House of Lords hearing, the Crown conceded, for the
purposes of deciding standing as a preliminary issue, that the
arrangement was illegal. The Divisional Court held that, as taxpayers
challenging the validity of other taxpayers' assessments, the Federation lacked 'sufficient interest'. This decision was reversed by a
majority (Lord Denning and Ackner LJ) on appeal.

LORD DENNING: [Their] grievance [is] that these 6000 Fleet Street casuals
have been given preferential treatment such as would not be accorded to any
other taxpayers [including] themselves . . . If their grievance stopped there, I
should have doubted whether they had a 'sufficient interest'. It seems to me
that the Revenue authorities should be allowed to negotiate with taxpayers,
and come to a settlement with them, without being harassed by complaints
from members of the public generally. It is most undesirable that every Tom,
Dick or Harry should be able to call the Revenue to account for their
stewardship, or to pry into their neighbour's tax returns. But . . . they [also]
think that the Fleet Street casuals are being given preferential treatment, over
and above that afforded to other taxpayers, because they have available the
weapon of industrial action open to them. [The Federation] have no
industrial muscle. They have no one against whom to strike . . .

If [they] cannot complain, there is no one else who can. The unlawful
conduct of the Revenue (assuming it is unlawful) will go without remedy. The
Revenue authorities will have obtained dispensing power without it being

authorised by Parliament. And that, by a defect in our procedure: because no one has a locus standi to complain. [So] I would allow the whole body of taxpayers a locus standi to complain. Assuredly the Attorney-General will not complain on their behalf. He never does complain against a government department . . .

I must confess that, if it were not for the [Crown's] concession . . . I should have been disposed to say that, as a matter of discretion, the application should be refused. But once the point emerges . . . whether the Revenue authorities have a dispensing power, then it is so important that . . . the court should be able to award the remedy on the application of a public-spirited citizen who has no other interest than a regard for the due observance of the law.

My conclusion is therefore that [they] are not busybodies. They are not spending their funds on this litigation out of spite or malice. They have a genuine grievance because, as they see it, the Fleet Street casuals are getting out of paying their back taxes: because of their industrial muscle.

Lord Denning blurs the traditional distinction between 'standing' and 'legality' by arguing that the Federation possesses 'sufficient interest' because the amnesty is illegal. This is something like the *Cinnamond* decision, where substantive considerations were invoked to determine what was fair procedure.

Lawton LJ, dissenting, kept the merits separate from the issue of access. In arguing for a restricted judicial role, he emphasized, unlike Lord Denning, the availability of non-judicial remedies, amongst which he included the right of a taxpayer to complain about his own assessment to the Special or General Commissioners of Tax (and then, on a point of law, to the courts), his MP, and the Parliamentary Commissioner. He pointed out that concern about the general conduct of the Revenue could be relayed to MPs or to the public via the press. Lawton LJ continued:

For [a sufficient] interest . . . there must be a connection with the subject matter of the application greater than that which citizens generally may have . . . A line has to be drawn somewhere. If this application is put on the side of the line where the federation want it to be, anyone's genuine concern for good and lawful government, whether at a national or local level, would be a sufficient interest to justify a judicial review. This would entangle the courts with administration in a way which would be inconvenient and unconstitutional. Such is the flexibility of our unwritten constitution that the lack of a remedy in the courts does not mean that justice may not be done elsewhere.

Those theoretical issues, avoided by the Law Commission, simply will not go away!

The Crown withdrew its concession before the law lords, who subsequently upheld the legality of the 'special arrangement'. But the judges (with the possible exception of Lord Fraser) were prepared to follow Lord Denning's example by breaking the orthodox division between standing and merits. They criticized the lower courts for determining the 'substantial interest' point solely as a preliminary question. Since it was tied to the merits, the two issues had to be considered together. The House of Lords held that, while the Divisional Court ought to have given leave to apply, it should have dismissed the application at the subsequent hearing:

LORD WILBERFORCE: There may be simple cases in which it can be seen at the earliest stage that the person applying for judicial review has no interest at all, or no sufficient interest to support the application; then it would be quite correct at the threshold to refuse him leave to apply. The right to do so is an important safeguard against the courts being flooded and public bodies harassed by irresponsible applications. But in other cases this will not be so. In these it will be necessary to consider the powers or the duties in law of those against whom the relief is asked, the position of the applicant in relation to those powers or duties, and the breach of those said to have been committed. In other words, the question of sufficient interest cannot, in such cases, be considered in the abstract, or as an isolated point: it must be taken together with the legal and factual context. The rule requires sufficient interest *in the matter to which the application relates*. This, in the present case, necessarily involves the whole question of the duties of the Inland Revenue and the breaches or failure of those duties of which the federation complains . . .

So far as the substantive law is concerned, this remained unchanged [by Order 53] . . . and the same preservation is contemplated by legislation now pending.[11] As to [the test of sufficient interest] I would state two negative propositions. First, it does not remove the whole, and vitally important question of locus standi into the realm of pure discretion. The matter is one for decision, a mixed decision of fact and law, which the court must decide on legal principles. Second, the fact that the same words are used to cover all the forms of remedy allowed by the rule does not mean that the test is the same in all cases . . . It would seem obvious enough that the interest of a person seeking to compel an authority to carry out a duty is different from that of a person complaining that a judicial or administrative body has, to his detriment, exceeded its powers . . .

[The income tax legislation] establishes that the commissioners must assess each individual taxpayer in relation to his circumstances. Such assessments and all information regarding taxpayers' affairs are strictly confidential. There is no list or record of assessments which can be inspected by other taxpayers. Nor is there any common fund of the produce of income tax in which income taxpayers as a whole can be said to have any interest. The produce of income tax, together with that of other inland revenue taxes, is paid into the Consolidated Fund which is at the disposal of Parliament for any purposes that Parliament thinks fit. The position of taxpayers is therefore very different from that of ratepayers [where] the amount of rates assessed on ratepayers is ascertainable by the public through the valuation list. The produce of rates goes into a common fund applicable for the benefit of the ratepayers. Thus any ratepayer has an interest, direct and sufficient, in the rates levied on other ratepayers; for this reason, his right as a 'person aggrieved' to challenge assessments on them has long been recognised and is so now in the General Rate Act 1967, s.69 . . .

The structure of the legislation relating to income tax, on the other hand, makes clear that no corresponding right is intended to be conferred on taxpayers. Not only is there no express or implied provision in the legislation on which such a right could be claimed, but to allow it would be subversive of the whole system, which involves that the commissioners' duties are to the Crown, and that matters relating to income tax are between the commissioners and the taxpayer concerned. No other person is given any right to make proposals about the tax payable by any individual; he cannot even inquire as to such tax. The total confidentiality of assessments and of negotiations between individuals and the Revenue is a vital element in the working of the system. As a matter of general principle I would hold that one taxpayer has no sufficient interest in asking the court to investigate the tax affairs of another taxpayer or to complain that the latter has been underassessed or overassessed; indeed there is a strong public interest that he should not. And this principle applies equally to groups of taxpayers: an aggregate of individuals each of whom has no interest cannot of itself have an interest.

That a case can never arise in which the acts of abstentions or the Revenue can be brought before the court I am certainly not prepared to assert, nor that, in a case of sufficient gravity, the court might not be able to hold that another taxpayer or other taxpayers could challenge them. Whether this situation has been reached or not must depend on an examination, on evidence, of what breach of duty or illegality is alleged.

[Lord Wilberforce reviewed the facts, which included evidence from the Revenue that, given 'the large number of potential taxpayers (about 25 million), the huge sums involved and the limitations on the Board's manpower . . . it is impossible for the Board to collect all the tax that is due, and that decisions have to be taken by way of "care and management" of the taxes to collect as much as is practicable, by cost-effective methods.' Discounting the suggestion that the amnesty had been conceded because of possible industrial action, Lord Wilberforce concluded:]

I fail to see how any court . . . could avoid reaching the conclusion that the Inland Revenue . . . were acting in this matter genuinely in the care and management of the taxes, under the powers entrusted to them. This has no resemblance to any kind of case where the court ought, at the instance of a taxpayer, to intervene. To do so would involve permitting a taxpayer or a group of taxpayers to call in question the exercise of management powers and involve the court itself in a management exercise. Judicial review . . . does not extend into this area . . . [So] the Divisional Court, while justified on the ex parte application in granting leave, ought, having regard to the nature of 'the matter' raised, to have held that the federation had shown no sufficient interest in that matter to justify its application for relief.

So Lord Wilberforce envisages a relaxed attitude towards applications for leave since only in 'simple' cases ought standing to be
denied. In other instances the courts are to investigate in enough
depth to establish, at the hearing stage, whether the applicant
possesses 'sufficient interest' in relation to the nature of the administrative function and the alleged illegality. However, Lord Diplock
disputed Lord Wilberforce's[12] claims concerning the limited impact
of Order 53. Lord Diplock argued that many of the older cases had
been swept away, so that a uniform, liberal test of standing had been
established:

LORD DIPLOCK: I should prefer to . . . dismiss the federation's application
. . . not on the specific ground of no sufficient interest but on the more general
ground that it has not been shown that . . . the Board did anything that was
ultra vires or unlawful. They acted in the bona fide exercise of the wide
managerial discretion conferred on them by statute . . .

The main purpose of the new Order 53 was to sweep away . . . procedural
differences [between the remedies] including, in particular, differences as to
locus standi . . .

As respects the claim for a declaration considerable reliance was placed [by
the Crown] on *Gouriet*. This decision is, in my view, irrelevant to any question
that your Lordships have to decide today. The defendant trade union in
deciding to instruct its members to take unlawful industrial action was not
exercising any governmental powers; it was acting as a private citizen and
could only be sued as such in a civil action under private law. It was not
amenable to any remedy in public law . . .

In contrast to this, judicial review is a remedy that lies exclusively in public
law . . . The language . . . of the new Ord. 53 shows an intention that on an
application for judicial review the court should have jurisdiction to grant a
declaration or an injunction as an alternative to making one of the prerogative
orders, wherever in its discretion it thinks that it is just and convenient to do
so, and that this jurisdiction should be exercisable in any case in which the
applicant would previously have had locus standi to apply for any of the
prerogative orders.

[Lord Diplock then reviewed the cases on prerogative orders and
associated himself with Lord Denning's stance in *Blackburn*'s case (above). He
pointed to the two-staged procedure of Order 53 and, focussing upon the
initial or 'threshold' stage, the application for leave to apply, continued:]

Its purpose is to prevent the time of the court being wasted by busybodies
with misguided or trivial complaints of administrative error, and to remove
the uncertainty in which public officers and authorities might be left whether
they could safely proceed with administrative action while proceedings for
judicial review of it were actually pending even though misconceived . . .

At the threshold stage, for the federation to make out a prima facie case of
reasonable suspicion that the Board in showing a discriminatory leniency to a
substantial class of taxpayers had done so for ulterior reasons extraneous to

good management, and thereby deprived the national exchequer of considerable sums of money, constituted what was in my view reason enough for
the Divisional Court to consider that the federation, or for that matter, any
taxpayer, had a sufficient interest to apply to have the question whether the
Board were acting ultra vires reviewed by the court. The whole purpose of
requiring that leave should first be obtained to make the application for
judicial review would be defeated if the court were to go into the matter in any
depth at that stage. If, on a quick perusal of the material then available, the
court thinks that it discloses what might on further consideration turn out to
be an arguable case in favour of granting to the applicant the relief claimed, it
ought, in the exercise of a judicial discretion, to give him leave to apply for
that relief . . .

   If, in the instant case, what at the threshold stage was suspicion only had
been proved at the hearing of the application for judicial review to have been
true in fact (instead of being utterly destroyed), I would have held that this
was a matter in which the federation had a sufficient interest in obtaining an
appropriate order, whether by way of declaration or mandamus, to require
performance by the Board of statutory duties which for reasons shown to be
ultra vires they were failing to perform.

   It would, in my view, be a grave lacuna in our system of public law if a
pressure group, like the federation, or even a single public spirited taxpayer,
were prevented by outdated technical rules of locus standi from bringing the
matter to the attention of the court to vindicate the rule of law and get the
unlawful conduct stopped. The Attorney General, although he occasionally
applies for prerogative orders against public authorities that do not form part
of central government, in practice never does so against government
departments. It is not, in my view, a sufficient answer to say that judicial
review of the actions of officers or departments of central government is
unnecessary because they are accountable to Parliament for the way in which
they carry out their functions. They are accountable to Parliament for what
they do so far as regards efficiency and policy, and of that Parliament is the
only judge; they are responsible to a court of justice for the lawfulness of what
they do, and of that the court is the only judge.

Although none of the Law Lords abandoned standing tests
altogether, the *Federation* case appears to represent a shift away from
the 'protection of the individual' view of administrative law towards
an expanded control theory which can encompass the interest in
administrative legality.[13] Lord Diplock is perhaps more expansive
than Lord Wilberforce. The latter, in stressing that the courts ought
not to go too far by interfering with 'managerial' decisions, bases his
decision on no sufficient interest. Lord Diplock rests his conclusion
on the absence of illegality and talks about 'vindicating the rule of
law'. The disagreement may be more apparent than real. There are
indications in Lord Diplock's speech that other taxpayers will only
possess a sufficient interest in 'flagrant and serious breaches of the

law'. And Lord Wilberforce is possibly more expansionist than first appears, because he contemplates intervention in cases of 'sufficient gravity', a phrase nowhere defined. So perhaps the best characterization of the *Federation* case is that it stands for a weakened version of the actio popularis, representing a judicial willingness to consider some, but not all, instances of administrative illegality.

The senior law lords also seemed to divide over the exercise of judicial discretion. Lord Wilberforce emphasized the primacy of 'legal principles', as manifested in the decided cases, over 'pure discretion'. Like Lord Denning in *Blackburn*'s case, Lord Diplock, who saw Order 53 as sweeping away the old distinctions, advocated liberal standing tests coupled with the use of discretion both on locus standi and the grant of remedies. This approach provides increased scope for judicial censure of administrative abuse of power although, at the end of the day, the individual aggrieved may receive no concrete remedy. Sunkin (see above, p. 267) argued that Lord Diplock's judgment in *O'Reilly* v. *Mackman* represented an assertion of judicial control over legal incursions into the administrative process. Given that standing requirements touch on the constitutional position of the courts (see below), is there perhaps a corresponding development here? Arguably Lord Diplock's approach also entails the transfer of discretionary power from administrator to judge. Is administrative arbitrariness reborn as judicial caprice? The commentators predictably divide. Griffith, discussing a number of student cases, including *Glynn* and *Roffey*, believes the refusal to grant remedies stems from prejudice common to judges and 'other, equally senior, members of society' (1977, p. 167). Wade (1977, pp. 456, 561) notes that a refusal to grant a remedy can, like a denial of standing, in effect validate an unlawful act and 'may make inroads upon the rule of law'. But he assures us that 'the judicial discretion in withholding remedies is very carefully exercised'.

Cane takes the argument one stage further. Since the key grounds of review are uncertain, the tying of locus standi to legality in the *Federation* case represents a shift away from rules:

It has turned the question of standing very largely into a matter of fact and discretion. The question of legality is a question of fact which must be decided from case to case. It is very difficult to make reliable concrete statements about the content of the vague formulae in which most of the law of *ultra vires* is couched. The law of natural justice is all a matter of fairness in the light of all the facts of the case [and] the vague, fact-relative standard of 'unreasonableness' lies at the bottom of review of the exercise of discretionary powers and of decisions on questions of fact . . .

The retreat from rules to facts which the *National Federation* case illustrates . . . can be taken too far. Even if it achieves nothing else, the discipline of justifying decisions in terms of rules forces courts to measure the consistency inter se of their decisions against a pre-announced bench mark. Decisions on the facts cannot be cross-checked in this way; the result, at the least, is a considerable measure of uncertainty in the law, and at the worst, a feeling that apparently inconsistent decisions are explicable in terms of unexpressed and undesirable value judgments. [Cane 1981, pp. 335–6.]

4 **Directions and objectives again**

You may think that we have unduly prolonged our discussion of dry and technical rules of procedural law. Important substantive issues lie behind the technicalities. Reich argued that courts are insufficiently receptive to new 'rights'. One way in which they decide which rights shall or shall not be protected is through the doctrine of locus standi. Again, traditional standing tests, which tend to vindicate material or personal interests, may be seen as part of a model of administrative law in which courts protect private *individuals* against the state. If, with Feldman, we perceive public law as being primarily concerned with 'remedying public wrongs', standing to sue ought to be swept away.

Feldman adopts a red light theory of administrative law: he wants to expand the 'interests' in respect of which the administration ought to be controlled. Those advocating the liberalization of locus standi may do so from an entirely different theoretical perspective. Stewart explains the American dilution of standing requirements as part of a judicially inspired trend away from the individual-oriented control model and towards one of *interest representation*. Society is here seen as encompassing a variety of disparate and conflicting interests. The function of administrative law is to open up the administrative process to these conflicts by ensuring adequate representation for all interests affected by agency decisions. In the following passage Stewart notes the significance of locus standi to this model. If facilitating increased participation in the administrative process is an object for the judiciary, then liberalized standing tests, allowing greater access to the courts, are required:

The judges have greatly extended the machinery of the traditional [control] model to protect new classes of interests. In the space of a few years the Supreme Court has largely eliminated the doctrine of standing as a barrier to challenging agency action in court, and judges have accorded a wide variety of affected interests the right not only to participate in, but to force the initiation of, formal proceedings before the agency. Indeed, this process has gone beyond the mere extension of participation and standing rights, working a fundamental transformation of the traditional model. Increasingly, the function of administrative law is not the protection of private autonomy but the provision of a surrogate political process to ensure the fair representation of a wide range of affected interests in the process of administrative decision . . .

Implicit in this development is the assumption that there is no ascertainable, transcendent 'public interest', but only the distinct interests of various individuals and groups in society. Under this assumption legislation represents no more than compromises struck between competing interest groups. This analysis suggests that if agencies were to function as a forum for all interests affected by agency decision making, bargaining leading to compromises generally acceptable to all might result, thus replicating the process of legislation. Agency decisions made after adequate consideration of all affected interests would have, in microcosm, legitimacy based on the same principle as legislation . . .[14]

The transformation of the traditional model into a model of interest representation has in large degree been achieved through an expansion of the class of interests entitled to seek judicial review . . . This growth has coincided with, and perhaps been shaped by, the expansion of the concepts of liberty and property that has been a response to large-scale government . . . Standing has been liberally granted to allow judicial enforcement of the requirement that agencies consider all such affected interests. [Stewart 1975, pp. 1670, 1712, 1723.]

This model implies a marked accretion in judicial power because courts can exercise substantial influence over access to the decision-making process. Extensions in control, as advocated by Feldman or attempted by Lord Denning, also imply an expanded judicial function. By way of contrast, Cane believes the tests of 'special damage', 'person aggrieved' or 'private legal right' to denote a quietist conception of the judicial role, which:

. . . maintains that the function of the courts is to enforce the law, and of the legislature and the executive to make it and in so doing to consider and give effect to the public interest. It sees the legislature as the proper forum for airing political issues and the political Attorney-General as the proper person to decide whether public rights ought to be enforced. It therefore gives the citizen the right to question what the administration has done only to the extent that his private rights are affected . . . The courts are there to adjudicate individuals' disputes, not to decide issues of policy. [Cane 1980, pp. 307, 316.]

So standing tests also lead us towards a consideration of 'proper' functions for the judiciary.[15] The retention of strict doctrines of standing may be urged by those who favour a restricted judicial role. Evans, in his edition of de Smith, writes:

It is not obvious that every member of the public should be entitled to vindicate the law by instituting legal proceedings ... First, it would be unwise to assume that the effect of the doctrine of binding precedent or the power of the courts to award penal costs against vexatious litigants would suffice to dam a flood of unmeritorious challenges to administrative action. Secondly, even if it is assumed that the litigant could establish some unlawfulness, it does not necessarily follow that power should be so distributed between the courts and the Administration as to allow the Judiciary to pronounce authoritatively on the legality of the conduct of the business of government whenever any member of the public chooses. Whilst the independence of the Judiciary from the political process is one of its most highly valued assets, it also limits its powers to interfere with the working of other branches of government. Thirdly, there is much to be said for the courts, as a matter of prudence, reserving their power and prestige for those occasions when they are moved by those upon whom the unlawful conduct of public authorities has tangibly impinged. Fourthly, there are obvious costs incurred in the institution of legal proceedings against public authorities – the expenditure involved in the administration of justice (including delays that may be caused to litigants with more immediate concerns) and the costs arising from the disruption of government. Whether it should be open to every member of the public to choose how to balance these costs against the benefit of disclosing some irregularity on the part of an agency of government is highly questionable. [de Smith 1980, p. 410.]

What role does Evans see for administrative law and how does his view of the functions of locus standi compare with Cane's?[16] Evans' fourth point illustrates how debate about the 'proper' functions of the judges encompasses not only politically-oriented controversies about their correct constitutional role but also interlinked arguments concerning the nature of the adjudicative process. We might add to Evans' concern with expense, earlier arguments concerning polycentricity and third party interests.

Cane does not determine how active or passive the courts ought to be nor at what quantum of interest standing requirements should be fixed. Instead he proposes changing the function of locus standi:

Standing rules should not be used as a mechanism for restricting the activities of the courts to adjudication and for presenting to the administration and the legislature the role of weighing competing interests in society. They should be used only to ensure that an appropriate application is before the court. [Cane, 1980, p. 327.]

But this does not lead him to advocate the abolition of all restrictions additional to the grounds of review. Rather he argues that decisions about the judicial role ought to be taken through an alternative and more appropriate limiting mechanism: *justiciability*. A judge ought to decline jurisdiction unless he considers that the courts are the most appropriate organ of government to deal with the dispute. For Cane (1980, p. 312), a doctrine of justiciability would include 'such matters as the availability of alternative and more convenient remedies, political questions, questions concerning the distribution of scarce resources and future rights'. The formulation might tie together some existing strands in administrative law. Cases like *Gouriet*, where an issue seen by the court as 'political' is left to the executive branch, and *Hendy*, where Scarman LJ recognizes the limitations of adjudication as a technique for dealing with the distribution of scarce resources, could both be viewed as amounting to determinations of 'non-justiciability'.

Cane sees several advantages in his proposal. It would permit a uniform test of standing. 'The law would gain in clarity and rationality if issues of standing were clearly separated from issues of justiciability' since the courts would have openly to articulate their proper role. The power to decide certain issues of justiciability would not, as in *Gouriet*, be allocated to the Attorney General, but rather to the courts. So Cane favours an expanded role for the judges because their 'proper' functions would become more self-defined. However, Cane does not claim to solve the central issues; he provides only a mechanism for doing so. We are left facing the fundamental question of what does constitute a 'justiciable' or 'non-justiciable' issue.

11
Discretionary justice?

> Our suspicion [is] that the rules governing judicial review have no
> more substance at the core than a seedless grape. [Gellhorn and
> Robinson 1975, p. 780.]

1 Justiciability

The division of power between judges and administration was, for
Jennings, an issue of central importance. Here the *Anisminic* case has
raised the legitimacy of judicial subversion of legislative provisions
and the *Malloch* affair the legitimacy of parliamentary nullification of
a judicial decision. The *Skytrain* affair involved difficult questions of
allocation of functions and the possibility of a clash between
government and judiciary. Now, with Cane's introduction of the
concept of 'justiciability', the issue must be tackled directly.

The judges to whom Cane's invitation was ostensibly extended
would no doubt regard such an approach as foolhardy. Theses on
adjudication are not a qualification for appointment to the English
bench – rather the reverse – and English judges are notably reticent
on the subject.[1] Indeed, Radcliffe (1967) advised his brethren to keep
their heads below the firing-line. Their attitude may, in part, be due
to the positivist tradition in which judges, in common with every
English law student, were until recently reared. Visiting England
twenty years ago, Davis felt that, in comparison with America,
English judicial review was restricted by an old-fashioned, positivist
corset:

The central [restraint] is the idea that seems to permeate the thinking of all
branches of the English legal profession – that judges have no responsibility
for reworking previously existing law in order that the needs of society may be
better served. The prevailing belief – to a degree that is astonishing to one
with a background in the American legal system – is that the task of judges is

limited to the application of previously existing law and does not extend either to a reexamination of case law with a view to improving it or to the making of policy choices in giving meaning to silent or unclear statutes. I do not say that English judges never give attention to the merits of issues that they are resolving; perhaps intelligent human beings are incapable of blindfolding themselves to that extent. What I do say is that English judges strive to avoid consideration of the policy aspects of the issues they decide and that in strikingly large degree they succeed. Not only that, but throughout the English legal profession the attitude runs very deep that judges should have no concern for policy – even when to an American observer the state of the law seems to be such that the only sensible approach to a particular problem is through a weighing of policy pros and cons . . . The typical judge, barrister, solicitor, teacher, or student responds with consternation to an inquiry into the soundness of the policies embodied in a judicial decision, and, if he persists, the inquirer is gently reminded that judges do not consider policy questions and that only Parliament can change the law; the task of the judge is wholly analytical – to discover the previously existing law, and to apply it logically to the case before the court. [Davis 1961, p. 202.]

Davis was arguing that the positivist position involved 'a considerable degree of intellectual dishonesty' or 'humbug' which made judicial decisions less 'efficient'. The denial of the policy dimension led judges artificially to narrow their consideration of policy, leading counsel in turn artificially to limit the scope of their argument and evidence. 'Judges who deal in policy problems only half-heartedly, who continually assert that the responsibility for policy does not lie with them, who pretend that they are not deciding policy issues – such judges are needlessly crippling themselves in whatever attempt they make to create a body of law that will satisfactorily serve the needs of living people' (Davis 1961, p. 216). He believed this weakened the position of judicial review in the British constitution.

Davis may have discounted the absence of a written constitution which could entrench the position of the judiciary and 'legitimate' judicial activity. In Chapter 2, we saw green light theorists dismissing the 'model of law' as an excuse for the hegemony of lawyers. But as long as the ideal of the balanced constitution remained intact it served as a valuable support for the judicial function.

Western institutional theorists have concerned themselves with the problem of ensuring that the exercise of governmental power, which is essential to the realisation of the values of their societies, should be controlled in order that it should not itself be destructive of the values it was intended to promote. The great theme of the advocates of constitutionalism, in contrast either to theorists of utopianism, or of absolutism, of the right or of the left, has been the frank acknowledgement of the role of government in society, linked with the determination to bring that government under control and to place limits on the exercise of its power. Of the theories of government which have attempted to provide a solution to this dilemma, the doctrine of separation of powers has, in modern times, been the most significant . . . [Vile, 1967, pp. 1–2.]

The balanced constitution or, as some would prefer to say, the doctrine of separation of powers, contains its own primitive division of labour; law-making is reserved for the legislature and policy for the executive. Judges are to interpret or declare the law, but they may neither legislate nor indulge themselves in policy-making. Thus Nonet and Selznick (above) were right to stress the link between the balanced constitution and legal positivism. In denying their policy-making function, English judges are expressing their view of their constitutional role. And as the notion of representative government increases in influence, so the law-making and policy-making dimension of judicial decisions becomes harder to admit. Twenty years after Davis, Ely made a similar point about the growth of 'interpretivism' (defined as 'about the same thing as positivism') in the American Supreme Court:

. . . [One] comparative attraction of an interpretivist approach . . . derives from the obvious difficulty [judicial activism] encounters in trying to reconcile itself with the underlying democratic theory of our government. It is true that the United States is not run town meeting style . . . But most of the important policy decisions are made by our elected representatives (or the people accountable to them). Judges . . . while they are not entirely oblivious to popular opinion – are not elected or reelected. Nothing can finally depreciate the central function that is assigned in democratic theory and practice to the electoral process; nor can it be denied that the policy-making power of representative institutions, born of the electoral process, is the distinguishing characteristic of the system. Judicial review works counter to this characteristic. [Ely 1980, p. 4.][2]

When Fuller (above, Chapter 4) states his belief that polycentric decisions should not be the subject of adjudication, he is making a statement about 'justiciability' with efficiency or technical competence in mind. We could describe this as a *qualitative* definition. It requires us to identify certain decisions as inherently or qualitatively suitable and unsuitable for adjudication. This is not an easy thing to do. Later, for example, you will meet the argument that judges can handle polycentric issues provided the policy dimensions are more openly admitted and a wider range of evidence admitted. Marshall, in his essay 'Justiciability' (1961) was forced to the conclusion that no dispute or issue was *inherently* justiciable. Perhaps for this reason Marshall found that the courts favoured procedural tests: e.g.

tribunal decisions are 'justiciable' because they are taken by judicial procedures. The approach has two disadvantages. First, it leads straight back to the 'judicial/administrative' dichotomy of Donoughmore, criticized in Chapter 1 for its circularity. Second, it is heavily reliant on precedent and tradition. It may be argued that the decisions of the Attorney-General or Metropolitan Police Commissioner cannot be reviewed because they have not been reviewed before and are not taken by judicial procedures. This sort of definition can hardly be regarded as conclusive. As Marshall points out (1961, p. 268), it may be easier for a judicial body to review decisions traditionally classified as 'judicial' but the rule is often broken by statute. Where it is broken, there is not necessarily any technical barrier to successful review. The courts would be perfectly capable of reviewing parole board decisions, though traditionally these are immune from review and are not taken by a 'judicial' procedure. Qualitatively, however, the decisions are broadly similar to those taken by a judge in sentencing, who would therefore be competent to review them. Similarly, in *Gouriet*'s case, the courts did not find much difficulty in the Attorney-General's reasons for refusing to bring a relator action. And in the *Blackburn* cases[3] the court was perfectly competent to review the decisions of the Metropolitan Police Commissioner to prosecute gaming clubs and vendors of pornographic materials; the question was whether review would be 'legitimate'.

At the end of his short survey, Marshall concluded that a general definition was like a 'will-o'-the wisp'. Summers criticized this defeatist attitude, but his own search for the chimera was hardly more successful. He had to conclude where he began:

If it is assumed that some disputes are more suited to one mode of settlement than to others, the problem of developing useful criteria for the allocation of disputes among these modes of settlement becomes paramount. Lawyers and jurists have not, however, devoted the attention to this problem that it deserves . . . [Summers 1963, p. 538.]

This concentration on efficiency in decision-taking loses sight of the constitutional dimension which reserves 'policy' for the executive or, more forcefully, for the elected representatives of the people. The constitutional approach requires a demarcation between 'justiciable' and 'political' issues. But Marshall, surveying the experience of the American courts in dealing with the doctrine of the 'political question'[4] is once more discouraging. He found (1971, pp. 110–11) 'a set of loosely related views' that some types of dispute are unsuitable for judicial resolution. The nature of the unsuitability, however, had 'not always been precisely defined', and the boundary line was 'obviously a misty one'. For Hailsham, on the other hand, the boundary line is clear. His test is largely one of method. On one side of the line falls the application of law to fact; on the other, policy with discretion. Hailsham does not believe that 'justiciable' issues must be apolitical in the sense of 'non-controversial' (compare Griffith, below) but he insists that:

What is left to the courts, however politically sensitive, should be genuinely justiciable, that is, dependent on the genuine ascertainment of facts, or upon the strict application of a clearly formulated rule of law, and not dependent on the subjective opinion of the individual judge. [Hailsham 1978, p. 106.]

Here 'justiciability' depends on the application of 'clearly formulated rules'. Similarly, a French writer has suggested that judicial review is only justified within these logical confines. Judicial review must never appear as an exercise of discretionary power; it 'makes sense only if the judge is in a position to enunciate or explain the rule on which his decision is based' (Kahn 1980, p. 525). Clearly we must go on to ask whether the 'rules' of judicial review are of this type. The greater the amount of judicial discretion, the more space for 'subjective opinion' and 'policy choices' which, for Hailsham, fall on the wrong side of the demarcation line. Thus discretion can involve judges in 'politics'. If you reread Lord Wilberforce's judgment in *Gouriet* (see above, p. 293), you will find a similar opinion voiced. Not surprisingly, Hailsham minimizes the amount of discretion or power of choice available to the English judge:

The possible range of options open to a judge in any given case is extremely narrow – far narrower in most respects than that available to judges on the continent of Europe or America. A judge in Britain is hedged about by a far more restrictive view of precedent than are they, and since most decisions nowadays consist in the interpretation and application of Acts of Parliament, it is even more important that the rules of construing Acts of Parliament followed by English and Scottish judges are far more rigid and limiting than in any country in the world not operating the British system. In addition, our traditional method of Parliamentary draftsmanship is so much more detailed than in any European country as to fetter judicial independence to an extent quite unparalleled elsewhere. Even on matters in which we are wont to leave a question to a judge's discretion, his use of it is subject to scrutiny by the pyramidal system of appeal to the Court of Appeal and the House of Lords who sit in panels of three and five and are therefore composed so as to counteract any individual idiosyncrasies in the lower tribunals or in one another. [Hailsham 1978, pp. 106–7.]

Today, the extreme version of 'slot-machine justice' has been discarded.[5] A majority of lawyers accepts the reality of judicial discretion, derived in part from the nature of the common law as a system of 'principles' deduced from cases. (Notice that in the following passage the author is not seeking to distinguish principles and standards as we did earlier:)

[In making] *rulings* on difficult points . . . [judges] do exercise choice. They create new standards for actual application in the instant case and for potential future application . . . they do [this] by way of interpretation of and extrapolation from existing legal standards. These standards are not all 'rules' in the specific sense of that term. Hence it is only ostensibly paradoxical to say both that judges in some degree *make* the law in hard cases, and yet that they do so by applying existing legal standards . . . Suppose that a legal system acknowledges the equitable principle that 'every wrong ought to have a remedy'. That is far more vague and general than say, the rule that 'a judge must impose a sentence of life imprisonment on any person over 18 years of age who is convicted of murder'. The general principle leaves the judge with a very wide discretion. The particular rule leaves him with no discretion at all. It sets a mandatory penalty. [MacCormick 1981, p. 129.]

We seem to be confronted here by a distinction between rules and principles. But we already know from Chapter 5 that rules may leave room for interpretative discretion or judgement:

A common error is the belief that one can devise a precise mathematical rule which will give objective certainty, so that all judges will apply identical tests and reach identical results in reviewing any agency action. This not only is impossible, but it is also a deceptively dangerous idea . . . [A rule] must be phrased in broad terms which leaves much to the discretion and good sense of the individual judge. The rule can give the conscientious judge some leads as to what to do, but it cannot give him a precise measuring tool . . . Attempts to do this are unwise and fraught with peril. [Kramer 1959, pp. 74–5.]

This is the opposite side of our discussion of administrative rule-making. Faced with Hewart's simplistic correlation of administration with discretion we found a complex process in which discretion was structured by rules and rules tempered by discretion. Faced with the simplistic picture of 'slot-machine' justice, we are forced to concede the existence of discretion in the adjudicatory process. Once this is acknowledged, the interest shifts to a secondary question. Remember Jowell's description (derived from Dworkin) of discretion as a continuum ranging from 'weak' to 'strong'. What sort of discretion do judges possess and how do they use it?[6]

The theory of 'weak' discretion represents only a small shift from the older positivist vision of a legal world of rules. Does Hailsham admit, for example, that judges have 'weak' discretion?. This is really Dworkin's own position. He admits that judges possess discretion but it is 'weak' discretion, structured by a hierarchy of principles, precedents, standards and other values, some of which are moral rather than strictly legal. It is an unreal world, but it is fair to say that Dworkin is describing an ideal to which he hopes judges can aspire.[7] Contrast MacCormick's view that judges possess 'strong' discretion because of the flexibility of the standards in which they trade. MacCormick believes that standards – once again MacCormick's use of this term differs from Jowell's – are indeterminate in character and ultimately subjective:

> Even if it be the case . . . that moral values and principles have some objective truth and universal validity, it remains also the case that people inveterately disagree about them . . . Political principles are . . . also subjects of inveterate disagreement. Legal systems result from a patchwork of historical assertions of contentious and changing political principles, political compromises and mere political muddles. That from which laws emerge is controversial, even if some or all of the controversies concern moral issues on which there may in principle be a single right answer. So the idea that judges have only a 'weak' discretion since their task is to 'find' *the* right priority ranking of legal principles and deduce from it *the* right answer is utterly unsustainable . . .
>
> In all cases, judicial discretion exists only within the framework of some predetermined standards. Where these standards are legal rules, the discretion extends only within rather a restricted field, though rarely eliminated completely. Where the rules give no guidance or give ambiguous guidance, recourse may be had to other standards of judgment. But since these standards are all less precise than rules, the discretion involved in interpreting and extrapolating from them is greater. [MacCormick 1981, p. 130.]

MacCormick introduces a second point. We should not assume that judicial discretion is *invariably* 'strong' or 'weak'. In the course of this book we have seen judges using discretion in many different circumstances. There is the discretion to disallow applications for judicial review, often informally administered. Equally generous is the discretion, openly avowed by the judges, to withhold remedies. In both cases the relative absence of guidelines and precedent allows a judge a discretion which may be thought to differ from the judgment or discretion used in selecting from a line of cases. In the study of ouster clauses, for example, there was less freedom of choice. Again, a judge, in interpreting statute, may possess either weak or strong discretion according to the degree of ambiguity created by the language.[8]

Furthermore, the attitude of individual judges towards their role may differ. Sometimes the variant attitudes are manifested in the same case. When you read the *Dorset Yacht* case, for example, contrast the attitude of Lord Reid, who relied on a general principle of civil liability applicable to different fact-situations unless there was good reason to exclude it, with that of Viscount Dilhorne, who deduced from the absence of decisions with similar facts that there could be no liability. Clearly he felt that he possessed only a 'weak' discretion, while Lord Reid freed himself from the restrictions of precedent.

Variations of this kind can also be traced over a period of time. It is important to remember that the principles of judicial review are judge-made not statutory; they were not suddenly born as a coherent system. In *Ridge* v. *Baldwin* Lord Reid said 'we do not have a developed system of administrative law – perhaps because until recently we did not need it'. Nearly 20 years later, Lord Diplock thought the position had changed. *O'Reilly* v. *Mackman* contains his personal apologia for the judges' handiwork and a catalogue of the leading cases which to him add up to a developed system of administrative law.[9] (Notice how both judges imply an equation between administrative law and judicial review.) Some writers argue that judicial review is cyclical; in some periods the judges are activist, in others they retreat from the fray and become passive.[10] Wade tacitly admits to a substantial measure of judicial discretion when he writes:

It would be wrong to say that [the judges] have invented new doctrines . . . and taken more power into their own hands. What they have done is to reactivate principles which have been embedded in the law for centuries, and to apply them with far greater confidence and vigour than they were willing to do 20 or 30 years ago. There has been little change in the law itself, but a very marked change of judicial spirit. [Wade 1980, p. 43.]

Thus judicial review is dynamic not static; principles can be expanded or retracted. Wade talks in terms of expansion and, writing two years later, Griffith agreed that 'the great wave of judicial interventionism which first lifted its snowy head some twenty years ago is still rolling forward' (Griffith 1982, p. 31). Other writers believe that the tide is turning or has turned.

Griffith does not accept that judges possess only weak discretion, confined to the 'application of law to facts'. They are easily able to carry out forays into political territory:

In our system for two principal reasons, the judiciary have a wide scope for the making of political decisions. First, statute law does not seek with any precision to indicate where, between Ministers and judges, final decision making should lie. Secondly, judges themselves, in the common law tradition of judicial creativity, frequently invent or re-discover rules of law which enable them to intervene and to exercise political judgment in areas that hitherto had been understood to be outside their province. In the event, for these two reasons, legislators and Ministers and public authorities are continuously being surprised to discover that, in the view of the judges, they do not have the powers they thought they had. [Griffith 1983, p. 55.]

He believes that the open-textured rules of judicial review leave too much discretion to judges. The holes in the doughnut are then filled with policy choices which derive from an inchoate judicial philosophy of political conservatism.[11] And he is concerned that judicialization of the political process will inevitably change the nature and scope of the debate. In the following passage he discusses the effects of introducing a justiciable Bill of Rights into the British constitution, an innovation which he does not favour:

One danger of arguing from rights is that the real issues can be evaded. What are truly questions of politics and economics are presented as questions of law.

[An] advantage in treating what others call rights as political claims is that their acceptance or rejection will be in the hands of politicians rather than judges and the advantage of *that* is not that politicians are more likely to come up with the right answer but that . . . they are so much more vulnerable than judges and can be dismissed or at least made to suffer in their reputation. Not only am I very strongly of the opinion that, in the United Kingdom, political decisions should be taken by politicians. I am also very strongly against any further judicialisation of the administrative process. [Griffith 1979, pp. 17–19.]

But if 'political issues' are to be excluded from the courts, they must first be identified. Here Griffith is not very helpful. All he can tell us is that political decisions involve 'the balancing of conflicts of interest between different groups in the community' (Griffith 1982, p. 311). Elsewhere, he has written: 'By political I mean those cases which arise out of controversial legislation or controversial action initiated by public authorities, or which touch important moral or social issues' (Griffith 1977, p. 52). But what does he mean by 'controversial action'? Arguably any action becomes controversial once it is contested.

We have here been talking in abstract terms. The next section contains a selection of cases concerning the review of discretionary power by courts, a development which Wade associates particularly with the last decade. Reading these cases you will be able to evaluate the points made here. Does the case law, for example, measure up to Kahn's expectations, strictly justifiable in terms of legal principle? Are the judges exercising powers which are discretionary in character and, if so, can their discretion be characterized as more or less 'strong' or 'weak'? Look closely at the concept of 'reasonableness' in *Roberts* v. *Hopwood*. What standards are used to measure reasonableness? Can these be described as legal principles or do they import value-judgements of a political nature? Watch closely to see how principles develop. An excellent example is provided by the concept of 'fiduciary duty' owed by a public authority to ratepayers. This evolves from an inexplicit mention in *Roberts* v. *Hopwood* through the 'fiduciary duty analogous to that of a trustee' (Jenkins LJ in *Prescott* v. *Birmingham Corporation* [1955] 1 Ch. 210) to the sophisticated 'public law' idea of the fiduciary duty to balance the competing interests of persons affected by an administrative decision or policy (Lord Diplock in the *Bromley* case). Test Griffith's definition of 'political questions'. Was the Transport (London) Act 1969 'controversial legislation'? At what point in time should the judgement be made? On Griffith's test, which of these cases is not 'political'?

2 Judicial review of administrative discretion: a case study

We give here two formulations by academics of the restrictions developed by the courts on the exercise by administrators of statutory discretion:

For more than three centuries it has been accepted that discretionary power conferred upon public authorities is not absolute, even within its apparent boundaries, but is subject to general legal limitations. These limitations are expressed in a variety of different ways, as by saying that discretion must be exercised reasonably and in good faith, that relevant considerations only must be taken into account, that there must be no malversation of any kind, or that the decision must not be arbitrary or capricious. They can all be comprised by saying that discretion must be exercised in the manner intended by the empowering Act. But it is for the court to say what intention shall be imputed to Parliament . . . Parliament cannot be supposed to have intended that the power should be open to serious abuse. It must have assumed that the designated authority would act properly and responsibly, with a view to doing what was best in the public interest and most consistent with the policy of the statute. It is from this presumption that the courts take their warrant to impose legal bounds on even the most extensive discretion. [Wade 1977, pp. 336–7.]

When Wade speaks of the presumption that Parliament did not

intend powers to be 'open to serious abuse', what does he mean? He goes on to use the words 'properly', 'responsibly' and 'in the public interest'. By what standards are these values to be measured? Remember the *Justice* 'Principles of Good Administration' and our suggestion that a good administrator would need to amplify these. Could an administrator use Wade's passage as a model of decision-taking? Does it present 'rules'? Compare the summary provided by the leading authority on judicial review. Do the passages correspond?

The relevant principles formulated by the courts may be broadly summarised as follows. The authority in which a discretion is vested can be compelled to exercise that discretion, but not to exercise it in any particular manner. In general, a discretion must be exercised only by the authority to which it is committed. That authority must genuinely address itself to the matter before it; it must not act under the dictation of another body or disable itself from exercising a discretion in each individual case. In the purported exercise of its discretion it must not do what it has been forbidden to do, nor must it do what it has not been authorised to do. It must act in good faith, must have regard to all relevant considerations and must not be swayed by irrelevant consider-ations, must not seek to promote purposes alien to the letter or the spirit of the legislation that gives it power to act, and must not act arbitrarily or capriciously. Nor where a judgment must be made that certain facts exist can a discretion be validly exercised on the basis of an erroneous assumption about those facts. These several principles can conveniently be grouped in two main categories: failure to exercise a discretion, and excess or abuse of discretionary power. The two classes are not, however, mutually ex-clusive . . . Nor, as will be shown, is it possible to differentiate with precision the grounds of invalidity contained within each category. [de Smith 1980, pp. 285–6.]

Some of these principles are derived from cases which have been discussed, e.g. the *British Oxygen* case. Below are extracts from some further cases. First deduce a principle from the case, then check it against de Smith's statement of the law. Ask yourself where on the line between 'rules' and 'discretion' the principle falls. How much discretion does (i) the decision-maker and (ii) the judge possess?

Roberts v. Hopwood [1925] AC 578

S.62 of the Metropolis Management Act 1855 empowered local authorities to pay to their employees 'such salaries and wages as . . . [they] may think fit'. Poplar Borough Council used these powers to pay rates considerably above the national average and to maintain them throughout a period of declining cost of living. Equal wages were paid to men and women for like work. Acting under s.247(7) of the Public Health Act 1875 the district auditor disallowed the sums as unreasonable and surcharged the councillors who controlled the council. The councillors conceded that their discretion could be challenged for bad faith. Their application for certiorari was rejected by the House of Lords:

LORD ATKINSON: It is but right and natural that the rate of wages should rise if the cost of living rises, because this tends directly to keep the purchasing power of the labourer's wage at what it was before the cost of living increased. The principle apparently adopted by the council, however, is that wages should rise if the cost of living rises, but should never go down if the cost of living goes down . . .

[It is stated] that 'the Council have always paid such a minimum wage as they have believed to be fair and reasonable without being bound by any particular external method of fixing wages, whether by trade union rates, cost of living, payments of other local or national authorities or otherwise'. Nobody has contended that the council should be bound by any of these things, but it is only what justice and common sense demand that, when dealing with funds contributed by the whole body of the ratepayers, they should take each and every one of these enumerated things into consideration in order to help them to determine what was a fair, just and reasonable wage to pay their employees for the services the latter rendered. The council would, in my view, fail in their duty if, in administering funds which did not belong to their members alone, they put aside all these aids to the ascertainment of what was just and reasonable remuneration to give for the services rendered to them, and allowed themselves to be guided in preference by some eccentric principles of socialistic philanthropy, or by a feminist ambition to secure the equality of the sexes in the matter of wages in the world of labour.

[These considerations] might possibly be admirably philanthropic, if the funds of the council at the time they were thus administered belonged to the existing members of that body. These members would then be generous at their own expense . . . A body charged with the administration for definite purposes of funds contributed in whole or in part by persons other than the members of that body, owes, in my view, a duty to those latter persons to conduct that administration in a fairly businesslike manner with reasonable care, skill and caution, and with a due and alert regard to the interest of those contributors who are not members of the body. Towards these latter persons the body stands somewhat in the position of trustees or managers of the property of others.

This duty is, I think, a legal duty as well as a moral one, and acts done in flagrant violation of it should, in my view, be properly held to have been done 'contrary to law' within the meaning of sub-s.7 of s.247 of the Public Health Act of 1875 . . .

LORD SUMNER: Persons who hold public office have a legal responsibility towards those whom they represent – not merely towards those who vote for them – to the discharge of which they must honestly apply their minds. Bona fide here cannot simply mean that they are not making a profit out of their office or acting in it from private spite, nor is bona fide a short way of saying that the council has acted within the ambit of its powers and therefore not contrary to law. It must mean that they are giving their minds to the comprehension and their wills to the discharge of their duty towards that public, whose money and local business they administer.

The purpose, however, of the whole audit is to ensure wise and prudent administration and to recover for the council's funds money that should not have been taken out of them . . . the auditor is not confined to asking, if the discretion, such as it may be, has been honestly exercised. He has to restrain expenditure within proper limits. His mission is to inquire if there is any excess over what is reasonable. I do not find any words limiting his functions merely to the case of bad faith, or obliging him to leave the ratepayers unprotected from the effects on their pockets of honest stupidity or unpractical idealism. The breach in the words 'as they may think fit', which the admitted implication as to bad faith makes, is wide enough to make the necessary implication one both of honesty and of reasonableness. It might be otherwise, if the express words were to be read as absolute and unqualified, but if they are to be read as subject to some qualification, I think that qualification must be derived from the purpose of the statutory audit, which is the protection of the ratepayers' pockets and not the immunity of spend-thrift administration.

What standards is the auditor to apply in assessing the 'reason-ableness' of expenditure? Laski criticized the open texture of the language used by the House of Lords in answering this question:

Lord Sumner does not provide us with definitions of words like 'proper' and 'reasonable'. Either there is some quantitative standard from which they may be deduced, or they mean only that due care has been observed in exercising the discretion. The first test does not exist; and since the House of Lords rejects the second, it can only mean that the courts admit that the real test is, in their view, the social ideal of the appointed official. And this, it may be suggested, was the perhaps unconscious end Lord Sumner had in view; for while he does not deny that the Auditor has no powers over policy, he defines policy in a manner which would otherwise be, I venture to think, almost unique as an example of misplaced judicial levity. He denies, first of all, that the elected members of local authorities 'are to be guided by their personal opinions on political, economic, or social questions in administering the funds which they derive from levying rates.' By whose opinion they are to be guided, he does not say. He admits that they are to decide matters of policy which he defines as 'such matters as the necessity for a urinal, and the choice of its position, provided no public or private nuisance is created.' It is difficult to draw from this any other inferences than that either Lord Sumner is not aware of the powers conferred on local authorities by Acts of Parliament or that he regards all policy with which he is in political disagreement as necessarily 'unreasonable'.

The test of reasonableness is, of course, one that it is seldom easy to apply in a court of law. For it always raises issues which in their nature are ultimately questions of opinion, and it tempts the judge to believe that he is simply finding the law when in fact he is really testing and rejecting other men's views by the light of his own. In arriving at the meaning of this conception, it is therefore urgent for the judge to be certain that he has surveyed the whole ground . . . Reasonableness does not mean what a court feels other men ought to believe. [Laski 1926, pp. 842–3.]

But Laski made a more important criticism of the decision. The district auditor, a non-elected official, was limiting the policy options of elected representatives and the courts were encouraging and participating in this encroachment on the political process. The courts, in other words, had interfered with the constitutional allocation of functions:

The Auditor, in fact, is in relation to the local authorities as the Comptroller and Auditor General in relation to departments of State. It is the latter's business to see that moneys authorized to be spent by Parliament are spent in good faith, without negligence, and upon objects of permitted expenditure. When that has been done, his functions cease, so far as Acts of Parliament define them. So, too, with the District Auditor. If a local authority, or its servants, be negligent or dishonest, if, further, they go beyond their powers, he is legally bound to make them pay. But if the actions involved are within the area of their competence, there is nothing on the statute book which suggests that he has a power of challenge.

The reasons for this limitation are clear enough. Could the Auditor go further, he could challenge the actions of an elected body, not on grounds defined by statute, but because he did not happen to agree with what it was doing. He would be seeking to replace its view of its duty by his own view. A person, that is, responsible to no one, could seek to destroy the policy of men who have been returned by the electorate to exercise, within the limits of law, the power confided to them. That would be a situation [both] inconceivable and intolerable. [Laski 1926, p. 838.]

The *Poplar* case was the culmination of a long dispute between central government and a local authority determined to introduce radical policies designed to alleviate the lot of the unemployed and low paid worker.[12] After *Roberts* v. *Hopwood* the council agreed to reduce wages to levels which 'remained more than 20 per cent above the prevailing rate for men and more than 50 per cent above that for women. Moreover, in terms of purchasing power they were worth much more than . . . when first introduced' (Branson, 1979, p. 220). Negotiations with the Conservative Minister, Neville Chamberlain, produced further reductions, the net effect of which was still that employees were better paid than in most London districts. In return Chamberlain cancelled the surcharge as he was empowered by statute to do. This ministerial decision was challenged in legal proceedings by the Poplar Municipal Alliance, a pressure group organized by employers to oppose Council policies, which claimed to be 'strictly non-political and non-sectarian, uniting all shades of opinion', though its secretary was a former mayor of Poplar and Conservative MP and it contested seats in local government elections. The decision was quashed by the Divisional Court in February 1927. Branson agrees with Laski:

Now the judgment over the Poplar wage case faced Chamberlain with another crisis which he would have preferred to sidestep. It had arisen because the judges had altered the law in a way never contemplated by Parliament. They had now done it twice in connection with Poplar, first depriving the council of its right to fix its wages and next depriving the Minister of his right to waive penalties, a right which he had exercised for half a century. They had, in short, filched the power of policy-making from elected representatives and put it in the hands of non-elected officials and judges. [Branson, 1979, p. 223.]

The Government then changed the law by introducing the Audit (Local Authorities) Act 1927 which provided that surcharge for sums in excess of more than £500 entailed automatic disqualification from office for five years. The ministerial power of waiver had gone. The Local Government Act 1933 consolidated the audit provisions, later ss.154–67 of the Local Government Act 1972, now ss. 11–36 of the Local Government Finance Act 1982. Follow these provisions in operation by reading *Asher* v. *Lacey* [1973] 1 WLR 1412, *Asher* v. *Environment Secretary* [1974] 2 WLR 466, the Housing Finance (Special Provisions) Act 1975, Mitchell, 'Clay Cross' (1974) *Pol. Quarterly* 165, and *Pickwell* v. *Camden LBC* (below).

Associated Provincial Picture Houses v. *Wednesbury Corporation* [1948] 1 KB 223

The Sunday Entertainments Act 1932 empowered local authorities to license cinemas for Sunday performances, subject to such conditions 'as the authority think fit to impose'. The defendants banned entry to children under 15. The plaintiffs sought a declaration that the condition was ultra vires.

LORD GREENE MR: When an executive discretion is entrusted by Parliament to a body such as the local authority in this case, what appears to be an exercise of that discretion can only be challenged in the courts in a strictly limited class of case . . . it must always be remembered that the court is not a court of appeal. When discretion of this kind is granted the law recognizes certain principles upon which that discretion must be exercised, but within the four corners of those principles the discretion, in my opinion, is an absolute one and cannot be questioned in any court of law. What then are those principles? They are well understood . . . The exercise of such a discretion must be a real exercise of the discretion. If, in the statute conferring the discretion, there are to be found expressly or by implication matters which the authority exercising the discretion ought to have regard to, then in exercising the discretion it must have regard to those matters. Conversely, if the nature of the subject-matter and the general interpretation of the Act make it clear that certain matters would not be germane to the matter in question, the authority must disregard those irrelevant collateral matters. There have been in the cases expressions used relating to the sort of things that authorities must not do . . .

I am not sure myself whether the permissible grounds of attack cannot be defined under a single head. It has been perhaps a little bit confusing to find a series of grounds set out. Bad faith, dishonesty – those of course, stand by themselves – unreasonableness, attention given to extraneous circumstances, disregard of public policy and things like that have all been referred to, according to the facts of individual cases, as being matters which are relevant to the question. If they cannot all be confined under one head, they at any rate, I think, overlap to a very great extent. For instance, we have heard in this case a great deal about the meaning of the word 'unreasonable' . . . [a word which] has frequently been used and is frequently used as a general description of the things that must not be done. For instance, a person entrusted with a discretion must, so to speak, direct himself properly in law. He must call his own attention to the matters which he is bound to consider. He must exclude from his consideration matters which are irrelevant to what he has to consider. If he does not obey those rules, he may truly be said, and often is said, to be acting 'unreasonably'. Similarly, there may be something so absurd that no sensible person could ever dream that it lay within the powers of the authority. Warrington LJ in *Short* v. *Poole Corporation* [1926] Ch.66 gave the example of the red-haired teacher, dismissed because she had red hair. That is unreasonable in one sense. In another sense it is taking into consideration extraneous matters. It is so unreasonable that it might almost be described as being done in bad faith; and, in fact, all these things run into one another . . .

It is true to say that, if a decision on a competent matter is so unreasonable that no reasonable authority could ever have come to it, then the courts can interfere. That, I think, is quite right; but to prove a case of that kind would require something overwhelming, and, in this case, the facts do not come anywhere near anything of that kind. [The] proposition that the decision of the local authority can be upset if it is proved to be unreasonable, really [means] that it must be proved to be unreasonable in the sense that the court considers it to be a decision that no reasonable body could have come to. It is not what the court considers unreasonable, a different thing altogether. If it is what the court considers unreasonable, the court may very well have different views to that of a local authority on matters of high public policy of this kind. Some courts might think that no children ought to be admitted on Sundays at all, some courts might think the reverse, and all over the country I have no doubt on a thing of that sort honest and sincere people hold different views. The effect of the legislation is not to set up the court as an arbiter of the correctness of one view over another. It is the local authority that are set in that position and, provided they act, as they have acted, within the four corners of their jurisdiction, this court, in my opinion, cannot interfere.

Are there two tests: (i) that the authority must act only after consideration of relevant considerations (the ultra vires test) and (ii) that the authority must not act 'unreasonably'; or did Lord Greene intend only one test? Is the court left with 'strong' or 'weak' discretion? Robson (1959, p. 204) thought that the decision demonstrated an 'indulgent attitude' and 'increasing recognition of the right of public authorities to determine matters within their jurisdiction without judicial interference or even scrutiny'. Do you agree? Now read *Prescott* v. *Birmingham Corporation* [1955] Ch. 210, a precedent relied on in the *Bromley* case (below). Are the cases distinguishable? Do they suggest 'strong' discretion, or cycles of interventionism?

> *Padfield* v. *Minister of Agriculture, Fisheries and Food*
> [1968] 2 WLR 924

The Agricultural Marketing Act 1958 established the milk marketing scheme. Producers had to sell their product to the Milk Marketing Board which periodically fixed prices on a regional basis. In case of dispute, s.19 provided a formal procedure. The Minister had to establish a committee of investigation consisting of a chairman and four or five members. If he received a complaint either from the public or from the representative consumers' committee, it could, 'if the Minister in any case so directs', be referred to the committee of investigation. On receipt of the committee's report, the Minister could, 'if he thinks fit so to do after considering the report', revoke or amend the scheme. A dispute arose over the basis of prices in the South Eastern region, producers in that area complaining that an additional element in the price fixed for their milk was too low since it did not adequately reflect increased costs in transporting milk from other regions. Since an increase paid to the complainants would be at the expense of other areas, the Board had declined to fix new prices. The Minister refused to refer the matter to the committee of investigation and the appellant (a South Eastern region producer) sought mandamus to compel a reference. By a majority, the House of Lords issued the order:

LORD REID: The Minister is, I think, correct in saying that the board is an instrument for the self-government of the industry. So long as it does not act contrary to the public interest the Minister cannot interfere. But if it does act contrary to what both the committee of investigation and the Minister hold to be the public interest the Minister has a duty to act. And if a complaint relevantly alleges that the board has so acted, as this complaint does, then it appears to me that the Act does impose a duty on the Minister to have it investigated. If he does not do that he is rendering nugatory a safeguard provided by the Act and depriving complainers of a remedy which I am satisfied that Parliament intended them to have . . .

[The Minister's reasons for refusing to refer the complaint were contained in a letter which stated that, if the complaint were upheld, the Minister would be expected to give effect to the committee's recommendations by laying a statutory order before Parliament. Lord Reid commented:]

If this means that he is entitled to refuse to refer a complaint because, if he did so, he might later find himself in an embarrassing situation, that would plainly be a bad reason. I can see an argument to the effect that if, on receipt of a complaint, the Minister can satisfy himself from information in his possession as to the merits of the complaint, and he then chooses to say that, whatever the committee might recommend, he would hold it to be contrary to the public interest to take any action, it would be a waste of time and money to refer the complaint to the committee. I do not intend to express any opinion about that because that is not this case. In the first place it appears that the Minister has come to no decision as to the merits of the appellants' case and, secondly, the Minister has carefully avoided saying what he would do if the committee were to uphold the complaint.

It was argued that the Minister is not bound to give any reasons for refusing to refer a complaint to the committee, that if he gives no reasons his decision cannot be questioned, and that it would be very unfortunate if giving reasons were to put him in a worse position. But I do not agree that a decision cannot be questioned if no reasons are given. If it is the Minister's duty not to act so as to frustrate the policy and objects of the Act, and if it were to appear from all the circumstances of the case that that has been the effect of the Minister's refusal, then it appears to me that the court must be entitled to act.

Lord Reid's final remarks might be expanded into a 'no-evidence' rule which means that, in the absence of any evidence to support the Minister's conclusions, the court may draw its own deductions and, if appropriate, will intervene.[13]

LORD MORRIS (dissenting): The language here is, in my view, purely permissive. The Minister is endowed with discretionary powers. If he did decide to refer a complaint he is endowed with further discretionary powers after receiving a report . . .

I cannot, therefore, accept the contention of the appellants that they had a right to have their complaint referred to the committee and that the Minister had a positive duty to refer it. The Minister, in my view, had a discretion. It was urged on behalf of the respondent that his discretion was in one sense an unfettered one, though it was not said that he could disregard the complaint. The case proceeded on an acceptance by the respondent that he was bound to consider the complaint and then, in the exercise of his judgment, to decide whether or not to refer it to the committee.

If the respondent proceeded properly to exercise his judgment then, in my view, it is no part of the duty of any court to act as a Court of Appeal from his decision or to express any opinion as to whether it was wise or unwise . . . A court could make an order if it were shown (a) that the Minister failed or refused to apply his mind to or to consider the question whether to refer a complaint or (b) that he misinterpreted the law or proceeded on an erroneous view of the law or (c) that he based his decision on some wholly extraneous consideration or (d) that he failed to have regard to matters which he should have taken into account . . .

Lord Morris then examined the evidence and decided that these criteria were not met. He therefore favoured dismissing the appeal. Which of these two opinions is preferable? Which is more in line with the *Wednesbury* case?

In the course of his judgment, Lord Reid also said:

If the Minister directs that a complaint by any of them shall be referred to the committee of investigation, that committee will make a report which must be published. If they report that any provision of this scheme or any act or omission of the board is contrary to the interests of the complainers *and* if not in the public interest, then the Minister is empowered to take action, but not otherwise. He may disagree with the view of the committee as to public interest, and, if he thinks that there are other public interests which outweigh the public interest that justice should be done to the complainers, he would be not only entitled but bound to refuse to take action. Whether he takes action or not, he may be criticised and held accountable in Parliament but the court cannot interfere . . .

After this decision, the Minister (Mr Cledwyn Hughes) referred the dispute to the committee of investigation which recommended change. The Minister told the House of Commons (HC Deb. vol. 781 WA, cols. 46–7) that he had declined to follow the report:

I have carefully considered the Committee's findings. I am satisfied that even if its recommendations were implemented within the framework of the regional pricing structure of the Milk Marketing Scheme, they would have a profound effect on incomes of milk producers in different parts of the country. Many of them, particularly those in the West of the country, would suffer significant losses. Moreover, if the principle that each and every producer should be paid according to his proximity to a liquid market were pursued to its logical conclusion, it would bring to an end the present system for the organised marketing of milk which has been so successful.

The Committee recognised that the wider questions of agricultural, economic and social policy involved in this matter were beyond the scope of its inquiry. These must, however, in my view be given full weight. After considering with great care all the issues involved, and the very wide implications of the Committee's recommendations, I have concluded that it would not be in the public interest for me to direct the Board to implement the Committee's conclusions.

Was this a valid exercise of discretion? On which cases did you rely to arrive at your conclusion and which 'tests' did you apply?

Criticizing *Padfield*, Austin accused the courts of arrogating to themselves discretionary power by ignoring a basic distinction between 'objective' and 'subjective' discretion.

The decision-maker's discretion is 'objective' where the source of his power imposes defined or ascertainable predetermined criteria by which, and solely by which, he must make his choice. The decision-maker's discretion is 'subjective', however, when the source of his power confers upon him the freedom to determine his own criteria for choosing between the alternative courses of action open to him. Subjective discretions are usually conferred by such phrases as 'if in his opinion', 'if he thinks fit', 'if he deems', 'if he considers' and numerous other similar expressions whose common feature is that they confer upon the decision-maker the freedom to set his own limits, to determine his own criteria . . .

That this distinction is a relevant one to make becomes apparent when it is realised that the application by the courts of the doctrine of substantive *ultra vires*, in reviewing discretionary powers, depends upon the existence in the empowering legislation of criteria against which the decision-maker's choice can be measured. In the absence of such criteria, the doctrine of substantive *ultra vires* is impotent. The courts have not expressly articulated this distinction, nor have they explicitly used it as a tool for the analysis of discretionary powers. But the earlier cases consistently show that this distinction underlies the decision whether a particular discretionary power is or is not reviewable for substantive *ultra vires*. However, some recent cases [like *Padfield*] have hinted at a disturbing possibility, namely that if the source of the power does not impose any objective criteria, the courts will imply such criteria; the disturbing element in this development is that the courts may simply be replacing their own subjective views for those of a person such as a Minister who is better qualified and equipped to exercise the power. In short, they may supply their own criteria rather than implying them from the terms of the empowering legislation. [Austin, 1975, pp. 152–4.]

Does this dichotomy provide a sound basis for review of administrative discretion? What function would remain for courts?

Education Secretary v. *Tameside MBC*
[1976] 3 WLR 641

In 1975 Tameside put forward for approval under s.13 of the Education Act 1944, a scheme for comprehensive education. This was approved. In May 1976, following a local election in which abolition of grammar schools was an issue, the Conservatives gained control. In June, the Labour Minister, Mr Mulley, was informed that Tameside would continue selective entry. S.68 of the 1944 Act provides that the Minister, if 'satisfied' that any local education authority has acted or intends to act 'unreasonably with respect to the exercise of any power conferred by the Act . . . may . . . give such directions as to the exercise of the power . . . as appear to him to be expedient'. Serving notice that this late change of plan 'would give rise to considerable difficulties' and was unreasonable, the Minister directed the Council on 11 June to operate a non-selective entry. The House of Lords unanimously refused his subsequent application for an order of mandamus to enforce this direction.

LORD DIPLOCK: My Lords, in public law 'unreasonable' as descriptive of the way in which a public authority has purported to exercise a discretion vested in it by statute has become a term of legal art. To fall within this expression it must be conduct which no sensible authority acting with due appreciation of its responsibilities would have decided to adopt.

The very concept of administrative discretion involves a right to choose between more than one possible course of action upon which there is room for reasonable people to hold differing opinions as to which is to be preferred. It has from the beginning to end of these proceedings been properly conceded by counsel for the Secretary of State that his own strong preference and that of the government of which he is a member for non-selective entry to all secondary schools is not of itself a ground upon which he could be satisfied that the Tameside council would be acting unreasonably if they gave effect to their contrary preference for the retention of selective entry to the five grammar schools in their area. What he had to consider was whether the way in which they proposed to give effect to that preference would, in the light of the circumstances as they existed on June 11, 1976, involve such interference with the provision of efficient instruction and training in secondary schools in their area that no sensible authority acting with due appreciation of its responsibilities under the Act could have decided to adopt the course which the Tameside council were then proposing.

It was for the Secretary of State to decide that. It is not for any court of law to substitute its own opinion for his; but it is for a court of law to determine whether it has been established that in reaching his decision unfavourable to the council he had directed himself properly in law and had in consequence taken into consideration the matters which upon the true construction of the Act he ought to have considered and excluded from his consideration matters that were irrelevant to what he had to consider . . .

It has not been seriously contended before your Lordships that the time available between June 11 and September 1, when the new term at secondary schools began, was insufficient to enable [selection] to be carried out effectively, if reasonable cooperation were obtainable from head teachers at the primary schools. However, three of the teachers' trade unions, including those to which the majority of head teachers of primary schools belonged, had threatened to withhold the cooperation of their members. So the question that the Secretary of State had to ask himself was: in face of the trade unions' threat that their members would refuse to cooperate was the council on June 11 acting unreasonably in not having abandoned by that date all plans for reintroducing selective entry to grammar schools in their area?

The letter of June 11 [containing the direction] contains no indication that the Secretary of State directed his mind to this question, let alone that he realised that it lay at the heart of what he had to decide . . .

The only passage capable of referring, even eliptically, to the unions' threat is the reference to the selection procedure being '. . . carried out in circumstances and under a timetable which raise substantial doubts about its educational validity.'

A relevant question to which the Secretary of State should have directed his mind was the extent to which head teachers would be likely to persist in a policy of non-cooperation if he himself was known to have declined to stop the council from proceeding with their plan. There is no suggestion in the [Minister's] letter, nor in either of the affidavits sworn on his behalf . . . that the Secretary of State ever directed his mind to this particular question or formed any view about it. Indeed, it is not until the second affidavit that it is disclosed that the teachers' trade unions had been writing directly to the department on the matter at all. It is not for a court of law to speculate as to how the Secretary of State would have answered that question had he directed his mind to it . . . Assuming, however, that he had formed the view that cooperation by head teachers was likely to be only partial so that the selection process would be liable to greater possibility of error than where full cooperation could be obtained, the Secretary of State would have to consider whether the existence of such a degree of imperfection in the selection system as he thought would be involved was so great as to make it unreasonable conduct for the council to attempt to fulfil the mandate which they had so recently received from the electors. Again, there is no indication that the Secretary of State weighed these two considerations against one another . . . In my view, the respondents have succeeded in establishing in these proceedings that the Secretary of State did not direct his mind to the right question; and so . . . cannot have directed himself properly in law.

Lord Wilberforce commented: 'A large number of parents had signed a petition against the 1975 proposals and no doubt supported the [Conservative] opposition. The opposition gained control of the council, and they considered themselves to have been given a mandate to reconsider their predecessors' education policy.' Was this relevant?

Now return to Lord Reid's judgment in *Padfield*. Does Lord Diplock's speech affect the 'no-evidence' test? Austin argues that a 'substantial evidence' rule developed along the lines of American law would be the best basis for a theory of review of discretionary power:

The most fruitful source of a new basis for review is the 'no evidence' ground, typified by the *Coleen Properties* case [below, Chapter 14] in which the Minister of Housing and Local Government was held to have acted without jurisdiction because the statutory reason for his confirmation of part of a local authority's requisition order was unsupported by evidence, none having been led on that specific point by the local authority at the public inquiry. The 'no evidence' rule is of course a form of jurisdictional review, its rationale being that the decision-maker must justify his finding of jurisdictional fact upon which his exercise of power is based. At present, the courts require no more than that there be some evidence, however slight, upon which the finding can stand. It is submitted that the courts could and should raise the standard of proof to that of a substantial quantum of evidence in support of the finding . . .

[Moreover] the substantial evidence requirement can be extended beyond the control of preliminary jurisdictional facts and can be applied to the whole of the decision-making process, even where the power is conferred in subjective terms, provided there is in all cases a duty to give reasons for a decision. Inevitably, reasons, even if disguised by the name of policy, must, in the individual case, be shown to be based on facts founded in evidence. The courts could and should test the substantiality of those evidentiary foundations. Thus, without questioning the merits of a decision-maker's subjective judgment, the courts could nonetheless require that there be substantial evidence to support the factual findings or assumptions upon which that judgment is based.

As to the test of substantiality, it is submitted that the correct test would be a modified form of that applied by magistrates in determining whether there are grounds for an indictment, namely, does the evidence led by the prosecution constitute a prima facie case against the accused. The modification would be that the court would consider the evidence *as a whole*, not merely the evidence in support of the decision-maker's findings or assumptions. This test, given the experience of the judiciary in assessing the weight and value of evidence, would provide a more objective and therefore more consistent ground for review than the present subjective purposive statutory construction, upon which the courts have founded their powers of review in recent years. [Austin, 1975, pp. 173–5.]

Compare the *Wednesbury* formula with an American definition of substantial evidence as 'more than a mere scintilla. It means such relevant evidence as a reasonable mind might accept as adequate to support a conclusion.'[14] In order to know whether a decision is based on substantial evidence, a court must see the evidence. What, to Lord Diplock, lay at the heart of the *Tameside* decision? Judging from his speech, what evidence on this issue was available (a) to the House of Lords and (b) to the Minister?

In *Tameside*, the court had to construe the intention of Parliament. Later, Palley wrote to *The Times* (23 August 1976); do you think this evidence of legislative history would have been helpful?

The word 'unreasonably' was deliberately inserted into the 1944 Act (by a government amendment in the House of Lords) to make it clear that the Minister could only interfere with LEAs in exceptional cases (*Hansard* (Lords) vol. 132, c.540–52, 861–4, 954–966; and *HC Deb.* vol. 402, c.955–967). Strong protest in the Lords at clause 93(2), which would have empowered the Minister to substitute his decision for those of LEAs in any circumstances he thought this was required, led to its omission and the insertion instead of what is sec. 68 . . . One thing is crystal clear: Parliament was unwilling to upset the balance of power as between central government and local government decision making on educational matters by giving the Minister power to substitute his own decisions for those of local authorities whenever he thought fit . . .

In reality the Tameside decision reiterates restrictions on the courts' own powers of interference. They may interfere with governmental decisions only in the limited circumstances in which a body acts 'unreasonably' or contrary to law. Had they given a looser interpretation to 'unreasonably', by allowing Mr Mulley a wide discretion to intervene, they would simultaneously have been extending their own powers because the formula defining their powers is the formula deliberately chosen to define his: Catch 22. Many administrative lawyers will regret this ruling because a wider meaning for 'unreasonably' . . . would have allowed the courts in future to touch on the merits of governmental decisions. The paradox is that they upset a particular minister's ruling, but strengthened the law limiting their own power to set aside ministerial decisions generally.

Do you agree that the House of Lords did not touch on the merits of the Minister's decision?

Bromley LBC v. *Greater London Council*
[1982] 2 WLR 62

The GLC, implementing a promise to electors in the election manifesto of the governing Labour councillors, reduced bus and tube fares by 25 per cent. This was done by a grant to the London Transport Executive which enabled the LTE to budget for a deficit. The grant was financed by a precept to all London boroughs to levy a supplementary rate of 6.1p in the pound. This supplementary levy raised the rates to a level at which loss of central government would be incurred under the terms of the Local Government Planning and Land Act 1980. Bromley, a Conservative-controlled borough, applied for certiorari to quash the precept. The council failed in the Divisional Court (Dunn LJ and Phillips J), but succeeded unanimously in the Court of Appeal. However the judgments were based on widely differing grounds; compare, for example, the 'narrow' opinion of Oliver LJ with Lord Denning's reliance on 'reasonableness' ([1982] 2 WLR 64). The Appeal Court decision provoked this exchange in the House of Commons (HC Deb. vol. 12, col. 418):

MR LYON (Lab.): Does the Prime Minister recognise the danger of the judges arrogating to themselves political decisions? Although it may be one thing to say that the council has exceeded its statutory power, it is quite another thing to say that, even if it had the statutory power, it acted unreasonably in balancing the interest of ratepayers and fare-paying passengers? In such circumstances, the judges were making political decisions and not judicial decisions.

MRS THATCHER: I wholly reject [that]. Judges give decisions on the law and the evidence before them. They do so totally impartially.

The House of Lords unanimously rejected the GLC's appeal:

LORD WILBERFORCE: The precept is attacked on two main grounds: (1) That it is beyond the powers of the G.L.C. as defined by the Transport (London) Act 1969. (2) That even if the G.L.C. has the necessary statutory powers, the issuance of the precept was an invalid exercise of its discretion under the Act. This ground itself may be divisible into two contentions (a) that the exercise of the G.L.C.'s discretion was unreasonable, or (b) that the G.L.C. when deciding to issue the precept did not take relevant considerations into account, or did take into account irrelevant considerations or misdirected itself as to the law.

Both of these grounds depend upon the fact . . . that the G.L.C., though a powerful body . . . is the creation of statute and only has powers given to it by statute. The courts will give full recognition to the wide discretion conferred upon the council by Parliament and will not lightly interfere with its exercise. But its actions, unlike those of Parliament, are examinable by the courts, whether on grounds of vires, or on principles of administrative law (those two may overlap). It makes no difference on the question of legality (as opposed to reasonableness – see *Tameside*) whether the impugned action was or was not submitted to or approved by the relevant electorate: that cannot confer validity upon ultra vires action . . .

The general duty of the G.L.C. is stated, in section 1, as being to develop and encourage measures which will promote the provision of 'integrated, efficient and economic transport facilities and services for Greater London'.

There has been a good deal of argument as to the meaning of these words, particularly of 'economic': no doubt they are vague, possibly with design. It has been strongly argued that the word means something like 'on business principles' but for present purposes I will take it to mean 'cost-effective', or 'making the most effective use of resources in the context of an integrated system' – the meaning most favourable to the G.L.C.

Section 3 gives the G.L.C. power to make grants to the L.T.E. 'for any purpose' and no doubt these words are wide enough to cover grants to revenue as well as for capital purposes. The section cannot, however, be read in isolation, and it is necessary to examine the rest of the Act in order to ascertain the framework in which this power is exercisable. Its extent and the manner in which it is to be exercised must be controlled by the fact that the G.L.C. owes a duty to two different classes. First, under its responsibility for meeting the needs of Greater London, it must provide for transport users: these include not only the residents of London, but persons travelling to and in London from outside (e.g. commuters) and tourists. Most of these will not pay rates to the G.L.C. Secondly, it owes a duty of a fiduciary character to its ratepayers who have to provide the money. These, it is said, represent 40 per cent only of the electorate and probably a smaller proportion of the travelling public: they would themselves, most likely, also be travellers. Most of the rates (62 per cent) have to be found from commercial ratepayers . . . These duties must be fairly balanced one against the other, see *Roberts* v. *Hopwood* [above] and *Luby* v. *Newcastle under Lyme Corporation* [1964] 2 Q B 64.

For Bromley, it is said that the executive must run its undertaking on business principles and so far as practicable must meet its revenue charges . . . out of fares and other available internal revenue. If it incurs a deficit in one accounting period, it must 'ensure', 'so far as practicable', that this is made up in the next accounting period . . .

The G.L.C. and L.T.E., on the other hand, while accepting that accumulated deficits have to be avoided, submit that the executive, in making up its revenue account, and in putting forward fare proposals, may take account of a prospective grant on revenue account from the G.L.C. . . .

They sought to reinforce this argument by reference to supposed Parliamentary intentions. It must, they argued, have been in the contemplation of Parliament that deficits would be incurred. Parliament may indeed have desired this, regarding transport as essentially a social service. Such deficits could only be made good by grants from the G.L.C. Parliament was content to leave the financing of them to the G.L.C., subject only to a prohibition against accumulated deficits.

To this argument, I have given careful consideration; it touches upon important issues of transport policy. There is indeed, and has been for some years, discussion, on the political level, as to whether, and to what extent, public transport, particularly in capital cities, should be regarded, and financed, as a social service, out of taxation whether national or local. We cannot take any position in this argument: we must recognise that it exists. But I am unable to see, however carefully I reread the Act of 1969, that Parliament had in that year taken any clear stance upon it . . .

In my opinion there are two clear provisions in the Act. The first . . . states the obligation of the London Transport Executive to make good a deficit in the year following a deficit year. This is an obligation, the meeting of which the executive is to ensure as far as practicable. In my opinion this points to the taking of action which it is in the power of the executive to take . . . The corresponding provision as regards the G.L.C. . . . recognises that the duty stated in section 7(3)(b) (to make up a deficit in year two) is one which 'falls to be complied with by the executive', and then obliges the council in performing its functions to have regard to that duty and take action which will enable the executive to comply with those requirements. Such actions might take several forms: the council might direct fares to be raised or services to be adjusted. Or the council could decide to make a grant. But it can only do that after it has 'had regard' to the executive's duty . . . The respective statutory obligations of the G.L.C. and London Transport Executive fit in with one another: the London Transport Executive must carry out its duty as defined in section 7(3): the G.L.C. cannot exercise its powers unless and until the London Transport Executive carries out that duty and must then do so with proper regard to its fiduciary duty to its ratepayers. If these constraints were not to exist, there would be no limit upon the power of the G.L.C. to make grants in aid of revenue, since the Act provides for no governmental control. I find it impossible, in the light of the previous history and of the far from definite language used, to accept that Parliament could have intended that this should be so. To say this is not to impose upon the London Transport Executive a rigid obligation to balance its accounts every year, nor . . . to maximise fares. There is flexibility in the words 'so far as practicable' and the obligatory establishment of a reserve gives room for manoeuvre . . . But, given this, it appears to me clear that neither the executive in making its proposals, nor the G.L.C. in accepting them, could have power totally to disregard any responsibility for ensuring, so far as practicable, that outgoings are met by revenue, and that the London Transport Executive runs its business on economic lines.

Lord Wilberforce distinguishes 'grounds of vires' from 'principles of administrative law'. What does he mean? Does the first term refer to statutory interpretation? He also distinguishes 'legality' from 'reasonableness'. Is the contrast once more between 'statute' and 'principles', or is he contrasting unreasonable exercise of discretion (contention (a)) with irrelevant considerations (contention (b))? Did Lord Greene intend this latter distinction? Why should the opinion of the electorate be relevant only to the question of reasonableness?

Now compare the reasoning of Lord Diplock:

The G.L.C., like other local authorities, is an elected body . . . Broadly speaking, the electors comprise all adults resident in Greater London, of whom about 40 per cent are also rate-payers. Apart from income-earning assets, the G.L.C.'s principal sources of revenue are (1) rates for which it issues precepts to the London boroughs, who are under a statutory obligation to levy rates upon the ratepayers in the amount specified in the precept, and (2) grants from central government funds. Some 62 per cent of the total amount of the income of the G.L.C. from rates is raised from ratepayers engaged in industry, business or commerce. They have no vote as electors. These structural characteristics of the G.L.C. need to be borne in mind in applying, as I think one must, a purposive construction to the sometimes opaque and elliptical language adopted in the Transport (London) Act 1969 . . .

When a statute speaks, as section 1 does, of a 'duty' of a local authority composed of democratically elected members, it is speaking of the collective legal duty of all those members acting through the ordinary procedure of debate and resolution, to make choices of policy and of action that they believe to be in the best interests (weighing, where necessary, one against the other) of all those categories of persons to whom their collective duty is owed. This will involve identifying the persons to whom the particular duty is owed, and in the event of a conflict of interest between one category and another deciding where the balance ought to lie. In the case of public passenger transport in Greater London those categories are: (1) potential passengers by bus and train in Greater London whether resident there or not; (2) residents in Greater London, who may be assumed to derive benefit from the general mobility of people living in or within commuting distance of Greater London resulting from the availability of a public passenger transport system, even though the particular resident may happen to make little or no use of it himself; and (3) ratepayers in Greater London, to the extent that they are required to contribute to the cost of the system. These three categories overlap but do not coincide. Most persons in category (2) will also be in category (1), and it will be convenient to refer to these as 'passengers', but . . . there is no such coincidence between either of these two categories and category (3), the ratepayers. They constitute only 40 per cent of residents and that 40 per cent bears only 38 per cent of the total burden borne by all ratepayers. The conflict of interest lies between passengers and the ratepayers.

I have left out electors as such, as constituting a separate category. A council member [who] fought the election on the basis of policies for the future put forward in the election manifesto of a particular political party, presumably considered that in the circumstances contemplated in the manifesto those policies were in the best interest of the electors in his ward, and, if the democratic system as at present practised in local government is to survive, the fact that he received a majority of votes of those electors who took enough interest in the future policies to be adopted by the G.L.C. to cause them to cast their votes, is a factor to which considerable weight ought to be given by him when participating in the collective duty of the G.L.C. to decide whether to implement those policies in the circumstances that exist at the time that the decision falls to be made. That this may properly be regarded as a weighty factor is implicit in the speeches in this House in *Tameside* . . . [But] when the time comes to play their part in performing the collective duty of the G.L.C. to make choices of policy or action on particular matters, members [must not] treat themselves as irrevocably bound to carry out pre-announced policies contained in election manifestos even though, by that time, changes of circumstances have occurred that were unforeseen when those policies were announced and would add significantly to the disadvantages that would result from carrying them out.

My Lords, the conflicting interests which the G.L.C. had to balance in deciding whether or not to go ahead with the 25 per cent reduction in fares, notwithstanding the loss of grant from central government funds that this would entail, were those of passengers and the ratepayers. It is well established . . . that a local authority owes a fiduciary duty to the ratepayers from whom it obtains moneys needed to carry out its statutory functions, and that this includes a duty not to expend those moneys thriftlessly but to deploy the full financial resources available to it to the best advantage; the financial resources of the G.L.C. that are relevant to the present appeals being the rate fund obtained by issuing precepts and the grants from central government respectively. The existence of this duty throws light upon the true construction of the much-debated phrase in section 1(1) 'integrated, efficient and economic transport facilities and services'. 'Economic' in this context must I think mean in the economic interests of passengers and the ratepayers looked at together, i.e. keeping to a minimum the total financial burden that the persons in these two categories have to share between them for the provision by the L.T.E. in conjunction with the railways board and the bus company of an integrated and efficient public transport system for Greater London . . . I think that the G.L.C. had a discretion as to the proportions in which that total financial burden should be allocated between passengers and the ratepayers. What are the limits of that discretion and whether those limits would have been exceeded if the only effect of the G.L.C.'s decision to instruct the L.T.E. to lower its fares by 25 per cent had been to transfer to the ratepayers the cost (amounting to some £69m) of the financial relief that was afforded to the passengers by the lowering of the fares is a difficult question on which the arguments for and against are by no means all one way. Fortunately I do not find it necessary to decide that question in the present appeals. It does not, in my view, arise, because the G.L.C.'s decision was not simply about allocating a total financial burden between passengers and the ratepayers, it was also a decision to increase that total burden so as nearly to double it and to place the whole of the increase on the ratepayers. For, as the G.L.C. well knew when it took the decision to reduce the fares, it would entail a loss of rate grant from central government funds amounting to some £50 million, which would have to be made good by the ratepayers as a result of the G.L.C.'s decision. So the total financial burden to be shared by passengers and the ratepayers for the provision of an integrated and efficient public passenger transport system was to be increased by an improvement in the efficiency of the system, and the whole of the extra £50 million was to be recovered from the ratepayers. That would, in my view, clearly be a thriftless use of moneys obtained by the G.L.C. from ratepayers and a deliberate failure to deploy to the best advantage the full financial resources available to it by avoiding any action that would involve forfeiting grants from central government funds. It was thus a breach of the fiduciary duty owed by the G.L.C. to the ratepayers. I accordingly agree with your Lordships that the precept issued pursuant to the decision was ultra vires and therefore void.

List the interests taken into consideration by Lord Diplock. Are there any further interests which in your view, ought to have been considered? You may find Stewart's analysis (above, p. 289) helpful here.

Let us pick up Davis's point that judges' attitude to policy is half-hearted, narrow and restrictive. Defending the *Bromley* decision extra-judicially, Lord Scarman draws a line between 'policy' and 'purposive interpretation':

Here, indeed, was policy-making by the courts: they forced a transformation of policy in the fares structure of the L.T.E. But the process by which they did it was, by the standards of judicial review developed in the post-war years, a legitimate judicial process. Judges may not act upon their own ideas of policy other than in the very restricted field of legal policy, a field which is more correctly described as that of legal principle. But, if it be possible to elicit the policy of a particular piece of legislation by studying it in its statutory context, and against the background of history, the courts will do so, and, when interpreting a statutory provision, use the policy thus elected as an aid in determining the true meaning of the statute. This is precisely what the Lords did in the fares case. The courts, therefore, will elicit and enforce policy, if it can be found by what Lord Diplock has called the purposive approach to statutory interpretation. But they will not give effect to their own subjective views on policy. [Scarman 1983, unpublished lecture.]

Commenting on the same case, Pannick was less well pleased with the performance of the House. He thought it ridiculous to embark on purposive interpretation without recourse to *Hansard*;[15] 'journalists seem to have little difficulty . . . in identifying extracts from *Hansard* which are germane to the appeal. Counsel should therefore be able to refer to parliamentary debates at the time the relevant legislation was enacted as one factor, amongst others, assisting the proper interpretation of the words of the Act.' He was equally concerned with the excessive importance attached to financial at the expense of 'social and other consequences'. Describing the reasoning as 'insular and pedantic' he concluded:

All the Law Lords emphasised the financial consequences to ratepayers if the GLC policy were to be upheld. But there is a paucity of reference to the social impact of the GLC's policy and the consequences of holding it unlawful; reduced passenger flow leading to even higher fares; an increase in road traffic causing more road accidents and greater pollution; a less frequent public transport service; and less jobs for London Transport staff. Nor is there any reference to the transport systems of other major cities in Europe, the subsidy of which was, no doubt, in the mind of Parliament in 1969. Whether or not the social and economic context and consequences of the decision argue against the substance of the Law Lords' judgment, it is objectionable that the judiciary should purport to construe admittedly ambiguous legislation without regard to the consequences of a decision for or against the GLC. [Pannick 1982, pp. 322–3.]

First let us take Pannick's point about statutory interpretation. *Hansard* would not have been conclusive nor perhaps even helpful. Although Members questioned the weight to be attached to the phrase 'efficient and economic', the debates were inconclusive. The Minister (Mr Marsh) introducing the 1969 Bill was not definite about the allocation of functions. He stressed the overall policy responsibility of 'the people of London through their elected representatives on the GLC'. He described clause 1, which empowered the GLC to draw up 'comprehensive' policies for transport taking into account 'the social and environmental problems', as the key clause. He clearly envisaged a measure of subsidy, because he said: 'The Council might wish . . . the Executive to run a series of services at a loss for social or planning reasons. It might wish to keep fares down at a time when costs are rising and there is no scope for economies. It is free to do so. But it has to bear the cost.' On the other hand, he described the obligation of the L T E 'to break even' as 'overriding' and, challenged on the question of subsidy, stated that it would certainly never be abused (see further, HC Deb. vol. 775, col. 1242 *et seq.*).[16]

Secondly, Pannick is asking judges to modify their procedures and techniques of decision-taking. This question is discussed further in the next chapters (see also Loughlin, above, Chapter 4). The aftermath of the *Bromley* case suggests that courts might be forced into evaluating evidence which they are ill-equipped to evaluate. Increasingly, their views on social and economic policy would be substituted for those of our elected representatives and their qualified advisers.

Later cases also suggest that the lower courts have not been swept away by Griffith's 'snowy wave of interventionism'. The initial reaction of the GLC to *Bromley* was to double fares. Later they produced new proposals (the Balanced Plan) in an effort to conform to the judgment while maintaining a policy of fares subsidy. The plan contained several options, of which the favourite was to return fares to the level at which they had been prior to the first reduction. Since there was uncertainty over the meaning of the House of Lords judgments and consequently of the legality of the 'Balanced Plan', a friendly action was brought to ascertain whether the new proposals were intra vires. In *R. v. London Transport Executive ex p. Greater London Council* [1983] 2 WLR 702, the High Court upheld the legality of the 'Balanced Plan'.

The legality of subsidies to public transport was again the subject of *R. v. Merseyside County Council ex p. The Great Universal Stores, The Times*, 18 February 1982. Woolf J. distinguished the case on the grounds that the text of the relevant statutes was different. He also contrasted the attitude of the respective councils; GLC had adopted a fixed policy of subsidy, Merseyside had been more flexible. In *R. v. GLC ex p. Kensington and Chelsea, The Times*, 7 April 1982, Kensington made an attempt to challenge the budgetary process leading to settlement of the GLC housing precept. With some reluctance, McNeill J granted leave to apply, though the application was disallowed. In the course of his judgment he remarked:

The issue on the special contingency balance is one for the political hustings and not for the court. It is a matter of real concern that the Divisional Court, exercising the power of judicial review, is increasingly . . . sought to be used for political purposes superficially dressed up as points of law. The proper remedy in such matters is the ballot box and not the court.

In *Pickwell* v. *Camden LBC* [1983] 2 WLR 383, the district auditor applied for a declaration that wages paid by the authority to manual workers following a strike, in excess of a nationally agreed settlement, were unlawful. Distinguishing *Roberts* v. *Hopwood*, the Court of Appeal held the settlement to be lawful on the ground that Camden had attempted to arrive at a fair settlement in all the circumstances and had not simply adopted a fixed policy, for example to accede to local union demands. The council disputed the fact that the wage increase exceeded the national average and the court heard evidence from their expert witness, Professor Metcalfe, an economist. Forbes J described the argument as 'more appropriate to economists than lawyers' and declined to venture any opinion, though he thought that 'the existence of so fundamental a divergence of opinion on a matter so important must cast some doubt on whether it can properly be said that no reasonable authority could possibly have acted as did Camden in this instance.'

Finally, in *R.* v. *Environment Secretary ex p. Brent LBC* [1982] QB 593, London councils successfully challenged the Minister's decision to withhold payment of the rate support grant on the ground that he had refused to listen to their representations before making up his mind. But when, after listening to representations, the Minister decided to maintain the original decision, a second application for review which included a claim for damages for breach of statutory duty was dismissed in *R.* v. *Environment Secretary ex p. Hackney LBC* [1983] 1 WLR 524. The lower courts do not see themselves as final arbiters of disputes over resource-allocation between central government, local authorities and ratepayers.

3 A seedless grape?

There is considerable agreement today among public lawyers that judicial review of discretionary power is itself discretionary in character. The leading authorities cannot sustain the case that judicial review is based on precise and clearly applicable rules. Wade, an ardent supporter of interventionist courts, is not greatly concerned. De Smith was torn between his desire to produce a definitive synthesis of the case law and his inner feeling that judicial review is discretionary and pragmatic.

Elliott, discussing Lord Scarman's judgments in *United Kingdom Association of Professional Engineers* v. *A CAS* [1980] 2 WLR 254 and *Engineers and Managers Association* v. *A CAS* [1980] 1 WLR 302, remarks on the 'open texture' of the so-called rules, describing the application of the *Wednesbury* formula in the modern cases as 'nonsense on stilts':

> Lord Greene's judgment . . . thought initially to have 'whittled down the requirement of reasonableness till it had all but disappeared', has been invoked recently not to uphold the actions of statutory bodies, but rather to invalidate them . . . This is hardly surprising: the principles that Lord Greene establishes – taking relevant considerations into account, ignoring irrelevant ones, acting reasonably and so on – are extraordinarily open textured, capable of meaning all things to all men. A crude conclusion from this history would be that the courts have been able to use the *Wednesbury* formula as a convenient rationalisation for varying policy decisions. However, Lord Scarman's belief that the *Wednesbury* language can be used as a test, no less, for deciding whether the judiciary should intervene in the exercise of discretionary powers must be examined. First, it is recognized that it is A.C.A.S.'s discretion and judgment that must determine the issues. It is an expert body, charged with a set of tasks by the statute: courts have neither the expertise nor a primary allocation of statutory power: they have neither the ability nor the legal justification to tell A.C.A.S. what it should do. The next step, the invention of the hypothetical doppelganger – the arbitration conciliation and advisory service charged with A.C.A.S.'s duties and responsibilities – involves some difficulty. In a case involving a local authority, the courts could imagine a substitute: there are, after all, lots of local authorities. There is however only one statutory arbitration conciliation and advisory service and that is A.C.A.S. So a hypothetical A.C.A.S. with an identical statutory framework and expertise to the real A.C.A.S. must be invented. Next, presumably, it must be decided what the hypothetical A.C.A.S. would have done. In other words, the hypothetical A.C.A.S. is the same as the real A.C.A.S. except for the fact that it is staffed by Law Lords. This difference is, one assumes, to be regarded as *de minimis*. What the hypothetical A.C.A.S. would have done is then compared with what the real A.C.A.S. in fact did. If the two results are the same, the challenge is dismissed: if different, the challenge is allowed although it is steadfastly maintained that A.C.A.S.'s job has not been performed for it. This is nonsense on stilts. [Elliott, 1980b, pp. 583–4.]

The problem is to find a formula for reform. Galligan is prepared to rely on judge-made formulae, though he advocates rather different principles. Judicial review for Galligan has two primary tasks: (a) the settlement of demarcation disputes between public authorities and (b) the enforcement of certain generalist principles of good administration. 'Review' entails regulation of the administrative process but never of the conclusionary reasons. Galligan deduces from this analysis that the courts should concentrate their attention on 'processes' designed to secure *democratic accountability* and *participation* by citizens in the democratic process.[17] Insistence on reasoned decisions would be for Galligan a vital step in this new type of review and one for which courts would be well fitted:

> It is a mistake to see the development of judicial review in terms of direct control of the substantive policy choices made by administrative officials. Activism in this direction is likely to breed conflict and controversy. The more suitable, and not less effective, course is to develop the general constraints on discretionary power. If we accept the importance of reasoned decision-making we accept certain values about the exercise of power, from which notions, such as equality of treatment, can be constructed. The requirement of reasoned decision-making involves those values which can be said in a real sense to be shared, and it is the extrapolation and development of these that provides an opening for both courts and administrative officials. For then it is not a case of the courts enforcing some set of controversial ends on the administrator, but a case of tapping the sources of genuine agreement. And after all these same sources provide the basis of all principles of good administration. [Galligan 1982, p. 274.]

If agreement over process and values were as genuine as Galligan believes, disputes over procedural fairness would never reach the courts. (Can you think of any cases which might be decided differently if Galligan's new emphasis were to be adopted?)

Scarman, too, believes in the possibility of consensus or, as he prefers to put it, in cooperation between judges and the executive. His recipe for judicial review is a new and looser style of legislative drafting leaving more room for 'purposive' interpretation by the judges:

> At present, the all too common approach of civil servants, Ministers, and legislators to the preparation of legislation is to make it judge-proof. And the basic position of the judiciary is that nobody, not even Parliament, has the right to tell the judges how to interpret statutes. They are the guardians of the law: not the slaves of a flickering legislative lamp.
>
> These attitudes will not change unless communications are improved. The judges have taken the first essential step towards co-operation by developing their principle of purposive interpretation. But it only works if the purpose, i.e. the policy, of the statute can be determined. Aids to interpretation are needed. If it should be possible to provide judges and the public with a guide as to the policy or purpose of a statute, it might be possible to do away with much of the very detailed drafting – the only plausible excuse for which is, I suggest, that it helps to prevent the judges from falling into error if they can understand it. If every statute was accompanied by an explanatory memorandum which was admissible as an aid but not binding in its effect, the quality of the work of judges and civil servants would be enhanced. Civil

servants would know that in deciding upon the meaning of ambiguous provisions the judges would at least know what was intended. And the risk of judicial misunderstanding of policy, which some (but not I) think arose in the GLC transport case, would be minimised. [Scarman 1983, unpub. lecture.]

Yet Scarman also realizes that courts have an important function as 'watchdogs empowered to compel compliance with the conditions to which executive power is subject'. If courts collaborate too closely with the administration, this function may go by the board. *R. v. Barnet L B C ex p. Shah* [1983] 2 WLR 16, a decision in which Lord Scarman was himself involved, illustrates this point.

Students who had lived in the UK for three or more years were refused grants for higher education on the ground that they were not 'ordinarily resident'. Using purposive construction, the Court of Appeal held that the phrase could have different meanings according to context and that 'ordinarily resident' for the purpose of paying tax was not the same as 'ordinarily resident' for the purpose of higher educational grants. Correcting this error, the House of Lords found it necessary to reprove the lower court for allowing 'their own views of policy and . . . the immigration status of the students' to intrude (Lord Scarman).[18] The decision, like that of *Hosenball* casts doubt on Scarman's thesis. Some applicants might argue that courts cooperate too closely with government already.

An alternative approach is to pin the judges down, structuring their discretion by rules. This is the solution preferred by Griffith, who proposes, in the light of the *Bromley* decision, that draftsmen should be instructed to include in new legislation express provisions as to justiciability, bearing in mind that matters within the area of policy and politics are 'appropriate for politicians and not judges'. But remember the *Anisminic* decision. That contained explicit provisions concerning justiciability. Could draftsmen render their provisions judge-proof?[19] Griffith also demands 'more positive, black-letter provision by statute which will define where the balance of public interest lies both in those situations where conflict is obvious . . . and where it is much less obvious but no less real'. Griffith's objective is to confine the ambit of judicial review. He believes that review should be confined to cases where public authorities 'act *ultra vires* in the narrow sense . . . [of exercising] powers not given them by statute'. He also believes that public authorities must abide by rules of procedure laid down 'by or under statute in accordance with natural justice'. Like Lord Wilberforce (above), Griffith sees a distinction between

346 LAW AND ADMINISTRATION

'narrow' and 'wide' ultra vires and he hopes to confine the second head of review to extreme cases, e.g. of corruption or bad faith. There is an ambiguity in his second proposal; it is not clear whether the rules of natural justice are to be observed by draftsmen or can be written by judges into statutory codes. *Furnell*'s case is a reminder of how important this distinction might prove. In any event, the curbs should be statutory; Griffith urges us to find 'a form of words which will positively state the grounds on which judicial control may properly be exercised' (Griffith 1983, pp. 58–9).

But could the principles of judicial review be transmuted into rules by a parliamentary draftsman? No attempt at codification has ever been made in England, though in Commonwealth jurisdictions it has been tried. S.5 of the Australian Administrative Decisions (Judicial Review) Act 1977 reads:

Applications for review of decisions
5.(1). A person who is aggrieved by a decision to which this Act applies that is made after the commencement of this Act may apply to the Court for an order of review in respect of the decision on any one or more of the following grounds:
(a) that a breach of the rules of natural justice occurred in connexion with the making of the decision;
(b) that procedures that were required by law to be observed in connexion with the making of the decision were not observed;
(c) that the person who purported to make the decision did not have jurisdiction to make the decision;
(d) that the decision was not authorized by the enactment in pursuance of which it was purported to be made;
(e) that the making of the decision was an improper exercise of the power conferred by the enactment in pursuance of which it was purported to be made;
(f) that the decision involved an error of law; whether or not the error appears on the record of the decision;
(g) that the decision was induced or affected by fraud;
(h) that there was no evidence or other material to justify the making of the decision;
(j) that the decision was otherwise contrary to law.

(2). The reference in paragraph (1)(e) to an improper exercise of a power shall be construed as including a reference to:
(a) taking an irrelevant consideration into account in the exercise of a power;
(b) failing to take a relevant consideration into account in the exercise of power;
(c) an exercise of a power for a purpose other than a purpose for which the power is conferred;

(d) an exercise of a discretionary power in bad faith;

(e) an exercise of a personal discretionary power at the direction or behest of another person;

(f) an exercise of a discretionary power in accordance with a rule or policy without regard to the merits of the particular case;

(g) an exercise of a power that is so unreasonable that no reasonable person could have so exercised the power;

(h) an exercise of a power in such a way that constitutes abuse of the power.

(3). The ground specified in paragraph (1)(h) shall not be taken to be made out unless:

(a) the person who made the decision was required by law to reach that decision only if a particular matter was established, and there was no evidence or other material (including facts of which he was entitled to take notice) from which he could reasonably be satisfied that the matter was established, or

(b) the person who made the decision based the decision on the existence of a particular fact, and that fact did not exist.

How precise are these provisions and how much discretion is left to the judiciary? S.5(1)(a), for instance, is an example of legislation by reference; it merely incorporates the common law into the statute, leaving future development for the judges. You have read many cases involving natural justice; can you define natural justice more precisely than this statute and instruct the judiciary when it is to be applied? And is natural justice static? There is nothing in the statute to inhibit judicial development of this elusive concept.[20] Is it desirable that there should be? S.5(1)(d) attempts to encapsulate the idea of 'narrow ultra vires'. In deciding whether a decision is or is not authorized by a given enactment the principles of statutory interpretation will naturally be invoked. Once again, the judge possesses significant freedom of manoeuvre. What precisely is 'bad faith' (s.5(2)(d)) or 'fraud' (s.5(1)(g))? Are these concepts (which Griffith also adopts) more precise than the standard of reasonableness? In the celebrated example of the red-headed schoolteacher, is s/he dismissed 'in bad faith' or 'unreasonably'? In other words, is unreasonableness only a gentle extension of bad faith? Is bad faith sufficiently elastic to encompass the vices listed in the Crossman catalogue of maladministration, e.g. 'turpitude, perversity, malice and corruption'? Is judicial review inevitably soft-centred, like a seedless grape? Or, if you agree with Griffith that judicial discretion has increased, is increasing and ought to be diminished, can you draft provisions which would effect this?

12
Compensation: private rights and public interest

1 Can't pay, must pay

Throughout this book, we have tried to look at administrative law from different angles. First, we took the traditional lawyerly view of administrative law as machinery for the control of government, and of judicial review as the centrepiece of administrative law. This conception was queried by green light theorists and, in Chapter 11, we found ourselves struggling with the elusive concept of justiciability, together with techniques by which judicial discretion could be structured and confined.

Next, we looked at law as a means by which policy objectives are attained as well as defined. Breaking the administrative process down into four functions of discretion, rule-making, adjudication and rule-application, we looked at each in turn. The final stage in this process was a detailed study of the application of statutory provisions for depreciation and home loss payments. Had we questioned the purpose of these payments we might have given the administrator's answer that they were designed to encourage home owners to move without fuss, and to lessen resistance to public works; in short, to grease the wheels of the administrative process and allow it to run smoothly. As Franks once remarked of the prevailing rates of compensation for compulsorily purchased land:

Much of the dissatisfaction with the procedures relating to land arises from the basis of compensation. It is clear that objections to compulsory purchase would be far fewer if compensation were always assessed at not less than market value. It is not part of our terms of reference to consider and make recommendations upon the basis of compensation. But we cannot emphasise too strongly the extent to which these financial considerations affect the matters with which we have to deal. Whatever changes in procedure are made dissatisfaction is, because of this, bound to remain. [Cmnd 218, para. 278.]

Politicians as well as administrators are alert to the uses of money payments in greasing the wheels. Discussing reform of the system of property ownership in capitalist society, Laski noted that the carrot was often preferable to the stick:

Extinction of rights by the payment of compensation seems to leave in full vigour a class of functionless owners. That is true; and in strict logic it is unjustifiable. But the life of a community must be adjusted to its experience and not to a strict logic. The sudden extinction of these legal rights would, if unaccompanied by compensation, probably result in an assault upon the government making the attempt. Men will sooner, as Machiavelli said, forgive the death of their relatives than the confiscation of their property. Nothing is so likely to poison the spirit of the body politic than the sudden disappointment of financial expectation . . . No investment is ever lost that maintains good-will; and in the transference to a new system, the more good-will we have the greater is the augury of its success. [Laski 1925, pp. 209–10.]

From this angle, 'compensation' is only one of many decisions about resource allocation and one which differs little from other decisions in the realm of economic planning. Suppose, for example, the government has to decide how best to rescue an essential but unprofitable industry. It could nationalize the concern, making provision for compensation to existing shareholders. The principle of compensation would here be conceded, but the amount would depend on the generosity or parsimony of the government and its view of the public interest. The post-war programme of nationalization did in fact proceed on this basis. Alternatively, the government might purchase a controlling interest in the concern, paying the market price, a difference which might be considerable. Or it might allow the concern to remain in private hands, providing funds in the form of development grants. In this case, shareholders would retain their property, in all probability enhanced in value by government intervention.[1] These are all questions of resource allocation; but some would see them as radically different answers to the same problem.

If compensation is simply a question of resource allocation, most of us would probably think of it as a political or governmental responsibility. We might go on to insist that Parliament, and more specifically the House of Commons, ought to take a hand in the decision. Once again, the influence of the seventeenth-century civil wars would be felt, though the constitutional tradition is probably a much longer one.[2] 'The fundamental principle that the Crown has no power to tax save by the grant of Parliament is . . . to be found in Magna Carta which, as Parliament itself has said, is declaratory of the common law . . . and legislation adds to its force, for the Bill of Rights, 1689, asserts that "Levying money for or to the use of the Crown by pretence of prerogative without grant of Parliament . . . is illegal" ' (Jennings 1957, p. 283). Remember Sir Peter Baldwin's defence of his department's refusal to make extra-statutory depreciation payments (see above, p. 247). His reference to a line of accounting not authorized by the Government is actually a pale reflection of these impressive constitutional principles though, in the particular circumstances, it may fail to convince.

There is an alternative approach. Lawyers tend to analyse problems in terms of 'rights' (Chapter 1); using the vocabulary of 'rights' we might argue that depreciation and home loss payments were more properly described as *compensation* for the injury to, or extinction of, a valuable property right. And we might distinguish the three methods of allocating resources to our 'lame duck' industry by saying that the first solution involved the extinction of a right while the second and third did not. This difference might have important consequences for the sums which would have to be paid in compensation. Again, there is nothing novel here. At least since the seventeenth century, western political theory and western political institutions have been greatly concerned with the protection of private property. The Declaration of the Rights of Man 1789, rated property second only to liberty[3] and its provisions are incorporated in many western constitutions, which accord constitutional protection to property as an over-riding, fundamental right. The tradition is affirmed by the title of Reich's essay, 'The New Property'. If you turn back to the quotation from Laski, dedicated socialist and green light theorist, you will find him talking in terms of property 'rights' and *A Grammar of Politics* contains a lengthy analysis of the topic.

But how, in a country without a written constitution, is property to be protected? One answer lies, of course, in Parliament. We know that, for Dicey, the other side of the equation was the common law: 'the general principles of the constitution are with us the result of judicial decisions determining the rights of private persons in particular cases brought before the courts'. Earlier we saw the courts intervening in two distinct ways to protect private property. The first was through judicial review. In *Laker*'s case, the court held that

Laker's licence could not be retracted, thus creating a valuable property right. In *Cooper* v. *Wandsworth Board of Works*, on the other hand, the plaintiff was complaining of a breach of the rules of natural justice, but he chose as his vehicle an action for trespass to land. The result was that the Board had to pay damages for the destruction of Cooper's house.

We are already familiar with amber-light theories which see as the central function of administrative law the balance of public and private interest. Compensation seems an equitable way of resolving such conflicts of interest. As administrative law theory slips into a median position, so one of its priorities becomes a system of adequate compensation for citizens whose interests have been injuriously affected by the growing power of the state.

Once again *Laker*'s case provides a useful illustration. We know that the courts intervened to protect Laker's property. Baldwin argued, however, that their intervention prevented the Government from implementing an important policy decision taken in the public interest and dislocated a sensitive administrative system. Amber-light theorists might suggest compensation as a way of adjusting the balance. The Government could implement its policy, subject to a legal right to compensation for abortive expenditure and even loss of profit. In Duguit's theory of public law (see above, p. 39), you will find that a similar view of compensation underlies his theory of the liability of the state.[4] Similarly, Garner and other English writers have argued that 'all modern societies require a special law of administrative liability capable of weighing public and private interests' (Garner 1978, p. 230).

At first sight this proposition seems unexceptionable, and it does not seem likely that the sums involved will be very great. Remember the claims for home loss and depreciation payments; very small sums were involved. Yet the annual cost of implementing the Land Compensation Act was estimated during the second reading debate at £65 million. Laker's expenditure amounted to £7 million, discounting loss of profit, and other individual court cases have involved enormous sums. The admittedly exceptional case of *Tito* v. *Waddell (No. 2)* [1977] 2 WLR 49 involved the British colony of Ocean Island (Banaba) on which phosphate was discovered. The islanders, at that time inexperienced in the ways of western capitalism, were persuaded to allow quarrying by the British Phosphate Commissioners. Small royalties were paid annually. Ultimately the island became uninhabitable and the Banabans had to leave. They felt that they had been unfairly treated and claimed compensation from the Crown. When negotiations broke down, they brought an action in the High Court, arguing that the Crown owed an equitable fiduciary duty to protect their interests and should make reparation in full. The argument is not preposterous; after all fiduciary duties have been acknowledged in other public law cases. But the cost of accepting this argument would have been very great. Ex gratia payments of approximately £9 million were made by the British and Australian governments after the islanders' claim had failed in the High Court.[5]

A legal right to compensation must have involved a far greater sum. And the case would also have established a precedent. Other acts of the British Government could have been called in question. In 1972, for example, the British Government leased the Indian Ocean island of Diego Garcia to the American government, allegedly in consideration of an offset of £11 million on Polaris submarines. The inhabitants were forcibly deported to Mauritius where they lived often in financial distress. Ten years later, £4.7 million was offered in compensation. Could it have been argued that the British Government owed a fiduciary duty or were legally liable to make full reparation?[6]

Our argument has obvious implications for Reich's theory of 'the new property'. Reich suggested that courts should extend their protection to new interests created by the expanding role of the modern state, e.g. to licences, rights to tender for contracts, welfare benefits, etc. By recognizing such interests as property, courts may be creating a right to compensation and incidentally a drain on public resources. The courts are not wrong to protect individual rights which are, at least partly, in their care. Resource allocation, on the other hand, is a governmental function. It is simply that from time to time the two functions conflict.

We are back with the central questions of allocation of functions and justiciability. Who will get compensation, and who will not, depends very much on the attitudes of the decision-maker. Property provides us with a key example. Griffith (1977, p. 107) believes that 'the attitude of the judiciary to legislation which seriously interferes with rights to the enjoyment of property – especially the ownership of land – has traditionally been one of suspicion. These rights have long been protected by the common law (which means the judges) and changes brought about by Acts of Parliament have not always been welcomed'. If such questions are submitted to courts under the guise of rights, answers different from those which might be given by politicians or administrators may be obtained.

For some writers, this conflict between resource allocation and individual rights, sometimes mirrored in a clash between the executive and the courts, is aptly described as a conflict of 'public' and 'private' interest. This terminology, together with some aspects of the conflict of interests, are discussed further in later sections.

2 Courts and the compensation principle

Civil law systems call the principle that private property should not be taken by the state for public purposes without compensation being made, the principle of 'eminent domain'. It is sometimes said that the common law does not recognize the principle. If this is true, it is somewhat surprising in the light of Griffith's comment. The cases which follow help to assess this; can you find a principle similar to 'eminent domain'? Do the courts go too far in protecting property or, as Wade alleges, not far enough?

A-G v. *De Keyser's Royal Hotel* [1920] AC 508
In 1914, Parliament passed the Defence of the Realm Act; this provided the Government with extensive powers, including regulatory powers, to prosecute the war. Acting under these powers, the War Office requisitioned the respondent's hotel to provide offices. It proved impossible to reach agreement over compensation. After the War, the respondents claimed compensation. The Crown sought to justify requisition by virtue of the prerogative powers. In this case compensation would be ex gratia. It was held that, for the duration of the statute, the prerogative powers of the Crown were in abeyance. The respondents were entitled to the statutory compensation. Lord Moulton pointed to a series of statutes authorizing requisition and providing for compensation. These were illustrative of important changes which had altered the position of the Crown. Wars, which had become more complicated, were paid for by the people through the legislature. Finally

... the feeling that it was equitable that burdens borne for the good of the nation should be distributed over the whole nation and should not be allowed to fall on particular individuals has grown to be a national sentiment. The effect of these changes is seen in the long series of statutes ... [which]

indicated unmistakeably that it is the intention of the nation that the powers
of the Crown in these respects should be exercised in the equitable manner set
forth in the statute, so that the burden shall not fall on the individual but shall
be borne by the community.

Hammersmith Railway v. *Brand*
(1869) LR 4 HL 171

The plaintiff owned a house which had been injuriously affected by
the construction of a railway. She claimed damages in nuisance for
depreciation of value and for obstruction of light and loss of amenity
through dust, smoke, vibration and noise. The construction of the
railway was authorized by private Act of Parliament subject to
conditions as to compensation contained in the Land Clauses
Consolidation Act 1845 and Railways Clauses Act 1845. The judges
were summoned to advise the House of Lords whether the common
law action in nuisance (which, if successful, might cause closure of the
railway) was available or whether it had been superseded by the
statutory rights of compensation. The House of Lords accepted the
view of Blackburn J that it had been superseded. The result was to
deprive the plaintiff of compensation because the statutes did not
apply to the case in point. Partly for this reason, Bramwell B (with
whom Lush and Willes JJ agreed) thought the common law action
could be maintained.

BLACKBURN J: I think that it is agreed on all hands that if the Legislature
authorizes the doing of an act (which if unauthorized would be a wrong and a
cause of action) no action can be maintained for that act, on the plain ground
that no Court can treat that as a wrong which the Legislature has authorized,
and consequently the person who has sustained a loss by the doing of that act
is without remedy, unless in so far as the Legislature has thought it proper to
provide for compensation to him. He is, in fact, in the same position as the
person supposed to have suffered from the noisy traffic on a new highway is at
common law, and subject to the same hardship. He suffers a private loss for
the public benefit.

Now the Legislature has thought fit to authorize the Defendants to make a
railway, and . . . 'to use and employ locomotive engines and other moving
power, and carriages and waggons to be drawn or propelled thereby.' And the
first question is, whether this is such a legislative authorisation of the use of
such power as to render all such consequences as inevitably attend it no
longer wrongful.

If this were a new matter I should think there was a great deal in what is
thrown out by Baron Bramwell in his judgment in the Exchequer Chamber in
this case; but the contrary [has been decided] . . . and if your Lordships were
to reverse those decisions the consequence would follow that any owner of a
house or field so adjacent to a railway that the inevitable disturbance from the

working of the line amounted to a nuisance might (at least where the railway has not been opened for twenty years) stop the working of the line. So large an amount has been invested in the belief that the trains might be run, even though some mischief to others was inevitable, that I think your Lordships will hold that even if the principle . . . was originally an error, it has long become *communis error*, and ought to be held to have made the law.

In my mind, therefore, the question is narrowed to this: do the compensation clauses in the statutes extend to the consequences of working the railway, and using the statutable powers for that purpose? Or are they confined to the *making* and maintaining of the railway and the works, and the using of the statutable powers for that purpose?

I must own that on reading the statutes I do not think that the Legislature deliberately excluded such claims. I think they were not in the contemplation of those who framed the statutes at all; and that if there are words used sufficiently large to embrace such a case it is by an unintended accident . . .

I can only repeat that in my opinion the onus lies on the Plaintiff to shew that the Legislature has given compensation, and I cannot find in the statutes any language which . . . expresses an intention to give compensation for such an injury.

BRAMWELL B: Now it is not supposable that in a private Act, for a particular company, an anomaly so great was to be introduced, as that an actionable nuisance might be committed with no common law remedy, and for the benefit of the company, that the profits might be larger if the nuisance was left without compensation. If it is said that compensation is given, then it is most surprising that in such private Act there is no provision for it in express words. And the same remark may be made on these general Acts. Why if the common law remedy was to be taken away, are there not express words to that effect? Why, if there is to be no action and no compensation, is so gross and anomalous an injustice inflicted when such pains are taken to give compensation for the slightest injury occasioned by the very fabric of the railway? It seems to me impossible that it can have been *intended* that this damage can be done without any compensation.

One reason only for such a state of things is given. It is said that the railway and the working of it are for the public benefit, and therefore the damage must be done, *and be uncompensated*. Admitting that the damage must be done for the public benefit, that is no reason why it should be uncompensated. It is to be remembered that compensation comes from the public which gets the benefit . . . It comes directly from those who do the damage, but ultimately from the public in the fares they pay. If the fares will not pay for this damage, and a fair profit on the company's capital, the speculation is a losing one, as all the gain does not pay all the loss and leave a fair profit. Either, therefore, the railway ought not to be made, or the damage may well be paid for. But farther, though if it were the law and practice to do individuals a damage for the benefit of the public without compensation no one in particular could complain when it happened to him, as every one would know that he held his property subject to being deprived of it or having it injured when it suited the public; still such a law and practice would be highly inconvenient and

356 LAW AND ADMINISTRATION

mischievous. It is, however, idle to discuss such a question, as the Legislature has acted under no such considerations. For if the public benefit is a good reason for damaging a man's property with compensation, so would it be for taking it without compensation. The Legislature has made the most careful and minute provisions for the payment of compensation for everything taken, and, indeed, for everything injuriously affected. And it is absurd to suppose that it was *intended* that if a house was damaged to the extent of £1 a year by its light and air being diminished compensation would be given, and that it should not be given where the damage was ten times as great, but was caused by the noise and vibration of the trains. Surely when a reasonable meaning can be given to the clauses relied on it should be adopted rather than one so unreasonable.

Wade criticizes the performance of the House. Did the judges consider 'the issue of personal sacrifice versus public benefit'? What other factors did Blackburn J consider?

It used to be the general rule that no compensation was payable to a person from whom no land was taken, however injuriously affected his property might be as a consequence of public works lawfully executed and operated, e.g. a motorway or an airport. An action for nuisance at common law is of no avail against the lawful exercise of statutory powers . . .

There was therefore an artificial contrast between those from whom part of their land was taken, and who were compensated for the injury to the remainder, and those from whom nothing was taken but who might suffer heavy uncompensated loss. This was an inducement to many people to resist projects for roads, airports and other public works by every possible means, thus causing many lengthy public inquiries into objections. Parliament made repeated attempts to secure for the community the increase of land values created by social development. But the loss of land values inflicted for the benefit of the community had to be borne in a great many cases by the owners upon whom it happened to fall 'for the greater good of the greater number'. In [the *Brand* case] the House of Lords held that the owner of a house beside a new railway, from whom no land was taken, had no right to compensation for damage caused by vibration from the trains. The legislation in question was so obscure that there was ample room for the issue of personal sacrifice versus public benefit to be considered. It was said that the common law contained the principle of sacrifice, since any landowner could dedicate a highway beside his neighbour's land, and ordinary user of the highway was not a nuisance. With this unconvincing analogy the House of Lords paved the way for technological progress at the expense of individual rights . . . [Wade 1982, p. 691.]

Belfast Corporation v. *O.D. Cars Ltd*
[1960] 1 All ER 65

The plaintiffs claimed compensation for refusal of planning permission on the ground of incompatibility with zoning requirements. They argued that s.10 of the Planning and Housing (Northern

Ireland) Act 1931 was unconstitutional in terms of s.5(1) of the Government of Ireland Act 1920 which prohibited the taking of property without compensation. The House of Lords held that the Planning Acts were not confiscatory in character. They were constitutionally valid.

LORD RADCLIFFE: I do not see how you can give a meaning to this phrase, 'taking without compensation', except by reference to the general treatment of the subject in the law of England and Ireland before 1920. A survey would, I think, discern two divergent lines of approach. On the one hand, there would be the general principle, accepted by the legislature and scrupulously defended by the courts, that the title to property or the enjoyment of its possession was not to be compulsorily acquired from a subject unless full compensation was afforded in its place. Acquisition of title or possession was 'taking'. Aspects of this principle are found in the rules of statutory interpretation devised by the courts which required the presence of the most explicit words before an acquisition could be held to be sanctioned by an Act of Parliament without full compensation being provided or imported an intention to give compensation and machinery for assessing it into any Act of Parliament that did not positively exclude it. This vigilance to see that the subject's rights to property were protected, so far as was consistent with the requirements of expropriation of what was previously enjoyed in specie, was regarded as an important guarantee of individual liberty. It would be a mistake to look on it as representing any conflict between the legislature and the courts. The principle was, generally speaking, common to both. Side by side with this, however, and developing with increasing range and authority during the second half of the nineteenth century, came the great movement for the regulation of life in cities and towns in the interests of public health and amenity. It is not an adequate description of the powers involved, so far at any rate as the United Kingdom is concerned, to speak of them as 'police powers'. They went far beyond that . . . Achieved by one means or the other, there is no doubt at all that the effect of them was to impose obligations and restrictions on the owner of town land which impaired his right of development, prohibited or restricted his rights of user and in some cases imposed monetary charges on him or compelled him to expend money on altering his property. Generally speaking, though not without exception, these obligations and restrictions were treated as not requiring compensation, though, of course, in a sense they expropriated certain rights of property . . . Only in a few special cases is compensation provided for the consequence of interference. No one, so far as I know, spoke of this as a 'taking of property' or treated the general principle of 'no taking without compensation' as applicable . . .

When town planning legislation came in eo nomine in 1909, the emphasis had, no doubt, shifted from considerations of public health to the wider and more debatable ground of public amenity. It may possibly have been for this reason . . . that the Act of 1909 included a comprehensive, though not exhaustive, 'injurious affection' section, the effect of which was to give property owners whose rights were interfered with in the cause of town planning a right to compensation for any damage that they suffered, subject to counter-claims for betterment and certain exclusions. This 'injurious affection' embraced an altogether wider category of injury than the 'injurious affection' that had been the subject of compensation under the Lands Clauses Consolidation Act, 1845 . . . What is important, I think, is to recognise that, though interference with rights of development and user had come to be a recognised element of the regulation and planning of towns in the interest of public health and amenity, the consequent control, impairment or diminution of those rights was not treated as a 'taking' of property nor, when compensation was provided, was it provided on the basis that property or property rights had been 'taken' but on the basis that property, itself retained, had been injuriously affected.

What interests in land are here classified as 'property' and when is property 'taken'?

> *Westminster Bank Ltd* v. *Beverley Borough Council*
> [1970] 2 WLR 645

The bank applied for planning permission to extend its premises. This application was refused by the council in its capacity as planning authority because the proposed extension would prejudice plans to widen the road behind the bank's premises. The council in its capacity as highway authority had not yet prescribed an improvement line under s.72(1) of the Highways Act 1959 nor was the land at that time designated for compulsory purchase in the development plan. The use of the planning procedures to safeguard the future widening of the road meant that the bank did not receive compensation; had the authority acted under the Highways Act compensation would have been payable. The object of the bank was to get an improvement line prescribed and avoid loss by 'planning blight'. It appealed against the refusal of planning permission to the Minister of Housing and Local Government. The Minister dismissed the appeal on the grounds that, as there seemed to be no doubt that the bank's land would eventually be required for the purpose of road widening, it would not be right to prejudice the local planning authority's scheme by permitting further development in front of the proposed new boundary of the road. The bank unsuccessfully sought an order, under s.179 of the Town and Country Planning Act 1962, to quash the Minister's decision. The House of Lords upheld the decision, but we quote also from the strong dissenting judgment of Salmon LJ in the Court of Appeal:

LORD REID: The appellant's argument is really founded on the principle that 'a statute should not be held to take away private rights of property without compensation unless the intention to do so is expressed in clear and unambiguous terms' . . .

I entirely accept the principle. It flows from the fact that Parliament seldom intends to do that and therefore before attributing such an intention to Parliament we should be sure that that was really intended. I would only query the last words of the quotation. When we are seeking the intention of Parliament that may appear from express words but it may also appear by irresistible inference from the statute read as a whole. But I would agree that, if there is reasonable doubt, the subject should be given the benefit of the doubt.

It would be possible to distinguish this statement of the principle on the ground that planning legislation does not take away private rights of property: it merely prevents them from being exercised if planning permission is refused. But that would, in my view, be too meticulous a distinction. Even in such a case I think we must be sure that it was intended that this would be done without compensation.

But it is quite clear that when planning permission is refused the general rule is that the unsuccessful applicant does not receive any compensation. There are certain exceptions but they have no special connection with street widening. If planning permission is refused on the ground that the proposed development conflicts with a scheme for street widening, the unsuccessful applicant is in exactly the same position as other applicants whose applications are refused on other grounds. None of them gets any compensation. So absence of any right to compensation is no ground for arguing that it is not within the power of planning authorities to refuse planning permission for this reason . . .

Parliament has chosen to set up two different ways of preventing development which would interfere with schemes for street widening. It must have been aware that one involved paying compensation but the other did not. Nevertheless it expressed no preference, and imposed no limit on the use of either. No doubt there might be special circumstances which make it unreasonable or an abuse of power to use one of these methods but here there were none . . . the authority had to choose whether to leave the appellants without compensation or to impose a burden on its ratepayers. One may think that it would be most equitable that the burden should be shared. But the Minister of Transport had made it clear in a circular sent to local authorities in 1954 that there would be no grant if a local authority proceeded in such a way that compensation would be payable, and there is nothing to indicate any disapproval of this policy by Parliament and nothing in any of the legislation to indicate that Parliament disapproved of depriving the subject of compensation. I cannot in these circumstances find any abuse of power in the local authority deciding that the appellants and not its ratepayers should bear the burden.

SALMON LJ (dissenting): At common law a man was entitled to do what he liked with his own, providing that in doing so he did not injure his neighbour. The complexity of modern society has made it necessary to introduce a multiplicity of statutory controls which have largely eroded this principle, some think unfortunately . . .

The courts, quite rightly, have no power to interfere with policy or administrative decisions merely because they do not agree with them. Policy and administrative decisions are clearly within the sphere of the executive alone. Accordingly, the courts are powerless to intervene to protect the private citizen unless the ministries concerned have exceeded the wide powers conferred upon them by Parliament or have abused those powers, for example, by a wholly unreasonable exercise of discretion. As the judge observed, however, we still live in a free society. We shall continue to do so only so long as the courts continue, as they have always done, to exercise the power they still possess of restraining any bureaucratic invasion of private rights which is not authorised by law . . .

Parliament has clearly manifested its intention in the Highways Act, 1959, that if a highway authority is to protect itself from having to pay an enhanced price in respect of land subsequently to be taken over for a road widening, it should do so by prescribing an improvement line so as to prevent the land being developed meanwhile, but that if it does so, it should do what would seem to the ordinary man to be fair and reasonable, namely, compensate the individuals who own the property concerned against the damage that their property will suffer as a result of that line having been prescribed. I for my part deplore the practice that appears to have grown up even before 1954, of using planning powers . . . for the purpose of defeating the manifest intention of Parliament expressed in the Highways Acts. The Highways Act, 1959, seems to me to prescribe the regular method to be adopted by the highway authorities if they wish to protect themselves against the extra expense to which I have referred.

To adopt the regular method of prescribing an improvement line would not prejudice the construction of the road in any sense except that it would cost the highway authority more money than this radical departure from the general law relating to highways, namely it would cost them the price of paying the landowners compensation for the damage which they might suffer by reason of the prescription of an improvement line. I do not think it matters much which way it is put. Whether one says that what was done amounted to a use or abuse of power to which no reasonable authority should be a party, or whether it is said . . . that it was done for an ulterior object, or whether it is described as an entire departure from the regular practice laid down under the Highways Act, it seems to me that it is quite unjustifiable in law. It was done solely to save the highway authority money by depriving the citizen of his statutory rights to compensation. I do not believe the powers under the Town and Country Planning Acts were ever designed to be used for that purpose.

What principle or principles of judicial review did Salmon LJ use to achieve his result? Contrast this with the judgement of Lord Reid. Does Lord Reid here regard planning legislation with 'suspicion'? Griffith (1977, p. 115) called the Beverley decision 'surprising'. In the light of this case study, do you agree? Before you make up your mind

finally, read *Hall* v. *Shoreham-by-Sea UDC* (see below, p. 495) and
Hartnell v. *Minister of Housing and Local Government* [1965] AC 1134.
The cases on which Griffith relies are *Lavender* v. *Minister of Housing and
Local Government* (see below, p. 484) and *Coleen* v. *Minister of Housing
and Local Government* (see below, p. 436).

3 Public and private interest

Wade's criticism of the *Brand* case is consistent with his view that one
function of administrative law is the protection of individual rights.
The *Brand* case is wrongly decided for Wade because the issue of
private sacrifice was not weighed against the *public benefit*. In the second
reading of the Land Compensation Bill, we find similar sentiments
expressed by Mr Rippon, introducing the Bill on behalf of the
Conservative Government (HC Deb. Vol. 847, cols. 35–7):

> The Bill seeks to strike a fair balance between the needs of the community and
> the rights of the individual. In recent years there has been a growing anxiety
> that in too many cases the balance has been tipped against the individual . . .
>   The Government's concern is two-fold. It is to ensure fairer compensation
> for those who must suffer from change and to make certain that damage to the
> environment is reduced through better planning. We are all agreed now that
> social costs and values have to be considered as well as direct costs and
> benefits . . .
>   It is perhaps with roads that the effects are most widespread and striking.
> The [DOE] and local highway authorities are currently building, preparing
> and planning major road schemes to a value of £4,370 million. Expenditure on
> new construction and improvement of major roads in Great Britain between
> now and 1977 is expected to exceed £3,000 million . . .
>   The result as we all know is the classic conflict between public and private
> needs. The White Paper[7] summed up the predicament in a fair way when it
> said:
>
> > The Government are committed to enhancing the quality of everyday life
> > in Britain. In so doing a balance must constantly be struck between the
> > overriding duty of the state to ensure that essential developments are
> > undertaken for the benefit of the whole community and the no less
> > compelling need to protect the interests of those whose personal rights or
> > private property may be injured in the process.
>
>   This dilemma is at the heart of contemporary political debate. Sometimes
> the State is seen as playing the role of a juggernaut, putting roads before
> homes, riding rough shod over the rights of individual citizens. At other
> times, the private owner is condemned for 'selfishly' holding up a much
> needed development. Yet nearly always, the conflict is not between public (or
> private) right and private (or public) wrong. It is a conflict of right with right
> – the public's undoubted right to have a new road or school or waterworks

and the private person's right to enjoy his home and garden, undisturbed.

Arguably, this traditional antithesis between public interest and personal or private rights is misleading. Like the adversarial procedure of law suits, it tends to suggest a one-dimensional equation. Government and administration represent one side while the individual represents his private interest. But the public is not a single entity with a single, identifiable interest and governments have to weigh the diverse claims of different sections of the community, no one of which is paramount. For example, the right of one citizen to purchase a council house may mean that another citizen cannot find a council house to rent. A new power station brings jobs and increased comfort for some; to others it brings destruction of the environment and loss of amenity. To create a legal *right* to purchase a council house or a *right* of compensation for 'loss' of environmental amenity automatically advances one claim at the expense of others.

When does the 'private person's right to enjoy his home and garden, undisturbed' of which Mr Rippon speaks, come into being? Millions of citizens do not own a home, let alone a garden. They live in industrial zones whose amenities consist of an atmosphere polluted by chemicals and in towns through which heavy traffic increasingly flows. On a purely legal analysis, they do not possess 'rights' to improvement of their environment, but their 'claims' are no less strong than those of people affected by new developments. As we recognize more interests in land, so the competing interests multiply, making the equation more difficult to solve. A plethora of committees and commissions has tried to grapple with the problem. Here the Uthwatt Committee, set up during the Second World War to report generally on the relationship between land values, development and compensation, expresses its concern at the rising cost of public development:

The price of land in the big towns and cities runs into very high figures. The effect is usually to make it impossible for the local authority concerned to carry out desirable improvements or impose any effective control of user with the limited resources at their command.

In addition to having to compensate on the basis of the value attaching to the land, acquisition in developed areas involves payment for the value of existing buildings which need to be demolished, and compensation to a trader for his removal expenses and for disturbance to his business. All these items have to be purchased before the land can be used for the purpose required in the interests of good planning. [Cmnd 6386 (1942), para. 31.]

Applying the traditional terminology of public and private interest to this passage, we might identify the individual's interest as being in compensation and that of the public in development. The lower the compensation, the more development is possible, so the public interest lies in keeping compensation low. But now let us bring in the Franks idea that adequate compensation does much to defuse dissatisfaction with compulsory purchase and planning procedures. There is an implication that *speed* is in the public interest and *delay* is not. Planning procedures delay development and development is in the public interest. Remember that Hartley and Griffith in discussing procedural fairness (see above, p. 80) equated speed and procedural simplicity with the public interest. Procedural protections, on the other hand, were in the interest of individuals.

Now the individual has acquired two interests: (a) in procedures and (b) in compensation. The first may help him to secure the second or the second may be used as a substitute for the first. Similarly, the public interest now has two facets. Development cannot occur if it is too expensive, hence (a) a public interest in limitation of costs; but development can be impeded by lengthy planning procedures, hence (b) a public interest in the prevention of delay. These two public interests may conflict. Moreover, the second *public* interest in more compensation was earlier classified as private.

In *The Ideologies of Planning Law* (1981, pp. 106–17), McAuslan describes the Land Compensation Act as a sham. On the surface, he says, the Act is greatly concerned with private interest; it provides for compensation where none was payable before. In reality, the concern is for the public interest, here defined as 'getting on with public development', in other words, our twin objectives of speed and low cost. McAuslan deduces this from detailed scrutiny of the financial provisions, where he sees concessions everywhere made to administrative convenience and to the financial interests of public authorities. He suggests incidentally that this unpalatable truth is often concealed by the grant of a discretionary power to pay or withhold compensation. 'There are limitations in the Act and discretions given where one might expect to find duties which can only be explained by this desire to minimize costs in the public interest even if this is at the expense of the individual property-owner.'[8]

McAuslan is greatly concerned with maximizing public participation in the planning process and he sees the Act as threatening this desirable objective:

The Act in some respects marked a reversal of policies encouraging public participation in the hope of reducing the time spent on dealing with the formal objections to schemes and plans for public development; it hung out instead the carrot of more compensation in the hope that this would lessen opposition and objection to public works and so speed development up.

We might go on* to identify a public interest in procedural fairness which may conflict with the public interest in speed. At this stage we could formulate a number of directly conflicting propositions:

(a) More compensation is in the individual interest. Less compensation is in the public interest because it permits more development.
(b) Less compensation promotes resistance to development. It is therefore against the public interest. More compensation speeds the development process. It is therefore in the private and public interest.
(c) More compensation tends to undercut the lengthy planning procedures which are designed to secure better planning and promote participation in the planning process. It is against the public interest.

So far we have assumed that development is always in the public interest, an assumption made throughout Mr Rippon's speech. But McAuslan criticizes the Act for assuming too easily that the 'overriding duty' of the state is to engage in public development which will make life 'comfortable, convenient and pleasant'. The extracts below are from a speech in which John Mackintosh MP examines the aims of the Offshore Petroleum Development (Scotland) Act 1975. Its main purpose was to facilitate oil drilling in the North Sea by streamlining the normal planning procedures. The Act also provided for compensation in terms of the Land Compensation legislation; in exchange it contained a 'no-nuisance' clause barring the common law right of action in nuisance. This speech contains some discussion of the pros and cons of development:

I support the Bill and its general application, and the desire as quickly as possible to get on with the benefits not just through taxation of the oil industry but through employment, spin-off and all the technology involved. But there is a tremendous danger with all these modern developments, in a community

*McAuslan does not classify participation rights as either a public or private interest. His thesis is that planning law has three ideologies: private interest, public interest, and public participation. This analysis is discussed in Chapter 14.

wanting it both ways – in other words, 'We want the end objective of the oil industry's wealth and prosperity and jobs, but we do not want the construction here. It and the pipelines and the refinery must go to another constituency'.

I have encountered this attitude towards electric power. One can well imagine the sort of language my constituents would use in 1982 if they found that they could not switch on their electric blankets. Yet they do not want an electric power station built next to their town. They want it somewhere else, and in some other way. Nevertheless, we have to accept that we need oil industry constructions and electric power stations, and that there is a generalised public interest which can only be fully expressed by people speaking broadly as representatives have to do, in the interests of the country at large. There is a great deal of time wasted in these planning procedures . . . which is not essential to the preservation of individual rights of the kind about which many of us are concerned – scenic rights, historic rights and so on . . .

Let us be clear what are the essentials that we must have in any procedure before the acquisition of land from private persons or trusts or bodies by the Government is to be acceptable to the public. . . The first essential is that there must be the possibility of cross-examination of the civil servants and officials concerned by independent persons. Without such cross-examination there would be no public confidence in the situation . . . It has become clear that some of the expertise quoted is not the expertise of the Government – who are reasonably impartial and interested in the public well-being – it is the expertise, at second-hand, of the developer – the oil company concerned . . .

I see that the Bill removes actions for nuisance. These can no longer hold against persons operating on these sites. Again, this seems to make an interdict impossible against polluters. I do not see why oil companies which go into bits of land of this kind should escape pollution control by way of the interdict action . . . Certainly the money that is to be made from these sites by the big oil companies should place a special obligation on them to avoid pollution and restore the sites. The old principle that the polluter must pay ought to be written into the Bill. [HC Deb. vol. 881, cols. 1144–8.]

We could now add a further proposition

(d) Less compensation is against the private interests of those whose property is purchased but in the private interests of developers who will carry out development.

Mackintosh also challenges ideas which we have met earlier in this book. We have talked so far as though individuals represented their own interests while the public interest was in the charge of government and its officials. This is the premise on which the *Gouriet* case was founded and which underlay the narrow rules of locus standi which restricted intervention to those individuals who showed an injury to a private right or material interest. But Mackintosh's view that scenic and historical interests belong to *individuals* is like the argument for extension of standing to sue to those whose intangible interests are affected. Mackintosh provides support for the idea that government represents the public interest when he says that governments are 'reasonably impartial and interested in the public well-being', but immediately undercuts his assertion by telling us that governments sometimes act on the advice and behalf of interested parties in invoking the public interest. On this view, another proposition emerges:

(e) Private interests are represented by individuals and public interest by government but government may act in the interest of individuals while individuals invoke the public interest.

The discovery that individuals may act to protect intangible interests casts doubt on Wade's tacit assumption that individuals act mainly for financial motives for which a pecuniary remedy is adequate. Individuals may sometimes prefer their common law remedy in nuisance to statutory compensation because they hope to obtain an injunction (interdict) which will bring the nuisance to an end. Here the tort action is being used to challenge planning decisions which cause damage to the environment. A 'no-nuisance' clause in a statute prevents this by partially ousting the common law jurisdiction of the courts. Rather than balancing public and private interests, compensation may be used to buy off individuals or groups of individuals who inconvenience government by challenging policy decisions. And we should not assume that governments always act impartially and for the public well-being while individuals act for motives of financial self-interest. How was ex gratia compensation described in the parliamentary debate which followed the *Malloch* affair (above, p. 279)? On some occasions, compensation might be thought to operate against the public interest by sheltering policy decisions from challenge through the legal process (this is really a variant of proposition (c)). Equally, however, we might argue:

(f) Compensation may be against the private interest when it facilitates the extinction of private rights.

These are clearly complex issues and we might now query whether Wade's formula of 'personal sacrifice' versus 'public benefit' will really suffice to produce satisfactory solutions.[9] A modern case which closely parallels *Hammersmith Railway* v. *Brand* illustrates some of the problems. The case concerned the development of Milford Haven as a tanker harbour and a site for oil refineries. Previously, the area had been rural in character. Then, one by one, large oil companies including Gulf Oil sponsored private Acts of Parliament authorizing the construction of giant oil-refineries. The Gulf Oil Refining Act 1965 made reference to the essential nature of the operations and authorized the compulsory purchase by Gulf Oil of 400 acres of land and the construction of necessary facilities. It did not specifically authorize the construction of a refinery nor did it contain provisions for compensation or a 'no-nuisance' clause. Planning permission was granted and a giant refinery built. Inhabitants of the village of Waterston began to suffer from noxious fumes, smells, vibrations and loud noises. They also lived in fear of explosion and fire. The plaintiff was one of 50 or 60 villagers who decided to challenge the operations by way of a common law action for nuisance. They claimed damages and an injunction. Gulf Oil applied for the action to be struck out on the grounds that statutory authorization existed for the activities. The Court of Appeal held on a preliminary point that the nuisance was not authorized but the House of Lords reversed the decision on the grounds that the statutory authorization covered the construction of the refinery and all necessary ancillary operations.

Allen v. *Gulf Oil Refining Ltd* [1979] 3 WLR 523 (CA);
[1981] 2 WLR 188 (HL)

LORD DENNING MR (Court of Appeal): I have considered this case on the construction of the statute according to the principles laid down in the railway cases of the 19th century. But I venture to suggest that modern statutes should be construed on a new principle. Wherever private undertakers seek statutory authority to construct and operate an installation which may cause damage to people living in the neighbourhood, it should not be assumed that Parliament intended that damage should be done to innocent people without redress. Just as in principle property should not be taken compulsorily except on proper compensation being paid for it so, also, in principle property should not be damaged compulsorily except on proper compensation being made for the damage done. No matter whether the undertakers use due diligence or not, they ought not to be allowed – for their own profit – to damage innocent people or property without paying compensation. They ought to provide for it as part of the legitimate expenses of their operation, either as initial capital cost or the subsequent revenue . . . I would suggest that, in the absence of any provision in the statute for compensation, the proper construction of a modern statute should be that any person living in the neighbourhood retains his action at common law; and that it is no defence for the promoters to plead the statute. Statutory authority may enable the promoters to make the installation and operate it but it does not excuse them from paying compensation for injury done to those living in the neighbourhood.

I realise that there is a difficulty about an injunction. No court would wish to grant an injunction to stop a great enterprise and render it useless. But the difficulty is easily overcome. By means of Lord Cairns' Act, the Chancery Amendment Act 1858, the court can award damages to cover past or future injury in lieu of an injunction . . .

So in this case I would hold that if there should be an explosion at this refinery, the defendants are bound to compensate those who are killed or injured or whose property is damaged: and it is no answer for the defendants to say, 'We are sorry. We were very careful. We used all the latest safety precautions. But yet it happened.' Justice demands that, despite those protestations, compensation should be paid by the defendants to those who suffered by the operations.

This is not a case of an explosion. But the principle is the same. It is damage done to the occupiers of houses by noxious odours, vibration and noise. Compensation should be paid to the owners and present occupiers of the houses on the lines of the compensation for 'injurious affection', in lieu of an injunction.

LORD WILBERFORCE (House of Lords): It is now well settled that where Parliament by express direction or by necessary implication has authorised the construction and use of an undertaking or works, that carries with it an authority to do what is authorised with immunity from any action based on nuisance. The right of action is taken away: *Hammersmith and City Railway Co.* v. *Brand*. To this there is made the qualification, or condition, that the statutory powers are exercised without 'negligence' – that word here being used in a special sense so as to require the undertaker, as a condition of obtaining immunity from action, to carry out the work and conduct the operation with all reasonable regard and care for the interests of other persons . . . It is within the same principle that immunity from action is withheld where the terms of the statute are permissive only, in which case the powers conferred must be exercised in strict conformity with private rights . . .

What then is the scope of the statutory authority conferred in this case? The Act was a private Act, promoted by the appellants, no doubt mainly in their own commercial interests. In order to establish their projected refinery with its ancillary facilities (jetties, railway lines etc.,) and to acquire the necessary land, they had to seek the assistance of Parliament. And so they necessarily had to satisfy Parliament that the powers they were seeking were in the interests of the public to whom Parliament is responsible. The case they undertook to make, which they had to prove, and which, as the passing of the Act shows, they did prove, is shown by the preamble. This recites 'increasing public demand for [the company's] products in the United Kingdom' and that 'it is *essential* that further facilities for the importation of crude oil and petroleum products and *for their refinement* should be made available' . . . It proceeds to recite the intention of the company to establish a refinery at Llanstadwell, that it was expedient that in connection therewith the company should be empowered to construct works including jetties for the accommodation of vessels (including large tankers) and for the reception from such vessels of crude oil and petroleum products therefrom: that it was expedient for the company to be empowered to acquire lands: and that 'plans . . . showing . . . the lands which may be taken or used compulsorily under the powers of the Act for the purposes thereof . . . have been deposited . . .'

I cannot but regard this as an authority – whether it should be called express or by necessary implication may be a matter of preference – but an authority to construct and operate *a refinery* upon the lands to be acquired – a refinery moreover which should be commensurate with the facilities for unloading offered by the jetties (for large tankers), with the size of the lands to be acquired, and with the discharging facilities to be provided by the railway lines. I emphasize the words *a refinery* by way of distinction from *the refinery* because no authority was given or sought except in the indefinite form. But that there was authority to construct and operate *a* a refinery seems to me indisputable . . .

The respondent's contention against this is a curious one. [She argues that] there is nothing but power to acquire lands. The construction of the refinery is left entirely to the promoters . . . and therefore the intention must be that they must construct it with regard to private rights . . .[10] This argument has remarkable consequences. It follows that if the plaintiff, or any other person, can establish a nuisance, he or she is entitled (subject only to a precarious appeal to Lord Cairns' Act) to an injunction. This may make it impossible for the refinery to be operated: that in turn would leave the appellants as the owners and occupiers of a large area of land which they have compulsorily acquired under the authority of the Act of 1965 for the purpose of a refinery, and which, in accordance with well known principles, they could not use for any other purpose.

Although Lord Wilberforce emphasizes statutory construction (compare his judgment in the *Bromley* case), he also affirms that Parliament is the judge of the public interest and refuses to reopen matters apparently raised during private bill proceedings. Is this allocation of functions correct? Should the courts intervene – as Lord Denning did – to weigh 'personal sacrifice'?

Compare the attitudes of the two judges to the award of an injunction. We have met this problem in the *Brand* case. Lord Denning believes that the injunction is a discretionary remedy; Lord Wilberforce believes that the discretion could be exercised only in exceptional cases. Is such a discretionary power desirable and in the public interest? One leading authority argues that it is.[11] Arguably, however, such discretions allow judges to intervene more directly in the administrative process.

Now suppose that damages are substituted for an injunction. How should they be calculated, in your view? Does your answer threaten the continuation of the oil refining activities?

How many 'interests' can you identify in this case? Which would you characterize as 'public' and which as 'private'? Which are 'material' and which 'ideological'? (see Stewart above, p. 228). Notice Lord Wilberforce's remark that the developers acted 'mainly in their own commercial interests'. We might conclude this section by saying:

(g) Development is not invariably in the public interest and compensation is not invariably in the private interest.

4 Polycentricity and indirect review

If, as Stewart argues, 'there is no transcendent public interest but only the distinct interests of various individuals and groups in society', we might go on to argue that courts should not for two reasons take 'public interest' decisions. First, these are really 'claims' of the type which Griffith argues are best reserved for the political process; second, we can see that decisions about the public interest are often polycentric issues of the kind Fuller suggested were unsuitable for adjudication. We might at this second, technical, level argue with Pannick or Gravells that courts should modify their decision-taking procedures to take on board resource allocation etc., but courts seem hesitant about their expertise in this area. In *Morgans* v. *Launchbury* [1973] AC 127, the House of Lords was discussing changes in the law of vicarious liability. Lord Pearson who, as chairman of the Royal Commission on Civil Liability and Compensation for Personal Injury, had considerable experience of the information needed for decisions in this field, expressed reservations. He thought the court had neither the requisite expertise nor the executive authority; the question was one for the legislature:

These questions of policy need consideration by the government and Parliament, using the resources at their command for making wide inquiries and gathering evidence and opinions as to the practical effects of the proposed innovations . . . Any extension of car owners' liability ought to be accompanied by an extension of effective insurance cover. How would that be brought about? . . . A substantial increase in premiums for motor insurance would be likely to result and to have an inflationary effect on costs and prices.

In the *Dorset Yacht* case, Lord Diplock expresses his concern that courts may not be in a position to weigh adequately the interests of parties who are not represented before the court. But this leading case also raised other familiar issues. Compare the attitudes of Lords Reid and Dilhorne to the virtual absence of precedent; what can you deduce about 'strong' and 'weak' discretion?

Home Office v. *Dorset Yacht Co. Ltd* [1970] 2 WLR 1140

Borstal trainees on an outside exercise on an island in Poole harbour absconded one night, boarded the respondents' yacht and caused damage. The respondents sued the Home Office as vicariously liable for the negligence of the officers in charge. Asked to rule on the preliminary point whether a duty of care was owed to the respondents by the officers, the House of Lords held by a majority that the Home Office could be liable.

LORD REID: In later years there has been a steady trend towards regarding the law of negligence as depending on principle so that, when a new point emerges, one should ask not whether it is covered by authority but whether recognised principles apply to it . . .

If the carelessness of the Borstal officers was the cause of the plaintiffs' loss what justification is there for holding that they had no duty to take care? The first argument was that their right and power to control the trainees was purely statutory and that any duty to exercise that right and power was only a statutory duty owed to the Crown. I would agree, but there is very good authority for the proposition that if a person performs a statutory duty carelessly so that he causes damage to a member of the public which would not have happened if he had performed his duty properly he may be liable . . .

Parliament deems it to be in the public interest that things otherwise unjustifiable should be done, and that those who do such things with due care should be immune from liability to persons who may suffer thereby. But Parliament cannot reasonably be supposed to have licensed those who do such things to act negligently in disregard of the interests of others so as to cause them needless damage.

Where Parliament confers a discretion the position is not the same. Then there may, and almost certainly will, be errors of judgment in exercising such a discretion and Parliament cannot have intended that members of the public should be entitled to sue in respect of such errors. But there must come a stage when the discretion is exercised so carelessly or unreasonably that there has been no real exercise of the discretion which Parliament has conferred. The person purporting to exercise his discretion has acted in abuse or excess of his power. Parliament cannot be supposed to have granted immunity to persons who do that . . . The present case does not raise this issue because no discretion was given to these Borstal officers. They were given orders which they negligently failed to carry out . . .

It was suggested that a decision against the Home Office would have very far-reaching effects . . . that it would make the Home Office liable for the loss occasioned by a burglary committed by a trainee on parole or a prisoner permitted to go out to attend a funeral. But there are two reasons why in the vast majority of cases that would not be so. In the first place it would have to be shown that the decision to allow any such release was so unreasonable that it could not be regarded as a real exercise of discretion by the responsible officer who authorised the release. And secondly it would have to be shown that the commission of the offence was the natural and probable, as distinct from merely a foreseeable, result of the release . . . I think that the fears of the appellants are unfounded: I cannot believe that negligence or dereliction of duty is widespread among prison or Borstal officers.

Finally I must deal with public policy. It is argued that it would be contrary to public policy to hold the Home Office or its officers liable to a member of the public for this carelessness – or, indeed, any failure of duty on their part. The basic question is: who shall bear the loss caused by that carelessness – the innocent respondents or the Home Office, who are vicariously liable for the conduct of their careless officers? I do not think that the argument for the Home Office can be put better than it was put by the Court of Appeals of New York in *Williams* v. *State of New York* (1955) 127 NE 2d. 545, 550:

> . . . public policy also requires that the State be not held liable. To hold otherwise would impose a heavy responsibility upon the State, or dissuade the wardens and principal keepers of our prison system from continued experimentation with 'minimum security' work details – which provide a means for encouraging better-risk prisoners to exercise their senses of responsibility and honour and so prepare themselves for their eventual return to society . . . The legislature has expressly provided for out-of-prison work, and its intention should be respected without fostering the reluctance of prison officials to assign eligible men to minimum security work, lest they thereby give rise to costly claims against the State, or indeed, inducing the State itself to terminate this salutary procedure looking towards rehabilitation.

It may be that public servants of the State of New York are so apprehensive, easily dissuaded from doing their duty and intent on preserving public funds from costly claims that they could be influenced in this way. But my experience leads me to believe that Her Majesty's servants are made of sterner stuff. So I have no hesitation in rejecting this argument. I can see no good ground in public policy for giving this immunity to a government department.

VISCOUNT DILHORNE (dissenting): Whatever be the reasons for the absence of authority,[12] the significant fact is its absence and this leads me to the conclusion . . . that we are being asked to create . . . an entirely new and novel duty and one which does not arise out of any novel situation.

I, of course, recognise that the common law develops by the application of well-established principles to new circumstances but I cannot accept that the application of Lord Atkin's words [in *Donoghue* v. *Stevenson*] . . . suffices to impose a new duty on the Home Office and on others in charge of persons in lawful custody of the kind suggested.

No doubt very powerful arguments can be advanced that there should be such a duty. It can be argued that it is wrong that those who suffer loss or damage at the hands of those who have escaped from custody as a result of negligence on the part of the custodians should have no redress save against the persons who inflicted the loss or damage who are unlikely to be able to pay; that they should not have to bear the loss themselves, whereas, if there is such a duty, liability might fall on the Home Office and the burden on the general body of taxpayers.

However this may be, we are concerned not with what the law should be but with what it is. The absence of authority shows that no such duty now exists. If there should be one, that is, in my view, a matter for the legislature and not for the courts.

LORD DIPLOCK: The analogy between 'negligence' at common law and the careless exercise of statutory powers breaks down where the act or omission complained of is not of a kind which would itself give rise to a cause of action at common law if it were not authorised by the statute. To relinquish intentionally or inadvertently the custody and control of a person responsible in law for his own acts is not an act or omission which, independently of any statute, would give rise to a cause of action at common law against the custodian on the part of another person who subsequently sustained tortious damage at the hands of the person released. The instant case thus lacks a relevant characteristic which was present in the series of decisions from which the principle formulated in *Geddis* v. *Proprietors of Bann Reservoir* was derived.[13] Furthermore, there is present in the instant case a characteristic which was lacking in *Geddis* v. *Proprietors of Bann Reservoir*. There the only conflicting interests involved were those on the one hand of the statutory undertakers responsible for the act or omission complained of and on the other hand of the person who sustained damage as a consequence of it. In the instant case, it is the interest of the Borstal trainee himself which is most directly affected by any decision to release him and by any system of relaxed control while he is still in custody that is intended to develop his sense of personal responsibility and so afford him an opportunity to escape. Directly affected also are the interests of other members of the community of trainees subject to the common system of control, and indirectly affected by the system of control while under detention and of release under supervision is the general public interest in the reformation of young offenders and the prevention of crime.

These interests, unlike those of a person who sustains damage to his property or person by the tortious act or omission of another, do not fall within any category of property or rights recognised in English law as entitled to protection by a civil action for damages. The conflicting interests of the various categories of persons likely to be affected by an act or omission of the custodian of a Borstal trainee which has as its consequence his release or his escape are thus of different kinds for which in law there is no common basis for comparison. If the reasonable man when directing his mind to the act or omission which has this consequence ought to have in contemplation persons in all the categories directly affected and also the general public interest in the reformation of young offenders, there is no criterion by which a court can assess where the balance lies between the weight to be given to one interest and that to be given to another. The material relevant to the assessment of the reformative effect upon trainees of release under supervision or of any relaxation of control while still under detention is not of a kind which can be satisfactorily elicited by the adversary procedure and rules of evidence adopted in English courts of law or of which judges (and juries) are suited by their training and experience to assess the probative value.

It is, I apprehend, for practical reasons of this kind that over the past century the public law concept of ultra vires has replaced the civil law concept of negligence as the test of legality, and consequently of the actionability, of acts or omissions of government departments or public authorities done in the exercise of a discretion conferred upon them by Parliament as to the means by which they are to achieve a particular public purpose . . . It is not the function of the court, for which it would be ill-suited, to substitute its own view of the appropriate means for that of the department or authority by granting a remedy by way of civil action at law to a private citizen adversely affected by the way in which the discretion has been exercised. Its function is confined in the first instance to deciding whether or not the act or omission complained of fell within the statutory limits imposed upon the department's or authority's disaction. Only if it did not would the court have jurisdiction to determine whether or not the act or omission, not being justified by the statute, constituted an actionable infringement of the plaintiff's rights in civil law . . .

In a civil action which calls in question an act or omission of a subordinate officer of the Home Office on the ground that he has been 'negligent' in his custody and control of a Borstal trainee who has caused damage to another person the initial inquiry should be whether or not the act or omission was ultra vires for one or other of these reasons. Where the act or omission is done in pursuance of the officer's instructions, the court may have to form its own view as to what is in the interests of Borstal trainees, but only to the limited extent of determining whether or not any reasonable person could bona fide come to the conclusion that the trainee causing the damage or other trainees in the same custody could be benefited in any way by the act or omission. This does not involve the court in attempting to substitute, for that of the Home Office, its own assessment of the comparative weight to be given to the benefit of the trainees and the detriment to persons likely to sustain damage. If on the other hand the officer's act or omission is done contrary to his instructions it is not protected by the public law doctrine of intra vires. Its actionability falls to be determined by the civil law principles of negligence.

Lord Dilhorne is concerned with legitimacy; he argues that extension of liability is for the law-maker, Parliament. Lord Diplock is more concerned with expertise; he is afraid that the decision may have hidden implications which may be left out of account. He suggests that the 'public law' test of ultra vires which leaves more scope for administrative discretion is better suited than the 'civil law' test of negligence for the determination of such issues. This terminology does not recommend itself to Lord Reid. He tells us that errors of judgement are not lightly to be equated with negligence but that a stage comes 'when the discretion is exercised so carelessly or unreasonably that there has been no real exercise of the discretion'. Where have you met this test before, and do the approaches of Lords Reid and Diplock differ substantially?[14]

In *Anns* v. *Merton LBC* [1977] 2 WLR 1024, Lord Wilberforce built on Lord Diplock's groundwork. The plaintiffs were owners of a block of flats found to be structurally unsound. Because the case was decided on a preliminary point, it was not certain whether the district surveyor had failed to inspect the foundations or whether his inspection had been insufficient, but the plaintiffs claimed damages for negligence in the exercise of the Council's statutory powers of inspection under the building regulations. Lord Wilberforce linked liability to the ultra vires principle. Discretion could be broken into 'an area of policy or discretion' in respect of which there could be no liability and an 'operational area' in which there could be liability where 'the act complained of lies outside the ambit of the power'. Like other conceptual classifications with which we are familiar – the administrative/judicial and void/voidable dichotomies for example –the distinction breaks down. Lord Wilberforce admits:

Although this distinction between the policy area and the operational area is convenient and illuminating, it is probably a distinction of degree; many 'operational' powers or duties have in them some element of 'discretion'. It can safely be said that the more 'operational' a power or duty may be, the easier it is to superimpose upon it a common law duty of care . . . A plaintiff complaining of negligence must prove the burden being on him, that the action taken was not within the limits of a discretion bona fide exercised, before he can begin to rely upon a common law duty of care.

Lord Diplock's concern in the *Dorset Yacht* case was that discretionary power should not be inadvertently fettered by a court which was considering the separate issue of negligence. Negligence liability may also indirectly affect resource allocation. Not only will public authorities have to weigh the benefit of inspection or open prisons against the chance of harm; they may also have to find funds to cover the loss caused, either themselves or through insurance. Noting the *Anns* case, Ganz (1977) argued that the escalation in claims on local authority insurers might be sufficient to inhibit local authorities from exercising important statutory powers. Some judges, like Lord Reid, discount the possibility. The circular issued by the Association of District Councils about participation in planning applications after adverse CLA reports shows that this is no idle fear. Chapter 15 contains a second circular warning planning departments that careless advice may give rise to legal liability.

As perfected in the later case of *Cocks* v. *Thanet LBC* [1982] 3 All ER 1135, the 'public/private' dichotomy is a useful conceptual tool for inhibiting such a development. Here the plaintiff brought an action for damages to enforce the statutory duty of the defendant authority owed to him under the Housing (Homeless Persons) Act 1977. The House of Lords held that there was no liability. The statute created two distinct types of obligation. At the decision-taking level there was a 'public law' obligation to execute the functions entrusted to the local authority but this did not give rise to individual rights. The 'private law' duty arose only at the operational level, in the unlikely event that a decision to allocate housing to a given individual had not been implemented.

The *Cocks* decision also has an important procedural dimension. Earlier homeless persons cases like *Thornton* v. *Kirklees MBC* [1979] 3 WLR 1, overruled by the House of Lords, were often test-cases designed to put pressure on local authorities to carry out their statutory functions. The tort action could be brought in the cheaper and more accessible county court. *Cocks* substituted Order 53 procedure in a majority of cases.[15]

In Chapter 10 we tried to evaluate test-case strategy. Linden (1973) sees an important role for tort law here. Like the ombudsman, tort law can open windows on the administration by subjecting secret processes to the glare of a full public trial. In this way it can become 'an instrument of social pressure upon centres of governmental, financial and intellectual power'. But Linden is writing of the North American experience. We can see that English courts are unwilling to see their procedures put to such a use. In *Allen*'s case, the House of Lords implied a 'no-nuisance' clause, while Lord Denning was willing to deny an injunction to successful litigants. Again, procedure, including cross-examination and discovery is, after *Cocks*, in the hands of the court (above, Chapter 9). Access to public documents is made more difficult still by the restrictive doctrines of public interest privilege and confidentiality, developed in a controversial fashion by the modern cases.[16]

Those to whom civil liability threatens administrative decision-taking may welcome such decisions. Those who, like Garner (1978) see administrative liability as a vital adjunct to a strong system of judicial review will probably be less happy. The courts have declined to create a right to damages in respect of illegal administrative activity and legislative intervention is now the only hope.[17] Arguably, to red light theorists, the public interest has once more triumphed.

5 Courts and Parliament: Burmah Oil

In Chapter 2, we described the *Laker* case as typical of the issues with which modern administrative law has to deal. Many of these recur in the Burmah Oil case. Here, Burmah Oil owned valuable oil installations in Burma. During the Second World War these were destroyed before the advancing Japanese on the orders of the British military authorities. After the war, ex-gratia compensation amounting to £11 million was paid by the British Government in respect of property loss caused to British individuals and companies in wartime Burma. Burmah Oil received nearly £5 million for 'reconstruction'. The word was carefully chosen; with the encouragement of the British Government, Burmah Oil was pursuing an action against the Government of Burma in the High Court of Burma and the British Government did not wish to prejudice the company's chances. But later it was explained that the sum was part of the total referred to above and that, although it was hoped that the money would be used in reconstruction, it was an out-and-out payment to Burmah to be dealt with as the company wished. Burmah got no compensation from the Burmese Government. It then re-opened negotiations with successive British Governments, who declined to find additional sums. Nearly 12 years later, when the English limitation period had expired, Burmah filed an action in Scotland claiming £31 million. The case went without trial to the House of Lords on a preliminary point.

The issue was that left undecided in *de Keyser*'s case: whether, in the absence of statute, the Crown had to pay compensation for the lawful exercise of its prerogative powers to requisition private property for the defence of the realm. A complicating factor was that Scots law was not necessarily identical with English common law because, as a civil law system, it recognizes the civilian principle of 'eminent domain'. For this reason the writings of Scots jurists were considered. Basing

themselves on a passage from Vattel, who distinguishes damage
caused in the face of the enemy (battle damage), where no compensation is payable, from damage caused in preparation for
hostilities, where compensation must be made, a majority of the
House held that Burmah possessed a claim to compensation. Lord
Upjohn's is a majority judgment, Viscount Radcliffe is dissenting.

Burmah Oil Co. Ltd v. *Lord Advocate* [1965] AC 75

LORD UPJOHN: In the *de Keyser* case much time was spent in researches into
early practice when the Crown compulsorily took the property of the subject,
with apparently negative results. For what it is worth, and it may not be very
much, that does seem to me on the whole to support the view that the Crown
did not take property without paying compensation. I would have thought
that had the contrary been the practice there would have been some clear
evidence of it. So . . . the practice of the Crown, so far as it can be ascertained,
and the course of statutory enactment at any rate from Napoleonic times
entitling the Crown to seize, use and destroy the subject's property supports
the view that this could only be done upon payment. Furthermore, it is clearly
settled that where the executive is authorised by a statute to take the property
of a subject for public purposes the subject is entitled to be paid unless the
statute has made the contrary intention quite clear . . .

Believing as I do in the great justice of the principle that if the Crown takes
the property of the subject for the public good whether for use or destruction
the Crown should pay for it, justice . . . demands that [Vattel's] second class
should be a limited one. No doubt in the actual battle the property of the
subject may be seriously damaged. It may be damaged by both sides and it
may be quite impossible to find out, indeed, how the damage did in fact arise.
But where even the day before the battle some property is razed to the ground
to provide some better field of fire, or something of that sort, is it unreasonable
to compel the Crown to compensate the subject for that loss providing he can
prove how it took place? . . . I would think that it was quite clear that the
destruction of the installations in this case fell within Vattel's first classification; it was done by way of precaution in the general prosecution of the
overall strategy. It was not done in the heat of battle.

VISCOUNT RADCLIFFE (dissenting): It is just in that distinction between
what is expected by public sentiment and what is actually obtainable by legal
right that our present difficulty lies. We know that by long tradition private
property appropriated for public use is treated as the subject of compensation
and we look to the Government to secure this, either by moving Parliament to
provide it or by some ex gratia payment which will afterwards receive
Parliamentary sanction. The recent war, for instance, gave us both the
Compensation (Defence) Act, 1939, which, speaking generally, was intended
to provide compensation to persons affected by defined acts in exercise of
emergency powers (including prerogative powers of the Crown) and the War
Damage Act, 1943, the purpose of which was to introduce a scheme of

insurance as cover against war damage due to enemy action.[18] The present case is strictly an anomaly because, relating to acts done in Burma outside the scope of the United Kingdom statutes and not . . . within the scope of any other statutes, it requires us to consider the acts of destruction as 'pure' prerogative acts without the control of legislative provisions that would obviously be available if the case were not wholly exceptional.

I cannot see that that circumstance entitles us to import into the common law a legal right that has not hitherto been recognised to exist. By what title do we do it? There is no principle of justice or equity made visible to us that has not by now been apparent for centuries: and if hitherto the justice of the matter has been administered through other channels, I do not think that there is any adequate reason to open the law courts to such claims. Indeed . . . the balance of public advantage and, perhaps, constitutional propriety argue against it . . .

Where war damage is concerned, the long-standing absence of any recognition that there is jurisdiction in the courts to award compensation is based on sound considerations of public policy. Such damage is a matter, being unpredictable in extent and range, that must be controlled by that department of the sovereign power that is responsible for the raising and expenditure of public money. There is not a legal line between those divisions of that damage that carry a legal right to compensation and those that do not. Damage inflicted by the enemy may be terrible individual loss, and it is certainly suffered in the common cause. Moreover, it is likely to fall with disproportionate weight on some citizens who suffer in that cause, a fact familiar in the last war to those whose homes or places of business were close to an object of strategic importance and so peculiarly exposed to air or missile attack. Damage inflicted by one's own side, accidentally or to prevent its capture and the enrichment of the enemy, does not seem to me different in kind unless the element of deliberation marks off the latter . . . And no one can find an equation between the personal loss that war inflicts and its inroads upon property . . .

None of this is an argument against the propriety or, indeed, urgent desirability of the state providing compensation schemes to take care, so far as possible, of all war damage, of person or property. But it is for those who fill and empty the public purse to decide when, by whom, on what conditions and within what limitations such compensation is to be made available. After all, states lose wars as well as win them: and at the conclusion of a war that has seen massive destruction, whether self-inflicted through the medium of a 'scorched earth' policy or inflicted by the enemy, there may well be urgent claims for reconstruction priorities that make it impossible in advance to mortgage the public treasury to legal claims for full individual compensation for such destruction as we have now to consider. Indeed, what in legal terms does 'compensation' mean in this case? The act of destruction was lawful, that is conceded . . . so we are not to think of damages and the legal rules for their assessment. Has the law any principle for measuring compensation as a legal right when an act has been done in circumstances so special that the ordinary conceptions of property do not apply to it? Can the state be asked to pay a requisition price for something for which there was at the time no conceivable purchaser? I do not think so.

Does the application of Vattel's classification to the facts produce a principle of law which satisfies you?

Immediately afterwards, with the acquiescence of the Opposition front bench, the Government introduced the War Damage Act which provided only:

1–(1) No person shall be entitled at common law to receive from the Crown compensation in respect of damage to, or destruction of, property caused (whether before or after the passing of this Act, within or outside the United Kingdom) by acts lawfully done by, or on the authority of, the Crown during, or in contemplation of the outbreak of, a war in which the Sovereign was, or is, engaged.

(2) Where any proceedings to recover at common law compensation in respect of such damage or destruction have been instituted before the passing of this Act, the court shall, on the application of any party, forthwith set aside or dismiss the proceedings, subject only to the determination of any question arising as to costs or expenses.

Not unnaturally, the retrospective element was a cause for concern. As in the *Malloch* case, it was seen to imperil the rule of law. Opening the debate on the second reading Mr MacDermot (Financial Secretary to the Treasury) explained why the step was being taken (HC Deb. vol. 705, cols. 1091–4):

The object of the Bill is to restore the common law of England and the law of Scotland to the position which was generally thought to exist before the decision and to provide that about 12 cases now pending . . . before the court are disposed of on the basis of the law as it has always been thought to be . . .

The whole question of compensation for damage and destruction inflicted during war presents serious problems for a country whose Government are anxious to secure equitable treatment for their people. The incidence of losses is arbitrary, but it has seemed right to the Government of this country that the burden should as far as possible be shared. Damage and destruction may arise partly from identifiable enemy action or from defensive action of our own forces, or it may arise in the course of actual fighting in which the side responsible for the particular damage may not be identifiable.

Moreover, the scale of losses in total wars in this century has been so formidable as to make the idea of their reparation in full impossible. Indeed, the depleted resources of the victorious countries after the exactions of recent wars have made restoration and rehabilitation on any scale a heavy burden, and, quite apart from damage to property, there has been an appalling toll of killed and wounded, leaving widows, children and disabled men to be supported. There has, therefore, emerged – no other satisfactory solution would have been possible – the concept of sharing the burden of losses in the country as a whole, on whatever scale the country as a whole can reasonably be held to afford.

    This carries two implications: first, there must be some equitable scheme for distributing such compensation as may be afforded in relation to the losses suffered by individuals; and, secondly, opportunity must not be left open to any special groups amongst those who have suffered loss to claim redress on a preferential scale. Any entitlement to compensation on an indemnity basis of common law would, in effect, give preferential treatment to those enjoying it . . .

    I am aware that many Members would readily accept the first part of the Bill, but would, nevertheless, feel anxiety about the proposal to give it retrospective effect. I fully share the view of such hon. Members about the general undesirability of retrospective legislation. There are, however, well recognised exceptions to the general rule against retrospectivity, and it is only because I am satisfied that this case falls clearly within these exceptions that I am moving the Second Reading of the Bill.

    There were two arguments for retroactivity. The first was that the sums involved were too large to be paid (Burmah was claiming £30 million and other claims might have totalled £200 million in S.E. Asia). The second concerned equality of treatment. Throughout the Far East claims had been dealt with in similar fashion. For example, in Malaya, the British Government had contributed £20 million to claims of £160 million and in Borneo £2.25 million to claims of £12.5 million. It was inequitable to allow people to accept compensation and then pay in full those who stood out for their legal rights. Do you agree?

    Here, from Mr Jenkin, is the constitutional argument against retroactive legislation. Would the compromise used after the *Atkinson* case concerning welfare payments to students (see below, p. 610) have been preferable here?

It has been said over and over again that ignorance of the law is no excuse if one commits a breach of the criminal code. In exactly the same way, ignorance of the law should never be used as a means of depriving a subject of his right to benefit under the law. Still more should we hesitate to legislate to make a retrospective interference with the rights of the subject when these rights have been judicially determined by the courts. We have strict rules about anyone's attempting interference with the judicial process, and very severe penalties for anyone who does. Indeed, one judge referred to it some years ago as 'poisoning the fount of justice at its source', and so it is.

    In exactly the same way, any retrospective interference with the judicial process is just as much a poisoning of the fount of justice, and none the less to be deplored, when it happens to be done by due legislative process. The French jurist Montesquieu based his celebrated doctrine of the separation of powers on the British constitution and as all constitutional lawyers know well, sadly misunderstood our constitution, but in one matter he was absolutely right, and that is, the separation of the powers of the Executive and of the Judiciary.

A Bill such as this, with the express intent to overrule retrospectively a decision of the House of Lords, is dangerous because it blurs that very necessary separation and legal safeguard. Parliament, I say, should be extremely chary of the way in which it exercises its powers in this regard. [HC Deb. vol. 705, cols. 1183–4.]

The retrospective element may have been unnecessary. Goodhart (1966, p. 114) observed that 'Parliament, by enacting the War Damage Act 1965 did the claimants a service, because although it deprived them of a claim which might have proved almost valueless when the time came to assess the damages, it saved them from unnecessary legal costs'. Lord Hodson (dissenting) had said, '. . . it would seem that the value of property that is about to pass, possibly forever, into the hands of the enemy must depend on the nature of the property and the chances of its survival and restoration, intact or damaged, to the pursuers [plaintiffs]'. Compare Lord Reid's view with Lord Radcliffe in dissent.

I am deciding nothing about the proper measure of compensation. The applicants appear to be claiming the full value of these installations in time of peace. I am holding that they are entitled to compensation, and it will be necessary to consider whether compensation must not be related to their loss in the sense of what difference it would have made to them if their installations had been allowed to fall into the hands of the enemy instead of being destroyed.

The *Burmah Oil* case is often represented as a clash of individual and public interests. What 'interests' can you identify? Which would you classify as 'public' and which as 'individual'? In the House of Commons Mr Wall (HC Deb. vol. 705, col. 1186) remarked:

It has been asked . . . why should one company get this large sum; why should the taxpayer finance big business? I understand that the stockholders of this company number 134,000, of which 131,000 are individuals, and that of those 131,000 95,000 hold stock worth £500 or less, so we are not really dealing with one large company, but with a large number of small individuals.

Remember Lord Diplock's warning in *Dorset Yacht*. Do you think the House of Lords identified the relevant issues and dealt adequately with them? Was there a 'right' answer? And was this a 'political question'? Finally, to what body should the ultimate decision have been allocated and was this achieved?

13
Administrative compensation

A main theme of Chapter 12 was the role of courts in decisions over compensation. Such an approach can be valuable. It is right to remember that the imposition on the sovereign state of an obligation enforceable in the courts to compensate for loss and injury caused to the subject has played a significant part historically in the struggle for civil liberty.[1] On the other hand, we do not want to tie the notion of compensation too closely to legal liability. Not every loss gives rise to legal liability. The Land Compensation Act was passed to fill precisely such a gap in the common law. And the common law normally insists that to be reparable loss should be attributable to the *defendant's* actions or that a relationship giving rise to *obligation* should exist between the parties. These requirements gave rise to difficulty in the *Dorset Yacht* case. The state may wish to recognize other obligations, interpreting 'compensation' much more loosely. For example, we might argue that industrial injuries compensation, today administered under the provisions of a series of National Insurance Acts which can be traced to 1911, but whose ancestor is the Workmen's Compensation Act 1897, is not properly 'compensation'. The state has not caused the injury and is therefore under no obligation to redress it. The scheme is really a system of compulsory insurance administered by the state and to which the state contributes. Yet the state does, in fact, recognize the obligation.

As we shall see, the analogy between legal liability and compensation can cut both ways. In the debates over criminal injuries compensation, for example, some speakers suggested that the state was under an 'obligation' to ensure the safety of its subjects; others saw the absence of legal liability as a reason why victims of violent crime should *not* be 'compensated' by the state. Proponents of 'compensation' for the victims of vaccine damage pressed the analogy with legal liability; the Government insisted that it was under no 'obligation' and that the 'payments' it was making were purely gratuitous. This point may be important in deciding what sort of scheme is to be established. An analogy to legal liability may suggest the inclusion of a formal method of adjudication. Gratuitous payments, on the other hand, may imply discretion and an administrative process. Similar reasoning prompts Atiyah's argument (below) that criminal injuries payments are analogous to welfare benefits such as mobility or invalidity payments and should be absorbed into the state's social security system.

Such arguments suggest that rational principles should underlie the allocation of 'compensation'. Public lawyers have devoted much time to the identification of a general principle of administrative liability, arguing, for example, that damages should always be available as a remedy for illegal administrative action.[2] Atiyah, however, is advancing the rather different case that political decisions should be rational. Admittedly, one of the aims of modern decision-taking theory has been to improve the quality (efficiency) of administrative decisions. Planners have for many years explored ways in which decisions can be made more 'rational', 'efficient' and 'cost-effective'. (Their ideas are explored in Chapter 14.) Similar ideas have influenced administrative law. Jennings thought efficiency an objective for administrative lawyers before the Second World War. Jowell later argued that courts may make a positive contribution to administrative decision-taking by encouraging the preparation of reasoned proofs and arguments. Pannick argued the reverse; administrative decision-taking techniques could lead to more efficient judicial decisions.

Lord Pearson's remarks in *Morgans* v. *Launchbury* (above) represent the opposite case. Contrasting the resources at the disposal of a court with those available to 'government and Parliament', Lord Pearson argued that the governmental decision could be more rational and efficient than that of a court. Is Fuller's case against judicial determination of 'polycentric' issues based on a similar assumption? And is the assumption correct, or is Griffith's picture of the political process as a series of bargains between competing interest groups more realistic? We can cite a rather extreme example. The Pearson

Commission on Civil Liability and Compensation for Personal Injury (Cmnd 7054 (1978)) closely resembled the Roskill Commission on the Third London Airport (below, Chapter 15). Chaired by a judge (Lord Pearson), but with members from many professions, the Commission had at its disposal a range of expertise and professional advice. It was able to commission research studies and take evidence from numerous individuals, professional bodies and interest groups. One of its recommendations was against the creation of 'special cases'. Lump-sum payments, for example, should not be made to compensate for the failure of the existing tort system. The case of slate quarrymen was expressly considered (Cmnd 7054, paras. 888–92). A year after publication of the report, Parliament passed the Pneumoconiosis (Workers Compensation) Act 1979, which provided for lump-sum payments to those disabled by pneumoconiosis and certain other industrial lung diseases *whose employers had ceased to carry on business.* So the state here acted as insurer for the tort system. The limited nature of the scheme, which applied to some recognized industrial lung diseases but not to others, led to accusations that a bargain had been struck by a weak Labour Government with Welsh Nationalist M Ps in exchange for support on other matters. The piecemeal nature of the arrangements was increased by the fact that the voluntary scheme operated by the National Coal Board for its own employees suffering from pneumoconiosis was not touched by the new Act. As you look further at a variety of administrative and political decisions to award 'compensation' you may like to reconsider arguments concerning adjudication and polycentricity.

Emphasis on the political stratosphere where decisions are taken by cabinet ministers and law lords is, in any event, misleading. Not every decision about compensation is taken by a High Court judge or by elected representatives, nor is every decision a high-visibility policy decision of the type referred to Royal Commissions. In Chapter 8, we found that public servants, although they queried the constitutional propriety of the practice, took decisions about compensation themselves. Both local authorities and central government have power to make ex gratia payments. In the case of local authorities, such payments can be challenged through the audit procedures; statute therefore makes provision for ministerial authorization to protect them from this danger. Central government is much freer. The Treasury Solicitor frequently recommends ex gratia payments in settlement of threatened legal actions. The PCA may also recommend payment after a finding of maladministration and departments may decide to make individual payments to meet exceptional 'hard cases'. Such payments usually need Treasury authorization and it is natural to find that the Treasury has issued guidelines on the subject (see Chapter 8, note 1). In this chapter several examples of such low-visibility decisions will be found. When, from time to time, they surface, we find that they are taken largely by civil servants with some input from ministers, but with little or no parliamentary control. Structured by unpublished departmental guidelines, the decisions are reminiscent of the official policy-making revealed by the Crichel Down scandal. Unless, like Griffith in his comment on that affair, we are content to trust the rectitude of civil servants, we need to scrutinize these decisions carefully. In examining informal compensation practices we are entitled to ask whether Davis's criterion of 'the miniature democratic process' is being met. Accountability is an important democratic value which, in this area, may receive insufficient recognition.

A majority of compensation decisions are, however, taken at the 'operational' level. These decisions may be appropriate for adjudication and require a measure of procedural fairness. The classic English court-substitute is a tribunal and we should expect to find many tribunals in this area. Today, for example, a minute percentage of claims for industrial injury reaches a court. The day-to-day work of assessment and compensation is handled by the DHSS, the bread and butter business of adjudication by National Insurance Local Tribunals (NILTs) from which appeal lies to Social Security (formerly National Insurance) Commissioners, a body of lawyers expert in the field.[3] So these tribunals are extremely busy; Table 1 (see p. 68) shows the volume of cases handled annually.

Some of the tribunals are formal. At one end of the spectrum is the Lands Tribunal. In Chapter 3 we described this tribunal as a paracourt. As such it has lost many of the advantages of tribunals. For example, McAuslan (1981, p. 112) complains of the delays; in order to challenge assessments, complainants have to forego compensation for some considerable time so that the need to take the case to the Lands Tribunal will deter all but 'the most determined or outraged from making a challenge'. The Lands Tribunal is also costly. The availability of legal aid has encouraged legal representation. One MP, during the debate on the Land Compensation Bill, claimed (HC Deb. vol. 847, col. 89) that his constituent, after a dispute and litigation lasting for ten years or more, had been awarded £50,000 by the tribunal. His costs amounted to £51,000. Even if these costs were paid for the individual by the state, they would seem disproportionate.

Other administrative procedures are more innovatory. One of the schemes chosen for study puts into perspective Ganz's statement that excessive reliance on the court model would stereotype administrative procedures. When the criminal injuries compensation scheme was debated by the House of Commons, some of the speakers like Sir Frank Soskice, a former Solicitor-General, wanted adjudication by courts. Perhaps fortunately, this view was disregarded. The chosen model, described in further detail below, is generally thought to function satisfactorily. Indeed, its procedures are under consideration as a possible prototype for reform of civil procedure, at least in personal injury trials. So here the tables are turned; public law techniques are forcing lawyers to rethink their own procedures.

The compensation schemes which follow are not typical. Indeed one might ask, typical of what? Like the untidy, unsupervised network of tribunals, compensation schemes have 'just growed'. They are hardly newcomers to the administrative scene. For example, in *de Keyser*'s case Lord Moulton referred to a Defence Act of 1842 which consolidated and repealed a series of Acts dating back to 1708 which contained compensation provisions. The Land Clauses Consolidation Act discussed in the *Brand* case dates to 1845. Lord Cairns made reference there to 'many hundreds of thousands of pounds – I might perhaps say millions of pounds' already paid out in compensation for 'injurious affection' of private property under this and the earlier private Acts which had been consolidated. Again, when the criminal injuries compensation scheme was debated in Parliament it was presented as a novelty; the second such scheme in the world, an abrupt change from the traditional civil law model. In fact, the Riot Damages Act, which provides state compensation for property damaged in the course of a riot, was passed in 1886. A committee set up in 1971 to review the Northern Irish criminal injuries scheme,[4] which differs from that for the rest of the country because property damage is covered, traced this legislation to a statute of Edward I which created a right in damages against local government hundreds and shires in respect of loss through robbery. The scale of state compensation has increased (£15 million was paid out after riots in Toxteth in 1981, and the NI criminal injuries compensation scheme in the same year paid out £36,523,503 in respect of property and £6,251,314 in respect of persons) but the principle is hardly novel.

From this proliferation of schemes, large and small, old and new, we have selected a handful for further study. Our choices are necessarily restricted by scale. For example, land compensation or industrial injuries are far too large to be dealt with here. But each scheme chosen raises one or more of the issues previously introduced. As you read on, you will find these issues, recapitulated below as questions, forming the framework of our studies.

(a) Who takes policy decisions to compensate and how are the decisions taken? What is the reason for compensation?
(b) If administrators take the decisions are they discretionary?
(c) How is administrative discretion structured?
(d) Is there machinery for adjudication? Is it an adequate court-substitute? Does the procedure improve on that of a court?
(e) Are there any external or internal 'controls'?

1 Criminal injuries compensation: a 'gesture of sympathy'

The criminal injuries scheme has never been placed on a statutory basis. The scheme was introduced in 1964 by a Conservative Government, with all-party support, as a response to pressure to 'do something for the victims of crime'. A working party was set up to consider what steps could be taken and, after two reports, a scheme was drawn up, the terms of which were announced to the House of Commons and published in *Hansard* and elsewhere.[5] In its first year of operation, 554 applications were received and £33,430 paid out in compensation. The number of claims has thereafter steadily increased. In 1974, when extension of the scheme was under consideration by a Home Office working party, £5,224,580 was paid out and more than 10,000 claims were received. In 1980–1, after the extensions, 20,613 claims were received and £21,462,464 paid out, an increase of 36.4 per cent on the previous year. These are sums for which statutory authorization is normally sought. Why then was it established on an ex gratia basis?

One answer seems to be that neither the working party, the Government nor speakers in the debates could devise an adequate principle of 'liability'. As Lord Denning pointed out in the House of Lords (HL Deb, vol. 245 cols. 272–8) the payments did not reflect the pattern of legal liability, nor was there clearly a moral obligation on the state to pay – at least, no obligation greater than that owed to motor accident victims, excluded from the scheme for reasons of cost and expediency.

Those who advocated the scheme made strenuous efforts to satisfy their critics. Amongst the arguments advanced by *Justice*, for example, was the idea that the state forbids resort to violence, discouraging the citizen from carrying arms or from taking the law into his own hands, yet imposes a general duty to help in bringing criminals to justice. These are parallels to *legal* liability. But legal liability extends to property damage which would leave government with a problem; how could property damage logically be excluded from the scheme? So the Government rejected any obligation, moral or legal, which might ultimately be used as an argument for extensive *legal* liability. The working party timidly concluded:

The proposition that the State has a duty to protect its members from unlawful violence and that if it fails to do so it should pay compensation. . . seems to us to be both fallacious and dangerous. Fallacious because we do not believe that the State has an absolute duty to protect every citizen all the time against other citizens: there is a distinction between compensation for the consequences of civil riot, which the forces of law and order may be expected to prevent, and compensation for injury by individual acts of personal violence, which can never be entirely prevented. It is true that nowadays the public generally are prohibited from carrying weapons to protect themselves, but it does not follow that the State has assumed the duty of protecting them everywhere and in all circumstances; the most it has done is to create an assumption that it will provide a general condition of civil peace. Dangerous, because acceptance of public liability for offences against the person could be the basis of a demand for acceptance of liability for all offences against property.

We can find no constitutional or social principle on which State compensation could be justified, but we think that it could nevertheless be based on the more practical ground, already in the minds of its advocates . . . that although the Welfare State helps the victims of many kinds of misfortune, it does nothing for the victims of crimes of violence as such, notwithstanding that they are largely deprived of the means of self-protection and in most cases have no effective remedy at law. There is an argument for filling this gap, based mainly on considerations of sympathy for the innocent victim, but falling short of acceptance of any bounden duty to mitigate the victim's hardship; and we think this argument more likely to appeal to the public than any more abstruse principles that might be formulated. [Cmnd 1406 (1961), paras. 17–18.]

Is there a 'constitutional or social' principle on which liability could be founded (see above, p. 39)? In the House of Lords, the

Bishop of Chester pursued the analogy with welfare payments (HL Deb. vol. 245, col. 268):

I believe that the justification for the claim is to be found in the spirit which underlies the whole of the Welfare State. We are learning more and more that we are indeed each other's neighbour, and that neighbourliness imposes an obligation upon each to care for the welfare of the other. So we consider it right and proper that in society the more fortunate should care for the less fortunate; that the wealthy should have an obligation towards the poor and the privileged towards the under-privileged. I think that we are learning this lesson especially in the realm of the responsibility for crime in society.

We might pause here to ask why 'sympathy' dictates compensation for physical injury but not for property damage. Or we might, like Atiyah, ask whether the welfare state does anything for anyone 'as such'. Criticizing the 'appeal to the public instinct' as 'a complete abdication of the role of legislator [which] might as well have been used to justify feeding Christians to the lions in ancient Rome or the burning of witches in medieval England', the author continues:

[The working party] never really came to grips with the crucial issue which was not whether victims of criminal violence ought to be compensated by the state, but whether there are any grounds for compensating such victims outside the normal processes of the welfare state. This question was only touched on in passing by pointing out that the welfare state did nothing for the victims of violence 'as such' – but the welfare state does nothing for anybody 'as such', whether as cancer victim, as widow or even as the victim of accident. What the welfare state does is to provide compensation for lost earnings, plus some compensation for disabilities if they are incurred at work . . . if the welfare benefits are inadequate, the right solution is to increase them; and if less money were devoted to special categories of unfortunates, it might be possible without much, if any, increased cost, to make the benefits perfectly adequate. [Atiyah, 1980, p. 297.]

This is Atiyah's argument for rational decisions. Classifying criminal injuries compensation as welfare payments, Atiyah asks for better benefits – a solution which, although he implies the contrary, would actually prove immeasurably more costly. (Figures which give some idea of the real cost of uprating benefits will be found in Chapter 18.) So the Government is saving cake while inviting applause for generosity. Atiyah sees this as illogical, but then, is it really impermissible for governments to create 'special cases,' justifying their behaviour by reference to public sentiment? Are they not elected to do precisely this? Such conduct may be the only path to progress, since otherwise every improvement will have to await reform of the whole. Here, in the debate which followed the introduction of the scheme in 1964, Sir Frank Soskice puts the case for 'special cases' (HC Deb. vol. 694, col. 1141):

... We cannot, in matters of compensation, obtain complete consistency ... It is said by some that it is the duty of the State to the citizen to maintain law and order and that, if the State falls down in the discharge of that duty and consequent harm results to the citizen, the citizen has at any rate a moral claim to compensation. I think that a difficult argument to accept. We are all 'the State'. The State, viewed as a kind of abstract conception remote and different from us, seems in the context we are discussing to be somewhat of an unreality.

We all collectively try to see that law and order is enforced. We set up a police force and public institutions, but we know in advance that we shall not succeed altogether. All we can do is to do our best to see that law and order on a broad scale is maintained. Therefore, it seems unreal to base a claim for compensation upon the assumed failure of the State or society at large to maintain law and order. That is not the basis on which we can proceed. The real basis is that as society evolves new situations are uncovered on which strong public feeling works.

In view of the increase in crimes of violence recently ... public sympathy is with the victims ... It says that as a matter of moral right they should be assisted in the only way in which, unfortunately, they can be assisted – by some monetary compensation.

A second reason for an ex gratia scheme was flexibility. The scheme was almost unprecedented, and the Government wished to be sure that it worked and could be adjusted. Moreover, they were uncertain how much it was going to cost. Announcing the institution of the scheme on an experimental basis, the Home Secretary, Mr Brooke, explained the government view, drawing justification from the absence of legal liability (HC Deb. vol. 694, col. 1129):

It is because of ... doubts about the extent to which the scheme will be needed, and because of the difficulty of ensuring in a pioneer scheme that public money is not wasted on undeserving or fraudulent claims, that the Government think that the sensible thing to do is to start on an experimental basis which can be modified later if necessary. We propose that compensation shall be paid *ex gratia* because, as the White Paper says, we do not think that the State can be held liable for injuries caused to people by the acts of others.

Ex gratia payment implies freedom of choice and some of the case law (below) suggests this. The reality is different. The Criminal Injuries Compensation Board (CICB), which administers the scheme, does not believe that it has unfettered discretion whether or not to compensate:

The use of the words *ex gratia* means that an applicant has no right to sue either the Crown or the Board for non-payment of compensation. But, in practice, the position is exactly the same as it would be if the Scheme was embodied in a statute with the words *ex gratia* being omitted. The Board's view of its legal obligation and duty under the Scheme is that, if an applicant's entitlement to compensation is established there is no power to withhold compensation. Furthermore, once entitlement to compensation is established, the Board regards itself as having no discretion to award any sum, save that which in the Board's opinion, would be awarded by a civil court for the same injuries, since the Scheme provides that compensation shall be assessed on the basis of common law damages. In order to ensure that the Board's assessments are broadly in line with awards in the courts, the Board undertakes assessment exercises in which judges and lawyers participate. [Cmnd 7752 (1979), para. 15.]

The Board is suggesting that the rules of the scheme are strict enough to render a statute superfluous. But in 1980, introducing a private member's bill which he later withdrew, Lord Longford argued (H L Deb. vol. 401, cols. 233–5) that the victims of crime were being treated as second-class citizens whose claims were 'not quite worthy of a full statutory scheme'. Compare the arguments which he puts here with the arguments of welfare lawyers (below, Chapter 18) for *entitlement* to benefit and welfare 'rights':

In wider terms, the establishment of a statutory system would command much more confidence among victims, and certainly could be used to promote much more effective publicity. As time went on a statutory board would no doubt be better placed to exercise influence on behalf of more generous treatment for victims.

Lord Longford makes an important point. The guidelines do differ from statute or regulations in that they can be amended from time to time without formality. (Later we will compare the amendment of social security regulations made under the 1980 legislation.) On 1 February 1983, for example, the Home Secretary used a parliamentary question to announce changes in the amounts of awards, ostensibly to bring them into line with changes in the civil law of damages on which awards are patterned. A new 'bereavement grant'[6] would be financed by lifting the limit below which claims cannot be made from £250 to £400, affecting an estimated 3–4,000 claims. On 3 March 1983, in an oral question, Mr Kilroy-Silk called this 'blatant hypocrisy', but there was no parliamentary recourse. Indeed, the changes were mentioned to the House only in passing (H C Deb. vol. 38 W A, col. 60).

When the scheme was first instituted, it was intended that the Board's decisions, because they were discretionary, should not be the subject of any appeal. It would seem too that judicial review was not anticipated, since the scheme was established under prerogative powers:

The board will be entirely responsible for deciding what compensation should be paid in individual cases and their decisions will not be subject to appeal or the Ministerial review. The general working of the scheme will, however, be kept under review by the government, and the board will submit annually to the Home Secretary and the Secretary of State for Scotland a full report on the operation of the scheme, together with their accounts. The report and accounts will be open to debate in Parliament. [Para. 3][7]

But para. 3 should not be taken at its face value. In *R.* v. *CICB ex p. Lain* [1967] 2 QB 864, the Divisional Court held that the Board, 'a servant of the Crown charged by the Crown, by executive instruction, with the duty of distributing the bounty of the Crown . . . came fairly and squarely within the jurisdiction of this Court'. No steps were taken to restore the original intention. Once again, inroads had been made on the scheme's discretionary nature.

We know that the scheme was not intended to give rise to 'entitlement' and the text reflects this. It is a 'code of practice' or guidelines meant to inform the public rather than to provide work for lawyers. The text is in two parts, 'the scheme' or rules of operation and 'the statement' intended 'for the benefit of applicants and their advisers as to how the Board are likely to determine applications'. In comparison to statute, the text is simple to construe and self-explanatory and, since the 15 members of the Board are lawyers experienced in personal injuries litigation, it might be expected that few problems would arise. Yet the text has been submitted to the courts for a ruling on a point of law on many occasions. Decisions are treated with great respect by the Board. They are summarized in the annual reports and referenced in the statement. Thus case law plays its part in structuring the scheme.

One case is interesting as showing a division of judicial opinion over the nature of the scheme. Para. 5 provides:

The Board will entertain applications for *ex gratia* payment of compensation in any case where the applicant . . . sustained . . . personal injury directly attributable to a crime of violence (including arson and poisoning) or to an arrest or attempted arrest of an offender or suspected offender or to the prevention or attempted prevention of an offence or to the giving of help to any constable who is engaged in arresting or attempting to arrest an offender or suspected offender or preventing or attempting to prevent an offence.

The question before the court in *R.* v. *CICB ex p. Schofield* [1971] 1 WLR 926 was whether a bystander knocked down accidentally during a struggle to arrest a shoplifter could claim under the scheme. A majority of the court thought that her injuries were 'directly attributable' to an arrest or criminal offence. Bridge LJ disagreed.[8] He thought:

the scheme, as the document is entitled which enshrines the rules for the board's conduct, is not recognisable as any kind of legislative document with which the court is familiar. It is not expressed in the kind of language one expects from a parliamentary draftsman, whether of statutes or statutory instruments. It bears all the hallmarks of a document which lays down the broad guidelines of policy.

Treating the CICB as an administrative authority subject to judicial review, he held that it would be wrong to intervene unless its interpretation was 'wholly untenable'. The CICB had given as its reasons that:

The purpose of the scheme is to compensate those who try to arrest an offender or who try to prevent the commission of a crime, or who assist a constable to do either of these things. It does not in our view cover bystanders who are accidentally injured by anyone who is engaged in the task of arresting an offender.

Bridge LJ thought this 'reasonably tenable'. If you agree with those who think that the rigid style used by statutory draftsmen obscures their meaning, you should look more closely at the text of the scheme. It does seem to balance clarity with flexibility. Its meaning is sufficiently clear to the layman yet detailed enough to structure the wide discretionary powers entrusted to the members of the CICB. But it does not solve every problem.

Unlike Lord Denning, who thought the absence of legal entitlement rendered ex gratia payments unsuitable for adjudication, the Government from the outset favoured formal adjudicatory methods. Apparently all those submitting evidence to the working party were agreed that claims for compensation should be determined by a judicial or quasi-judicial body. The Government's choice fell on the CICB. As you read on, ask yourself how you would classify these procedures. Do you agree with Sir Frank Soskice that a court or tribunal would have been preferable?

The first stage in the application process is to submit a claim which is initially processed by a single member of the Board using documentary evidence. Application forms are available on request. About 75 per cent of applications are resolved at this stage; the remaining 25 per cent are set down for a hearing by a three-member panel at the request of the applicant or on reference by a single member. In fact, about 19 per cent of these requests are later withdrawn. This procedure helps to keep down administrative costs. A single member application cost about £105 in 1982/3 while hearings averaged about £290 in addition. These figures do not allow for legal costs, but legal representation is the exception not the rule.

The hearing is not an appeal 'but a renewal of the application which is heard and decided *de novo* before 3 members of the Board . . . [who] are not bound by the single member's decision' (Cmnd 5791, para. 7).

The procedures at hearing are published in the scheme. It is up to the applicant to 'make out his case' and he may do this in person or through 'a friend or legal adviser'. Procedure will be 'as informal as is consistent with the proper determination of applications', and hearings are generally in private, though the Board has a discretion to admit observers. Here from an early report is a description of procedure. Pick out the inquisitorial features. Note that the case law supplements the Board's *own* precedents in structuring discretion. Many of these decisions are published in the annual reports.

Our hearings are held in private and have been conducted informally. We have not considered ourselves bound by the rules of evidence. The applicant is called upon to prove his case on the balance of probabilities.

Most of the applicants have conducted their own case but in a few cases we have had the assistance of counsel, in some the assistance of a solicitor and in others that of a Trades Union official representative. Clear presentation of difficult facts and law by professional advocates has from time to time been of considerable value to us in reaching a decision.

A legally qualified member of the Board's staff appears as advocate at each hearing. He acts as a friend of the Board rather than as a party to the dispute. He presents all the facts and arguments which are relevant whether they are favourable or unfavourable to the applicant's case. He also draws the attention of the Board to its previous decisions and to the decisions of the courts. In some cases he challenges the case put forward by cross-examination, by the evidence he calls and by his submissions of law. In others, the evidence he calls and the arguments he puts forward may tend to establish the applicant's case. So even when the applicant's case is not put forward by a professional advocate, the risk of it not being fully put before the Board is greatly reduced.

We have no power to compel witnesses to attend hearings to give evidence and they frequently refuse to do so, or fail to appear. Thus, in cases where an applicant's share of responsibility has to be considered, his evidence may stand uncontradicted. We cannot say in how many cases we would have reached a different conclusion if further evidence had been available. It is probable, however, that the evidence of those who were compelled to come against their will would be of little value. Furthermore, if the assailant had been acquitted it would be hard to compel him to give evidence a second time to support his acquittal. [Cmnd 3117 (1966), paras. 31–2.]

The documentary procedures help to reduce delay. Yet recently the Board was concerned because it was accumulating a backlog. Look at the figures in the following extract; even in 1979/80, 74.8 per cent of applications were resolved within the year. Notice the explanation for the apparent rise in cases which were not.

Despite a higher figure of resolutions than ever before, cases are taking longer to resolve. The increased processing time is, naturally, of concern to the Board which is dependent on outside bodies for the vast majority of its information; delays in this area automatically protract the time taken to resolve applications. However, the temporary establishment of a small arrears unit during the year has achieved an increase in cases resolved and has also permitted a greater concentration of effort on applications in which (often because the injuries are extensive) protracted enquiries are necessary and complex matters arise. Although this has had the satisfactory effect of increasing the resolution rate in cases which have been on hand for over 12 months, it also tends to convey a misleading picture in the table [of time taken to resolve cases]

	1979–80 %	1978–79 %	1977–78 %
Up to 3 months	1.8	3.5	7.5
3–6 months	22.7	29.0	40.8
6–9 months	31.6	37.3	31.5
9–12 months	18.7	17.4	13.0
Over 12 months	25.2	12.8	7.2

... Problems of this nature are frustrating in that they tend to negate successful efforts in other parts of the Office, often achieved by the regular review and adaptation of working procedures to meet changing circumstances. Any interruption of the smooth flow of work creates an increase in the number of time consuming enquiries received from applicants who, understandably, are concerned about the progress of their case. The overall effect of this is to delay still further consideration of work on hand. [16th Report of CICB, Cmnd 8081 (1980), para. 32.]

In 1981 the CICB made inroads in its backlog (about 1,500 cases). But its inquisitorial procedures take time (e.g. in collecting information from outside bodies) and by 1983 the backlog was 3,440 cases (see Cmnd 9093 (1983), p. 4).

Here Lord Longford describes inquisitorial procedure (HL Deb. vol. 401, col. 235):

Today there is much that we cannot discover, including, of course, the reason why claims are turned down. I went as a claimant's friend (the claimant was not allowed legal aid) before an appeal tribunal not long ago. The claim had already been turned down once after it had been examined on paper without the applicant being seen by anyone. This time a high official of the board (who must be deemed to have had a good deal to do with turning down the original claim) appeared in person against my friend. The result seemed like a foregone conclusion, and certainly the verdict went against us. No reasons were given. There was no appeal to the court. Under a statutory scheme it would be more likely that justice would be done, and far more likely that it would be seen to be done.

Here Lord Longford makes four points; test them against the Franks recommendations. He complains (a) that the Board was both judge and prosecutor; (b) that the Board gave no reasons for its decision; (c) that the proceedings were private and (d) that he could not appeal. The evidence of the annual reports and the case law is that the Board does give reasons, adequate as a basis for judicial review. Is it true to say that there is 'no appeal to a court'? Has Lord Longford misunderstood the inquisitorial style of the Board's procedures? And is there a case for privacy here? Remember that the Council on Tribunals exceptionally conceded the case for private hearings, e.g. in vaccine damage tribunals. Hearings before SBATs are also private. The Board is not a 'court', which can confer immunity from civil liability on witnesses. Its decisions involve findings of criminality in incidents which have not always come to trial; some victims may complain of domestic violence. The Board explains that it will have 'power to publish information about its decisions in individual cases; this power will be limited only by the need to preserve the anonymity of applicants and other parties' (Scheme, para. 24).

The establishment of machinery for adjudication operated by lawyers has meant a steady progress towards formality and entitlement, tempting the courts to fill the major gap by creating a right to judicial review. Yet we might argue – like the Home Office working party set up to review the scheme in 1974 – that little is gained by the extra-statutory format. The working party thought the external controls unsatisfactory and proposed a short statute to regularize the position. It was 'anomalous that the Board's decisions should continue not to be subject to a formal avenue of appeal'. They recommended substitution of appeal on a point of law to the High Court. They also thought the CICB should be brought under the supervision of the Council on Tribunals 'in accordance with the general principle that all new statutory tribunals should come under the jurisdiction of the Council'. Finally, 'the administrative aspects of the work of the Board and its staff [should] be made subject to the supervision of the PCA'.

Ought we to be concerned that the 'short statute' has not so far materialized?[8a] Lord longford thought so:

The most obvious advantage of a statutory scheme would be that in the last resort there would be an appeal to the courts and much of the mystery that inevitably attaches to a bureaucratic scheme of the kind that we have today would be dissipated.

His last point is important. We said earlier that the scheme was thought to be working well. On reflection, we should have said that we know of no evidence that it is not. One effect of the traditional, narrow, focus of administrative law on courts and tribunals may be that administrative procedures are not properly tested by research studies.

2 Vaccine damage: 'A sad and sorry policy'?

Vaccine damage payments are in some senses an offshoot of the thalidomide tragedy. Thalidomide was a tranquillizer which, prescribed at a sensitive stage during pregnancy, was shown to damage the foetus. Marketed in the U K by Distillers Ltd, the drug led to the birth of children with severe congenital deformities. The affair exposed serious weaknesses in the English legal system. Settlement took ten years or more, during which time the children had been supported in part from a charitable fund administered by Lady Hoare, to which the Government had contributed. Thalidomide victims faced a number of legal problems, including doubt whether the common law acknowledged rights in an unborn child.[9] It was hard to prove a causal link between deformity and administration of the drug. There were also practical problems in obtaining evidence and access to confidential documents or even in getting legal aid. The affair is sufficient in itself to cast serious doubt on Linden's picture of 'tort law as Ombudsman'. Without the help of the *Sunday Times* and determined M Ps, notably Mr Ashley, settlement could never have been achieved.

The thalidomide tragedy provided a climate of sympathy from which the vaccine damage campaign benefitted. It also provided a pool of expertise on which to draw. The Association of Parents of Vaccine Damaged Children was formed which received support from M Ps, especially Mr Ashley, by now a seasoned campaigner for the disabled. Alive to the possibilities inherent in Europe, the group sponsored an unsuccessful complaint to the European Commission on Human Rights. It lodged a complaint with the PCA. Adjournment debates and parliamentary questions were used systematically by MPs to forward the campaign.

Vaccination is not compulsory in Britain but is strongly encouraged by government and must be provided free at the request of a parent by a local health authority. The vaccination most likely to cause adverse reactions is that for whooping cough (pertussis), but an epidemic of whooping cough can be serious. Before routine vaccination in 1957, 85,000 cases and 88 deaths were notified; in 1973, when 79 per cent of children were being vaccinated, 2,500 cases and two deaths were notified. Thus the DHSS, which is responsible for health education and coordination of the vaccination programme, had good cause to be alarmed when, by 1976, pertussis vaccination had fallen to 38 per cent (now 35 per cent). A principal cause of this fall was fear that adverse reaction might cause irreversible brain damage or severe disability. The risk, about 1 in 10,000 vaccinations, had been widely publicized, in part due to the campaign by the Association.

The legal problem for vaccine damaged children is partly similar to that encountered by thalidomide litigants: causation. Many young babies suffer spontaneously from fits, a major symptom of vaccine damage. It is equally difficult to pin liability to any sufficiently proximate act or omission. Negligence in the preparation or administration of the vaccine could found liability, though the burden of proof is heavy. The alternative would be to show negligence by the DHSS in the exercise of its advisory and supervisory functions. Clearly, the reasoning of *Anns* v. *Merton LBC* might create difficulties here. In a House of Lords debate, for example, Lord Campbell stated that if the DHSS were negligent, 'having regard to the fact that it recommended such vaccination but failed to warn the parents and failed to tell them of the contra-indications . . . this would not give rise to any liability whatever, because if a discretionary power is exercised *bona fide* within the ambit of the statute, the law gives no redress' (HL Deb. vol. 436, col. 1242). Do you agree with this statement of the law?

Plaintiffs also face severe procedural problems. Access to medical records is not easy, there are difficulties in obtaining statements from NHS employees and of overcoming reluctance by professionals to give evidence against their colleagues. These problems are accentuated by the fact that everyone concerned is likely to be in the employ of the NHS or the powerful government department responsible for it. In one adjournment debate, an exasperated MP (Mr Adley) described litigation with the NHS as 'sparring with a gigantic octopus' (HC Deb. vol. 928, col. 1245).[10]

Can public law techniques come to the aid of litigants in this position? The complaint referred to Sir Idwal Pugh by the Association fell into two parts: the first concerned information available to doctors and parents concerning adverse reaction, the second involved investigation of four test-cases from 380 recorded by the Association.

His dual function as PCA and Health Services Commissioner (HSC) gave Sir Idwal access to the records of the DHSS and the Scottish Home and ∙Health Department (SHHD), regional practitioners and health visitors. He was in no doubt over the departments' advisory functions; compare his attitude to that, for example, of Lord Diplock in *Dorset Yacht*:

The issue in this investigation has been the way in which the policy for whooping cough vaccination has been administered. In this I have found the role of the Departments to be central, although the Departments have sought to limit and in a sense to minimise their role . . . [They] give the appearance of thinking that [this] consisted of transmitting scientific and expert opinion . . . I believe that the role and therefore the responsibility, of the Departments is much more fundamental. The expert committees which they have set up . . . certainly provide the Departments with advice of high quality: and they take responsibility for that advice. But the responsibility for accepting that advice, for deciding whether alternative and differing views should be consulted or accepted, and for transmitting that advice with the authority of the Departments, lies and can only lie with the Departments. Indeed I have seen that at all points the Departments' Chief Medical Officers were involved in considering the advice . . . and that Ministers were consulted before the advice was transmitted . . . Since 1963, the Departments have indicated in their circulars and booklets addressed to doctors that there are reservations about whooping cough vaccination for some children. With the passage of time these warnings have become more positive . . . Bearing in mind that Departmental literature was not the only source of guidance available to doctors, I conclude that the Departments acted reasonably in this respect . . . [But] I have found no evidence that, until the Association . . . raised the issue in 1974, the Departments had given any thought to the advantage of adding . . . advice that went further than a suggestion that parents should consult a doctor or clinic . . . In this respect at least parents should have had better information. The parent is in the best position to observe the child's reactions and I think the Departments missed an important opportunity of helping doctors, and of safeguarding against unwitting administration of repeat injections in unsuitable cases . . . The latest leaflet does this . . . [but it] was published only recently. The responsibility for the administration of policy on whooping cough vaccination rests squarely on the Departments. I consider that they have not fully recognised this responsibility in the past. The responsibility falls, in broad terms, into two parts: the provision of information to doctors through medical channels and the provision of information direct to the public . . . I consider that the Departments must accept a large measure of responsibility and I believe that they should have recognised earlier the desirability of alerting parents, as they have now done. [HC 571 (1976/7), paras. 51–62.]

The PCA was less forthright in his investigation of the specific cases. Case A he decided fell outside his jurisdiction as involving 'clinical judgement.'[10a] Case B also involved clinical judgement but the PCA thought that in any case the health visitor concerned was not to blame as the departmental literature would not have enabled her to recognize epilepsy as a contra-indication. In case C clinical judgement was also involved, though again the PCA saw no reason to criticise anyone. His sole criticism was addressed to the fact that an appointment card had been sent to parents whose child had already been hospitalized; and the computerized system made this unavoidable. Case D involved a conflict of evidence between a mother and a health visitor, both of whom were interviewed by the investigators. The PCA felt unable to resolve the difference between the mother's recollection and that of the visitor. 'The evidence does not entitle me to criticize the health visitor's performance or the Health Board's procedures.'

In the light of the cases in Chapter 12, could legal liability be founded on anything in this report? Can you connect Sir Idwal Pugh's concern for publicity with an earlier PCA report?

Now let us return to the political campaign. The Government response to the thalidomide tragedy was to set up the Pearson Commission on Civil Liability and Compensation for Personal Injury. One response to the vaccine damage campaign was to refer the question to Pearson. The Association presented evidence. In its report, the Commission recommended absolute liability in tort to any child injured through the administration of a vaccine on the recommendation of a central government department or a local authority. The burden of proof would remain on the plaintiff to show causation. But Pearson was worried that this would create an anomalous exception. There are about 100,000 severely disabled children in the country and significantly Pearson (para. 1501) went outside its terms of reference to recommend a weekly payment of £4 (at 1977 rates) to *all* children 'suffering from a long term mental or physical handicap (but not necessarily a permanent one) which causes the child's performance or development to fall far below those of other children of the same age'.

In the meantime, the Labour Government had intervened. The Health Minister, Mr Ennals, announced an 'interim compensation scheme'. A payment of £10,000 would be made to any severely disabled child (or adult since the scheme was retroactive to 1947) who 'on balance of probabilities' had suffered vaccine damage. The payment would be without prejudice to existing rights in tort or indeed to the pending recommendations of the Pearson Commission.

Why did the Government step outside the normal rules of civil liability to accept responsibility in this exceptional case? The Minister described the scheme as 'a way in which the community as a whole has sought to share a responsibility for the hardship which has fallen upon [these children]' (HC Deb. vol. 949, col. 977). Welcoming the Bill on behalf of the Opposition, Dr Vaughan implied a 'special case' or obligation:

A child is vaccinated partly for his own protection but also for the sake of society . . . Society has asked for children to be vaccinated and the Government representing society have endorsed the procedure. It is therefore right that society should shoulder some of the responsibility when the procedure goes wrong. [HC Deb. vol. 962, col. 40.]

Here, from Fleming, is the argument against 'special cases'; but can you recall a theory of governmental responsibility which could accommodate the case of vaccine damage?

In what way, one might ask, were the thalidomide children more deserving of public generosity in Britain than the 1,000 other handicapped children born every week or the 100,000 severely handicapped children under sixteen who must be content with the benefits of the general social security program? For that matter, how are we to justify the disparity between the . . . grants . . . of £10,000 to serious vaccine victims and the £54,000 that were eventually awarded to each of the thalidomide children? . . . Special compensation plans . . . suggest a potentially serious problem of injustice. If the current treatment of a given class of victims is altered so that it better conforms to that afforded some other similarly situated victims, the change will at the same time place the altered class out of harmony with yet another class of similar victims. [Fleming 1982, p. 319.]

The 'special case' of vaccine damage provides several examples of such discrimination. For example, the scheme can affect a claim for welfare benefits. £10,000 takes the recipient over the £2,000 capital sum which is the threshold for SB claims. The DHSS at first required the surplus capital to be used before a beneficiary under the scheme could claim benefit. After it was pointed out that the Minister had undertaken to the House that this would not occur, the policy was changed. Later, however, the more generous policy was reversed by a new Minister, Mr Boyson, who denied that there had been any change in the rules and blamed the misunderstanding on an unnamed civil servant. The effect is to deprive poor claimants of their awards at the age of 16. Again, the scheme creates 'hard cases' because it is restricted to those who can prove 80 per cent disablement; with 75 per cent disability a child receives nothing. To many this seems arbitrary and unfair. But the limitation corresponds to that imposed by social security legislation generally (e.g. for invalidity benefit) and Dworkin (1979, p. 334) argues that it is justified by administrative convenience. 'The answer is that lines must be drawn somewhere: from the point of view of speed, simplicity and cost and in accordance with the Pearson theme that payments are confined to the severely disabled.' Compare the attitudes of the PCA and the DHSS to rationing in the Invalid Tricycles cases.

The Vaccine Damage scheme is formal and the rules leave administrators with a minimum of discretion. By the Vaccine Damage Payment Act 1979, the Minister must make a payment of £10,000 if he is satisfied that an application meets the conditions of entitlement set out in ss. 1 and 2. Review of ministerial decisions by an independent tribunal, subject to the Council on Tribunals, is provided. Procedural details are contained in the Vaccine Damage Payments Regulations SI No. 432/79 which have been referred to the Council. An information leaflet is published by the DHSS and applications are made on a claim form available from local offices.

When the scheme was initiated, the DHSS anticipated about 700 awards at a cost of £7 million, spread over several years. By June 1981, 2,716 claims had been received; 338 claimants were able to satisfy the Minister at the initial stage; 1,362 claimants, of whom 79 withdrew, went on to a tribunal. Of the 1,103 cases then determined, 308 were successful (HC Deb. vol. 7, WA col. 112). By August 1982 when 2,797 claims had been received, Melville and Johnson calculated that 13 per cent of claims succeeded at the initial stage. Of the 60 per cent of unsuccessful claimants who went on to a tribunal, 28 per cent succeeded; 708 payments had been made – a success rate of 26 per cent (*The Guardian*, 1 December 1982).

A renewed campaign followed publication of these figures.[11] The first line of attack concerned the Government's failure either to implement the Pearson recommendations (above) or to increase the

£10,000. The arbitrary, fixed sum was compared to the sums paid to
the victims of crime and patterned on civil damages. Lord Winstanley
argued (HL Deb. vol. 436, col. 1244) that vaccine damage was a
'special case', meriting full state responsibility:

> ... where parents take specific action, medically, in relation to their children,
> on the advice of Government, not necessarily in the specific interests of the
> child but in the interests of the community as a whole, then one ought to
> accept that society has a greater responsibility than it might have towards the
> occurrence of serious damage in other ways.

Attacks were also made on the tribunals. The chairman is a
qualified lawyer who sits with two medical assessors. By s.4(4) of the
1979 Act, their decision is to be conclusive unless the Minister agrees
to reconsider on the ground of material change in circumstances or
mistake of fact (s.5). But the tribunals are subject to the Tribunals
and Inquiries Act 1971, which provides appeal to the High Court on a
point of law.[12] Thus the tribunals are relatively formal. Yet Lord
Campbell argued (HL Deb. vol. 436, col. 1243) that *the Minister*
should not have played any part in the process of adjudication 'upon
delicate and intricate matters concerning the welfare of children
which, by tradition, properly lie within the province of the courts of
law'. Remember the reasons given by Wade (above, p. 71) for
preferring tribunals to courts. The question for a tribunal to decide
here is whether the claimant is or was before his death 'severely
disabled' as a result of 'the vaccination to which the claim relates'.
Would you allocate the decision to a tribunal or to a court? Why?

The *Guardian* article pointed to variations between the seven
regional tribunals, alleging that 38 per cent of claims succeeded in
Nottingham against 18 per cent in Edinburgh. The authors argued,
too, that the tribunals were less than independent. 'The closing of
institutional ranks can be impossible to overcome, for, with the sole
exception of the chairman of the tribunal, every person with whom
the claimant has to deal is likely to be employed by the DHSS'
(Melville and Johnson, *The Guardian*, 1 December 1982). A parliamentary question by Mr Ashley produced Table 10 which reveals the
full extent of variation. Asked to take steps to rectify the discrepancies, Lord Trefgarne, speaking for the Government, gave the
classic constitutional reply, 'Vaccine Damage Tribunals are independent adjudicating authorities and it would be inappropriate for
me to comment on their decisions' (HL Deb. vol. 438, col. 1318).

Earlier, Dworkin had foreseen a difficulty which may account for

Table 10. Vaccine Damage Tribunals 1979–82

Tribunal	1979		1980		1981		1982*	
	Number of cases reviewed	% successful	Number of cases reviewed	% successful	Number of cases reviewed	% successful	Number of cases reviewed	% successful
Belfast	0	—	40	20	6	17	3	0
Cardiff	13	8	118	25	18	44	7	14
Edinburgh	8	25	70	19	36	14	8	50
Leeds	15	27	83	25	16	31	7	14
London	33	36	307	25	84	35	17	47
Manchester	13	38	133	31	20	35	4	50
Nottingham	12	33	123	41	26	31	15	47

Source: HC Deb. Vol. 35, WA cols. 291–2.
* To 15 October.

the low success rate. The Act required the Minister to be 'satisfied' but it failed to relax the civil standard of proof. The applicant must show 'causation', on which civil actions frequently founder, on a balance of probabilities. The DHSS was placed in an awkward dilemma:

It is possible for the [DHSS] to deny most claimants on the ground that causation cannot be proved – but that is not the intention; if evidence is accepted too readily then the parties may be satisfied, but the practice may go well beyond the authority of the Act . . . if causation is admitted for one purpose, how can the DHSS deny causation in later civil proceedings against them, without also confessing that the Act was being administered too liberally? The Government's extra-statutory attempt to be generous creates an impossible dilemma. [Dworkin 1979, p. 335.]

We might argue that an informal, ex gratia, administrative payment would meet Dworkin's objection by releasing the department from its dilemma. The success rate might improve but then again, it might not. Discretion is a two-edged sword.

3 The Employment Act: 'the Minister's say-so'

Between September 1974, when the 'closed shop' provisions of the Trade Union and Labour Relations Act 1974 became operative and August 1980 when they were amended by the Employment Act 1980, a number of people were dismissed from their jobs for not being members of a trade union in a closed shop. The 1980 Act prohibited dismissal for refusal to join a union in a 'closed shop' in certain circumstances. 'Unfair dismissal' in contravention of these provisions can be referred to an industrial tribunal which has power to award compensation. This is not a state compensation scheme and the provisions are purely prospective. But Sched. 1 of the Employment Act 1982 provides that the limited class of employees dismissed during the currency of the 1974 Act may retroactively file a claim for compensation from the Department of Employment. Because the closed shop is particularly controversial, this small compensation scheme generated more political heat than any which has so far been mentioned. The Opposition attacked it as retrospective legislation which was discriminatory and unfair. The Government replied that the scheme was necessitated by the judgment of the European Court of Human Rights in *Young, James and Webster* v. *UK* (1982) 4 EHRR 38, in which the dismissal by British Rail of non-union employees who refused to join a union after a closed shop was declared at their work-place was held to be a breach of the Convention. As a settlement had been negotiated, however, the three applicants did not themselves fall under the scheme.

By Sched. 1 of the 1982 Act, the Employment Secretary may 'if he thinks fit' pay to any person who satisfies criteria set out in the schedule, an amount 'not exceeding that specified.' Para. 3 links the sum payable to the sums which would have been awarded if the claimant could have sued successfully for wrongful dismissal and para. 2 limits claims to those who, during the life of the 1974 legislation, 'did not bring or brought but did not succeed in' a complaint of unfair dismissal but could have succeeded under the provisions of the 1980 legislation. Applications are to be made in writing to the Minister who may, if he thinks fit, refer them to an 'appointed person'. Where this is done, the applicant will be allowed to make representations, including oral representations, if he so wishes (para. 6). The Minister must take into account both the assessor's report and any previous findings of an industrial tribunal, but neither binds him. The assessor actually appointed by the Minister is an experienced barrister, recently retired as Solicitor to the Department of Employment (Mr John Billam).

Opposition fury might be dismissed as an over-reaction. After all, the scheme was strictly limited; an estimate of £2 million to a limited class of 400 people was mentioned, though if one reason for choosing administrative procedures is cost, then the estimated sum of £250,000 for administration of this tiny scheme seems unduly high. But the Opposition did raise serious points about accountability. The Act did not grant the Minister unlimited discretion, as it set out the conditions of entitlement, but it did permit him to disallow a claim without giving any reason and without appeal. The Opposition insisted that the function was *judicial*. Proper adjudicative machinery was essential. A one-man tribunal sitting in secret would not do:

The hearings would be analogous to industrial tribunals. Most of the terminology has been borrowed directly from that of industrial tribunals . . . The scheme is a new type of industrial tribunal operated by one man with his friends, his dogs or whatever, as assessors. In industrial tribunals names are published, and many of those applying will be people who have already been before industrial tribunals and given their names, but this time they will not have to give their names. It is all most peculiar. [HC SCG 1981/2, col. 271.]

Mr Mikardo thought the Minister would benefit from a proper tribunal in another way:

I am not saying that Ministers ought always to seek to hide behind the skirts of an organisation in order to avoid responsibility for their decisions. It would be wrong to say that. Ministers have to stand up and be counted on their decisions and carry the can if they turn out to be bad decisions. But we are dealing here with a subject that has aroused very strong emotions. It is an emotive matter, and people with a sense of grievance one way or the other will feel it very deeply and will kick up about it. I should have thought that . . . it would make sense for the Secretary of State to be able to justify a decision in either direction . . . either to give or refuse. It would also make sense if he could justify his decision on the basis that it arose from advice that he was given by a competent person or persons. [SCG 23 February 1982, cols. 51–2.]

The Government replied that privacy was essential. Claimants might be deterred from making claims by fear of reprisals. They cited the precedent of the CICB which, Opposition members pointed out, was hardly analogous because 'although criminal injuries payments are discretionary, if a person is not satisfied with the award given by the single adjudicator, he has a right to appeal to what amounts to a tribunal of three people, who will consider the merits of the case [and] anyone can be told who has been awarded compensation, how much and why'. The Government spokesman (Mr Alison) relied on the absence of legal entitlement to justify the absence of a tribunal. 'No new rights, obligations or liabilities are imposed of the sort which a judicial tribunal is normally regarded as the appropriate forum to consider, examine or determine' (HC Deb. 25 February 1982, col. 54). Adjudication would cause unnecessary delays. 'Because the principle of disbursing public funds, has been endorsed enthusiastically by a majority of more than 100, it would be time consuming, irrelevant and illogical to impose a judicial tribunal.' In any case, adjudication was not entirely disbarred. 'An applicant who was aggrieved by the way in which the statutory discretion was or was not exercised could apply to the High Court for judicial review in certain circumstances.' The Opposition lowered its sights. Mr Varley asked:

. . . that, in this unprecedented situation, a once-for-all report should be made to the House of Commons listing the names of the individuals who have benefited, the compensation, the grounds on which the payments have been made, the names of their former employers, the trade unions to which they did not wish to belong and the reasons for their dismissal. I should have thought that that was a request to which the Government could accede.

[It was] said that it would be possible to table parliamentary questions. I know that there is much more discretion about what goes into a parliamentary answer. Certain information can be withheld on the basis of confidentiality, but it is the same with the report. Information could be withheld there if there were good reasons . . .

What really alarmed me was the Secretary of State's suggestion that in no circumstances would he give information along the lines requested by my hon. Friends, or commit it to a report . . . If the Government refuse . . . I suspect that the Select Committee on Employment will, during the next 15 months, want to know from the Secretary of State what arrangements he has made for compensation. [SCG, 11 March 1982, cols. 282–3.]

Mr Tebbit (Employment Secretary) replied that he would be 'happy and willing to answer parliamentary questions about amounts of money disbursed and the number of people to whom it is disbursed'. The only issue was that of confidentiality; like the Chancellor with tax payments, he declined to provide names.

By June 1983, 435 applications had been received and 54 awards made totalling £261,086 (*The Guardian* 21 June 1983). Ewing and Rees (1983) found the investigatory procedure speedy, efficient and just. But they still felt the precedent was dangerous. The constitutional arguments should be evaluated carefully. Was the Minister's function judicial? Was confidentiality essential or was there, as the Opposition suggested, an exact parallel to a claim of unfair dismissal before an industrial tribunal and, if so, should the decision have been entrusted to the normal system of industrial tribunals? Did the sums involved require a greater measure of accountability to Parliament?

4 Absconding prisoners: 'free insurance'?

Although no reference to this is made in the *Dorset Yacht* case, the Home Office has, since 1950, accepted limited responsibility for damage done by absconders from open prisons and borstals. Shortly after the decision, a complaint made to the PCA revealed the existence of the ex gratia scheme. The complainant lived about 17 miles from a borstal. She complained that the Home Office had refused to compensate her when her garden gate was damaged by an absconder. The PCA's report revealed:

The Department have informed me that they do not accept any general responsibility for damage caused by borstal absconders. They have explained that the Courts have held that in certain circumstances they can be held liable for the damage done by borstal trainees when absconding, but there must have been negligence on the part of someone in the service which led to the escape. The underlying concept is that it is Government policy, based on the public interest, to train borstal boys in conditions which permit absconding and it is therefore right for the public to accept the risks inherent in this policy. But, they say, it ceases to be right when, owing to an accident of geographical

location, an individual member of the public is exposed to greater risk than
the public at large. It has therefore been the policy of the Department, since
1950, to pay compensation on an *ex gratia* basis to members of the public who
suffer loss or damage to their property as a result of offences committed by
absconders, only where the damage occurs in the neighbourhood of the
borstal (and provided also that the loss or damage is not covered by
insurance) . . .

It seemed to me . . . that, although the complainant lived outside the area
which the Home Office accept as the neighbourhood of the borstal, the
damage occurred during the course of the actual pursuit from the borstal, and
the two boys could not in any way be said to have made good their escape. I
therefore suggested to the Department that there might be grounds for
treating her claim as a special case and I asked them whether they would be
prepared to reconsider their decision. The Department informed me that they
could find no grounds for paying her compensation without being prepared
to pay claims at a similar distance from the establishment in future. But they
said that as a result of my investigation they had decided to bring forward a
review of the policy which had been asked for by the Minister of State, with
particular reference to the definition of 'neighbourhood' in relation to penal
establishments. I therefore decided to delay completion of my investigation
until the Home Office had carried out their review . . .

The Home Office have now informed me that they have completed their
review of the policy. They say that in general the compensation scheme has
worked well; and they still consider that *ex gratia* payments should be limited
to claims arising in the vicinity of the establishment. But for a variety of
reasons, including the fact that absconders have become more mobile since
1950, now that transport is more widely available and more of them are able
to drive, the Department have decided that the area which constitutes the
'neighbourhood' of a borstal shall be interpreted more liberally. [HC 42
(1973/4), p. 112.]

The PCA started from departmental guidelines. He did not
question them, but asked the department to treat the complainant as
a 'special case'. Was this because of jurisdiction (see above, p. 201)?
The department refused – compare the attitude of the same PCA and
of the DHSS in the Invalid Tricycles cases – but voluntarily
reviewed the guidelines. Does anything suggest that the terms of the
scheme as set out below postdate the review?

The Department does not admit any legal liability to make compensation in
respect of private property stolen or damaged by inmates when escaping.
However ex gratia compensation will be paid in respect of such loss or
damage subject to the following requirements:

(a) Only cases occurring in the neighbourhood of the institution from which
the escape was made will be considered.
(b) No payment is made when the loss or damage is covered by insurance
except in cases involving damage to cars etc., where compensation may be

paid in respect of 'no claim' bonus.
(c) Escapes from outside hospitals, working parties or from escort when proceeding on transfer are treated in the same way as escapes from actual penal establishments.

['Neighbourhood' is to be interpreted 'as reasonably as possible' and its extent will 'differ from establishment to establishment'.]

We have described the PCA as a window on the administration. Who is able to look through the PCA's window? Are Megarry's worries about the secrecy of 'administrative quasi-law' still justified? Remember that the PCA now publishes only a selection from his investigations.

When the case was reported to the Select Committee, it seemed surprised. Mr Buck doubted the propriety of the payments which he described as 'free insurance'. The Principal Officer (Sir Arthur Peterson) felt that the sums paid out were too small to cause concern and the purpose was reasonable (HC 268 (1974), p. 16):[13]

It was to get people to accept more readily the setting up of an open borstal in their neighbourhood and I would say that the amount of money paid out has been very well justified over the years . . . it has enabled borstals to be set up in different parts of the country which might otherwise not have been set up and the expense of the Government in having to maintain borstal boys would have been greater.

The Committee was apparently satisfied, saying (HC 268 (1974), para. 30):

Your Committee welcome this departure from the neighbourhood principle towards a wide and more generous policy in accepting liability for compensation. This is yet another example of a general improvement in administrative practice assisted by the investigation of an individual case by the Commissioner.

Do you agree? Do you consider that the payments here rest on adequate authority? What further steps could be recommended? Lord Diplock was hesitant about making policy in *Dorset Yacht*, do you consider this administrative policy-making more or less satisfactory? If you look carefully at the PCA's report, you can see at what level the policy decision was taken.

5 Compensating the innocent: 'clean hands'

The state is not legally liable if, as a result of a miscarriage of justice, someone is wrongfully convicted and imprisoned. S.2(5) of the Crown Proceedings Act 1947 provides that the Crown shall not be liable for the torts of its judicial officers. Judges also enjoy a wide measure of personal immunity. Briefly, the immunity extends to all official acts done within the limits of jurisdiction and, in the case of a court of record, to cases where the judge inadvertently exceeds his jurisdiction.[14] This rule leaves someone who has been wrongly convicted without remedy, otherwise than in an exceptional case. An action against the police or prosecuting authorities for wrongful arrest or malicious prosecution, though theoretically possible, is in practice difficult to maintain.[15]

With other compensation schemes, the departments concerned have been able to provide a rough estimate of the extent of the problem. Here it is more difficult. The Home Office has told the House of Commons that it receives about 2,600 petitions annually for review of criminal conviction, but the majority of these concern motoring offences. *Justice* estimated that there might be 200–300 'serious', miscarriages, defined as those involving custodial sentences. The figures produced to the Home Affairs Committee (HAC) by the Home Office did not seem to the Committee to support this conclusion. In the decade 1972–81, there were 34 references to the Court of Appeal by the Home Secretary involving 46 defendants of which 21 cases succeeded. There were 2,247 free pardons with 1,331 remissions of custodial sentence (HC 421 (1982/3), pp. 2–5, App A Tables 1–4). In the same period, there were 47 payments totalling £341,473.00, so compensation in such cases is by no means automatic. Everything depends on the discretion of the Home Secretary, exercised with the advice and support of the 12 members of C5 division of the Home Office.

It is not easy to piece together, from parliamentary questions, a select committee report and other sources, a complete picture of the scheme. Pieces of the puzzle seem always to be missing, the statistics do not tie up and Home Office officials themselves seem unclear how the scheme operates. Brandon and Davies in their book *Wrongful Imprisonment* (1967) found it hard to obtain any information. In the 1970s, pressure mounted, partly in the wake of the *Confait* case, where the wrongful conviction of three young men occasioned by police malpractice resulted in a formal inquiry. Largely due to the efforts of the constituency MP, Mr Chris Price, a free pardon and compensation were finally obtained.[16] The Home Affairs Committee in its report 'Miscarriages of Justice' (HC 421 (1982/3), p. vi) regretfully accepted the views of witnesses that the chances of such a fortunate outcome to a petition 'must sometimes depend less on its intrinsic merits than on the amount of external support and publicity that it was able to attract. In practice the Home Office decision to act may depend upon the amount of pressure that is brought to bear on the Home Secretary by people of influence.' One result has been to open the compensation process to wider public scrutiny and also, it seems, to attract more applications.

In 1971, an investigation by the PCA attracted the attention of the Select Committee. The complainant had been acquitted in 1967 after a retrial, with new evidence, ordered by the Court of Appeal. By then he had served nearly the whole of his 12 months' sentence. He claimed compensation, which was refused, as there were no grounds for thinking that there had been 'negligence or default by the police or the prosecution'. The PCA was told that the Home Office had decided in 1968 not to review its arrangements:

The Department decided that so long as the onus of proof remained upon the prosecution, it would be difficult to justify automatic compensation on acquittal, and that any procedure allowing for the payment of compensation only in selected cases would involve an invidious discrimination which would reflect upon those not compensated. [HC 261 (1970/1), p. 127.]

This was disingenuous. As the Principal Officer (Sir Philip Allen) explained to the Select Committee, ex gratia payments were sometimes made, though there were only five cases in the last three years:

There is no general statutory power saying that because a man has spent so much time in custody, he can be given compensation for that purpose. But we have with Treasury agreement over the years made ex gratia payments in certain circumstances and have had to devise rules in accordance with which those payments are made . . . [HC 513 (1970/1), p. 70.]

Here the implication is that only those who have spent time in custody are eligible. Summarizing the 'rules', Sir Philip divided the cases into two categories. Where there had been a free pardon, compensation was automatic, because 'the state has gone so badly adrift and the man has suffered so much, that compensation is payable quite apart from any question of negligence'. Today we know that for all practical purposes the claimant must have proved his innocence to obtain a free pardon:

. . . a Free Pardon is . . . normally only recommended when there are not merely doubts about the defendant's guilt but convincing grounds for thinking that he was innocent. Nor is it sufficient for this purpose that the defendant is merely 'technically' innocent of the offence. It is a long-established policy that the Free Pardon, as an exceptional act of grace, should be confined as far as possible to those who are morally as well as technically innocent. This 'clean hands' doctrine implies that the Home Secretary must be satisfied . . . that in the incident in question the defendant had no intention of committing an offence and did not in fact commit one. [HC 421 (1982/3), p. 3.]

Sir Philip's second class was where the Court of Appeal had acquitted. Here compensation could be made in cases (a) of particular hardship or (b) of mishandling by the state. It was customary here for ministers to pay rather than stand on their legal rights. Asked whether the Home Office should seek statutory authority, he replied:

This is so small that I do not think that anyone takes objection to this being handled ex gratia in this way. If we were to go in for this in a big way on some sort of routine basis, one would need statutory powers.

This was one reason why cases of remand in custody pending trial followed by an acquittal were not covered by the arrangements. A considerable problem would be created by the 2,000 or more cases each year. Today this embargo remains. Thus the Home Affairs Committee was told that compensation was never made in these cases – though later it emerged that three payments had been made in the period 1979–81! The Committee thought this anomalous, but was told by a Home Office spokesman (HC 421 (1982/3), p. 25) that:

So far at any rate the community through its governments has been prepared to provide for ex gratia compensation only in the limited range of cases we described in the memorandum.[17] To go further than that and to provide for compensation from the state to everybody who having been fed into the criminal justice system through a prosecution is ultimately acquitted would be a very big step.

Notice here that *government* rather than *Parliament* is said to represent the community. And the decision-taking described here is hardly Davis's miniature democratic process. Policy decisions are secret, though parliamentary questions can elicit the 'rules'. And are they 'rules'? Here are the principles set out by the Minister of State (Dr Summerskill) in 1977. The statement is not complete. Is it accurate? No-one, not even the departmental officials, seems sure what the 'rules' are and whether they are being observed consistently. Does the second paragraph suggest anything about the continuity of administration?

If someone thinks that he has grounds for compensation, his legal remedy is to pursue the matter in the civil courts by way of a claim for damages. In exceptional circumstances, however, the Home Secretary may authorise an ex gratia payment from public funds, but this would not normally be done unless there had been some misconduct or negligence on the part of the police or some other public authority . . . Our legal system provides that in criminal cases the onus of proof rests upon the prosecution, and as long as an accused person is not required to prove his innocence it is difficult to justify automatic compensation on acquittal. Nor does it seem possible to discriminate between acquitted defendants except on the ground that where there has been public default it is right that the State should make some recompense.

What other criteria for selecting deserving cases could be adopted? Any other procedure for allowing compensation in selected cases only would involve invidious discriminations that might reflect upon those not compensated. The implication would be that the person whose claim was rejected was somehow regarded as being less innocent than the successful claimant. It is for this reason that the Home Secretary confines the making of ex gratia payments to cases in which the circumstances are compelling and where there has been some default by public authority. [HC Deb. vol. 929, cols. 835–6.]

There is little room in this discretionary scheme for adjudication but, in 1976, the Home Secretary (Mr Jenkins) introduced a hint of independence and openness. The practice was now said to be that, after a decision to compensate was taken, the facts would be submitted to an independent assessor, the Chairman of the CICB, for assessment of the figure to be offered. The Home Secretary is not bound by the advice but in practice it has always been followed. The important concession was that from now on 'the claimant or his solicitor should be informed of the factors which would be taken into account by the assessor, that he should have the opportunity of making personal representations to the assessor and that he should subsequently be given an explanation in broad terms of the basis on which the assessment had been made'. The statement, published as a written answer (HC Deb. vol. 916 pt 2, WA cols. 328–30), details the informal procedure. The assessment is based on written submissions prepared by the Home Office on which the claimant is allowed to comment. His representations are annexed to the memorandum and an interview is available if either the claimant or assessor wishes for one.

The statement also lists the heads of damage, an important concession, as a main complaint has always been that the sums offered are arbitrary, inconsistent and parsimonious. Compensation can cover pecuniary loss including legal costs and expenses incurred in consequence of detention, damage to character or reputation and hardship, including mental suffering etc. But there is still a great deal that we do not know. For example, we do not know the price of a reputation, although the Chairman of the CICB has talked un-officially of a baseline figure of £5,000 for a year in prison for a person of good character. The requirement of good character is not explicitly spelled out by the statement, a fact criticized by one member of HAC (Mr Lyon), who remarked that the most important element in assessment would usually be bad character, yet this was not made plain! The Home Office officials were satisfied. The assessor, they told the Committee, always produced a fully reasoned statement and the claimant was almost always represented. So the informal procedure was 'very much open' for the claimant. 'Character' may explain discrepancies in cases published in a *Justice* report (below). Meehan, pardoned after a confession showed that he was innocent of murder, was offered only £7,500 for seven years imprisonment. At the other extreme is the case of Preece, convicted of murder on the evidence of a Home Office forensic scientist which was later discredited when the official was suspended, and awarded £70,000. Perhaps this settlement reflected possible civil liability? Yet all awards are meant to be patterned on civil liability and punitive or exemplary awards are expressly excluded by the statement. It is all speculation; the anonymous statistics published by the Home Office tell us nothing.

How could we restructure this wide and virtually uncontrolled area of discretionary power? Several patterns have been presented. The Oregon parole model of formal rules openly published and combined with review procedure is one solution. Another is simply to add these cases to the criminal injuries scheme, submitting the modifications to Parliament as is customary. Here are two further models. The first was recommended by the HAC to provide a review of conviction, though not compensation.

The HAC thought the Home Office should filter off both the trivial (motoring) offences and the hopeless appeals. The remainder should be submitted to an independent review body composed of:

... up to a dozen members, under a legally qualified Chairman, appointed either by the Home Secretary or the Attorney-General. Though the membership should include a proportion of criminal lawyers, legal ex-perience ought not to be regarded as the sole qualification. The review body would distribute the casework among its members according to the size of the task involved. While we imagine that in many instances it would be sufficient for a single member to study the appropriate papers, the more controversial papers might be allocated to a panel of three persons. In all cases the conclusions would need to be endorsed by the review body as a whole.

We consider that the review body should be given a very wide measure of discretion as to the procedures they may choose to adopt in any individual case. Once supplied with the facts . . . and such documents as were already available to the Home Office, the review body would decide for themselves what further inquiries were necessary and how or by whom any additional information should be gathered . . . We would expect that, in the majority of cases, the review body would be able to assess the evidence without the need for a formal hearing. They should, however, be empowered . . . to hold a full hearing with legal representation on both sides, and also to recommend the award of legal aid . . . It would also be normal practice for the Home Office to supply the parties concerned with a copy of the reasoned judgment of the case which the review body had submitted to the Home Secretary. [HC 421 (1982/3), pp. xi–xii.]

The Government rejected the idea of a review board on the ground that 'miscarriages of justice which occur within the judicial system, should, so far as possible, be corrected by that system, which itself embodies high and long-established standards of openness and independence' (Cmnd 8856, p. 3).

The approach of *Justice* (1982), dealing only with compensation, was more traditional. They asked for an 'Imprisonment Compensation Board' closely modelled on the CICB, with a legally qualified chairman and members appointed by the Lord Chancellor. Its proceedings would be private, though observers could be admitted, and reasoned decisions would be given. The Board would be entirely responsible for deciding what compensation should be paid and its decisions would not be subject to ministerial review or appeal save to the High Court by way of judicial review. It would report annually to Parliament. *Justice* did not want to tie it down too tightly: 'it is clearly desirable that the Board should be flexible in its approach'. This was partly because they did not want to restrict the right to apply. Claimants who had (a) been granted a free pardon or (b) whose conviction had been quashed on appeal, should have an unrestricted right to apply, and a person acquitted at trial after detention in custody a right conditional on a certificate from the trial judge. Below are *Justice*'s own proposed guidelines (1982, pp. 19–20):

Guidelines for the Imprisonment Compensation Board
(a) After the Board has accepted a claim as falling within its jurisdiction and being worthy of consideration it may refuse or reduce compensation if it considers that:
(i) a conviction has been quashed on grounds that the Board regard as being a mere technicality;
(ii) it would be inappropriate in view of the imprisoned person's conduct in respect of the matters which led to the criminal proceedings;

(iii) the applicant has failed to give reasonable assistance to the Board in its efforts to assess compensation.

(b) In respect of paragraphs (a)(i) and (a)(ii) above, the Board will normally only consider evidence which was advanced at the trial or at the hearing of the appeal, except that it may consider and take into account matters which have come to light in the course of a subsequent investigation.

(c) Where the applicant's claim is accepted as coming within the provisions of the scheme the Board will grant compensation for:

(i) expense reasonably incurred in securing the quashing of the imprisoned person's conviction;

(ii) loss of earnings by the imprisoned person or any dependent person where such loss is a direct consequence of the imprisonment;

(iii) any other expenses or loss which are reasonably incurred upon imprisonment either by the imprisoned person or any dependent person;

(iv) pain suffering and loss of reputation suffered by the imprisoned person or by the imprisoned person's dependants.

The Board will reduce any award by the amount of any other compensation or damages already received by the claimant.

(d) Compensation will not be paid if the assessment is less than £250.

(e) A person compensated by the Board will be required to undertake that any damages, settlement or compensation he may subsequently receive in respect of his wrongful imprisonment will be repaid to the Board up to the amount awarded by the Board.

Remember the arguments against allowing tribunals to proliferate. How close is this proposal to the CICB model? Should this new jurisdiction be allocated to the CICB? Why is *appeal* to the courts, in your view, precluded? Is this desirable? Compare the view of the Home Office working party on criminal injuries compensation. Note the views of the HAC on non-legal membership. What might be the advantages of a tribunal over this 'administrative' board? Do you agree with the Government that judicial errors should be corrected by the judicial system? If so, should a right of action against the state be created?

On p. 388, we set out some questions which we thought relevant to administrative compensation. By now, you will be able to answer some of them. Can you go further to deduce 'general principles' of the type which traditional administrative law favours? Should every decision to refuse 'compensation' be appealable, for example, and can you define 'compensation' with sufficient precision? Are tribunals inherently preferable to boards and what value-judgements shaped your answer? Or is every situation a 'special case' demanding functionalist treatment?

14
Planning and participation

1 The planning process

Opening a generalist study of planning, Hall (1982, p. 1) points out
that the word is ambiguous and difficult to define. Its divergent
meanings are, however, connected. 'Planning' may mean simply a
scheme for accomplishing an objective or purpose, in which case it is
an operational technique or method. In this sense, few human
activities are today carried out without planning:

We talk about planning the economy to minimize the swings of boom and
slump, and reduce the miseries of unemployment; we hear about a housing
plan and a social-services plan. Industry now plans on a colossal scale: the
production of a new model of a car, or a typewriter has to be worked out many
years in advance of its appearance in the shops . . .
Whether labelled free enterprise or social democratic or East European
socialist or Maoist, no society on earth today provides goods and services for
its people, or schools and colleges for its children, without planning. One
might regret it and wish for a simpler age when perhaps things happened
without forethought; if that age ever existed, it has gone for ever. [Hall 1982,
p. 4.]

Although planning in this general sense is frequently a 'private'
activity, it cannot be denied that modern governments are primarily
elected to 'plan'. Planning is today an output function of government
comparable to rule-making or rule-application, and an important
method of policy formulation and decision-taking. The study of
governmental planning of this type could be approached in two ways.
First we could adopt the theoretical angle chosen in Chapter 5 for our
study of rule-making, in which case our subject would become the
theory of decision-taking. Thus, Hall (1981, p. 1), defining planning
as 'a set of *processes* whereby decision-makers engage in logical
foresight before committing themselves', lists the stages in decision-
taking as: problem definition, problem analysis, goal and objective

setting, forecasting, problem projection, design of alternative solutions, decision processes, implementation processes, monitoring, control and updating. In short, he depicts planning as a continuous process, the product of a discrete intellectual discipline with its own methodology whose distinctive vocabulary we would need to learn.

We might on the other hand, adopt a functionalist approach by selecting for study a limited area of governmental activity, e.g. housing or education, and making an 'in-depth' study of policy formulation and decision-taking therein. We might, for example, study London's transportation problems. We would then be in a better position to decide whether the decision in the *Bromley* case was 'wrong' and to assess the argument that the House gave the wrong 'weight' to the factors which prompted the G LC's policy of heavily subsidized fares. Hall (1981) makes just such a study of two of the more controversial aspects of London's transportation: the projected third airport which has never materialized and the piecemeal strategy for London's motorways. These case studies are designed to illustrate the approach of modern, western society to the output of 'public goods', by which we mean goods – like defence, schools or hospital facilities – which can be produced and consumed only on a collective basis.

The second meaning to planning is locational or geographical. 'Planning' here refers to a '*physical plan* showing the distribution of activities and their related structures (houses, factories, offices, schools) in geographical space' (Hall 1981, p. 2). So 'planning' is town and country planning. Once again, the term may be widely or narrowly construed. We might confine ourselves to 'land use planning', treating social issues primarily as the context in which spatial planning occurs. For example, changing patterns of family life may affect the country's housing needs or the rise in car ownership may mean a shift from inner urban to suburban life. The term 'regional planning', on the other hand, commonly denotes 'economic planning'. Spatial planning will here be only one dimension of the plan. Later we shall see that there is some dispute amongst planners whether land use planning is sensible or even feasible except in the context of wider economic and social plans.

Physical or geographical planning can also be approached functionally. For example, we could make a case study of government's policy for 'New Towns' or study the development of a particular new town like Stevenage[1] or of an 'Urban Development Area' like

Merseyside or the London Docks. A study of this type would help us to understand why locational planning tends to broaden out from the limited notion of the use of physical space. For example, consider two major planning applications (a) to allow the reprocessing of nuclear waste at Windscale (1977) and (b) to install a new type of pressurized water nuclear reactor (the PWR) at Sizewell (1983). Ostensibly separate decisions about the use of land in different areas of Britain, they are fairly obviously linked by the common thread of nuclear energy policy. But nuclear energy brings into consideration conventional energy resources. The Windscale and Sizewell decisions may thus be connected with other decisions hotly contested on environmental grounds, to permit extension of mining activities in the picturesque Vale of Belvoir (1980).[2] Again, security and defence are relevant considerations because the vulnerability to guerrilla attack of nuclear installations and transport facilities for nuclear waste are issues of public concern. And in his study of the Windscale decision, Breach (1978, p. 122) goes much further, arguing that the whole of the 'mainstream environmental dialectic' was relevant. He describes this dialectic as a live discipline drawing together 'the work of economists, anthropologists, statisticians, life-scientists and others'. Although it possesses the common theme of respect for global ecology or 'instructions for the care and maintenance of a small planet', it is highly specialized and technical, ranging from 'plant genetics to ekistics, agronomy to energy strategy, wildlife protection to resource conservation, population theory to pollution abatement'. Clearly it is not an easy matter to accommodate issues of this type within the planning process. You may indeed feel that such decisions cannot be made at all unless some way is found to narrow the issues and the arguments. This is a constantly recurring theme in planning and one which arises particularly in the context of the planning inquiry.

Provided that we do not adhere too slavishly to our divisions, it is convenient to divide post-war planning into three main phases.[3] Each results from an overhaul of the system and is marked by the report of a royal commission or advisory committee which found expression in statute. Our first phase dates from the post-war reconstruction and ends in the late 1960s with the report of the Planning Advisory Group (PAG) and legislation in 1968, later consolidated as the Town and Country Planning Act (TCPA) 1971. The second phase ends in the late 1970s with the Dobry Review of the Development Control System and a further review by the Expenditure Committee of the House of

Commons. The third phase is inaugurated by the Local Government, Planning and Land Act (LGPLA) 1980.

The basis of the modern planning system is a series of statutes passed in the immediate post-war years. The experience of war was an eloquent testimony to the need for land use planning, while the devastation of many cities provided a challenge to planners as well as an opportunity for planning. For example, in 1943, the Coalition Government commissioned from Patrick Abercrombie, a leading planner of the day, a regional development plan for the whole of the Greater London area. Equally, however, the post-war legislation embodied experience of the inter-war period of depression, founded on the report of the Barlow Commission,[4] which was established in 1937 to consider the problems posed by the uneven distribution of industry throughout the country. The Commission reported in 1940. The report was not unanimous but the members were agreed on a greater measure of national and regional planning to promote the dispersal of industry, too narrowly concentrated in the Greater London area. An extension of the existing statutory powers was recommended, together with further studies to establish what measures might be appropriate. The response of the Coalition Government was to establish committees. The first, chaired by Lord Justice Scott, considered land use in the rural areas.[5] A second, chaired by Lord Reith, then Minister of Works, considered the dispersal of population from crowded conurbations into 'New Towns'.[6] A third, chaired by Lord Justice Uthwatt,[7] was commissioned to inquire into land values. It faced two linked problems: compensation for land purchased compulsorily and betterment, by which is meant rises in land value resulting from development. Uthwatt's radical proposals for the nationalization of all undeveloped land were never implemented, a compromise solution which was less politically controversial being selected as the basis of compensation under the Town and Country Planning Act 1947. In Chapter 12 we saw how land value raises politically divisive and contentious issues fundamental to the organization of society. As with industrial relations legislation, the prescriptions of one government are regularly swept away by the next; for example, the Community Land Act 1975, a determined effort by the Labour Government to secure development value for the community, was promptly repealed by the incoming Conservative administration of 1979. We do not need to describe the arrangements for compensation,[8] but we do need to bear in mind the extent to which this question of land values lies concealed behind the planning system.[9] This will become more apparent when in Chapter 15 we discuss the topic of planning gain and planning bargains.

The recommendations of these various committees, in the main, reached the statute book. The Distribution of Industry Act 1945 provided some control over the location of new industry. The New Towns Act 1946 provided the means for establishing new towns and New Towns Corporations to run them. The National Parks and Access to the Countryside Act 1949 laid the foundations for rural conservation. Finally, the Town and Country Planning Act 1947 established the general machinery of planning.[10]

The 1947 system had two main aspects, sometimes described as 'positive' and 'negative'. 'Positive planning' refers to the obligation of the planning authority, first imposed by TCPA 1947, to draw up a general development plan for its area. In contrast to the post-war system of social assistance, which is organized on a national basis (below, Chapter 18), the planning system has never been centralized. True, a new Ministry of Town and Country Planning was charged with the task of devising and coordinating national policy on land use and development but the Ministry's functions, although they should not be underplayed, were essentially supervisory. Approval was required for development plans and the Minister decided planning appeals, but the mechanics of planning were left to local authorities, i.e. the existing counties and county boroughs. The Act required every planning authority to prepare and submit by July 1951 a development plan for ministerial approval. Development plans were to be reviewed quinquenially. The format of the plan was closely regulated by the Town and Country Planning (Development Plan) Regulations 1948. Based on detailed maps, the plan was precise, specific and complicated. It regulated the uses to which land could be put, zoning the area for various purposes. Planning was spatial planning.

To ensure that the plan was implemented, authorities relied on 'negative planning' or development control.[11] All 'development', defined as the carrying out of building, engineering, mining or other operations in, on, over or under land, or the making of any material change in the use of any buildings or other land, after 1947 required the permission of the local planning authority. The legislation provided for the Minister to create exceptions to this general principle by statutory instrument. This was done in the General Development Order which specified classes of 'permitted development' and the Use Classes Order which permitted certain 'changes of use' (the *Belfast Corporation* case (above, p. 356) illustrates how this system is intended to work). In granting or refusing planning permission, the planning authority was required to have regard to the provisions of its development plan. Thus the two facets of planning interlock and development has been described as 'the business end' of the planning system (Grant 1982, p. 145).

A number of factors contributed to the discontent which, by the mid-sixties, was felt with the planning process. Some do not really concern us here: for example, that a system designed to cater for public sector development, was being asked to cope with one in which private sector development predominated or that society's behaviour patterns refused to conform to the predictions of the planners. More relevant to our general theme are complaints which concerned the administrative process. Here we find something of a contradiction. We have described the planning system as decentralized, but it was also highly centralized at the stage when planning appeals and development plans had to be referred for ministerial decision and approval. The detailed format of the development plan combined with inadequate resources both in the Ministry and in the planning departments of the counties and county boroughs, to overload the system. Local authorities took many years over the survey and analysis on which their plan was based. A further two-three years might elapse in securing departmental approval. Many quinquennial reviews never took place.[12] Plans became outdated and the system proved inflexible. Grant (1982, pp. 83–4) describes a situation in which both local authorities and the Ministry found it advantageous to by-pass the formal system. Development plans tied the hands of planning authorities in deciding planning applications and, as they became out of date, this might be disadvantageous. S.36 TCPA 1947 allowed authorities to disallow development in the absence of a completed plan on the basis of the policies likely to be included in the plan; thus pending adoption of a plan, the authority had more discretion. Grant feels this was 'doubtless a factor inhibiting enthusiasm for speedy plan preparation in some cases'. The Ministry's reaction to its own shortcomings was also to rely on discretion. 'Authorities were discouraged from using the machinery of the Act, and steered instead towards the use of non-statutory policies . . .

which would fill policy gaps on an interim basis, pending full review of the statutory plan.'

Together with a feeling that development plans did not accurately reflect the rapidly changing social scene, came changes in the planner's attitude to his own discipline. We have described the development plan as based on a detailed map, hence as relatively static. By the 1960s, a more fluid planning sequence, influenced by the new science of cybernetics, was becoming fashionable.[13] The new system was based on a continuous flow of information subject to an ongoing process of evaluation. Goals, objectives and policies represented diagrammatically replaced the map. At the same time, 'planning' broadened out in two ways. First, the aspirations of the planner extended beyond purely spatial objectives. Describing with 'a certain amount of unease' one leading planner's metaphor of 'a helmsman steering the city', McAuslan (1974, p. 140) cites a definition from a prestigious group of environmental planners which many would find still more unnerving:

We use the word planner because it is convenient and short. But we mean by it a person contributing to urban governance through the planning process . . . whatever his precise role in the managing system (he may be a politician, a director, a manager, an analyst, a model builder); whether he is engaged within or without a statutory planning process (planners may be in community organisations for instance); whether a member of a professional institute or not; and regardless of the particular field with which he is concerned (it may be the physical environment, economic development, education, the local authority budget or organisation itself – and so on) . . . [Centre for Environmental Studies, 1973, p. 10.]

Secondly, and perhaps in consequence, planning needed to be carried out over wider areas. There was a feeling that the locally based planning system could not deal with problems of national transportation or of regional economic growth. Such ideas produced pressure for a reform of the local government system (see below) which proceeded parallel to reform of the planning system. Contemporary visions of the planning process merged, under the common influence of planning theory, with contemporary trends in city management, urban government and regional planning.[14]

In 1965, the Minister of Housing and Local Government (Mr Crossman) called together a Planning Advisory Group (PAG), described in his *Diary* (vol. 1, p. 81) as a 'stunningly able and successful group of town clerks, treasurers and planners . . . working . . . with the Ministry's planning officials on a drastic revision of all planning procedure'. The PAG was invited to recommend changes. Its report was published as *The Future of Development Plans* (1965).

The PAG saw the system as too centralized. Ministerial approval was required on too many occasions. The format of the development plan was also defective. The plan was at one and the same time too detailed and not detailed enough:

It has proved extremely difficult to keep these plans . . . forward looking and responsive to the demands of change . . . They have tended to become out of date in terms of technique in that they deal inadequately with transport and the inter-relationship of traffic and land use; in factual terms in that they fail to take account quickly enough of changes in population forecasts, traffic growth and other economic and social trends; and in terms of policy in that they do not reflect more recent developments in the field of regional and urban planning . . . On the other hand, the development plans have not provided an adequate instrument for detailed planning at the local level . . . They give little guidance to developers beyond the primary use zoning. They make no contribution to the quality of urban design or the quality of the environment . . . [PAG 1965, paras. 1.16–1.3]

Before we try to evaluate the planning procedures introduced in 1968 and consolidated by TCPA 1971, it is convenient to provide a brief outline of the new system.[15] The development plan was now divided into two stages. First there is a *structure plan*, which is the responsibility of the county or metropolitan authority and, in the case of London, the GLC. S.7 TCPA 1971 provides that the structure plan shall be based on a survey. It is to be a written statement of policy which may include diagrams and illustrations, though not normally a map. In preparing the plan, the county planning authority must, by s.6, consult district planning authorities, new town development corporations and other relevant bodies. S.9 then provides for the structure plan to be submitted to the Minister who must consider objections and also appoint a person or persons to hold an examination in public (EIP) (see below, Chapter 15). The Minister may also consider the views of any other person or planning authority. He must give reasons for approval or rejection of the plan.

The second aspect of positive planning is the *local plan*. Local plans are normally the responsibility of district authorities and are based on the authority's detailed proposals for 'the development and other use of land' but including management of traffic and 'measures for the improvement of the physical environment' (s.11(3)). A district plan may be prepared for the whole of a planning area. It may also be prepared for an 'action area' in which positive steps for development or improvement are to be taken. More specific plans, e.g. for traffic management, can also be prepared. Local plans are all based on maps and a written statement and, by s.11(9), must conform generally to the (proposed) structure plan. In preparing the plan, the authority must consider objections and, where objections are made, must, by s.13(1), cause a public local inquiry (PLI) or other hearing to be held by a person appointed by the Minister. In contrast to the structure plan, not every local plan requires ministerial approval; s.14(3) provides for submission of copies of the plan to the Minister who *may direct* that the plan shall not have effect unless approved by him.

S.23 of TCPA 1971 requires planning permission to be obtained for all development and all uses other than those specified in the General Development and Use Classes Orders. We should note here that local authorities, statutory undertakers and the Crown possess important privileges which are often the subject of complaint because they enable the requirements for participation to be evaded. An example can be found in the *Covent Garden* case below. Planning applications are normally decided by district planning authorities which can enforce the development control system by serving 'enforcement notices', but s.35(1) allows the Minister to 'call-in' planning applications for decision by himself. This procedure may be used in cases of local controversy or disagreement between local authorities. It may also be used for issues of national importance (e.g. Windscale).

An applicant for planning permission must, by s.27, notify all persons other than himself who are owners of the land of the proposed development. In certain cases of unneighbourly development (e.g. building of public lavatories) or of development in conservation areas, he must also give notice to the public generally. The planning authority can grant or refuse permission and must take into account any representations that it has received. Appeal against a refusal or conditional grant of planning permission lies to the Minister, whose decision on the merits is final; appeal on a point of law lies by s.245 to the High Court. It is important to bear in mind how limited are the rights of 'objectors' to participate in development control procedures. Only the applicant can appeal to the Minister. At the request of the applicant or the planning authority, an inquiry may be held before a person appointed by the Minister, though the parties may waive this right and proceed by exchange of written representations.[16] Today this is done in over 70 per cent of appeals. Only the applicant, the planning authority and persons who must be notified under s.27 have a right under s.29 to appear at the inquiry; other persons can make statements etc. only with the permission of the inspector. After an inquiry either the inspector makes recommendations to the Minister who determines the appeal or, in about 80 per cent of cases, the appeal is delegated to the inspector for decision at the inquiry. Only the public authority and those who have a substantial interest in land to be developed have 'rights' to be represented in this procedure. Later we shall see that these restrictions are extremely contentious.

This loosely-woven system is knit together and coordinated by the functions of the Minister. He may disallow structure plans in the interests of government policy; call in local plans for approval if it seems desirable; call in key planning applications and, on appeal, over-ride the decisions of local planning authorities. The system is also knit together by ministerial circulars issued to planning author-ities by the DOE which, in sharp contrast to many immigration restrictions (see below, Chapter 17) are published and available to the general public.[17] The circulars have several functions. They may explain complex statute or regulations and alert planning authorities to changes in the law; this can be valuable to authorities with small planning departments. Others are designed to secure uniformity in administrative procedure. For example, structure planning was governed by the TCP (Structure and Local Plans) Regulations SI No. 1486/74 (now revoked by SI No. 555/82). The regulations were explained and amplified in a key circular No. 98/74, which instructed authorities on the format to be used in preparing structure plans. Again, the statutory requirements for consultation between planning authorities are minimal (below). Circ. No. 74/73 (now replaced by No. 2/81) stressed that district councils were to be 'closely involved with structure plan work, and committed to following it through in their local plan and development control work'. The circular emphasized that the process must be a continuing one:

It is not just a question of considering whether and, if so, what adaptations of existing machinery might suffice. Nor is it enough to rely simply on the formal consultation, important though this is, required by statute or regulations.

The function of this circular was to coordinate the system.

Other circulars advise local authorities how to exercise their own powers. For example, in the *Beverley* case (above, p. 358), reference is made to a ministerial circular, actually No. 696/54 issued by the Ministry of Transport. The circular advised authorities how to

coordinate their planning powers with powers under the Highways
Acts. A controversial paragraph read:

The Minister will no longer entertain applications for grant in respect of
expenditure incurred by councils in meeting claims for compensation payable
in consequence of the prescription of building and improvement lines.

The Bank argued that, in choosing to act under TCPA rather than
under the Highways Act, the Council had been motivated by
improper and irrelevant financial considerations. The circular had
tied its hands. Bearing in mind the discussion of 'administrative
quasi-law' in Chapter 5, consider the effects of this circular on local
authority practice. Was it 'mandatory' in character? In the Court of
Appeal, Salmon LJ felt that it was intended to have this effect. In his
dissenting judgment, he paraphrased the circular to read:

You would be very stupid to prescribe an improvement line under the
Highways Act, because that will involve you in paying the compensation to
property owners which Parliament has given them for the damage which they
may suffer by such a line being prescribed. In the past, of course, you have
been able to rely on getting the money back, or a large part of it, from the
central government; but you can by pass the Highways Acts and treat them as
a dead letter, because you can rely on the planning authority in fact to impose
an improvement line by refusing planning permission; that will deprive the
property owners of any of their rights to compensation. Accordingly you are
just throwing money away which you will not get back from us if you
prescribe the line under the Highways Acts.

The House of Lords, however, thought that the circular was purely
advisory. Viscount Dilhorne said: 'I am prepared to assume that [the
authority] were influenced by it, but I see no grounds for concluding
that they were improperly influenced. If they should have exercised
their powers under the Highways Act, and were deterred from doing
so by this circular, then it could be said that they were improperly
influenced.' But, reflecting on the legislative process, he did wonder
whether Parliament, in enacting the relevant legislation 'was unaware of this advice'.

Yet another use of circulars is to advise local planning authorities of
ministerial or departmental attitudes, thus preventing inadvertent
clashes of policy between the centre and the periphery. This is
particularly helpful in suggesting how planning appeals may be
decided. One such circular, 'The Use of Conditions in Planning
Permission' (No. 5/68), surfaced in the case of *Newbury District Council
v. Environment Secretary* [1980] 2 WLR 379. The Council had attached
a condition to planning permission that buildings being used as a

store or repository would be demolished at the end of a limited period. Later we shall see that conditions must be reasonably related to the planning permission. The Council argued that the Minister, in holding its condition to be unreasonable on appeal, had relied heavily on the circular, which was inaccurate. The House of Lords, upholding the Minister's decision, found that he had interpreted the legal provisions correctly. But Lord Fraser called the circular 'erroneous in law' and the House agreed in thinking that the Minister's decision, if based on it, would have been wrong. Notice that in this case, the circular was challenged by the planning authority and contrast the more typical situation in the *Beverley* case where the administrators were accused of treating as 'binding' what the judges agreed in thinking 'advisory'.

Writing only three years after the inception of this system, McAuslan (1971, p. 268) described the PAG report as 'a totally new approach to planning which has as its future aim the turning away from its emphasis on land use and design and towards an emphasis on the techniques and skills of foreseeing and guiding change'. For him and for other writers, the new system was designed to facilitate consideration of wider objectives. Jowell and Noble, for example, entitled their survey of the first structure plans (see below) 'planning as social engineering'. S.6(3) of the TCPA 1971 permitted social and economic policy to figure directly in the structure plan. The planning authority was enjoined to consider (a) the principal physical and economic characteristics of the area (b) population distribution and composition (c) communication, transport and traffic as well as (d) any other relevant considerations, including (e) such matters as the Minister might direct. The relationship between 'social engineering' and 'spatial planning' is described in Circ. No. 4/79:

The development plan system calls for a broad and open consideration of planning problems taking account of physical, economic and social aspects and allows authorities to adopt a flexible approach to the way they treat and present the contents of their plans. In particular the Memorandum [annexed to this circular] calls attention to considerations which are now given emphasis in development plans – the integration of land use and transport planning; measures for improving the environment; the relationship with regional planning; the resources likely to be available for carrying out development; and social considerations. The preparation of structure and local plans will bring together these considerations and match them with specific initiatives requiring special attention such as policies for inner city urban areas.

Yet Jowell and Noble were forced to conclude that the new approach had never materialized, for which they blamed the influence of the DOE:

[Our] conclusion is . . . that despite the recommendations of the [PAG], and the desired shift towards broader criteria and a 'corporate' element in planning, the official view is that social and economic criteria may not be reflected in concrete policies and proposals in structure plans. While broader considerations can influence the choice of policies and proposals, and may justify their choice, those policies and proposals must themselves refer to land use and land use alone.

One of the aims of the PAG recommendations was that the new Development Plans would provide a 'positive brief' for development, that structure plans should not be merely mechanisms for negative regulation but form part of a system of directive planning. This function of structure plans appears to have been restrictively interpreted by the Secretary of State at approval stage . . . It is clear . . . that the hopes for the positive role of structure planning foreshadowed by the PAG are unlikely to be realised. [Jowell and Noble 1980, pp. 308–9.]

The new system had come under pressure in other ways. A key problem lay in the administrative structure. The PAG had intended that both plans would be designed by the same authority and, had the recommendations of the Redcliffe-Maud Commission on Local Government in England (Cmnds 4039, 4040 (1969)) been implemented, this would have been the case. For most of the country, the Commission favoured a unitary structure of local government in which the units were to be significantly larger than previously. But the Local Government Act 1972, introduced by a Conservative Government, did not adopt this approach. Throughout most of the country a two-tier system of counties and districts or boroughs was introduced.[18] The result was, as we have seen, that county councils became the planning authority with responsibility for structure plans while local plans and development control were both handled by district councils. A further and quite unintended split had been introduced into the planning system. To complete the picture, an expanded Department of the Environment with wider powers and functions was set up in 1970. The exact division of responsibility between county, district and the DOE is complex and delicate.

'Planning as social engineering' also created resource problems. Departmental circulars reflect both this concern and a certain suspicion of the advanced techniques required for systems analysis. Circ. No. 98/74 urged planning authorities to:

. . . do no more work than is required to enable them to provide the reasoning underlying, and the justification for, their eventual choice of policies on their key issues . . . The use of sophisticated techniques should be considered in the light of the contribution they can make to decision-taking (i.e. to the choice of policies as against the need for economy in terms of time and money).

This was replaced by Circ. No. 4/79 which shows some disillusion with the experience of structure plans and once more emphasizes the resource problem:

Unnecessary work must be eliminated . . . the aim is to maintain valid structure plans but to avoid treating this task [i.e. renewal of the structure plan] as a major one calling for large staff resources.

As with the 1947 system, there are complaints of inflexibility and of delay. For example, the statutory local plan is not mandatory; s.11(1) of the TCPA 1971 provides that the local planning authority 'may, if they think it desirable, prepare a local plan for all or any of that part of the area'. Some authorities think the statutory procedures too cumbersome and prefer to rely on the development control system. By the mid-seventies, this too was under attack on grounds of delay. In 1974, George Dobry QC was asked to review the system[19] and in 1977 the Expenditure Committee of the House of Commons made a further review.[20] Whether or not the system was too slow is largely a value-judgement. The Expenditure Committee felt that it was and produced a statistical mountain in support of that view. The Dobry review stressed that 'in most cases quality of decision is more important than speed, and streamlining must not become a euphemism for omission of proper checks'. Although the controls were 'sometimes liable to be exercised in far too rigid and bureaucratic a manner' and should be applied by authorities 'with as light and human a touch as the best of them do', planning control was essential. Dobry saw delay as 'the price we must pay for democratic planning of the environment', though he proposed major reforms, many of which proved unacceptable at the time.

There were (and are) no doubt grounds for complaint, but the changes introduced in the third planning phase had political motives. The planners' assumptions which underlay the PAG report were antithetical to the new radical conservatism whose influence was beginning to make itself felt. Development control entailed major incursions into the concept of private property. In America, Dunham (1964, p. 28) invited a reassessment of the 'relationship of city planning to private property and liberty'. Scruton (1980, p. 164) objected to the managerial conception of local government in which large units, financed in the main by central government and dependent on national parties were no longer truly 'local' but had become a bureaucratic extension of central government. This made 'a nonsense of planning law'.[21] These views may be reflected in the desire to 'streamline the cities'.

For some, LGPLA 1980 inaugurates a new planning era, whose hallmark is impatience with development control, and commitment to private development and economic development.[22] It may be that the structure plan will be a more modest document with limited objectives. Sched. 14(1) provides that a structure plan shall in future consist of a written statement formulating the local planning authority's policy and general proposals 'in respect of the development and other use of land in that area (including measures for the improvement of the physical environment and the management of traffic)'. The statement may contain only such other matters as the Minister prescribes and is to be illustrated by a diagram. The plan is to be accompanied by an explanatory memorandum which will not itself require approval. Thus social policy may be used to explain planning choices but not to dictate future development. In addition, the more specific local plan is to take priority over the general structure plan (Sched. 14(10)(d)) which may ultimately favour district at the expense of county planning authorities.

At the same time, provision was made for Urban Development Areas in which planning controls can be relaxed and the planning process speeded up in the interests of urban regeneration. Merseyside and the London Dockland became the first such areas. The concept undercuts local democracy, as many planning functions are exercised by Urban Development Corporations whose members are appointed by the Minister (ss. 135, 136). Sched. 32 of LGPLA 1980 in some ways goes further, allowing the Minister to designate 'enterprise zones' or 'no go areas' in which planning controls can be lifted and other financial inducements held out to developers.[23] To this can be added the general provisions of s.88, which also dispense with the need for a public inquiry into the local plan in certain cases. Amendments to the development control system were made by the General Development (Amendment) Order 1981, which removes applications from the system by exempting some 'householder development' from control. Other changes were administrative; delegation of appeals to inspectors continues and a new circular (No.

22/80) aimed at 'a general speeding-up of the system' urges planning authorities to proceed where possible by way of negotiation in preference to time-consuming, formal appeals.

For some this streamlining of the planning process is irrelevant in an era of financial restriction when development is in decline. Circ. No. 22/80, for example, goes to the lengths of exhorting authorities 'to ensure that development is only prevented or restricted when this serves a clear planning purpose and the economic effects have been taken into account'. Others feel that community participation could be seriously undercut by this legislation which will begin to bite if and when the recession comes to an end. This view is epitomized by a passage from a discussion paper by the Council for the Protection of Rural England (CPRE), a major environmental pressure group:

> Since 1979, Ministers have repeatedly castigated the planning system as a source of unacceptable cost and delays to the development industry. Developers have echoed, increasingly vociferously, the criticism that planners, and by implication local planning authorities, have had too little respect for the financial considerations important to the construction industry. Such attitudes are hardly new. What is new is their elevation to axioms of national planning policy . . . Redefinitions of planning are now being floated which discard the emphasis on 'control' and 'guidance' which have been so valuable in past decades in preventing the erosion of England's countryside . . .
>
> CPRE has been closely involved in the evolution of Britain's town and country planning system over the past 50 years . . . Far from being negative, it has in fact been thoroughly positive. The fact that so much of the character and quality of the English countryside remains intact is a tribute . . . to the planning system and to the efforts of local authorities who have safeguarded rural amenities in the face of remorseless pressures for urban development.
>
> But the country now faces the prospect of a growing convergence between the planning system and the private development industry. Developers are achieving new freedoms at the expense of long-established and widely accepted policies of restraint . . . Official restrictions on most forms of new development have been eased . . . in all but the most sensitive areas . . . The Government acknowledges that the planning system is being refashioned to create a more sympathetic climate for developers. But Ministers deny that new green field sites will be developed increasingly as a result . . . We disagree . . . There is little in the public record[24] to suggest that Mr Heseltine [then Environment Secretary] or his advisers have taken account of the cumulative implications of their recent initiatives for the future character of the English countryside. [CPRE, 1981, pp. 5–6.]

2 The decision-makers

In Chapter 12 we suggested that it was misleading to talk as if 'the public interest' was homogenous. The decentralization which we have been at pains to emphasize provides the opportunity for a wide range of interactions, for friction and for divergence of interest in the planning process. The interests of the various planning authorities, responsible to different electorates, different populations, urban and rural, and often of different political persuasions, clash. They may clash again with the interests of non-representative bodies, themselves disparate in character and interests. New Town Development Corporations are established under the 1946 Act (consolidated in 1981) and appointed by the Minister to undertake development and exercise planning functions in a particular new town. Urban Development Corporations today exercise similar functions in inner cities. Statutory undertakers, such as the Central Electricity Generating Board (CEGB) the British Airports Authority (BAA) or regional water authorities exist to carry out a single function on a national or regional basis. One organ of the state may oppose another: for example, at the 1983 inquiry into the need for a fifth terminal at Heathrow Airport London, BAA opposed proposals for extension put forward by the state airline, British Airways.

Sometimes the DOE and the Minister act as an umpire between these various agencies, which may have the support of other ministries, for example, Energy or Agriculture. The DOE is not a single entity either. Its regional offices may develop regional loyalties; this point is illustrated in the Tyneside investigation (see below). Nor do the interests of politicians and bureaucrats always coincide. In a large metropolitan county or city or a rich, industrial county, the planning department may itself be accounted a bureaucracy and sociologists have described bureaucratic 'ideologies' which are promoted alongside or even instead of those of the agency.[25] These administrative agencies have ongoing relationships and one of the problems of administrative law has been to secure a sufficient share of the action for the individuals and members of the public who appear on a part-time basis and in 'walk-on' parts. The traditional answer of administrative law is the rhetoric of rights and procedural protections for 'individuals'. As usual, the reality is more complex. In Chapter 15, we shall find developers, typically corporations, negotiating and bargaining with the planners. We shall also find citizens banding together to strengthen their position by forming interest groups: amenity and conservation societies, community and housing associations etc. All the typical manifestations of the political process are present.

Earlier, we described planning as a discrete academic discipline which drew upon the skills of several professions (e.g. architects, engineers, statisticians, demographers, economists). These professions have their own expertise and methods of analysis. We mentioned, too, the influence of the new academic discipline of cybernetics. If, as red-light theorists do, we see the aim of administrative law as control of the administration, the possibility of clash between the two professional elites of lawyer and planner would be of relevance. Until recently, Goldsmith tells us, planners were not alert to the possibility of dissension. They saw themselves (like lawyers) as neutral, skilled advisers whose objectives were apolitical and uncontroversial:[26]

The view that planning is, above all else, a political activity in the broadest sense has only recently and grudgingly been accepted by the planning profession itself. In part this was because the professional ideology was essentially one that claimed that planning was objective, technical, and as such non-political. For most of its history, the profession believed that there was no disagreement in society about goals, and that the means by which these goals are achieved could be decided by the technical methods available to the planner. [Goldsmith, 1980, p. 126.]

In practice the values of planners and lawyers often conflict. The Crichel Down affair involved just such a clash when Andrew Clark QC criticized policies developed in the Ministry of Agriculture and the methods used in their execution (Cmnd 9176 (1954)). In *Coleen Properties* v. *Minister of Housing and Local Government* [1971] 1 WLR 433, Tower Hamlets LBC declared two rows of houses to be clearance areas under the Housing Act 1957. S.43(2) empowered them also to acquire adjoining land on the ground that it was 'reasonably necessary for . . . the satisfactory development . . . of the clearance area'. The Council sought to acquire an adjoining property in good condition. At the inquiry, it declared the acquisition to be 'reasonably necessary' but produced no further evidence. The inspector reported against the acquisition, but the Minister disagreed on the ground that 'by the very nature of its position, the exclusion of this property must seriously inhibit the future development of the rectangular block of land . . . in which it stands.' The Appeal Court held that insufficient evidence had been produced to support the contention that acquisition was reasonably necessary. Sachs J made short work of planners' priorities, saying:

It is, of course, clear that the premises in question are at the corner of a rectangular island . . . From [the] plan it is quite plain that when developing the rectangle it may well be convenient to have the corner site included in the development, so as perhaps to make it more homogeneous. It is plain that to get possession of it and include it in the development may well be 'a tidy idea' according to the canons of Whitehall. It may be that it is better from the point of view of looks. But all that is not enough. It must be reasonably *necessary* for the satisfactory development or use under consideration.

In *The Ideologies of Planning Law* (1981), McAuslan develops the idea of the clashing values of different interest groups, discovering three competing 'ideologies':

Firstly . . . the law exists and should be used to protect private property and its institutions; this may be called the traditional common law approach to the role of law. Secondly, the law exists and should be used to advance the public interest, if necessary against the interest of private property; this may be called the orthodox public administration and planning approach to the role of law. Thirdly, the law exists and should be used to advance the cause of public participation against both the orthodox public administration approach to the public interest and the common law approach of the overriding importance of private property, this may be called the radical or populist approach to the role of law. [McAuslan 1981, p. 2.]

Compare these definitions with the discussion in Chapter 12; has McAuslan discounted the possibility of overlap? With which group(s) do you associate the 'ideologies'? Can you see any link with red and green light theories?

If we were to trace this argument into the area of judicial review, we would be retreading ground already covered in Chapters 11 and 12.[27] It is more appropriate here to track the 'ideology of participation'. This is not easy. Introducing the standard bibliography, Barker (1979, p. vii) compares participation with an amoeba, forever changing shape and putting out 'false feet' which may indicate a change of direction. 'The size of its academic and practical literature and the inherent importance of the fields (whether city planning, housing, schooling or wider environmental issues) across which it has moved in recent years combine to make a survey of its anatomy rather more taxing than keeping track of the amoeba's uncertain intentions.' In the next section, we try to track the amoeba.

3 Citizen participation

McAuslan describes the 'ideology of participation' as both radical and populist, a description only partly justified. As we shall see, by undercutting traditional democratic institutions, arrangements for a more direct form of participation may have the effect of increasing the influence of the more articulate. Yet the movement for 'citizen participation' in planning reflects a wider dissatisfaction with political institutions.[28] It is easy to see from Reich's description of American corporatism (see above, p. 48), how demands for citizen participation might grow out of his disillusionment with the corporate state. In Britain R. Barker (1978, p. 208) discusses a similar shift in post-war socialism. He records a shift away from 'managerial conceptions of public ownership' and renewed interest in earlier theories – such as 'guild socialism' – which made the citizen something 'more than a claimant on resources and an occasional elector'.[29] The movement for worker participation in industry provides a parallel to that for community participation in planning.

If, for the moment, 'planning' is given its wide meaning of a method of decision-taking, we sense a feeling of impotence. In modern technological societies, decisions are taken out of the hands of the people and reserved for an elected élite and its expert advisers. For Fagence, this is an inescapable dilemma for modern democracy:

As society has developed, and has become culturally and technologically sophisticated, there has grown an insistence that decision-making should be infused with a more democratic expression. Thus, within the last decade or two modern society has tended to advocate the simultaneous growth of participatory democracy and expertise in decision-making. Clearly it is not possible to maximise both of these value preferences; it is not that they are exclusive and incompatible one with the other, but that they are capable of neutralising each other with the result that the decisions made are less than satisfactory to the demands of the participants and the technical require-ments of the problem to be solved. Despite these antagonisms, the tensions in society dictate that meaningful attempts should be made to reshape the traditional decision-making processes to accommodate strategies of citizen participation; the movement of such advocacy has gained a momentum which is now irresistible, and it has attracted a high emotional content so that any denial of opportunities for citizen involvement is challenged as a betrayal of democratic tradition. [Fagence 1977, p. 3.]

Benn's *Arguments for Democracy* are more radical and populist. He attacks the authoritarian structure of British government, in which a façade of ministerial responsibility and representative government shelters a virtually unaccountable civil service. For Benn, decisions are reserved for a powerful élite, the populace being divested of all power of decision and control:

Despite all that is said about British democracy and our traditional freedoms, the people of Britain have much less control over their destiny than they are led to believe; far less than they are entitled to expect and demand; and a great deal less than they had a generation ago. In short, the powers which control our lives and our future have become progressively more concentrated, more centralised, more internationalised, more secretive and less accountable. The democracy of which we boast is becoming a decorous facade behind which those who have power exercise it for their own advantage and to the detriment of the public welfare . . . The extent to which we have all been effectively disenfranchised has been concealed from us, so that the blame for our frustrations has been directed into harmless and divisive channels. [Benn 1982, p. 4.]

Sewell and Coppock identify a feeling of alienation. Modern government is increasingly remote from the citizen and the communications are breaking down:

Pressure for an expanded role for the public in planning is rooted in both philosophical and pragmatic considerations. The former is related primarily to the general belief in democratic societies that the individual has the right to be informed and consulted and to express his views on matters which affect him personally. In modern representative government reliance is placed upon elected representatives, who provide a channel of communication between the governors and the governed, and upon various traditional techniques such as the ballot box, public inquiries and letters to officials or to newspapers. This system works well when the interests can be identified, when those affected can articulate their views and when channels of communication are well-known to the individuals involved. It works less well when it is difficult to determine precisely whose interests would be affected and when people do not have to convey their views. In recent years there has been growing concern that the public – or at least significant segments of it – has developed an increasing feeling of alienation towards governmental decision-making. Sometimes there are no channels of communication for the transmission of information or the expression of views, and even where they exist, the public may not know about them or they may seem ineffectual. In some instances a profound distrust of the entire system has developed. [Sewell and Coppock 1977, p. 1.]

The authors go on to list the following methods of interest representation: (1) public opinion polls and surveys; (2) referenda; (3) the ballot box; (4) public hearings; (5) advocacy planning (below); (6) letters to editors or public officials; (7) pressure groups; (8) protests and demonstrations; (9) litigation; (10) public meetings; (11) workshops or seminars; (12) task forces. How many have you met already in this book? Which would you classify as administrative law techniques?

By the mid-sixties 'citizen participation' was being advanced as an all-purpose remedy for a society which, political scientists stressed, was still sharply divided into 'haves' and 'have-nots', a situation which traditional democratic methods had done little to ameliorate.

Arnstein (1969, p. 216) pointed out that it was in danger of becoming a fashionable catch-phrase. 'The idea of citizen participation is a little like eating spinach: no one is against it in principle because it is good for you.' But there was 'a critical difference between going through the empty ritual of participation and having the real power needed to affect the outcome of the process'. Arnstein's celebrated 'ladder of participation' was designed to expose the extent to which consultation and participation procedures were a sham. 'The ladder juxtaposes powerless citizens with the powerful in order to highlight the fundamental divisions between them.'

Eight Rungs on a Ladder of Citizen Participation

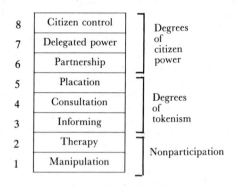

Types of Participation and 'Nonparticipation'
A typology of eight *levels* of participation may help in analysis . . . The eight types are arranged in a ladder pattern with each rung corresponding to the extent of citizens' power in determining the end product.

The bottom rungs of the ladder are (1) *Manipulation* and (2) *Therapy*. These two rungs describe levels of 'non-participation' that have been contrived by some to substitute for genuine participation. Their real objective is not to enable people to participate in planning or conducting programs, but to enable power-holders to 'educate' or 'cure' the participants. Rungs 3 and 4 progress to levels of 'tokenism' that allow the have-nots to hear and to have a voice: (3) *Informing* and (4) *Consultation*. When they are proffered by power-holders as the total extent of participation, citizens may indeed hear and be heard. But under these conditions they lack the power to insure that their views will be *heeded* by the powerful. When participation is restricted to these levels, there is no followthrough, no 'muscle', hence no assurance of changing the status quo. Rung (5) *Placation*, is simply a higher level tokenism because the groundrules allow have-nots to advise, but retain for the powerholders the continued right to decide.

Further up the ladder are levels of citizen power with increasing degrees of decision-making clout. Citizens can enter into a (6) *Partnership* that enables them to negotiate and engage in trade-offs with traditional powerholders. At the topmost rungs, (7) *Delegated Power* and (8) *Citizen Control*, have-not citizens obtain the majority of decision-making seats, or full managerial power. [Arnstein 1969, p. 217.]

. Arnstein applied her analysis to a number of US Federal social programmes. She described 'rubberstamp advisory committees' and certain 'neighbourhood councils' without legitimate function or power as 'manipulative'. 'Group therapy' masked as 'citizen participation' was 'both dishonest and arrogant'. Arnstein instanced campaigns to clean up unsavoury housing estates which diverted tenants from attacking more important questions like arbitrary eviction. Only on the top two rungs of Arnstein's ladder was there any genuine transference of power. As you read further about efforts at 'participation in planning' remember to evaluate them by Arnstein's ladder. Are particular groups in the community particularly prone to find themselves respectively on the top or bottom rungs? Evaluate Jowell's thesis (above, Chapter 3) that adjudication is a method of participation in decision-taking; on which rung(s) would you place it? Remember in chapters 18 and 19 to compare the extent to which the poor participate or receive representation in the social security system.

Much of the pressure for participation came from inside the planning profession. By the mid-sixties 'aesthetic' theories (below) were giving way to 'advocacy planning' or 'pluralistic planning', originating in America.[30] Gans, for example, emphasized the need for planners to become 'goal oriented' and 'consumer oriented'. They should accept that the public must decide the goals, a concession which Gans regarded as a change of direction. 'Planning began as a reform movement, not a client-centred service, and when predispositions conflicted with the requirements of planning ideology, they were rejected' (Gans 1968, p. 20). Planning had reflected predominantly the middle-class 'predispositions' of the planner. But society was pluralist and pluralism was valuable. The planner should present the public with viable 'choices' and the public should be allowed to make the choices:

Goals and values arise out of the opportunities and restraints which are encountered in everyday life, and different age and class groups inevitably have different goals and values. The planner ought to respect these and give people the opportunity, resources and freedom to choose what they want to do. [Gans 1968, p. ix.]

The new school was questioning the accepted view of planning. Early planning, with its origins in slum clearance and public housing schemes was paternalistic. It was assumed that the residents of 'slums' would prefer aesthetically superior accommodation, and, in any event, they were not people to whom planners and officials were accustomed to listen. Even if 'participation' meant only education and explanation, McAuslan saw it as a step forward:

Residents in the Housing Action Areas are . . . almost by definition, not part of the 'normal' or 'standard' population, an HAA will be likely to have a concentration of 'households likely to have special housing problems for instance, old age pensioners, large families, single parent families or families whose head is unemployed or in a low income group.' These are not the sort of people whom administrators would expect to have views or ideas to contribute on future living conditions or life-styles. Indeed, explaining *to* them what is to be done *for* them rather than just doing it represents a significant step forward in respect of participation in implementing programmes for this class of person. [McAuslan 1981, p. 35. The quotation is from Circ. No. 14/75.]

Dennis, contributing to the argument valuable studies of community reaction to housing clearance schemes in Sunderland, raised the important theoretical question of the state's right to intervene, previously assumed. Dennis defined a 'public issue' in three ways. First, it was one in which individual interests conflicted with other people's interests to the point where the first must be restricted; thus houses which are structurally unsafe can be pulled down. Second, a public issue was one which involved public goods like sewers, roads or airports. Third, a public issue meant 'public concern for members of the community who are suffering in some way'.[31] If, like sewers, roads and airports, homes were public goods, then public intervention was always justified. But if housing involved a public issue only in the third sense, the wishes of the local community must be paramount:

The claimants of power over standards of housing consumption beyond the level at which the public element is clearly discernible view the home . . . as if it were a public property in this second sense, like an airport. The design and location of a major airport, however, is a matter which affects millions of passengers very directly. It is so socially and technically complex that it cannot be created except by a large team of highly trained experts. It is difficult, however, to accept the home as 'public' in this sense at all. The home is the paradigm of all that is broken from the public world and absorbed into the pattern of the private and unique life of each family . . . [In the third sense] public intervention is simply meant to make life more pleasant for the people who are otherwise at a disadvantage. Obviously, then, this sort of argument for replacement is plausible only if life *is* made more pleasant for the inhabitants of the condemned dwelling. The best judge (some would say the only possible judge) of whether a change of circumstances has this result is the person himself. There can be little sense in a policy which is justified by reference to its beneficial effects, if the 'beneficiaries' experience the results as hardship. [Dennis 1970, pp. 359–60.]

Dennis drew two deductions from his analysis. First, participation in the real sense should increasingly become an essential ingredient of the planning process and, second, that those who lost 'in the clearance areas for the public good must not be left to bear an inequitably large share of the cost'. (Compare his analysis with the arguments of Wade in Chapter 12, or Duguit in Chapter 2.)

Damer and Hague (1971, p. 217) list five factors which were influential in persuading planners that public participation was generally a 'good thing': (a) the example of American planning experience; (b) the social ethic of planning, by which is meant 'the strong tradition of social commitment and idealism inherent in our planning'; (c) a general growth of interest in participatory rather than representative democracy; (d) a history of bottle-necks and hold-ups in the administrative processing of plans; (e) a general growth of interest in the urban environment promoted by the fact that planning proposals were now affecting large numbers of articulate social groups which were protesting vigorously.

It is not surprising then to find both the PAG and Dobry accepting participation as a 'good idea'. But the high-water mark of participation in official thinking is probably the Skeffington Report, *People and Planning* (1969). The Skeffington Committee was set up in 1968 to advise the Minister on 'the best methods, including publicity, of securing the participation of the public at the formative stage in the making of development plans for their area'. The Committee first defined its terms:

(a) Participation – We understand participation to be the act of sharing in the formulation of policies and proposals. Clearly, the giving of information by the local planning authority and of an opportunity to comment on that information is a major part in the process of participation, but it is not the whole story. Participation involves doing as well as talking and there will be full participation only where the public are able to take an active part throughout the plan-making process. There are limitations to this concept. One is that responsibility for preparing a plan is, and must remain, that of the local planning authority. Another is that the completion of plans – the setting into statutory form of proposals and decisions – is a task demanding the highest standards of professional skill, and must be undertaken by the professional staff of the local planning authority.

(b) The Public – We do not think of the public solely in terms of the community as it shows itself in organised groups. We regard the community as an aggregate comprising all individuals and groups within it without limitation.

(c) Publicity – We use the word 'publicity' to mean the making of information available to the public. Basically this information will be fact, argument and explanation. Publicity alone is not participation; but it is the first essential step towards it. [Skeffington, 1969, para. 5.]

Skeffington went on to recommend a considerable investment in promoting public participation and interest in the planning process. As you read on, try to situate the proposals against Arnstein's ladder and check the recommended techniques against Sewell and Coppock.[32] The first, publicity stage would involve the use of the media to broadcast information. There would also be exhibitions at which opinions could be expressed, and the public would be encouraged not only to participate through surveys but to help in the conduct of the surveys. Thus the public would be provided with 'choice'. Some of the Committee's proposals were still more populist. For example, it thought that planning authorities should employ community officers 'to secure the involvement of those people who do not join organisations' (para. 80). It recommended the establishment of community forums to:

. . . provide local organisations with the opportunity to discuss collectively planning and other issues of importance to the area. Community forums might also have administrative functions, such as receiving and distributing information on planning matters and promoting the formation of neighbourhood groups. [Skeffington, 1969, p. 45.]

Dismissing previous efforts as 'information' rather than 'consultation', Skeffington envisaged a continuous dialogue between public and planning authority, stressing the advantage for the latter:

Where information comes too late and without preliminary public discussion there is the likelihood of frustration and hostility. It may be that the plan produced is the one best suited to the needs of the community but the reasons for decisions do not emerge, nor are people told why superficially attractive alternatives have been put aside. This failure to communicate has meant that the preparation of a plan, instead of being a bridge between the authority and the public, has become a barrier, reinforcing the separation that springs up so easily between the 'them' of authority and the 'us' of the public . . .

Representations should be considered continuously as they are made while plans are being prepared; but, in addition, there should be set pauses to give a positive opportunity for public reaction and participation. Local planning authorities should concentrate their efforts to secure participation at two stages. These stages apply to both structure and local plans and are (a) the presentation following surveys of the choices which are open to the authority in deciding the main planning issues for the area in question and (b) the presentation of a statement of proposals for the area in question.

Where alternative courses are available, the authority should put them to the public and say which it prefers and why. [Skeffington, 1969, p. 47.]

The Skeffington report has been described as naive.[33] Damer and Hague commented (1971, p. 223): 'The Report barely conceals an ideological stance aimed at defending the professional prerogatives of the planning profession'. They developed their point by a citation from Skeffington: 'We have never forgotten that planning is a means and not an end; and that its purpose is to set the framework within which houses, roads and community services can be provided at the right time and in the right place.' Damer and Hague take this passage to imply a commitment to a *consensus* view of planning in which participation served a particular educational function. Conflicts between the planner and his public were due not to difference in life-style or goals (see Gans, above) but to a misunderstanding of the planner's viewpoint. Participation would allow the planner to achieve his goals more easily in an atmosphere of 'greater understanding and cooperation rather than [of] a crescendo of dispute' (Skeffington, para. 20). Damer and Hague were pessimistic about the probable outcome. Disillusion would set in when consensus was not achieved –as it never can be – while the less articulate classes of society would still be excluded from the debate.

Long, in an extended case study of community participation during the preparation of the West Cumberland structure plan, argues that there has never been any commitment in the British planning system to radical or populist ideals in the senses of offering the public 'a series of choices', commitment to pluralism (Gans) or helping people to exercise increased control over their lives (McAuslan). He postulates several objectives for participation procedures in the British planning system. Long sees the 'ideology of participation' as essentially administration-oriented. First, it is invoked to further the planner's goal of rational and scientific decision-taking by allowing the planner to solve problems by moving to a consensual 'correct' answer. If participation were not an element in planning, the planning process might degenerate into a discourse between experts conducted in terms of 'a highly specialized scientific language and terminology'.

Consider, for example, Breach's 'mainstream environmental dialectic'; is this a discourse in which the community can easily participate? Second, participation has 'educative' functions,[34] allowing the planner to absorb interested and influential sections of the community into the planners' 'own internal validation process' (compare this with Prosser or Blake and Gillespie (above, Chapter 3) discussing the use of tribunals to 'legitimate' administrative decisions).

The recognition of a need for a participation element in planning may have been a response to the potential danger of 'narrow technicism', or in other words, that the planner might become too divorced from the public and should therefore be continually reminded of the public's existence. Alternatively, the Government [in framing the TCPA 1971] may have accepted that the public would constitute a danger to the operational efficiency of the new system. Participation could thus be viewed as an attempt to educate the public in planning matters and thereby absorb the interested sections into the planners' own internal validation process. [Long, 1975, p. 75.]

Finally, Long considers and rejects the hypothesis that participation procedures are a 'citizen safeguard' akin to the system of administrative tribunals or the Ombudsman:

This is clearly a myth – *public participation is not a citizen safeguard and nor was it intended to be.* The concept as embodied in [TCPA 1971] conferred no new rights on the citizen. Representations to planning departments could be made before the passing of the Act just as easily as they could afterwards, the only slight extension was that planners were required to consider these representations. Both PAG and Skeffington saw public participation primarily as a public relations exercise concerned with reducing opposition to planning proposals by *raising the level of public consent,* thereby contributing to the drive for speed and efficiency. [Long, 1975, p. 78.]

Let us look at informal participation at the initial stage of plan preparation in the light of these strictures. (The formal processes of the inquiry and public examination are dealt with in Chapter 15.) Ss. 8 and 12 of the TCPA 1971 require a planning authority to advertise the proposals of its draft structure/local plan and listen to representations. In the case of structure plans, the authority is enjoined by s.8(1) to take 'such steps as will in their opinion secure adequate publicity'. By s.8(3) the planning authority must enclose a statement explaining the steps taken to implement s.8(1) and the Minister can approve the scheme only *if he is satisfied* with the steps taken. If he is not satisifed, he may return the plan with a direction as to what further steps should be taken (s.8(4)). Suppose the Minister refused to intervene; are the provisions legally enforceable? No particular persons are designated for consultation. The chances of success in an application for review are highly speculative.[35] These deficiences persuade Damer and Hague (above) to dismiss the provisions as 'a public relations exercise designed to damp down opposition'.

But even a public relations exercise can be taken seriously. Circ. No. 52/72 ('Development Plan Proposals: Publicity and Public Participation') emphasized the Government's commitment to Skeffington's recommendations. It explained the absence of detailed statutory provisions by reference to Skeffington's view that 'participation should not be a formalised or rigid process but should be flexible enough to meet all types of need'. Local planning authorities were urged to go *beyond* the basic requirements and to deal with them imaginatively:

The Secretaries of State believe that publicity and public participation are essential factors in the new development plan system and they fully support them. They take this opportunity to stress how important it is, in embarking on that new system involving new concepts, to seek the views of the ordinary citizen and to listen to them. If the policies to be embodied in the plans are to be understood and generally accepted, and if the proposals in them are to be implemented successfully, the authorities must carry the public with them by formulating, for public discussion, the aims and objectives of the policies and then the options for realising these aims and objectives. Giving the public the opportunity to participate in the formative stage will, when handled with skill and understanding, not only make the plan a better plan but also do much to improve relationships between the planning authorities and the public. Participation is a two-way process.

Is this provision participatory in the sense that transference of power and cooperative decision-making is envisaged? Is the public to be presented with genuine choices? Or is participation seen as an aid to 'efficient' planning? The circular contains other provisions which confirm the suspicions of critics like Long or Damer and Hague. For example, para. 5 deals with the question of delay:

The overall time taken on plans is important: constructive participation should help both to improve their quality and relevance, and to keep the period for preparing and approving them within an acceptable timetable.

This leaves a great deal to the discretion of the local planning authority.[36] For example, the Beresfords surveyed the participation exercises conducted by the Wandsworth LBC in connection with the local plan. In 1977, a draft plan was produced by a Labour council 'with a reputation for being radical and progressive'. After completion of the participation exercises, the council changed hands. A new plan was prepared by the Conservative Council and 'validated' by a new participation programme. The researchers saw an apparent contradiction:

If we take the public participation . . . at its face value, then what Wandsworth council has done . . . is to overturn what local people said they wanted as embodied in a modified Labour Borough Plan. On the other hand, this council will be able to say, and doubtless will be saying, that it has carried out the obligations to ensure public participation and that the resulting plan which it will produce will be based on what local people want. [Beresford 1980, p. 412.]

For the researchers, the answer lay in the style of the second round of participation, which demonstrated the indifference of the Conservative administration to the ideal of participation. But we might simply deduce that 'the people' had changed their minds and registered their feelings at the local election.

If participation is viewed as an exercise in public relations, or in information and education, then the experiments of the last decade might be accounted a reasonable success. Insofar as participation exercises are intended to present real choice from which an agreed solution results, the verdict must be more doubtful. And if by participation we mean power sharing and community decision-taking, many would argue that it has never yet been tried. Here the experience of the Home Office Deprivation Unit is directly relevant. The Unit cooperated with local authorities to establish 12 Community Development Projects. Each had an 'action team' employed by the local authority, designed to raise the level of consciousness and stimulate the community's capacity for self-help. Three inner area studies were commissioned to discover what the housing preferences of residents of Birmingham, Liverpool and Southwark really were. The CDPs formed a joint editorial team to publish its reports. In *Gilding the Ghetto* (p. 4) the teams exposed

the real contradictions at the heart of the CDP notion. As the teams began in earnest to work and organise with local tenants and action groups over questions of housing or welfare rights they found themselves drawn into direct conflict with councillors and officials of the local authorities – the very people, who, in part at least, were their employers.

CDP reports also criticized government policies. In 1976, after the team published *Cutting the Welfare State (Who Profits?)*, the Home Office closed the unit. Responsibility for inner urban areas was transferred to the DOE.[37] Government policy changed, and the change found expression in the more recent concept of the Inner Urban Development Area and the Enterprise Zone (above).

This is important in evaluating the movement for 'citizen participation' in planning. The planner's perception of members of an amenity or community group as 'respectable' has the effect of opening up the planning process to them. This is another factor favouring those who already have their feet on the ladder to power:

Quite clearly, many planners see some groups as somehow important, or as having something to contribute to the planning process, and as such treat these groups very differently from the way in which other sections of the public are treated. Full reports of survey, rather than summaries, as well as technical reports, are sent to such groups, whereas they may be available only on request or at a price to the ordinary man in the street. Special meetings may be arranged for such groups, so that they may consult with the planners on a more personal basis; indeed, some of these groups may be incorporated into the planning process by virtue of their membership of something like a consultative panel. [Goldsmith, 1980, p. 74.]

In earlier chapters we described the use of pressure groups for interest representation. We have seen them active in the political process (Chapter 12) and using 'test-case strategy' (Chapter 9). Some of these groups (like the American Sierra Club) were 'amenity groups', the characteristic pressure group of the planning process. Some amenity groups, like the CPRE (see above) operate on a national basis or like Friends of the Earth, internationally. Others, like the Petersham Amenity Society (see below) have a purely local base. Many small groups, representing different interests, may operate inside a single community.

Although McAuslan used the words 'radical and populist', later in his book he describes the participation movement as devastatingly middle-class.* He records (1981, p. 54) some research conducted into the composition of the Petersham Amenity Society by one of his students.[38] The relevance lies in the fact that the Petersham Society was able to stage a well-organized objection to a planning application which ended in the High Court.

The Petersham case involved a planning inquiry into a building which, it was alleged, would be visible from and would spoil the celebrated view over the Thames from Richmond Hill. The amenity society had no statutory right to appear at the inquiry but was permitted by the inspector to give evidence. Later it wished to

*The precise meanings attached to 'middle-class', 'working-class', etc., by sociologists is not reflected in planning literature where the words may mean no more than 'articulate', 'well-off', 'poor', etc.

challenge the report and appealed on a point of law. The question arose whether it had locus standi. In earlier cases, the statutory formula of 'person aggrieved' had been restrictively interpreted (above, p. 290). In *Turner* v. *Secretary of State for the Environment* (1973) 28 P and CR 123, it was held that the amenity group had locus standi by virtue of the fact that it had been allowed to appear at the inquiry and was from then on 'aggrieved' by the inspector's decision. The ruling did not greatly benefit the society because Ackner J found against it on other points, but the case was heralded as a break-through by public lawyers generally, who saw in it the possibility of introducing the American 'class action' into English law. The point made by McAuslan is that the society was able to 'play the administrative law game' because it boasted amongst its membership 'a large number of members of the upper crust of the establishment, the peerage and the diplomatic corps'.

More general confirmation of McAuslan's point is contained in Barker's survey for the Civic Trust (1976) of amenity groups registered with them. Of Barker's respondents, 66 per cent agreed that their members tended 'to live in the neighbourhoods with the best standards of layout and amenity', while 78 per cent agreed that few of their members were council housing tenants, students, nurses or even young unmarried people. 43 per cent reported a pre-ponderance of members in the 'relevant' professions of archi-tecture, planning, law and design. A later, more comprehensive survey of the impact of environmental groups by Lowe and Goyder amply confirms the earlier finding. They found (1983, p. 10) that members of environmental groups are predominantly middle class, often upper middle class. The professions predominate; probably less than one third of members do manual work. Membership also tends to be concentrated in the home counties. The authors point out, however, that American studies show a considerable level of *support* among all groups for the aims of amenity groups. And in *Cublington: A Blueprint for Resistance* (1973), Perman attempts a rough breakdown of the participants in the Wing, Cublington and Stewkley action groups formed to fight the choice of Cublington as London's third airport. He compares his findings with the results of the official sociological survey at the Foulness site commissioned by Roskill from the University of Essex and concludes that the Berkshire movement was more working class. Perman admits that the organizers of WARA (the Wing Airport Resistance Association) came from the profes-

sional classes and included a barrister. But he insists that support for
the movement came from the community as a whole, citing in support
a card-indexed petition from 62,000 supporters. Again, by focusing
on amenity groups, and ignoring housing or other community
associations, Lowe and Goyder may have distorted the picture.
Dennis has documented a relatively successful attempt at community
participation in Millfield, a working-class area of Sunderland, though
he warns that the area may be atypical because 'the homogeneity,
solidarity and lack of social and geographical mobility of the
inhabitants facilitates community action' (Dennis 1972, p. 34).
Arguably, however, amenity societies, whose interests are generally
aesthetic and who see themselves as apolitical, cannot be said to speak
for or be representative of the whole community. Perhaps it is not
surprising if they prefer a 'sweetheart relationship' with government
or the local planning department,[39] and 'lose the name of action'.

Different techniques of protest are recorded in accounts of the
opposition to the GLC's development scheme for Covent Garden
after the fruit and vegetable market was resited in Nine Elms.[40] The
GLC had far-reaching proposals for the area including a major road
scheme and new office developments. The residents, a majority of
whom lived in cheap housing, did not wish to move. Under the
leadership of Brian Anson, a disenchanted member of the GLC's
planning department, the Covent Garden Community Association
(CGCA) was formed to fight the proposals.

After a public inquiry into the GLC's proposals, the scheme was
partially rejected. The Minister (Mr Rippon) expressed the view that
the GLC should secure greater public participation through consultation. In response, the GLC created the Covent Garden Forum,
comprising nine residents, nine businessmen, nine service workers
and three property owners elected by people who live, own property
or work in the Garden. Is this the type of 'community forum'
Skeffington had in mind? The Forum still meets regularly on an
advisory basis and two representatives attend meetings of the GLC
Covent Garden Committee. What happened next illustrates how
certain groups may favour methods of protest which do not oblige
them to work within the confines of existing political structures. The
CGCA participated in the first Forum elections. After experience of
the Forum's methods of operation, it withdrew its members, arguing
that the Forum was unable to pressurize the authorities effectively
and would dull the effectiveness of the CGCA. Amongst reasons

given were that the CGCA had no patience with lengthy debate and study, or with efforts to appease interests whose legitimacy they did not accept. Although the CGCA is usually quoted as a successful working-class protest movement, Anson is less sanguine. He insists:

It is said that victories have been won in Covent Garden during the last ten years. That may be so, but they have come at a price and that price has been paid not by the British Government nor by the middle class who now dominate the area, but by those who have always paid in Covent Garden – the indigenous working-class community. [Anson 1981, p. xv.]

In the light of this comment, consider an important case which formed part of the CGCA campaign. The Covent Garden Committee recommended that certain premises in James Street should be allocated for housing use with studios or workshops at ground-floor level. In March 1977, at a PLI into the draft local plan, a GLC representative confirmed this use, which was not contested. Subsequently, when the GLC had changed hands, the reconstituted GLC Covent Garden Committee was presented with an alternative plan for offices on the site. The GLC Planning Committee passed a resolution granting 'deemed planning permission' for this new office site, which dispensed them from the need to hold another public inquiry. *Covent Garden Community Association* v. *GLC* [1981] JPL 183 was an application for judicial review by CGCA on the ground that the statutory procedures appropriate to a change of plan had not been followed and the requirements of natural justice had not been observed. In short, the community had been deprived of its right to object and to participate in this important planning decision.

Although the action failed on its merits, the judge showed understanding of the difficulties of community groups of this kind. Holding that the group had locus standi to apply for judicial review, Woolf J reasoned that the only alternative legal redress was a relator action:

Before being joined as a relator, the Attorney-General required an indemnity as to his costs and this the applicants were not in a position to give. Furthermore, in such proceedings the applicants would need to seek an interim injunction and this they were not in a position to obtain because they could not give the necessary undertaking as to damages.

This decision is not only important because it extends the law of locus standi in planning cases. A note [1981] JPL 187 calls it 'a recognition by the courts that questions of public interest cannot be left entirely to public bodies even elected ones and . . . an important concession to the ideology of public participation'. The case also illustrates how community action groups may utilize administrative law procedures. This is not the first case of its kind. In *Elliott* v. *Southwark LBC* [1976] 1 WLR 499 owner/occupiers in a slum clearance area applied for declarations in an attempt to reopen the case for rehabilitation rather than demolition. Another similar case is *R.* v. *Hammersmith LBC ex p. People Before Profit* (1982) 80 LGR 322. Here the applicant was a local action group which sought to challenge the Council's decision to reject recommendations made after a PLI by the inspector broadly favourable to the group's suggestions. Again a judge held that the group had locus.

We should not rush to the conclusion that participation is 'planner-oriented' and élitist or that opportunities for participation, informal and formal, will simply increase the representation of 'middle-class' groups. We might, for example, meet this difficulty by increasing the opportunities for other groups to participate through community action and community development projects. Or we might have uncovered another problem of 'unmet legal need'. On the other hand, we should not assume lightly that more participation is always 'a good thing'. Skeffington was not concerned that existing constitutional arrangements would be endangered. The Committee thought that western democracy might be entering a new phase; 'There is a growing demand by many groups for more opportunity to contribute and for more say in the working out of policies which affect people . . . Planning is a prize example of the need for this participation, for it affects everyone. People should be able to say what kind of community they want and how it should develop.' By 1974, Dobry was expressing himself more cautiously:

The public can make a valuable contribution to decision making so long as consultation is properly channelled and kept within reasonable bounds. But I do not think that the decision itself can be made by the public through appropriate participation. Because one tends to talk about 'the public interest' or 'the public view' one can be led into thinking that all that is needed is to sound out the public; find out what their view is, and implement it. The fact is that there will be almost as many views as there are individuals or groups consulted . . .

In general local authority members should be the main channel for public involvement. There is evidence that neither the public nor many of the elected representatives fully appreciate that this is the basis of the democratic process which should be in control of planning. [Dobry, 1974, paras. 4.19–4.20.]

Hill amplifies this, remarking that citizen participation and popular control 'inevitably involve new kinds of representative institutions':

It is very difficult to envisage systems of popular democracy operating in relation to institutions whose activities affect large numbers of people, without some representational system developing. With such representational systems would come the potential for the development of oligarchy . . .

The representatives would become involved in the details of decision making, and would be drawn close to the full-time officials, in such a way that problems of alienation from the rank and file, whom they represented, could arise. Again, therefore, when our system of representative government is attacked, or when the character of the existing distribution of power is considered, it would be helpful if critics would make clearer the probable character of the alternatives they envisage. 'Participation' and 'popular democracy' can too easily be fine but empty slogans which do not contribute to an effective attack on contemporary reality, because they relate it to an ideal which cannot be translated into a concrete form. [Hill 1976, pp. 233–4.]

(Compare Hill's argument with that of Griffith concerning adjudication as a substitute for the political process, above, Chapter 10.)

By 1979, Ash was asking whether it was time to bury Skeffington. She reported (1979, p. 136) that many local authorities had become 'disillusioned about the possibility of involving the public'. The Association of County Councils was asking for a return to the statutory minimum requirements. Two years later, a new circular was issued, said by the DOE to represent 'a change of policy based on experience gained since 1974'. Under the heading 'public participation' Circ. No. 28/1981 advised planning authorities:

15. The contribution of the individual citizen and interest groups to the preparation of structure and local plans remains one of the central features of the development plan system. The statutory requirements now are:

    (a) to give publicity to the matters proposed to be included in the plan and in the explanatory memorandum and

    (b) to give those interested an adequate opportunity to make representations about matters proposed to be included in the plan [and] to consider those representations . . .

16. The view of the Secretary of State is that those requirements are adequate and that planning authorities should not normally need to do more. Only one stage of publicity and public participation will normally be necessary for a plan or an alteration and a period of 6 weeks for the making of representations on the draft plan should be adequate, though authorities may consider representations received outside this period . . . authorities

may undertake further work but . . . should be satisfied that the further work and delay that [is entailed] is further justified.

The Royal Town Planning Institute noted the changing political climate in a major reappraisal of public participation since Skeffington by a working party reporting in 1982. There was a 'divergence between the desire of the public for more participation and that of the Government for less . . . Too often public participation is being equated in local and central government circles with delay, excessive cost and inefficiency.'[41] The RTPI insisted that public participation was essential for the healthy future of local representative democracy. Their report had two recurrent themes: participation as negotiation or bargain; and access to information or open government in the planning process. In the bargaining model, participation is 'akin to a bargaining process involving the local authority and organised interest groups within a given set of rules.' The report continued:

The adoption of a 'bargaining' perspective to public participation must . . . recognise the inequality of access to the processes through which decisions are made. We need to ensure that the largest or strongest groups in society do not dominate at the expense of minorities or those who are unable readily to express themselves as well as the others . . . The bargaining process between a public authority and those affected by its actions can never be a wholly open and equal one, but it is possible to propose measures for making it more open and explicit, and more equal in terms of access and bargaining power, and this is what our proposals attempt to do.[RTPI para. 2.6.]

Thus some proposals tried to increase 'grass-roots' participation, for example by the establishment of Community Planning Councils (CPCs) whose members would be nominated by accredited voluntary organizations such as amenity groups, existing bodies such as Trades Councils and Chambers of Commerce, and local authorities. How 'representative' or 'oligarchic' would such a body be? CPSs would have statutory rights to be consulted and of access to information and other proposals stressed the need for access to information by the interested public. The report recommended improvements in the formal machinery for participation. It insisted also that a national code of practice to standardize informal procedures which would set out the rights and responsibilities of all parties at every stage of the plan was essential.

We are left asking whether there is room for McAuslan's third ideology. Has citizen-participation failed us or has it never properly been tried?

15
Planning: profit before people?

Participatory decison-making and participation theory formed the central theme of the last chapter. We listed possible objectives for participation, watched the growth of the participation movement and tried to estimate its successes and failures. We also considered the uses and abuses of informal participation techniques. Now we turn to formal procedures, the traditional preserve of administrative law. But as you read on, do not forget what has gone before. Ask yourself how far the procedures are intended to and do secure participation. If they do, who participates? And question the value of participation by reference to Arnstein's ladder.

Our first two sections suggest tightening legal 'control'; in short, judicialization from within and without. But by now we are alive to the possibility of administrative counteraction. We are familiar with 'rules within rules' (Chapter 5), and have seen the administration resort to prerogative powers and informal bargains (Chapter 1). To some, 'planning bargains' are another example of the 'retreat from legalism' and 'cheque-book planning' epitomizes the unacceptable face of corporatism, to others 'negotiated development' is the ultimate aim of citizen-participation. These contrasting views are discussed in the last section.

1 Planning inquiries: on from Franks

By 1955, when the Franks Committee was appointed, inquiries were a well-established feature of the administrative scene. But administrative law found difficulty in accommodating inquiry procedure, which seemed to balance perilously between 'judicial' and 'administrative'. The purpose of an inquiry was to gather information and ascertain the strength of public feeling; it was, in short, advisory. For the department, the inquiry was merely one stage in an administrative process which might interrupt relationships with other administrative agencies. For the public on the other hand there seemed little point in an inquiry if its result was preordained.

For McAuslan, Franks was a turning-point in British administrative history because its recommendations tipped the balance away from the administration-centred idea of the inquiry as a small part of a continuing administrative process towards a 'private interest' ideology. It laid the foundations on which the participation movement could later build. McAuslan sees two recommendations as specially important: the publication of the reports of inspectors and officials inside the ministry and the introduction of statutory rules of procedure:

Between them they have decisively shifted the balance in public local inquiries in the land use planning field from the inquiry process as being merely one part, albeit the most public part, of the administrative process of reaching a decision on a planning issue, to being the forum in which a much greater degree of public participation can take place, in which a decision is increasingly being reached and through which the courts can exert a much greater control on the planning process, usually but not always in the interests of, and in accordance with, the ideology of private property. Just as the absence of statutory rules ensured in inquiries, and ensures in the public examination [EIP], that the administrators retain complete control of the process and organise it in accordance with the ideology of public interest, so the presence of statutory rules even more than their content has removed control of the process from the administrators and vested it in the courts. [McAuslan 1981, p. 47.]

The tension between these two views of the inquiry as 'administrative' or 'adjudicatory' is one important theme of the post-Franks era. Another is the tension between formality, with statutory procedures, and informality. McAuslan suggests that informality favours the administration while formality favours both private interests and participation. Later we shall find contrasting views.

One celebrated decision illustrating the view of the inquiry as an administrative process is *Arlidge*'s case (above, p. 26). Another, equally famous, is *Franklin* v. *Minister of Town and Country Planning* [1948] AC 87. This case concerned the procedures used before the designation of Stevenage, a rural area of Hertfordshire, as the site for a new town under the New Towns Act 1946. Anticipating the passage of the Act, the Minister (Mr Silkin) addressed a packed meeting in Stevenage, where he confirmed that the project would go forward with or without the cooperation of local people. When he said that he would carry out his duty even if people were 'fractious and unreasonable' he was met by shouts of 'Gestapo!'

Stevenage was duly designated as the site for a new town after the Bill became law and a public local inquiry was held after objections had been received. The inspector's report summarized the objections and, shortly afterwards, objectors learned that the Minister had decided, after considering the report, to confirm the designation order. Franklin and others applied for the order to be quashed on the ground that the Minister was biased when he considered the order and had not, as required, considered the objections fairly and properly. The House of Lords upheld the Minister's decision. Lord Thankerton, reading their unanimous judgment, used the traditional classifications to support the administrators' view of the function of the inquiry. Compare his reasoning with that in *Arlidge*'s case:

LORD THANKERTON: In my opinion, no judicial, or quasi-judicial duty was imposed on the respondent, and any reference to judicial duty, or bias, is irrelevant in the present case. The respondent's duties under [the New Towns Act] are . . . purely administrative, but the Act prescribes certain methods of or steps in, discharge of that duty . . . It would seem . . . that the respondent was required to satisfy himself that [the scheme was sound] before he took the serious step of issuing a draft order. It seems clear also, that the purpose of inviting objections and . . . of having a public inquiry, to be held by someone other than the respondent, to whom that person reports, was for the further information of the respondent in order to [facilitate] the final consideration of the soundness of the scheme of the designation . . . No judicial duty is laid on the respondent in the discharge of these statutory duties, and the only question is whether he has complied with the statutory directions to appoint a person to hold the public inquiry, and to consider that person's report . . .

The use of the word 'bias' should be confined to its proper sphere. Its proper significance is to denote a departure from the standard of even-handed justice which the law requires from those who occupy judicial office, or those who are commonly regarded as holding a quasi-judicial office, such as an arbitrator . . . The respondent having no judicial duty, the only question is what the respondent actually did, that is, whether in fact he did generally consider the report and the objections . . . Nothing said [at the meeting] was inconsistent with the discharge of his statutory duty when subsequently objections were lodged, and the local public inquiry took place, followed by the report of that inquiry, genuinely to consider the report and the objections.

In the *Franklin* case, Lord Thankerton expressed understanding of

the inter-departmental relationships involved in the planning process. The Minister, he thought, would have 'made elaborate inquiry
into the matter and have consulted any local authorities who appear
to him to be concerned, and obviously other departments of the
Government, such as the Ministry of Health, would require to be
consulted'. The extent to which the establishment of an inquiry can
be allowed to interfere with these relationships is a thorny problem for
administrative law. In one celebrated pre-war case, the Jarrow
Corporation embarked on an ambitious programme of slum clearance in the course of which a public inquiry had to be held on behalf of
the Minister. When he read the inspector's report, the Minister was
inclined to think that a settlement between the corporation and
owners of affected property might be negotiated. A departmental
deputation visited Jarrow and met corporation spokesmen. The
owners were neither invited to attend nor to comment on correspondence. The Minister later confirmed the provisional clearance
order under the Housing Act 1930. In *Errington* v. *Minister of Health*
[1935] 1 K B 249, the Court of Appeal quashed the order for breach of
natural justice:[1]

MAUGHAM LJ: It has been suggested that the main object . . . of the public
inquiry, is to afford publicity in the local press which may in some way affect
the decision of the Minister. That is not . . . by any means the only reason for
requiring a public local inquiry to be held. The obvious implication is, that at
such an inquiry the two sides may be heard. . . The public inquiry is of the
nature of a quasi-judicial inquiry in which, although the rules of procedure of
a Court of Justice may not be followed, the ordinary principles of fair play
have to be observed. . . The question whether the Minister, after such an
inquiry has been held and after a report has been made, can then proceed . . .
to hear ex parte statements from one side or the other in the absence of those
whose obvious desire it would be to controvert them is precisely similar to the
question whether, after holding a public local inquiry or after having caused a
public local inquiry to be held of a quasi-judicial character, the Minister can
then hold a private inquiry of his own to which one party only is admitted.
That seems to me to be a very extraordinary result . . . especially in . . . a case
in which the rights of property owners are being affected without compensation . . . In my judgment . . . the officials committed an error of
judgment in allowing the results of the public inquiry to be supplemented by a
quasi-private inquiry, plus ex parte statements made to the Minister, without
any repudiation of that being the right course.

In the first edition of his textbook, Wade showed understanding of
the difficulties created for administrators:

The decision was received without enthusiasm in Whitehall; and one must
admit that this mixture of administrative and judicial responsibilities makes

it difficult for the Ministry to fulfil their functions. As soon as an objection is lodged, they must either give up their normal dealings with the local authority, or else they must allow the objectors to intrude into the daily work of the department. When the inquiry has been held, the Ministry cannot refer back to the local authority without reopening the whole subject of the inquiry. What makes the position seem artificial is the idea that the local authority is a party to the dispute, and that the Minister is an independent judge. In fact, the two authorities are working – or should be working – hand in glove, one at the local and one at the national level. Both are wielding administrative power and there is no real difference in the nature of their activities. [Wade 1961, p. 153]

Franks was asked to consider 'the working of such administrative procedures as include the holding of an inquiry or hearing by or on behalf of a Minister . . . and in particular the procedure for the compulsory purchase of land.' In the event, the evidence received related almost entirely to the latter head and Franks decided to concentrate on it. In contrast to the administration-centred view of the inquiry as a stage in the administrative process, Franks could be said to have viewed the administrative process as the *context* of the inquiry.

To Franks, all inquiries seemed to involve the classic conflict between state and individual, public and private interest. They set out to find a reasonable compromise in the light of their guiding principles of openness, fairness, impartiality:

All [enquiries] involve the weighing of proposals or decisions . . . made by a public authority . . . against the views and interests of individuals affected by them . . . All culminate in a ministerial decision, in the making of which there is a wide discretion and which is final. Because of the importance of these common features it is reasonable to consider the various procedures together when formulating a broad approach to them . . . The intention of the legislature in providing for an enquiry or hearing in certain circumstances appears to have been twofold: to ensure that the interests of the citizens closely affected should be protected by the grant to them of a statutory right to be heard in support of their objections, and to ensure that thereby the Minister should be better informed of the facts of the case. [Cmnd 218, paras. 267, 269.]

Notice how this statement of objectives mirrors the tension of the *Errington* case. Objectors prefer to make their case before an adjudicator who will hold the ring and see fair play. But a minister who wishes to know what people are thinking, might find an *inquisitorial* procedure which finds room for negotiation and informal discussion more helpful.

Franks' own conclusions concerning responsibility for policy suggest that 'participation' did not occur to the Committee as a major objective for the inquiry. They reported that inability to get access to ministerial policy was a 'major source of public grievance', but their proposals were not particularly radical. For example, they recommended that departmental witnesses should be available for questioning, but that they should be protected from 'questioning on matters for which Parliament is the right forum' (paras. 314–20). Moreover, statements of policy could not be allowed to fetter the Minister's future freedom of action:

> We recognise that broad policy is something for which a Minister is answerable to Parliament alone and we have no wish to suggest that these statements of policy should be automatically open to debate in the restricted forum of an enquiry. The Minister should be free, when issuing a statement of policy, to direct in writing that the whole or certain parts of it are not open to discussion at the enquiry . . . This power would avoid useless discussions of policy in the wrong forum, but the manner of its exercise would itself be open to criticism in the right forum – Parliament . . . Policy is, by its very nature, evolutionary and . . . a Minister's policy . . . may change after the enquiry. In such an event it would be unreasonable to bind the Minister to his previously issued statement, but the letter conveying his final decision should draw attention to and clearly explain the change of policy . . . [Cmnd 218, paras. 288–9.]

In this respect Franks could be described as 'public interest oriented' or perhaps merely traditionalist in constitutional matters. Generally, however, as with tribunals, Franks opened the door to judicialization within and without: within, through procedural rule-making and the formalization of inquiries, without, through the supervisory activities of courts and of the Council on Tribunals. Grant (1982, p. 610) attributes 'a dramatic change of approach' to three procedural reforms: (a) the right of appeal on a point of law to the High Court; (b) the requirement of reasoned decisions, first given effect by the Inquiries Procedure Rules 1962 (SI No. 1424/62); and (c) the introduction of procedural codes. 'The cumulative effect of these reforms was that a great deal of ministerial decision-making became subject to detailed legal rules, the scope of which was often – as with the duty to supply reasons – quite uncertain, and yet compliance with which was often a precondition to the making of a valid decision.' Compare McAuslan's views.

Inevitably, Franks confirmed the planning inspector's arbitral position and, if the recommendations had been fully implemented, the process might have gone further still. As with tribunal chairmen,

Franks hoped that inspectors would be appointed by the Lord Chancellor. In fact they are still appointed by, and attached to, the DOE. Wraith and Lamb tell us that inspectors:

... are recruited (by the normal methods of advertisement) almost wholly from outside government service, at a point when they have established themselves in other careers; no one would be recruited before his late thirties and a more usual age would be over 45. The requirement, apart from personal qualities, has normally been a professional qualification in surveying, town planning, architecture or civil engineering and the main sources of recruitment have been from local government service and private professional practice. [Wraith and Lamb 1971, p. 181.]

Although Franks treated planning inquiries generally, we ought not to assume that they always serve the same purpose. Both *Arlidge* and *Errington* concerned the taking of property, in which the owner clearly has an interest and where he may regard 'the state' as an adversary. Public local inquiries set up to hear objections before the approval of local plans are not so obviously adversarial. Perhaps they should not be seen as a fight between objectors and the authorities although, as we shall see later, they often are. Planning appeals are often of minimal interest to anyone other than the applicant and, where an inquiry is held, the Minister more often than not delegates his powers.[2] The inspector's position then becomes equivocal: is he an arbitrator or a ministerial representative?

From time to time a planning appeal inquiry develops dimensions of public policy: e.g. the Windscale inquiry. It is hard to classify this as an issue between 'the state' and 'an individual'; indeed the fight may be between the community and a powerful corporation. Sometimes the developer may have ministerial backing, sometimes the relationships are more complex, but the procedure is seldom 'three-cornered', as in the court model. Think too about the issues which might arise at a PLI or an inquiry into a 'called-in' planning application like that at Windscale. Are they the same as those raised by the normal planning appeal? What skills might an inspector require? Is access to departmental policy and information desirable? Is it more important to stress the inspector's 'independence'? In 1978, after a major review of trunk road procedures, the department conceded (Cmnd 7133, (1978)) that inspectors in trunk road inquiries should be nominated by the Lord Chancellor, though approved by the Minister. Does this concession suggest to you that Franks was right? Bear the point in mind when reading *Bushell*'s case (below).

Discussing inquiries into the siting of electricity installations (e.g. pylons, generators or power stations) Drapkin points out that inquiries serve purposes apparently not considered by Franks. How many objectives can you find in this passage? Is there consensus over these objectives by all the groups concerned?

The public inquiry is a continuous tug of war between substance and procedure. Natural justice now requires that objections be fairly aired. Fairness requires procedures of a quasi-judicial nature, which leads objectors to believe that the decision is also limited by the judicial process. Since no such limitation exists, conflicts in expectations arise . . .

Objectors are concerned about something. This includes local residents, whose property is directly affected, and local amenity groups, whose intentions are admirable, but who (according to some critics) are unable to see the national necessities at stake. These feelings may have detrimental consequences, both for the Government and for the Board. Therefore, from the decision-maker's perspective, the inquiry is seen as a means for 'neutralising public opinion', 'doing something about local hostility and resentment', or allowing the public to 'let off steam'. This may be useful for the decision makers, but, in context, it is misleading the participants. The emphasis on impartiality, and quasi-legal atmosphere nurture the expectation that participation may influence the decision. The resulting conflict of expectations undermines the theory of public participation here. [Drapkin 1974, pp. 239, 244.]

Allan, a planning inspector, has expressed his belief that the inspector's task is 'not to formulate policies or determine their merits, or even interpret policies except in the limited sense of translating them into terms of land use. His primary job is to determine how far the given framework of policy should be applied in the particular case.' Not surprisingly he went on to argue that planning appeal inquiries were more successful than those inquiries where the issues were allowed to broaden out. As you read this passage, ask yourself whether Allan sees his role as 'judicial' or 'administrative' (remember the definitions used by the Donoughmore Committee). How does participation ideology fit in?

It is my belief that in principle the customary procedures of the conventional planning inquiry, into an appeal, or a called-in application, for example, are eminently suitable for the limited purpose of applying given policies to a specific proposal, and that difficulties only begin to arise as the objectives of the inquiry begin to extend well beyond these limits; in attempting to deal effectively with alternative proposals for example, or to seek the best solution rather than merely avoid the unacceptable, or to formulate or even debate the merits of broad planning policies. Increasingly, in the bigger, more contentious inquiries the tendency is to explore the economic and social factors that influence policy or to attempt to evaluate both strategy and planning techniques. This takes the Inspector outside his more normal role. [Allan 1974, p. 4.]

Franks had demanded a statutory code of procedure drafted by its independent councils on tribunals. The role of the actual Council on Tribunals in procedural rule-making is directly comparable to its experience in the tribunal field. It has devoted much of its time to the scrutiny of procedural rules and the result has been increasing procedural formality. Today procedure at planning appeal inquiries is governed by the Town and Country Planning (Inquiries Procedure) Rules 1974 (S I No. 419/74). Reg. 10(1) apparently vests a wide discretion in the planning inspector: 'Except as otherwise provided . . . the procedure at the inquiry shall be such as the appointed person shall in his discretion determine'. Nevertheless, the rules themselves are a detailed procedural code. For example, they provide that notice of an inquiry must be published (Reg. 5); statements are to be served on applicants and documents discovered (Reg. 6); the persons entitled to appear are listed and a right to counsel specified (Reg. 7).

Judicial review of planning decisions had always been a possibility, but some of the cases already quoted illustrate an underlying judicial hesitation about augmenting statutory planning procedures or insisting on conformity with a judicial model. The requirements of the Tribunals and Inquiries Acts 1958 and 1971 stamped judicial intervention with the seal of official approval. The statutory rules opened the inquiry process to increased court 'control'. Case law increasingly stipulated that the Minister in deciding planning appeals should adopt the judicialized style of decision-making with which we are familiar from previous chapters. The conceptual vocabulary of lawyers, distinguishing, for example, 'fact', 'law', 'policy', 'opinion', appeared in the cases. It was held that the Minister's decisions ought to be based on the inspector's findings of fact, that they must be supported by 'sufficient evidence' or that a decision to differ from the inspector's recommendations should be justified in an adequately reasoned letter of decision[3]. An article by a principal in the planning department of the D O E shows how judicial decisions have an influence in planning appeals wholly disproportionate to their number:

Much time must now be spent in a painstaking checking operation to make sure that every fact has a clear source in the report and relates to a matter which has been argued at the inquiry and that the conclusions and the recommendation flow from the facts. One must be absolutely sure that an Inspector is not basing a fact or conclusion on something he has seen with his own eyes (which used to be thought the reason for his inspection of the site) which has not been discussed at the inquiry. The Minister has, in fact, submitted to judgment in a case because the decision was partly based on the fact that the Inspector noticed at the site inspection that the site was detached from the main part of a district by a busy road. No one denied that it was, but the appellants argued that they had not had the opportunity to comment on the traffic objection. The same principle also applies to plans. A challenge has been made because an Inspector, comparing two plans both handed in at the inquiry noticed discrepancies. Avoidance of this type of challenge places an added burden on decision officers who must now do a check on the 'mechanics' of the decision-taking process instead of just concentrating on the planning merits. In written representations cases care must be taken to base the decision on matters that have been argued and not on matters deduced from the representations.

There is also a ground for challenge if it is held that the Minister has failed to take certain matters into account. This puts an added responsibility on Inspectors who must make certain that their report faithfully records the cases put, as well as on those drafting the decision letters . . .

The Department is swift to act upon Court decisions. A law student who worked with me for a time said he was amazed to find how conscious we were of the power of the Courts when so few of our cases were actually challenged. This is true, for we must behave as though every decision is going to be challenged even though only a handful of cases a year are. [Payne 1971, pp. 116–17.]

Although the rules are not mandatory at PLIs, they serve as a model and are followed as closely as possible. In 1977, the DOE issued an informal 'Code of Conduct' ('Local Plans: Public Local Inquiries', Circ. No. 68/77). This is now published as a booklet available to the public. Bruton, Crispin and Fidler (1980, p. 381) (henceforward Bruton *et al.*) in a series of studies of PLI procedures describe a consistent trend to formalization and assimilation of PLIs to appeal inquiries. There is some discretion, e.g. to allow un-programmed contributions, but cases are formally presented, witnesses are called and cross-examined by counsel and formal rights of reply accorded: 'Formal, but non-statutory, is the convention.' Think about the purposes of the local plan. Is the PLI primarily for 'participation' or to protect the interests of property-owners who may be affected? And does your answer affect the choice of procedures? Bruton *et al.* concluded (1982, p. 286) that there was a 'high level of satisfaction with the fair, orderly and impartial conduct of PLIs to date and a clear need for flexibility in procedures given the wide range of objections and objectors.' There were textual advantages to the informal code; it was 'written in a language which would be inappropriate in a statutory instrument but which is right for the job in hand, providing a clear, informative and readable written guide to procedures which is especially valuable to objectors'. You will be able later to compare the experience of the S B regulations and 'Hand-book' (below, Chapter 19). A final advantage to the inspectorate lay in the fact that there was no basis for an appeal on the ground that the code had not been followed.

On the other hand, the authors were concerned by the absence of truly independent assessment in a process where the P L I inspector reports to the planning authority which makes the final decision. In the following extract, notice the implication that planning authorities may avoid the more formal procedures wherever possible:[4]

The evidence from [our] research demonstrates that the public at present does not trust the local authority to sit in judgment on its own plan proposals; the public almost unanimously feels that the final decision on local plan policies should be taken by the Secretary of State – after all 'The Minister is the only person sufficiently remote from the issue to be objective'. Indeed . . . some means of arbitration is essential in those situations where none of the parties in the debate are prepared to make concessions.

The obvious way to resolve this problem is to change the role of the P L I so that it becomes more of a judicial than administrative event; to centralise the final decision. However, this would undermine the concept of the deter-mination of local plan issues at the local level; it is not in step with current government thinking; it would require a change in the law and it would be strongly opposed by the local authorities . . .

Yet the problem of credibility and the ultimate legitimacy in the eyes of the public remains. How can this be achieved whilst still retaining the present administrative functions of the plans P L I? . . . Ironically, one of the perceived defects with the local plans P L I – the additional time required to process a local plan through to statutory adoption – may contribute to [its] natural evolution into more of a judicial/arbitral role . . . Local authorities . . . resort to statutory local plans only in situations where formal support is considered necessary in the face of complex conflicting interests which cannot be resolved through the local political processes . . . In these situations, the inspector's role will in reality be a quasi-judicial one. The local authority in the face of conflicting interests will make the independent third party responsible for taking what will be unpopular decisions for some and will thus accept the inspector's recommended modifications. [Bruton, Crispin and Fidler 1982, pp. 285–6.]

On the other hand, the authors feel that the increasing use of lawyers, though in the main favoured by the inspectorate, threatens the use of inquiries as a forum for citizen participation. But Lavers, discussing the experience of a small PLI at Lewes, without lawyers, comes down on the other side:

> Without lawyers the Inspector is likely to have to do most of the questioning which he requires to maximise his information. At many inquiries the Inspector finds that taking notes is all that he has time for. If lawyers are no longer there to do the questioning, the Inspector must formulate and ask the question, and listen to the reply, while noting both question and answer. Some Inspectors may refuse to do this or be unable to do so to their own satisfaction. They may depend upon council officers and objectors to undertake the questioning. This will either involve laymen imitating their perception of lawyers, almost certainly with an inferior technique, or cross-examination will be replaced by a series of simply factual questions, often of a technical kind.
>
> Lawyers are more than familiar with the judicial type of procedure; their whole presentation of a case is moulded by it and they have a shared tradition which ensures conformity and uniformity. Every objector, and indeed every council official coming to an inquiry for the first time, will have to be guided through the first session at least and possibly prompted throughout. At Lewes, some objectors were as heedless of formality at the end of the proceedings as they had been at the beginning . . .
>
> The Inspector's ease of understanding may suffer considerably from the removal of lawyers. The rambling irrelevance of some statements at EIPs suggests that to discover what is the nub of an argument an Inspector may have to undertake, during and after an Inquiry, that sifting of material which a lawyer would usually have completed before it began. Unrepresented objectors frequently cause this problem anyway, but to make everyone unrepresented is to multiply the problem for the Inspector. [Lavers 1979, p. 519.]

Payne, describing a personal appearance as an objector at a planning appeal inquiry, does not agree:

> I attended an inquiry as the owner of a property near a large garden that was to be developed with houses. The only questions in dispute were the density and access . . . I was horrified to find that the appellant, the authority, [and] neighbours . . . were all represented by counsel, who behaved throughout as though they were engaged in criminal proceedings. The two younger ones even prefaced most of their questions with 'Would you mind telling the *Court* . . . ?'. The atmosphere was so tense with counsel competing with each other to ask the witnesses the most penetrating or discomforting question, that I for one could not have risen to my feet to speak . . . I felt at the end . . . that the lot of the individual had been worsened as a direct or indirect result of the very procedure that is designed to protect their interests. No doubt the Council on Tribunals (who have pressed the point) and lawyers would say that this proves that legal aid should be available at inquiries, but I consider that they should be conducted in such a way that any appellant or third party should feel perfectly capable of conducting their own case. [Payne 1971, p. 114.]

Here is a dilemma. On the one hand, we have escalating judicialization with the panoply of lawyers, costs, legal aid, rules of evidence and procedure and reasoned 'judgments' (compare tribunals). On the other hand, we find flexibility but without 'rights' or procedural protection. This parallels the debate over welfare 'rights' and tribunals.

Some authorities have pioneered experiments which might in time be substituted for the 'judicialized' PLI. Jewell was present at such a meeting in Enfield, described as a cross between a 'public participation exercise' and a 'formal inquiry'[5] and expressed satisfaction with 'the kindly and sympathetic way the meeting was conducted'. Notice, however, that the chairman was the distinguished planner, Sir Colin Buchanan, with wide experience of planning inquiries:

> The meeting proved to be an arena for genuine public debate. So often in the inquiry system the major emphasis is on the main protagonists – the local planning authority and the appellants, the authority and the statutory objector, whilst the role of the so-called third parties is in practice a minor one slotted into the inquiry at convenient times. Yet, in many cases it is the third parties who are going to be the main beneficiaries or otherwise of a proposed development ... At many inquiries ... there is considerable frustration amongst the public not only that the lengthy submissions and cross-examinations by the major parties dwell on matters of abstruse details but also that their own contribution is often ignored ... The Enfield Town meeting indicated that the public have a great deal to contribute and achieve considerable satisfaction from being fully and actively involved in the debate. In addition, it increases their confidence in the decision-making process. [Jewell 1979, p. 221.]

There is a strong case for informality at small-scale inquiries of this type, especially if community participation and consensual decisions are seen as objectives of the planning process. At the opposite end of the scale, we also find dissatisfaction with the formalized 'Big Public Inquiry.' For example, the Roskill Commission sat for four years, at a cost of £1.5 million, employed its own research team, devised its own methodology and, in addition, held four local inquiries, one on each projected site. Roskill's conclusions were jettisoned before the ink was dry on its pages and Perman argues that it merely delayed an inevitable 'political' decision. In its own jargon, the Commission was hardly cost-effective:[6]

> [One] local effect of the Commission's long-winded and heavily judicialised procedures was that it forced the amenity groups to put all their eggs into the one basket of legal argument and to refrain for two years from political campaigning. On a number of occasions, Mr. Justice Roskill made it plain

that the Commission took a dim view of any attempt to side-step the complex arguments about cost/benefit and to resort to any form of political search for a solution . . .

The inquiry involved a number of difficult areas of government policy which had not at the time been subjected to anything like full political debate . . . [The people concerned] knew instinctively that their fates could be settled only by a political decision and . . . they showed a strong desire to force this decision into the open by means of demonstrations . . . The WARA [below] leadership was reluctant to let this happen and for some time there was a gulf between some of the association's more frustrated supporters and the leadership . . . This partly explains the great outpouring of popular feelings . . . once the Roskill inquiry was out of the way and the issue had become unequivocally a political one. [Perman 1973, pp. 174–5.]

Amenity groups like WARA, the pressure group set up to contest the choice of Cublington for the third airport, may find the cost of appearing at a major inquiry prohibitive. Because it decided that its case must be presented to the Roskill Commission 'on an equal footing with the local authorities and other public bodies', WARA briefed leading counsel. The cost of legal and technical representation amounted to £43,713 which had to be met from subscriptions and other fund-raising activities. Naturally, this has created a movement for costs to be awarded to objectors at planning inquiries on a more generous basis.[7]

A second example is that of the Layfield inquiry into the Greater London Development Plan (GLDP), the last of the old-style development plans. This was the largest inquiry ever held in Britain (a record now under threat at Sizewell). The 19,997 objectors made 28,392 objections and 326 appearances. The inquiry lasted almost two years – a total of 237 sitting days. The panel thought the forum quite unsuitable for discussion of a complex development plan (under the 1968 legislation, this would have been a structure plan).

The GLC have, in some respects shown a commendable willingness to accept criticism . . . But on occasions they showed a reluctance to do so, and throughout the Inquiry they were hampered by the procedure of cross-examination and reply which invariably encourages defensive attitudes and puts a higher premium on answering back than on self-analysis. The GLC were, no doubt, understandably concerned lest any change they proposed in the submitted plan would lead to an even longer Inquiry and further representations. [Layfield 1973, para. 2.15.]

For the objectors, McAuslan (1981, pp. 40–1) sees the GLDP inquiry as a limited success; 'despite the weight of expertise on the side of the GLC, the weight and cogency of many of the objections and their sheer volume impelled the panel to recommend extensive modifications to the plan'. For the panel and for the planners, it was a frustrating experience. The issues could not be satisfactorily separated one from another. The cumulative effect of incoherent and repetitious evidence made the planners, if anything, less responsive. The delays inherent in large inquiries lead the planners in two directions; either they come increasingly to rely on informal planning, or they must experiment with substitutes for the inquiry – hence the 'new structure plan procedures' referred to by Layfield.

Expressions of dissatisfaction were heard again after the planning appeal inquiry held at Windscale when the Minister 'called in' an application by British Nuclear Fuels to erect a plant for the reprocessing of irradiated oxide nuclear fuels. Mr Justice Parker, with two technically qualified assessors, chaired an inquiry which lasted for six months and finally formed the basis for a parliamentary debate.[8]

Neither the experts nor the objectors were satisfied with the legal framework of the Windscale inquiry. The experts felt that their highly technical arguments were distorted by translation; 'lawyers "intervene" between experts, losing arguments for want of knowledge' (*Nature*, vol. 272, 9 March 1978). For the objectors, the Windscale inquiry was a tiny corner of the debate on nuclear policy. Parker J did not exclude this debate, indeed he let it range more widely than Franks could have envisaged, but the objectors thought him ill-informed. 'During the hearings, he showed himself (quite honestly and openly) to be ignorant of much of the mainstream environmental dialectic' (Breach 1978, p. 192). Further, the cost to the environmental groups was enormous, faced as they were by the resources of the government and the nuclear industry. Friends of the Earth, which sustained a major share of the objectors' campaign, incurred costs of £50,000, raised by an appeal.

The statutory alternative is the 'Planning Inquiry Commission' (PIC). S.48(2) of TCPA 1971 provides for the establishment of a PIC to consider planning proposals which (a) involve issues of national or regional importance and which 'require evaluation, but a proper evaluation thereof cannot be made unless there is a special inquiry for the purpose' or (b) where the 'technical or scientific aspects are of so unfamiliar a character as to jeopardise a proper determination of that question'. The PIC consists of a chairman and two to four members and is to use a two-stage procedure. The first stage is comparable to a royal commission, where evidence is submitted by interested parties and considered by the Commission informally. At the second, specific proposals are listed at a public local inquiry in the usual way. The PIC has never yet been tried and is therefore hard to evaluate. It may be, however, that the experience of the Roskill Commission provides some pointers to latent problems.[9]

For those whose aim is participatory decision-making, it is important to penetrate the decision-making process at a much earlier stage. Specific proposals on which planners have expended energy, time and resources are infinitely harder to contest. Thus the authors of 'The Big Public Inquiry' (1979) (a working party of *Justice* and the Outer Circle Policy Unit) propose a 'project inquiry' (PI). A PI would be instituted at the time when a formal application for planning permission is likely, but *before* there has been too great an investment in the proposal. A PI would consist of a chairman and six to nine members appointed by a minister. The first stage would be investigatory, relying on an exchange of written material between the parties and the panel on a confidential basis. The second stage would be an inquiry 'with the important difference that all the "evidence" which is so laboriously led, cross-examined and re-examined . . . will already have been put in long since, and have become familiar to everyone taking a serious part in the inquiry . . . This stage will take far less time, and cost far less money, than at any public inquiry.' The authors envisage a third stage, when the panel's report would be debated in Parliament and a decision taken.

The RTPI working party (above) also considered 'The Big Public Inquiry'. They felt that inquiries were often instituted before there had been sufficient public debate, 'even though the policy underlying the project may well have been developed over many years of deliberation within government and semi-autonomous public agencies'. (Return to Perman, (above, p. 470); does this reflect his objections to Roskill?)

The RTPI suggested that need should be first evaluated by a select committee.[10] Then a 'Project Assessment Commission' (PAC), consisting of five commissioners, would be set up. The PAC would use investigatory procedures and would have powers to commission research. It would consider alternative solutions to the problem and might hold inquiries to determine whether given sites were more or less appropriate. Finally, a site-specific inquiry into detailed siting, design and land take would be held. The public would be permitted and encouraged to participate by providing information at every stage and the PAC would possess powers to 'specify the information' which they required from the government and the promoter (RTPI 1982, paras 6.8–6.31).

But Parker, describing his experience of Windscale, felt that the two-stage project inquiry would be unprofitable. Everything would need to be repeated at the second stage. The proposals would be 'a recipe for discontent and inefficiency' and Parker preferred the existing, site-specific inquiry:

Amongst other things the [PI is] against an adversary system which I regard ... as being highly desirable when one is holding a public enquiry ... Suppose a Tribunal of an Inspector and two Assessors. One of the Assessors thinks of a question to ask and he asks it. He gets an answer which he thinks is satisfactory. In the absence of the adversary system that is an end of it. But if the question has been asked by an advocate under the adversary system his expert behind him will or may urge him, on getting the answer, to continue to probe, and the matter will then be more thoroughly investigated. Scientists on the whole don't much like being cross-examined by lawyers and consider that differences between them should be resolved by some other means. But I remember very well a very eminent scientist having suffered two hours of cross-examination ... saying to me afterwards, 'It would be a very good idea if everybody who was about to present a scientific paper were cross-examined ... Half the papers wouldn't be presented at all and the other half would be a damned sight better.' It is a process which is very unpleasant if you are at the wrong end of it but it is exceedingly efficient at getting quickly to the real guts of a problem. Of course the Tribunal, even where the procedure is basically adversary, must have a power of investigation and it must exercise it, but with this qualification I think the adversary system serves the public better than any other. [Parker 1982, pp. 54–5.]

Before you go on to consider the structure plan EIP, think carefully about the inquiry. What are the advantages and disadvantages of adversarial procedure? What, if anything, can lawyers contribute? You can test your opinions by visiting a planning inquiry; they are public and open. You can even test yourself against the lawyers by making an objection. And is the difference between the PI, the PIC and the PAC purely nominal? Do they sit happily inside our existing political framework? Are they utopian visions of a planning system in which decisions are always rational and conflict does not exist?

2 Examination-in-public

Section 9(3) of TCPA 1971 (as amended) provides that the Minister must, before approving a structure plan, appoint a person or persons to hold an E I P. In practice, a panel of an independent chairman and two members is appointed:

The Chairman of the panel is an independent figure – usually a planning lawyer, an academic or a retired civil servant – while the other two members are drawn respectively from the planning inspectorate, so as to inject experience of implications for appeals, and from the appropriate joint regional office of the D O E and Transport, to bring to bear familiarity with the region concerned. The regional office also has an important role in inviting representations and objections, in selecting the issues to be examined at the E I P and arranging them on an agenda, in inviting representatives of particular interests to appear at particular sessions, and in preparing daily summaries of the proceedings. [Friend, Laffkin and Norris 1981, p. 445.]

Objectors may be invited to participate in the E I P, but it is doubtful if they have any enforceable legal right, or indeed locus standi, to challenge the Minister's decision because he is not required 'to secure to any local planning authority or other person a right to be heard at any examination . . . and the bodies and persons who may take part therein shall be such only as he may, whether before or during the course of the examination, in his discretion invite to do so.' The participants are selected by the Minister for 'the effectiveness of the contribution which, from their knowledge or the views they have expressed, they can be expected to make to the discussions of the matters to be examined'. So experts rather than the objectors control the E I P.

A code of practice, published by the D O E as a booklet entitled 'Structure Plans: the Examination in Public' (1973) governs procedure, which is modelled on that of an academic seminar. Those who have attended a number of structure plan examinations as observers, like Bridges and Vielba who conducted a survey for the Institute of Judicial Administration,[11] have generally found the experience disappointing. They felt that 'the hoped for round-table probing discussion' had not been achieved. Examination hearings still tend to be formalised, with most discussion directed through the chair and little direct interplay between participants. Contributors were often cut short and the discussion of many topics was superficial. The proceedings observed were dominated by official bodies and commercial interests and *alternative* planning strategies were only discussed when powerful central or local government bodies disputed the submitting authorities' preferred strategy in a fundamental way. (Locate this description on Arnstein's ladder.)

Darke, examining the case of the S. Yorkshire structure plan, agreed. Scrutiny of the list of participants led him to the conclusion that industry and commerce were over-represented while environmental groups had a poor chance of being invited to participate. The ministerial discretion was open to serious abuse in this respect. In comparison with inquiry procedures, the EIP was neither open nor democratic. His argument will be familiar:

What is rationalised as an expedient measure could be used to de-politicise controversial issues and ensure a commitment to central Government policies and opinions. Planning inquiries are quasi-judicial in the sense that the Minister has the final right of decision. Traditionally any objection could be heard and could be seen to be heard. Under the Code of Practice for [EIPs] this right has been lost. The principle that detailed matters are not appropriate so that some areas of debate are closed off, together with selection of participants, means that the EIP can be managed and directed in a way which was not possible under the old arrangements.

Contrast the proceedings at recent major roads and environmental planning inquiries where no such limitations have applied and where public opinion has been vociferously expressed, with the growing experience from EIP's. The common conclusion is that the EIP tends to be highly technical, given over to public bureaucrats and raises little interest from the public. [Darke 1979, p. 34.]

In a more cynical account, Friend, Laffkin and Norris (Friend *et al.*) place the structure plan examination firmly in the context of the corporate state. The examination is an 'arena' in which political dramas are enacted and positions staked out in a wider political game:

For all its apparent drama, the EIP can be seen as no more than one landmark in a more continuous kind of 'policy game' which is played out over time among the three levels of government, with interventions by the various other interests which can claim a legitimate stake in matters of land-use policy. Over the years during which a structure plan is being prepared, and again over the years that follow, the leading participants have many opportunities to reach accommodation on issues of controversy both minor and major, and to adapt to new circumstances as they arise. Thus the patterns of inter-governmental conflict, bargaining and co-operation over land-use matters can shift repeatedly both before and after the EIP takes place. In this context some of the structure plan policies, and the postures struck by spokesmen at EIPs, can be seen as dramatized attempts to assert often familiar political or territorial interests in the hope that the Secretary of State's response will be as advantageous as possible to the party concerned. Thus EIPs may present in a heightened form fundamental issues to do with the legitimacy of various perspectives on the use of land, and the sovereignty of elected local authorities. Simultaneously, they may provide opportunities for compromise and adjustment between authorities over more detailed matters, particularly where less formal channels of communication have become restricted for political or other reasons . . .

Nevertheless, the EIP is significant in that it provides an arena for the clash of interests over unspecified future schemes that one or other of the participants might at any time wish to pursue. The threat here is that, through the wording of its general policy position, one authority might pre-empt the position which another organization might wish to take over some particular development proposal at some later time. Such threats of pre-emption can often be challenged by casting doubt on the assumptions used to justify the policy in the face of changing conditions and attitudes, shifts in national policy and arguments stressing the inherent complexity of the interrelationships between land-uses. However, it was noticeable in the EIPs which were studied that these challenges were not made as forcibly as they might have been; even allowing for the constraints of the EIP format, it seems that there is often an implicit, and sometimes explicit, mutual understanding in which authorities accommodate to each other's interests in the pursuit of shared ends. [Friend, Laffkin and Norris 1981, pp. 453–4.]

With academic opinion largely favouring the view that the EIP is less participatory, more capable of being manipulated and less protective of the interests of those directly affected,[12] it is surprising that Hampton and Walker (1976, pp. 34–5) should find favourable public reaction to the Teeside/Cleveland EIP in 1975. They questioned 28 respondents, including eight members of the general public, who had attended a public inquiry as well as the EIP. They reported comparisons between the EIP and public inquiry to be generally favourable to the former. Only the commercial concerns were generally unfavourable, their complaints centring on (a) the lack of detail in the structure plan and (b) the absence of any chance of cross-examination. One speaker felt that the structure plan depended largely on unchallengeable assumptions. Of 19 respondents who included suggestions for reform, 12 asked for less formality and more open discussion. There was criticism of the way in which the Chairman limited the discussion. Some requests were made for small-group discussion.

In an unusual case,[13] structure planning and development control were the subject of a complaint to the PCA (HC 799 (1979/80), p. 23) by an amenity group. The complaint arose out of an application to build a food processing factory in the district of N. Tyneside MBC. The district was minded to allow the application and the draft structure plan, which was about to proceed to EIP, zoned the area for industrial use. Objections including three petitions had been received to this proposal. When the application came in, the regional office of the DOE at once issued a direction under Art. 10 of the General Development Order to prevent the district from granting planning permission without ministerial authorization. Later this direction was cancelled on the Minister's orders and he refused to 'call in' the application. These decisions formed the subject of the complaint, with an ancillary complaint – quickly dismissed by the PCA – of misleading advice which had prejudiced the amenity group by persuading it to reserve its objections for the EIP. The PCA was sympathetic to the idea that the ministerial decision had pre-empted the result of the EIP but, although he had interviewed the Minister, he was not entitled to question the merits of a discretionary decision:

I am satisfied that there was no statutory obligation on the part of the local planning authority to refer the planning application to the Department, nor on the Secretary of State to call it in for decision by him. It was open to the Department to call it in if they saw fit and there is evidence in the Department's files that this possibility was considered when they became aware of the concern expressed by a county councillor . . . on the possible pre-emption of a decision on the draft Structure Plan. But the Department have explained to me not only that it is exceptional for them to . . . intervene in local planning matters (a point I was aware of from other investigations and one the principle of which I see no reason to criticise), but also that if they do it is in order primarily to deal at a public inquiry with matters of fact of wider public importance (for example public safety) than local residents' amenity objections, however worthy these may be in the local context. For my part I see no reason to question the view, confirmed to me by the Secretary of State himself, that there were no proper grounds for calling in this particular application.

Officials in the Northern Regional Office, however, were concerned . . . that if the local planning authority granted the permission sought in the early months of 1980 'the proposed [EIP] would be negated . . . and it would appear to the public that the Secretary of State's decision on the [Structure Plan] had been pre-judged . . .' This seems to me to have been a worthy reaction on the part of officials and I certainly cannot criticise their decision to make use of powers available to them to issue a Direction which would have the effect of giving everyone concerned time to consider all the implications carefully. In doing this they were not taking the ultimate decision on the planning application out of the hands of the local planning authority: they were simply requiring them to hold their hand until the Department said they could go ahead. In their letter to the local planning authority they said, indeed, that the Direction was issued 'in order not to prejudice the Secretary of State's consideration of the Tyne and Wear Structure plan . . . Until the report of the Panel conducting the [EIP] been received . . . it would be premature to determine the current application'.

The cancellation of this Direction did not have and never would have had the effect of depriving the Association of the benefits of a public inquiry into the planning application. They would have had that only if the Department had called in the application. As it was not called in they had no statutory right to a public inquiry because a local planning authority are not required to hold one before deciding an application in front of them.

There is the question, however, whether the local planning authority's decision on that application before the [EIP] of the draft Structure Plan, and before the Secretary of State's consideration of the Panel's report on that [EIP] prejudiced the public's right to have their objections to that Plan fully heard and, if so, whether there was an obligation on the Department to prevent that happening. At first, as I have explained, officials thought it would and that there was. But the Department tell me that it is not normal for an area as small as the 50 hectares allowed in the draft Plan for possible industrial use, let alone one as small as the 16 hectares required by the company, to be the subject of detailed consideration by the Secretary of State in the context of a Plan laying down no more than general guidelines over an area of hundreds of square kilometres. The Department say that structure plans and their [EIPs] are primarily concerned with major issues such as Green Belts and the siting of such controversial things as nuclear power stations, and that it would be quite wrong for day-to-day detailed planning decisions to be held up simply because decisions on the wider issues had not yet been taken . . .

I cannot find that in allowing the planning application to be dealt with at a local level the Department were depriving the public in general, or the Association in particular, of their full rights to express and have publicly considered their views on the Structure Plan as a whole. Nor can I reasonably find that within that context the Association had a right to have a decision on the application held up, or that the Department were under any obligation to ensure that it was held up.

This extract gives a good impression of the way in which planning decisions are taken in the DOE. What was the departmental view of the functions of an EIP? What light does the affair shed on 'citizen-participation' in planning? Does it support the views of Friend *et al*?

3 Insider dealings

Notice the number of insider dealings in the course of the *N. Tyneside* case between regular participants in the planning game (e.g. the DOE, its regional office, county and district councillors, etc.). These dealings make it particularly difficult for outsiders to find out what is going on. Cases like *Errington* (above) or *Lavender* (below) represent the attempt of courts to deal with this difficulty. The *N. Tyneside* affair can also be linked with the *Franklin* case (above) because in both cases the formal inquiry procedures seemed to the objectors to have been pre-empted.[14] The problem for the public is accentuated by the complexity of the planning process and the legal provisions which govern it. Both points caused the RTPI working party concern:

As far as possible the public should have access to the information that councillors and officers have had in preparing a plan, they should also be informed when work on a new plan or review of a plan is beginning and be able to contribute at certain stages . . . The public must also have opportunities for challenging existing policies and proposals which local authorities have no current intentions to change. These participation rights should apply to *all* policies . . . Details of how the public can participate should be published; they should know where they stand if there is to be equitable bargaining between government and the public . . .

Although planners are familiar with the different components of the planning process and the way they fit together, we cannot expect this of the public . . . The public get very confused by the different stages in the statutory planning process; to them issue definition, options and draft plans are somewhat artificial and unpredictable divisions. It must seem strange to the public that one year they may be consulted many times on different plans or projects and then not be consulted at all for, perhaps, four years. We feel planning policy should be discussed and debated on a more regular basis. This does not necessarily imply that the policies have to be changed every time they are discussed; simply that they need to be looked at regularly . . . and not just when the local authority decide the time is right to change them . . .

The public should have access to all policy documents (whether statutory or non-statutory) used by a local authority: a list of these documents should always be available in conjunction with the register of planning applications. In addition the public should have access to any information used in preparing the documents. [RTPI 1982, paras. 4.4–4.16.]

These recommendations run counter to a long tradition concerning access to official information and responsibility for policy. The materials which follow deal with two problems: (a) the extent to which 'policy' can be challenged at a planning inquiry, and (b) the extent to which normal administrative relationships can be interrupted by a planning inquiry. Before you read them, reread the Franks Committee's recommendations (above, p. 462). Several external agencies are involved. Are their attitudes consistent? Are their solutions more satisfactory than those of the planners and administrators involved?

(a) The Chalkpit affair
Buxton was the owner of land in a predominantly agricultural area which he used for breeding pigs and ponies. He was interested in creating a nature reserve. Gravel and sand extraction was carried out on neighbouring property, whose occupiers put in an application to

quarry chalk. The application was refused by the local authority. The applicants appealed to the Minister who caused a local inquiry to be held. The Inspector recommended that the appeal be dismissed. He gave as his reason that 'the production of chalk from this site is likely to result in dust being blown on to adjoining land with serious detriment to the present use of the land'. Without reopening the inquiry or affording opportunities for comment, the Minister consulted MAF and allowed the appeal. Speaking for the Government, Viscount Kilmuir maintained that the procedure complied with the recommendations of the Franks Committee, which had distinguished 'factual evidence' from 'expert advice' (HL Deb. vol. 230, cols. 740–4):

New factual evidence which ought to be disclosed could not include technical or other advice given by Government officials on the issues raised at the inquiry and on the weight to be attached to evidence submitted there. Ministers must be free to seek such advice, and cannot be obliged to disclose the advice tendered to them by officials before they come to a decision. The Minister must inform himself, on the best advice available to him, on the right conclusions to be drawn from the argument, and those interested in the application cannot expect to be brought into this process; always provided that if any new factual evidence . . . or any new issue which may affect the decision – is brought to his notice that must be disclosed for comment before he reaches a conclusion . . .

The Government do not consider that there is any distinction to be drawn between experts who may happen to be in the Department of the deciding Minister and experts in another Department. The way in which the work of Government happens to be organised is neither here nor there for this purpose. In the case under consideration no new factual evidence, no new issue, was brought to the Minister's notice. He simply received confirmation of the appellants' argument that chalk from the appeal site would make a useful contribution to the area, and advice on the argument which had taken place at the inquiry about the damage which the chalk might be expected to cause; and his advice was that on this point the inspector's conclusion could not be supported, given the conditions which were to be imposed.

Buxton appealed to the High Court to reverse the Minister's decision for error of law. In *Buxton* v. *Minister of Housing and Local Government* [1961] 1 QB 278, he was held not to have locus standi. A complaint was then referred to the Council on Tribunals which found the Government explanation unsatisfactory. The matters referred to experts 'should have been brought to a head at the inquiry'. The Council published a special report on the subject of new evidence, recommending two new rules:

(1) Where the Minister proposes to disagree with the inspector's recom-

mendation either because of some factor not considered at the inquiry or because he differs from a finding of fact made by the inspector, he will notify the parties to the appeal of his disagreement and the reasons for it and afford them an opportunity for making comments and representations in writing before finally making his decision.

(2) Where the Minister proposes to depart from the inspector's recommendations because of (a) fresh evidence on a question of fact, or (b) fresh expert evidence (including expert advice) or (c) the introduction of a fresh issue, the inquiry should (if any of the parties so desire) be re-opened and the new evidence or issue should be produced at the re-opened inquiry. [AR 1961, App. D.]

The Government accepted the report. In the House of Lords debate which followed its publication, Lord Chorley argued that the problem lay in the definition of 'policy' (HL Deb. vol. 239 cols. 1146–7):

It seems to me that the Council on Tribunals has found a way out of that, because if the matter is one of policy, the policy must be known to the Minister from the start, and if the policy is made clear at the very beginning then it will be quite impossible for these suspicions to arise in the way that they did at a later stage.

I would not . . . say that a civil servant should go down to an inquiry and subject himself to cross-examination on policy. Surely it would be impossible for the Government to accept a view of that kind. National policy clearly is not a subject on which civil servants should be cross-examined. There is no doubt a shading-off between national policy and agricultural advice which may be on the borderline of policy; and no doubt on some point of that kind it is feasible for a civil servant to be cross-examined by counsel in the light of expert evidence which he himself is calling and the advice which he has received in his brief. But I would suggest that it is not possible to go beyond that. But if the policy is made perfectly clear at that stage it cannot afterwards be said that, after all the evidence has been given, the speeches have been made and the inspector has drawn up his report, then, in some hole-and-corner way, policy is brought in and the inspector's report to the Minister is overriden.

The Inquiries Procedure Rules 1974 (SI No. 419/74) now provide:

12 (2) Where the Secretary of State –
    (a) differs from the appointed person on a finding of fact, or,
    (b) after the close of the inquiry takes into consideration any new evidence (including expert opinion on a matter of fact) or any new issue of fact (not being a matter of government policy) which was not raised at the inquiry;
and by reason thereof is disposed to disagree with a recommendation made by the appointed person, he shall not come to a decision which is at variance with any such recommendation without first notifying the applicant, the local

planning authority and any [party] who appeared at the inquiry of his disagreement and the reasons for it and affording them an opportunity of making representations in writing within 21 days or (if the Secretary of State has taken into consideration any new evidence or any new issue of fact, not being a matter of government policy) of asking within 21 days for the reopening of the inquiry.

(3) The Secretary of State may in any case if he thinks fit cause the inquiry to be re-opened, and shall cause it to be reopened if asked to do so in accordance with the last foregoing paragraph . . .

If these rules had been operative, ought the Chalkpit inquiry to have been reopened?

(b) The Packington Estate affair

In 1965, a second complaint handled by the Council on Tribunals reached a less successful conclusion. Islington Council prepared a scheme for redevelopment of old houses in Islington as a new housing estate. There was considerable opposition from residents' groups who wanted the area to be rehabilitated and not redeveloped. Planning permission was refused by the planning authority (the GLC) and, on appeal to the Minister, an inquiry was held. The Inspector favoured rehabilitation but the Minister dismissed the appeal on the ground that he was not satisfied that rehabilitation was preferable to redevelopment. Later, discussions took place between the Ministry, the GLC and Islington about a modified scheme; the objectors were not represented. A complaint was referred to the Council on Tribunals, who asked for a meeting with departmental officials. A date was set but, immediately before, the Council was informed (a) that Islington had submitted a fresh planning application to the Minister, unknown to the objectors, and (b) that this application had been approved. The Council submitted a special report to the Lord Chancellor:

The Council do not suggest that at any stage the Minister exceeded his powers. Nevertheless they consider that the complainants have real reason to feel aggrieved.

It will be seen that in seeking to justify the procedure adopted the Ministry contend, and the complainants deny, that the Minister upon consideration of the inspector's report decided that the future of the area must lie in redevelopment rather than in rehabilitation . . .

If the Minister did intend to decide initially in favour of redevelopment the Council consider that the decision letter of 23rd July 1965 was ineptly expressed and likely to mislead the complainants.

But the real grievance of the complainants is . . . that they were denied the opportunity of taking any part in the proceedings on the second application. They were rightly allowed to contest the first application and secured its rejection; and the second application was so closely connected with the first that it was, in substance, a further stage in the same proceedings. By being excluded at that stage altogether the complainants were, as the Council think, less than fairly treated.

The Council have assumed that the Ministry are correct in suggesting that the second application was substantially different from the first. If, as the complainants maintain, the two applications were substantially the same, the complainants have the further grievance that one or other of the decisions must have been wrong.

Whatever the truth of the matter, there has been apparent unfairness to the complainants. Openness, fairness and impartiality – the hall-marks of good administration – are not enough, if they are not all apparent. [AR 1965, App. A, p. 28.]

After the Report was published the Minister (Mr Crossman) made a statement to the House of Commons. We give some extracts from the debate (HC Deb. vol. 724, cols. 403–6):

MR CROSSMAN: When I came to consider the recommendation I sympathised with those who found the area attractive and who saw its potential for improvement. But the case against rehabilitation was strong. I was impressed by the expense and difficulty of achieving a really good result by these methods; and I had to take account of the 100 extra dwellings that redevelopment would produce . . .

Following this, the borough council made a second application . . . for a revised scheme of redevelopment, and this was referred to me for decision. I could at my discretion have held a second inquiry on this application. But since the objections to redevelopment and the arguments for rehabilitation had been thoroughly discussed at the first inquiry, I came to the conclusion that in this case it was reasonable to dispense with a second inquiry.

I have thought [the Council's] criticism over very carefully indeed and appreciate the motive which is, of course, to ensure that decisions are not taken without fully ventilating the facts and giving objectors the fullest opportunity for protest. In this case, I am clear that nothing would have been gained by a second inquiry that would have justified the months of delay. Having satisfied myself, therefore, that the revised scheme was a good one, I granted planning permission for it . . .

Even when it is not legally necessary . . . a Minister should always choose an inquiry where it is necessary either to elicit the facts or to enable people to protest. But, once that has been done, the need to inquire must be balanced against the need not to have intolerable delay . . . The biggest single complaint which I receive from the construction industry is that planning procedures are causing intolerable delays . . .

MR LUBBOCK: . . . does [the Minister] not think that the advocates of rehabilitation should at least have been given the opportunity of expressing a view on whether or not the criteria set out in his first decision letter had been satisfied by the new scheme? Is he aware that many people, not only in Islington, but in other parts of the country, are very worried about the way in which these far-reaching planning decisions are deliberately concealed from the public until it is too late for them to make any objection?

MR CROSSMAN: If I had thought that there was any suggestion of concealing a planning decision from the public I would have been shocked. There was no suggestion of concealing a planning decision. On the contrary, it had been subjected to a long investigation.

Does the explanation satisfactorily answer the Council's points? What similarities are there to *N. Tyneside?*

(c) **Lavender (H.) & Son Ltd** v. **Minister of Housing and Local Government** [1970] 1 WLR 1231

The company applied for planning permission to conduct gravel-extracting operations on part of a farm in an area (the Waters reserve) of high-quality agricultural land. The planning authority refused permission and appeal was made to the Minister. A public inquiry was held at which the only substantial objection was that of the Minister of Agriculture. The Minister dismissed the appeal saying:

It is the Minister's present policy that land in the reservations should not be released for mineral working unless [MAF] is not opposed to working. In the present case the agricultural objection has not been waived, and the Minister has therefore decided not to grant planning permission . . .

WILLIS J: It seems to me that by adopting and applying his stated policy the Minister has in effect inhibited himself from exercising a proper discretion (which would of course be guided by policy considerations) in any case where the Minister of Agriculture has made and maintained an objection to mineral working in an agricultural reservation. Everything else might point to the desirability of granting permission, but by applying and acting on his stated policy I think the Minister has fettered himself in such a way that in this case it was not he who made the decision for which Parliament made him responsible. It was the decision of the Minister of Agriculture not to waive his objection which was decisive in this case, and while that might properly prove to be the decisive factor for the Minister when taking into account all material considerations, it seems to me quite wrong for a policy to be applied which in reality eliminates all the material considerations save only the consideration, when that is the case, that the Minister of Agriculture objects. That means, as I think, that the Minister has by his stated policy delegated to the Minister of Agriculture the effective decision on any appeal within the agricultural reservations where the latter objects to the working. I am quite unable to accept that in these circumstances, the public inquiry could be justified . . . as giving the Minister of Agriculture the opportunity to hear the case and, if he thought right, to waive his objection. Unless there was a real chance that he would do so – and it seems to me clear beyond question that there was not – the inquiry was quite futile.

The Minister had erred in two ways: (a) he had improperly delegated his discretion, and (b) he had fettered his discretion. Which cases establish (b) as a ground for review? What might follow the quashing of a planning decision (see *Padfield's* case above, p. 329)? Compare Viscount Kilmuir's view of departmental advice; which do you prefer?

Some years later, a complaint was made to the PCA that a rugby club had to pay development tax on sale of its ground because of delay in deciding its application for a new site (HC 302 (1979/80) p. 11). The DOE had received a strong objection to the application from MAF with the result that the application was called in for a public inquiry. The club asked for an early decision as new laws on development tax were soon to come into force. The inspector recommended approval, concluding that 'because of the generally high quality of land in the area . . . the chances of finding available equally suitable land of lower agricultural value . . . were small'. The DOE referred this decision to MAF for comment. The ensuing inter-departmental negotiations took more than a year. The PCA found maladministration causing injustice, but he did not recommend an ex-gratia payment. Do you agree with his reasoning (below)? Did the DOE 'reach a planning decision lawfully'? If not, could the DOE be held liable in damages (above, Chapter 12)? Do you agree with the PCA that the outcome was 'satisfactory'?

I recognise that in a case where there are conflicting Departmental interests it is only realistic to accept that inter-departmental discussion and resolution of any real difference of opinion must take time, particularly when one Department considers an issue of principle to be involved . . . Nevertheless I think that, given the relative simplicity of the facts and the issues on which the difference of opinion arose, to allow a year to elapse before that decision was reached and issued was unreasonable and excessive to a degree which constituted maladministration . . . I have considered whether the mal-administration shown in this case caused the club any significant injustice calling for a remedy more tangible than the Department's apologies. [The club contends] that, as a result of the delay, they incurred a liability of over £88,000 in development land tax whereas given a more expeditious decision they might have had to pay in development gains tax only a little more than £74,000 . . . I do not consider that . . . [the Department] were obliged in their handling of the case to take the club's taxation anxieties specifically into account. Their obligation was to reach a Planning Act decision lawfully, fairly and with due regard to good planning practice and established government policies, after resolving any difference of opinion that might arise with other government departments about the application of those policies to the particular case. This obligation also included, in my view, a general duty of reasonable expedition having regard to all the circumstances of the case, but not a special duty of expedition by reference to the particular financial calculations or speculations of the applicants concerned.

In any event a more expeditious decision could as easily have gone against the club as in their favour. And they decided to use the planning permission they did eventually get, just as they had decided to apply.for it in the first place, on their own responsibility and at their own risk. Accordingly I do not consider their bad tax luck in this case to have been part of the Department's responsibility as decision-makers, whether quick or slow, under the Planning Act.

(d) **Bushell** v. **Environment Secretary** [1980] 3 WLR 22

At an inquiry held into draft schemes for the constitution of motorways under s.11 of the Highways Act 1959, objectors wished to question witnesses for the DTp on the accuracy of traffic predictions contained in a departmental publication known as the 'Red Book' and used as the standard basis for predicting traffic growth. The inspector disallowed the questions. Before the Minister issued his decision, but after the inquiry, a revised method was used. The Minister refused to reopen the inquiry to allow challenge. The appellants applied for the Minister's decision to be quashed on the grounds (a) that the refusal to allow cross-examination was a breach of natural justice and (b) that the Minister had taken into account new evidence (i.e. the revised methods of traffic calculation and the question of 'need') which had not been disclosed to the objectors. The argument was accepted by the Court of Appeal, whose decision was reversed by the House of Lords, Lord Edmund-Davies dissenting.

LORD DIPLOCK: The subject matter of the inquiry is the objections to the proposed scheme that have been received by the minister from local authorities and from private persons in the vicinity . . . whose interests may be adversely affected. The purpose of the inquiry is to provide the minister with as much information about those objections as will ensure that in reaching his decision he will have weighed the harm to local interests and private persons who may be adversely affected by the scheme against the public benefit which the scheme is likely to achieve and will not have failed to take into consideration any matters which he ought to have taken into consideration . . .

The Highways Act 1959 being itself silent as to the procedure to be followed at the inquiry, that procedure . . . must necessarily be left to the discretion of the minister or the inspector appointed . . . or partly to one and partly to the other. In exercising that discretion, as in exercising any other administrative function, they owe a constitutional duty to perform it fairly and honestly and to the best of their ability. [Lord Greene's judgment in *B. Johnson & Co (Builders) Ltd* v. *Minister of Health* [1947] 2 All ER 395] contains a salutary warning against applying to procedures involved in the making of administrative decisions concepts that are appropriate to the conduct of ordinary civil litigation between private parties. So rather than use such phrases as 'natural justice' which may suggest that the prototype is only to be found in procedures followed by English courts of law, I prefer to put it that . . . the only requirement . . . is that [procedure] must be fair to all those who have an interest in the decision . . . whether they have been represented at the inquiry or not . . .

What is fair procedure is to be judged not in the light of constitutional fictions as to the relationship between the minister and the other servants of the Crown who serve in the government department of which he is the head, but in the light of the practical realities as to the way in which administrative decisions involving forming judgments based on technical considerations are reached. To treat the minister in his decision-making capacity as someone separate and distinct from the department of government of which he is the political head and for whose actions he alone in constitutional theory is accountable to Parliament is to ignore not only practical realities but also Parliament's intention. Ministers come and go; departments, though their names may change from time to time, remain. Discretion in making administrative decisions is conferred upon a minister not as an individual but as the holder of an office in which he will have available to him in arriving at his decision the collective knowledge, experience and expertise of all those who serve the Crown in [his] department . . . The collective knowledge, technical as well as factual, of the civil servants in the department and their collective expertise is to be treated as the minister's own knowledge, his own expertise . . . This is an integral part of the decision-making process itself; it is not to be equiparated with the minister receiving evidence, expert opinion or advice from sources outside the department after the local inquiry has been closed . . .

A decision to construct a nationwide network of motorways is clearly one of government policy in the widest sense of the term. Any proposal to alter it is appropriate to be the subject of debate in Parliament, not of separate investigations in each of scores of local inquiries before individual inspectors up and down the country upon whatever material happens to be presented to them at the particular inquiry over which they preside. So much the respondents readily concede.

At the other extreme the selection of the exact line to be followed through a particular locality by a motorway designed to carry traffic between the destinations that it is intended to serve would not be described as involving government policy in the ordinary sense of that term. It affects particular local interests only and normally does not affect the interests of any wider section of the public, unless a suggested variation of the line would involve exorbitant expenditure of money raised by taxation. It is an appropriate subject for full investigation at a local inquiry . . .

Between the black and white of these two extremes, however, there is . . . a 'grey area'. Because of the time that must elapse between the preparation of any scheme and the completion of the stretch of motorway that it authorises, the department, in deciding in what order new stretches of the national network ought to be constructed, has adopted a uniform practice throughout the country of making a major factor in its decision the likelihood that there will be a traffic need for that particular stretch of motorway in 15 years from the date when the scheme was prepared . . . Priorities as between one stretch of motorway and another have got to be determined somehow. Semasiologists may argue whether the adoption by the department of a uniform practice for doing this is most appropriately described as government policy or as something else. But the propriety of adopting it is clearly a matter fit to be debated in a wider forum and with the assistance of a wider range of relevant material than any investigation at an individual local inquiry is likely to provide; and in that sense at least, which is the relevant sense for present purposes, its adoption forms part of government policy . . .

I think that the inspector was right in saying that the use of the concept of traffic needs in the design year *assessed by a particular method* as the yardstick by which to determine the order in which particular stretches of the national network of motorways should be constructed was government policy in the relevant sense of being a topic unsuitable for investigation by individual inspectors upon whatever material happens to be presented to them at local inquiries held throughout the country.

LORD EDMUND-DAVIES (dissenting): The inspector could – and should – disallow questions relating to the merits of government policy. But matters of policy are matters which involve the exercise of political judgment and matters of fact and expertise do not become 'policy' merely because a department of government relies on them. And, as the Franks Committee had put it in 1957: 'We see no reason why the factual basis for a departmental view should not be explained and its validity tested in cross-examination . . . The general law may, I think, be summarised in this way: (a) In holding an administrative inquiry (such as that presently being considered), the inspector was performing quasi-judicial duties. (b) He must therefore discharge them in accordance with the rules of natural justice. (c) Natural justice requires that objectors (no less than departmental representatives) be allowed to cross-examine witnesses called for the other side on all relevant matters, be they matters of fact or matters of expert opinion. (d) . . . the only restrictions on cross-examination are those general and well-defined exclusionary rules which govern the admissibility of relevant evidence . . . Beyond those restrictions there is no discretion on the civil side to exclude cross-examination on relevant matters'. And there is a massive body of accepted decisions establishing that natural justice requires that a party be given an opportunity of challenging by cross-examination witnesses called by another party on relevant issues.

Then is there any reason why those general rules should have been departed from in the present case? . . . The parameters of the inquiry, as agreed to by the department representatives, embraced *need* as a topic relevant to be canvassed and reported upon . . . While I am alive to the inconvenience of different inspectors arriving at different conclusions regarding different sections of a proposed trunk road, the risk of that happening cannot, in my judgment, have any bearing upon the question whether justice was done at this particular inquiry.

In the light of Chapter 14, do you agree with Lord Diplock's view of the functions (a) of the local inquiry and (b) of the Minister? Test his view of the inquiry against Arnstein's ladder. Is Lord Diplock's view of cross-examination compatible with that of Parker (above)? What are the consequences of this case for participation theory?

Do you agree with Lord Diplock's view of the relationship between the Minister and his officials?[15] Compare this passage with Viscount Kilmuir's views (above); are the different approaches significant for the planning process? Would you classify traffic need assessment methods as 'government policy' (Lord Diplock) or 'fact and expertise' (Lord Edmund-Davies)?

4 **Negotiated planning**

One view of *Bushell*'s case is of the latest in a series of battles to open up the planning system and make decisions more 'democratic' and 'participatory'. But the case suggests also that the price of participation may sometimes be greater than we are prepared to pay. The inquiry lasted 100 days. The inspector's report was made in June 1975 and the Minister's decision in August 1976. To reopen the inquiry would increase the delay. The judicial proceedings were lengthy as well as costly. Sir Douglas Frank QC gave judgment on December 1977 and the Court of Appeal in July 1979. The hearing before the House of Lords lasted seven days and judgment was given in February 1980. The formal part of the process had taken about five years. This may or may not satisfy the advocates of participation, but it is likely to invoke a hostile response from other actors in the planning process. Mr Crossman (above) mentions complaints of delay from 'the construction industry'. Payne (above) describes the efforts of administrators to avoid giving grounds for legal action. Below she describes how the PCA has helped to make administrative processes less flexible, a reaction which may help to generate more complaints of delay. Remember Holdsworth's list of possible responses to CLA investigations (above, Chapter 7). How do Payne's reactions compare?

There had been a question of maladministration by omission (happily not eventually upheld) because I, writing to a colleague, had used a piece of internal shorthand that meant a lot to us but nothing to the Commissioner's staff. I think what affected my morale so badly was the thought that my career could be blighted by the fact that although I had read and digested all the papers on the file and looked at the plans, because this was something I did every time, it did not occur to me to record the fact. It seemed to me for a while, that no decision I took could be good enough. It requires a certain amount of nerve to take any type of decision and appeal decisions sometimes take a considerable amount of it. Unless you are reasonably confident that you know what you are doing and that those above you normally regard your judgment as sound, you cannot act alone. The initial impact of the Commissioner's investigations caused a crisis of confidence and . . . that caused cases to be put upwards for decision. However, cold common-sense (which dictated that one had to carry on) and bracing messages from above, helped to redress the damage.

I think that there is now much less tension about the Commissioner's activities. Both sides are now much better at it, for the Commissioner's staff are more familiar with our language and we are writing all minutes on the assumption that they will be read by outsiders and spell out simple facts that we would not formerly have insulted the intelligence of the recipient by mentioning . . .

[Previously] we had not thought it necessary to write unnecessary explanations on the file when all the emphasis was on speed and the decision letter gives one's reasons for the decision. It might be good for us to have to explain ourselves but it all takes time (and paper!). [Payne 1971, pp. 116–17.]

Complaints about planning, though not of inquiry procedure, which is the responsibility of the DOE, have from its inception formed a large part of the caseload of the CLA. In its first year (1974/5), 202 out of 473 complaints concerned the planning process. Stungo, a London planning officer who felt that 'sooner or later all planning departments can expect to be involved in a complaint to the Commission', decided to investigate reactions to investigation of other London planning departments. Some officers thought the work involved disproportionate to the triviality of the complaint, but many disagreed. It was generally felt that the likelihood of complaint increased paperwork because 'There is a conflict between the need on the one hand to deal expeditiously with planning applications and, on the other, to deal with every case carefully so as to avoid a situation which could give rise to a complaint being made.' The author concluded that some office procedures needed to be reconsidered and finished with some practical hints how to avoid investigation. Planners should pay more attention to complaints from 'people living next to or in the vicinity of proposed developments', check all facts, insist on fuller drawings and remind applicants that development must conform to approved plans. The tension between speed and thoroughness which led to mistakes would still remain (Stungo 1976, p. 725).

In the light of a rise in planning complaints to 34 per cent (724) of all C L A complaints by 1978/9, Hammersley thought the impact of investigation was for many planners 'a traumatic experience' and advised planners to 'stick to the rules':

Whether it is a counter query, a letter, an application or whatever – all need to be logged, processed and answered; alternatively if the authority wishes to take some action (including decisions on application), it must exercise its discretionary powers for consultation in a systematic manner. There should be comprehensive, but plain, rules which everyone – the public, the councillors, junior and senior planning officers – has access to, understands and operates. This point has been made on many occasions by the ombudsmen themselves. [Hammersley 1980, p. 27.]

But Hammersley noted with disapproval another argument which was emerging to the effect that large numbers of trivial decisions led inevitably to mistakes and maladministration. The fear of error and perhaps of compensation was thus undercutting the 'system of development control by creating an argument for redefinition of the boundaries to exclude small-scale developments which produced the bulk of complaints'. One way to achieve an efficient administrative system is to abolish it!

We can link these developments with the discussion in Chapter 14 of participation techniques after Skeffington. We know that officials were encouraged during the seventies to respond helpfully to the public with advice and information. The Dobry Report, for example, stressed the need for information to speed up the planning process, talking of 'hot lines' to local authority offices. Dobry also emphasized the need for advice.

Many planning authorities do offer advisory services to planning applicants, answer questions about the need for planning permission and are generally prepared to be helpful. What is the position if the advice or assurance is misleading, the applicant acts on it and then finds that planning permission is not forthcoming? Obviously, there is a possibility of legal liability (above, Chapter 12). Another danger is that the local authority may find itself bound or, in technical terminology, 'estopped'. In *Lever Finance* v. *Westminster LBC* [1971] 1 QB 222 this occurred. The developer's architect telephoned the council and asked whether he would be allowed to vary his plans by siting a house nearer to the neighbour's boundary. He was told by the planning officer that he could. Later, there were objections and the council's planning committee tried to overrule their officer. The Court of Appeal held that the council were estopped by the planning officer's assurance that a further planning application was not necessary for the variation. Their powers had effectively been delegated and although an 'exchange of notes' might have been desirable it was not necessary 'to clutter the files of architect and authority alike with a mass of additional paper'. Consider the implications of this for community participation.

Soon afterwards, an article appeared in the Local Government Review, listing the precautions which ought to be taken by the prudent planning officer. 'Make it absolutely clear, in writing, that any expression of opinion is just an expression of opinion, does not and cannot bind the local planning authority, and does not and cannot constitute a grant of planning permission or s.53 determination unless it is so expressly stated in writing' (Samuels 1975, p. 430). In response, this advice was circulated:

An unrecorded conversation can be misinterpreted and could lead to court proceedings, claims for compensation or complaints to the Ombudsman. Because of this and after discussion with Group Leaders, it has been decided that:

(a) When telephone enquiries are made as to whether planning permission is required, the member of staff who answers the call should inform the enquirer that permission is probably required if, from a description of the proposals this appears to be so. In all other cases, the officer must tell the enquirer to write a letter briefly setting out the proposals. Alternatively, the officer can send the appropriate forms to the enquirer. *In no circumstances should an officer state, over the telephone, that permission is not required . . .*

When applicants come to the office, it is reasonable to tell them whether or not permission is likely to be granted for a particular proposal. However, officers must stress that the view expressed is their personal opinion and the final decision rests [with the planning authority].

Not all courts favoured the doctrine of estoppel and the legal position was obscure.[16] In the later case of *Brooks and Burton* v. *Environment Secretary* (1977) 75 L G R 285, Lord Widgery showed that he was not indifferent to the danger that a useful public service might be inhibited if the courts allowed the doctrine to grow too quickly. Here a company purchased a site for light industrial purposes on being told by the local authority's planning department that planning permission would not be necessary if they carried on the vendor's business of manufacturing concrete blocks 'as the previous occupiers had done'. Without applying for permission, they greatly expanded the business, manufacturing concrete blocks outdoors, until complaints were received. An enforcement notice alleging material change of use was made and confirmed by the Minister after an inquiry. The Divisional Court refused to accept that the planning authority was estopped by the earlier conversations with planning officers.

LORD WIDGERY LCJ: There has been some advance in recent years of this doctrine of estoppel as applied to local authorities through their officers, and the most advanced case is . . . *Lever Finance Ltd* [above] . . . It no doubt is correct on its facts, but I would deprecate any attempt to expand this doctrine because it seems to me . . . extremely important that local government officers should feel free to help applicants who come and ask them questions without all the time having the shadow of estoppel immobilising their authorities by some careless remark which produces such an estoppel. So far as the present case is concerned, I am completely satisfied that this question of fact . . . as to what representation was made to the company, has been resolved by the Secretary of State in favour of the planning authority. There was plenty of evidence upon which that conclusion could be reached, and it being a matter of fact it is not . . . for us to interfere.

Like those described in the Home Loss study, these interactions are complex. Courts do not only 'control' the administrative process, they also react to it. Compare *Brooks and Burton*, for example, with *ex p. Hendy* (above). And things are not always what they seem. In the 'private interest' oriented case of *Lever Finance*, where did the private interest lie?[17] Could we say that the 'ideology of participation' lost out when neighbouring landowners were deprived of their right to object?

We have met the argument that participation helps produce 'efficient' planning decisions, yet the delays sometimes occasioned by participation procedures are one factor in provoking a 'retreat from legalism'. Under the 1947 system, Grant described departmental approbration for informal discretionary planning practices. Today Bruton and Nicholson (1983, p. 433) record that 'many of the practitioners involved in formulating and implementing local planning policies have grown disenchanted with statutory local plans . . . and in consequence are turning towards a wide range of non-statutory instruments'. The authors advise the DOE to drop their hostile attitude; informal planning appears 'to fulfil genuine local needs' and is here to stay. In a circular which explains the new appeals system, 'Planning and Enforcement Appeals' No. 38/1981, the DOE stressed the advantage of informal procedures in development control:

Before a disappointed applicant for planning permission lodges a planning appeal . . . there should be consultation and negotiation between the parties and other bodies or individuals affected. Discussions of this kind can often resolve difficulties more quickly and cheaply than appealing. An appeal is intended to be, and should remain, a last resort.

Those who see participation as leading to consensus are likely to see negotiated planning as a desirable objective (remember Arnstein's ladder). Those who see the planning process as essentially conflictual[18] will not be surprised to find planning regulated by negotiation and bargain, necessary for dispute-resolution. (Compare Griffith's picture of the political process.) Sometimes the bargains are structured, as when a negotiated solution to a planning dispute emerges from an EIP or PLI. Sometimes the bargains are unstructured. Look back at the *Ostler* case (above, p. 108). Negotiations affected Ostler's 'private' interests unfavourably – you may think that they were also against the 'public interest' in that they undercut the process of participation and gave rise to suspicions of improper conduct by officials, though they were later cleared by the PCA (HC 524 (1976/7), pp. 16–18). Formal inquiries, like courts, are open to the public; negotiations are not always so accessible (consider the *Tyneside* case in this context).

Although we know something about the officials and public bodies involved in planning, we have not thought much about the 'private' side. The typical complainant in planning matters is revealed by CLA reports as an owner/occupier aggrieved by development on nearby land. But think of the planning case law cited so far: the 'typical' litigant is a corporation or development company. Very large sums may turn on the result of individual planning applications. For example, the value of 'green belt' land which cannot be used for commercial purposes may be multiplied beyond belief if the planning authority can be persuaded to make an exception and grant planning permission – as the new draft circular urges them to do.[19]

Prizes like this may tempt applicants to play the 'law game' to its bitter end. On other occasions and in other situations the developer may gain more from negotiation and concession. Sometimes one party, sometimes the other is in the stronger bargaining position. This may reflect the current political climate. For example, the Community Land Act 1975 provided planning authorities with a bargaining counter. A period of recession in which authorities are encouraged actively to seek development and a government which favours the private sector may tip the balance. And in the corporate state, 'public' and 'private' often combine. For example, local authorities may contract with private developers, enter into joint development enterprises or form a company. Then the planning authority will have acquired an interest in the financial viability of development which may affect its attitude to planning permission. The possibility of corruption cannot be ruled out. But we should not assume that all local authorities support the market philosophy. Some may seek to secure for the public (financial) advantages which are not permitted by the legislation through the indirect means of contract and covenant. Negotiated planning may be welcomed by private developers as a means of enabling them to cut through red tape. It may be equally welcome to public authorities as a means of speeding the administrative process and avoiding challenge in the courts. They may also hope to achieve 'planning gains'.

Before we can understand 'planning bargains' we need to look briefly at the circumstances in which planning authorities can control development and the use to which land is put. Remember that not all development needs planning permission (above). There are restrictions too on the planning conditions which may be imposed by the authority. S.29(1) of TCPA 1971 authorizes local authorities to 'grant planning permission, either unconditionally or subject to such conditions as they think fit'. The courts long ago intervened to impose limitations on this 'subjective' discretion.[20] In *Hall* v. *Shoreham UDC* [1964] 1 WLR 240, the principles applicable were summarized under three heads: (a) the conditions imposed must fairly and reasonably relate to the provisions of the development plan and to planning considerations affecting the land; (b) they must fairly and reasonably relate to the permitted development; (c) they must not be so unreasonable that it can be said that Parliament clearly cannot have intended that they should be imposed. Later cases confirm this formulation, which was approved by the House of Lords in *Newbury District Council* v. *Environment Secretary* [1980] 2 WLR 379.

The *Hall* case itself offers an interesting contrast to the *Beverley* case (above, p. 358). The planning authority attached to planning permission a condition obliging the developer of an industrial site to construct, at his own expense, a feeder road on to the main road allowing access, where appropriate, to traffic from neighbouring developments. The Court of Appeal was told that different procedures under the Highways Act 1959 could have been used. It found the planning conditions attached to the permission would allow the authority to 'obtain the benefit of having the road constructed for them at the plaintiffs' expense, on the plaintiffs' land, and without the necessity for paying any compensation in respect thereof'. Willmer LJ continued:

Bearing in mind that another and more regular course is open to the defendants, it seems to me that this result would be utterly unreasonable and such as Parliament cannot possibly have intended . . . [It is a well-known principle] that a statute should not be held to take away private rights of property without compensation unless the intention to do so is expressed in clear and unambiguous words. I can certainly find no clear and unambiguous words in the Town and Country Planning Act 1947 authorising the defendants in effect to take away the plaintiffs' right of property without compensation by the imposition of conditions such as those sought to be imposed.

Is this judgment compatible with that in the *Beverley* case? Was the plaintiffs' land 'taken'?

Local authorities possess powers and often obligations to provide services – such as roads, sewerage or lighting – for local residents. The *Hall* case makes it difficult to obtain from developers a contribution to these costs, often called 'the costs of the infrastructure', by the imposition of conditions. Particularly in a period of pressure on local authority funds, planning authorities may be tempted to negotiate an agreed 'contribution' to these, and other development costs. The authority gains a financial advantage. It may, in addition, obtain extra facilities such as open space or off-street parking spaces. This is what we mean by 'planning gain'. In the definition of the Property Advisory Group (1981, para. 2.01), 'A planning gain accrues when, in connection with the obtaining of a planning permission, a developer offers, agrees or is obliged to incur some expenditure, surrender some right or concede some other benefit which could not, or arguably could not, be embodied in a valid planning condition.' But the bargain is not necessarily as one-sided as the *Hall* decision suggests. The development may not be able to proceed at all unless the funds for infrastructure are available, while the profits from the development today benefit the developer and the community only indirectly through the taxation system.

Grants of planning permission and the validity of attached conditions may be challenged in several ways. The first line of attack is through the Minister. For example, if a landowner believes planning permission to be invalid, he may refuse to abide by the conditions imposed, in which case an 'enforcement notice' may be served by the planning authority. This may be contested in an appeal to the Minister. Similarly the Minister has a statutory power under s.53 of the TCPA 1971 to determine whether or not permission is actually necessary. But the Minister's decision may in both cases be challenged by way of judicial review. In *Pyx Granite Ltd* v. *Minister of Housing and Local Government* [1958] 1 QB 554, [1960] AC 260, a developer applied for planning permission in terms of a private Act of Parliament. The Minister refused permission, whereupon the developer asked for a declaration that permission was actually unnecessary. Although the Minister argued that his decision was final, neither the Court of Appeal nor the House of Lords agreed and the declaration was granted. So the developer or landowner can avoid the danger of illegality by testing his course of action before embarking on it. This does not mean, however, that his remedy in the courts is barred if he does receive planning permission and acts on it. If at a later stage he wishes to argue that planning permission was unnecessary, he will still be allowed to do so. The point is established by the *Newbury* case (above).

R. v. *Hillington LBC ex p. Royco Homes* [1974] QB 720 is important because it allows the system of ministerial appeal to be short-circuited. Royco had applied for permission to build dwelling houses. The authority granted outline permission subject to conditions that (a) the housing should be built to local authority standards and (b) the first occupiers should be taken from the authority's waiting list. Royco applied for certiorari to quash the permission on the ground that the conditions were void and for mandamus to order the authority to reconsider the application according to law. Although Royco could have appealed to the Minister, the court held that prerogative orders would lie. Lord Widgery warned that this was an exceptional procedure because normally ministerial appeal, which could deal with merits as well as law, would be more convenient. But the court here went on to hold that the conditions imposed were so unreasonable that no reasonable authority could have reached them. There was an error of law and the conditions would be quashed, bringing the whole planning permission down. So the 'planning gain' which Hillingdon sought could be obtained here only by informal agreement with Royco. Royco, on the other hand, was left without planning permission. Both parties therefore stood to gain from negotiations.

Planning agreements may be arrived at in a number of ways. A developer might rely on informal representations, similar to those made in the *Lever Finance* case or a binding contract might be concluded. The parties might also enter into a 'Section 52 agreement'. S.52 TCPA 1971 authorizes a planning authority 'to enter into an agreement with any person interested in land in their area for the purpose of restricting or regulating the development or use of the land, either permanently or during such period as may be prescribed by the agreement.' The purpose of this section is to ensure that such agreements run with the land like restrictive covenants.

Jowell, who was among the first to notice the growth of 'planning bargains', was quick to relate it to corporatism, a philosophy which Jowell described as being 'shared by all present political parties' and as concerned with 'results rather than the maintenance of legal rights or interests'.[21] Although Jowell was concerned for individual interests, he also identified a threat to the 'public' interest. (Can you link his view to the theories of administrative law discussed in Chapter 2?).

The model of rules presents development control as involving decision according to ascertainable guides. The courts have ruled that ulterior purposes may not be achieved through development control powers. Yet planning through agreement appears to evade the criteria and permit what the courts forbid. Agreement of this kind appears to release the naked power that procedural justice attempts to restrain. Undue influence, collusion, and the abuse of discretion all seem on the surface to be encouraged by a practice which seems close to a barter, or a sale of planning permission. [Jowell 1977, p. 70.]

Other lawyers were more concerned with private interests. Ward, for example, maintained that inequality of bargaining power might lead to unconscionable bargains:

I do not believe it is enough for the local authority to say, as some do, that the developer voluntarily enters into the planning bargain. This argument presumes that a local authority is entitled to bargain with its development control powers. This is not the case and never has been. The system of development control is not intended for use in this way. In any event there is not a true and open bargaining position between a local authority and a developer – the market is unbalanced – the local authority holds most of the cards and whenever one party has such a distinct negotiating advantage the other party will almost always end up paying over the odds. Bearing in mind that, as the law stands at present, a landowner is *entitled* to planning permission for any development of his land to which there is no substantial planning objection, it is incumbent upon a local authority to be exceedingly careful how it goes about the business of bargaining for planning gain. [Ward 1982, p. 80.]

The 'voluntary' nature of one apparent planning bargain had to be considered in *County and District Properties* v. *Horsham U D C* (1970) 115 E G 1399. The plaintiffs had applied for planning permission on a site in the centre of Horsham. No local plan existed at the time. During negotiations, the plaintiffs made a payment of £6,000 to the council, probably as a commuted payment for facilities in the council carpark but also in expectation of planning permission. Some years later, when planning permission still seemed far away, the plaintiffs reclaimed the money. The council now argued that the sum was a gift made in accordance with s.139 of the Local Government Act 1972 and not reclaimable. Paull J held that it must be returned:

> The fact was that the money was paid over on the understanding that detailed planning permission would duly be issued on a site . . . which the plaintiff had acquired for redevelopment purposes. To describe such a sum of money as a gift was . . . a complete misuse of the word 'gift' and a misunderstanding of [the section which] contemplated a charitable gift by a charitably-minded person to benefit a district. It did not mean money paid as an inducement for the favourable consideration which, if granted, would put large sums of money into the donor's pockets. The last thing in the plaintiff's mind was charity. This was a final desperate attempt to get detailed development plans passed by the Council.

Generally speaking, however, a developer who enters a planning bargain may find himself deprived of legal protection. Informal agreements are covered by the doctrine of estoppel (above), a most uncertain shield. However, formal contracts are not necessarily safer for the developer because of the principle that a public authority cannot by contract fetter the future use of its statutory powers, a doctrine which applies equally to s.52 agreements.[22] This is well illustrated by *Windsor B C* v. *Brandrose Developments Ltd* [1981] 1 W L R 1083 and [1983] 1 W L R 509 (C A).

No development plan was in existence when, in 1976, Windsor granted permission to Brandrose to develop, subject to a s.52 agreement which permitted the necessary demolition of certain buildings if the site was to be developed. In 1979, before demolition had occurred, the council incorporated the site into an existing conservation area. The council now sought a declaration that demolition would require planning permission and an injunction. S.52(3)(a) provides that nothing in the section or an agreement made thereunder can restrict the exercise of planning powers provided they are exercised in accordance with the development plan. In the absence of a plan, Fox J held that the agreement was valid and that planning permission was not needed before demolition. On appeal, however, it was held to be 'trite law' that a statutory body with public duties to perform cannot lawfully agree not to exercise its powers at a later date.

We have considered possible disadvantages to 'private' and 'public' interests. By 1980, Heap and Ward were concerned that third parties might suffer from 'cheque-book planning':

The temptation to forsake sound planning principles for commercial advantage is obvious and it is not made any easier for the local planning authority to resist by the fact that negotiations for these planning bargains are almost invariably conducted in secret. There is usually no opportunity for members of the public to express a view on what is going on and there is no right of appeal available to a third party who objects to the terms of the bargain made in his name by the local planning authority. Although the courts have in the past expressed themselves willing to control the exercise of discretion by public authorities it is by no means certain that it would be possible for a third party, even one with the necessary energy and resources, to bring such a matter before the courts. [Heap and Ward 1980, pp. 636–7.]

Predictably, the fashionable nostrums of administrative law were prescribed. Suddards (1979, p. 665) presented the 'case for new legislation'. A short statute would 'ratify the whole idea of planning by agreement, permit it, and in effect give it respectability' – an objective which not everyone would share. The statute would go on to determine what constituted reasonable planning gain and provide an arbitrarial procedure to determine difficult cases. The author felt the Lands Tribunal would be an appropriate forum because it has 'the advantage of being totally accepted in terms of valuation techniques. It is an easily accessible and speedy authority to appeal to' (compare McAuslan, p. 386 above). What other machinery for outside scrutiny might be suitable?

The Minister commissioned a report from a Property Advisory Group which identified the 'problem of planning gain' as arising *only* where a planning authority 'tries to incorporate into the proposed development some element of public benefit or advantage which the developer, left to his own devices, would not have volunteered'. (Do you agree?) They went on to conclude that planning gain was acceptable only in exceptional circumstances. Their examples included the provision of a necessary infrastructure or public services necessitated by development or the cost of increasing existing public buildings or services (a health centre, school or fire station) to cope with an influx of population on the developer's land. (Would such conditions in any event meet the criteria laid down by courts?) Some central control was necessary, but a 'formal and elaborate' Code of Practice was not. The Report ended by suggesting the following guidelines to be set out in a ministerial circular (para. 9.01):

(1) When a local authority receives an application for planning permission, it should be considered on its own merits, and as a whole.

(2) If the proposal is one to which no legitimate planning objection can be raised, the authority should grant permission.

(3) If there are objections to the proposal which can be overcome by the imposition of valid planning conditions, permission should be granted subject to those conditions.

(4) If there are objections to the proposal which, but for some technical legal objection, could be overcome by the imposition of a valid planning condition, the local authority should be willing to grant permission subject to the developer's entering into an agreement, under Section 52 . . . or other powers, which will overcome the legitimate planning objection.

(5) If the application is a 'mixed' application which contains a number of elements, some of which are, by themselves, objectionable, but others of which promote positive planning advantages, the separate elements should be looked at individually as well as collectively so that, in the final result, the decision on the application, which must be a decision on the application as a whole, will achieve a just balance which cannot be characterised as the mere 'sale' of development rights.

The Report largely failed to satisfy the academic lawyers. Grant, for example (1982, p. 374), tersely remarked that it 'failed to grasp the economic forces from which planning gain arises, and failed therefore to give full consideration to how the phenomenon might be brought under control'. The Law Society reacted more favourably, recommending extra guidelines, including one which required *publicity* for proposals which involved planning gain. The DOE's response was to issue (after consultation) a circular (No. 22/83) which recognizes that planning gain is here to stay and attempts only to formulate simple guidelines. Planning gain is acceptable where it:

(1) is needed to enable the development to go ahead e.g. provision of adequate access, water supply and sewerage and sewage disposal facilities; or

(2) in the case of financial payments, will contribute to meeting the cost of providing such facilities in the near future; or

(3) is otherwise so directly related to the proposed development and to the use of the land after its completion, that the development ought not to be permitted without it, e.g. the provision, whether by the developer or by the authority at the developer's expense, of car-parking in or near the development or of reasonable amounts of open space related to the development; or

(4) is designed in the case of mixed development to secure an acceptable balance of uses.

The gains must also be 'fairly and reasonably related in scale and kind' to the benefits derived by the development. How far does this represent the Property Advisory Group proposals?

The circular went on to state that the cost to the developer must be 'reasonable'. For example, the developer must not be asked to subsidize the taxpayer by providing the infrastructure needed for development to start. Alternative methods of finance (e.g. by charging the public) must also be considered. This proposal prompted D. J. Hughes to argue (1983, p. 7) that the circular was 'over-cautious, imprecise and woolly'. He especially deprecated introduction of the 'essentially fluid and imprecise common law notion of reasonableness', a happy hunting ground for litigants in other areas of the law. He too advocated legislation.[23]

But remember that circulars are not binding, a problem once more highlighted in *Richmond-upon-Thames L B C* v. *Environment Secretary, The Times*, 16 May 1983. The 'action area' plan for Richmond stipulated that office developments in the action area must provide some planning gain. Accordingly, Richmond refused permission for a small development which seemed to provide no gain. At an inquiry, the inspector over-ruled their refusal, saying that the requirement in the action area plan conflicted with departmental policy evidenced by the Property Advisory Group's report. Upholding the inspector's decision on other grounds, Glidewell J held that the inspector had made an error of law in preferring the report to the formal requirements of the action area plan.[24] Planning gain could in future be legitimated by incorporation as a requirement of local plans. Consider the advantages and disadvantages of this approach.

In Chapter 5, we met Reiss's argument that advocates of 'the model of rules' ignored the way in which people behave. In these chapters, we have tried to see how the planning game is played. Sometimes the players stand on the letter of the law and their legal rights. Often, however, they seek to bypass rules and cut red tape. In the immigration process, you will see these 'games' taken further.

16
Immigration control: a developing process

In the *Home Loss* study (Chapter 8) we traced a series of complex and protracted interactions between ombudsmen, parliamentarians, local authorities and departments. The study was based on a relatively simple model of rules and discretion. Visualize the two areas within the inner rings of a target. The bulls-eye or inner core represents the zone of entitlement inside which claimants satisfied the prescribed criteria and received compensation. We portrayed this as formal and rigid. The requirements imposed were statutory and we concentrated on those, like the time limit provisions, which approximated more closely to rules than discretion, although others (e.g. the condition that the claimant be 'permanently displaced') left officers with a margin of judgement or interpretation. The surrounding area denotes those cases where, although the claims failed to satisfy the statutory criteria, administrators were prepared to meet them by exercising discretion, e.g. to sanction ex gratia payments by local authorities. In effect the ambit of the compensation schemes was extended. We learnt not to assume that administrators exercise their discretion in an unstructured manner. The distinction between core and periphery lay not so much in the rigidity of the criteria adopted as in the informal nature of the rules in the outer zone together with the lack of public scrutiny, only partially corrected through PCA investigations.

In the area of immigration control relating to non-EEC nationals, which is the subject of the next two chapters, we find a more complicated relationship between rules and discretion. Here the inner core is less solid. The Immigration Rules, which supposedly set out the practice to be followed, are not in the form of statutory instruments and their precise legal status remains elusive. Important elements of control, e.g. work permits and special vouchers for British Overseas Citizens, lie outside the Rules; they are administrative schemes where rule-making is conducted in varying degrees of secrecy. So the core is diffuse. Again the Immigration Rules often appear to leave officials considerable freedom of manoeuvre. But the picture is complex because the Rules themselves are structured and confined in two ways. First there are 'rules within rules' contained in the Instructions issued to officials by their superiors. These give further guidance to officers about how to exercise their discretion, and set out the operating procedures. Secondly, there is adjudication; rules can slowly emerge through precedent. On some matters restrictive interpretation of the Rules by the Immigration Appeal Tribunal (IAT) has gradually bled out much of the original discretion. However, in many cases, the issues are primarily factual and appeals are determined without much recourse to precedent. Here administrative practice is particularly important because the appeals system performs only a limited checking function.

If the core of immigration control is elusive, so too is its periphery. Whether a case is covered by the Rules or an administrative scheme, the Home Secretary will on occasion exercise a discretion 'outside the rules' for the immigrant's benefit. Sometimes this is done in discretionary fashion on a one-off basis, elsewhere practice has crystallized into rules of varying rigidity and formality. In turn, this dispensing power encourages immigrants and their organizations to bring pressure on the Minister through demonstrations, petitions, resort to the media and, in particular, representations by M Ps and peers, a constitutional device often ignored by public lawyers. This happens not only when campaigns are mounted on behalf of groups of immigrants or where, as is the case over substantial areas of immigration control, external scrutiny by tribunals and courts is non-existent or heavily circumscribed. Even where full rights of appeal to a tribunal exist, there is significant and apparently increasing resort to informal, political procedures. One reason is the progressive tightening of the Rules by government amendment and tribunal interpretation; if the bulls-eye is covered up, the archer must aim for the outer zone. Another is disillusionment with the appeals system whose procedures are thought to stack the cards in favour of exclusion.

We might compare the development of planning bargains. Although immigrants are rarely in a position to negotiate, in both instances we see a shift away from formal procedures towards more fluid, flexible processes. In both, the old informal procedures supplement the formal systems but have not wholly supplanted them. And the different lurches towards informality raise familiar issues of restricted external scrutiny and accountability. In immigration control, these permeate the inner core because the Instructions structuring the Rules, like the old informal S B Codes (Chapter 18), are confidential. We will have to move back into Griffith's 'dark and windowless' areas of administration.

1 Extending control

In 1903, by recommending powers to exclude and deport 'undesirable' aliens, the Royal Commission on Alien Immigration (Cd.1741), established in response to the influx of mainly Jewish immigrants fleeing the pogroms of Eastern Europe, paved the way for the modern precursor of current legislation, the Aliens Act 1905.[1] This statute was a moderate affair, granting the Home Office severely restricted powers and imposing external scrutiny. Those already here could only be deported following a court recommendation after a criminal conviction or where, within 12 months of their arrival, a magistrate found them to be destitute, living in insanitary conditions due to overcrowding or wanted for an extraditable crime. Of those seeking to enter, only 'undesirables' (lunatics, the destitute, previous deportees and fugitive offenders) might be excluded and then only if they were steerage passengers arriving on 'immigrant ships' (vessels carrying 20 or more steerage passengers). Those excluded might appeal at the ports to tribunals, the Immigration Boards, which overturned the authorities' decision in 38 per cent of cases heard.[2] The Permanent Under-Secretary at the Home Office, Sir Edward Troup, was clearly dissatisfied, considering the Act:

. . . from the administrative point of view one of the worst ever passed. The limitation of the control . . . opened very wide doors for the admission of undesirables: and . . . decisions [to exclude] were constantly over-ridden by the statutory appeal boards in a way that made effective enforcement of the restrictions almost impossible. [Troup 1925, p. 143.]

Sir Edward did not have long to wait. Anticipating war, the department prepared a draft scheme and in due course the Aliens'

Restriction Act 1914 was rushed through Parliament in a single afternoon. The statute was an enabling Act, conferring on the Crown massive rule-making powers exercisable by Order in Council. In turn the Aliens Restriction (Consolidation) Order 1914 (SR and O No. 1374) granted the Home Secretary almost unlimited powers to exclude and deport aliens, whether 'enemy' or 'friendly', without providing for external scrutiny (an omission which the courts refused to supply). This became the established pattern of controls over aliens, lasting, in the guise of the annually renewed Aliens' Restriction Amendment Act 1919 and the Aliens Order 1953 (SI No. 1671), until the 1970s, although in certain deportation cases there were later informal hearings before first the Aliens' Deportation Advisory Committee (above p. 76) and then the Chief Metropolitan Magistrate. The Home Secretary's powers were often couched in discretionary terms, for example under the 1953 Order he could deport an alien where he 'deems it to be conducive to the public good' and vary leave to enter 'in such manner as he thinks fit'. In practice the discretion was structured by instructions to officials but these, which by 1967 were 400 pages long, remained secret. Thornberry (1963, p. 431) thought the scheme, however sympathetically applied in practice, bore the imprint of its birth: 'As might be expected of legislation conceived in anger in a time of war or emergency the powers conferred by it are, in comparison with peacetime legislation, draconian.' Remember to assess this comment after reading about the Immigration Act 1971.

Of course, millions of aliens were given leave to enter under the scheme, for example as visitors or students. Many were allowed to work. After the Second World War the Government, believing Britain to face an acute labour shortage, encouraged the entry of European labour.[3] During 1946–51 a net immigration of several hundred thousand European nationals took place, and eventually recruitment was systematized into a work permit scheme. These workers were contract labourers; as aliens their admission and continued stay depended on a temporary permit limited to a specific job with a named employer.

Meanwhile successive governments had pursued an open-door policy towards 'British Subjects' who retained the common law rights of those owing allegiance to the Crown to enter, stay and leave free from control. The British Nationality Act 1948 dealt only with citizenship. Responding to Dominion demands for their own citizenship laws, Parliament divided the status of British Subject, held by all peoples of the Empire, into local citizenship units linked to each independent Commonwealth country. For Britain the local citizenship was of the 'UK and Colonies' and the legislation specified how this might be obtained, e.g. by place of birth, descent from a citizen, naturalization (for aliens) and registration (for Commonwealth citizens). But in 1948 all British Subjects, whatever their local citizenship, remained immune from exclusion and deportation, and might settle if they wished.

Throughout the 1950s, government and industry facilitated their entry. From 1948 on, partly in response to recruiting campaigns, there was a steady influx of British Subjects, first from the West Indies and then from the Indian sub-continent, the Home Office estimating the net immigration, for the years 1955–60 inclusive, as 161,450 and 50,190 respectively.[4] From 1960 onwards, however, 'immigration', often treated as synonymous with black and coloured Commonwealth immigration, became a major political issue.[5] Harold Macmillan's Conservative Government introduced the first immigration controls on British Subjects. The Commonwealth Immigrants Act 1962, which contained no provision for appeals, gave Immigration Officers powers to refuse admission or to impose conditions, for example, about the duration of stay, and empowered the Home Secretary to deport following a court recommendation after a criminal conviction. But many remained exempt, namely those born in the UK, holders of UK passports and those, e.g. wives, included in the passports of persons falling within the first two categories. In short, the controls caught British Subjects of independent Commonwealth countries such as India, and the mainly non-white peoples of remaining colonies who could not satisfy the prescribed conditions. Later the Home Secretary (Mr Butler) explained why he considered the legislation necessary:

Size was the essence of the problem. The number of Commonwealth immigrants from the under-developed countries . . . rose from 21,000 in 1959 . . . to 136,000 in 1961 . . . It was, to put it mildly, questionable whether we should be able to absorb largely unskilled immigrant labour in such huge and uncontrolled numbers. Moreover they were concentrated in particular areas . . . where a great influx of newcomers inevitably imposed strains on local services and even provoked isolated anti-racial manifestations . . . I was by 1961 persuaded that the rise of racial tension could be avoided only if it were anticipated. [Butler 1971, p. 206.]

If numbers were the name of the game,[6] the 1962 Act proved, at first, counter-productive; rumours of impending controls fuelled the sharp rise in immigration referred to by Mr Butler. But it soon had an impact. The legislation restricted entry for settlement to holders of employment vouchers (and their families) issued under an administrative scheme by the Ministry of Labour. Initially the quota of vouchers was fixed at 51,000 per annum and divided into three categories covering specific job offers, skilled and unskilled workers. The last was quickly reduced and then abolished by the incoming Labour Government in its White Paper of 1965 'Immigration from the Commonwealth' (Cmnd 2739), which also imposed a quota of 8,500. Mr Hattersley, like Mr Butler, justified restrictions as necessary for the improvement of race relations: 'Without integration, limitation is inexcusable; without limitation, integration is impossible.'[7] By 1967 the number of Commonwealth citizens admitted as workers had fallen to 4,978 from 30,125 in 1963 although the number of their dependants entering had increased to 52,813 from 26,234.

Further restrictions were then directed at the many East African Asians who had escaped the 1962 controls. They had not opted for the citizenship of newly independent countries like Kenya and Uganda but to remain citizens of the UK and Colonies, often obtaining UK passports from British High Commissions. In 1966, some 6,800 East African Asians used these passports to enter the UK and in 1967 this figure doubled as many Kenyan Asians, faced with Africanization policies, chose to leave. Labour promptly enacted the Commonwealth Immigrants Act 1968 which extended controls to holders of UK passports issued overseas who were not born, naturalized or adopted in the UK and without a parent or grandparent who could satisfy these conditions. Once again legislation was tied to an administrative quota scheme. Those newly restricted could only settle in Britain if the head of the household held a 'special voucher' issued by a British post overseas. Initially the quota was 1,500.

Meanwhile the Wilson Committee, established by Labour to consider a system of appeals, had reported in 1967 (Cmnd 3387) in favour of tribunals. Perhaps its reasoning was ambiguous, but in the context of tightening control some critics saw the new external scrutiny as a 'sop to liberal outrage' or, like Blake and Gillespie (Chapter 3), as a procedural device legitimating government policy. Certainly the ensuing Immigration Appeals Act 1969, which judicialized parts of the system, had another important consequence for the administration of control. Under previous legislation many aliens and all Commonwealth immigrants could choose either to turn up and ask to be admitted or to secure entry clearance (visas for aliens and entry certificates for Commonwealth citizens) from UK entry clearance officers (ECOs) in their country of departure. An entry clearance did not guarantee admission but would indicate to immigration officers at ports of entry that the holder appeared qualified to enter. Wilson stressed its advantages, particularly where officers had to verify the age and familial relationships of Commonwealth citizens seeking to enter as dependent relatives. Those refused would be saved the cost and strain of a wasted journey while local officers were better placed to investigate difficult cases. But the Committee declined to recommend compulsory entry certificates. Many aliens did not require visas and 'it would be out of the question to impose on Commonwealth citizens the same requirement under another name' (Cmnd 3387, para. 70). Labour thought the unthinkable. Mr Callaghan, the Home Secretary, argued (HC Deb. vol. 782, col. 1631): 'it would be more humane and lead to improved efficiency if those with claims to settle here have their cases scrutinised and decided before they set out.' Thus the 1969 Act made entry clearance for Commonwealth dependants compulsory; decision-making had been partially shifted overseas.

Such was the backdrop to the Immigration Act 1971.[8] The 1960s legislation had blurred the previous sharp division between aliens and British Subjects, but the two legal regimes remained distinct and in certain respects Commonwealth immigrants remained better off. In particular those entering with employment vouchers under the 1962 Act still possessed vestiges of their former status. Although they had lost the right to enter, once in they could settle free from all controls and were not dependent, like aliens, on temporary permissions to work. The 1971 Act changed all this. The distinctions between aliens and controlled Commonwealth citizens were phased out and the latter placed on the same footing as foreign workers. Both were only able to enter for a specific job and were reliant on it for continued residence. Only after four years could they apply to settle.

But for a comprehensive immigration policy, the Government must also consider many other cases, for example, visitors and the families of those already settled here.[9] Not surprisingly the 1971 Act does not contain the specifics. Instead Parliament set out the definition of 'patrials' who, exempt from control, were given the 'right of abode', listed the grounds for deportation and specified certain criminal offences connected with immigration control, e.g. overstaying limited leave and illegal entry. It then largely delegated to the Home Secretary the policy function of determining the criteria by which 'non-patrials', who required leave, could enter and remain.

There were two broad categories of patrial. First, citizens of the 'UK and Colonies' who were (a) born, adopted, registered or naturalised here or (b) the child of a parent so qualified or (c) settled and ordinarily resident here for five years. Secondly, Commonwealth citizens who were (a) born to a parent who was a citizen of the 'UK and Colonies' by birth or (b) the wife of a patrial as defined above. These provisions did not involve express discrimination, but in practice the British Subjects controlled were generally non-white. Evans (1976, p. 38) commented: 'insofar as patriality reflects links with the United Kingdom through family, it works one way. It favours the descendants of emigrants, but not the families of recent immigrants'.

Although the Immigration Act 1971 still governs immigration control, the nomenclature of 'patriality' was swept away by the British Nationality Act 1981 which replaced the citizenship laws of the 1948 legislation. It is now 'British Citizens' who possess the 'right of abode'. Former citizens of the 'UK and Colonies' are subdivided into three categories: 'British Citizens', 'British Dependent Territories Citizens' (BDTCs) and 'British Overseas Citizens' (BOCs) (e.g. the East African Asians). Although important changes are made in the future acquisition of citizenship,[10] at the moment of commencement the Act had little effect on the scope of immigration control. No non-patrials obtained the right of abode while nearly all patrials either became 'British Citizens' or retained their existing right of free entry.[11]

2 Published rules

The statutory responsibility of the Home Office for immigration control is divided by s.4 of the Immigration Act 1971 between two tiers. Power to grant or refuse entry is dispersed to individual immigration officers working at the ports, while the Home Secretary is given the power (in practice exercised by officials in the Ministry's Immigration and Nationality Department) to vary pre-existing leave and to grant leave to remain. But the statute does not specify *how* the examples will demonstrate, other, more specific, provisions entail discretionary power confined and structured to widely differing degrees. According to Lord Roskill in *R*. v. *Immigration Appeal Tribunal ex p. Alexander* [1982] 1 WLR 1076, the courts are forced to abandon their usual canons of interpretation:

... these [Rules] are not to be construed with all the strictness applicable to the construction of a statute or a statutory instrument, they must be construed sensibly according to the natural meaning of the language which is employed.

What do you think he means?

Here are some provisions concerning control on entry. Para. 17 of the 1983 Rules prescribes the conditions which a prospective visitor must meet:

[He] is to be admitted if he satisfies the immigration officer that he is genuinely seeking entry for the period of the visit as stated by him and that for that period he will maintain and accommodate himself ... without working or recourse to public funds ... But in all cases leave to enter is to be refused if the immigration officer is not so satisfied, and in particular, leave to enter is to be refused where there is reason to believe that the passenger's real purpose is to take employment ...

In theory, para. 17 is mandatory: the officer 'is' to admit or 'is' to refuse. But rule-application is not so simple. Interpretation may be necessary for example of the phrase 'recourse to public funds'.[13] The facts must be ascertained. Since the Rules are generally silent about the administrative procedures to be followed, there remains freedom to determine how the evidence will be collated and tested, subject to the duty to act fairly imposed in *Re H.K.* (see above, p. 80). Because para. 17 does not specify the criteria relevant to the assessment of intention, the factors to be considered must be chosen before the individual officer decides whether they produce 'satisfaction' or 'reason to believe'. Here there is clearly room for subjective impression.

Compare the 1980 Rules dealing with returning residents:

56. A Commonwealth citizen who satisfies the Immigration Officer that he was settled [here] at the coming into force of the Act, and that he has been settled here at any time during the two years preceding his return, is to be admitted for settlement. Any other passenger returning ... is to be admitted for settlement on satisfying the Immigration Officer that he was settled [here] when he left and that he has not been away for longer than two years.

57. A passenger who has been away ... too long to benefit from the preceding paragraph may nevertheless be admitted if, for example, he has lived here for

control the Executive – to be farmed out to bodies which are remote from political control'. In Standing Committee (HC SCA 1968/9, cols. 69–78), Mr Clegg expressed concern that the tribunals might carry out a policy different from the Minister's. And Mr Buck, in terms reminiscent of Donoughmore, suggested that the appellate authorities be confined to matters of fact and law since exercising discretion involved policy considerations suitable for determination by a minister responsible to Parliament and not by a 'judicial' or 'quasi-judicial' body. Replying, Mr Rees was dismissive. He characterized the delegation of discretion as minimal, arguing that it was 'no larger than in some functions assigned to ordinary courts' and that Parliament would retain overall control of policy through its formal rule-making powers. In advance, it was 'impossible to draw up a book of rules . . . covering all possibilities'. Flexibility and, thus, discretion were integral to this administrative process.

In Chapter 3 we met the argument that rules might emerge from adjudication, with a resultant loss of flexibility. Some critics believe that this describes exactly the evolution of immigration appeals:

> Established essentially as an administrative system and not as a judicial one the immigration appeals system has nevertheless created for itself a body of legal precedent and intentionally deprived itself therefore of discretion which could benefit appellants. [Runnymede 1981, p. 24.]

The implication here is that the diminution of discretion has worked one way, serving to tighten controls. The appellate authorities, especially the precedent-forming IAT, have not merely umpired according to pre-existing rules but have actively developed Home Office policies to limit immigration. In short, they have not played a 'neutral' role. UKIAS (UK Immigrants Advisory Service), the government-funded agency which represents most immigrants at appeals, agrees. Its annual reports contain repeated complaints, e.g. 'the [IAT] went on pursuing the policy of narrowing the scope in the interpretation of immigration rules to the disadvantage of the immigrant' (AR 1978/9, p. 27); 'after ten years the precedents . . . leave us little room for manoeuvre' (AR 1979/80, p. 27); and 'the strictness of the rules and the development of immigration law have contributed towards a formal and rigid system in which compassion and the awareness of cultural differences appear to have little place' (AR 1981/2, p. 4). UKIAS also criticizes what might be called reverse test-case strategy: 'frequently Home Office appeals to the [IAT] are designed to provoke observations from the Tribunal which establish precedents for the rejection of future applications in similar cases' (AR 1977/8, p. 36). Two can play the legal game. Summing up, the deputy director of UKIAS, Ahmed Ali, expressed concern that what had been informal hearings seeking after the facts had become formal proceedings focused on (restrictive) precedent. As the system solidified, so the mode of argumentation changed:

> With immigration control getting tighter and the adjudicators tougher, an appellant today has less chance of winning an appeal than he had in earlier years when the adjudicators had greater flexibility in the application of rules to a particular case and were not as much fettered by precedents and directives as they are today. They are assuming to a significant extent the role of case lawyers in so far as the immigration rules and their interpretation are concerned and this is to be regretted ... The [IAT] is embarking on a rule making process which, if it goes on unchecked, could seriously undermine the immigration appeal system. [AR 1977/8, pp. 37, 39.]

This process resembles but is different from that described by Nonet (Chapter 3). He analysed a regulatory agency's drift towards adjudication; here formalization involves shifts in the adjudicative process. Compare Ali's criticisms of the unhelpful precedents of the IAT with Titmuss' distaste for 'legalism' (below, p. 588).

Let us consider some ways of reducing discretion. In *Mahmoudi* v. *SSHD* [1981] Imm. AR 130, M entered as a visitor but then enrolled on an English language course. One issue was whether visitors could apply for variation of leave to study. (Students do not require entry clearance.) Para. 90 of the 1980 Rules provided:

> People admitted as visitors or students or for other temporary purposes have no claim to remain here for any other purpose ... In particular, except [for marriage and settlement after four years' residence] applications to remain are to be refused where the application is to remain for a purpose for which an entry clearance is required. Applications to remain for other purposes (not including employment, which is dealt with in [para. 91]) may be granted ... unless it appears that the applicant is attempting to remain permanently.

The IAT dismissed M's appeal:

> [The appellant] argued that if ... a visitor could not change to any other category it would be against the intention of the rules and he submitted that the first sentence must mean that a student can apply for any other temporary purpose but not a permanent purpose, that is as a businessman or for settlement ...
> We [disagree]. We note that the previous rules ... specifically provided for a visitor to be granted leave to stay in this country in some other temporary capacity, as for example, an 'au pair' girl or student, but such provision has not been repeated in the [1980 Rules]. Paragraph 90 provides that 'people admitted as visitors or students ... have no claim to remain here for any other

purpose'. These words appear unambiguous, and we see no reason to construe the rule as meaning 'for any permanent purpose'.

This decision created another no-switching provision. Applying the Rules, officers and adjudicators could not choose to let a visitor become a student. As a matter of interpretation, do you agree with the Tribunal's determination? Notice the legalistic reasoning; in formulating policy the IAT does not discuss the purpose of the Rule. K. C. Davis might label its approach 'inefficient'.

Here are two lines of precedent illustrating how the IAT may confine and structure discretion. We examine first decisions on para. 57 (above). In *Costa* v. *SSHD* [1974] Imm. AR 69, a Cypriot woman had been resident in the UK between 1963 and 1966, and, except for one sister, all her close relatives lived in Britain. She was readmitted as a visitor in 1969 and later sought to be treated as a returning resident. The tribunal treated the 'example' contained in para. 57 as a guideline, extracting from it the 'underlying principle' that the person 'must show strong connections with this country by a combination of length of residence and family or other ties.' Characterizing the case as borderline, the IAT relied on the catch-all provision, now para. 97 (above), to uphold the refusal to admit as a returning resident because the applicant had overstayed her visitor's leave by 18 months. Subsequently, in *Gokulsing* (24987/78 (1632) (unreported)), the IAT held a second set of criteria relevant to the exercise of discretion under para. 57. Not only, as the 'example' indicates, must an officer consider UK links, he must also examine the reasons for the delayed re-entry. Thus 'civil disturbance, personal accident or sickness' preventing re-entry within two years would be 'good external factors to be considered'. In *ECO, Dacca* v. *Armat Ali* [1981] Imm. AR 51, the applicant was unable to return from Bangladesh in time because a local court order restrained him until court proceedings, which eventually took six years, were completed. The IAT allowed him to enter; para. 57 should be operated flexibly since its purpose was 'to avoid injustice or undue hardship which might arise from the inflexible non-discretionary provisions of [para. 56]'.

Contrast *ECO, Kingston* v. *Peart* [1979–80] Imm. AR 41. P, a single man and a Jamaican citizen born in 1920, came to England in 1955 and remained for 20 years before returning to Jamaica because of his widowed mother's illness. Unable to make the family's smallholding pay, he invoked para. 57 after two years nine months absence. The ECO refused entry clearance, saying that P did not fall within the specified example because he had not lived here 'for most of his life'. On appeal the adjudicator distinguished the test developed in *Costa*; if an applicant could satisfy the example, 'he is entitled to entry clearance whether or not there are family or other ties present'. And, overruling the ECO, the adjudicator argued: 'it is proper to say that a single man who has worked here for 20 years has spent the majority of his adult life here, and therefore it is proper to say that he has indeed lived here for most of his life'. The ECO appealed. P contended that he had been a good member of the community, had strong connections notwithstanding that he had no family here, and was unable to return within the prescribed period because of his mother's ill health. The IAT held against him:

On looking at [para. 57], the wording of the example therein contained appears to be quite clear and unambiguous. 'Most' means greatest in amount and to ascertain whether a person has spent most of his life in this country it is necessary in fact to do a mathematical calculation and the mathematical calculation in this case shows that [P] has not lived here for most of his life . . . We do not agree [with the adjudicator] that because he worked here for 20 years he had to 'all intents and purposes' been here for most of his life . . . The adjudicator has imported the word 'adult' into the rule and in doing so . . . he was in error.

Do you agree that the wording is 'clear and unambiguous'? Notice how P's other arguments are ignored, although the previous determinations had held some of them relevant. The IAT (and apparently the ECO) transforms the 'example' into a condition which must be met, thereby undermining an apparently 'strong' discretion to the immigrant's disadvantage.

Secondly, we consider the IAT's interpretation of the phrase 'normally to be refused' in the old para. 5 (above). In what circumstances would the tribunal require the Home Office to exercise its discretion to refer, so allowing the Department of Employment to determine whether the proposed employment should be approved under the work permit scheme? In *Tally* v. *SSHD* [1975] Imm. AR 83, T was admitted as a visitor. A depot manager of British Rail later sought permission to employ him as a diesel fitter. The Home Office denied the application without referring, and the IAT rejected T's argument that BR's request for his skilled services took him out of the 'normal' category:

There is . . . nothing uncertain about what is meant by 'normally' . . . it means 'in the normal way or usually'. The fact that British Rail had vacancies for craftsmen at the Diesel Maintenance Depot did not constitute an abnormal situation which warranted a departure from the terms of para. 5.

In *Nicolaides* v. *SSHD* [1978] Imm. AR 67, the Home Office refused, without referring, N's application to work as a baker of pitta bread. The employer argued that without N the small family business would be in difficulties; the conditions and Greek ambience meant that 'no-one English would want [the job]'. Expanding on *Tally*, the IAT chose the set of criteria relevant to referral decisions:

> The 'normality' or otherwise of a situation has to be looked at primarily in the context of the applicant's circumstances; and the circumstances of the employer – if considered at all – are only a minor consideration . . . The main purpose of the immigration rules is to control, and to deal with the circumstances of, immigrants: the rules are not intended to deal with industrial matters. If it were otherwise, and serious inconvenience to an employer could be regarded as an important consideration, a visitor would only have to choose his employer carefully to defeat the intention of the rules and the situation could lead to unfairly discriminatory treatment as between one applicant and another.

Meanwhile in *SSHD* v. *Stillwagon* [1975] Imm. AR 132 the IAT had constructed a test of the applicant's circumstances. CBS Records wished to employ S on a long-term recording contract, describing her as 'a singer of unique and extraordinary talent' who would generate work for a considerable number of English backing musicians. Rejecting her appeal under para. 5, the tribunal accepted the Home Office's submission that to warrant referral 'there must be exceptional circumstances, such as strong personal and compassionate reasons or reasons involving an aspect of vital public interest'. How does this test compare with the *Tally* formulation? Are there other possible interpretations of the word 'normally'? Consider subsequent applications of the test. In *SSHD* v. *Sarwar* [1978] Imm. AR 190, a visitor sought to remain as a qualified teacher of the Islamic religion employed by the Muslim Educational Trust. She would instruct 130 Muslim girls at four secondary schools; unsuccessful attempts had been made to recruit a suitable teacher from the local community. The IAT thought that a matter of 'vital public interest' was involved and stipulated referral. However, in *SSHD* v. *Pereyra* [1978] Imm. AR 13, P, a Pakistani citizen, entered as a visitor accompanying his elderly mother, who possessed the right of abode. Unable to walk far and suffering from giddy fits, she could not look after herself. The IAT held that these were not 'strong compassionate reasons' meriting referral:

> [Although] the applicant and his mother are certainly deserving of sympathy

by reason of the mother's infirmity, this is not necessarily a question of splitting up a mother and her son since, however less comfortable it may be for her in Pakistan, it would be open to her to return there with the applicant.

This line of cases illustrates the restrictive precedent-forming process to which critics like Runnymede object. The IAT constructs a test nowhere mentioned in the Rules, selects the relevant criteria and applies its own test in later cases. Might we conclude that the no-switching provision introduced in 1980 represented little change? Under para. 5 the tribunal had enacted a standard so demanding that almost all applicants were already bound to fail.[17]

Yet the solidification is intermittent. Determinations like *Armat Ali* show how particular IAT panels may resist pressure to reduce discretion. The process is occasionally reversed. For example, *Mahmoudi* v. *SSHD* was overruled by the IAT in *Adebeshin* v. *SSHD* [1982] Imm. AR 71, at the joint request of UKIAS and the Home Office. The decision had upset the department's policy which was only to stop people coming to Britain and later working. And solidification has not progressed equally on all fronts. Here are some decisions about deportation for breach of condition under paras. 154, 156 and 158 (above). Whether the proper balance was struck is a value-judgement, just like the determinations themselves. In *SSHD* v. *Yuksel* [1976] Imm. AR 91 the adjudicator found no compassionate circumstances but allowed an appeal against deportation because the political situation in Cyprus made the appellant's return there inappropriate. The IAT reversed this decision, emphasizing that the 'relevant factors' in para. 156 must relate to the two basic criteria set out in para. 154. Weighing these, the tribunal accepted that 'compassionate circumstances' might arise from the political conditions obtaining in the country of return but held on the facts that these did not outbalance the 'public interest' (which it did not attempt to define). In *Ali* v. *SSHD* [1978] Imm. AR 126, the appellants used deception to obtain entry, overstayed and carried on business in breach of their entry conditions. They unsuccessfully appealed against deportation to Kenya, pleading that two children had been born here and the wife was expecting a third and that as persons of Indian extraction they feared racial and political persecution resulting from 'Africanization' policies. The IAT indicated that the greater the misconduct, the larger the 'public interest' in deportation. 'Africanization' was not itself sufficient to justify their fears and the wife's imminent confinement could be taken into account by the Minister in considering when to implement the deportation decision. In *Bano* (61659/80 (1949) (unreported)), B was a schizophrenic whose entry had been secured through her relatives' deception. Most of her family were in Britain and those in India could not look after her. The IAT held that excluding B would be so inhumane as to outweigh the serious misconduct. In *Murderris* (4694/79 (1690) (unreported)), M was 13 when, in 1973, he entered from Cyprus with his parents. They had no claim to stay and were removed in 1979. Since M remained, it was decided to deport him but, being now over 18, he could not be excluded as a 'family member'. The IAT upheld the adjudicator's decision that the 'compassionate circumstances' outweighed the 'public interest': M was in the middle of further education, his grandparents who were here lawfully would look after him and as a child he bore no responsibility for his parents' actions in 1973.

A significant feature of these decisions is their individuated character. Precedents were barely mentioned and the tribunal focused on the particular facts. One reason why the IAT has left the open-textured weighing process largely unstructured is suggested by *Jordan v. SSHD* [1972] Imm. AR 201. Two Anglo-Indian brothers who had overstayed appealed against deportation. They came from a family with long traditions of service in British India, had close relatives in the UK and their employment prospects in India were poor. The adjudicator, noting their Indian upbringing, single status and lack of dependants in Britain, dismissed the appeal. The IAT agreed:

In weighing the 'public interest' against any compassionate circumstances the aim, under [para. 154] is 'an exercise of power of deportation that is consistent and fair as between one person and another'. Were the appellants to be permitted to remain in this country for the reasons [suggested] it could hardly be said that such action would be 'consistent and fair' as between them and the many persons subject to United Kingdom immigration control whose circumstances and background are similar to those of the appellants.

Did the tribunal misconstrue para. 154? The IAT in any case is ill-equipped to apply it. Only Home Office administrators who see all the deportation cases can aim realistically at 'consistent and fair' treatment (subject to different governments' views about how the underlying balance should be struck):

The Tribunal could not, however it decided cases, achieve the objective of 'fairness and consistency' between one person and another because not every

deportee appeals so it does not see every case. There is no practicable method
by which it can monitor or control Home Office standards of fairness and
consistency unless it does see every case. [Blake 1983, p. 36.]

Was Mr Buck (above) right after all?

Ahmed Ali states that the reduction of discretion has diminished
the immigrant's chances on appeal. The retention of discretion by the
appellate authorities is no guarantee of success either. Decisions like
Bano and *Murderris* on deportation for breach of conditions are rare
and, as Table 12 demonstrates, the success rate in appeals against
deportation is extremely low. Forced to second-guess what is
'consistent and fair', the adjudicators usually accept the department's
viewpoint. Again Table 11 reveals only a marginal fall in the
percentage of appeals allowed of those allowed and dismissed. It does
not follow that the solidifying tendencies are unimportant. The
statistics cannot measure the effect of increasing rigidity on the
decision-making process as a whole. Precedents can possess marked
'ripple' effects. Nevertheless Ali's conclusion is only partly borne out.
A deeper truth emerges: rules or discretion, immigrants' appeals
usually fail. No latter-day Sir Edward Troup has complained about
the decisions handed down by the present tribunal system.

Table 11. Appeals to Adjudicators 1970–81

	Total disposals	No jurisdiction	Withdrawn	Dismissed	Allowed	Allowed as % Allowed Dismissed
1970	350	–	6	293	51	14.8
1971	2,443	–	294	1,688	461	21.6
1972	4,114	–	800	2,610	704	21.2
1973	5,292	20	869	3,652	751	17.1
1974	7,666	13	2,085	4,634	934	16.8
1975	10,937	17	3,291	6,327	1,302	17.1
1976	12,412	682	3,302	7,131	1,297	15.4
1977	11,671	743	2,557	7,098	1,273	15.2
1978	11,455	174	2,357	7,569	1,355	15.2
1979	13,176	67	3,106	8,437	1,566	15.7
1980	16,599	58	4,153	10,381	2,007	16.2
1981	18,010	26	4,161	11,589	2,234	16.2
Total	114,125	1,800	26,981	71,409	13,935	16.3

Source: 'Evidence', p. 153.

Table 12. Appeals to Adjudicators by Selected Categories 1977–81

Category	Year	Total disposals	No jurisdiction	Withdrawn	Dismissed	Allowed	Allowed as % Allowed/Dismissed
Refusal of entry clearance	1977	6,579	5	1,286	4,183	1,105	20.8
	1978	6,339	–	1,128	4,015	1,196	23.0
	1979	7,361	1	1,425	4,572	1,363	23.0
	1980	9,912	2	2,106	6,069	1,735	22.2
	1981*	10,452	1	1,974	6,677	1,800	21.2
Refusal to vary leave to enter	1977	3,157	724	956	1,377	100	6.8
	1978	3,035	160	917	1,865	93	4.7
	1979	3,782	46	1,327	2,279	130	5.4
	1980	4,506	43	1,653	2,639	171	6.1
	1981*	4,498	21	1,607	2,698	172	6.0
Decision to make Deportation Order	1977	535	2	102	416	15	3.5
	1978	520	3	50	461	6	1.3
	1979	447	2	72	355	18	5.0
	1980	414	2	75	310	27	8.0
	1981*	299	1	47	232	19	7.6
Giving of Removal Directions (for illegal immigrants)	1977	93	1	11	81	–	0.0
	1978	110	–	10	100	–	0.0
	1979	118	1	14	102	1	1.0
	1980	119	1	11	107	–	0.0
	1981*	130	–	14	116	–	0.0

Source: HL Deb. vol. 405, cols. 1670–2; HL Deb. vol. 426, col. 1188.
* 11 months to 30 November.

Table 13. Immigrants' Appeals to the Immigration Appeal Tribunal 1970–81*

	Total disposals	No jurisdiction	Withdrawn	Dismissed	Allowed	Allowed as % Allowed/ Dismissed
1970/1	117	–	11	74	32	30.2
1972	166	–	24	96	46	32.4
1973	152	4	25	93	30	24.4
1974	203	2	50	105	46	30.5
1975	190	4	73	79	34	30.1
1976	603	32	140	333	98	22.7
1977	257	16	51	151	39	20.5
1978	342	7	91	207	37	15.2
1979	311	11	83	171	46	21.2
1980	392	36	110	167	79	32.1
1981	510	38	118	290	64	18.1
Total	3,243	150	776	1,766	551	23.8

Table 14. Home Office Appeals to the Immigration Appeal Tribunal 1970–81*

	Total disposals	No jurisdiction	Withdrawn	Dismissed	Allowed	Allowed as % Allowed/ Dismissed
1970/1	41	–	6	16	19	54.3
1972	52	–	8	23	21	47.7
1973	41	–	4	19	18	48.6
1974	44	–	12	8	24	75.0
1975	58	–	27	9	22	71.0
1976	136	2	47	31	56	64.4
1977	70	–	15	15	40	72.7
1978	95	2	20	24	49	67.1
1979	74	2	7	25	40	61.5
1980	80	3	23	28	26	48.1
1981	88	4	18	28	38	57.6
Total	779	13	187	226	353	61.0

Source of Tables 13–14: 'Evidence', p. 154.
* Figures in Tables 13–14 relate to appeal cases (which may include several individual appeals).

4 A decision-making chain

Using these statistics, critics argue that immigration appeals are defective. Besides developing restrictive precedents, they constitute an ineffective check on administrators' decisions. 'To many appellants . . . the appeals system was only a "rubber stamp" to endorse the decision against which appeals are lodged' (UKIAS AR 1977/8,

p. 36). The complaints sometimes echo the detailed and empirically based criticisms of SBATs to which social scientists have devoted considerably more attention. For instance, there is the membership. IAT members are appointed by the Lord Chancellor's Department but, contrary to the Franks' model, adjudicators are chosen by the respondents, the Home Office. Adjudicators have received little or no training – after a one-month induction course in 1970 there were no further exercises during the next seven years. Many have no recent experience of the countries from which most appeals originate. Some of the more recent appointees are ex-UKIAS representatives or are from ethnic minorities. But many of the original adjudicators were ex-colonial civil servants, some of whom JCWI (Joint Council for the Welfare of Immigrants), quoting from their judgments, has accused of racial and political prejudice.[18] Mr Ennals, director of UKIAS, put it in milder tones for the Home Affairs Committee (HC 90–11 (1981/2), herein 'Evidence', para. 326): 'I am sure that all adjudicators are totally objective. It is just that some are more objective than others.'

There are other, more specific bones of contention. For example, UKIAS (AR 1981/2, p. 8) claims that the tribunals' exercise of discretion to grant leave to appeal to the IAT is more liberally exercised when the Home Office appeals. In another departure from Franks, immigration appeals are now the only major tribunal system from which there exists no appeal on a point of law to the courts. This partly explains the very high proportion of judicial review cases involving immigrants. Forced to use Order 53 procedure, they must obtain leave, while cross-examination etc. and remedies are discretionary. In most cases, the Immigration Appeals (Procedure) Rules (SI 1684 of 1972) place the burden of proof (expressed as the balance of probabilities) on the immigrant. These Rules grant adjudicators wide discretion over the general conduct of proceedings. As a consequence 'the way in which such hearings are conducted can differ widely . . . allowing some adjudicators to work in a way which is mainly adversarial and others to lean towards [an] inquisitorial approach' (Runnymede 1981, p. 22). As with SBATs, there is no settled practice.

However there are important differences between the two tribunal systems. Unlike SB, most appellants here are represented. Following the Wilson Committee's recommendations, UKIAS, a non-statutory voluntary body, was established to provide free advocacy in immigration appeals. In addition, U K I A S makes representations to ministers (below, Chapter 17), deals with welfare problems (e.g. finding immigrants accommodation) and provides advice. It also lobbies M Ps against immigration restrictions and participates in research projects, training for E C Os and advisory services overseas.

The organization has its detractors. Although controlled by an Executive Council representing voluntary and statutory bodies concerned with immigrants' welfare (e.g. the British Council of Churches, the Indian Workers Association and the C R E), U K I A S is almost entirely government-funded. So radical critics, seeing immigration appeals as a legitimating and depoliticizing device can point to the Service as an illustration of *official* interest in making the appeals system work. From this viewpoint, its increase in funding, during a period of financial stringency, from £533,000 in 1980/1 to £721,000 in 1982/3 is not surprising. Its annual reports suggest, if not cosy relationships, then cooperation with immigration officers and, especially, with the appellate authorities and Home Office presenting officers. Working primarily within the system, 'cordial relations [with] the Adjudicators and staff at the Immigration Appeals must be maintained' (A R 1981/2, p. 30). Indeed its first chairman, Lord Foot, saw U K I A S (A R 1977/8, p. 4) as 'an organisation which fights its battles without rancour', a label which few campaigning organizations would relish.

However this may be (and its more recent annual reports indicate greater dissatisfaction with the administration of immigration controls culminating in vociferous criticism before the Home Affairs Committee (below)), U K I A S plays a pivotal role in immigration appeals, representing about 55 per cent of all appellants. Indeed solicitors and law centres have found it difficult to muscle in because detailed knowledge of immigration law has remained concentrated in the department, U K I A S and J C W I, the most powerful immigrants' pressure group. Many I A T and nearly all adjudicators' decisions go unreported, unindexed copies being available only at the Supreme Court Library and Law Society in London. Only comparatively recently have books begun to synthesize the precedents in detail.[19]

U K I A S is crucial in another sense. S B claimants have the right to be present and heard when their appeal is determined. Most immigrants do not. By ss.13 and 16 of the Immigration Act 1971 certain rights of appeal can only be exercised from abroad although the hearing takes place in Britain. These include persons removed from Britain as illegal entrants, persons without work permits or entry clearance denied entry at the ports and applicants refused entry clearance overseas who, Table 12 reveals, comprise over half of all appellants. In their absence family and friends must appear, frequently relying on UKIAS for advice and representation. Lawyers, with their traditional concern for fair procedures, may find these truncated appeals offensive. Decisions which can divide families are taken without the appellant being present to put his case. However, truncated appeals can be seen as facilitating the working of present controls and discouraging abuses of the Act. The aim of localizing many decisions might be frustrated if immigrants could come to Britain and appeal, while the Home Office, in its discussion document 'Review of Appeals under the Immigration Act 1971', contended:

To confer a right of appeal before removal on an illegal entrant would place him in a more favourable position than people who seek to enter lawfully but who are refused entry and can only exercise their right of appeal [from abroad]. Where the illegal entrant was apprehended in the act of seeking to enter, or even shortly afterwards, such a result would be manifestly unfair. It would not be practicable to extend rights of appeal before removal to everyone without quite unacceptable extra demands on resources. Such a situation would in any case be exploited by those who had no claim to enter but would seek entry nevertheless in the knowledge that by appealing they could at least stay in the country until their appeal was determined. Detention would ensue in these cases where the passenger could not be relied on not to disappear. [Home Office 1981, para. 20.]

The appeals system is only part of the decision-making chain. To understand fully the difficulties facing appellants in truncated appeals we must digress to the stage of primary decision-taking. We will focus on the largest category of truncated appeals, applications to enter from the wives and children under 18 of men already settled in Britain. By paras. 46–50 of the 1983 Rules, such persons must be admitted provided certain conditions are met, for example, that the sponsor will maintain and accommodate them. These dependants must possess current entry clearance so their eligibility is tested by ECOs working overseas. We will consider administrative procedures in the Indian sub-continent where most applications of this nature are made.

Once an application for entry clearance is received, the applicant is placed in a queue of persons waiting their turn for interview at the relevant British post. Each High Commission operates non-priority and priority queues, the latter comprising those cases deemed worthy of early resolution. In Pakistan, for example, the priority queue includes about half of all applicants, involving children under ten, first wives without older children, 'urgent compassionate cases', etc. Applicants are asked to provide at interview documentary evidence substantiating their claimed relationships to sponsors, for example marriage certificates and personal correspondence. In practice, however, little weight is attached to applicants' documents, since ECOs are wary of false documentation in countries where, until comparatively recently, there existed no comprehensive obligatory systems of registering births, marriages and deaths. Instead, officials use an elaborate and lengthy system of questioning, the 'discrepancy' method of interviewing. If, for example, the applicant is a wife, she will be asked, through an interpreter, detailed questions about the family tree, her marriage ceremony and the family's home, village, work, etc. Her answers will be compared for discrepancies with those provided by the sponsor in Britain and by any relatives or friends who accompanied her to interview. The ECO may then try to resolve any discrepancies which have arisen by arranging a 'confrontation' between interviewees or by deferring the application for further enquiries locally (e.g. visiting the applicant's village) or for further investigation by Home Office officials in the UK. Otherwise, at the end of the interview, the ECO will grant or, with his immediate superior's approval, refuse entry clearance, depending on the magnitude and number of discrepancies disclosed.

In its report on British posts overseas, 'Review of Overseas Representation' (1977), the now defunct Central Policy Review Staff (CPRS), popularly known as the Government's 'Think Tank', described the objective of this 'highly complex system of processing' as being to detect and deter persons seeking to enter the UK by false pretences. Mr Callaghan (above) justified decision-making abroad as 'more humane' and 'efficient'. Interested pressure groups discern less reputable motives. First, they criticize the administrative delays. At their peak, the waiting periods for first interview in the non-priority queues have been Bangladesh 38 months (1974), Pakistan 23 months (1980) and India 16 months (1976). At the end of 1982 the periods were 16 months, 11 months and 14½ months respectively. Additional delays will ensue if the ECO defers the application. In Bangladesh a further nine months delay has not been uncommon between referral to Home Office officials and re-interview. The situation in JCWI's view (Evidence, p. 58) 'is dictated . . . by deliberate policy rather than by necessity'. The delays are not accidental: this is immigration control through bureaucratic procrastination. Some applicants may give up while others may be deterred from applying. And in *R*. v. *Secretary of State for the Home Department ex p. Zamir* [1980] 2 WLR 357 the Court of Appeal held that where an applicant has ceased to be eligible for admission by the date of decision he is not entitled to entry clearance. So a child, aged 16 when the application was made, who had to wait three years for interview, would be unable to invoke the under 18 rule and would have to satisfy the stricter criteria for entry over that age. Although para. 12 of the 1983 Rules now provides that eligibility is not lost solely for this reason, some delayed applicants may marry or cease to be 'dependent'.

Critics also contend that the administrative procedures outlined have operated unfairly, serving to deny many genuine dependants entry. The following statistics indicate wide fluctuations.

Table 15. Refusal rates for applicants seeking entry clearance for immediate settlement as wives and children 1977–81 (in percentages)

	New Delhi		Bombay		Islamabad		Dacca	
	Wives	Children	Wives	Children	Wives	Children	Wives	Children
1977	7	23	+	7	14	26	47	65
1978	3	27	+	6	20	33	28	45
1979	3	35	1	17	24	36	23	42
1980	6	40	1	16	22	32	23	37
1981	8	30	2	12	20	30	21	33

Source: 'Evidence', p. 213.
Note: 'Refusal rate' denotes the number of refusals divided by the sum of refusals and grants.
+ = less than 0.5 per cent.

In 1973 Runnymede sponsored field research in Pakistan, involving attendance at interviews, discussions with ECOs and trips to the localities where many applicants lived. The researchers concluded that the burden of proof was pitched far too high. Applicants were required to prove their claimed relationship not on the balance of probabilities or even beyond all reasonable doubt but 'beyond any doubt whatever'. The interviewing sessions were long and gruelling when most applicants had never attended an interview of any kind before. The standard of interpretation was poor and led to many misunderstandings which ECOs might construe as discrepancies. And discrepancies were inevitable because the questions were sometimes ambiguous or were capable of being answered in more than one way. For example, the answer to the question 'which side of your house adjoins the neighbouring house?' depends on which you consider to be the left and right of your house, which in turn depends on which way you are facing at the time. Similarly, the apparently innocuous inquiry 'how many rooms does your house have?' elicited the observed response 'two – and a veranda'. The researchers commented:

This is perhaps the most difficult question to answer and causes more suspicion than anything else. The lady had stated that there were two rooms (which were the main rooms) but in fact there were a lot more. The applicant's dilemma is whether to include or exclude the following: veranda, sitting room, small side rooms, kitchen, rooms where animal food is kept, rooms where animals are kept, a room where fodder is stored [etc] . . . Also a farm is run jointly by an extended family but at home each nuclear family may have a separate dwelling within the main house . . . Should these rooms be counted or not? Any discrepancies in this statement will count heavily against the applicant, because an [ECO] will argue that if the [interviewees] cannot agree on the number of rooms in the house, there must be something wrong. [Runnymede 1974, pp. 9–10.]

The interviewing system requires officers applying the Rules to make subjective assessments about the credibility of claimed relationships. Although the researchers found no general agreement about how many discrepancies officers would overlook, they concluded that the 'overwhelming concern' of ECOs was to prevent the issue of entry clearance to persons not strictly eligible. There was exclusion by administration:

If it is desired to reduce the number of people entering this country, the honest way to do it is by changing the law to disqualify the category one wishes to exclude, not to make the attainment of their rights as difficult as possible. We have never yet countenanced the permanent separation of families, but if we are to do so now, let us do so openly . . . The process . . . does not work effectively, at least as a method of arriving at the truth; its main effect is to discourage people. [Runnymede 1974, p. 28.]

Runnymede returned to the sub-continent in 1976, examining 58 cases where wives and children had been refused entry clearance *and* had appealed unsuccessfully. In most cases the ECO gave more than one reason, the most frequent grounds being discrepancies in domestic circumstances (49 cases), discrepancies in the family tree (24), suspicion and/or evidence of false documents (32) and medical reports concerning age (9). Following village visits, document checks, interviews and detailed attempts to explain discrepancies, the researchers concluded that 55 applicants had a genuine right of entry, two were fraudulent and one case was inconclusive. They saw as causes of erroneous decisions the lack of documentary evidence, clerical errors, mistranslations, over-reliance on children's evidence and the atmosphere in interviewing rooms which, by making applicants nervous, prompted wrong and/or short answers. ECOs, they argued, should be more prepared to step outside interviewing rooms and into the villages. The fresh evidence caused 30 of the decisions to be reversed. The researchers commented:

[Our] findings . . . demonstrate fairly conclusively that the elaborate entry clearance and appeals system set up by the British Authorities is failing to separate the genuine from the fraudulent dependant and that as a result, significant numbers of wives and children of men settled and working in this country are being denied the right to join their husbands and fathers here. [Runnymede 1977, p. 8.]

In the same year, the CPRS was concerned with the quality of decisions and of staff:

Because so much interpretation [of evidence] is involved it is inevitable that subjective judgments are made. To make the right judgments considerable knowledge is required of the local culture and economic conditions. We suspect that this knowledge is often rather limited. The misunderstandings and errors of judgment that occur make the interviewing system inaccurate. [CPRS 1977, p. 166.]

Yet despite the well-substantiated complaints, the CPRS recommended modifications, not abandonment. Interviews were often the only reliable source of evidence, so well-trained ECOs (who should possess 'racial tolerance; intelligence; good judgement; a friendly and outgoing manner; an interest in the cultures of other peoples; patience; and resilience') should use superior interviewing techniques (shorter sessions, better trained interpreters, a more relaxed atmosphere, etc.) to produce more reliable decisions.

Four years later, the Home Affairs Committee was listening to complaints from UKIAS and JCWI identical to Runnymede's.[20] UKIAS claimed:

[A] strenuous search for discrepancies has become almost an obsession . . . The standard of objectivity in assessing the reality or otherwise is declining every day . . . The administrative policy on immigration in the context of the Indian sub-continent reflects an approach that thousands of genuine persons may be allowed to suffer but one dishonest one may not be allowed to enter the [UK] ['Evidence', p. 91.]

But the HAC, in its report 'Immigration from the Indian Sub-Continent' (HC 90–1 (1981/2), hereafter 'Report'), gave the system a relatively clean bill of health. Although the central ingredient – the heavy reliance on a discrepancy model of interviewing – remained largely untouched, procedures had evolved. There were some village visits to assess doubtful cases, better local advisory services etc. Waiting times would soon be drastically reduced because queues were being cleared. The number of applications from wives and children was in decline (from 23,280 in 1977 to 13,130 in 1981) and had been overtaken by the rate of processing (21,040 in 1981). Criticisms of the present staff's approach were unfounded and unfavourable research was outdated. The all-party Committee felt able to conclude after a nine-day visit by some members:

However the system may have operated in the past . . . at present we found a strong commitment by ECOS and their seniors to recognising the difficulties facing applicants in proving their relationships, and in some circumstances giving them the benefit of any doubt. [The officers] do a first class job in extremely difficult circumstances . . . Some eligible people may . . . be kept out, but equally some who are not eligible will slip through the net. We are convinced that neither result is the objective of those operating the system. ['Report', paras. 48, 50.]

The Government expressed delight but its response to suggestions for improvement was less positive. The Committee had recommended that the Government fund a UKIAS representative to help Bangladeshi applicants fill in forms and arrange adequate documentation. It also wanted extra resources for more village visits. The Government refused both requests. Visits, although useful, were 'costly in time and resources and, although some increase in their frequency may be possible, the particular circumstances of a case must continue to be the criteria for undertaking such enquiries, which cannot become the norm' (Cmnd 8725, p. 10).

Whichever you care to believe, these variant descriptions of entry clearance procedures emphasize the importance of organizational objectives and restraints for administrative law. The economic context is equally apparent. Governments take policy decisions about the resources allocated to particular administrative processes. Truth does not always come cheaply, if at all. Remember too that courts determine far fewer immigration cases than ECOs; analysis of judicial decisions, the traditional concern of administrative lawyers, is barely relevant in comparison with the impact of ECO decisions.

We can now make a related point about 'truncated appeals' before adjudicators.[21] The point is important because in Chapter 6 we suggested that more attention be paid to documentary and inquisitorial procedures. The issues in truncated appeals are primarily factual and evidential involving, typically, doubt over the credibility of a claimed relationship. Administrative practice is particularly important here because on appeal it is difficult to correct official errors at the initial rule-application stage. In 1981, one-third of all applicants for immediate settlement were refused entry clearance, of whom about three-quarters appealed. Although the success rate was the highest of all immigration appeals, it was still only 22.1 per cent (23.9 per cent in 1980). There is either a lot of fraud or else many genuine appellants fail to prove their entitlement.

Truncated appeal procedures revolve around an 'explanatory statement' based on the ECO's report which, under the procedural Rules, must be a 'written statement of the facts relating to the decision . . . and the reasons therefore.' At the appeal hearing this document becomes the cornerstone of the Home Office case since presenting officers rarely expand upon it. Subject to their cross-examination, the applicant's sponsor gives oral testimony trying to explain the discrepancies. Other evidence, for example applicants' letters commenting on interviews, may be introduced.

Critics focus on the explanatory statement.[22] It is based on translations of oral comments and is prepared months after interview, frequently not by the ECO involved but by an official in the UK working from the ECO's notes. Again, although varying widely in quality, explanatory statements are not dispassionate collations of all 'the facts'. Runnymede (1974, p. 26) has called them: ' a farrago of suggestions, accusations and statements of fact' culled selectively to count against the applicant.

It is not only the appellant's absence which makes such explanatory statements difficult to rebut; ECOs working overseas are also unavailable for cross-examination. So these officials know they will never have to justify their actions personally in open proceedings. Their statements are not given on oath and, since discovery of documents is here linked to the appearance of witnesses, the full interview file will not be open to inspection. Thus an appeals procedure involving presenting officers, (state-subsidized) representatives and adjudicators, which is in form largely adversarial, omits many of the ingredients which lawyers, trained on court procedures, would consider essential. Neither party to the initial decision participates. Recently U K I A S has tried to circumvent these difficulties by developing a new role for its advisory services operating in Pakistan and Bangladesh. Previously they gave applicants assistance filling in forms etc.; now:

> ... the majority of U K I AS Counsellors as well as C R Os and solicitors write to the Overseas Advisory Service for field reports to check the claimed relationship of the appellants to the sponsors ... The field trips are conducted most efficiently and comprehensively. The integrity and cogent value of these reports is often upheld by the Adjudicators and Tribunal. [A R 1981/2, p. 17.]

But U K I A S lacks the money, transport and manpower to do the job comprehensively and the Government (Cmnd 8725, p. 9) will not fund expansion of this *investigative* input into appeal determinations. Levin (1980, p. 180) comments: 'with the best will in the world, the adjudicator will rarely be confident that his decision is based on the real facts because of the nature of the evidence put before him and the fact that it is not adequately tested.'

5 'Reforming' immigration appeals

By now you may think the immigration appeals system needs 'improvement'. Yet strengthening one link of a decision-making chain is hardly a complete solution. The administrative procedures on which an appeals system rests may dictate the outcome of appeals. Perhaps, like S B (Chapter 19), the real challenge lies in getting the initial decision right. U K I AS (A R 1981/2, p. 5) comments: 'the solution lies in a more rigorous investigation at the source, i.e. in the village itself'. This, however, government seems loath to introduce.

In any case what does 'improvement' mean? From their different perspectives, commentators may stress different 'problems' with the same administrative procedures. Analysing immigration appeals, lawyers might be concerned by the departures from Franks and might wish to impose more court-like procedures by developing legal aid, discovery of documents, cross-examination etc. Radical critics who believe that the appeals system exists to depoliticize immigration and legitimize restrictive controls, might disagree. Changing appeals procedure could not cure the 'real evil' of government immigration policy while increased legalization might even be counter-productive.

The present Conservative Government has largely resisted suggestions by the H A C designed to make the appeals system more accurate. Ignoring an adjudicator's opinion ('Evidence', p. 161) that conducting truncated appeals properly would require a flying court hopping from country to country, the Committee proposed more modestly that there should be (further) experiments with tape-recordings. The Government agreed, though it was felt that applicants would probably be disconcerted. An interim recommendation that notes of each question and answer should be appended to explanatory statements met with less success. It would 'require considerable additional resources and generally delay entry clearance procedures' (Cmnd 8725, p. 11). The (secret) guidance to ECOs on the preparation of appeal statements would be 'reviewed' instead. A third request that adjudicators should be explicitly instructed to apply the balance of probabilities test drew the reply (Cmnd 8725, p. 12):

An adjudicator is independent and classed as a Tribunal under the . . . Tribunal and Inquiries Act 1971 . . . Adjudicators have consistently applied . . . the balance of probabilities, and the [IAT] has been vigilant in upholding this . . . A number of appeals are allowed in which discrepancies have not been resolved.

How does the Government's response to criticisms of Vaccine Damage Tribunals (Chapter 13) compare? Are Mr Bell's sentiments (above) borne out?

The Home Office made suggestions for reform in its discussion document on appeals. Here again 'delay' was the excuse or justification for reform.[23] Delays were seen as advantageous to those seeking temporary extension of stay but unfair to dependants waiting to appeal from abroad. More important perhaps, the appeal system cost £4.5m per annum to operate. There were two ways to 'rationalise' appeals:

The first is to rationalise the substantive rights of appeal set out in [the 1971] Act . . . The second is to revise the procedure rules so as to ensure that scarce resources of manpower and accommodation are devoted to the most serious issues which arise and that time is not wasted on less important matters.

Although implementation of the measures put forward [here] might produce in due course a net saving in expenditure and manpower, the main aim at this stage is to make maximum use of the existing resources in order to speed up the hearing of appeals and thus to reduce the number of outstanding cases. [Home Office 1981, paras. 5–6.]

Translated, the first form of 'rationalization' meant withdrawing some existing opportunities to appeal and resisting pressure to introduce others. But the main procedural reform envisaged was to determine some appeals without oral hearings. The Home Office proposed continuing existing procedures where the law or facts were in dispute or where the exercise of discretion was in issue, e.g. where compassionate circumstances were pleaded against proposed deportation. But where paragraphs of the Rules 'lay down requirements which are so clear-cut that it should normally be readily apparent whether or not they are met', adjudicators should decide on the case papers, save where they found 'compelling reasons' not to do so. In Chapter 14, we saw that a majority of planning appeal decisions are today decided on the papers. Is this documentary procedure to become a blueprint for administrative justice? (See also Chapter 19.)

The Home Office proposals are significant for what is omitted. There is no mention of 'openness, fairness and impartiality', the procedural criteria which Franks constructed to evaluate the work of administrative tribunals. Instead, assessing performance in terms of cost and speed of processing, the document highlights disagreement about what constitutes 'improvement' and 'good administration'. It is concerned with notions of 'efficiency' and not of 'justice'. Under departmental review at the end of 1983 following criticisms from *Justice*, JCWI, etc.,[24] the document's message for administrative lawyers working in the 1980s is that their concerns may seem parochial to those involved in a wider political or economic debate.

Immigration control: secondary systems

At first sight the changes wrought in the administration of immigration control since 1969 appear substantial. Previously aliens faced wide discretionary powers structured only by secret guidelines and with little external scrutiny. Today the published Immigration Rules are subject to Parliamentary veto while appeals and judicial review supply a measure of judicialization. But looking more closely, we found that the Immigration Rules left many gaps to fill and, since rule-making by adjudication was patchy, that certain discretionary powers remained relatively unstructured. And we saw how the ECOs' fact-finding function was subject only to limited checking further up the decision-making chain. Administrative practice and procedure took on significance as we discovered that officials *retained* substantial choice and freedom of manoeuvre. In this chapter we develop the theme by focusing on informal aspects of immigration control, ending with a study of illegal entry where the courts have had an important role to play.

M Ps are well aware that the administrative process is flexible. In a recent Supply Day debate (HC Deb. vol. 26, cols. 633–704), Mr Hattersley (Labour) unsuccessfully moved the motion: 'this House regrets the increasingly repressive operation of immigration regulations'. He complained:

The Home Secretary is responsible for the general hardening of attitudes in the immigration services which has come about either as a result of direct ministerial instruction or because the policies and attitudes of the Conservative leadership have indirectly permeated down through the Home Office.

The notion of change within existing parameters will be familiar. Compare Wade's suggestion (p. 318 above) that a transformation of 'judicial spirit' describes recent developments in judicial review. The secrecy surrounding the immigration service makes Mr Hattersley's claim difficult to assess. In any case, to Conservatives, Labour's charge of 'repression' would translate as the 'firm control' promised in the Government's election manifesto. We suggest reading the debate to decide whether the Opposition made out its case and because it catches the flavour of many Parliamentary debates on immigration.

Whatever the conclusions, the debate underlines the importance of administration to immigration control. Earlier, in the context of entry clearance, we saw Runnymede complaining about 'dishonest' bureaucratic techniques used to deter potential applicants. Some critics see these as a general characteristic of immigration control under successive governments:

> The economy no longer needs immigrant workers from the Commonwealth and their dependants are seen as a drain on state resources. To legislate for repatriation or to divide families would be politically unacceptable. By effectively curtailing the few rights immigrants have left under recent legislation, administrative practice fills the gap between what is politically acceptable and what is required by dominant interests in the economy. [Community Development Project 1977, p. 28.]

From this viewpoint, administration is an important method of securing official goals. Compare Prosser's suggestion (p. 587 below) that one function of discretion in SB has been to disguise, and so facilitate, the operation of certain policies.

With immigration control, such arguments take a particular twist. Restrictions on Commonwealth citizens were introduced against a background of concern about non-white immigration. Critics complain that, in addition to the legal concepts (like patriality and British Citizenship) being weighted against ethnic minorities, the *administration* of control is carried out in racially discriminatory fashion. For example, UKIAS ('Evidence', p. 91) 'strongly feels that persons from the Indian sub-continent are being treated unfairly both by the ECOs abroad as well as by the Immigration Officers at the ports of entry. [They] are discriminated against simply on the basis of their origin.' In a sustained critique of discrimination in immigration law and practice, Grant and Martin (1982, p. 350) stress the scope for prejudice: 'the wide areas left to the subjective discretion of very junior officials [are those] into which racial discrimination can so easily enter'. Familial relationship provided one example. Another is the application of para. 17 (p. 513 above). The most common ground for port refusals is that the immigration officer is 'not satisfied' that the visitor 'is genuinely seeking entry for the period of the visit as stated by him'. Table 16 reveals that the proportion of refusals to passengers admitted varies enormously.

Table 16. Passengers Refused by Nationality 1980

Nationality	Proportion refused	Nos. refused	Nos. admitted
Old Commonwealth	1 in 4100	174	714,000
USA	1 in 2780	649	1,800,000
New Commonwealth and Pakistan	1 in 140	6,252	869,000
India	1 in 150	1,239	190,000
Bangladesh	1 in 125	192	24,000
Pakistan	1 in 80	1,040	83,000

Source: 'Evidence', pp. 85–6. (The statistics following in the text are also from this source).

Under para. 20 of the 1980 Rules, a period of six months entry 'will normally be appropriate' for a visitor and 'the period should not be restricted to less unless this is justified for special reasons – for example . . . if his case ought to be subject to early review by the Home Office'. In their secret instructions (below) immigration officers are told to admit for a shorter period where there are doubts about a visitor's intentions but insufficient evidence to justify refusal. The proportions of visitors during October 1980–March 1981 *not* admitted for six months (overwhelmingly those considered 'doubtful' cases) was: USA 1 in 165; Old Commonwealth 1 in 100; New Commonwealth and Pakistan 1 in 8; India 1 in 10; Bangladesh 1 in 9; Pakistan 1 in 6. Again, the Immigration Act 1971 empowers immigration officers to detain passengers pending further examination, a decision to grant or refuse entry and, after refusal, a decision to remove. However 'temporary admission' (usually subject to conditions about residence and reporting to the police) can be granted instead. In 1979 the percentages of all persons whom the authorities detained at the main Harmondsworth Detention Centre were as follows (the percentages of all persons admitted are shown in brackets): USA 1.4 per cent (16.4 per cent); Old Commonwealth 0.5 per cent (7.1 per cent); India 16.8 per cent (1.6 per cent); Bangladesh 3.9 per cent (0.2 per cent); Pakistan 15.7 per cent (0.8 per cent). Statistically we might conclude that an Indian passenger was nearly

30 times more likely to be refused entry at a port than an Old Commonwealth passenger, about 10 times more likely to be characterized as 'doubtful' and nearly 160 times more likely to be detained at Harmondsworth.

Of course, the department may possess statistics demonstrating that visitors of certain nationalities tend to overstay more than others. If so, these have not been published and whether they could justify such differential treatment is another matter. More generally, official secrecy obscures the precise nature and extent of any discrimination. Although there is a substantial and rapidly expanding use of computer records,[1] it was only after intense criticism that the Government withdrew from its current Data Protection Bill a provision exempting data required for 'the control of immigration'. There are no equivalents here to the annual reports on the police presented to Parliament by H M Inspectorate of Constabulary. And although complaints can sometimes be made to the PCA, his (published) forays into the area have been (like judicial review) limited and sporadic.[2] Thus complaints about the conduct of officials are usually investigated by the immigration service itself, successive governments having resisted pressure to establish a separate independent complaints procedure (see for example the adjournment debate moved by Miss Richardson (HC Deb. vol. 963, cols. 213–24)).

In Chapter 1 we noted the use of administrative agencies to supply a measure of 'independence' or distance from government departments. Such agencies might, like the PCA, act as advocate for individuals. Similarly, we noted a tendency for administrative law to be used to settle disputes between different organs of the state. It is interesting in this context to see how the CRE has stepped in to investigate the immigration service, announcing in 1979 a formal inquiry into the 'arrangements made for the enforcement of the Immigration Act 1971 with special reference to the equality of treatment afforded to persons of different racial groups'. The investigation would be detailed and wide-ranging, involving interviews with officials, sample surveys of decisions, examination of secret departmental files and instructions, evidence from outside organizations, etc. It would extend to administrative delays and the appeals system, including the decisions handed down. Not surprisingly the Home Office expressed concern: a quango proposing to bite the hand which funds it. Woolf J refused the department's application for a declaration that the investigation would be ultra vires (read *Home*

Office v. *Commission for Racial Equality* [1981] 2 WLR 703). At the end of 1983 the CRE was working on its report. However its terms of reference preclude questioning the substance of controls:[3] the CRE is concerned only with the application of statute and the Rules. Critics like the Haldane Society (1983, p. 2) warn against so divorcing administration from its legal and political context, arguing that since the immigration service operates within a framework which defines non-white immigration as the 'problem', it is hardly surprising to find immigration officers going 'about their business with the assumption that their purpose is precisely to keep black people out'.[4] From this viewpoint racial discrimination within the service is likely to continue, whatever the findings of the CRE's investigation.

1 **Rules within rules**

We begin with the incident which sparked off the CRE inquiry. In 1979, it emerged that an Indian lady, as part of the investigation to determine whether she was the genuine fiancée of a man living in Britain and so entitled to enter, had been vaginally tested by immigration officials at Heathrow to see whether she had borne children or had sexual relations. In the uproar which followed, the CRE expressed particular concern because such tests were apparently directed at certain ethnic groups. As Miss Richardson put it (HC Deb. vol. 963, col. 215): 'they are racially discriminatory because they have been carried out on women who come from a cultural background which places particular emphasis on female modesty – in other words, on Asian women'. Replying, the Home Secretary (Mr Rees) announced that virginity tests were being abandoned at home and abroad.

The case highlighted the use of medical techniques in immigration control where no questions of infectious disease etc. are involved.[5] Similarly Runnymede's second investigation into entry clearance procedures in the Indian sub-continent revealed that in some of the nine cases where the applicant was refused as not being of the age claimed, X-rays of children's bone structures were used. *The Guardian* (8 February 1979) also reported that some Bangladeshi women were X-rayed to determine their age and identity. Once again there was public disquiet (especially about the health risks involved), culminating in a resolution passed by that most powerful of interest groups, the British Medical Association, characterizing medical examinations performed solely for administrative purposes as 'unethical'. Mr Rees announced an internal departmental inquiry conducted by his chief medical adviser, Sir Henry Yellowlees. In his report, *The Medical Examination of Immigrants* (1980), Sir Henry considered X-rays a 'fairly accurate and acceptably safe way of estimating the age of children'. Meanwhile the Government issued directives (which emerged six months later in response to a written question: HC Deb. vol. 980 WA, col. 355) halting X-rays on adults. Sir Henry changed his mind about accuracy when confronted with a critical report, *The Use of X-Rays for Age Determination in Immigration Control* (1981) prepared for the Opposition peer Lord Avebury. The Home Secretary (Mr Whitelaw) subsequently announced (HC Deb. vol. 18 WA, cols. 279–80) that X-rays for administrative purposes had been abandoned.

The various tests were never mentioned in the Immigration Rules nor, until there were complaints, were they ever debated in Parliament. They were carried out under statutory authority to examine passengers in accordance with secret Home Office instructions. Sched. 2, para. 1(3) of the 1971 Act recognizes a *second* form of departmental rule-making:[6]

In the exercise of their functions ... immigration officers shall act in accordance with such instructions (not inconsistent with the immigration rules) as may be given them by the [Home Secretary] and medical inspectors shall act in accordance with such instructions as may be given them by the [Home Secretary].

The *General Instructions to Immigration Officers* and the *Instructions to Medical Inspectors* need not be presented to Parliament nor are they binding on tribunals and the courts. In theory, para. 1(3) renders the General Instructions inferior to the Immigration Rules; where the two conflict, immigration officers are released from their duty to obey the Instructions. Of course there are many other bits of confidential paper flying about. Home Office presenting officers have their own instructions, as do ECOs and the staff working in the Immigration and Nationality Department. The *Interim Staff Instructions* keep junior officials abreast of recent developments. One function of this sophisticated communications network is to fill in the gaps left by the published Rules. The medical tests provide an illustration: the Rules themselves are silent about the operating procedures to be followed when testing the credibility of a claimed relationship.

Here are some more practical examples of these 'rules within rules'.

First some guidance about interpreting the Rules. Para. 56 permits the return within two years of those 'settled' in the UK (above, p. 513). Before 1978 Home Office practice was to readmit provided the applicant possessed indefinite leave to remain. However, the Labour Government considered that some people were abusing the Rules by preserving their status through short visits judiciously timed just before a two-year absence occurred. Without announcing the change, it tightened control by circulating a reinterpretation of para. 56. Taking the point that to be 'settled' a person must be 'ordinarily resident', applicants were required to demonstrate ordinary residence in the UK during the period before leaving. As a consequence about 150 people a year, who thought they possessed entitlement, were either denied entry or, more often, admitted with leave for six months whereupon the time-limit might, as a matter of discretion, be removed. Eventually, after widespread protests (see, for example, HC Deb. vol. 9, cols. 793–800), the Minister of State (Mr Raison) announced a reversion to previous policy. The department would be 'saved much unnecessary work' while 'a considerable and needless source of aggravation' for applicants would be removed (HC Deb. vol. 26, col. 694). Once again the alteration was made by *instruction* and only became crystal-clear in the 1983 edition of the Rules.

Secondly, some confining and structuring of discretion. We have already met one example, the directive to officers telling them when to admit visitors for less than six months. Yet even this 'rule within a rule' accords officials considerable freedom of manoeuvre and, if prejudice enters its application, the instruction itself, like others which have become available, does not prescribe overt racial discrimination. Under para. 79 of the 1983 Rules 'any passenger . . . who appears not to be in good health or appears to be mentally or physically abnormal, should . . . be referred to the medical inspector'. Para. 80 then provides: 'where the medical inspector advises that for medical reasons it is undesirable to admit the passenger the immigration officer should refuse leave to enter unless he considers admission warranted by strong compassionate reasons'. The Medical Instructions structure the apparent discretions, providing guidance about what is 'undesirable'. Inspectors are advised to report serious communicable diseases, mental disorders, senility and 'conduct disorders' e.g. 'alcoholism, drug addiction, abnormal sexuality' etc. But junior officials still retain *judgment*, for example the term 'abnormal sexuality' is not defined.[7]

Other glossing instructions are more specific. In 1968 (HC Deb. vol. 769, cols. 189–91), the Minister of Health told MPs that the Government considered the activities of the Church of Scientology socially harmful. Using the Aliens legislation it would prevent foreign nationals from coming to Britain to study and work in the church (*Schmidt's* case (above, p. 85) was a consequence). The ban survived the restructuring of immigration control. Thus in *Van Duyn* v. *Home Office* (No. 2) [1975] 3 All ER 190, an EEC national unsuccessfully challenged a refusal to give leave to enter before the European Court of Justice. As her rejection slip indicated, the Minister had dispatched a general and standing instruction telling immigration officers to exercise their discretion to refuse leave on the ground that exclusion would be 'conducive to the public good':

You have asked for leave to enter the United Kingdom in order to take employment with The Church of Scientology but the [Home Secretary] considers it undesirable to give anyone leave to enter . . . on the business of or in the employment of that organisation.

Finally, consider the instructions to ECOs on the application of para. 57 (above, p. 513) operative in 1978. The following are the 'examples' of 'special circumstances' which officers were to consider when deciding whether to re-admit:

(1) Where a person's return has been delayed due to circumstances beyond his control.
(2) Where a person travels abroad for lengthy periods by reason of his occupation but has close domestic ties with the UK.
(3) Where a person goes abroad with a particular employer, remains in his service or wishes to return with him.
(4) Where a person goes abroad as an employee of a British firm or in the service of the UK government.
(5) Where a person goes abroad for long periods of study or wishes to rejoin his family here.
(6) Where a person goes abroad for a prolonged period of medical treatment not available here.

So para. 57, which read alone accords 'strong' discretion, is structured through adjudication *and* the communication of further illustrations. What scope is there now for fact-finding and interpretation respectively? You may think the 'examples' obvious cases for readmittance. But they can tempt officers to reason negatively that because an applicant's case is not covered he should be excluded. Could the applicant in *Peart's* case (see above, p. 521) satisfy any of the 'examples'? How do these compare with the results of the precedent-forming process?

All our practical examples influence substantive determinations about entitlements, yet some are easier to challenge than others. For example, applicants can appeal about the exercise of discretion under para. 57, but in *Al-Tuwaidji* v. *CIO, London (Heathrow) Airport* [1974] Imm. AR 34 the IAT held medical inspectors' judgments conclusive. Again (after the event), resort may sometimes be made to the courts: the Indian woman vaginally examined claimed damages for assault and the Government settled out of court. Was the Home Office on safe legal ground when it reinterpreted para. 56?

The degree of secrecy surrounding these informal practices varies. The restrictions placed on scientologists were debated in Parliament and received widespread press coverage. Some instructions trickle out through parliamentary questions, media leaks, official statements etc. No doubt many remain secret. One consequence is that outside expertise is concentrated further in the case-work agencies who monitor departmental decision-taking. Ironically, the Home Office uses JCWI to disseminate information about administrative practice to immigrants; for example, the reversion to pre-1978 policy on returning residents was announced first in a letter to the group.

The lack of openness introduces questions of accountability and democratic control similar to those raised by low-visibility compensation schemes (Chapter 13) but highlighted by the controversial nature of medical testing for administrative purposes. Its past incidence remains unclear. Lord Trefgarne has stated (HL Deb. vol. 426, col. 1114) that about 700 children were X-rayed in the Indian sub-continent during 1981. Mr Rees assured Miss Richardson that only one or two virginity tests had occurred at the ports during eight years, but JCWI (AR 1978/9, p. 5) pointed to 34 known to have been carried out in India on adult daughters whose claim to entitlement depended on their being unmarried. Since Mr Rees also claimed that ministers were unaware of vaginal examinations, the traditional control of ministerial responsibility – as in Crichel Down – seems to have broken down. Yet the identity and ranking of the civil servants who authorized these tests remain hidden by the fiction. Might we conclude that trusting to officials' 'rectitude' is, in the context of immigration control, a little far-fetched? Certainly Miss Richardson (HC Deb. vol. 963, col. 217) complained that MPs could not participate if the rules were secret:

When so much power lies in the hands of relatively junior officials, it is essential that we know the nature of the detailed guidance. If the guidance is unacceptable, we can campaign to change it. If it is reasonable, public opinion will be reassured and we shall know when the cases are brought to us whether the guidelines have been breached in any way.

Mr Rees replied:

I have read through the instructions [to immigration officers] again today. One of their purposes is to deal with abuse, and undoubtedly it would be wrong to publish some of the information that is given in those instructions. It would only help those who want to abuse immigration control . . . I do not believe that . . . anything would be achieved by such publication.

From the department's viewpoint one advantage of instructions is their flexibility. A lawyer may consider the Rules relatively informal, a civil servant who knows that amending them gives Opposition M Ps an opportunity to berate his minister thinks otherwise. And 'there are instructions which would have to be amended because they would be unacceptable if. . . known to the world at large' (Grant, *The Guardian*, 10 May 1982). Secretive administration allows government to secure goals politically difficult or impossible to achieve through the democratic process. No doubt Mr Rees understood this as well as K. C. Davis.

2 Selective enforcement

Earlier we mentioned that the Minister may sometimes relax the formal Rules in favour of immigrants. The Instructions' second function is to inform officers when and how this may be done. Once again we begin with some practical illustrations.

First, a refusal to adopt a tribunal interpretation. After *Mahmoudi* v. *SSHD* had frustrated the Government's policy by establishing that visitors could not apply under para. 90 for variation of leave to study, presenting officers were instructed not to cite it until the department could find another case (*Adebeshin*) with which to have it over-ruled.[8] Here departmental policy was more liberal than the precedent. Secondly the practice of not requiring strict proof when applying the Rules. Under para. 46, a child's admission to join a single parent for settlement depends, where both parents are living, on that parent having 'had the sole responsibility for the child's upbringing' unless 'there are serious and compelling family or other considerations which make exclusion undesirable'. However Mr Raison (H C Deb. vol. 976 W A, col. 220) has announced a dividing line: the exclusion of children under 12 will automatically be regarded as 'undesirable' without further enquiry provided certain conditions about care and accommodation are met. How does the pre-1978 application of para. 56 compare? Thirdly a departure from the Rules. Para. 46 makes no provision for the situation where, after a marriage has broken down, a child's parent remarries and the child subsequently seeks entry to join the step-parent rather than the natural parent. Occasionally the Department will exercise 'discretion outside the Rules' and allow the child in.[9] Next a breach in an apparently mandatory rule. Earlier we remarked that the no-switching provision, para. 91, left officials little leeway when applying it. But this does not deny the existence of further rules structuring the *non-enforcement* of para. 91. Indeed given extra-statutory tax concessions and the Home Loss affair, we might almost anticipate them. Taken at face value, para. 91 prevents foreign students from working in Britain on the completion of their studies without leaving and applying for a work permit from overseas. However, in 1982 a Home Office letter to the Committee of Vice Chancellors and Principals of universities (the CVCP) announced an administrative concession concerning appointments to academic posts:

Officials and ministers ... recognise that rigid adherence to the 'no switching' principle could lead to the [UK] losing people who could serve the national interest in both the academic and industrial worlds. As a result a measure of administrative flexibility was introduced. In formulating the line we took we had to be careful not to adopt a policy which could be seen as a wilful disregard of the wishes of Parliament ... We accept that, when it is in the general interests of the [UK] to allow an overseas student to use his qualification here, the hurdle in the Immigration Rules should not prevent the Department of Employment from considering whether their approval can be given.

These examples illustrate the variety of administrative tactics for playing games with rules. But they affect only a few people. At the other extreme lies the ministerial exercise of discretion in favour of a class of persons who did not qualify under the Rules: the 10,000 Cypriots displaced by the Turkish invasion in 1974 who were admitted or allowed to remain on a year-by-year basis with the normal prohibition on employment removed.

The admission of foreign husbands and fiancés provides another example. The Conservatives extended control in the 1980 Rules. Under paras. 50 and 117 the husband or fiancé of a woman settled here could only qualify to enter or remain through marriage if the wife was a citizen who was born here or had a parent born here. Further, permission would be denied if there was, either on application or at the end of a probationary year, 'a reason to believe' that (a) the marriage was entered into primarily to obtain admission, or (b) one of the parties no longer had any intention of living with the other as spouse, or (c) the parties to the marriage had not met, or (d) the husband had before the marriage remained in the U K in breach of the immigration laws or been the subject of deportation proceedings, or (e) the marriage had been terminated. Perhaps as many as 2,000 applicants a year were caught by these provisions.[10] But several hundred men were allowed to settle by the exercise of discretion outside the Rules. Selective enforcement on this scale tempted bureaucrats to systematize; special procedures and (unpublished) criteria were established for dealing with these cases. Policy was formulated centrally in B2 division of the Home Office which distributes guidance to ECOs through the Instructions. This was supplemented in lawyer-like fashion by bulletins synthesizing the results of recent administrative decisions. ECOs referred to B2 any cases requiring further inquiries while the division checked the determinations which individual officers made.

Let us consider the ramifications of discretion outside the Rules.[11] Its use is not authorized explicitly by the Immigration Act 1971 but is recognised implicitly by s.19(2).[12] This provides that when adjudicators determine appeals:

> ... no decision or action which is in accordance with the immigration rules shall be treated as having involved the exercise of a discretion by the [Home Secretary] by reason only of the fact that he has been requested by . . . the appellant to depart . . . from the rules and has refused to do so.

Yet we saw that s.3(2) places the Home Secretary under a mandatory duty to lay before Parliament 'statements of the rules . . . laid down by him as to the practice to be followed in the administration of [the] Act'. Arguably this means *all* the rules and not just some of them. Might we conclude that successive ministers have acted unlawfully by not laying the instructions functioning as 'rules within rules' or to guide departures from the Rules? Much hinges on the word 'practice'. We must (arbitrarily) fix the point on Dworkin's sliding scale of rules and discretion at which decision-taking crystal-lises into it. One-off determinations might be thought permissible whereas consistent courses of action (e.g. the admission of children under 12) might not.

However this may be (and there is no reported decision), s.19(2) performs another function, insulating the informal elements of immigration control from the appeals system. It prevents successful recourse to the adjudicator on the ground that although the authorities' decision against the applicant was in accordance with the Rules, the Minister should have departed from them.[13] In *SSHD* v. *Glean* [1972] Imm. AR 84 the IAT overturned an adjudicator's decision that, contrary to the Rules, 'natural justice' dictated that a foreign husband should not be excluded when his immediate family had the right to live here. In *Tosir Khan* v. *ECO, Dacca* [1974] Imm. AR 55 the IAT brushed aside the appellant's complaint that he but not others had been refused admission outside the Rules following civil disturbances in Bangladesh. In short, adjudicators must apply the Rules and *only* the Rules although they sometimes recommend a departure from them. For legal recourse applicants are left with the (unlikely) prospect of convincing a judge that the Minister has failed to take relevant considerations into account etc.[14]

We learn that although decisions against applicants contrary to the Rules can be corrected by appeal or judicial review, the department retains a largely unchecked discretion to dispense *benefits* by waiving the formal provisions. The two sides of immigration control must not be divorced. All the actors concerned (pressure groups, adjudicators, officials etc.) work on the basis that Ministers can and sometimes will depart from the Rules. When restructuring the scheme, government saw this as a key component importing, according to Mr Rees (HC SCA 1968/9 cols. 69–78), the necessary flexibility and political responsibility. The department can exercise compassion in individual 'hard' cases.

We might take this further. 'Compassionate' decisions create no fixed precedents. Standing concessions can be revoked at any time simply by rewriting the Instructions. And techniques of selective enforcement can facilitate strict formal rules. Political opposition to controls coalescing around particular cases can be diffused by departing from the Rules while Ministers can justify imposing tighter restrictions by promising that deserving cases will be considered sympathetically. Mr Raison told the HAC: 'The [Rules] are tight so it is possible, if there is really an overwhelmingly strong case for doing so, to make exceptions' ('Evidence', p. 137). The discretion is highly functional.

The administrative process is dynamic. Increasing resort to discretion outside the Rules implies a *withdrawal* from the formal structures of rule-making and adjudication devised by the Wilson Committee. As, for example, the scope for admitting foreign husbands within the Rules diminishes, emphasis shifts from what we have termed the open 'core' of immigration control to its shrouded 'periphery'. And judicializing and formalizing parts of the administrative process can tempt officers to use alternative informal techniques. Rendering procedural restraints watertight is not so easy: discretion may just keep moving along. We saw this phenomenon in the rise of planning bargain. Here, in the letter to the CVCP, we find administrators prizing the new-found freedom which, ironically, the no-switching provision in the Rules allows them. Given the nature of the Rules, what do you think of the argument?

The use of a degree of flexibility is possible by the exercise of discretion outside the Immigration Rules and, by its very nature, discretion is a matter for which all-embracing guidelines cannot be set down. Were it possible to set down definite guidelines they could be written into the Rules with the attendant rights of appeal against adverse decisions.

We can now make a related point about appeals. Disillusionment with procedural inadequacies, the restrictive interpretations handed down and participation limited within the confines of rules established by government can prompt immigrant organizations to shift case work away from appeals and towards inducing departures from the Rules. Here they adopt the various tactics used by pressure groups to force government's hand, in particular a distinctive feature of immigration control, the channelling of representations to ministers through MPs and peers. JCWI, which characterizes (AR 1976/7, p. 2) the appeals system 'as a farce in which [we do] not willingly collude', cut back on representation from 145 cases in 1978 to 73 in 1980 (primarily involving significant points of law and disputes relevant to current campaigns) because (AR 1978/9, p. 11) 'the inadequacy of the system meant that a large amount of staff time was being devoted to efforts which are unproductive'. UKIAS (AR 1977/8, p. 3) has stated: 'It has [become] more difficult to win appeals than before . . . leaving the making of representations to Ministers and the Home Office a more fruitful line of approach on behalf of many of our clients.' More recently, UKIAS commented: 'Whilst we have not yet become disillusioned with the Appeals system we are, increasingly, making representations to the Home Office for the many persons who cannot qualify under the [Rules], but whose circumstances warrant exceptional consideration' (AR 1981/2,

p. 4).[15]

In Chapter 3, we saw that adjudication, like rule-making, ranged from the informal to the formal. Administrative lawyers tended both to confine their studies to more formal adjudicatory techniques such as tribunals and to press increasingly for formality. Here we can see a formal method of adjudication supplemented by an informal one. The Home Office recognizes representations by MPs as a constituent element of the scheme: ministers have issued instructions that no steps should be taken to remove someone from the country while these are still being considered. Earlier we remarked that while judicialization focuses attention on individuals, the political process tends to the collective. Here the political process is being used in individual cases.

Some representations involve cases where there is no right of appeal, e.g. if a work permit or special voucher has been denied (below). Others concern applicants who can only appeal from abroad, especially where 'temporary admission' is sought for persons without entry clearance excluded at the ports or alleged to be illegal entrants. And others, as Mr Raison (HC Deb. vol. 26, col. 691) described, supplement directly immigration appeals:

We have created a remarkable system. The decisions involved are considered and reconsidered in a way which is not matched in any comparable sphere where a judicial or quasi-judicial system operates. By and large, when an appeal tribunal operates, and certainly when the courts are involved, that is the end of the line. With immigration cases, the decisions of the adjudicators and the tribunal may be a prelude to a prolonged series of appeals by hon. Members to Ministers.

We know relatively little about this informal system. A single case can engender many letters and these may be, like test-case strategy, one tactic in a wider campaign. The relief sought and obtained varies: the 'positive gains' achieved in the 38 out of 90 cases surveyed by Runnymede (1981) ranged from having a deportation order revoked to being released from prison to marry. Certainly the procedure can absorb significant amounts of MPs' time, especially if they sit for constituencies with large immigrant communities. One member from Central London informed Runnymede that the correspondence and interviews involved constituted approximately 20 per cent of his constituency workload (itself about half his total work). The Home Office ministers' postbag is correspondingly full to overflowing. In 1981 Mr Whitelaw and Mr Raison dealt with about 10,500 letters from MPs concerning immigration and nationality cases (HC Deb. vol. 26, col. 691). To this could be added representations received from other quarters and correspondence about policy in general.

In practice the departmental strain is borne largely by the Minister of State and his private office of five or six civil servants. There is then a relatively high degree of ministerial input into individual decisions. And just occasionally this politicization of the administrative process causes ministers difficulties when defending controversial decisions. They cannot, as Lord Trefgarne could with vaccine damage (Chapter 13), disclaim personal responsibility. The vitriolic parliamentary and media attacks on Mr Raison's successor, Mr Waddington, for sending back Mr Papasoiu, an illegal entrant said to have made many attempts to flee Romania, provide a striking if exceptional illustration of what may follow. (See, for example, HL Deb. vol. 440, cols. 1523–49 and HC Deb. vol. 40, cols. 518–25.)

The use of informal political techniques has a further consequence: the outcome may depend more on the effectiveness of the campaign waged than the merits of the particular case. In turn there may be unequal treatment of applicants in similar situations. The nature of certain cases renders them more susceptible to successful campaigning than others. For example, public attention is generally easier to focus on the plight of someone threatened with deportation than, say, of a person denied entry clearance overseas. Out of sight in the Indian sub-continent, out of mind. Some MPs will be more interested in immigrants' affairs than others and members may even hold varying degrees of sympathy for different ethnic groups. They possess absolute discretion whether to pursue constituents' cases and, if so, with what vigour: 'the refusal by an MP to take up a case or pursue it as well as he might other cases, whether accentuated by dislike of the constituent, his colour, his politics or the nature of his problem, is something which can be challenged only in the political arena' (Winetrobe 1982, p. 152). We find members (HC Deb. vol. 26, cols. 647, 683) disagreeing about their constitutional responsibilities:

MR STOKES: I do not send every case to the Government. If I did, government would become impossible. I use my judgment first. Every hon. Member must use his judgment and not be bullied by anyone about him.

MR CLINTON DAVIS: I [find] astonishing the suggestion [that] hon. Members . . . have the right to sit in judgment to determine issues that more properly should go to the Minister. I do not accept that criterion for dealing with cases. No hon. Member has sufficient time to investigate all these matters in depth. Many of the cases, particularly where there are language difficulties, require an inordinate amount of preparation to ensure that every reasonable point is put to the Minister.

Summing-up, JCWI (AR 1981/2, p. 11) complains: 'Discretion is often a remedy open only to those with access to good advice, a good MP, or substantial media and neighbourhood support.' Compare the HAC's conclusions about the department's propensity to act on miscarriages of justice (see above, p. 413).

Ministers, too, have expressed dissatisfaction. Soon after taking office, Mr Raison (*The Guardian*, 9 August 1979) floated the idea that MPs' representations should be restricted. And in a change of practice the Home Office sometimes declined to listen to representations other than those made by the constituency MP (see e.g. HC Deb. vol. 969, cols. 30–2). Recently, Mr Waddington, giving as reasons delays and repetition, wrote to all MPs stating that henceforth this would be normal procedure (*The Guardian*, 25 July 1983). Opposition MPs protest that the practice places a greater premium on possessing a 'good' representative, but Mr Whitelaw (HC Deb. vol. 26, col. 646) has characterized it as part of the general convention that members do not meddle in others' constituency affairs.

Speaking to UKIAS on 12 April 1980, Mr Raison declared:

I still have concern about the extent to which the working of the appeal system is overlapped by representations from [MPs]. There is certainly no question . . . of appeal to the Minister being regarded as . . . a last resort. Very often I find that . . . representations to me or the Home Secretary are seen as an alternative or additional avenue through which a case may be pursued. Representations are made while there is a right of appeal which has not been exercised. Or they may be made alongside the exercise of the right of appeal. Often I am entreated to anticipate the outcome of appeal proceedings. And sometimes, although the appellate authorities have thoroughly reviewed a decision and upheld it, I am asked to set it aside, not because there is any new evidence or any special factor which was not previously known, but simply because the decision is unfavourable and therefore unwelcome.

This does not . . . mean that I am not willing to accept representations [nor that MPs] should not make [them]. This is a legitimate part of their duty to represent their constituents' interest. What I do believe is that the appeals system should be recognised as the means by which disputed matters of fact and eligibility under the Rules should normally be resolved. The system was after all set up by Parliament for exactly this purpose.[16]

Without detailed information[17] about the breakdown of representations, we cannot assess this statement statistically. In any case, the Minister could be said to want to eat his cake and have it: to selectively enforce without being overburdened with petitions for mercy. Representations are *concomitant* with the power of departing from the Rules. It is hardly surprising to find JCWI and, to some extent, UKIAS reorientating their case work in this direction as the Rules tighten through amendment and interpretation. JCWI has scant sympathy for ministers, believing the heavy workload to be the product of their own policies. Just as from this viewpoint the way ahead on immigration appeals does not entail reducing appeal rights, so limiting representations will not 'improve' the administrative process:

> The solutions to [Mr Raison's] desire to reduce the over 1000 immigration cases his office deals with each month lie in his own hands. MPs would complain less about delays if delays were reduced. Relatives would seek MPs' intervention less often if there were fewer arbitrary and manifestly unjust refusals by immigration officers. The exercise of ministerial discretion would be sought less often if the Immigration Rules were drafted with a real respect for family life. The decisions reached in the existing appeals system would be accepted more often if it met minimum standards of impartiality and proper judicial procedure. Alleged illegal entrant cases would come before the Minister less often if the Home Office ceased to attempt their removal without disclosure of the evidence against them or any hearing on the facts [see below]. There would be no need to press the Minister's office for temporary release from detention so often if the immigration service did not persist in detaining passengers who are in fact highly unlikely to abscond. [AR 1978/9, p. 3.]

To conclude this section, try evaluating the discretion to depart from the Rules coupled with representations from the viewpoint of (a) individual applicants, (b) JCWI, (c) the department. Whatever your conclusions, we think you will agree that in the practical world of administration 'weighing' the strategic advantages and disadvantages of a particular procedure can be extremely difficult. And can you think of any other relevant considerations which we have omitted to mention?

3 Beyond the rules

So far we have focused on the application and selective enforcement of the Immigration Rules which we discovered were, if not the tip of the iceberg, then only a limited guide to policy and administration. Yet there are also important areas of control lying wholly outside the formal provisions. Earlier, for example, we saw that para. 45 of the 1983 Rules was quite straightforward about the entry for settlement of those former U K P Hs who are now British Overseas Citizens. With a special voucher (S V) they must be admitted, without one they must be refused. However, the criteria determining whether a voucher is issued in the first place are not incorporated in the Rules; indeed they are not available in any published document, dribbling out instead through indirect means. Another function of the confidential Instructions is to inform officers how to exercise discretion in those parts of immigration control which the Rules do not reach.

Let us consider the S V scheme in more detail. Entitlement is restricted to B O Cs with no other citizenship considered to be under 'pressure' to leave their country of residence. Vouchers can be issued to single persons of either sex over 18 but otherwise only to persons regarded as 'heads of household' (which does not include married women unless the 'disability' of the husband prevents him from being so regarded). Applications, which are processed by E C Os working overseas on a fairly rigid 'first come, first served' basis, are accepted only in the country of 'normal residence'. There is an annual quota of vouchers which has been raised gradually from 1,500 to 5,000. A portion of this global figure is retained centrally for distribution to B O Cs in countries like Pakistan and Malaysia, who are considered as individuals to be under pressure to leave. The remainder is then subdivided into separate quotas for countries where the Government thinks B O Cs are automatically under 'pressure'. From the scheme's inception, these have included East African countries pursuing Africanization policies. In 1972 a separate quota was established to cover the many East African Asians who, desperate to move but unable to obtain vouchers promptly, had gone to live in India.

The aim, as the Home Office ('Evidence', p. 5) puts it, is 'to facilitate . . . entry at a controlled rate'. Successive governments have reaffirmed that U K P Hs excluded under the Commonwealth Immigrants Act 1968 will be allowed to settle, but the quota slows down their admission. The effect is accentuated because unused vouchers from one country's allocation are not redirected to places where demand is high. Up until 1975 there were lengthy queues in East Africa where the number of U K P Hs applying greatly exceeded the vouchers made available. But, following the declarations of admissibility by the European Commission of Human Rights in the *East African Asians* case,[18] these were cleared by increased quotas and today vouchers are virtually obtainable on demand in this area where, in any case, demand is largely exhausted. However, in India, where the quota is 600, the waiting time between application and voucher issue has risen from three years in 1977 to over six years in 1982, when there were 4,930 outstanding applications. Although recently the number of new applications has fallen below 600, the HAC ('Report', p. xxvii) computed that at present rates of progress it will take 12 years to clear the backlog. Globally the results are striking: the number of vouchers issued falls well below the 5,000 figure, declining from 3,590 in 1976 to 1,350 in 1980.

Critics stress the hardships which BOCs, delayed in the Indian queue, face. Employment opportunities are restricted for non-Indian citizens, currency controls apply and the uncertainty about when a voucher will be issued makes it difficult to plan for the future. JCWI, which conducted field research in 1981, complains that claim forms are too complex, replies to enquiries are unhelpful, applicants are required to travel long distances for medical examinations, etc. JCWI (1981, p. 15) also believes that 'the unwritten rules applied in the voucher scheme are consistent mainly in producing whatever result is least favourable to the applicant'. For example, it cites cases where East African-born BOCs, who had travelled to India for education and then returned, were informed that they could not apply for vouchers in East Africa but must queue in their new country of 'normal residence'.

The complaints about delay and insensitive administration in India echo the criticisms levelled against entry clearance procedures. With SVs, there is a new twist. There has been no external scrutiny of the application of criteria which, in any case, have never been presented to Parliament. In short, from the applicant's viewpoint, the scheme has been wholly arbitrary.

First, no appeal lies from refusal of a voucher. In *Shah* v. *SSHD* [1972] Imm. AR 56, an East African Asian UKPH who was eligible for a SV but had not yet obtained one, tried to short circuit the quota system by entering as a visitor and then asking for permanent settlement. His request was denied because he had no voucher and, when he appealed, counsel for the Home Office argued, 'special vouchers for those in East Africa could not be issued in the [UK]'. Dismissing the appeal, the IAT held that the method of issuing special vouchers lay outside its jurisdiction and that the refusal to grant permanent settlement could not be questioned since it was in accordance with the Rules. Counsel's use of the phrase 'could not' is interesting; translated, it means 'would not'. Since the voucher scheme is purely administrative, there is no legal restriction on issuing vouchers in Britain. Just occasionally this is done. Recently, for example (JCWI, AR 1982/3, p. 3), a Dr Patel was refused entry clearance to visit his ailing father after the British post, having telephoned the hospital, decided that the illness was not serious. A fortnight later the father died and Dr Patel was then denied entry at the airport, only obtaining temporary admission after MPs' representations. Eventually, following widespread newspaper publicity and protests, Mr Raison granted Dr Patel a voucher allowing him to remain and support his widowed mother. We might characterize this as another 'departure from the rules', always remembering that here there are no formal Rules, only internal departmental instructions.

The absence of appeal was reiterated in *R*. v. *ECO, Bombay ex p. Amin* [1980] 1 WLR 1530. A female UKPH married to an Indian citizen was denied a voucher because she was not a 'head of household'. She claimed a right of appeal to an adjudicator, arguing that vouchers were 'entry clearance' as defined by the 1971 Act. However the Divisional Court distinguished the two, holding that while entry clearance was only evidence of a person's eligibility, vouchers constituted the factual basis of admission. Lord Lane CJ stressed the practical limits of adjudication:

[Counsel for the minister] submits . . . that . . . the special voucher system is outside the appellate system because it is not properly subject to the ordinary idea of an appeal. For example, if the present case were to go to an adjudicator, how would he set about the difficult problem of substituting his own discretion for that of the people (a) operating the scheme at the centre, and (b) distributing this scheme at the periphery? One can see that there would be very great difficulty indeed. In fact it is hard to see in most cases how he would be able to substitute what he thought was right for what those operating the scheme thought was right.

The nature of the applicant's challenge is significant. On appeal she wanted the 'head of household' criterion rewritten. Lord Lane is saying that the *rule-making* function should be allocated to administrators taking a global view and not to adjudicators focusing on the particular case before them. However, the denial of jurisdiction also means that BOCs cannot contest *rule-application* by junior officials, arguing that the criteria have been misinterpreted or improperly applied. The House of Lords, by a majority, has recently confirmed the Divisional Court's views ([1983] 3 WLR 258).

Secondly, departmental discretion has remained untouched by

judicial review. Although in the *Amin* case Lord Fraser approved the authorities' concession that the courts could intervene, the Court of Appeal has refused to do so. In *Re Javeed Iqbal Bhatti* (7 September 1981, unreported), a UKPH resident in Kenya was refused a voucher because his birth in Pakistan also made him a citizen of that country. Subsequently he was refused admittance as trying to enter for settlement without a voucher. Claiming that the birth in Pakistan had happened during a visit by his parents and that he had not been back since he was a baby, the applicant contended that the Nairobi High Commission had misconstrued the criteria and (somewhat desperately) that 'any scheme of this kind excluding persons . . . who have got dual nationality arising from the accident of birth, is a scheme which offends against concepts of natural justice and which ought to be supervised by [the courts]'. Refusing leave to apply for judicial review, the Court of Appeal held that neither the administrative criteria nor their application were justiciable. According to Lawton LJ, the Minister, when setting up the voucher scheme,

. . . was exercising prerogative powers of the Crown. He was exercising that right which the Crown has always had to say who is and who is not to be allowed into the [UK] if they have not got a legal right to be here . . . This scheme . . . does not arise from any provision of an Act of Parliament . . . It follows therefore . . . that this Court has no jurisdiction to interfere with the terms of the . . . scheme made by the Secretary of State or how it is administered by High Commissions overseas.

In addition, the PCA has been unable to investigate. Sched. 3 of the Parliamentary Commissioner Act 1967 exempted official action taken overseas from scrutiny while s.6(4) required that the complainant be resident in the UK. These provisions also insulated entry clearance procedures from review. For example, when an applicant in Pakistan complained of misleading advice and of having to wait months for interview, the PCA (HC 281 (1974), p. 126) declared the actions of the immigration authorities in Islamabad outside his jurisdiction. For critics, Mr Callaghan's partial shift of decision-making overseas has allowed officials to stiffen controls by administrative tactics, in particular delay, which, if they were used in the UK, might constitute maladministration.

Recently, the jurisdictional limitations have been altered. When the PCA scheme was established two main reasons were put forward to justify the exclusions: that the actions of officials abroad often depended on the decisions of foreign governments over which they had no control and that the PCA would be faced with considerable difficulties and expense when investigating complaints overseas. Sir Idwal Pugh, however, assured his Select Committee (HC 615 (1977/8), p. xiv) that he could do the job and would pay due regard to the realities of international relations. The Committee duly recommended cutting-back Sched. 3 and allowing 'British citizens' not resident in the UK to complain. The Parliamentary Commissioner Order 1979 (SI No. 915) amended Sched. 3, bringing within the PCA's jurisdiction action taken overseas 'in relation to a citizen of the [UK] and Colonies with the right of abode.' This formula was then repeated in the Parliamentary Commissioner (Consular Complaints) Act 1981 which amended s.6(4). Persons so qualified but resident abroad can now complain. However the administration of immigration control overseas remains largely immune. Entry clearance applicants will usually be foreign nationals. The 'right of abode' condition prevents BOCs, who were citizens of the UK and Colonies, from complaining about the SV scheme. This was quite deliberate. The Government resisted Opposition backbench amendments designed to protect 'British subjects without citizenship' (now BDTCs and BOCs). Mr Blaker (Minister of State, Foreign and Commonwealth Office (FCO)) explained the Government's stance in Standing Committee (HC SCB 1980/1, cols. 12–5):

We have already to cope with the situation . . . of long queues at consular offices of [UKPHs] and . . . people seeking entry certificates, and we have to recognise that the wider we extend the number of people who are potential complainants the greater will be the potential burden on not only the staff of the Parliamentary Commissioner but also on the staffs of our . . . offices . . . overseas . . . If . . . they are to have to write up a large number of cases for the Parliamentary Commissioner, I fear that the queue will become even longer . . .

In present circumstances, we cannot contemplate increasing the staffs of our missions overseas and, indeed, we are doing our best to examine those staffs closely to see whether they can be reduced to effect economies.

Not all administrative practices beyond the Rules exist in a world as closed as the SV scheme. Like the 'rules within rules', the degree of openness varies. Take the Work Permit scheme, for example, whereby a British employer who wishes to employ a foreign national must apply in the UK to the Department of Employment for permission. This is a central element of immigration control and in recent times of high unemployment successive governments have imposed stricter limitations on the issue of permits. Under para. 27 of the 1983 Rules those seeking admission for employment without one must be refused entry unless certain exemptions apply. But, as with SVs, the criteria determining whether the essential document is issued are not contained in the Rules. And there is no appeal to an adjudicator against the Department of Employment's refusal to issue a permit or renew an existing one (read *Pearson* v. *IAT* [1978] Imm. AR 212). On the other hand, the terms of the administrative scheme are published in leaflets available from the department and major amendments, although not presented formally, are announced in Parliament by ministers.

Our final illustration is a particularly controversial aspect of control. S.33 of the 1971 Act defines an 'illegal entrant' as 'a person unlawfully entering or seeking to enter in breach of . . . the immigration laws [including] a person who has so entered'. Sched. 2, providing for arrest without warrant and detention pending examination etc., empowers the immigration authorities to summarily remove such persons from the UK. However, unlike most deportation decisions, the factors relevant to deciding whether or not to exercise the discretionary power to expel are not incorporated in the Immigration Rules and their 'balancing' in any particular case is not subject to appeal. Instead the department uses informal criteria and procedures. Thus Mr Raison informed the HAC (HC 89 (1980/1), paras. 25–34) that illegal immigrants would not be removed where the Home Office, with knowledge of the facts, had previously granted permanent settlement and that while officers handled many cases, he reviewed personally those concerning Commonwealth citizens entering before 1971 and also most of those involving MPs'

Table 17. Persons dealt with as having entered the UK illegally 1976–82

	Detected	Removed as illegal immigrants	Allowed to stay indefinitely	Allowed to stay for limited time	Allowed to stay–entered before 1973	Illegal status not established
1976	390	270	25*	10*	15*	NA
1977	810	490	50	40	30	60
1978	940	540	130	40	15*	60
1979	990	590	220	50	5	25*
1980	1,620	910	360	80	–	40
1981	990	650	230	70	–	NA
1982	1,260	610	240	190	–	NA

Source: Control of Immigration Statistics 1982 (Cmnd. 8944), Table 15.
* Approximate.

representations. Such disclosures apart, the balancing process remains shrouded in secrecy. Table 17 illustrates how the number of removals grew from 1976 on, culminating in 1980 when the authorities removed 910 persons as illegal entrants and allowed 360 to stay permanently.

Before choosing whether or not to remove, the Home Office must determine that the person is an illegal entrant. Against this decision there is a right of appeal to an adjudicator but, under s. 16 of the 1971 Act, it can only be exercised from abroad after the appellant has been removed. Table 12 demonstrates the futility of appealing against removal: during 1977–80 only one out of 390 appeals succeeded. Critics find it impossible to believe that serious mistakes have not occurred. Refer back to the department's arguments against allowing an appeal before removal (p. 531 above). JCWI observes:

The Home Office remains incapable of acknowledging that it is not infallible: it refers consistently to those who might be granted a right of appeal before removal as 'illegal entrants' and not 'alleged illegal entrants'. This is all the more remarkable since Home Office statistics [see Table 17] show a significant number of people wrongly detained as illegal entrants: over 180 people . . . in 1977–80 are listed as 'illegal status not established' . . . This is the extent of the error even when alleged illegal entrants are denied a hearing on the facts at which they can give evidence. The incidence of injustice among the 2530 persons removed as alleged illegal entrants in those four years can only be guessed at. [JCWI 1981, p. 4.]

This comment must be read against the background of a judicially inspired expansion of the illegal entry concept. In *R. v. Governor of Pentonville Prison ex p. Azam* [1973] 3 All ER 765, the law lords held that the removal powers contained in the 1971 Act (which came into force on 1 January 1973) applied retrospectively. This caught Commonwealth citizens who, under the Commonwealth Immigrants Act 1968, had entered illegally between 1968 and 1972 and had achieved a status of irremovability through the expiry of statutory time-limits on expulsion. Successive governments took action to mitigate the decision. Mr Carr, the Conservative Home Secretary, agreed to consider individual cases on their merits (HC Deb. vol. 857, cols. 1205–12). Mr Jenkins, the Labour Home Secretary, later declared a general amnesty (HC Deb. vol. 872, cols. 637–46):

I shall not direct the removal of any Commonwealth citizen or citizen of Pakistan who entered illegally before 1st January 1973. Those in this category will, on application to the Home Office and verification of the facts, be given indefinite leave to remain . . . My decision does not extend to those who were not adversely affected by the retrospective provisions in the Act of 1971 and so does not apply to foreign nationals other than citizens of Pakistan [which had previously been in the Commonwealth] or to people who entered lawfully but then overstayed.

Similarly, when the courts (below) began including fraudulently-obtained admission within the definition of illegal entry, Mr Rees (HC Deb. vol. 940 WA, cols. 125–8) extended Mr Jenkins' amnesty to those caught by *Azam* who had entered by employing deception. Mr Rees also announced a cut-off date of December 1978 for applications under the concessions and stressed that applicants had to prove they qualified.

Consider the implications of Labour's schemes. Officers would interview the applicant and any supporting witnesses and verify documentary evidence before making their decision. Table 17 denotes a number of persons who were allowed to stay as entering before 1973. These were immigrants who were detained but then released because they could regularize their position under the amnesties. Table 18 reveals that many more came forward before the authorities caught up with them and that significant numbers were declared ineligible (and so subject to removal). Once again there was informality: in Mr Jenkins' words, the department 'condoned by administrative action illegality'. The amnesties were not included in the Immigration Rules and there was no appeal against an adverse decision on, say, a disputed issue of fact like the date of entry. In *Purewal* v. *ECO, New Delhi* [1977] Imm. AR 93, the appellant had been expelled as an illegal entrant and was then refused entry clearance in accordance with the Rules. He appealed, claiming to be eligible under the amnesties. Declining jurisdiction, the IAT held the schemes to be an exercise of the Minister's discretion outside the Rules and that s.19(2) of the 1971 Act prevented review of what in effect was a refusal to depart from them. Further in *Birdi* v. *SSHD* (1975) *The Times*, 12 February, the Appeal Court emphasized that although the amnesties were not wholly devoid of legal effect because, by creating a 'legitimate expectation' that genuine applicants would be allowed to stay, they grounded the duty of procedural fairness, judicial review of individual decisions was circumscribed because no 'rights' were conferred. Suppose a similar scheme was established today. Could it be challenged as fettering the statutory discretion to remove? (Refer back to the *British Oxygen* case above, p. 149). And if so, by whom? (Consider the *Federation* case above, p. 300).

Table 18. Applications processed for Regularization of Position in the U K 1974–80

	Under announcement of 11 April 1974		Under announcement of 29 Nov. 1977	
	Granted	Ineligible	Granted	Ineligible
1974	410	180	–	–
1975	810	160	–	–
1976	330	120	–	–
1977	130	120	10	5*
1978	70	10	270	110
1979	60	20	190	60
1980	30	–	80	10

Source: Control of Immigration Statistics 1980 (Cmnd. 8199), Table 16.
* Approximate.

In a series of cases beginning in 1976, the courts held that illegal entry occurred where the immigrant submitted himself to examination but obtained admission by telling lies etc. His leave to enter was vitiated by the fraud. For example in *R. v. SSHD ex p. Maqbod Hussain* [1976] 1 WLR 97, an entrant who admitted having presented another person's passport was considered to have entered illegally. Again in *R. v. SSHD ex p. Claveria* (22 November 1979, unreported), the Divisional Court held the administrative work permit scheme to have indirect legal consequences. A Filipino woman was held liable to removal because the existence of her children had been concealed when she obtained a permit as a resident domestic, one of the conditions being that the holder should have no such dependants. These decisions surprised even the Home Office which admitted (HC 89 (1980/1), paras. 4–6) that it had not believed the removal power to arise in such cases. At the time of the 1971 Act much attention had been focused on clandestine entry, and it had been generally assumed that the (open-ended) definition of illegal entry was confined to the case where persons had avoided passing through immigration control.

One way to avoid the truncated appeals procedure was to apply for habeas corpus. A successful applicant established the right to remain. But judges expressed extreme reluctance to review departmental decisions. On a habeas corpus application the court must determine whether the jailor has power or 'jurisdiction' to detain the applicant. Nicol (1981, p. 23) identifies three possible tests.[19] First, the 'wholly subjective' where it suffices that the Minister honestly believes he has power to detain (see, for example, the majority judgment in *Liversidge* v. *Anderson* [1942] AC 306). Secondly, the interventionist 'wholly objective' test where the court declares the detention illegal unless the facts on which the power rests exist. (See *Eshugbayi Eleko* v. *Administrative Authority for the Government of Nigeria* [1931] AC 662.) This will be familiar as the notion of 'jurisdictional fact' (Chapter 4). In this context, the detention would only be justified if, after enquiring into the matter, the court determined that the applicant actually was an illegal entrant. The third test lies between the previous two: the judges do not interfere provided the Minister has 'reasonable grounds' to believe that the necessary facts exist. Applied here, the immigrant may be detained and removed not for what he did, but for what the Home Office (reasonably) thinks he did. From 1977 on, this approach found favour in illegal entry cases (see e.g. *R.* v. *SSHD ex p. Choudhary* [1978] 3 All ER 79). And writing in 1981, Nicol could find no instance of the courts declaring the Home Secretary's belief unreasonable.

These various developments were confirmed and taken further in *Zamir* v. *Secretary of State for the Home Department* [1980] 2 All ER 768. In 1972, Z, aged 15 and unable to speak or read English, applied as a dependant son to join his father who was settled here. It took the British post in Islamabad three years to issue an entry clearance, a delay not exceptional in the Indian sub-continent. Three months later Z married in Pakistan and the following month arrived alone at Heathrow. By this time he was 18 and the Rules then in force required children over 18 to qualify for admission in their own right, although an unmarried and dependent son might be admitted in certain circumstances. Z was not asked about and did not disclose to the immigration officer at Heathrow the fact of his marriage. He was granted indefinite leave. Two years later, Z applied to bring in his wife and child and this prompted the department to make enquiries about his initial entry. Z vigorously asserted that he had not appreciated the significance of his marriage (which removed the basis of his claim to admission) and JCWI on his behalf contested the Home Office's statement that he would have received a handout in Islamabad informing him of it. Z was detained as an illegal entrant pending removal and a unanimous House of Lords (which reiterated that illegal entry was not confined to clandestine entry) refused his application for habeas corpus.

LORD WILBERFORCE: It is for [the applicant] to show that his detention is unlawful . . . Two questions of law arise . . . The first is what is the basis for any judicial review if the Secretary of State, or an immigration officer acting on his behalf, concludes that there has been deception . . . The immigration officer in deciding whether or not to grant leave is performing an administrative duty in a statutory and parastatutory framework. It follows that the decision can only be reviewed . . . on the normal principles applicable to such decisions, of which those [relevant here] are that there was no evidence on which he could reach his decision, or that no reasonable person in this position could have reached it.

If . . . this is the position [regarding] leave to enter, it must also be the position as regards decisions to remove . . . It would be absurd to apply different principles as regards . . . a decision to allow entry [and] a decision that the permission to enter was vitiated . . .

It has been challenged by counsel for the applicant. The present [case] is, he submitted [one] where the exercise of power, or jurisdiction, depends on the precedent establishment of an objective fact [and] it is for the court to decide whether that precedent requirement has been satisfied . . . The [case law] he claimed, marked a departure from this principle which should now be reinstated . . .

I am of opinion that the whole scheme of the Act is against this argument . . . The immigration officer . . . has to consider a complex of statutory rules and non-statutory guidelines. Often there will be documents whose genuineness is doubtful, statements which cannot be verified, misunderstandings as to what was said, practices and attitudes in a foreign state which have to be estimated. There is room for appreciation, even for discretion.

The Divisional Court . . . on judicial review of a decision to remove and detain, is very differently situated. It considers the case on affidavit evidence, as to which cross-examination, though allowable, does not take place in practice. It is . . . not in a position to find out the truth between conflicting statements: did the applicant receive notes, did he read them, was he capable of understanding them, what exactly took place at the point of entry. Nor is it in a position to weigh the materiality of personal or other factors present . . . to the mind of the immigration authorities. It cannot possibly act as, in effect, a court of appeal as to the facts on which the immigration officer decided. What it is able to do, and this is the limit of its powers, is to see whether there was evidence on which the immigration officer, acting reasonably, could decide as he did . . .

The second legal question [is] what is the standard of the duty owed by persons . . . seeking leave to enter? The Act itself sets no standard . . . The immigration officer [the applicant] says, could have asked him if he was married, or if his circumstances had changed, but he did not. The applicant's only duty was to answer, if asked; he was under no duty to volunteer information. I do not accept this contention: indeed it cannot be too strongly repudiated. At the very lowest, an intending entrant must not practice a deception. It is clear on general principles of law that deception may arise from conduct, or from conduct accompanied by silence as to a material fact. It can be no answer to a claim that such deception has occurred to say that no question was asked . . . I would, indeed, go further than this, a point so far left open . . . In my opinion an alien seeking entry . . . owes a positive duty of candour on all material facts which denote a change of circumstances since the issue of the entry clearance. He is seeking a privilege; he alone is, as to most such matters, aware of the facts: the decision to allow him to enter . . . is based on a broad appreciation by immigration officers of a complex of considerations, and this appreciation can only be made fairly and humanely if, on his side, the entrant acts with openness and frankness . . .

The present case is . . . disposable under any test. The applicant was not candid in not revealing . . . his marriage, a clear change of circumstances which was most material to the immigration officer's decision . . . It is one thing to seek to enter as a child dependent on a resident father, quite another to enter as the head of a household and prospective family . . . The immigration officer had ample grounds for deciding that there had been deception vitiating the permission to enter.

Condemnation of this decision was widespread. The positive duty of candour meant that entrants, many of whom were not fluent in English, had to disclose all facts considered 'material' on matters where the law was frequently complex and not easily accessible. The penalty for non-compliance might be arrest, imprisonment and expulsion. Since the issue would not have arisen had the official at Heathrow asked Z whether he was married, the duty to disclose was said by Blake (1980, p. 773) to place 'a premium upon incompetence by the immigration officer. He need ask no questions, raise no queries, challenge no facts, probe no statements'. Where was the incentive to eradicate sloppy administration if immigrants could always be removed for not volunteering the relevant information? Critics mourned the death of habeas corpus. Lord Wilberforce had placed the burden of proof on the applicant, rejected review based on 'jurisdictional fact' and stated that the Divisional Court could not go very far in scrutinizing the facts. The last was a self-imposed limitation – compare O'Reilly v. Mackman – which influenced the likely outcome; without detailed inquiries it was virtually impossible for applicants to prove the department had no 'reasonable grounds'. The judges were attacked for abrogating their responsibility to protect personal liberty by effectively allocating to the executive decisions about who could be detained and removed. Nicol saw a constitution very different from that beloved of red light theorists:

In liberal mythology, the courts are independent, a bulwark between the citizen and the government . . . The illegal entrant cases are a damning indictment of [this]. Not only did the courts fail to stand up to the government but with barely a dissenting judgment they approved extensions of the executive power which not even the Home Office ministers thought they could assert . . . By affirming [these] powers which were at best ambiguous and by emasculating habeas corpus . . . the courts demonstrated to whom Lord Denning's imperative 'Trust the Judges'[20] was really addressed. The Home Office could rest assured that it would be protected by the courts. [Nicol 1981, p. 43.]

The aftermath of this line of cases illustrates once more how complex the interaction of courts and administrators can be. Despite representations by MPs, Z was removed to Pakistan from where he unsuccessfully appealed (*Zamir* (73894/81) (unreported)). The Chief Adjudicator thought that seen in context, 'the entire business . . . stinks of deception'. Z's father had entered illegally in the 1960s, his mother had tried passing off a second boy as her son, Z had used a bogus birth certificate and, having obtained entry clearance, 'quickly [got] married and maintained a discreet silence'. Further, whether or not Z received the relevant handout, 'to anyone who has observed at close quarters in Islamabad (as I have) the activities and knowledge of immigration rules of Pakistan immigration advisers, it is inconceivable that [Z and his mother] did not know of the importance of marriage in the rules governing admission'. The IAT refused leave to appeal.

JCWI, acting for Z, did not give up so easily. Test-case strategy 'European-style' was still available.[21] In *Zamir* v. *UK* (1983) 5 EHRR 242 the Commission, following *Uppal* v. *UK (No. 1)* (1979) 3 EHRR 399, held that Art. 6 of the European Convention on Human Rights ('the right of a fair trial . . . of a person's civic rights and obligations or of criminal charges') did not catch administrative proceedings like deportation and removal. However, it declared admissible Z's other complaints. First, since the illegal entry concept was too unpredictable to be 'law', it fell foul of Art. 5(1) ('no one shall be deprived of his liberty save . . . in accordance with a procedure prescribed by law'). Secondly, under Art. 5(4) ('everyone who is deprived of his liberty shall be entitled to take proceedings by which the lawfulness of his detention shall be decided speedily by a court and his release ordered if the detention is not lawful'), habeas corpus was inadequate. It was too slow (Z waited two months for bail and another three months for a full hearing) and the test of 'reasonable grounds', was insufficiently probing. In late 1983 the Commission adopted its report, attempts at a 'friendly settlement' having failed.

JCWI (AR 1979/80, p. 3) ascribed the sharp rise in removals

from 1976 on to the expanded definition of illegal entry and to a hardening of official attitudes. It criticized 'the lengths to which the Home Office has been prepared to go in seeking [illegal entrants] out, even at the cost of the unlawful arrest and detention of people lawfully settled here'. For example, there were widespread complaints that the police regularly checked the immigration status of members of ethnic minorities with whom they came into contact for other reasons. Mr Whitelaw (HC Deb. vol. 977 WA, cols. 552–3) issued guidelines to Chief Police Officers, advising them to avoid any action which might be construed as harassment of immigrants. Particular concern was expressed about alleged 'fishing expeditions' whereby the police, hoping to net some illegal entrants, detained groups of people for questioning. This time Mr Whitelaw issued a circular tightening up the procedures used in joint operations by the police and the immigration service (see HC Deb. vol. 995 WA, col. 884).[22]

Meanwhile a campaign was being waged to minimize the impact of *Claveria*.[23] Potentially there was a marked 'ripple' effect since the Home Office (HC 89 (1980/1), p. 3) knew of over 250 cases, mostly involving Filipino women, to which the judgment applied. Local community groups were formed to lobby on behalf of individuals, while as part of a national campaign, parliamentarians, churchmen, trade union leaders etc., made representations to ministers that the class of persons be allowed to stay on compassionate grounds. Once again the administrative process became highly *politicized*: for immigrants' groups the campaigning approach to case work was essential since the law was cut and dried against them. Eventually about two-thirds of the women were permitted to stay.

The campaign also prompted inquiries by the HAC (HC 89 (1980/1), paras. 1–38). Mr Lyon (Labour) pressed for a general amnesty covering all those caught by the judges' new interpretation. Mr Raison replied:

If you are asking whether [ministers] exercise discretion in cases like this and whether there are occasions when we do not remove illegal entrants, then . . . the answer . . . is: yes, very frequently . . . But what we feel basically is that when the courts have said that something is the law, the natural responsibility . . . on the part of the Home Office, is to accept the readings of the court . . .

We are not after all talking about retrospective legislation. There was retrospective legislation arguably in the 1971 Act and that led to the amnesty . . . We are talking about the interpretation of the law by the courts, which is . . . a different matter . . . The basic point . . . that deception is just as much a reasonable ground for saying entry is illegal, is one which is actually rooted in commonsense . . .

It really does not seem . . . acceptable for the Home Office simply to say there is this whole string of court judgments to which we [will] pay no regard. I think we try to operate this flexibly and sensitively and try to look very carefully at individual cases.

How do these arguments compare with those made by officials justifying only limited ex gratia payments for time-barred HLP claims? Is the point about retrospectivity convincing? Miss Richardson sought a lesser concession. Given the small numbers involved and the fact that many had already been allowed to remain, could not all the Filipino women stay? Mr Raison had an answer for that too:

If you gave an amnesty to a particular, very much publicised, category of illegal entrants by deception, there would be a very great many other people who were illegal entrants by deception who would say, 'Why that category and why not us as well?' [They] would say that this one group had really received privileges which others had not received.

The deception cases gave the department a way to bypass the criminal law. S.26 of the 1971 Act makes it an offence punishable with imprisonment to employ false representations when obtaining admission. As an alternative to removal, the authorities could obtain a conviction and, following the court's recommendation, deport. However, as Mr Raison acknowledged (HC 89 (1980/1), para. 14), it was far easier to use administrative powers: 'it is a remarkably difficult thing [to prosecute] because the essence of illegal entry by and large is absence of evidence and . . . of proof.' In *R. v. SSHD ex p. Mohammed Anwar* (19 January 1978, unreported), the Divisional Court, applying the 'reasonable grounds' test on habeas corpus, countenanced an immigrant's removal for being a bogus dependant son although an earlier prosecution had collapsed when the department's witnesses changed their stories. Criminal trials of alleged illegal entrants became virtually unknown.

There was also a retreat from formal rule-making and adjudication. Persons overstaying a limited leave can be deported but they can stay and be heard at their appeals. After *Zamir* they might simply be removed if there were reasonable grounds for believing they had entered intending to overstay. In *Tariq Tareen* (55850/79(1745) (unreported)), the IAT held it had no jurisdiction to hear an alleged overstayer's appeal against deportation if it determined that he had entered illegally. Since the appellant possessed no leave, there was nothing to overstay. He had to be removed.

However, the lower courts, as they did with the *Bromley* case, began to restrict the influence of *Zamir*. In *R. v. SHDD ex p. Iqbal and Hussain* (1982) 132 NLJ 297, the Court of Appeal held the positive duty of candour to arise only where the applicant knew the concealed facts were material. There was official disagreement about when deceit was 'material' to an officer's decision. The department (HC 89 (1980/1), p. 2) thought the deception must be 'sufficient to influence an immigration officer to grant leave which he would otherwise have been bound to [refuse]'. Adjudicators went further, declining juris-diction to hear appeals where the deception secured leave which might have been refused. The upshot was *R. v. SSHD ex p. Jayakody* [1982] 1 All ER 461. Treating J as an overstayer, the department refused an extension of stay. The adjudicator, considering J to be an illegal entrant, held he had no right of appeal. An immigration officer then decided to remove J. The Home Office supported J's application to quash the decision and the Court of Appeal granted it, preferring the department's view of materiality. In *R. v. Immigration Adjudicator ex p. Bowen and Akhtar* (1982) *The Times*, 8 April, a similar clash between Home Office and appellate authorities was also resolved in the department's favour. B appealed against a refusal to let him remain to take employment. A appealed against a refusal to let him stay as a businessman. In both cases the IAT declined jurisdiction, deter-mining that entry had been obtained by deception. Aiming to maximize control over the decision-making process, the department once again supported applications for judicial review. Granting these, McNeill J overturned *Tariq Tareen*. Adjudicators and the IAT could only decline jurisdiction if the appellant had acted unlawfully *and* the Minister chose to treat him as an illegal entrant. The appellate authorities' refusal to accept the department's treatment of some illegal entrants merely as overstayers frustrated the administrators' 'power to under-enforce' which was a 'necessary and appropriate' facet of the administrative process.

The courts also started to doubt immigration officers' claims to infallibility.[24] In *R. v. SSHD ex p. Shahzan Noreen* (26 November 1980, unreported), a returning resident's passport was stamped with indefinite leave for which she was not qualified. Six years later she returned from another visit abroad but was refused entry, the chief immigration officer taking the view that, given the questions which should have been asked at interview, she must have deceived his officer (who could remember nothing of the incident) to obtain the indefinite leave. In essence the issue was who should bear the risk that administrative procedures might break down. Donaldson LJ intervened:

> In my judgment, the one factor of which [the CIO] has not taken any account . . . is the possibility that in the hurly-burly of Heathrow an immigration officer could make a mistake and put the wrong stamp on a passport. I can well understand his being reluctant to reach such a conclusion. Loyalty between immigration officers is a very desirable characteristic, but nevertheless . . . if you look at this objectively there is no evidence whatsoever of any deception . . . All that can be said is that if you eliminate the possibility of any human error by [the immigration officer], if you make that assumption, then you are driven ineluctably to the conclusion that [the applicant] deceived him, but for my part I do not think that any [CIO] can reasonably put on one side as virtually impossible human error by the immigration officer. Once you take that into account then the balance is all one way in view of the seriousness of the charge . . . and the tremendous change in [the applicant's] status . . . I do not think that this was a reasonable decision which can be upheld.

The stage was set for the conjoined appeals reported as *Khawaja* v. *Secretary of State for the Home Department* [1983] 1 All ER 765. Khawaja told an immigration officer that he wished to enter for a visit. It emerged later that he had already married a UK resident and accompanied her on the incoming flight (before entering through separate control channels). He was detained as an illegal entrant. Following *Zamir*, the Appeal Court declined to interfere. His counsel sought leave to appeal, arguing the case could be distinguished. Granting leave, the Appeals Committee of the House of Lords took the unusual step of inviting contentions that *Zamir* was wrongly decided and scheduled sufficient time for these to be heard. The Committee then added to the hearing list *Khera*'s case. Khera, who had entered as a dependant son, was detained (pending removal) for not having disclosed his marriage when he obtained entry clearance. Although it reaffirmed that illegal entry included obtaining admission by deception, the House of Lords rejected the positive duty of candour and, invoking the rarely exercised power to overrule its own decisions, liberalized the use of habeas corpus. Khera's appeal was allowed since there was no evidence of fraud. Khawaja's was dismissed because the evidence against him was considered overwhelming. Lord Bridge instanced the 'blatant lie' about his true intentions and Lord Fraser commented: 'deception may arise from silence as to a material fact in some circumstances; for example, the silence of Khawaja about . . . his marriage to [X] and the fact that she had accompanied him on the flight . . . were capable of constituting deception, even if he had not told any direct lies to the immigration officer.'

LORD SCARMAN: In *Zamir* deception was proved . . . It was not necessary, therefore, for the House to consider whether even where there is no deliberate deception . . . a positive duty of candour [is owed]. It is certainly an entrant's duty to answer truthfully the questions put to him and to provide such information as is required of him . . . But the [1971] Act goes no further. He may, or may not, know what facts are material. The immigration officer does, or ought to, know the matters relevant to the decision he has to make . . . To allow officers to rely on an entrant honouring a duty of positive candour . . . would seem perhaps a disingenuous approach to the administration of control: some might think it conducive to slack rather than to 'sensitive' . . . administration . . . I reject the view that there is a duty of positive candour and that mere non-disclosure . . . of material facts in the absence of fraud is a breach of the immigration laws [within s.33].

[Lord Scarman then made jurisdictional fact the basis of review:]

I am convinced that the *Zamir* reasoning gave insufficient weight to the . . . fundamental . . . consideration that we are here concerned with, the scope of judicial review of a power which inevitably infringes the liberty of those subjected to it. This consideration . . . outweighs . . . any difficulties in the administration of immigration control to which the application of the principle might give rise . . .

The *Zamir* decision would limit judicial review where the executive has decided to remove someone . . . to the '*Wednesbury* principle'. This principle is undoubtedly correct in cases where it is appropriate [but] it cannot extend to the interference with liberty unless Parliament has unequivocally enacted that it should . . . The principle excludes the court from substituting its own view of the facts for that of the authority . . .

Faced with the jealous care our law traditionally devotes to the protection of . . . liberty . . . I find it impossible to imply into the statute words [which] would . . . take the [removal power] out of the 'precedent fact' category . . . If Parliament intends to exclude effective judicial review of the exercise of a power in restraint of liberty, it must make its meaning crystal clear.

LORD BRIDGE: I have no doubt that when a person detained . . . as an illegal entrant [has a] leave to enter and remain here which is valid on its face the onus lies on the immigration officer to prove the fact that the leave was obtained by fraud . . . The [difficult] question . . . concerns the standard of proof required to discharge that onus. I was at first inclined to [the criminal law standard] that proof is required beyond all reasonable doubt. But . . . the civil standard of proof by a preponderance of probability will suffice, always provided that, in view of the gravity of the charge of fraud . . . and of the consequences which will follow if it is [made out], the court should not be satisfied with anything less than probability of a high degree. I would add that the inherent difficulties of discovering and proving the true facts in many immigration cases can afford no valid ground for . . . relaxing the standard of proof required. If unlimited leave to enter was granted perhaps years before and the essential facts relied on to establish the fraud alleged can only be proved by documentary and affidavit evidence of past events which occurred in some remote part of the Indian sub-continent, the courts should be less, rather than more, ready to accept anything short of convincing proof. On the other hand it must be accepted that proof to the appropriate standard can, and in the vast majority of cases will, be provided, in accordance with the established practice of the Divisional Court, by affidavit evidence alone. I understand all your Lordships to be agreed that nothing said in the present case should be construed as a charter to alleged illegal entrants who challenge their detention and proposed removal to demand the attendance of deponents to affidavits for cross-examination. Whether to permit cross-examination will remain a matter for the court in its discretion to decide . . . The cases will be rare when it will be essential, in the interests of justice, to require the attendance for cross-examination of a deponent from overseas. If the alleged illegal entrant applying for [judicial review] files an affidavit putting in issue the primary facts alleged against him he will himself be readily available for cross-examination, which should enable the court in the great majority of cases to decide whether or not he is a witness of the truth.

It is too early to state the precise consequences of the turnabout. The lower courts must flesh out the circumstances in which deception arises from silence and – as with *O'Reilly* v. *Mackman* – when cross-examination and discovery will be permitted. Truncated appeals against removal may decline as applicants turn to habeas corpus. Even so, alleged illegal entrants will not have the jury trial enjoyed by individuals arrested and detained for criminal offences as serious as fraud. If the refutation of the duty to disclose means that the department must deport and not remove in certain cases, the low success rate in deportation appeals suggests the end-results will often be the same.

We have learnt not to assume a simple correlation between judicial determinations and administrative actions. Commenting on *Khawaja*, Mr Waddington (*The Guardian*, 26 February 1983) declared: 'in practice the judgment has not made any difference'. It was not likely to result in the readmission of persons removed under the former regime and the department had reviewed 30 cases where removal was suspended pending *Khawaja*, concluding that in none of them was there now a right to stay. Immigration officers, he said, gathered high standards of evidence and their decisions would stand examination by the courts. About this, of course, only time and the judges can tell.[25]

18
Social assistance: attacking discretion

1 Poorhouse to safety net

To quote the present Director of the Child Poverty Action Group (CPAG) 'Supplementary benefit is supposed to provide you with enough money to make ends meet without difficulty but many people find that it does not' (Lister 1974a, p. 17). The number of people who discover this is steadily increasing. The Department of Health and Social Security (DHSS) today handles some 25 million social security claims and makes 1 billion payments. (The term 'social security' is generally used to describe cash benefits such as pensions, national insurance, sickness and disability or unemployment benefit, whether means tested, contributory or otherwise. 'Social Services' provide benefits in kind, like subsidized housing, education and medical treatment.) Nine million of the claimants are old-age pensioners and there are 13 million children for whom child benefit or family income supplement is payable. Thirty additional benefits – invalidity, mobility or attendance allowance, for example – involve 1.5 million claimants. There are 4 million people claiming SB, a figure which has climbed from just under 3 million at the end of 1979 and 1 million in 1947. Including dependants, approximately 7 million people were estimated in December 1982 to be living on SB (HC Deb. 19 April 1983, WA col. 76). The term 'supplementary benefits' in our domestic legislation is a reference to the fact that social assistance can be additional to social security payments. 'Social assistance' is the international euphemism for state payments to the needy.

How 'poverty' is to be defined and whether it is absolute or relative to the general standards of life in any society is, as you might expect, an extremely contentious question. We shall not attempt to tackle the question, on which there is a substantial literature.[1] Whatever the answer, if we take the standard rate of SB to represent the poverty line, many state benefits have been allowed to slide below it. For example, on 22 November 1982, the basic rate of unemployment benefit was £25 or £40.45 for a claimant with an adult dependent. For a single householder, the SB rate was £25.70 (or £32.70 on the long term rate) and £41.70 (£52.30) for couples. The basic rate of pension was £32.85. Whether these are described as 'relative' or 'absolute' poverty, they are hardly lavish.

In 1982, 1.6 million pensioners were claiming SB with an additional 87,000 over pension age but not pensionable. In other words, just under one half of all SB claimants had reached retirement age. The other main categories of claimant are the sick and disabled (238,000); the unemployed (1.7 million); widows under retirement age (16,000); and one-parent families (upwards of 415,000 families).[2] All these figures are approximate.

The SB scheme as we know it today derives from legislation of 1966 modified and consolidated by the Supplementary Benefits Act 1976 and substantially revised and amended by the Social Security Act 1980. It is this revision which forms the subject matter of Chapters 18 and 19. Although the 1966 legislation for the first time introduced a standard rate of entitlement to supplementary pension or allowance for 'every person in Great Britain of or over the age of 16 whose resources are insufficient to meet his requirements', the scheme was still largely discretionary. The Act retained an important power to supplement the standard rate of benefit in exceptional or urgent cases. S.3(1) authorized a single payment 'to meet an exceptional need'. Such payments were known familiarly as 'ENPs'. S.4 allowed the statutory provisions to be overridden 'in an urgent case'. Para. 4 of Sched. 2 allowed additional allowances ('ECAs') to be made for 'exceptional circumstances' (e.g. medical diet or extra heating for young children). These discretionary powers were vested in the Supplementary Benefits Commission (SBC) and exercised on its behalf by benefit officers working in the local offices of the DHSS. Today this administrative agency has been eliminated, but during its short lifespan it played a central role in the revision.

The objectives of the official bodies (the SBC and DHSS) did not necessarily coincide with those of the unofficial 'poverty lobby' – an informal grouping of politicians, welfare lawyers and pressure groups working in the interests of the poor – also working for reforms. Both sides were, however, agreed that administrative discretion should be replaced by a model of rules, rights and entitlement. This is the pattern adopted by the Social Security Act 1980.

The legislation which we have taken as our starting point has a long ancestry. SB replaced national assistance, administered under the National Assistance Act 1948. This in turn replaced unemployment assistance, administered under the Unemployment Assistance Act 1934. These were national schemes. Behind them lie a succession of Poor Law Acts, dating to the Poor Relief Act of 1601 which consolidated systems of parochial relief introduced by the Tudor monarchs. The celebrated 'Poor Law' was many times patched and repatched before a major reform was set in motion in the wake of the Napoleonic Wars and implemented by the Poor Law Amendment Act 1834, with which the names of Nassau Senior and Edwin Chadwick are closely associated.[3] The long tradition is significant because the parsimonious spirit of poor law relief has proved strikingly resistant to change, an obstacle which has to be borne in mind by administrators and by the poverty lobby alike if they are to avoid backlash. For example, if you followed up our reference to the background of *Roberts* v. *Hopwood*, you will already know that the case was a battle in a war of attrition between the central government on the one hand, and the Labour controlled Poplar Council with the Board of Guardians on the other. The latter were responsible for administering the workhouses and the local system of 'outdoor relief' or cash benefits. Particularly contested was the principle of 'less eligibility' which meant that public assistance must always remain below the wages paid to the poorest worker. This can be traced directly to the Poor Law reforms of 1834.

Edwin Chadwick's Poor Law left two fatal legacies for modern administrators. First was the idea that poor relief was the end of the road; it was available only to those for whom no other form of relief was available. This idea was echoed in the Beveridge Report, *Social Insurance and the Social Services* (Cmnd 6404, 1942), which formed the basis of post-war social assistance. Beveridge called national assistance a *safety net* and the social security system was itself 'one part only of a comprehensive policy of social progress'. The Beveridge Plan aimed to lift as many groups as possible off national assistance. First, full employment was an essential precondition for success; work was a right, but it was also an obligation. Second, mandatory social insurance would allow the notional purchase of pensions and other benefits (such as unemployment or maternity benefit). Third, personal social services would provide for fairer income distribution through the provision of medical, educational and housing facilities to all citizens. The safety net of national assistance would catch only a few minnows in its meshes.

Assistance will be available to meet all needs which are not covered by insurance. It must meet those needs adequately up to subsistence level, but it must be felt to be something less desirable than insurance benefit; otherwise the insured persons get nothing for their contributions. Assistance therefore will be given always subject to proof of needs and examination of means; it will be subject also to any conditions as to behaviour which may seem likely to hasten restoration of earning capacity. [Cmnd 6404, p. 141.]

Very closely linked with the 'safety net' and 'less eligibility' is the idea of stigma. Chadwick himself once said, 'I wish to see the Poor House looked to with dread by our labouring class and the reproach for being an inmate in it extend downwards from father to son.' McDonagh (1977, p. 120) describes the Victorian poor law as 'cheap, poor, grudging and wasteful; and the original brand of the broad arrow could never be altogether effaced . . . Though ever fainter, [it] was ineradicable so long as the poor kept pride. It would require an altogether new beginning in formal style, and in the rhetoric of right and citizenship before this wound could heal'. Donnison, Chairman of the SBC in 1976–80, links stigma with *social control* (see above, Chapter 1) when he remarks (1982, p. 9) that 'from the start this service was concerned both with peoples' welfare (preventing them from starving) and with controlling their behaviour (preventing disorder, and encouraging paupers to earn their own living). It still is.' Piven and Cloward take this last point much further, arguing that the *primary* objective of poor relief in all capitalist societies is social control. A pool of labour is essential to the economic structure of such societies and welfare systems are designed to secure such a pool without any fundamental reforms in the structure of society. Welfare law 'regulates the poor' by

defining and enforcing the terms on which different classes of men are made to do different kinds of work; relief arrangements, in other words, have a great deal to do with maintaining social and economic inequities. The indignities and cruelties of the dole are no deterrent to indolence among the rich; but for the poor man, the spectre of ending up on the welfare or in the poor-house makes any job at any wage a preferable alternative. [Piven and Cloward 1971, p. xvii.]

Thus one reason for the means test and for the discretionary elements in public assistance was to reinforce the image of charitable relief and, with it, the claimant's sense of shame.

Two ways in which the poor can be protected from stigma and persuaded to claim and accept state payments willingly are first, as Beveridge recommended, that they can be lifted out of the safety net into the domain of contributory benefits. In this case their contributions create in them a sense of entitlement. It must be realized, however, that the entitlement is partly notional.[4] Contributions would never be enough in an inflationary period to purchase the benefits provided. A massive injection of funds would by now be necessary to lift large numbers of people from the 'safety net'. In 1979, the SBC calculated that it would cost 13.6 billion at 1977 level to lift all of the pensioner claimants from the scheme. This would double social security expenditure. It would cost £350 million to remove even three-quarters of the one-parent families (*Response*, p. 11). Since 1980, the number of people on SB has risen, while the real value of many benefits has been eroded by the Social Security (No. 2) Act 1980, which changed the arrangements by which benefits were automatically uprated in line with inflation.[5] The necessary sums are unlikely therefore to be forthcoming in the foreseeable future.

A less costly alternative, for which welfare lawyers pressed in the early seventies, is to introduce the 'rights rhetoric' into the system. Obviously a massive injection of funds would again be necessary to produce a real improvement for those on the poverty line. But the SBC certainly hoped that such a change would help them to solve the problem of unclaimed benefits which by 1976 was seen as serious. In a survey of 'take up', the SBC estimated that 20–30 per cent of those entitled to claim were not claiming and that as much as £240 million was left unclaimed annually.[6] The belief that SB was 'some sort of charitable handout' was blamed and the SBC relied on 'the transition from discretionary rules of thumb to firm regulations' to solve the problem (Cmnd 8033, 1980, p. 113).

In addition to the problem of stigma, the 'safety net' concept creates a problem of coordination. Since the demise of the SBC in 1980, the DHSS administers the SB scheme through its local offices on a national basis. But not all social security payments are administered by the DHSS; unemployment benefit is the responsibility of the Department of Employment and rent and rate rebates (later housing benefits) were administered by local authorities, whose social workers sometimes have access to other discretionary funds. This is a continual source of difficulty. People feel that 'the welfare' should know what benefits they are receiving and to what they are entitled.

It is difficult to know, first, what benefits are available and, secondly, which service is responsible for which payments. For example, who should pay the bill for electricity used to run an expensive kidney machine (below)? Although the sums involved are often small, they may mean a lot to someone trying to make ends meet on S B and often unable to invest time, money and energy in traipsing from one office to another. The Community Development Project underlines the consequences for claimants in *Limits of the Law* (1977, p. 40):

People forced to depend on means-tested benefits do not only have to cope with the supplementary benefits office. To attempt to obtain what you may be entitled to it is also necessary to tour the Housing Department (rent rebate), the Treasurer's Department (rates rebate), Education Department (school meals, school uniform, educational maintenance grant), and the Social Services Department (help for the sick and disabled, nursery provision, help with bills). This process is not just time consuming and frustrating. The extensive administrative divisions mean that all too often needs are left unmet. Departments with overlapping *powers*, but not *duties*, frequently deny their responsibility, while acknowledging the need. Precisely because need is not acknowledged to be the remit of any particular department, the claimant has no recourse within the structure to any appeal mechanism.

The administrative law machinery is not always well suited to such complaints. S B A Ts, for example, frequently hear from appellants that information given to one department was not passed on to another. There is little they can do because s.20 of the Supplementary Benefits Act 1976 entitles the Minister to recover sums paid in consequence of misrepresentation or failure to disclose any material fact whether the claimant has acted 'fraudulently or otherwise'. Once again the obligation to know the rules rests on the public rather than the administration (compare the Home Loss study and the immigration service). Some tribunals have tried to mitigate hardship by a legalistic interpretation of this section: for example, by holding that over-payments resulted from departmental carelessness and not from the claimant's non-disclosure.

Lack of departmental co-ordination generates many complaints to the PCA – you will find a typical case below – but he seldom secures more than an apology. You will also find below a CLA complaint involving lack of liaison between the housing officers of a local authority and the DHSS, and a High Court ruling on the residual obligations of the SBC. But the DHSS does not see itself as a 'collection agent' to fight frontier disputes with other authorities. Donnison explains why. Can you find references to 'stigma' and 'less eligibility'?

The development of the supplementary benefits scheme has repeatedly led us – for the worthiest reasons – into providing help which might better come from neighbouring services . . . [I am not saying] that these problems are really the responsibility of other departments: we are *all* responsible, and it is a disgrace to each of the departments concerned if the public suffers from confusions and conflicts between us. The question we have to consider is whether we should do our best to help our claimants cope with every aspect of their lives and all the public services on which they may depend, or whether we should confine ourselves to providing an assured minimum income. We should bear in mind that the SBC 'passport' which the first alternative would confer on our claimants might encourage some services to regard them as second-class citizens deserving second-rate treatment. We must also remember that many of the working poor, who never get a penny from us, also have difficulty in buying school uniforms, paying for their housing, visiting their relatives in hospital . . . and so-on – and they resent it when they find our claimants get help with such things at their expense. [Donnison 1976, pp. 350–1.]

The complex arrangements and multiplicity of benefits available also creates a problem of 'unmet legal need'. The sums involved are often so small that the incentive for practitioners to specialize in this field is correspondingly less. Again, courts may be unwilling to encourage litigation where they feel that sums involved are trivial. The result has been that good legal advice has not always been available. In the Hamlyn lectures for 1974, Scarman was blaming practitioners for their ignorance of a system which 'is not only complex but pervasive; it enters into the life of everyone, and is a major factor in the lives of millions' (Scarman 1974, p. 35). The next Hamlyn lecturer, then chief National Insurance officer, made a similar point about national insurance tribunals. He thought it wrong 'from the public point of view that claimants for substantial sums should not be legally represented simply because most of the legal profession are not interested' (Micklethwait 1976, p. 5). The situation has since improved. There are good textbooks[7] and welfare law finds a place on many legal syllabuses. Law Centres, the Free Representation Unit and the CAB have tried to provide legal services while CPAG and the Legal Action Group provide training for practitioners. Collectively, and through their members, these bodies are today among the most articulate representatives of the poverty lobby.

We have begun to collect reasons why in the mid-seventies a reform movement was gathering momentum. Generally speaking, the target was administrative discretion, though the motives of the reformers were by no means the same. If we look briefly at the way in which the scheme was administered under the 1966 and 1976 Acts, we can point to the main areas of discretion and the objectives of the protagonists become clearer.

A claim for SB was made in writing and decided by a benefit officer working in a local DHSS office. A successful claimant was entitled to a payment at a standard rate, prescribed from time to time. He could also apply for an ECA or an ENP. In 1978, when they came to review the system, the DHSS explained how the discretionary powers were divided between the SBC and benefit officers:

Clearly the SBC cannot themselves make millions of decisions a year about the entitlement of individuals to benefit. They are responsible for the general direction of the scheme and they lay down guidance to the tens of thousands of the Department's staff in local offices throughout the country who actually take the decisions in individual cases. These staff are accountable direct to the Secretary of State for those parts of the supplementary benefits scheme for which he has retained responsibility in the legislation. For the major part of their job, however, the staff in local offices are responsible through the Department to the SBC, to follow the instructions or guidance which the SBC have laid down under their duties or broad discretionary powers ('Commission discretion'); and also for the exercise by individual officers of their own judgement and discretion in a particular case ('officer discretion'). This last discretion is in effect the delegation by the SBC of decision-making powers in millions of cases to their agents in local offices. [*Social Assistance*, 1978, pp. 20–1.]

By 1975, when the SBC published its first report, SB was no longer a safety net nor was it a residual form of benefit. By now, 8 per cent of the total population was claiming SB, and the sum of £1,200 million paid out in benefit represented 13 per cent of social security expenditure and 2.3 per cent of the national expenditure. Worse, the claimants came from classes whom Beveridge intended to exclude. The SBC explained why this was likely to remain as a constant feature of the scheme:

Britain now has growing numbers of old people, one-parent families, students, and unemployed school leavers . . . The growing numbers of one-parent families have had a marked impact on the supplementary benefits scheme. In 1948 they were not even identified as a separate group in the statistics of the National Assistance Board. In 1967 there were 142,000 lone parents receiving supplementary benefit. By 1977 they had increased to 326,000 – about 11 per cent of all our claimants, or, with their dependants, nearly one in five of all the people supported by the scheme. Over 40 per cent of all one-parent families are thought to rely on supplementary benefit and their numbers are still growing. Of all the children in families living on supplementary benefit 52 per cent are now in one-parent families. In the absence of alternative provision, it is clear that on present trends more and more one-parent families will have to look to supplementary benefit for support . . .

In 1948, 71 per cent of the unemployed depended solely on unemployment benefit, and only 16 per cent received national assistance. By 1977, only 33 per cent were managing on unemployment benefit alone, and 49 per cent were receiving supplementary allowance. The unemployed now constitute over 22 per cent of all supplementary benefit claimants, whereas in 1966 they accounted for only 7 per cent. But the real effects of this change are even more striking. Most unemployed claimants receive supplementary benefit for relatively short periods between jobs, so that the number of claims made over a year is very much larger than the number getting benefit at any one time. For example, at the end of 1977, 22 per cent of the people receiving benefit were unemployed, but the unemployed accounted for 67 per cent of the 5,776,000 claims received during the year. The whole character of the service and the morale of its customers and staff depend heavily on its capacity for meeting the needs of the unemployed fairly and efficiently. The scheme faces mounting difficulties in doing this. People who have lost their jobs may be faced with immediate and pressing financial worries, but to get the money they need, more and more of them must undergo the complex process of registering for work, claiming unemployment benefit, and then undergoing a detailed means test to qualify for supplementary benefit. They then depend upon a service which provokes a lot of public dissension, much of it focused particularly on the unemployed claimant . . .[8]

The 1,738,000 pensioners receiving supplementary benefit are the largest group of claimants in the scheme. The Pensions Act of 1975 offers the best prospect of reducing their numbers. But the full effects of this legislation will not be felt for many years . . . At the end of 1977 the average supplementary pension was £7.65. To replace this by a bigger contributory pension, whether by credits or by a straight increase in the basic pension, would cost £2.7 billion a year, which is equivalent to about 20 per cent of social security expenditure at November 1977 rates. Even this would still leave a lot of pensioners on supplementary benefit. To lift all but a few off means-tested pensions would cost far more – about £13.6 billion at November 1977 levels. That would double total social security expenditure.

The industrial structure of Britain is undergoing fundamental changes which have not yet come to an end. These changes in balance of the economy, coupled with the low growth rates of recent years, have led to growing unemployment, and no-one can confidently predict a return to the 'full employment' experienced in the generation ending in the mid-sixties.

These developments, together with the failure of national insurance benefits to support people when they are out of work, have vastly increased the numbers of unemployed people who need to claim supplementary benefit. [*Response*, paras. 2.2–2.6, 3.7.]

If you think about the discussion in Chapter 5, you will see that a scheme on this scale could never be left simply to 'officer discretion'. Decisions would be disparate and too many complaints of discrimination would be received. In fact, benefit officers' freedom of choice was limited by administrative instructions issued by the SBC dictating the way in which officer discretion should normally be exercised. These instructions added up to an unpublished, confidential 'code of practice', known unaffectionately to welfare lawyers, who were familiar with its contents since the CPAG had come into possession of complete copies, as the A and AX codes. The public had to rely for guidance, however, on a resumé of SBC practice published as the *Supplementary Benefits Handbook*.

For the administration, this system had the advantage of flexibility; policies could be withdrawn at will and in secret. On the other hand, remember the principle that discretion must not be fettered by the application of fixed policies (see further below); this rule rendered the status of the code uncertain. Welfare lawyers, by way of contrast, saw little good in the unpublished, secret rules. Their secrecy made them hard to attack and was in principle undemocratic. By now, you know enough about immigration procedures to take Bradley's comparison with a pinch of salt:

The present unsatisfactory position of the A-Code, and the limited and not always informative contents of the *Supplementary Benefits Handbook* should both be superseded by a new Benefit Code. This should contain a full statement of the policies and rules which the Commission has issued for the administration of the scheme: and it should be laid before Parliament for scrutiny, in a manner similar to that in which instructions to immigration officers are at present laid before Parliament under the Immigration Act 1971 . . . It is this kind of open rule-making that the American administrative lawyer, K. C. Davis, had in mind when he said, 'Rulemaking procedure is one of the greatest inventions of modern government'. Yet in 1971 . . . Titmuss quoted this remark in a complex defence of the Commission's own secret rulemaking procedures – when it is plain that Davis had in mind published rules made by an open procedure which included consultation with affected interests. [Bradley 1976, p. 118.]

Prosser (1977, p. 59) takes this argument somewhat further by arguing that secrecy and discretion were designed to disguise the contradictions inherent in the scheme and to divert attention from the need for reform. Thus the discretion was highly functional in political terms (compare McAuslan's criticisms of the Land Compensation Act). But to the administrators discretion had come to seem dysfunctional. Research conducted by the SBC and published in its annual reports[9] showed that discretion was expensive to administer. SB absorbed more staff time than other areas of social security (e.g. pensions) and the discretionary areas of SB absorbed more staff time, generated more appeals and were the cause of more errors (below) than the area of standard entitlement. Even after the revision, SB remains an expensive service to administer because it is means tested and the entitlement is complex. In 1979/80 the administrative cost of the SB system was £323 million or 13 per cent of the benefits; by 1981/2, this had fallen to £507 million or 10 per cent of the benefits (HC Deb. 27 April 1983, WA cols. 353–4). Unemployment benefit in 1981/2 cost £380 million to administer or 9.4 per cent of total benefit (HC Deb. 28 April 1983, WA col. 402).

We can summarize the argument as it stood in the late 1970s by saying that discretion was seen by administrators to be inefficient. On the other hand, welfare lawyers did not welcome it either.[10] Partington (1980a, p. 621) summarized the main anti-discretion arguments:

(i) it leads to inconsistent decision-taking, both by officials and appeal tribunals;
(ii) it leads to arbitrary decision-taking;
(iii) it leads to undesirable social control by officials;
(iv) it diverts attention from more fundamental issues, e.g. the adequacy of the basic levels of supplementary benefits payments;
(v) it encourages feelings of stigma in claimants;
(vi) it prevents claimants understanding how the SB scheme works;
(vii) it leads to some claimants being jealous of others.

In an influential article, Titmuss admitted that the British social security system was imperfect. But he warned of the dangers of moving too far in the direction of rules and legally enforceable rights. A legalistic system might prove less humane in the long run. The essential problem 'was to find the right balance between general rules and individualised justice'. Relate this passage to the arguments which conclude Chapter 5. Do the discretionary areas of immigration control provide 'flexible, individualized justice'?

[A welfare system] needs an element of flexible, individualised justice for two fundamental reasons. First, because as far as we can see ahead and on the basis of all we know about human weaknesses and diversities, a society without some element of means-testing and discretion is an unattainable ideal. It is stupid and dangerous to pretend that such an element need not exist; that all will be resolved by the automatism of negative income tax, the money market, consumerism and the lawyer. Secondly, we need this element of individualised justice in order to allow a universal rights scheme, based on principles of equity, to be as precise and inflexible as possible. These characteristics of precision, inflexibility and universality depend for their sustenance and strength on the existence of some element of flexible, individualised justice. [Titmuss 1971, p. 131.]

Wilding, writing for social workers, agreed that benefit officers were often unjustly blamed for a poor performance which resulted largely from the overloading of the system, a problem for which rules would not necessarily provide a panacea. Contrast the argument with our earlier argument that discretionary powers of selective enforcement enable the rules to be stricter:

Most of the necessary improvements in the administration of supplementary benefits can be brought about by improvements in training, in managerial supervision and in communications between the Commission and its staff . . . The alternative of elaborating and publishing the rules and instructions seems a lot less attractive from the point of view of the claimant's interest. It is a fallacy to believe that discretion can be virtually abolished in this field . . . The effect of multiplying rules is not to abolish discretion but to transfer it to a narrower and less fruitful area. As rules define, moreover, they necessarily also restrict. If the Commission attempted precisely to define the circumstances in which help could be given, it would have to rule some circumstances and some categories of claimants out. But it is certain that among them there would be some cases of genuine and pressing need. Rules will not tell you which they are, but the local officer, looking at all the circumstances of each case, will get at least some of them right. [Wilding 1975, pp. 61–2.]

But the case for rules was gaining ground. The question was, what sort of rules? In 1978, the DHSS published a review of the scheme entitled *Social Assistance*. In the same year, the SBC independently published its *Response*. *Social Assistance*, which ultimately formed the basis for the 1980 reform, showed the DHSS hesitating over the degree of formality appropriate to their needs. Compare the department's solution with those adopted in the immigration service or in the employment field. Are the circumstances similar or dissimilar? Do the arguments cover Partington's points?

We . . . think it essential that the detailed rules and practices of the scheme should be set out publicly in a sufficiently authoritative form for them to be followed consistently by both the officials administering them and the appeal tribunals. This . . . might be done in regulations, which would be binding on the adjudicating authorities and would secure greater consistency. The SBC's policies regarding the use of its existing discretionary powers are already codified in instructions to local officers (many of which are summarised and set out in the Handbook) and these could be transferred to regulations without materially affecting the substance of the scheme. Discretion would have to remain but it should be used to deal with cases which cannot appropriately be covered by general rules. There are at present far too many basic rules in the scheme which depend on the exercise by the SBC of its discretionary powers. We think these should all be given statutory force . . .

An alternative course to putting most of the scheme's rules and practices into regulations would be to confine the regulations to the basic rules of the scheme, and to deal with more detailed matters in some less formal and binding document than regulations. This could be a Code of Practice, such as is coming into use in other fields. Adapting this to our purposes, we should need to provide for a Code of Supplementary Benefit policy which would be laid before Parliament, and to which the adjudicating authorities would be required to have regard. Such a code would not be fully binding; but it would be public and exposed to Parliamentary discussion, and it would leave a measure of flexibility which would be lost if all the details of the scheme had to be submitted to regulation-making procedures.

We find great attraction in the idea of a Code of Practice, which would ensure that decisions in particular cases were more clearly based on publicly-known rules which would influence – though not bind – the appeal authorities and would avoid the proliferation of regulations and amending regulations needed if the more detailed features of the scheme were embodied in statutory form. Such an approach also seems likely to permit the drafting of the rules in language more accessible to claimants and their advisers, and we think this an important consideration for a social assistance scheme. In the reshaping of the scheme we recommend that this approach should be explored further, as should the possibility of putting both the basic and more detailed rules in the Code. [*Social Assistance*, paras. 3.13–3.15.]

In the event, formality won. The Social Security Act 1980 contained 26 powers to make regulations which were in due course made. This decision had its effect on the movement for reform of SBATs which were, during the same period, equally under attack. SBATs had been specifically exempted from the Franks recommendations. They operated as 'a case-committee' (some said a teaparty) checking the benefit officer's findings of fact and use of discretion. Even if these tribunals were adequate in a discretionary framework, they could not survive the change to a model of rules. As we shall see in Chapter 19, rule-making and judicialization were inevitably linked.

One final, general point needs to be made. Remember Jowell's warning that rules are only as good as the policies which infuse them.

Donnison, who played a leading part in the reforms, emphasizes (1982, p. 21) that they were conceived in a period of optimism about the objectives of the welfare state which he describes as one of *central consensus*, 'originally derived from progressive thinking of the period before the first world war, gradually fashioned into a central consensus by the experience of depression and two world wars, and made economically viable by the long post-war boom in the advanced economies of the world.'[11] The assumptions of the central consensus allowed for a measure of income redistribution through the social services. 'Although inequalities in income would persist, their harsher effects could be gradually softened by a "social wage" (consisting of social services distributed with greater concern for social need)'. The process of social engineering would be financed through progressive taxation, but consistent economic growth 'would produce the resources to create a fairer society without anyone suffering on the way'. The central consensus was acceptable to the trade unions and labour movement. A succession of Conservative Governments also acquiesced in these objectives to a limited extent.

For Donnison and others, the consensus ended abruptly with the election of 1979. It was replaced by a new ethos in which the welfare state was seen as an element in national decline. For Scruton (1980, p. 183) the rationale of the welfare state is social control. 'Poverty and indigence are powers at large in the state. Not to relieve them is to foster resentment . . . Yet to relieve want is one thing, to make all men equal in respect of it another.' Welfare is described as 'a compulsory form of charity' imposed on the professional classes. Scruton also challenges Reich's case for 'the new property':

In fostering the illusion of a 'natural' right to home, health, wealth and comfort, the state erodes both the individual's will and its own authority. The state becomes a kind of machine, a centre of distribution, an alien object which sometimes grants, and sometimes withholds, what is thought of as an independent right. [Scruton 1980, p. 50.]

Mesher, anticipating the massacre of the welfare state, described a new and hostile ethos of 'scroungermania' in which:

One explanation of [the moral degeneration of the nation] was the existence of the welfare state itself. This finds expression particularly in the writings of Dr. Rhodes Boyson: 'In . . . an irresponsible society no-one cares, no-one saves, no-one bothers – why should they when the state spends all its energies taking money from the energetic, successful and thrifty to give to the idle, the failures and the feckless . . . Not only is the present welfare state inefficient and destructive of personal liberty, individual responsibility and moral

growth, but it saps the collective moral fibre of our people as a nation'[12] . . .
The symbol of moral degeneration has been the scrounger. Concern about
malingering has of course existed as long as assistance has been given, but in
the late seventies scrounging became defined as a serious social problem . . .
the approach was summed up in Mrs Thatcher's denunciation of the 'Why
Work? Syndrome' which evokes an image of claimants living comfortably and
irresponsibly off the dole, their own and workers' moral fibre sapped and the
nation's efficiency damaged. [Mesher 1981, pp. 120–1.]

A reform conceived in one political era was born into an altogether
different world. Concern for take-up of benefits was replaced by
concern for the elimination of fraud. Departmental resources were
diverted into this area.[13] Stigma was back in fashion. If we feel that
dysfunctional discretion was replaced by dysfunctional rules, the
blame does not necessarily rest with administrative law.

2 The Supplementary Benefits Commission

Like the Council on Tribunals, the SBC, which was established by
the Ministry of Social Security Act 1966, was a part-time body,
consisting of a full-time chairman, a deputy chairman and about six
members. Unlike the Council, it did not employ its own staff and
again unlike the Council, its advisory functions were purely secondary. In the House of Commons, the Minister of Pensions (Miss
Herbison) spoke of the Commission as 'a source of advice to the
Minister on many social problems'; it would also 'assist the Minister's
programme of research into those problems' (HC Deb. vol. 729, col.
340). In practice, however, the executive functions of the SBC were
its real business. There is a contrast here with its predecessors. The
pre-war UAB employed its own staff, fixed benefit rates and
published an annual report to Parliament. During the first ten years,
Donnison argues, the SBC was less independent than the Board.
This affected its working methods. Can you make any comparisons
with (a) the CLA (b) the Home Office handling immigration
complaints and (c) the Council on Tribunals?

At every stage since then the Board's successors have been incorporated more
deeply into the workings of their parent department and their legal powers
have been reduced. By the 1970s, the SBC's staff all belonged to the DHSS;
they produced, till 1976, no annual reports. Parliament fixed the rates of
benefit on the recommendations of the Government . . . Unlike its predecessors, the UAB and the NAB, the SBC no longer managed its own
service, and had no authority to tell other people how to do so. The only
executive power it retained was its responsibility for the discretionary parts of

the system . . .

Whatever private pressures they may have exerted, and whatever private disagreements they may have had, the Commission in public defended virtually every feature of the system . . . Usually the Commission avoided public contributions to debate altogether, preferring to respond individually, humanely and privately to cases as they arose – to the flow of problems referred for advice by staff in the front line, letters from M Ps (The Chairman answered about 4,000 a year), protests from pressure groups and the like.

The Commission's officials preferred to work in this way. They had to serve their Ministers and a semi-independent Commission. That would become a tricky job if the Commission were ever to begin flexing their muscles and disagreeing publicly with the politicians . . . The Commission could exert a good deal of influence if they were determined to do so. But they could only make decisions about the 'discretionary benefits' which together accounted for only one pound in every £20 paid out. They could do no more than advise about the rest of the system. The staff, who were all DHSS civil servants, were ultimately accountable to the government, not the Commission. [Donnison 1982, pp. 15–17.]

Working with Richard Hayward, then Chairman, the Minister (Mrs Hart), had in 1968 formulated the role of the SBC as being to present reports on its activities, drawing the Minister's attention to any questions which, while outside the Commission's formal responsibilities, interacted upon them and gave the Commission cause for concern. It was also to comment on departmental proposals which might substantially affect the Commission's exercise of its discretionary powers.[14] In 1975, the SBC was suddenly asked to take on a new role when the Minister (Mrs Castle) asked it to resume the pre-war practice of publishing independent reports prepared in consultation with the Secretary of State and her advisers, but not necessarily with her approval. The research function was strengthened by the appointment as Chairman of an academic who was willing to take on an independent policy-making function:

The Secretary of State for Social Services in announcing the appointment of Professor David Donnison as Chairman of the Commission said 'I . . . propose to restore the practice of a separate Annual Report by the Commission in which in addition to the usual statistical material, they would be free to comment on developments and express views about priorities'. This then, is to be more than a report containing factual information about the administration of the supplementary benefits scheme and family income supplement although it does, of course, include this. It is primarily intended to enable us to account for our responsibilities each year by reporting on our work and the numbers and needs of the people whom we have tried to help, and to set out our views about existing and future policies which affect our claimants and others whose situation is similar . . .

The Commission also acts as an advisory body to the Secretary of State and helps to promote relevant research into a range of social problems. In announcing the present Chairman's appointment the Secretary of State emphasised this role by saying 'I intend to make greater use of the Commission as an advisory body in referring issues to them for advice and report (which would ordinarily be published) and in looking to them for ideas on research in their field and on priorities for development of policies as and when resources permitted and more generally for promotion of studies of future development of social policies'.

We intend that our Annual Reports should play a vital part in developing our wider, advisory role. In them we will comment on current developments and give our views about priorities for the future. By this means we hope to convey our thinking to a wider audience and stimulate a constructive discussion of issues arising in this particularly sensitive area of public policy. [Cmnd 6615, paras. 1.1, 1.3.]

This extended mandate involved the SBC in split responsibilities. It could advise on policy but was not *responsible* for it, nor could it get its policies implemented. On the other hand, it was responsible for implementing a scheme whose terms it might not approve or might even have advised against. From the following passage, how autonomous does the SBC seem?

The Commission does not have responsibility for the basic provisions governing eligibility for benefit. The scale rates for personal requirements are fixed by the Government of the day. They are varied ('uprated') by regulations made by the Secretary of State, which require an affirmative resolution of both Houses of Parliament and it has become customary for these upratings to take place at the same time as the Government uprates national insurance benefits. It is the Act, not the Commission nor the Secretary of State, which lays down the rules for the assessment (and taking into account or disregarding) of resources; and other provisions such as the cohabitation rule, the disqualification of strikers from benefit in respect of their personal requirements and a system of appeals (and formerly the wage stop, which was ended under 1975 amending legislation). All these provisions can be amended only by Act of Parliament, not by regulations. The Commission is responsible for their application in individual cases, through the guidance issued to local officers, but we have no powers to abolish or change them and can do no more than express our views to Ministers when we think it is right to do so on the desirability of reforming the law . . .

Expenditure on benefit is borne on the Supplementary Benefits Vote which is administered by the Department of Health and Social Security . . . The cost of administering the supplementary benefits scheme is met from the Department's [vote] . . . Our Chief Adviser is an official of Deputy Secretary rank, who is supported by two Under-Secretaries and their staff, all of whom are made available to the Commission by the Secretary of State whom they also advise.

The Department of Health and Social Security is responsible for the recruitment, training and management of the staff who carry out our policies at Regional and local level . . . The Chairman and Commission members visit Regional and local offices to meet the staff and talk to them about their work, as often as they can . . . and Commission members frequently visit training centres, address training courses and join in discussions with the staff attending them. [Cmnd 6615, para 1.4.]

In this passage, you can see the SBC exercising an executive function. This it did in two ways: by rule-application and by informal rule-making. A system of rules within rules emerged over a period of time in which the open rules were glossed by secret instructions. The cohabitation rule to which reference is made provides an illustration. Today this means that the resources of a couple 'living together as husband and wife' must be aggregated. This statutory phrase replaced the earlier 'cohabiting as man and wife' on the advice of the SBC given in its report 'Living together as Husband and Wife' (1976). The operation of the previous rule had produced a stream of complaints of departmental 'snoopers'. Benefit officers were accused of depriving women of their benefit on the evidence of anonymous letters and of otherwise acting oppressively. The SBC had published a previous report in 1971 and monitored its effects in 1974. The Minister then referred the matter again to the SBC for new advice. The SBC concluded:

In view of all the criticism that has been levelled at the cohabitation rule, the Commission examined the rule itself, conscious that the implementation of such unpopular legislation is a thankless task for the staff who sometimes have to make distasteful enquiries and give unwelcome decisions to claimants . . . Like the Finer Committee on one-parent families, the Commission would be glad if the rule were not necessary, but it considered that what it said in its 1971 report and what the Finer Committee echoed in its own report, is still true: namely that 'it cannot be right to treat unmarried women who have the support of a partner . . . better than if they were married' . . .

The report emphasises that the operation of the rule causes no trouble in the majority of cases . . . But the Commission must be concerned about the minority of cases where hardship may result and the report carefully reviews the guidance given to the staff both as to the nature of a husband and wife relationship and as to the way in which cases should be dealt with. Revised procedures are proposed which are designed to ensure that all claimants affected are fully advised about the meaning of living together as husband and wife and that interviews with these claimants are conducted by experienced officers with suitable training and in an atmosphere of mutual confidence. Special measures are to be adopted for dealing with doubtful cases where . . . the relationship may be a merely temporary one . . . In circumstances like these . . . officers are to be instructed that they should take into account the stability of the relationship and allow the couple a little time to decide whether they wish to remain together once the consequences of their doing so for the claimant's entitlement to benefit have been explained . . . The full implementation of [these] proposals will depend upon suitable trained staff being made available, but the Commission hopes that it will not be long delayed. [Cmnd 6615, para. 3.19.]

Subsequently, the SBC's informal guidelines on cohabitation were printed in the Handbook. Para. 2.10 lists the criteria which are to be taken into account. The couple must be (a) members of the same household and (b) living together in a stable relationship. Evidence of (c) financial support or (d) a sexual relationship is normally required. The presence of a child of the union (e) or public acknowledgement (f) creates a presumption of a husband and wife relationship. Open publication of these 'guidelines' has several advantages. It acts as a guide to benefit officers and helps to provide uniformity. It is useful to a tribunal in checking an officer's decision. It helps claimants to work out their entitlement. Clearly in this example the SBC exercised a useful 'firewatching' function.

The SBC used its powers on occasion to question the rules which it was asked to administer. The 'wage-stop' was a modern version of the 'less eligibility' rule. It meant that the allowances payable to an unemployed claimant must not be allowed to rise above the level of the net weekly earnings plus any other income which he would notionally receive if he were engaged in full time work in his normal occupation. In 1967, when the rule affected up to 35,000 claimants, the SBC questioned its utility in a special report 'Administration of the Wage Stop'. The rule was difficult to administer and involved benefit officers in arbitrary decisions, a problem which they solved by adopting the basic wage for local authority manual workers as the standard of eligibility. Taking an opposite angle from that customarily adopted, the report called the rule 'a harsh reflection of the fact that there are many men in work living on incomes below the supplementary benefit standard'. In 1975, by which time only 6,000 claimants were affected, the end of the wage-stop was secured and the SBC expressed its pleasure:

The end of the wage stop was widely welcomed as a relief to some of the most deprived families in the community. For the Commission it removed one of the unhappiest duties which fell to it under the Supplementary Benefit Act. [Cmnd 6615, para. 3.2.]

But the SBC used its advisory function to promote broader measures of reform. The first annual report set out 'the ideal to which [the SBC] would like to see policies directed', including removal of large groups of claimants from the 'last-resort means-tested, labour-intensive' SB service. But this raised important issues of resources which were for the Government rather than a quango to solve. The SBC reported a new governmental initiative, the germ of the 1978 review:

The questions we are posing raise very large issues for government, with implications going well beyond the Commission's own direct area of responsibility. The view government takes of them is bound to reflect wider opinion about the kind of scheme we should as a community provide for the support of our poorest members – and be prepared to pay for. We hope that by promoting more public discussion of these issues in our annual reports we can help to work out fresh approaches to their problems. Certainly they will have to be faced, for they will not go away. We are very encouraged to know that the Secretary of State for Social Services has already accepted our view that special attention needs to be given to them, and has decided that a small team of staff should be set up so that the DHSS can review, in consultation with us, the issues we have begun to raise. We warmly welcome this and look forward to associating ourselves with the work. [Cmnd 6615, para. 2.37.]

Try to compare these extracts with the work of the Council on Tribunals. Which body is the most autonomous? What factors do you see as enabling the SBC to make a substantial contribution to research and policy-making? Is this the type of body which Robson or *Justice* hoped for in the tribunals field? Then compare the SBC with other advisory bodies such as the Planning Advisory Group, the Skeffington Committee or a royal commission. Was it more or less independent?

Discussing the SBC's executive function, we identified a potential for firewatching. The SBC used research techniques to monitor the quality of decision-taking by its officers. In 1978, for example, a subgroup was set up 'to examine and review the quality of service . . . and relevant aspects of the organisation and management of local offices, deployment of staff, staff training, office facilities, etc; to consider any implication for the commission's policy and to make recommendations . . . as appropriate' (Cmnd 7725, p. 62). Their study showed that 17.5 per cent of all decisions contained errors of some kind. Further analysis proved that 55 per cent lay in the area of discretion. A special scrutiny of heating addition cases showed that 45 per cent of all errors occurred here and this was shown to be due to recent administrative changes which had been introduced to the rules of practice. Twenty-five per cent of all errors occurred 'in areas of work where the rules are most intricate and it seems clear that errors occur to a considerable extent because of the complexity of the rules staff have to apply.' This was a powerful argument for simplicity.

Now we can compare the advantages of firewatching and fire-fighting. The SBC because of its responsibilities for staff training and its close relationship with the DHSS, was able to implement changes of practice aimed at improving performance. Indeed, their anxiety for administrative efficiency led ultimately to changes in the law. A court could hold an error to be 'negligence' and award damages; whether this would influence administrative behaviour is questionable. The PCA might label an error 'maladministration'. Complaints to the PCA might reveal a number of such errors occurring in a single area, suggesting a need for reform. The PCA could take the matter up with the DHSS and ask for reports but, unlike the SBC, the PCA cannot act on its own initiative nor can he monitor subsequent practice to check the effectiveness of reform.

An early assessment of the PCA's performance in this area points to the advantages of a quasi-autonomous body like the SBC. Partington (1975) suggested that the PCA lacked general expertise in the field and was unfamiliar with the system. Do you think this view is fair, given secondment of departmental staff to the PCA's office? How does Partington see the PCA's role?

Despite the fact that in the cases which have come before him he has been able to discover that little things are going wrong all the time, and that occasionally major blunders occur, the PCA's caseload is at present extremely small. Unless the number of SB cases increases dramatically, he and his staff will not be able to get a broad view of this area of administration. They will be unlikely to see the welfare implications of the cases that do come before them; nor will they understand the frustrations caused to claimants by SB administration which lead them to complain of victimization and rudeness. Again, the effect of the PCA on the Department as a whole will remain extremely limited.

Even if the PCA and his staff develop their own knowledge of problems in this area, their effectiveness will be muted if there is no system of following up the results of conclusions he has reached. In this regard, the Select Committee of the House of Commons needs to examine in more detail the impact which the PCA is making at local office level. [Partington 1975, p. 167.]

In cases where the PCA is dissatisfied with office organization, he may be unable to obtain an adequate response. For example, in one complaint (HC 524 (1977/8), p. 148) where the DHSS failed to refund an applicant's national insurance contributions, the PCA recorded lamentable inefficiency:

No action was taken by the Department's local office on the application for a refund of contributions for some three months . . . And when they did send the papers to the Refunds Group in Newcastle the local office failed to deal with the outstanding waiver of liability for Class 2 contributions and the small earnings exception. As a result . . . the client was asked to return a contribution card which had already been in the Department's possession for seven months. Even after the solicitors had explained what had happened about the card, she was still sent a reminder warning her of possible prosecution if the card was not returned. The Department have explained to me that, in the first half of 1977, the local office concerned was considerably in arrears, with some 2,500 items requiring attention, and the work resulting from the first year's operation of a new contribution system was being handled by inexperienced staff. As for the delay in the office of the Refunds Group, the Department have explained that they had to establish the value of contributions paid by the client from 1970/71 onwards and that this required reference to archives for earlier documents and to the computer system for more recent contributions. I know from other cases I have investigated that the Refunds Group were also under severe pressure from having to deal with a totally unexpected number of applications following the introduction of the new scheme. Nevertheless, for reasons which I have been unable to establish, the Refunds Group took three months to get the information they required and another month passed after it had been obtained before payment was made.

The only remedy forthcoming in the case was an apology and we have no way of knowing whether the PCA demanded administrative reforms or asked for further reports.

Again, let us consider Partington's point that the PCA was unsympathetic towards the problems of claimants. In a recent annual report, Sir Cecil Clothier recorded the receipt of a number of complaints of the conduct of departmental fraud investigators. He did not seem to take the complaints too seriously.[15] Remember that accusations of a criminal offence are being made and compare the earlier SBC reports on cohabitation.

In three [cases] it was alleged by the complainants that they had been threatened, frightened or otherwise ill-treated during interviews with the members of the regional special claims control teams which had been set up by the department in response to increased concern about abuse of the social security scheme. But although I found in each case that matters had in some minor respects been mishandled and that individual fraud and special claims control staff had on occasion acted hastily or without giving the claimant as full an explanation of what they were doing as he was entitled to expect, I did not in any instance uphold the main complaint.

I can understand that a claimant may find it alarming when it is suggested that his claim is in some way irregular and when it is pointed out that to make a false statement claiming benefit is a criminal offence for which he may be punished. But in my view the department have a clear duty to investigate any suggestion that a person has, by deception, obtained more from public funds than was his proper due and in none of the cases I have investigated where there has been such a suggestion have I found reason to criticise the department's methods of discharging their duty in this respect. [HC 257 (1982/3), p. 11.]

Subsequently, the Minister (Mr Rossi) ordered an internal inquiry after which the procedures of the Specialist Claims Control unit were regulated by an internal circular (FIG 21) that outlawed the more questionable practices of fraud investigators, reminding them of the legal constraints of 'Judges rules'.

Towards the end of their life, the SBC tried to establish an 'interest-representation' function, asking the Government whether 'the Commission might, for example, report regularly on the needs of the poorest people in the country, on the services that might be specifically designed for them, and on the policies in this field' (Cmnd 7382, p. 3). This suggests a role more nearly akin to that of a political adviser, though one provided with extensive research facilities and access to the system. Whether the SBC could have performed this function adequately[16] we shall never know, because in the end its indeterminate status proved unacceptable to the Government which thought that 'issues or policy should be decided by Ministers and Parliament, rather than a non-elected body such as the Supplementary Benefits Commission' (Cmnd 7773, p. 2). Perhaps this development could be linked with the vogue for quangocide.

Ss. 6(2) and 9 of the Social Security Act 1980 abolished the SBC and replaced it by the Social Security Advisory Committee (SSAC). This is a more traditional institution, reminiscent in its composition of the Council on Tribunals. It is a part-time body consisting of a chairman and 12 members appointed by the Minister. The first Chairman (Sir Arthur Armitage) is again an academic, though without experience in the field of social administration. It has no executive responsibilities and no access to the system. Its functions are to give 'advice and assistance' to the Minister in connection with the discharge of his functions. The Minister may refer matters to it or assign to it other duties and it must normally be consulted on the content of new legislation or regulations. The SSAC is not necessarily uncritical of government policy; for example, it has called the SB rates inadequate and asked for them to be increased. Recently it has severely criticized impending cuts in housing benefit. But it remains to be seen whether the SSAC, whose remit covers the whole area of *social security*, possesses the expertise to make effective policy proposals or the will to articulate vigorously the interests of the poor.[17] Prosser (1983, p. 67) fears that the inadequacy of the secretariat will prevent the SSAC from exercising a 'truly critical role'. The work will have to be done by the organizations who are regularly consulted by the SSAC before its recommendations are made.

If the SBC seems in retrospect to have been relatively effective, we should not overrate its achievements. In the last report, it sees its advantages as institutional. Its semi-autonomous status allowed it to:

(a) have direct access to Ministers; (b) initiate enquiries as well as respond to Ministers' questions; (c) make independent reports after consulting Ministers; (d) have easy working relations with officials and ready access to all levels of the system; (e) have a Chairman devoting most of his time to the job; (f) have some staff who work mainly with us; (g) prompt and influence research through the normal DHSS mechanisms; and (h) have the help of a policy inspectorate carrying out research directly for us. [Cmnd 8033, para 7.6.]

We have to remember, however, that all the advances were made during Donnison's period of 'consensus' when the Ministers concerned were broadly sympathetic to the reforms and to the SBC's working methods. Administrative lawyers, always inclined to place too high a value on procedures and processes, might deduce that this position could be institutionalized by a statutory regime. An unsympathetic government could quickly neutralize such an institution. It could ignore unfavourable reports (compare the experience of the Council on Tribunals). It could use its powers of patronage to create a body whose advice would be more congenial. No political or administrative system is static. Personal and political factors should never be underrated.

3 Participation through pressure groups

The claim of the SBC to represent the interests of the poor would certainly be disputed by 'the poverty lobby'. Equally, the claims of the poverty lobby may be treated with scepticism by officials. One research team was told by an official, 'We are not happy that the one-parent groups are speaking for their clients. The membership is more likely to contain middle class vocal lone parents not the working class'. Another official thought that 'there is no really representative group in the social security field. CPAG doesn't really talk for anyone – the Claimants Union are probably the least representative of all' (Whiteley and Winyard 1983, p. 19).

In Chapter 4 we met Prosser's argument that the poor lacked political clout; the question is how to supply it. One answer is to appoint an administrative agency – the CRE or SBC – to act as spokesman. Another is to provide funds for more autonomous bodies like UKIAS or the CAB to represent individuals and to sponsor political campaigns. Many would argue that such a course is paternalistic and that welfare claimants must band together in groups like the Claimants Union to provide their own non-professional tribunal representation and to speak for 'the poor'. In recent years, efforts have also been made to 'raise the consciousness of the poor' and to work through existing community associations or political groups.[18] The CDP describes one of the more successful campaigns:

Several projects have helped, or have attempted, to establish claimants unions. But faced with the powerful individualising and demoralising effects of the social security system, have found that such groups have run into difficulties in sustaining their activities and have never involved more than a small minority of claimants. Where projects have given support to organis-ations with wider interests, they have met with more success ... It is significant too, that the more successful 'take-up' campaigns have been those which took advantage of an existing network of community organis-ations.

The greater the change sought, however, the bigger and stronger the organisation needed to bring this about. Here is another example of a campaign built out of frustration with traditional 'welfare rights' approaches. In May 1975, a group of community workers and tenants' representatives set up the Campaign Against High Heating Costs in Newcastle. Heating costs were rising far faster than supplementary benefit rates, people's debts were increasing, and for many the only resort was not to use essential fuel for heating and cooking. Information workers had of course encouraged people to claim extra payments from the DHSS or seek assistance from the Social Services Department, but with little success. The situation was made worse by the power given to the Gas and Electricity Boards to disconnect the supplies of debtors rather than pursuing the normal remedy of taking civil action in the county court. The CAHHC has held a number of public meetings to organise support for a ten-point charter. Tenants' groups, environmental groups, unions involved in power supply, social work agencies were also contacted and in October 1975 the campaign affiliated, to the national 'Right to Fuel Campaign'. A big public meeting was held in February, laying the basis for a united campaign, undertaken with support from local MPs and Newcastle Trades Council. Publicity reached its peak in April when a local Fuel Action Week was held.

As a result of this and other action throughout the country, the government was obliged to at least look at the problem. A new code of practice has been produced by the Department of Energy which makes some concessions. One major significance of the campaign was how it managed to involve active trade unionists. An issue which had initially been a simple income maintenance problem of claiming an additional heating allowance had been developed to encompass the broader issues of fuel policy. Trade unionists working in the industry were equally concerned about the effects of a fuel policy over which they had no control. Similarly other union branches and trades councils were able to see the significance of the campaign to their own and their members' interests and fully supported it. [Community Development Project 1977, pp. 40–1.]

The claim of pressure groups does not necessarily rest on their representative character. Pressure groups work for, as well as with, the poor. It is easier for administrators to consult and collaborate with an identifiable organization (though this may be a danger) and it is easier for the public to participate through pressure groups. Outstanding in the field of income maintenance pressure groups is CPAG. Whiteley and Winyard (1983, p. 4) were told by a senior civil servant that its sustained opposition to means-tested benefits in the 1970s 'created a climate in which "it was no longer respectable within the department to propose a new means tested benefit" '. The same authors found that CPAG was rated both by official and unofficial groups as highly effective and admired for its professional expertise. A later study reaches the opposite conclusion, believing that CPAG's efforts have been largely ineffectual and relating its 'lack of sustained influence' directly to its unrepresentative nature. CPAG's goals are not widely supported by the poor:

Indeed, the incidence of 'scrounger-phobia' [and] the electoral backlash feared by Labour ministers in the 1960s if more aid was given to claimants . . . suggest that the public at large do not share CPAG's views or support its stand. In this sense the civil servant has perhaps been able to claim a wider mandate than the group and his concern to achieve the 'national' interest may, accordingly, be more defensible than the apparently sectorial demands of CPAG. [McCarthy 1983, p. 220.]

As we have seen already, the legal process may be used as part of a political campaign. In the late 1960s, English welfare lawyers, influenced by the work of the American Civil Rights movement, turned to test-case strategy. Their experience has been described by Hodge and Prosser who concluded that welfare test-cases failed largely on two counts: (a) judges were not anxious to operate in any area which they regarded as 'discretionary' and 'involving trivial issues' and (b) the administrative reaction to test-case strategy was unexpected (though Hodge admits that perhaps it should have been anticipated). Reread pp. 269–74 before reading the materials which follow.

Who won what? Test-case strategy examined[19]

Example 1. In *R.* v. *Greater Birmingham Appeal Tribunal ex p. Simper* [1973] 2 WLR 709, S was in receipt of SB at the long-term rate, including an ECA of 35p for heating in terms of para. 4 of Sched. 2 of the 1966 Act which provided that 'in determining whether to award benefit in accordance with para (1)(a) of this para (a) regard shall be had to the provisions made by this schedule for additional requirements . . .' After two years, she became entitled to an extra 50p for additional requirements under para. 12. The benefit officer, acting on the authority of an SBC directive, offset the ECA, paying only 15p extra. This decision was confirmed by the SBAT. S applied successfully for an order of certiorari.

CUSACK J: [Counsel] has argued that what is happening is that in interpreting para 4(2)(a) the commission, affirmed by the tribunal, has laid down a hard and fast rule meaning that where two sums are involved, one under para 4 and one under para 12, there must always be a deduction. His submission is that that is not the correct interpretation of para 4(2)(a) which leaves the matter . . . at discretion. He says that the provisions of para 4(2)(a) are intended to avoid duplication . . . but that that does not mean that there must always in every case, without the exercise of any discretion, be an arithmetical deduction of the one sum from the other, as has occurred in this case.

[Counsel] on behalf of the Ministry . . . has suggested that the correct interpretation is that para 4(2)(a) is mandatory, not simply in the sense that the commission must pay attention to it but in the sense that a deduction must be made . . .

My interpretation of these regulations is that para 4(2)(a) means that a discretion is to be exercised; that is to say, it is intended that the person making a determination of the sum of money due should exercise a broad judgment to ensure that in fact there is no overlapping, but that he ought not to proceed simply on a rule of thumb that exact deductions should be made.

After the *Simper* decision, Lewis complained that it was being disobeyed by the SBC and ignored by SBATs:

There is a postscript to the *Simper* judgment which exposes the fallacy in the argument that the rejection of legal involvement is the retention of individualised justice. The offending action taken by the Commission in that case was the deduction of a weekly heating allowance from the standard long-term addition. After the judgment the Chairman of the SBC wrote to the Heating Action Group thus:

This deduction will now be made under our discretionary powers rather than as a matter of statutory obligation as hitherto.

It is difficult for a lawyer to resist the conclusion that such flagrant abuse of power by a body wielding such influence can only be restrained by a more realistic injection of legal technique into the decision-making process, particularly when, at the time of writing, ten out of eleven appeals conducted by the CPAG since the judgment have upheld the Commission's decision to deduct. [Lewis 1973, p. 277.]

Do you agree that the SBC letter contravenes the *Simper* judgment? Are the SBAT appeals to which Lewis refers necessarily wrongly decided? Prosser (1983, p. 62) thought: 'a legislative response to change the law would in principle be justified, for . . . it seems clear that the intention behind the legislation in question had been that such an automatic deduction would be made. Moreover, individual justice in the way implied by the decision would have been administratively impracticable.'

Shortly afterwards the PCA received the following complaint (HC 49 (1974/5), p. 85) about the presentation of a case by the DHSS to a SBAT. The PCA was precluded from investigating the decision itself but had this to say about the administrative actions concerned:

In her complaint to me the complainant contends [inter alia] that officials are disobeying 'case law' by offsetting 50p of a long-term addition to her weekly grant against her special needs, although it was announced in a BBC broadcast that this would cease after 1 October 1973, in accordance with a ruling of the High Court. The Department tell me that, before 1 October 1973, supplementary benefit payments included, for pensioners and for certain long-term recipients, a standard addition to their normal requirements, known as the 'long-term addition'. Up to age 80 this addition amounted to 60p of which 50p was intended as automatic provision for special expenses not included in the normal scale requirements. Where a claimant had special expenses that exceeded 50p a further addition was made. There was thus in these cases an offset of 50p against the sum total of any special expenses . . . The effect of [the High Court] ruling was that offsetting the long-term addition against special expenses was held not to be mandatory – as the Department had previously assumed – but a matter of discretion; the offset could be made in full, in part, or not at all. The Department tell me that the policy of the Supplementary Benefits Commission was reviewed in the light of this ruling but it was decided, having regard to the purpose for which the long-term addition was intended, not to change their off-setting practice.

From 1 October 1973 the National Insurance and Supplementary Benefit Act introduced, in place of the former long-term addition, new long-term scale rates which included a margin of 50p for special expenses, and made off-setting of this margin mandatory in all but three types of special expenses.

In the complainant's case only one of her special expenses is not subject to off-setting, namely her extra heating expense. The Department's papers show that an addition on this account of 6op a week is allowed in full in the calculation of her requirements for supplementary benefit. The off-setting element of 5op has been applied to her three remaining special expenses (paragraph 4) which total £1.27 a week, leaving a net addition for these items of 77p to her weekly requirements.

I conclude that the Department have not acted in disobedience of case law in deciding the amount to be allowed for special expenses in the complainant's case.

Offsetting is now dealt with by Reg. 13(5) of the Supplementary Benefits (Requirements) Regulations (SI No. 1299/80), which provides:

Subject to paragraph (6), where a long-term rate for normal requirements is applicable to the claimant under regulation 7, amounts shall only be applicable to him under Part II of Schedule 3, other than paragraphs 8 and 11, to the extent that in aggregate they would, but for this paragraph, exceed 5op.

The Handbook (7th edn 1981) gave the following translation of the legal provisions (in the 1982 edn the paragraph is reworded):

Where the long-term rates are payable
5.3 [Additional requirements] can be awarded only to the extent that they exceed the margin of 5op included in the long-term scale rates for extra expenses. (This margin is called the 'Available Scale Margin' or ASM). There are, however, exceptions to this rule. The ASM is not taken into account when awarding:
   1. age additions for the over 80s
   2. additions for blindness
   3. additions for extra heating or central heating
   4. any addition for a dependent child for his special diet, his attendance expenses, his extra baths, heavy wear and tear of his clothing, or his expenses in visiting a patient in hospital.

5.4 The method of calculating an AR where the long-term scale rates are payable is therefore as follows: the special expenses of the beneficiary, his partner, and his dependants – apart from the exceptions mentioned in paragraph 5.3 – are added up and the ASM is deducted. The remainder, plus any special expenses payable in respect of the exceptions, form the AR. When someone getting a supplementary allowance qualifies for the long-term scale rate, the margin of 5op for extra expenses replaces up to 5op of any AR he *may have (apart from the exceptions referred to in paragraph 5.3)*.

Example 2. In *R.* v. *Preston SBAT ex p. Moore and Shine* [1965] 1 WLR 624, M was a married student with two children. He claimed benefit in the summer vacation at the end of his course on the ground that his grant was spent. The SBC refused, arguing that the grant must be allocated over one year, and M therefore possessed 'notional resources'. S who shared a flat with fellow students each contributing equally to expenses, claimed to be treated as a 'householder . . . directly responsible for household necessities and rent'. M and S applied for certiorari to quash the decisions of the SBAT for error of law on the face of the record. The orders were refused by the Divisional Court and their appeals dismissed by the Court of Appeal.

LORD DENNING MR: If this were to be regarded as a strict point of law, there is much to be said for Mr. Shine's contention. Under the Interpretation Act 1889, singular includes plural. So 'householder who is' includes 'householders who are'. And these four students, being *jointly* responsible for household necessities and rent, are all four householders. It makes no difference in law that gas and electricity bills were sent in the name of one of them only. That was a mere matter of convenience which did not affect the responsibility of all four of them.

This seems to me a good instance where the High Court should not interfere with the tribunal's decision, even though it may be said to be erroneous in point of law. It cannot be supposed that each one of these four should each have the full allowance as if he was responsible for the whole. Nor even that one of them . . . should have the full allowance. The better way of administering the Act is to hold that none of the four gets the allowance as being the householder: but that each should be regarded as a lodger contributing towards a householder's commitments. Each should get an allowance in respect of his contribution to the rent: . . . and each may be granted a special addition under paragraph 4(1)(a) to take account of the exceptional circumstances. That is what the tribunal allowed to Mr. Shine. It was a reasonable way of administering the Act on a point which was not covered by the Schedule.

Principles on which the Court should interfere

It is plain that Parliament intended that the Supplementary Benefit Act 1966 should be administered with as little technicality as possible. It should not become the happy hunting ground for lawyers. The courts should hesitate long before interfering by certiorari with the decisions of the appeal tribunals. Otherwise the courts would become engulfed with streams of cases just as they did under the old Workmen's Compensation Acts . . .

The courts should not enter into a meticulous discussion of the meaning of this or that word in the Act. They should leave the tribunals to interpret the Act in a broad reasonable way, according to the spirit and not to the letter: especially as Parliament has given them a way of alleviating any hardship. The courts should only interfere when the decision of the tribunal is unreasonable in the sense that no tribunal acquainted with the ordinary use of language could reasonably reach that decision . . . Nevertheless, it must be realised that the Act has to be applied daily by thousands of officers of the commission: and by 120 appeal tribunals. It is most important that cases raising the same points should be decided in the same way. There should be uniformity of decision. Otherwise grievances are bound to arise. In order to ensure this, the courts should be ready to consider points of law of general application. Take these two cases. In Moore's case, [counsel] raised an important point on the meaning of the word 'resources'. Did it mean actual resources, or notional resources? It applied to all students seeking educational grants. It was very right for the High Court to give a ruling upon it. In Shine's case, [counsel] raised an important point on the meaning of 'householder' when there were two or more joint tenants. It applied to all students sharing a flat when all were directly responsible for expenses. Were all entitled to the householder's allowance? Or only one? Or none? It is very desirable for this point to be authoritatively decided. So we have decided it. But so far as Mr. Shine's £50 grant is concerned, that is of small importance, though of general application. So the High Court should not be troubled with it.

The Court of Appeal did decide that resources meant 'notional' resources. Did it decide the meaning of 'householder' or did it decide that the SBC was not bound by the strict meaning of the law? Can an interpretation of statute be 'broadly reasonable' or must it be correct? Compare Lord Denning's decision in *Pearlman*'s case (see above, Chapter 4). Are the decisions compatible? Henry Hodge, who acted in this case, explains his objectives and describes CPAG's disappointment at the result:

An attempt was made by CPAG in that case to educate the Court of Appeal as to the general position of supplementary benefit claimants, their numbers and the way the Appeal Tribunal system worked. Counsel attempted to show the court how the supplementary benefit system exists only on the fringes of the ordinary legal system. The court was not interested . . . An attempt was made to take the case to the House of Lords but they refused to intervene saying that no general principle was involved. It was difficult to avoid the conclusion that despite knowing the problems faced by people on supplementary benefit and the inadequacies of the tribunal system, Lord Denning and his colleagues in the Court of Appeal were not interested in assisting. The further more general conclusion was that the courts were not interested in the legal rights of the poor. [Hodge 1979, p. 247.]

Regulation 5(2) of the Supplementary Benefit (Requirements) Regulations (SI No. 1299/80) provides a new definition. Would Shine be a 'householder' today?

. . . a householder is person, *other than a partner*, who –
(a) under Part IV of these regulations (housing requirements) is treated as responsible for expenditure on items to which any of those regulations other than regulation 23 (non-householder's contribution) relates or, if the household incurs no such expenditure, is the member of the household *with major control over household expenditure*;
(b) does not share such responsibility or control with another member of the same household; and

(c) is either not absent from the home or whose absence is for a period which has not yet continued for more than 13 weeks.

Example 3. In *R.* v. *Barnsley SBAT ex p. Atkinson* [1977] 3 All ER 1031, A was a student in receipt of minimum education grant of £50. He applied for SB in the summer vacation. The SBC treated as 'notional resources' a proportion of the parental contribution to his grant which was not in fact made. The same ruling was applied to all students as a 'class'. They deducted a further figure of £1 under para 4(1) of Schedule 2 of the 1966 Act which provided: 'Where there are exceptional circumstances . . . (b) a supplementary allowance may be reduced below the amount so calculated or may be withheld; as may be appropriate to take account of those circumstances.' CPAG advised that the case would not succeed but A applied in person for certiorari. The order was withheld by the Divisional Court but granted by the Court of Appeal.

BRIDGE LJ: The real question which falls for decision on this part of the case . . . is whether voluntary payments can properly be treated as resources at all for the purpose of Schedule 2 of the Act. The answer to that question in the handbook to which we have referred is in the affirmative. It is said in paragraph 27:

> . . . The Commission under their discretionary powers normally ignore payments made by relatives, friends, or charities for, and provision in kind of, items regarded as not covered by supplementary benefit . . . but regular and substantial provision in kind is normally taken into account.

The applicant submits that this is wrong and that no payment received by a claimant in cash or kind to which he is not entitled as of right ought to be treated as part of his resources. There is no definition of 'resources' in the Act. Giving the word its ordinary English meaning, we think that it is clearly proper to treat a regular cash allowance from a parent to a student or the regular provision for him of maintenance in the family home during vacations as part of the resources of that student.

The question then arises how the amount of a student's resources of this character is to be calculated. Clearly it would be impracticable for the commission, who have thousands of such claims to consider, to investigate the circumstances in detail in each case. They must at least be entitled to adopt some reasonable rule of thumb as a prima facie guide to the assessment. On that basis it is difficult to think of a better practical rule than one starting from a presumption that a parent whose income is sufficiently large to reduce his student son's or daughter's local authority grant below the maximum will be at least sufficiently generous to make up the difference. This must, we think, have been the basis on which the commission, in the first place, determined a notional attribution to the applicant of a yearly resource of £58 available for his maintenance in the vacations. The applicant submits, however, that when the matter came before the tribunal, this basis of calculation was not treated as giving rise to a mere presumption as to his resources, but as an inflexible rule to be applied regardless of the actual amount of any allowance or other provision for his maintenance made by his parents. If this was indeed the approach of the commission or the tribunal, then we think it was wrong. It should, in our judgment, be open to a student claimant to satisfy the commission or the tribunal, if he can, that his parents, for some reason, either cannot or will not make up his local authority grant to the level of a full grant. We recognise that the onus of establishing such a claim would be a heavy one, and that the commission or the tribunal would be fully justified in examining any such claim with suspicion. But that is not to say that it can be dismissed out of hand . . .

We would, however, go further and base our rejection of the commission's special treatment of students on a wider ground. It cannot be right, in our judgment, for the commission, or the tribunal on appeal, to invoke the discretion under paragraph 4(1)(b) to justify discrimination against a whole class of persons. We use the word 'class' in this context, not in the narrow social sense, but as equivalent to 'category'. The trend of contemporary legislation, and indeed of generally accepted contemporary social attitudes, is firmly opposed to such discrimination. Wide as the phrase 'exceptional circumstances' may be, it must, in our judgment, have been used here in reference to the particular circumstances of individual cases. For these reasons we think that the commission and the tribunal, if they deducted £1 from the claimant's weekly benefit on the ground that the fact of his being a student was an 'exceptional circumstance' acted on an erroneous principle which justifies the intervention of the court.

This case applies a general principle of administrative law to the welfare area. What is the principle and in which leading case can you find it?

A full account of the aftermath of this case is given by Prosser (1983, pp. 63–5). Immediately after the decision, clauses were inserted into a bill, conveniently before Parliament, which ultimately became ss. 14 and 15 of the Supplementary Benefits (Miscellaneous Provisions) Act 1977. This legislation (a) removed the narrow effect of the decision, by permitting the Minister to make regulations to modify the parent Act by treating 'notional' parental contributions as 'resources'; the SB (Students) Regulations 1977 effected this change; (b) allowed the SBC to deal with cases on a class basis by defining as exceptional a case which 'falls within a class of case the circumstances of which are exceptional'; and (c) saved 'any decision substituted or to be substituted for a decision quashed by an order of a court made before March 4 1977'. What was (c) intended to achieve and why? (See above, pp. 380–2).

Reg. 4(4) of the Supplementary Benefit (Resources) Regulation S I No. 1527/81 now provides:

Notwithstanding that it is not actually made, a student shall be treated as possessing any contribution in respect of the income of any other person which a Minister of the Crown or an education authority takes into account in assessing the amount of the student's grant or award unless the student is:
(a) a single parent;
(b) a partner; or
(c) a disabled student.

Apply this regulation to the facts of *Atkinson*'s case.

Example 4. S.1(3) of the Supplementary Benefits Act 1976 excludes from the ambit of the scheme 'medical, surgical, optical, aural and dental requirements'. In *R. v. Peterborough SBAT ex p. SBC* [1978] 3 All ER 887, the Divisional Court held that the SBC could not avail itself of its discretionary power to make an ENP, to cover treatment given by an osteopath. Osteopathy is not available through the National Health Service. But in *R. v. W. London SBAT ex p. Wyatt* [1978] 1 WLR 240, W and his wife were disabled. The local authority and DHSS provided electrically operated equipment for their use, but refused to meet the running costs. The SBC refused an application for an ECA on the ground that s.1(3) of the 1976 Act excluded payments for 'medical' requirements. The decision was upheld by the SBAT. W applied successfully for certiorari.

MAY J: In my view, without considering each particular piece of equipment separately, the purpose for which it is used, and it may well be by whom it was originally supplied, it cannot be said that the running costs of these special aids must all come within the phrase 'medical requirements' in section 1(3) of the Supplementary Benefits Act 1976. Some may; some may not. But I think that it was wrong for the tribunal to refuse to take into account the running costs of these special aids on the basis that in any event and on any view these must fall within the provisions of section 1(3). Thus, in my judgment, on the face of the tribunal's decision alone this application must succeed.

I would add this. As has been said in argument, supplementary benefit is the ultimate source of financial assistance which, subject to the provisions of the Act, is available to the ordinary citizen who may need it. For instance, for medical purposes it is available, if at all, only after recourse has been had to the National Health Service . . . It is available, if at all, only after the provisions of the relevant equipment itself under other legislation which applies to the local authorities. But if and to the extent that in circumstances such as the present these electrical running costs cannot be obtained from any other authority, I think it only right that one should seek to construe the Supplementary Benefits Act 1976 if one can in such a way that these costs are within its scope either as a 'requirement' not excluded under section 1(3), or, alternatively, under paragraph 4 of Schedule 1 to the Act of 1976.

In so far as this last statutory provision is concerned, our attention was drawn to . . . the *Peterborough* case [where] the court had to consider sections 6 and 7 of the earlier Act of 1966, which have now effectively become sections 1(3) and 3 of the Act of 1976. Section 3 permits the commission to make a lump sum payment rather than weekly payments in exceptional circumstances, and, as Michael Davies J. held on section 7 of the earlier Act in the *Peterborough* case, in considering whether or not to make such a lump sum payment rather than a weekly one, which is the normal basis of operating the supplementary benefits scheme, I think that the 'requirements' referred to in section 1(3) are to be disregarded.

But the *Peterborough* decision did not deal with, and in my judgment ought not to be treated as applying to, paragraph 4 of Schedule 1 to the Supplementary Benefits Act 1976. I think that that provides the Supplementary Benefits Commission with the ultimate discretion to make exceptional payments if it considers it appropriate, and that when they are considering whether or not to do so they are not restricted by the provisions of section 1(3) of the Act of 1976.

To resolve the apparent conflict between these decisions, the SBC might have appealed. Instead it issued a circular to benefit officers and tribunal chairmen:

The Commission have considered how their policy should be adjusted . . . in the light of the recent judgment, i.e. how they should exercise the discretion which, under that judgment, they have to make ECAs for medical, surgical, optical, aural or dental requirements. They accept that their primary role is income maintenance, and that they are an agency of last resort. But they do not accept that anything which costs claimants money is the concern exclusively of the Commission, or that wherever another potential source of help has failed to provide it, the Commission should necessarily help. The Commission's views are as follows:

(a) First, the Commission would not wish to exercise their discretion so as to make available to their claimants private medical treatment or facilities when there is a free, comprehensive NHS available to the population as a whole. The Commission consider that to make private treatment and facilities available in this way would be to discriminate unreasonably in favour of their claimants and would be a misuse of public funds.

(b) Secondly, although the Commission accept fully the special importance of health services they do not see charges made for, or costs arising from, services provided by other agencies in connection with a person's health as any different in principle from charges and costs in connection with services provided by local authority social services, housing and education departments . . . Thus the expectation should be that the Commission will not normally use their discretionary powers to shield claimants from costs, arising out of the provision of another agency's services, which other people on low incomes have to tolerate . . .

[The Commission consider that] (a) An ECA should not be awarded where the cost is for private medical treatment; (b) An ECA should not be awarded where the cost is a charge imposed by another authority having power to waive that charge or is an expense which could be met by another authority under its own powers.

Partington (1979, p. 5) argued that the letter of the law was not broken because the instructions do not actually 'defy the clear words of the judgment'. (Do you agree?) But he questioned 'whether this kind of internal statement about new principles for the exercise of a discretion is a proper method for making such a policy known' concluding that it was 'a matter of regret, at least, that more publicity was not given to the statement'. On the other hand, circulation of the internal administrative document to tribunal chairmen was improper:

Given that there was considerable dissatisfaction amongst officials about the *Wyatt* decision, and that the internal statement ... was available, the temptation to circulate this document together with the judgment obviously proved overwhelming. This attempt to influence tribunal chairmen would seem to contravene both the principle of the rule of law and the concept of the independence of tribunals. [Partington 1979, p. 6.]

Relate to May J's remarks a CLA investigation, *Westminster* (Inv. 446S of 17/3/82), in which Baroness Serota found the Council guilty of maladministration causing injustice because an officer placed Mr A (the complainant) in accommodation costing £49 a week and led him to believe that the difference between that and his benefit income of £47.10 a week would be made good by the DHSS. The DHSS did not in fact increase his benefit. The applicant was legally entitled to 'advice and appropriate assistance' under the Housing (Homeless Persons) Act 1977. The Commissioner felt that the Council's Homeless Persons Unit should have behaved more sensibly and expressed the hope

that they will seek to improve the liaison arrangements between the HPU and the DHSS offices in the Council's area so that clearer and firmer advice and assistance can in future be given to those who find themselves in Mr A's position.

Para. 1(d) of Sched. 2 of the Social Security Act 1980 amended s.1(3) of the SB Act 1976 by adding to the end of subsection (3) the words: 'and regulations may provide that the requirements which by virtue of this subsection are not included in a person's requirements include or exclude prescribed requirements'. However, neither the SB (Single Payments) Regulations, No. 985/80, nor the SB (Requirements) Regulations (above) dealt specifically with the point. In R(SB)52/83, a Tribunal of three Social Security Commissioners was specially convened to consider the impact of the new legislation on medical requirements. Two applications for single payments for an orthopaedic mattress and repairs to a hearing aid were concerned. The DHSS argued that these were 'medical requirements' barred by s.1(3). The Tribunal held that s.1(3) barred allowances for 'requirements', but not single payments. The case-law (above) was distinguishable. It did not deal with the 1980 scheme and the Commissioners now exercised a co-ordinate jurisdiction to that of the High Court before 1980. So High Court precedents were persuasive, not binding. But the SBATs to whom the cases were remitted were firmly reminded of the 'stringent requirements' of reg. 30 and of 'need' (reg. 3). Within a week SI No. 1630/83 had been laid before Parliament without reference to the SSAC and come into force. Reg. 6(2) of the Single Payments Regulations (now No. 1528/81) was amended to exclude any 'medical, surgical, optical, aural or dental need'. A prayer to annul failed.

The results of 'test-case strategy' in SB clearly did not justify the time and resources expended by the promoters. Indeed, the end-product may be no more satisfactory to the individual than that produced by the thousands of letters which arrive each year in the postbags of the DHSS or of sympathetic MPs. Nor did the attempt at 'administration by adjudication' secure a long-term influence on policy. High court rulings could be ignored by tribunals or nullified by unpublicized instructions. Here was a further argument for incorporating policies into binding rules which could be attacked directly by those working for reform.

Some successful interest groups concentrate their efforts on working quietly as 'insiders' to develop 'a sweetheart relationship with the government'. Others concentrate their attention on the political process. They actively lobby MPs and work to stimulate public opinion. Their propaganda campaigns can be influential. In Chapter 12, for example, we saw that the campaign for vaccine damage payments centred on Parliament. Others, like JCWI, divide their efforts between representation and more general political campaigning. CPAG never regarded test-case strategy as more than a small part of its work. For example, Mr Ennals, Labour's Minister for Social Services, regarded CPAG's propaganda campaign as a factor in the defeat of the Wilson government in 1970. He also describes how such campaigns may be used by Ministers for their own purposes, e.g. to suggest to Cabinet colleagues that wide public support exists for a policy which is being pushed.[20]

More important, perhaps, pressure groups provide services which enable private members to play a full part in the law-making process. When you read extracts from the Committee stage of the Health and Social Services and Social Security Adjudication Bill in Chapter 19, you will see how important this is. Opposition and private members have to be well briefed on the implications of complex legislative provisions sometimes deliberately shrouded in impenetrable, technical language. The demise of the SBC removed a partly independent body which could provide the facts and figures necessary to contest the proposals of government departments. Its place is, to a certain extent, filled by the CPAG, which has contributed a steady stream of well-researched pamphlets to the literature of poverty; and by other bodies. Backbench members can be, and some are, very well briefed on the subject of welfare benefits. Yet even then Prosser (above) feels that the lobbying effort taking place on behalf of the poor is far less than that on behalf of other groups who may be affected by legislative change. With the death of the SBC the poor arguably lost a powerful friend at court.

19
Social assistance: dysfunctional rules?

1 The optimum point?

Advocates of rule-making to structure discretionary power maintain that discretion should never be entirely eliminated but that an optimum point exists on a scale between rules and discretion. The test of an efficient administrative process becomes whether this balance has been achieved.

In the old scheme, we met *agency discretion* to make policy and give instructions how the powers were to be exercised; and *officer discretion* in the application of the policies. The second term can be confusing. Bull (1980, p. 67) identified three separate types of officer activity: 'interpreting rigid rules, taking decisions in areas where it is deemed inappropriate to have such rules, and using their freedom to depart, in exceptional circumstances, from these rules.' We are familiar with these types of discretion. The first we have elsewhere called judgement and the third, selective enforcement, a terminology which, for convenience, we shall continue to use here. The new scheme does not banish 'discretion'. We shall find, however, that agency discretion has expanded its empire at the expense of officer discretion and that 'judgement' has largely replaced Bull's second type of officer discretion, which we shall call 'unstructured discretion'. It is this difference which leads those who, like Professor Titmuss, find legalism as great a threat as discretion, to argue that rule-based schemes are inflexible.

The three main uses for discretion in the old scheme were: (a) to award ECAs, (b) to make ENPs, and (c) to deal with urgent cases. The new scheme deals with each situation in like manner: first, statute provides that prescribed payments shall be made in pre-scribed circumstances; secondly, regulations are made which prescribe both circumstances and payments in exhaustive detail. The regulations are of different types. Some require only routine classification; others preserve marginal room for judgement; others again preserve discretionary power at officer and agency level. Much officer discretion is still imbedded in the rules. We find constant allusion to standards: 'necessary', 'essential', 'exceptional', or 'reasonable'. The familiar discretionary formula 'in the opinion of the benefit officer' also recurs throughout the rules. So benefit officers possess significant freedom of manoeuvre.

Because we made very similar points about the text of the Immigration Rules we shall not analyse the SB regulations in great detail.[1] Summarizing their many defects, we might say first that they are extraordinarily complex. It is easy for even an experienced welfare lawyer to miss relevant provisions. This point has been made by the senior chairman (below). When they have been unearthed, many regulations are difficult to interpret. Look, for example, at the SB (Resources) Regulations (SI No. 1527/81), which deal with the calculation of a claimant's income, notional income and capital resources. These raise complex questions of property, tax and matrimonial law suited to a Chancery judge rather than to benefit officers or lay tribunals. One such point was referred under the original regulations (SI No. 985/80) to a Social Security Commissioner (see below) on appeal. In R (SB) 7/81, the Commissioner, Mr Rice, expressed the view that the regulations were badly drafted and should be amended. They did not seem to cover the point of lump sums awarded by a court in lieu of maintenance. The amended regulations (above) are quite as difficult to construe. As we shall see, this has some bearing on the composition of tribunals. Equally, it suggests an increased need for legal aid and advice. A young wife, stranded in the matrimonial home with young children and no means of subsistence, needs a solicitor more than a social worker.

Secondly, the regulations display the worst characteristics of English statutory draftsmanship. What do we mean by 'openness'? Look back to p. 606. Is this opaque regulation 'open' in the sense that the claimant can discover his entitlement, or only in the sense that it is published? The distinction has consequences. To interpret the text, the claimant has to turn to the Handbook and the benefit officer to a departmental manual of practice issued by the Chief Supplementary Benefit officer (CSBO). Unlike the A-code which it replaces, the new S-code is published and is available to claimants. 'Guidance' on interpretation of regulations previously published by the CSBO is now incorporated in the S-code. There are, however, also unpublished, internal, instructions circulating to officers which deal with controversial topics: one example, the internal memorandum concerning fraud procedures, has already been mentioned. We can never be sure that published rules are more than the tip of the iceberg.

Thirdly, the regulations are often too specific; e.g. items for which a single payment can be awarded are listed and the precise sum payable may also be prescribed. If an item is inadvertently omitted or the sum payable needs to be raised, amending regulations must be made and laid before Parliament. Like the Forth Bridge, the regulations are constantly undergoing repair. Bradley argued (above) that this open process was democratic. Arguably, it represents a devaluation of the parliamentary process. If amending regulations are used for such trivial purposes, MPs may cease to take the procedure seriously. Important policy changes can then be slipped through unnoticed and might prove in practice as hard or even harder to challenge than a more flexible 'code of practice', which could be administratively amended by the department. One well-known example is that of a Commissioner's decision (R(S)7/78) which allowed invalid housewives to claim benefit where they were 'unable to perform normal household duties'. Three days after the decision, unfavourable to the SBC's interpretation, was made, it was nullified by amending regulations, laid while Parliament was in recess and not referred to the National Insurance Advisory Committee. The subterfuge failed to deceive MPs, who moved a prayer for annulment after the recess. The Government promised a review, but no policy change resulted. (Compare p. 614.)

Now let us follow the point that much officer discretion is still embedded in these rules which are less 'rigid' than Bull (above) implies. For example, Reg. 19 of the Single Payments Regulations (above) permits a single payment to be made 'in respect of expenses of essential internal redecoration to a claimant's home'. The officer discretion preserved here was interpreted by 'Guidance' to mean that 'the redecoration must be necessary to prevent insanitary conditions or deterioration of the internal structure, e.g. badly peeling or torn wallpaper may harbour germs or be followed by damage to plaster'.

A case reached the Social Security Commissioner in which an aged widow with restricted mobility claimed for wallpapering her kitchen on the ground that 'it hasn't been done for 5 years and needs it badly'.

A benefit officer reported that the paper was faded and rubbed but not dirty, torn or peeling. He refused a single payment and his decision was upheld by an SBAT. The Commissioner (Mr Edwards-Jones) ruled (Decision R(SB)10/81):

... it is clear that the ... officer regards 'essential' as [meaning 'indispens-ably requisite']. But I am as a matter of construction satisfied that this is too rigorous a meaning to accord it in the context of the Single Payments Regulations.

There are a number of other uses of the word 'essential' as a qualifying term elsewhere in the Single Payments Regulations which assist me in construing regulation 19, as I do, as using 'essential' to mean 'necessary' in the sense in which luxuries are differentiated from 'the necessaries of life' and as importing a requirement of substantial need, judged by the modest general standard of living to the provision of which the award of supplementary benefit is directed; but falling short of a requirement of being 'indispensable' if life is to be sustained ... or of so rigorous a test as is imposed by regulation 30 of the same regulations which enables discretionary payments to be made *outside* the range of specific needs catered for by the preceding regulations only if payment is 'the only means by which serious damage or serious risk to ... health or safety ... may be prevented ...'

[In] simple cases of the present nature a Tribunal must in my judgment be entitled to bring its own knowledge of life and people to bear in such respects as recognising that an elderly widow of impaired mobility, living on her own in modest circumstances, is likely to spend a great deal of her time in her kitchen and to become seriously depressed by increasing shabbiness and drabness of the decoration short of a state of degeneration in it dangerous to hygiene or physical health – although clearly the need must be much more substantial than a mere whim for a fresh colour scheme, and my decision in the present case imports no general principle warranting replacement of items which though still serviceable have become shabby ...

The Commissioner is urging a flexible, 'common sense' approach to the facts. The Guidance was later amended to take account of the judgment. Notice that it is drafted in terms of 'rules'. In your view, does the Guidance correctly interpret the Commissioner's decision?

The Commissioner has pointed out that the word 'essential' can have different interpretations in different circumstances. In the vast majority of situations the presence of faded paintwork and wallpaper worn around doorways and light switches is likely to have very little effect upon the occupants of the accommodation. When considering claims under regulation 19 in such circumstances, 'essential' should be interpreted as 'necessary to prevent insanitary conditions or deterioration of the internal structure'.

However, in the case of someone suffering from a condition such as severe depression, or of an elderly or seriously disabled person who is confined to the home or unable to leave it alone, the state of the internal decoration can have a very marked effect. In these circumstances a single payment should be considered where the poor state of the decoration is clearly causing the claimant concern.

Generally, the broad, flexible officer-discretion of the type favoured by Titmuss and Wilding has been, at least in theory, destroyed. Urgent cases are prescribed and single payments can be made only 'to a person who is entitled or would if he satisfied prescribed conditions be entitled to a supplementary pension or allowance'. The over-arching, fall-back power is supplied by Reg. 30 of the S B (Single Payments) Regulations which authorize a single payment where 'in the opinion of a benefit officer, such a payment is the only means by which serious damage or serious risk to the health or safety of any member of the assessment unit may be prevented'. Whether this regulation is discretionary in the broad sense used by Titmuss is dubious because, where the conditions are met, and only where they are met, the Regulation provides that a payment *shall* be made (compare para. 17 of the Immigration Rules, see above, p. 513). Clearly, however, it permits subjective officer-discretion which, in the interests of uniformity, has been structured by Guidance issued by the CSBO. That 'serious damage or risk' is to be restrictively interpreted is made clear by examples which range from that of elderly, frail adults without winter clothing to battered wives who have left home in their night clothes.

In practice, however, some tribunals have refused to accept this restrictive Guidance and use Reg. 30 in much the same way as ENPs were used under the old scheme, to allow people who had existed for a long time on the poverty line to add expensive items like winter coats to their wardrobe once in a while. Benefit officers have found themselves appealing in cases where Reg. 30 was used, for example, to award trousers to a claimant who already had one pair, or shoes to a claimant whose shoes leaked.[2] Although more generous than the Guidance, the Commissioners' decisions have not wandered too far in the direction of luxury. The Commissioner (Mr Watson) said in R(SB)5/81 (the case of the leaking shoes), 'Shoes that let in water seem to me to present an obvious risk to health. Damp is an insidious cause of ill-health.'

A different Commissioner (Mr Rice) disallowed the trousers, but set out the following guidelines in R(SB)6/81. Compare the extract with R(SB)10/81 and with the judgment in the *Moore* case (above, p. 607).

In approaching questions of the construction and scope of reg. 30, I bear in mind that it is clearly intended as a 'long-stop' discretionary provision, enabling a single payment to be made in cases of exceptional need which cannot otherwise be met and when the consequences of deprivation are likely to be serious. These considerations suggest that the regulation should be broadly, rather than over strictly, construed . . . The exercise by the benefit officer or Appeal Tribunal of the discretion to make a single payment under it would not be disturbed unless upon no reasonable view could the circumstances have enabled the discretion legitimately to be so exercised.

These claims concerned a single pair of shoes and trousers. Again, the regulations have been amended to allow for single payments for the purchase of an electric iron, inadvertently omitted from the text originally laid before Parliament. Think about Titmuss's defence of discretion. Would he approve this continual process of rule-making, appeal and rule-making or would he regard it as pathological legalism? The regulations are not quite what the claimant would have hoped for. They are too complex for him to calculate his entitlement easily. They create a need for skilled legal advice which may not be met. The technicality of the language creates uncertainty, increasing the scope for judgment and with it the chance of appeal. From the departmental viewpoint, such appeals waste time and resources. And rules, like discretion, can be turned to the purpose of social control. Throughout the Acts and Regulations, for example, changes have been made which diminish the assistance available to strikers and their dependants. Partington (1980), describing the changes, made two points. First, the changes were deliberate governmental policy, designed at one and the same time to peg the levels of expenditure on SB while also removing the disincentive for strikers to return to work. This he saw as politically controversial because social security law is being used to further external objectives. Arguably:

. . . the social security system should remain broadly neutral in its effect [and] should provide assistance for those who are in need without inquiry as to the causes of that need . . . It should not be used by the state to support employers by, in effect, driving back to work employees who have a legitimate grievance against their employers. On the other side, it is argued that it is not a proper use of public finance to fund industrial disputes. [Partington 1980b, p. 243.]

Secondly, although some of the changes were well publicized and debated by Parliament, others were less well publicized because they were contained in regulations. For example, would MPs necessarily notice that members of an 'assessment unit' lose their entitlement to heating allowances where any member of the unit is on strike (Reg. 12(2)(a) of the Requirements Regulations)? Again, Reg. 6(1) of the

SB Single Payments Regulations provides:

Notwithstanding anything in these regulations, in particular regulation 30 . . .
(b) no single payment shall be made where any member of the assessment unit is a person whose requirements fall to be disregarded to any extent by virtue of section 8 of the Act (persons affected by trade disputes).

The overarching provision does not arch over the families of strikers, even where a serious risk to their health or safety is involved. Such punitive provisions could have proved extremely controversial if packaged together in statutory form. The changes represent conscious governmental policy decisions, and to this extent, they are democratic. But they are partly concealed behind formalistic legal language and 'legislation by reference'. This may be the reality of the democratic process, but it is hardly what Davis had in mind.

2 Judicializing the tribunals

Our study of adjudication showed that the two functions of administration and adjudication blend imperceptibly. Moreover, the reasons for placing a particular decision-taking process on one or the other side of the line are often complex. SBATs are the direct successors of National Assistance Tribunals (NATs), established under the National Assistance Act of 1948. These in turn are based on the tribunals which existed under the Unemployment Assistance Act 1934. The genesis of those tribunals has already been described (Prosser, p. 77 above).[3] Herman, an American sociologist who surveyed the work of SBATs in 1969 classified them as 'administrative'; their decisions were a natural extension of administration:

It was anticipated in the legislation creating the National Assistance Board in 1948 that no matter how well the assistance programme were to be administered, a machinery would be needed for those claimants who felt they had been treated unjustly to seek a different decision. Accordingly, that Act provided for the creation of tribunals with broad powers to hear and decide appeals . . . Similar tribunals had existed under the Unemployment Assistance Act of 1934 and it was entirely consistent with previous British administrative experience to rely upon tribunals to fulfil this function. Since 1911, with the extension of statutory rights in such fields as social security, health, housing, and planning, a need had been recognized to provide a suitable instrument to resolve disputes between individuals and public bodies responsible for the administration of these programmes. [Herman 1972, pp. 13–14.]

The role of the tribunal was relatively simple. It could be compared to a teacher listening to a prefect's complaint about a pupil; he is concerned with the facts but he is not likely to question the school rules. Similarly, tribunals were not necessarily independent of departmental policy. Perhaps surprisingly, the Franks Committee accepted this departmental view of NATs as a 'case committee' which would take a second look at decisions to see that the official got it right. They thought NATs operated satisfactorily (perhaps they meant that they received no grave complaints). They went on to decide that NATs were 'special' and excepted them from their requirement of openness; 'if any or all of these appeals were to be held in public many applicants might be deterred from appealing or even from applying for assistance and the purpose of the legislation might thus be frustrated' (Cmnd 218, para. 180).

There were other signs that Franks did not regard NATs as 'machinery for adjudication'. They did not create an appeal to the High Court on a point of law. They made no recommendations about legally qualified chairmen. Their only real concession was the admission that 'legal representation should be permitted to the applicant who can satisfy the chairman of the Tribunal that he cannot satisfactorily present his case unless he is allowed to employ a lawyer' (para. 183). You can see how these features might help to disguise dissatisfaction with tribunals. Claimants were not legally represented and were hardly likely to know of prerogative order procedure. Neither lawyers nor journalists were present to articulate dissatisfaction.

No major questions about function or structure were raised about SBATs during the passage of the 1966 legislation. And in 1971, in the first edition of the Handbook, Lord Collison, then Chairman of the SBC, wrote:

The Commission is grateful to all who act, in whatever capacity, as friendly counsellors to claimants and hope that this Handbook will make a major contribution, not only to removing misunderstanding where it exists, but also to intensifying and extending positive co-operation with anyone advising, representing or helping claimants ... The concept of co-operation, in the Commission's view, goes to the heart of a successful operation of the scheme.

Five years later, the climate had changed decisively. Bradley (1976, p. 101) quoting this passage, described the functions of SBATs as being

... to decide *disputes* which the administration of social security has thrown up, disputes which break the surface because a citizen is sufficiently aggrieved by the official decision to appeal against it. It is an important function of tribunals to be able to settle such disputes in an impartial and fair manner. If their decisions are to be accepted, they must observe certain minimum standards both of procedural and of substantive justice . . .

Think about this disagreement. Is Collison denying that 'disputes' can arise over SB? Is Bradley saying that disputes must be resolved by a certain procedure if the solution is to give satisfaction? Or is he questioning 'the concept of co-operation'?

The difference is important if we are not to slip into unquestioning acceptance of our own court model. Perhaps no area of administrative justice has received so much attention as SBATs. The trend of academic opinion has been to assume that tribunals are machinery for adjudication which must conform to the trilogy of fairness, impartiality and, to a limited extent, openness. Yet negotiation, conciliation or advice could be valid elements in resolving disputes which our adversarial model of justice leads us to undervalue. On the other hand, we might accept that conciliation is a valid objective and still maintain that conciliation requires a *conciliator*. This is particularly the case when a dispute arises between a citizen and a powerful department of state because of the disparity of knowledge, resources and status between the parties. In this situation 'co-operation' may mean that pressure is brought to bear on the citizen to accept a solution which an impartial observer would regard as unacceptable. This realization underlies the French idea of the ombudsman as a 'mediator' who will intervene on behalf of the less powerful party to effect a reconciliation between the citizen and the administration.

Experiments with conciliation techniques in England include the areas of race relations and also of industrial relations where ACAS today possesses important negotiatory and conciliatory functions.[4] The Rent Act 1965 provided for the appointment of rent officers who would try to persuade landlords and tenants to accept a fair rent. If you think about Mr Crossman's attitude to tribunals (above, Chapters 4 and 6), it is not surprising to find him saying:

We need to create a new level where landlord and tenant can be brought together, accept a fair rent, and never go to the real tribunal . . . at all. To achieve this, to dispel the atmosphere of litigation and forensic dispute, I have provided in the rent officer someone to help them before they are committed to fight it out before a tribunal. [HC Deb. vol. 710, col. 49.]

This attitude towards dispute-resolution, which infused the original tribunals in the social assistance field, is arguably missing from Bradley's formulation. As tribunals have increasingly been formal-

Table 19. Appeals to SBATs 1975–81

	Appeals	Withdrawn or not admitted	Revised without tribunal hearing	(%)*	Cases heard by tribunals	Decisions revised by tribunals	(%)†
1975	68,975	12,029	24,187	(35)	32,759	6,568	(20)
1976	101,112	22,131	23,856	(24)	55,125	10,450	(19)
1977	114,734	23,531	28,307	(25)	62,896	12,071	(19)
1978	115,467	21,079	32,080	(28)	62,308	12,526	(20)
1979	94,178	16,510	27,029	(29)	50,639	10,840	(21)
1980	94,481	17,547	27,579	(29)	49,355	10,914	(22)
1981	108,570	24,145	34,561	(32)	49,864	8,862	(18)

*Of all appeals.
†Of all hearings.

ized and judicialized, so this dimension has diminished. We shall return to this point.

Now let us see what happens when a claimant contests a decision made by a benefit officer. You will see from Table 19 that by no means every appeal reaches a SBAT. This is because the decisions of a benefit officer are not 'final and binding' in the same way as those of a court. Section 14(2)(d) of the 1976 Act, with para. 4 of the SB (Determination of Questions) Regulations 1980 (which re-enacts earlier provisions), permit the substitution of a revised decision where there has been an error of law or fact or a change in material circumstances. So any appeal sets in motion an internal administrative review designed to see whether the decision was correct or ought to be varied. In 1968/9, with the help of the SBC, a study was made of the internal review procedure by Coleman, an outside lawyer.

The procedure described by Coleman started with a written complaint. This led to a review by the DHSS area office. Usually a visit followed. The case was then discussed with the area office manager. Then, if the original decision seemed to be incorrect or in need of revision, it was superseded by a new decision. If the decision was maintained and the appeal pressed by the claimant, a fresh investigation was carried out, normally by a special welfare officer from the regional office. Occasionally, if an important point of policy seemed to arise there might be a referral to the SBC headquarters. So every decision appealed was reviewed twice or even three times in the style of a 'case conference' and with the possibility of a visit before it reached an SBAT. The success rate was relatively high. Using Coleman's figures (1971, p. 6), of 26,096 determinations which went to review, 23.2 per cent were resolved by an administrative decision and 11.2 per cent were withdrawn. Of those which went on to an SBAT, 52.8 per cent were decided in favour of the SBC and 12.8 per cent were revised (usually in the claimant's favour). So the internal review was an important filter. Table 19 confirms that this picture was not atypical.

Coleman made two general comments about the review process: first, he thought that the number of revisions reflected adversely on the quality of the initial decision-making and secondly, that the inadequate standard of the initial process gave those with the strength of purpose to question a determination a high chance of success. After watching the administrators at work, Coleman made no criticisms of their integrity or impartiality, though he did favour a further inquiry into withdrawn appeals. We know, for example, that some claimants are satisfied only when they receive a proper explanation of their position, which may occur only when the case reaches a higher level in the hierarchy. Others feel that their appeal is not worth the trouble, particularly if they find work shortly afterwards. But Coleman wanted to eliminate the possibility that claimants felt under pressure from officials to withdraw good appeals and to assess the need for independent advice. Is this similar to Bradley's point about 'co-operation'? Remember that Coleman was discussing a largely discretionary system. Are his arguments equally applicable to a model of rules? Can you think of any reasons why officer-discretion may be used more/less cautiously than the discretion of relatively senior officials? What might be achieved by a favourable finding at regional level?

Those who act for or advise dissatisfied claimants must recognise that the administrative pre-hearing process is as important as any hearing before a tribunal . . . In particular it would appear that in cases concerned with the exercise of discretion under the 'A' Code, the review carried out by the regional office may be particularly significant. After all, an SBAT is not a tribunal which can claim to be the repository of any great technical expertise, and since it is confined to the very general language of the Act and the regulations, its decisions on the exercise of the discretionary powers are likely to be arrived at by a process of analysis which is obscure. On the other hand, the regional office, and to a lesser extent the area office manager, are experts, who have the accumulated experience of the 'A' Code upon which to draw. At the same time . . . they may be less subject to pressure to interpret their discretions strictly than are the ordinary territorial executive officers. In fact, in a case where an adviser feels that there is good reason for the exercise of a discretionary power in the claimant's favour, reconsideration of the case by the area office manager, and hopefully the regional office, might well be the real object of an appeal. [Coleman 1971, p. 10.]

This procedure needed revision when the SBC was abolished and in 1980 a new procedure was introduced by which a vetting section of the DHSS regional office scrutinized the papers, difficult cases being referred to a 'Special Cases Officer', who is more experienced than the benefit officer. Internal review of this type is an economical way to rectify errors. The procedure acts as a sieve and, if the rate of error is really of the order of 10 per cent (above), then you may see an advantage to the claimant in automatically appealing; appeal is, after all, free! Despite the opportunity for internal scrutiny, numbers of cases still reach tribunals which contain elementary mathematical or factual errors. These are normally presented for rectification by the Presenting Officer. It is doubtful whether members would notice them, although good chairmen check and question the arithmetic. Currently, however, the DHSS is reducing the role of regional offices. After two experiments in which appeals were prepared and presented by area offices instead of by regionally based presenting officers, this system is to be adopted nationally. All these changes eliminate an important stage in the appeals procedure, placing a heavier burden on the SBAT.

The traditional antipathy to administrative appeals and pre-occupation with tribunals makes it hard for us to recognize this internal review as an appeal. Probably we should classify it as the administrative spadework necessary for the appeal. In Chapter 6, however, we were critical of the Council on Tribunal's lack of interest in inquisitorial procedures. Can we see in this internal review the embryo of a new, inquisitorial and documentary review procedure? Evaluate it in the light of Bradley's remarks. Is the procedure, or could it be made, sufficiently independent? And does consumer satisfaction depend on a 'day in court'? The assumption is often made that appellants prefer an *oral* hearing. Fulbrook (1975, p. 12), in an admittedly small sample of 38 interviews, found that some appellants had neither expected a tribunal hearing nor intended to appeal. 'The overwhelming feature of [the] response was the obvious bewilderment at the whole tribunal process and what it involved' (see further below).

Perhaps the answer depends partly on the quality of the hearing. Hearings are normally private, permission to observe being granted only in exceptional cases. The emphasis has always been on informality. When a claimant enters an SBAT, he ought to see facing him across a table the Chairman seated between the two members. He and his representative sit opposite. The clerk sits to the side. The presenting officer should sit beside the claimant to emphasize their equal status, though in many London tribunals he sits opposite to the clerk, giving the impression that he is an officer of the tribunal. Every member, the clerk and the presenting officer should have with them the 'Yellow Book', a formidable volume issued by the DHSS which contains all relevant statutes, regulations and guidance. They should also have the procedural guide, issued by the DHSS, but written for them by senior chairmen, after discussion with the Council on Tribunals (see above, p. 191). The Chairman should also have summaries of relevant High Court precedents and Commissioner's decisions. These publications are a relatively recent introduction, the importance of which is not yet always appreciated.

Researchers in the early seventies who attended tribunals regularly were depressed by what they found. Tribunals were heavily dependent on the officials, including the departmental presenting officer. The Franks Committee had favoured informality, but they also warned (para. 64) that informality without rules of procedure might produce 'an unordered character which makes it difficult, if not impossible, for the tribunal properly to sift the facts and weigh the evidence'. This was an apt description of SBATs, where ignorance of the simplest legal ideas, such as who ought to prove what or how things are to be proved, was common. Members received no training at all, staff received minimal training and legally qualified chairmen were exceptional. Unaware of the need for independence or procedural protections, tribunals were inclined to give free rein to prejudice: for example, the 'cohabitation' rule was too often interpreted to deprive women who 'behaved immorally' of benefit.

Lewis argued that Titmuss had underestimated the advantages of legal input, praising the 'traditions of English lawyering which can, at its best, rise to lending order to administrative processes without ever meddling.' Something further had to be done:

[The tribunals] appear to operate in marked contrast to the national insurance local appeal tribunals which are usually a model of balancing informal expertise with order and legality. This point is made to indicate that criticism of supplementary benefit tribunals is not based upon comparisons with courts of law but is made within a framework of acceptance of the valuable job performed by administrative tribunals at large. Nor is the objection to underdeveloped legal technique an attempt to promote the claims of the legal profession to intellectual leadership of the 'welfare rights movement'. It is simply that the system of appeals from the SBC is vastly important, that it is not operating upon the basis of anything resembling objective standards, that such a state of affairs works to the ultimate detriment of claimants and that some of the fault is a lack of legal expertise. [Lewis 1973, pp. 258–9.]

Discretion was once again a target. SBATs examined the discretionary decisions of benefit officers on their merits and could 'substitute for any decision appealed against any determination which a benefit officer could have made' (see, now, s.15(1)(c) of the SB Act 1976 as amended). Before 1980, benefit officers were in practice guided by the unofficial codes. SBC policy was not binding on the 'independent' tribunals (e.g. the *Wyatt* case, above). Observers were concerned by the way in which the power of choice was exercised. Either the tribunal tended to accept SBC policy unquestioningly or it gave free rein to personal prejudices.

Here the composition of the tribunal was important. The SBAT was and is still supposed to represent the community. Chairmen were appointed by the Minister from a panel approved by the Lord Chancellor. They did not need legal qualifications. Of the two members, one is selected by the Minister from a panel nominated by trade unions and other representative organizations, the other is appointed by the Minister from a list of people 'with knowledge or local experience of people living on low incomes'. In practice, such members are often drawn from social service organizations such as the CAB, or local chambers of commerce. In an unofficial survey published by CPAG, Lister (1974b) found that, in the London area at least, members were unrepresentative of the population at large. Women and ethnic minorities were under-represented; 'there is, as in many such lay bodies, a clear bias towards men in the higher age and social class groups'. Equally, they were unrepresentative of claimants. There was a danger that tribunals would fail to recognize claimants' difficulties and might, as a group, possess prejudices which they did not recognize and could not restrain.

The indeterminate nature of the 'rules' then came into play with lack of training reinforcing any latent bias. Tribunals tended to turn for advice to the clerk, an officer of the tribunal though not a member, and the presenting officer, technically the departmental representative and theoretically equal in status with the claimant. Regular appearance in tribunals and access to departmental policy gives these officials of the DHSS a misleading appearance of expertise and may even suggest objectivity. But presenting officers are not legally trained. Their advice on the meaning of statute and regulations and their knowledge of High Court decisions may be partial. The dangers were exposed by the Bell survey conducted on behalf of and with the co-operation of the DHSS.[5] Bell concluded (1975, pp. 10–12) that presenting officers did not understand their role; some could more aptly be described as prosecuting officers. Presenting officers needed to be of high calibre and properly trained if they were to balance their conflicting duties of 'adviser' and 'presenter'. Lister also thought that tribunals misinterpreted the role of the presenting officer. Think about the implications of her remarks for 'adversarial' procedures in informal tribunals:

> Obviously, as the members pointed out, presenting officers vary; some are kind, others are more aggressive. What is alarming is that the members of the tribunal should look for impartial guidance to someone who in fact represents one side of the dispute and that his views on a case should carry such weight. What the presenting officer usually gives them is the [SBC's] interpretation of the law on which the original decision has invariably been based . . . the presenting officer is constantly stressing what is 'policy' and 'normal practice'. In addition to the damaging implications that this holds for the independence of the tribunal, there is also a danger that where a friendly relationship has grown up between the tribunal and the full-time presenting officer, this could be offputting for the claimant. [Lister 1974b, p. 14.]

A further problem was created by the fact that non-lawyers do not always recognize the lawyer's hierarchy of rules. In other words, some tribunals did not realize that SBC directives and codes of practice (the A and AX codes) were 'quasi-law', which could not fetter either the benefit officer or the tribunal. As one member remarked to Lister (1974b, p. 36) 'We're guided by the clerk and presenting officer as they've got the information. We've got to be careful. Parliament makes the rules not the man behind the counter or us.' Tribunals did not have access to such case law as existed and, without legal qualifications, might have found it hard to interpret. Lister found that members misunderstood both the extent of their jurisdiction to make a new decision and the nature of their powers. SBATs saw their function as something nearer to a review than an appeal and they were, quite naturally, encouraged in this view by presenting officers.

Clerks could not be relied on to redress the balance. Clerks are not legally qualified. They are seconded to tribunals from regional DHSS offices for a period of service and may later be absorbed again into the administrative work of the department. And clerks, unlike presenting officers, remain with the tribunal while it is deliberating and after the appellant and his representative have left.

Lister found that clerks played a crucial role as a source of advice and information. Some clerks intervened of their own accord in proceedings where they felt the tribunal was going wrong. Some members claimed that clerks 'frequently tried to influence the tribunal's decision in favour of Commission policy and that some Chairmen automatically accepted what [they] said'. Worse still, some clerks were allowed to draft the tribunal's decisions and reasons. Some members relied wholly on the clerk, feeling 'that in view of the clerk's presence they did not need to know the law themselves'.

Although she did not recommend a specific reform, Lister concluded:

The tribunal's dependence on the clerk for guidance in dealing with the cases that come before it clearly represents a grave threat to its independence. How can a tribunal claim to be independent when its thinking is moulded by an employee of the Department whose decisions are the subject of the appeal? The instructions issued to clerks are not made public but it is known that they have been revised in recent years in an effort to restrict the clerk's role. Clerks are now instructed not to take an active role at the oral hearing and to divert any questions tactfully to the appellant or presenting officer. This, however, is no solution to the problem for it means that at the hearing the presenting officer who is even more committed to the Commission's case, is made responsible for interpreting the law to the tribunal. And it ignores the fact that the clerk's main influence is exercised at the deliberation when the appellant and presenting officer are no longer there to answer questions. [Lister 1974b, p. 16.]

These imbalances could have been partially rectified if claimants were represented. Some support for this statement comes from the correlation shown by Table 20 between success rates and representation (legal or otherwise). (Success rates also correlate with attendance; only about 7 per cent of appellants who neither attend, nor are represented succeed in their appeal.)

It may be that the adversarial procedures in which we traditionally put our faith do not function particularly well in the absence of lawyers. As Table 20 shows, legal representation is still exceptional.[5a] If claimants are unrepresented, the chairman is bound to intervene in proceedings. Yet the parties present their case using the adversarial plan. The presenting officer, who normally opens the case, is both departmental advocate and unofficial legal adviser, though the procedural guide has attempted to deal with this, warning (para. 32) that 'The Benefit Officer who presents the case to the Tribunal is not a servant of the Tribunal, and the Tribunal is not bound to accept his interpretation of the law'.

This procedural guide, first issued in 1977, was revised for the DHSS by the senior chairmen (below) and reissued in 1981 (see also Chapter 6). This and the extension of training has done something to standardize procedures and make them fairer since Lister wrote, but the claimant is still at a disadvantage. For example, he may not know what to prove nor how to prove it and may arrive at the hearing without essential documents and not understanding the function of the tribunal. A more sensible system might allow the chairman to sift papers in advance, deciding what had to be proved, advising applicants what to bring with them in the way of proof and calling on

Table 20. Attendance and Representation at SBATs 1979–81

Accompanied and/or represented by	Year	Appeals heard (i)	Appellant attended (ii)	Appellant absent (iii)	Favourable decisions			
					Appellant attended (iv)	% of (ii)	Appellant absent (v)	% of (iii)
Social/ welfare workers	79	2,224	1,934	290	1,057	55%	159	55%
	80	2,528	2,197	331	1,174	53%	147	44%
	81	2,858	2,442	416	1,132	46%	168	40%
Unions, voluntary organizations	79	1,760	1,580	180	713	45%	70	39%
	80	2,155	1,915	240	846	44%	113	47%
	81	2,366	2,168	198	886	41%	79	40%
Solicitors	79	300	252	48	96	38%	13	27%
	80	308	233	75	109	47%	17	23%
	81	419	363	56	131	36%	17	30%
Friends and relatives	79	7,532	5,923	1,609	1,906	32%	534	33%
	80	7,774	6,215	1,559	2,040	33%	458	29%
	81	7,886	6,680	1,206	1,722	26%	272	23%
Neither accompanied or represented	79	38,823	16,479	22,344	4,670	28%	1,622	7%
	80	36,590	16,774	19,816	4,687	28%	1,323	7%
	81	36,335	17,971	18,364	3,558	20%	897	5%

Source of Tables 19–20: SBC Annual Report 1979 (Cmnd. 8033), Tables 13.1, 13.2; DHSS Internal Working Paper (1982).

the presenting officer to provide adequate support for his view of the facts. The procedural booklet only hints at the problems when it says (para. 51):

If the claimant is neither present nor represented the Tribunal must endeavour to arrive at a balanced view of the case by hearing the Presenting Officer and any witnesses and by putting questions to them which the claimant might have been expected to put had he been present. It is particularly important in every case that the Benefit . . . Officer's decision should be critically examined.

How is this to be done when the only statement of the appellant's case may be a short statement in his notification of appeal? On occasions this might say as little as: 'The officer is wrong and I want to protest. I have only the clothes I am wearing and I haven't enough money to live.' The evaluation of the facts then depends entirely on the record made by the benefit officer, who is not present at the hearing. Even if the appellant is present in person, conflicting stories are hard to resolve. As with immigration, tribunals set up to establish the facts are often not in a position to do so.

As you read on about the reforms which are leading us inexorably down a path to the courtroom, ask yourself if it is the right path. Ought we to have spent more time in developing an inquisitorial model? In the course of this book, have you come across any suitable models? Could the SBC's internal review procedure be adapted to replace tribunals?

The Bell Report was an important stage in the move to judicialism. It recommended a 3-stage programme. Stage 1 was designed to strengthen existing tribunals, for example by appointing legal practitioners as 'Senior Chairmen' to supervise tribunals and institute training schemes. Some of these improvements have just been described. Stage 2 aimed to improve on existing tribunals by a planned programme of judicialization: for example, Bell recommended legally qualified chairmen, better provision for representation and a higher calibre of member with strong commitment to the work. Stage 3 would bring the integration of SBATs with NILTS but, as a halfway measure, the appeals system would be restructured to allow a second appeal on a point of law to National Insurance Commissioners who would be given jurisdiction in both sets of tribunals and rechristened 'Social Security Commissioners':

(i) At present no further right of appeal exists from decisions of SBATs to a second-tier appeal body. Furthermore, they are excluded from Section 13 of the Tribunals and Inquiries Act 1971 which provides for an appeal on a point of law to the High Court.[6] They are subject to review by certiorari but in fact this is a limited, complex and inaccessible remedy. The operation of these tribunals is kept under general review by the Council on Tribunals but although the Council has been much concerned with the problems discussed in this paper, it is an advisory body and has no power to alter any tribunal decision. Taking all the research findings into consideration I find no justification for leaving SBATs in a position in which they are virtually uncontrolled. A second-tier appeal body should, I submit, be treated as a matter of urgency and priority. The only reason this recommendation is placed in Stage III is that until the decision-making of SBATs and their recorded, reasoned decisions can be substantially improved it would be difficult, if not impossible, for a superior appellate body to do its work . . . I recommend extending the jurisdiction and title of the National Insurance Commissioners to constitute them the second-tier appellate authority. At the earliest possible moment a right of appeal to them on points of law from decisions of SBATs should be granted.

(ii) The second issue is bound up with the first and for this reason has been left to Stage III. The lack of a body of reported decisions is a serious weakness in supplementary benefit adjudication. I do not see how this can be remedied without a second-tier appeal structure. The National Insurance Commissioners have great experience and expertise in building up a body of 'caselaw' in national insurance. There are differences between national insurance and supplementary benefit adjudication but I am convinced the Commissioners would be able to differentiate and would speedily make an impact by their reported decisions. [Bell 1975, pp. 24–5.]

A majority of these proposals – e.g. training schemes and appointments – could be implemented administratively but the 1980 legislation provided the new appeals structure. Ss.14 and 15 of the Social Security Act 1980 provide for appeal on a point of law with leave to the newly constituted Social Security Commissioners, some of whose decisions you have already read,[7] and thence with leave again to the Court of Appeal.[8] To support this, the appeals rules[9] provided for the tribunal to record its reasons and findings of material questions of fact. Dissenting opinions must be recorded. This prevents the chairman or the clerk from recording the decision when the members have gone home. Subsequently, the procedural handbook stressed the importance of those provisions (paras. 71–2):

On the form with which the Tribunal is provided for recording its decision is a space labelled 'Tribunal's unanimous/majority decision'. This is not a space simply for a 'rubber stamp decision'; it is an important space and in it the Tribunal's decision should be fully, intelligibly and accurately set out. It is not enough merely to say 'decision revised' or 'appeal dismissed' . . . it is what leads to that result that matters . . . Similarly, in the case of a majority decision not only must it be clearly and unambiguously stated precisely what that decision is, but the dissentient member's opinion should also be recorded. The wording should be such that neither the claimant nor the Benefit/Supplement Officer is left in any doubt as to what the Tribunal has decided. A proper recording of decisions is absolutely essential.

It is elementary that a party to proceedings should be able to understand why a decision has been given against him and the reasons for it. Thus, it would plainly be inadequate simply to record as the reason for dismissing an appeal that: 'On the facts found, the Tribunal held that benefit is not payable' . . . Nobody could possibly understand from such statements why, or on what basis, the Tribunal came to those conclusions . . . A Commissioner has recently stated that it is of the utmost importance . . . that the Tribunal should identify the regulation(s) pursuant to which any award is made. Identification should extend to the paragraphs and sub-paragraphs, as well as to the regulations relied upon . . . The law with which appeal tribunals are now faced is both new and complex. It is only too easy to fall into error. The exercise of pinpointing the precise provision or provisions relied upon greatly concentrates the mind – and thereby reduces the possibility of error.[10]

How are Bell's hopes for regulation of the tribunals by a system of precedent working out? Clearly the Commissioners' tribunal is more accessible than the High Court. Between 1977 and 1980, there were 150 appeals under s. 13 of the Tribunals and Inquiries Act. In the first 12 months of the new procedure, there were 945 applications for leave to appeal to the Commissioners, 100 of which came from the DHSS. A substantial volume of precedent is being built up and, as the last extract shows, it can serve to regularize procedure, as well as to rule on the interpretation of the regulations. The Commissioners are specialists who understand the operation of the SB system. Yet despite the greater independence of the Commissioners, complaints have already been heard from welfare lawyers that appeals from the DHSS receive preferential treatment and are heard more quickly than those of the average claimant. Official statistics provide some confirmation.[11] The large number of appeals also enables the DHSS to indulge in 'test case strategy', selecting their most favourable cases for appeal.

The elementary nature of the procedural booklet tells you something about the standard of SBAT chairmen. Practising lawyers would (or should) not have to be told those things. There have been moves towards appointing legally trained chairmen. In 1977, 12 per cent of chairmen were legally qualified; by appointing lawyers to vacancies, the total had crept up to 26.4 per cent in 1982. The regional variation was a cause for concern, however. In two of the London regions only two out of 20 (10 per cent) chairmen were legally qualified in contrast to the North West and Northern regions where 11 out of 22 (50 per cent) and 12 out of 29 (41 per cent) were legally qualified. Five senior chairmen had been appointed on a regional basis. Their function was to monitor tribunals and to supervise training. By 1982, they were assuming a 'watchdog' function. Bull describes an informal meeting between CAB and CPAG workers and three senior chairmen. Notice the continuity with complaints recorded by Lister or Bell. Compare the description of this informal, hierarchical system – regional controllers are DHSS employees – for handling complaints with our earlier assessment of the Council on Tribunals. What might the advantages and disadvantages be?

The main complaints received on the performance of tribunals have been about overbearing chairmen; biased chairmen or members; and inadequate recording of decisions. We are assured that most chairmen have welcomed such feedback: 'The thinking chairmen will welcome any way of helping them to understand their role under the new legislation'.

In the past, many of such complaints found their way to the Lord Chancellor's office, sometimes via the Council on Tribunals . . . Those complaints that still reach this destination are now being forwarded to senior chairmen. Not only does this mean that the on the spot watch dogs . . . are able to have a word with the alleged offenders; it is worth bearing in mind that these complaints are being handled by persons who are going to play a major independent role in the great overhaul, due in 1984, of SBAT membership.

Senior chairmen have also been given a major say in the appointment and removal of SBAT clerks. Again, they may find it appropriate to have a direct word with allegedly errant clerks – most commonly when they are accused of interfering – or they may refer the matter to the Regional Controller . . .

If we might have contemplated, before September 1980, referring complaints about SBATs to the Lord Chancellor's office . . . so might we have thought, perhaps, of the Ombudsman as a way of redressing grievances against clerks and local offices. So why go to the new watchdogs instead? One answer is *speed*: as one senior chairman sardonically put it, 'you can be told faster that nothing can be done'. But he was underselling his potential. He and his colleagues can also boast *proximity*. Remember that they know all the regional controllers and all the SBAT chairmen . . . This does enable them to have a quick, informal word. This will sometimes lead to instant improvements; at the very least, it could help the long term pruning of SBATs. [Bull 1982, p. 14.]

Let us summarize the position in 1982. There had been a sharp shift from discretion to unduly complex rules. Procedural improvements were in hand, though slow. Legally trained chairmen were gradually being appointed. There was some training, though training was not obligatory and there was too little. The system was still relatively informal. What more could be done? And what would claimants want?

Claimants are not often consulted though one or two 'opinion polls' have been taken.[12] Not surprisingly, they show that claimants' feelings about tribunals are very much influenced by success or failure. But two factors which seem to produce a feeling of disadvantage in many claimants are (a) a tribunal which seems out of touch with claimants' problems and (b) the lack of a representative. Milton, for example, identified a general feeling:

> that current tribunal membership is inappropriate because members lack the relevant experience and knowledge upon which to base decisions. Age, for example, may be important not simply in terms of the 'generation gap', but at a very practical level in as far as members may be out of touch with the commitment and financial responsibilities of the appellant at his or her particular point in the life-cycle. Many appellants are actually ignorant of where tribunal members are drawn from and have a tendency to class them as judges or lawyers, and 'local worthies', i.e. people very much out of touch with their own day-to-day experiences. [Milton 1975, p. 134.]

Bell recorded that appellants preferred to be represented by social workers,[13] because they allowed appellants to participate in presenting their own case. She also confirms Milton's finding that claimants

> felt more deeply about lay members than about any other single aspect of their experience. In attaching importance to lay membership they had definite views about their role as well as expectations about their performance. As seen by respondents, members should play an active and *enabling* role towards the appellant by showing sympathetic understanding of his problem, by listening, asking relevant questions, drawing him out, and generally helping him sort out his case. They were able to distinguish this enabling role from that of an advocate. Moreover, they clearly wanted ordinary people as panel members – particularly people with first-hand knowledge and experience of the kinds of problems and conditions experienced by supplementary benefit claimants . . . What they wanted was a full and rather informal hearing of their grievance with the tribunal playing a definite enabling role towards them and in which all would play an active part. [Bell 1975, p. 18.]

These studies were conducted before the move from discretion to rules and we cannot know whether a new survey would reproduce the same results. They stand as a warning, however, against making assumptions about the *objectives* of the tribunal system. Lawyers tend to define fairness in terms of procedure, and rate success or failure in terms of money payments to their client. Perhaps not every client sees tribunals in this light. A tribunal hearing may be a platform for political protest, an opportunity to participate in decisions which concern one's life or even a chance for a chat. Formalization undercuts these objectives. (Of course, you may feel that this does not matter because these are inappropriate aims for a tribunal system.)

Although the 1980 reforms made no changes in membership, in other respects they moved towards formality. The Health and Social Services and Social Security Adjudications Act 1983 moves still more sharply towards the court model. The Act provides for N I L Ts and S B A Ts to be amalgamated. Decisions as to benefit will from now on be taken by an 'adjudication officer' – you may see this change of title as significant – and appeal will lie to a Social Security Appeal Tribunal (S S A T). Para. 8 of Sched. 4 empowers the Lord Chancellor to appoint a president and regional and full-time chairmen for the tribunals. These appointments will be offered to barristers or solicitors of not less than ten, seven and five years standing respectively. The greater independence of the tribunals is recognized by the fact that staffing, including the post of clerk, will now be the responsibility of the President with consent of the Minister and Treasury. Further appeal will continue to lie to the Social Security Commissioners and Court of Appeal.[13a]

The debates on this measure, which was considerably amended during its passage, are interesting because they bring out familiar divisions about the purposes of tribunals. They remind us both of the green light theorists' suspicion of the 'legal hegemony' (see Robson, Jennings, Chapter 2) and of the long tradition of Labour Party hostility to courts and lawyers, demonstrated in Crossman's attitudes to Rent Tribunals, R A Cs and rent officers (above). The Bill originally provided for members to be drawn from a panel appointed by the Minister to represent the area and with 'knowledge or experience of conditions in the area'. Both this provision and the new arrangements for legally qualified chairmen were hotly opposed by the T U C and the Labour opposition, which set down a series of amendments. In committee, Mr John (Labour) argued that tribunal members should be 'representative'. Compare this extract with Bell's findings about the expectations of claimants:

[The Appellant] should be adequately represented and have a fair and sympathetic hearing. We shall therefore seek to write into the Bill . . . that there shall be representatives on the tribunal who can help and sympathise with the appellant and understand his point of view. The rule is still that people are unrepresented. They represent themselves and are often confused by procedures and by the doctrine of precedent that is increasingly being applied. It would help them if members of the tribunal were to have a knowledge of their conditions and their welfare. [HC SCB, 19 April 1983, col. 58.]

Although there is a reference to 'adequate representation' here, the opposition members are not thinking in terms of lawyers and an extension of legal aid. Indeed, they went on to argue that legal expertise is not the sole criterion for a good chairman. At first they argued for the retention of good chairmen who did not possess the requisite legal qualification. When the Government refused to concede, they tried to insist that newly appointed chairmen should include some knowledge of social security law amongst their qualifications. One opposition member (Dr Thomas) expressed great suspicion of 'mini-courts' and of the legal profession. He argued that, in the transition to regulations, the original purpose of tribunals was being overlooked. How far does his argument parallel that of Titmuss? Is it relevant to our earlier discussion of 'inquisitorial' and 'adversarial' procedure? Compare the speaker's views with those of Bell and Milton:

Surely the one feature we do not wish to transmit to places where people are appealing on benefits which they feel they are being denied is the atmosphere of the courtroom . . .

The Minister . . . says that, in addition to being familiar with proceedings, a lawyer has the 'ability to cope with the maze of regulations which form the background to the claims'. The Minister is assuming a great deal in coupling those two factors. They are totally different. Surely people could familiarise themselves with the complex background regulations without having had any experience of a courtroom. One might say that the less experience that the chairman has of a courtroom the more fairly would the appellant be able to put his case, and the easier and more familiar the atmosphere in which he does so. I do not understand why we are to have such sweeping changes. Why are former members . . . being cast aside for the new-style members? Why are the people who served on these tribunals for so long suddenly being cast aside? Their experience is treated as being of no value whatsoever now that we are to have lawyers. I am very suspicious about why the Government are bringing in such rigid arrangements. [HC Deb. SCB, 21 April 1983, col. 645.]

The disagreement was overtaken by news of an election. In order to secure passage of the measure, the Government conceded changes in the method of appointing members. Para. 7 of Sched. 8 provides that appointments are to be made by the President from two area panels, the first composed of 'persons who appear to the President to represent employed earners', the other composed of persons who either 'represent employers and earners other than employed earners' or 'who appear to him to have knowledge and experience of conditions in the area and to represent persons living or working in it'. Before making appointments to the panels, the President may listen to recommendations from committees and organizations, particularly those representing employers and employed earners. This triumph may be short-lived. Clause 9 of a new Health and Social Security Bill proposes to restore the single panel, eliminating all reference to employers and earners.

3 After the welfare state?

The administrative process is never static and the process of administrative reform cannot end abruptly in 1980 or 1983. The welfare state is in transition, perhaps even dissolution,[14] and changes in ideological climate must inevitably be reflected in the social system. Recently the Second Permanent Secretary at the DHSS, Sir Geoffrey Otton, described in an unpublished public lecture the parameters inside which his department has to work. For the clientele, the paramount consideration is 'prompt and accurate delivery of benefits'. For the highly unionized and low-paid work-force, improved conditions of service are important:

[Claimants] are exercised about their rights, when they feel they have paid for them through their contributions, and will pursue us endlessly – and for years – if they think the system is not giving them all they should get, however small the sums may appear. They are concerned with fairness, and want to know why they get less than other people, and why scroungers aren't stopped and they tend to exert a pressure for expansion of the schemes in ways that lead to more expenditure, more manpower, and often more complexity.

The DHSS staff serving them are predominantly a junior work-force, not highly paid. They are expected to administer a mammoth and intricate scheme, which has only been made manageable for them by being broken down into small components, each of which is the subject of a mass of detailed instructions. Much of the work is repetitive. Much of it entails face-to-face contact with the public – which is often rewarding but can be the reverse, and stressful. We expect a great deal of this army of junior staff . . . They suffer the disadvantages of the front-line troops in any large organisation; they see only their own part of the task and do not comprehend the whole . . . They are subjected to a mass of instructions and communications. They get the rough end of the job: policy authorised by Parliament or Headquarters ends up with them, and they have to deal with the new tasks and problems it creates and with the public reaction to them.

As society changes, so administration must change.[15] For example, cash payments have today been superseded by cheques and post office giros. Again, by 1982, the DHSS had found that claimants preferred postal claim forms to personal application for benefits. A DHSS official thought the introduction of the new postal claims marked 'a move away from the predominantly home visiting service of national assistance days, through the crowded waiting rooms of the discretionary SB scheme to a pattern of working that is much more suited to the new codified scheme' (Hughes 1983, p. 12). Perhaps some of the side-effects were not foreseen. In 1980, for example, local authorities campaigning against social security and social service cuts turned their attention to the problem of 'take-up'. Strathclyde alone issued 100,000 'post-free' envelopes inviting recipients to claim directly from the DHSS, an exercise which allegedly resulted in weekly benefit increases of £1.3 million and single payments of £3 million in the region before the 1980 Act took effect.[16] In 1982, a complaint to the PCA involved a similar campaign (HC 44 (1983–4), p. 55). The claimant had completed a postcard which was passed to a special section set up to control correspondence arising from the campaign. He subsequently called at the local office in person and submitted another claim. The PCA considered that the confusion and delays which marked the case arose largely from the claimant's own conduct but partly from the department's failure to link the two claims. Since he was told that the local office had received 2,700 postcards during the campaign and still had to give priority to existing claims, together with the annual programme of benefit uprating, he was not disposed to be critical.

An administrative change to postal claims can do as much to combat stigma and promote 'take-up' of benefits as the legal rhetoric of 'rights' and 'entitlement'. On the other side of the counter, a management survey[17] has suggested that delegation of decision-making to local offices would produce a better service and a more contented workforce. Hughes (1983, p. 12) believes that localization is only possible because 'the model of rules' protects individuals against arbitrary and inconsistent decisions. An internal survey of the operation of the Single Payments Regulations undertaken as part of a regular monitoring process confirmed that staff preferred working within a framework of rules and felt that public relations had consequently improved. If you think about the skeleton SB system outlined in Chapter 5 you will see how the pattern of administration has changed. In the model of rules, internal controls may be more important that adjudication.

The current preoccupation with efficiency and value for money creates administrative problems for a management faced with a growing clientele. To provide the sort of service which the public wants and which its political masters are demanding, the DHSS, like other government departments, is increasingly dependent on new technology.[18] The objective is joint administration of all social security benefits. The adjudicatory machinery of the 1983 Act has just such a development in mind.

The demand for administrative justice and the preoccupation with rulemaking are in their own way both responses to the welfare state. Today we stand on the threshold of a new age dominated by information technology which may demand a totally different response from administrative law. For instance, a computerized information-retrieval service could soon link local offices of the DHSS and Department of Employment to a central databank based on a personal social security record. The micro-computer or silicone chip allows benefits to be quickly and accurately calculated at the touch of a button. Ultimately, such aids could revolutionize the administration of social security benefits, disposing of a large proportion of appeal work. Tribunals which 'take a second look at the facts' would be largely outmoded. Similarly, poor co-ordination would no longer be excusable. Could it then be right to impose on the subject the obligation to produce relevant facts to the administration?'

The new technology is beginning to impinge on the legal profession. In *R.* v. *Boundary Commission for England ex p. Foot* [1983] 2 WLR 456 the High Court, asked to review the operations of the Boundary Commission in redrawing the electoral map of Britain, found itself faced with an extensive computer analysis.[19] In the rating cases (above, Chapter 11) courts have been asked to evaluate forecasting techniques increasingly used in economic planning. *Pickwell*'s case typifies a traditional reaction. Judges have been heard to complain, too, that data retrieval systems allow cases to be indiscriminately cited and that copying facilities force them to read volumes of irrelevant material. But the new technology can be used more positively. For example, a computerized retrieval system allows complex regulations to be indexed, making it easier to trace the relevant law. Word processors can mechanically standardize the use of technical terms through a complex set of regulations, or recall previous relevant statute and regulation in order that it may be correctly listed and repealed. The all-pervasive model of rules might at least be made more symmetrical by recourse to modern technology.

These are largely beneficent developments, but for those who see administrative law as the control of executive power, the computer age affords an alarming prospect. Modern technology offers governments a terrifying accretion of power, centralized in the hands of a few technical experts.[20] The language of legislation, for example, will have to be translated into computer language.[21] Does this mean that the expertise of the lawyer will be superseded by that of the technologist? Certainly mechanically calculated benefit printouts will be harder to challenge than the doubtful arithmetic of junior officials.

Both Otton and Hughes (above) tell us that the time saved by mechanical aids will be used to improve the service. For instance, the DHSS has been experimenting with phone-in advisory offices, mobile exhibitions to encourage take-up and the provision of Prestel display screens for personal calculations of benefits in local offices. Administrators are venturing on to the traditional terrain of welfare lawyers.[22] We need to pause and consider these developments. Hewart's view of administrative decision-taking would hardly have been more favourable if he had learned that decisions were taken by a robot. It is no surprise then to find voluntary organizations like the CAB experimenting with the microcomputer.[23] Monopolies of information and technology are dangerous. Unlike other countries, Britain, as yet, has no freedom of information legislation, no adequate data privacy legislation and no statutory right of access to one's 'administrative record'. Yet standard administrative law texts which devote many pages to the doctrine of Crown Privilege usually contain no more than a glancing reference to these glaring omissions. We do not want to find that cradle to grave welfare services are matched by cradle to grave surveillance. If the administrative process is dynamic, then administrative law must match and anticipate its dynamism.

Notes

Abbreviations of periodicals

We have included here only abbreviations difficult to trace in a library.

ABAJ	American Bar Association Journal
Am. Soc. Rev.	American Sociological Review
BJLS	British Journal of Law and Society
CLJ	Cambridge Law Journal
CLP	Current Legal Problems
H and P Rev.	Housing and Planning Review
JBL	Journal of Business Law
JPL	Journal of Planning and Environmental Law
JSPTL	Journal of the Society of Public Teachers of Law
JSWL	Journal of Social Welfare Law
ICLQ	International and Comparative Law Quarterly
ILJ	Industrial Law Journal
LAG Bulletin	Legal Action Group Bulletin
LQR	Law Quarterly Review
MLR	Modern Law Review
NILQ	Northern Ireland Legal Quarterly
NLJ	New Law Journal
OJLS	Oxford Journal of Legal Studies
PL	Public Law
Sup. Ct Rev.	Supreme Court Review
T and CP	Town and Country Planning

Chapter 1: Red light theories

1   *A Grammar of Politics* (1925), p. 578

2   In *The Constitutional History of England* (1908), pp. 533–5, Maitland, discussing an earlier definition from Holland (*Jurisprudence*, p. 363), called the distinction one of convenience. The definitions are used by Griffith and Street, *Principles of Administrative Law* (3rd edn 1965), pp. 2–3, though the authors remark that the distinction is arbitrary.

3   See e.g. Maitland, 'A Historical Sketch of Liberty and Equality' in *Collected Papers* (1911), Vol. 1, p. 1; Pollock, *Essays in the Law* (1922), Nos. 2 and 3, pp. 31–110.

4   Mitchell, 'The Causes and Effects of the Absence of a System of Public Law in the United Kingdom', [1965] *PL* 95; Nevil Johnson, 'Law and the Polity', Ch. 8 of *In Search of the Constitution* (1978); Diplock, 'Administrative Law: Judicial Review Reviewed', (1974) 33(2) *CLJ* 233.

5   Dimock, *Law and Dynamic Administration* (1980), where a useful bibliography is to be found.

6   Students unfamiliar with the history of modern political ideas will find Barker, *Political Ideas in Modern Britain* (1978) an invaluable aid.

7   The classic exposition is Corwin, 'The "Higher Law" Background of American Constitutional Law', 42 *Harv. LR* 149 and 365 (1928–9) and 'The Debt of American Constitutional Law to Natural Law Concepts', 25 *Notre Dame Lawyer* 258 (1950), reprinted in Loss (ed.), *Corwin on the Constitution* (1981).

8   See, on the first point, MacCormick, *Legal Reasoning and Legal Theory* (1978), Ch. 9. On the second, see Summers (below) and Rumble, 'The Legal Positivism of John Austin and the Realist Movement in American Jurisprudence', 66 *Cornell LR* 986 (1981), where the views of Twining, *Karl Llewellyn and the Realists* (1978) are also discussed.

9   Hart, 'Philosophy of Law and Jurisprudence in Britain (1945–1952)', 2 *Am. J. Comp. Law* 355 (1953); Cotterell, 'English Conceptions of the Role of Theory in Legal Analysis', (1983) 46 *MLR* 681.

10   Some of the reasons why this is so are to be found in Summers, 'Pragmatic Instrumentalism in Twentieth Century American Legal Thought – A Synthesis and Critique of our Dominant General Theory about Law and its Use' (1981) 66 *Cornell LR* 861; Fuchs, 'Concepts and Policies in Anglo-American Administrative Law Theory', (1937–8) 47 *Yale LJ* 538. See also Arnold, 'Trial by Combat and the New Deal', 47 *Harv. LR* 913 (1934). Contrast Dickinson, *Administrative Justice and the Supremacy of Law* (1927).

11   You can follow these ideas in Nonet and Selznick, *Law and Society in Transition: Toward Responsive Law* (1978); David Miller, *Social Justice* (1978); Kamenka and Tay, 'Beyond Bourgeois Individualism: the Contemporary Crisis in Law and Legal Ideology', in *Feudalism, Capitalism and Beyond*, ed. Kamenka and Neale (1975). See also E. P. Thompson, *Whigs and Hunters* (1975), pp. 258–69.

12   Maitland, op. cit., p. 501 called us 'a much governed nation', while in *Law and Public Opinion in England* (1905; pp. 64–5 of 1962 edn), Dicey divided the nineteenth century into periods, choosing 1870 for the beginning of collectivist influence on legislation.

13   For an introduction see O. McDonagh, 'The Nineteenth-Century Revolution in Government: A Reappraisal', 1 *Historical Journal* (1958) 52; H. Parris, 'The Nineteenth Century Revolution in Government: A Reappraisal Reappraised', 3 *Historical Journal* (1960) 17. And see H. Parris, *Constitutional Bureaucracy* (1969); O. McDonagh, *Early Victorian Government* (1977) and 'Pre-transformations: Victorian Britain' in Kamenka and Tay (eds.), *Law and Social Control* (1980).

14   Ziegert, 'A sociologist's view', in *Law and Social Control*, pp. 60, 63, attempts a definition. See further Higgins, 'Social Control Theories of Social Policy', (1980) *Jnl Soc. Pol.* 1; Green, 'Arguments for Liberty: A Reply to Tony Benn', (1982) 53 *Pol. Quarterly* 418.

15   See also Barry, 'The New Liberalism', 13 *Brit. J. Pol. S.* 93 (1983); Ryan, 'The New Libertarians: a Gauntlet to both Left and Right', 56 *New Society* (1981) 427.

16   R. Bendix, *Max Weber: an Intellectual Portrait* (revised 1962). See also Kamenka and Krygier (eds.), *Bureaucracy* (1979).

17   Aucoc, *Conférences sur l'administration et sur le droit administratif* (3rd edn 1885), intro No. 6, p. 15, quoted in Dicey, *Law of the Constitution* (1885), pp. 332–3. Dicey was better versed in the subject of French administrative law than were many of those who came after him. See his later views in '*Droit administratif* in Modern French Law', (1901) 17 *LQR* 302.

18   For Dicey's later views, see 'The Development of Administrative Law in England', (1915) 31 *LQR* 148. Here Dicey admits that there has been 'a considerable step towards the introduction among us of something like the *droit administratif* of France' but maintains that the jurisdiction of 'ordinary law courts' in cases of breach of the law by public officials 'is fatal to the existence of true *droit administratif*'.

19   Daintith, 'Regulation by Contract: the New Prerogative', (1979) 32 *CLP* 41 explains why, and read Ganz, [1978] *PL* 33, and Ferguson and Page, [1978] *PL* 347 for further examples. See also *Town Investments* v. *Department of the Environment* [1977] 2 WLR 450, noted Harlow, (1977) 40 *MLR* 728.

20   Laski, 'The Responsibility of the State in England', (1919) 32 *Harv. LR* 447; C. K. Allen, *Law and Orders* (3rd edn 1965), pp. 316–48.

21   For a different definition again, see H. W. R. Wade, *Constitutional Fundamentals* (1980), pp. 46–53. The case law is discussed in B. Markesinis, 'The Royal Prerogative Re-Visited', (1973) 32 *CLJ* 287.

22   For further comment see Harlow [1980] *PL* 1, Bevan, 'Is Anybody There?', [1980] *PL* 431.

23   Mitchell, op. cit., n. 4. Kahn Freund, 'Common Law and Civil Law – Imaginary and Real Obstacles to Assimilation' in *New Perspectives for a Common Law of Europe* (1978), pp. 158–63, contrasts the two approaches.

24   See also the Introduction to the 9th and 10th edns of Dicey, by E. C. S. Wade. An excellent retrospective is F. H. Lawson, 'Dicey Revisited', (1959) 7 *Pol. Studies* 109 and 207.

25   Compare the views of Lord Chancellor Hailsham, *The Dilemma of Democracy – Diagnosis and Prescription* (1977), especially Ch. XVI.

26   For a recent analysis, see Williams, 'The Donoughmore Report in Retrospect', (1982) 60 *Pub. Admin.* 273.

27   The Donoughmore Committee made important recommendations on the subject of delegated legislation which are dealt with in Chapter 5.

28   For fuller treatment see D. Foulkes, *Administrative Law* (5th edn 1982), pp. 11–52.

29   See also Street, 'Quasi-Government Bodies since 1918' in Campion (ed.), *British Government since 1918* (1950).

30   McCrudden, 'The Strategic Use of the Law' in *A Review of the Race Relations Act 1976* (Runnymede Trust, 1979). For another study of a regulatory agency, see his 'Law Enforcement by Regulatory Agency: The case of Employment Discrimination in Northern Ireland', (1982) 45 *MLR* 617.

31   Nevil Johnson, 'Accountability, Control and Complexity: Moving Beyond Ministerial Responsibility' in Anthony Barker (ed.), *Quangos in Britain* (1982).

32   See the Pliatzky Report on Non-Departmental Public Bodies, Cmnd 7797 (1980).

Chapter 2: Green light theories

1   Griffith, 'The Teaching of Law and Politics', (1982) 16 *The Law Teacher* 1, and Dimock (1980), p. 69, both make this point.

2   See 'The Path of the Law', (1897) 10 *Harv. LR* 457.

3   Hume, 'Jeremy Bentham and the Nineteenth-century Revolution in Government', 10 *Historical Journal* (1967) 361; Finer, 'The Transmission of Benthamite Ideas' in G. Sutherland (ed.), *Studies in the Growth of Nineteenth Century Government* (1972).

4   Duguit's main works in this field were *Traité du droit constitutionnel* (5 vols., 1911) and *Les transformations du droit public* (1913). Laski translated the latter under the title of *Law in the Modern State* (1921) and our extracts are drawn from his translation. See also 'The Law and the State', (1917–18) 31 *Harv. LR* 1.

5   And also in American texts. See, for example, J. Hart, *An Introduction to Administrative Law with Selected Cases* (1st edn 1940), where the author defines administrative law as 'all the law that controls the adminis-

tration as well as that *made by* the administration' [our italics] and states that 'the subject matter that administrative law takes as its focal point is public administration'. Dimock (1980) contains a survey of the development of American administrative law with a bibliography.

6   'Courts and Administrative Law – The Experience of English Housing Legislation', (1935) 49 *Harv. LR* 426; *Housing Law* (1st edn 1935).

7   A fuller account of the Crichel Down case is given by Griffith, (1955) 18 *MLR* 557. See also Report of the Clark Inquiry, Cmnd 9176 (1954); HC Deb. vol. 530, cols. 1182–302.

8   Robson, *Justice and Administrative Law* (3rd edn 1951), pp. 426–9; Jennings, 'The Report on Ministers' Powers', (1932) 10 *Pub. Admin.* 348.

9   See Pollock, 'Government by Committee in England', *Essays*, (1922), pp. 110–41; Wheare, *Government by Committee* (1955). Modern developments are discussed in Ganz, *Administrative Procedures* (1974). See also Fox, *Public Participation in the Administrative Process*, Law Reform Commission of Canada (1979).

10 On the history of concern for the individual inside the Labour Party, see Gwyn, 'The Labour Party and the Threat of Bureaucracy', (1971) 19 *Pol. Studies* 383. On Laski, see Ekirch, 'Harold J. Laski: The Liberal Manqué or Lost Libertarian?', 4 *J. of Libertarian Studies* 139 (1980).

11 This is the theme of his Hamlyn Lectures, *English Law – the New Dimension* (1974).

12 A fuller discussion can be found in Middlemas, *Politics in Industrial Society* (1979), Ch. 13, 'Corporate Bias'; Birnbaum, 'The State Versus Corporatism', (1982) 11 *Politics and Society* 477 discusses different models. See also Martin, 'Pluralism and the New Corporatism', (1983) 31 *Pol. Studies* 86. Booth, 'Corporatism, Capitalism and Depression in Twentieth-century Britain', (1982) 33 *British Journal of Sociology* 200, argues that corporatism has never taken root. See also Middlemas, 'The Supremacy of Party' and 'Rout of the Tory Wets', 10 and 17 June 1983, *New Statesman*.

13 See Kamenka and Tay, 'Social Traditions, Legal Traditions' in *Law and Social Control* (1980), or 'Beyond Bourgeois Individualism: the Contemporary Crisis in Law and Legal Ideology' in Kamenka and Neale (eds.), *Feudalism, Capitalism and Beyond* (1975).

14 Shonfield cites as an example the case of *R. v. Brixton Prison Governor ex p. Soblen* [1963] 1 QB 829. The case is strongly criticized by P. O'Higgins, (1964) 27 *MLR* 521. See also C. Thornberry, 'The Soblen Case', (1963) 34 *Pol. Quarterly* 162. Compare this case with the later case of *Hosenball* in Chapter 3.

15 And see Winckler, 'Corporatism', (1976) 17 *European Journal of Sociology* 17; Daintith, 'Public Law and Economic Policy', (1974) *JBL* 9; Adler

and Asquith, 'Discretion and Power' in *Discretion and Welfare* (1981). See also Page, 'Public Law and Economic Policy: the UK Experience' (1982) 9 *BJLS* 225.

16   Wade, *Constitutional Fundamentals* (1980), pp. 43–7, argues that the power to designate was not a prerogative power but 'merely a piece of administrative action on the international plane'. The cancellation was, in his view, ultra vires.

Chapter 3: Adjudication and the allocation of functions

1   See, for example, planning appeals (Chapter 14).

2   See Polanyi, *The Logic of Liberty* (1951). See further Weiler, 'Two Models of Judicial Decision-Making', 46 *Can. Bar Rev.* 406 (1968).

3   The best discussion is in the American literature where the 'substantial evidence' rule has allowed courts to examine a wider range of policy issues and technical evidence than is customary in Britain. For an introduction see Stewart, Bryse and Breyer, '*Vermont Nuclear Power Corp.* v. *Natural Resources Defense Counsel Inc.*: Three Perspectives', 91 *Harv. LR* 1802 (1978) and also Beatson, 'A British View of *Vermont Yankee*', 55 *Tulane LR* 435 (1980–1).

4   See Bull, 'School Admissions: A New Appeals Procedure', (1980) *JSWL* 209. Bull identifies a related problem. If an adjudicator's decision can communicate itself outwards, previous determinations can affect the one he has to take. If the relevant resources are already used up, an adjudicator cannot award what is not available.

5   See further Galanter, 'Why the "Haves" Come out Ahead: Speculations on the Limits of Legal Change', (1974) *JLS* 95.

6   Fulbrook, Brooke and Archer, *Tribunals: A Social Court?* (Fabian Tract No. 427, 1973), p. 1.

7   But tribunals are not a novel constitutional development. See, for example, Arthurs, 'Rethinking Administrative Law: A Slightly Dicey Business', (1979) 17 *Osgoode Hall LJ* 1, on the plethora of commissions and tribunals which existed in the nineteenth century.

8   Because they vary so much there is no simple definition of 'administrative tribunals'. See Farmer, *Tribunals and Government* (1974), pp. 2–5, 184–94; and also Lowe and H. F. Rawlings, 'Tribunals and the Laws Protecting the Administration of Justice', [1982] *PL* 418.

9   Quoted in Nicol, *Illegal Entrants* (JCWI and Runnymede, 1981), p. 15.

10   The Immigration Appeals Act 1969 had provided a statutory procedure in such cases but the Rudi Dutschke case resulted in its substitution by the procedure outlined in the text. See further Hepple, 'Aliens and Administrative Justice: The Dutschke Case', (1971) 34 *MLR* 501.

11 But see for an opposing view, Stone, 'From Principles to Principles' (1981) 97 *LQR* 224.

12 See, for example, the student cases of *Ward* v. *Bradford Corporation* (1972) 70 LGR 27; *Herring* v. *Templeman* [1973] 3 All ER 569; *ex p. Roffey* (below, p. 285); *Glynn* v. *Keele* (above); *Patel* v. *University of Bradford Senate* [1979] 2 All ER 582; and for trade unions, *Lawlor* v. *Union of Post Office Workers* [1965] Ch. 12; *Leary* v. *National Union of Vehicle Builders* [1971] Ch. 34; *Edwards* v. *SOGAT* [1971] Ch. 354; *Breen* v. *Amalgamated Engineering Union* [1971] 2 QB 175; *Roebuck* v. *National Union of Mineworkers (Yorkshire Area) (No. 2)* [1978] ICR 676. See also the speech of Lord Wilberforce in *Calvin* v. *Carr* (below).

13 Mention of the 'Brandeis brief' invokes the more generous evidential rules of American law to which reference is made in note 3 (above).

14 There is a long tradition of refusals by courts to review the exercise of the Home Secretary's discretionary powers over aliens: see de Smith (1980), pp. 164–5; *R.* v. *Halliday* [1917] AC 260; *Liversidge* v. *Anderson* [1942] AC 206. Lord Denning himself participated in the similar decision of *R.* v. *Brixton Prison Governor ex p. Soblen* [1963] 2 QB 243. See further, Chapter 17.

15 Other cases which could profitably be used to expand the sample include *Wiseman* v. *Borneman* [1971] AC 297; *Re Pergamon Press Ltd* [1971] Ch. 388; *Maxwell* v. *Department of Trade and Industry* [1974] QB 523; *Chief Constable of the North Wales Police* v. *Evans* [1982] 1 WLR 1155; *Attorney-General of Hong Kong* v. *Ng Yuen Shiu* [1983] 2 WLR 735.

Chapter 4: Judicialization from within and without

1 For those unfamiliar with the grounds of judicial review, the Australian codification (p. 346) provides a convenient summary.

2 In Chapter 11 we discuss statutes which seek to restrict judicial review indirectly by casting the relevant decision-making power in subjective terms, e.g. through the formula 'if the Minister is satisfied'.

3 Other time-limitations on obtaining judicial review are imposed by the general limitation periods and the Rules of the Supreme Court (Chapter 9).

4 Now s.14 of the Tribunals and Inquiries Act 1971. The saving reference to the FCC has been deleted and is now contained in s.3 of the Foreign Compensation Act 1969 (below). See also the British Nationality Act 1981, s.44 (noted [1982] *PL* 179).

5 For a brief historical account, see de Smith (1980), pp. 400–2. The Australian codification (see note 1) does not require the error of law to appear on the record.

6 The Lord Chancellor, after consultation with the Council, may make an order exempting a class of tribunals from this requirement. The

section does not specify the quality of the reasons to be given. In extreme cases, where the reasons provided are uninformative or unintelligible, the courts have ordered tribunals to give sufficient reasons. See e.g., *Givaudan* v. *Minister of Housing and Local Government* [1966] 3 All ER 696.

7   In the earlier case of *Smith* v. *East Elloe RDC and John Campion* [1952] CLY 59, an action for trespass against the Council succeeded. But in *Smith* v. *Pywell, The Times*, 29 April 1959 an action for conspiracy against the town clerk and a ministry official failed. See further Ganz, 'Malicious Exercise of Discretion' [1964] PL 372.

8   Compare Griffith (1979), p. 19 who denies the very notion of 'constitutional principle': 'The constitution of the United Kingdom lives on, changing from day to day, for the constitution is no more and no less than what happens. Everything that happens is constitutional. And if nothing happened that would be constitutional also.'

9   From Wade, the Chairman of the Bar Council and the President of the Law Society; *The Times*, 1 and 4 February 1969.

10   See further Weaver, 'Herbert, Hercules and the Plural Society: A "Knot" in the Social Bond', (1978) 41 *MLR* 660, 670–80.

11   To take this further, read Craig, 'Representations by Public Bodies', (1977) 93 *LQR* 398, advocating a varied judicial approach to the problem of estoppel and informal representations made by public bodies. What form of contextualism does he contemplate?

12   S.107 provides: 'no judgment or order of any judge of county courts . . . shall be removed by appeal, motion, certiorari or otherwise into any other court whatever, except in the manner and according to the provisions in this Act mentioned.'

13   Eveleigh LJ, who agreed with Lord Denning in finding jurisdictional error, did not claim to abolish non-jurisdictional errors of law. Rather he argued that the relevant error of law was jurisdictional.

14   But see H. F. Rawlings, 'Jurisdictional Review after Pearlman' [1979] *PL* 404, arguing that the analysis may be confined to situations where conflicts of interpretation in lower courts need settling.

15   The analysis also gets rid of the anomaly, disclosed by *Punton* v. *Ministry of Pensions and National Insurance (No. 2)* [1964] 1 WLR 226, that a declaratory judgment is not effective for a non-jurisdictional error of law.

16   Lord Diplock's analysis of *Anisminic* did not obtain clear majority support. Lord Keith adopted it but Lord Scarman made no comment. Lord Edmund-Davies, reiterating the Privy Council's view in *South East Asia Fire Bricks Sdn. Bhd.* v. *Non-Metallic Mineral Products Manufacturing Employees Union* [1980] 2 All ER 689 that the law had been correctly stated by Geoffrey Lane LJ (dissenting) in *Pearlman*, did not treat administrative bodies and inferior courts separately, but took a

general distinction between jurisdictional and non-jurisdictional errors. Lord Salmon considered that *Anisminic* was 'confined to decisions made by commissioners, tribunals or inferior courts'; i.e. he explicitly rejected a distinction between administrative bodies and inferior courts. Lord Diplock's approach was adopted in *R.* v. *Surrey Coroner ex p. Campbell* [1982] 2 WLR 626.

Chapter 5: Getting things taped

1 The various proposals and reforms are discussed by Byrne in 'Parliamentary Control of Delegated Legislation', (1976) *Parl. Affairs* 366, where references to all the Reports can be found. The Report of the Joint Committee on Delegated Legislation (the Brooke Report) is HL 184, HC 475 (1971–2). This Report was instrumental in securing some reform. And see Norton, *Commons in Perspective* (1981); Miers and Page, *Legislation* (1982), pp. 155–66.

2 Beith, 'Prayers Unanswered: A Jaundiced View of the Parliamentary Scrutiny of Statutory Instruments', (1981) *Parl. Affairs* 165, briefly cited in our text.

3 For the establishment of these departmental committees, see 1st Report from the Select Committee on Procedure (1977–8) HC 588 (1977–8) and HC Deb. vol. 969, cols. 33–224. For expansion of the argument in the text see Nevil Johnson, 'Select Committees as Tools of Parliamentary Reform: Some Further Reflections' in Walkland and Ryle (eds.) *The Commons Today* (1981). And see Ann Davies, 'Reformed Select Committees: the First Year', *Outer Circle Policy Unit* (1981).

4 *R.* v. *Sheffield Crown Court ex p. Brownlow* [1980] 2 WLR 896, Lord Denning MR discussing *Buchanan* v. *Babco* [1978] AC 141. See also *Nothman* v. *Barnet LBC* [1979] 1 WLR 67; *Newbury District Council* v. *Environment Secretary* [1980] 2 WLR 379.

5 *The Process of Legislation*, Cmnd 6053 (1975), especially pp. 27–30, 56–70, noted Drewry, (1975) 46 *Pol. Quarterly* 443. See also *Renton and the Need for Reform*, Statute Law Revision Committee (1979).

6 Dale, *Legislative Drafting: A New Approach* (1977), argues for simpler language. See also Drewry, 'Legislation' in Walkland and Ryle (above); Zander, *The Lawmaking Process* (1980), pp. 1–34.

7 The draftsman's perspective is presented in Miers and Page, pp. 83–93; Bennion *Legislative Drafting* (1981).

8 Allen is discussing *Blackpool Corporation* v. *Locker* [1948] 1 KB 349 (where a court cut down unpublished circulars which dealt with property requisition) and *Lewisham Borough Council* v. *Roberts* [1949] 2 KB 608.

9 See also Duff and Findlay, 'Jury Vetting – the Jury under Attack', (1983) 3 *Legal Studies* 159.

10   Vile, *Constitutionalism and Separation of Powers* (1967), pp. 315–50, citing Almond and Coleman (eds.), *The Politics of Developing Areas* (1960).

11   See the review by Bradley, 'Research and Reform in Administrative Law', (1979) 13 *JSPTL (NS)* 35. For examples, see Lewis and Livock, 'Council House Allocation Procedures: Some Problems of Discretion and Control', 2 *Urban Law and Policy* (1979) 133; Freeman, 'Rules and Discretion in Local Authority Social Services Departments: The Children and Young Persons Act 1963 in Operation', (1980) *JSWL* 84; Bull, 'School Admissions: A New Appeals Procedure', (1980) *JSWL* 209.

12   Davis' influence is attested by the essays in Fogel and Hudson (eds.) *Justice as Fairness, Perspectives on the Justice Model* (1981). English works treating the same topic are Galligan, 'Guidelines and Just Deserts: A Critique of Recent Trends in Sentencing Reform', [1981] *Crim. LR* 297; Wilkins, 'Sentencing Guidelines to Reduce Disparity', [1980] *Crim. LR* 201. The Home Secretary's discretion was recently debated by the House of Lords: HL Deb. 14 Dec. 1983, cols 310–38.

12A Forst (ed.), *Sentencing Reform: Experiments in Reducing Disparity* (1982), contains a detailed account of the Oregon scheme. See also Dickey, 'The Promise and Problems of Rulemaking in Corrections: the Wisconsin Experience', (1983) *Wisconsin Law Rev.* 285.

13   For a fuller account, see the Annual Reports of the Parole Board, (HMSO), or Hall Williams, 'Parole in England and Wales: A Success Story', 10 *Univ. of Toledo LR* 465 (1979).

14   Compare the courts' attitude to prison discipline and parole. In *R.* v. *Board of Visitors of Hull Prison ex p. St Germain* [1978] 2 WLR 42, it was held in a landmark decision that the rules of natural justice applied to the Board in hearing disciplinary charges. The Appeal Court extended control and set out guidelines concerning legal representation in *R.* v. *Board of Visitors of Wormwood Scrubs Prison ex p. Anderson*, *The Times*, 9 November 1983. In contrast, the courts have refused to extend their supervisory jurisdiction to the 'administrative' process of parole in *R.* v. *Home Secretary ex p. Gunnell*, *The Times*, 3 November 1983, as well as in *Payne*'s case. See also *R.* v. *Dilworth*, *The Times*, 13 November 1983.

15   See particularly Crozier, *The Bureaucratic Phenomenon* (1964).

16   Particularly 'The Model of Rules 1 and 2' in *Taking Rights Seriously* (1977).

17   Wheale, *Equality and Social Policy* (1978).

18   *Judd* v. *Ministry of Pensions* [1965] 3 All ER 642 and HC 72 (1972), para. 29, p. 8.

19   The cases are discussed further by Ganz, 'The Role of the Ombudsman in Welfare Law' in Partington and Jowell (eds.), *Welfare Law & Policy* (1979), pp. 117–29. Compare cases of industrial grants considered by

Ganz, *Government and Industry* (1977), pp. 35–45, where the *British Oxygen* case is also discussed.

20   See also Molot, 'The Self-Created Rule of Policy and Other Ways of Exercising Administrative Discretion', (1972) 18 *McGill LJ* 310.

21   This case should be compared to *Stringer* v. *Minister of Housing and Local Government* [1970] 1 WLR 1281; *Cumings* v. *Birkenhead Corp.* [1972] 1 Ch. 12. See also the situation where policy is formulated by another department: *Lavender* v. *Minister of Housing and Local Government* [1970] 1 WLR 1231 (p. 484). Contrast *Sagnata Investments* v. *Norwich Corporation* [1971] 3 WLR 133.

22   The text of the Act is reproduced in Schwarz and Wade, *Legal Control of Government* (1972). See also Gellhorn and Byse, *Administrative Law: Cases and Comments* (7th edn 1979), pp. 178–248. Recent developments in US rulemaking procedures are discussed by Asimow, 'Delegated Legislation: US and UK', (1983) 3 *OJLS* 253. See also Chapter 3, note 3.

23   See, for example, Strauss, 'Rules, adjudications and other sources of law in an executive department: reflections on the interior department's administration of the mining law', 74 *Col. LR* 1231 (1974).

24   The Education Act 1968 regularized the position, providing that s.13 procedures were to extend to amalgamations etc., but that questions arising were to be 'determined by the Minister'. The Education Act 1980 substitutes new procedures.

25   The rule that a public authority cannot fetter its discretion by contract or otherwise contract out of its statutory duties derives from *Birkdale District Electricity Supply Co. Ltd* v. *Southport Corp.* [1926] AC 35, here cited by Lord Denning. See further *Attorney-General of Hong Kong* v. *Ng Yuen Shiu* [1983] 2 AC 629.

26   But compare *Bates* v. *Lord Hailsham* [1972] 1 WLR 137, where Megarry VC, discussing the rule-making functions of the Law Society, confined the *Liverpool* case to its facts. And see Jergesen, 'The Legal Requirements of Consultation', [1978] *PL* 290.

27   Gellhorn, 'Public Participation in Administrative Proceedings', 81 *Yale LJ* 359 (1972), is a classic American source. See also Collins, 'Public participation in Bureaucratic Decision-Making: A Reappraisal', (1980) 58 *Pub. Admin.* 465.

28   Cmnd 7497 (1979), pp. 72–9. See also Manning, 'The Social Control of Police Work' and James, 'Police–Black Relations: The Professional Solution', in S. Holdaway (ed.), *The British Police* (1979); Cain, 'On the Beat' in S. Cohen, *Images of Deviance* (1971) and 'Police Professionalism: Its Meaning and Consequences', 1 *Anglo-American LR* 217 (1972).

29   Hill, 'Social Workers and the Delivery of Welfare Benefits' in Partington and Jowell (eds.), *Welfare Law and Policy* (1979); Freeman,

op. cit. n. 11; Lister, 'Patching Up the Safety Net', CPAG No. 31 (1977).

30   See also *Vestey* v. *IRC (No. 2)* [1979] Ch. 198, 203–4; David Williams, 'Extra Statutory Concessions', [1979] *British Tax Review* 137; Sumption, 'Vestey v. IRC', [1980] *British Tax Review* 4.

31   See further Harlow, 'Administrative Reaction to Judicial Review', [1976] *PL* 116, 131; Report of the Public Accounts Committee, HC 300-I (1970/1), pp. 408–10.

Chapter 6: Firefighting to firewatching: the Council on Tribunals

1   All paragraph references are to the Report of the Franks Committee on Administrative Tribunals, Cmnd 218 (1957).

2   It must be remembered that Franks wanted the Council to handle appointments (para. 133), an additional argument in favour of the Lord Chancellor's office. It never assumed this task.

3   The actual arrangements for Scotland are a little different. The Council's Scottish Committee deals with any tribunals special to Scotland. Our description is confined to England.

4   Under the Tribunals and Inquiries Act 1971, the Council is to have not more than 15 nor less than 10 members. These are to be appointed by the Lord Chancellor and the Lord Advocate. The PCA is, by virtue of his office, a member of both the Council and the Scottish Committee. At present, excluding the PCA, the Council has a membership of 15.

5   A. D. Rose, 'The Council on Tribunals – Need for a New Direction', (1979) unpublished thesis, University of London, p. 32. The study draws on information provided to the author by the Council's staff.

6   Wraith and Hutchesson (1973), pp. 300–6, see the absence of a career structure as a serious weakness of the British tribunals' system. They are not in favour of secondment from government departments and prefer the institution of a common tribunals' service to provide staff (e.g. clerks, presenting officers) throughout tribunals. Such an arrangement could include the Council on Tribunals.

7   Statistical material concerning the Council's jurisdiction over statutory inquiries is included in this chapter. See Ch. 15 for two case-studies.

8   Compare the attitude of the Select Committee and the first PCA (Sir Edmund Compton) to procedure and merits, discussed in Chapter 7.

9   The saga is recorded in the *LAG Bulletin*: Nov. 1979, p. 247; Dec. 1979, p. 276; Feb. 1980, p. 27. See also June 1980, p. 127.

10   Rules of Parliamentary procedure limit criticism of judicial decisions: Erskine May, *Parliamentary Practice* (19th edn 1976), pp. 368–468;

Wade and Phillips, *Constitutional and Administrative Law* (9th edn), pp. 319–21.

11　A similar problem involving the Commission for Racial Equality was discussed by the Home Affairs Committee of the House of Commons: see HC 46 (1981/2). The CRE was criticized for emphasizing its 'promotional' work (e.g. publication of tribunal decisions, advisory work, etc.) at the expense of law enforcement and investigation, which had fallen into arrears. The CRE was also criticized for intervening in controversial 'political' matters, which might undermine confidence in its impartiality. Compare also the CLA (below).

12　See further Bell, 'Social Security Tribunals – a General Perspective', (1982) 33 *NILQ* 132, 138–9.

13　See, further, Report of the Law Society and Comments and Recommendations of the Lord Chancellor's Advisory Committee (1973–4), (HC 20 (1974/5)); AR of the Council on Tribunals for 1972/3 (HC 82 (1973/4)), and 1974/5 (HC 679 (1975/6)). In its 33rd Report (HC 137 (1982/3)), the Committee called for legal aid in immigration cases and before Social Security Commissioners.

14　The (Benson) Commission on Legal Services devoted much space to consideration of legal services in tribunals. The Council gave evidence favouring the extension of legal aid to all tribunals in which legal representation was permitted. The Benson Commission recommended expansion of legal aid, of the 'green form' advisory scheme and of lay representation: Cmnd 7648, Vol. 1, Ch. 15 (and see Lawrence, 'Solicitors & Tribunals', [1980] *JSWL* 13). The Legal Aid Act 1979 extended the advice scheme but full legal representation was extended only to Mental Health Review Tribunals (see HC 64 (1982/3), paras. 3.30–3.34). See now 'The Government Response to Benson', Cmnd. 9077.

15　See further Gellhorn, 'Administrative Procedure Reform: Hardy Perennial', 48 *ABAJ* 243 (1962).

16　Some further ideas are contained in Ison, 'Small Claims', (1972) 35 *MLR* 18, 27–31. French administrative law procedure is briefly described in Brown and Garner, *French Administrative Law* (3rd edn 1983), Ch. 5. See also 7th AR (1982/3) of the Australian Administrative Review Council, pp. 28–9.

17　For a further account see Farmer, *Tribunals and Government* (1974), pp. 113–23. Street (1975) contains an unflattering portrait of rent tribunals.

18　Doig, 'Public Bodies and Ministerial Patronage', (1978) *Parl. Affairs* 1; Davies, 'Patronage and quasi-government: some proposals for reform' in Anthony Barker (ed.), *Governments and the Networks of Public Policy Making* (1982).

19　Of the six Chairmen, Sir Hugh Ross served only four months, Lord

Reading (1956–60) was a lawyer and politician, Lord Tenby (1961–7) a retired politician, Lady Burton (1967–73) a writer, broadcaster and, later, politician interested in consumer affairs, Lord Tweedsmuir (1974–81) a politician with experience in foreign affairs and administration. The new Chairman, Lord Gibson-Watt, was once Minister of State at the Welsh Office.

20   The Australian solution is more in line with Robson's wishes. An Administrative Appeals Tribunal can review tribunal decisions *on their merits*: see Hall, 'Aspects of Federal Jurisdiction: The Administrative Appeals Tribunal', (1983) 57 *Aus. LJ* 389. The Administrative Review Council has a general supervisory mandate and may, *inter alia*, recommend new tribunals.

21   See, for Sweden's justice ombudsman, Sten Rudholm, 'The Chancellor of Justice' in Rowat (ed.), *The Ombudsman* (1965) and Anderson, 'Judicial Accountability: Scandinavia, California and the USA', (1980) 28 *Am. J. Comp. Law* 393.

22   This aspect of the Conseil's work is well described in Rendel, *The Administrative Functions of the French Conseil d'Etat* (1968) or Freedman, *The Conseil d'Etat in Modern France* (1961).

Chapter 7: Ombudsman techniques

1   A number of ombudsmen-like institutions were established in Britain during 1967–74: Parliamentary Commissioner for Administration (1967); Northern Ireland Parliamentary Commissioner and Northern Ireland Commissioner for Complaints (1969); National Health Service Commissioners in England, Wales and Scotland (1972/3); Commission for Local Administration in England, Wales and Scotland (1974).

2   Mitchell, 'The Ombudsman Fallacy' [1962] *P.L.* 24, preferred to bridge the gap by developing judicial controls along the lines of the French Conseil d'Etat.

3   See Herman, 'Adjournment Debates in the House of Commons', 26 *Parl. Affairs* 92 (1972); Medawar, *Parliamentary Questions* (Social Audit, 1981).

4   See e.g. Morrell, *From the electors of Bristol* (Spokesman Pamphlet No. 57, 1977); Norton, 'The Importance of M P-to-Minister Correspondence' (1982) 35 *Parl. Affairs* 59. See also Chapter 17 on M Ps' constituency work concerning immigration.

5   Stacey, *The British Ombudsman* (1971) describes the setting-up of the PCA.

6   The first four PCAs have been Sir Edmund Compton, a former Comptroller and Auditor-General; two senior civil servants, Sir Alan Marre and Sir Idwal Pugh; and a lawyer, Sir Cecil Clothier QC.

7 Compare *Sachsenhausen* (Chapter 13) where Mr Brown, the Foreign Secretary, stated (HC Deb. vol. 758, cols. 112–16) that although he did not accept the PCA's finding of maladministration (HC 54 (1967/8), p. 65), it would be wrong, having established the office, to reject his findings.

8 See Gregory, 'The Select Committee on the Parliamentary Commissioner for Administration 1967–1980', [1982] *PL* 49.

9 For an early study of the MP filter, see Cohen, 'The Parliamentary Commissioner and the "MP Filter" ', [1972] *PL* 204.

10 See further Marshall, 'Maladministration', [1973] *PL* 32.

11 See Foulkes, 'The Discretionary Provisions of the Parliamentary Commissioner Act 1967', (1971) 34 *MLR* 377. For a description of the PCA's overlap with adjudicatory mechanisms and other external monitors, see Bradley, 'The Role of the Ombudsman in Relation to the Protection of Citizens' Rights', [1980] 39(2) *CLJ* 304. See also Verkuil, 'The Ombudsman and the Limits of the Adversary System', [1975] *Col. LR* 845.

12 The dispute between Committee and government is long-standing. As early as 1969 (HC 385 (1968/9)) they disagreed about the personnel exclusion. The cycle repeated itself in 1979/80: see HC 593 (1979/80) and Cmnd 8274.

13 See Chapter 17 for similar government reluctance to let the Commission for Racial Equality scrutinize the Immigration Service.

14 The CLA is a collegiate body, with three commissioners responsible for different parts of England and with the PCA as an ex officio member. So far there have been five commissioners: Baroness Serota, Mr Harrison, Mr Cook, Mr Mackenzie-Johnson and Professor Yardley. See generally on organization and structure, Lewis and Gateshill, *The Commission for Local Administration – A Preliminary Appraisal* (RIPA, 1978).

15 Sir Idwal Pugh (HC 157 (1977/8), p. 7) saw his office 'as having two functions. One is the statutory one of investigating individual complaints and, where appropriate, recommending remedies for individual injustices sustained through maladministration. The other is to draw attention to lessons which should be learned from such individual cases and applied to improving administrative practice generally.' For general descriptions by Sir Cecil Clothier, see 'The Efficacy of the Parliamentary Ombudsman' in *Parliament and the Executive* (RIPA, 1982) and 'The Work of the Health Service Commissioner', (1983) 51 *Medico-Legal J.* 8.

16 See, for example, AR, 1978/9 for the views of Baroness Serota (p. 109) and Mr Harrison (p. 115). Nor can we assume that different holders of an office operate in the same way. For instance the first PCA, Sir Edmund Compton, was criticized for adopting a cautious approach,

not dissimilar to the CLA's search for consensus. However, Gregory and Hutchesson (1975, p. 652) contend that the institution needed time to grow: 'Such is the entrenched power of the Administration that an external critic setting out to work against it rather than with it might very well have found himself isolated and largely ineffectual, however much enthusiasm his flamboyant efforts generated among the on-lookers.' The recent replacement as CLA Chairman of Baroness Serota, formerly a Minister of State, with Professor Yardley, a lawyer, may presage a change of direction. The 1982/3 Annual Report is more lawyer-like in approach.

17   In 1981/2 the average time from the receipt of a complaint to the issue of a CLA investigation report was 38 weeks, the lowest figure since the initial year of operation. In 229 cases up to 1981/2 (27 per cent of the total) more than six months elapsed between the date of a report and the date when the commissioner could signal satisfaction with the outcome. The system is not particularly cheap. Mr Cook (AR 1982/3, p. 60) estimated the average direct cost of dealing with each enter-tainable complaint as £223.

18   Maria Colwell, aged seven, was returned from local authority care to her mother and subsequently killed by her step-father. See 'Report of the Committee of Inquiry into the Care and Supervision Provided in Relation to Maria Colwell' (DHSS, 1974).

19   Compare *Rootkin* v. *Kent CC* [1981] 2 All ER 227; noted (1982) 45 *MLR* 87. See also Crawford, 'Where Judges Fear to Tread . . . ?', [1982] *JPEL* 619.

20   See, for example, the White Paper, 'Efficiency and Effectiveness in the Civil Service' (Cmnd 8616 1982), which announced the Financial Mangement Initiative designed to improve the allocation, manage-ment and control of resources in central government. Cmnd 9058 is the first report on progress. See also Loughlin, 'Local Government in the Welfare Corporate State', (1981) 44 *MLR* 422, on the Conservative Government's conception of 'effective management' in local authori-ties.

21   See Danet, 'Toward A Method to Evaluate the Ombudsman Role', (1978) 10 *Admin. & Soc.* 335; also Gwyn, 'The Ombudsman in Britain: A Qualified Success in Government Reform', (1982) 60 *Pub. Admin.* 177.

22   See further Burgess, 'Whose side is the Ombudsman really on?', (1983) *New Society* 55.

Chapter 8: Passing time, or how administrators apply the rules

1   There are no statutory procedures governing ex gratia payments by government departments, but the internal civil service accounting

procedures normally involve Treasury consent, though this may sometimes be dispensed with. In 1960–1, the procedure was explained to the Public Accounts Committee (see HC 252 (1960/1)). The guidelines are published in the 'Epitome of the Reports from the Public Accounts Committee (1938–1969)', HC 187 (1969/70), pp. 426–31. A short account of the procedure is given in Harlow, *Compensation and Government Torts* (1982), pp. 119–20.

2   Baroness Serota, in a case (Inv. 3969S of 21/11/77) involving a complaint that Kent County Council had failed to comply with its statutory duty to provide sufficient land for gypsies' accommodation, emphasized that, while a failure to fulfil a statutory duty raises a presumption of maladministration, that presumption is rebuttable: 'My task . . . is to consider the facts against what is reasonable and practicable for the County Council in the circumstances of each particular case and there may be good reasons why such a failure does not amount to faulty administration.'

3   These were Norwich's reasons ([1982] 2 WLR 580, 587) for not deploying more resources in order to meet the Secretary of State's nine-month deadline for completing all outstanding council house valuations: 'We are trying to keep a balance between the need not to increase our staff costs, and the various claims on resources . . . which in the Council's judgment cannot be neglected, as they would have to be if the . . . target were to be met . . . It simply will not do . . . to neglect the problems of the homeless, and other statutory housing obligations – and the work we are doing to create employment . . . just to enable a relatively small number of people, who are already comfortably housed, to buy a property a few months earlier than they otherwise could, when they will lose nothing by waiting.'

4   At the end of 1983, the CLA was still awaiting the Government's final decision.

Chapter 9: Judicial review: the tip of the iceberg?

1   Habeas corpus procedures differ from the rest. For a description, see R. J. Sharpe, *The Law of Habeas Corpus* (1976), Ch. 10.

2   But see the *Federation* case (p. 300).

3   However, in Sunkin's survey (1979), most Applications for Judicial Review involved only the prerogative orders; 31.6 per cent were certiorari applications, 22.8 per cent mandamus and 15.8 per cent certiorari and mandamus combined. Our follow-up survey (1982), conducted before *O'Reilly* v. *Mackman* (p. 264), produced figures of 33.7 per cent, 10.1 per cent and 26.8 per cent respectively.

4   See Rules of the Supreme Court (Amendment No. 4) 1980, SI No. 2000, amending the 1977 Order 53. The applicant can request an

oral hearing. If dissatisfied with a judge's decision on the papers, he can also renew his application by applying for an oral hearing.

5   For Office working purposes in 1980, composite applications were double-counted where the remedies were of equal 'weight', a 'commonsense' approach being used where applications included all available remedies.

6   For comment see Beatson and Matthews, (1978) 41 *MLR* 437 and Harlow, [1978] *PL* 1. The provisions were translated into statutory form by ss.29–31 of the Supreme Court Act 1981. See Jacob, 'The Supreme Court Act 1981', [1981] *PL* 452.

7   The cases involving declarations and injunctions, whether sought individually or in conjunction with other remedies, accounted for only 5.1 per cent and 6.3 per cent of Sunkin's sample (1979). In our 1982 survey the figures were 13.9 per cent and 4.4 per cent. The move towards centralization may cause these figures to rise. Cmnd 9065, Table 1.4, contains (in bare outline) the 1982 statistics.

8   See Blom-Cooper, 'The New Face of Judicial Review: Administrative Changes in Order 53', [1982] *PL* 250.

9   S.31(6) of the Supreme Court Act 1981 provides that a court may refuse leave or final relief if it considers that there has been undue delay in making the application and that to grant relief would cause substantial hardship or substantially prejudice the rights of any person, or would be detrimental to good administration. See further, *R.* v. *Merseyside CC ex p. Great Universal Stores* (*The Times,* 18 February 1982).

10   Crown Proceedings Act 1947, s.28.

11   See also *Uppal* v. *Home Office* (*The Times,* 11 November 1978); *Lambert* v. *Ealing LBC* [1982] 2 All ER 394; *Bousfield* v. *North Yorkshire CC* (*The Times,* 4 March 1982).

12   See p. 332, for the test of Substantial Evidence.

13   For conflicting views see Harlow, ' "Public" and "Private" Law: Definition without Distinction', (1980) 43 *MLR* 241 and Samuel, 'Public and Private Law: A Private Lawyer's Response', (1983) 46 *MLR* 558. See also Cane, 'Standing, Legality and the Limits of Public Law', [1981] *PL* 322.

14   It was held, following *R.* v. *British Broadcasting Corporation ex p. Lavelle* [1983] 1 WLR 23, that the Supreme Court Act 1981 did not extend the scope of the prerogative orders so as to include the decisions of domestic tribunals. See also *R.* v. *East Berkshire Health Authority ex p. Walsh, The Times,* 15 November 1983.

15   Thrasher, 'The Concept of a Central-Local Government Partnership', 9 *Policy and Politics* 455 (1981), provides an introduction to the (substantial) literature on principal-agent and partnership models of

central-local relations. See, further, R. Rhodes, *Control and Power in Central-Local Government Relations* (1981); M. Elliott, *The Role of Law in Central-Local Relations* (1981). See more generally, G. Jones (ed.), *New Approaches to the Study of Central-Local Government Relationships* (1980). The illustration in the text can be taken much further because neither 'central' nor 'local' government need be viewed as a homogeneity; see, e.g., Heclo and Wildavsky, *The Private Government of Public Money* (2nd edn 1981).

16 Reported by Hansen, 'Litigation, A Strategy for Fighting Racial Discrimination?', (1981) *LAG Bulletin* 229, p. 231.

17 We encountered this technique in the aftermath of *Anisminic*. In Chapter 12 we meet it again, in its retrospective guise, with the *Burmah Oil* case.

18 Reduction may be described briefly as a Scottish writ approximating in effect to certiorari in England.

Chapter 10: Rationing judicial review

1 See de Smith (1973), p. 335. See also 'Report of the Justice Committee on Administrative Law' (1966), paras. 36–8.

2 See on the exercise of remedial discretion in relation to the existence of alternative remedies, *R. v. Hillingdon Borough Council ex p. Royco Homes Ltd* [1974] 1 QB 720. See also *R. v. Knightsbridge Crown Court ex p. Marcrest Properties Ltd* [1983] 1 WLR 300 on 'technical' errors of law.

3 For another case where the court deployed the void/voidable distinction to avoid administrative inconvenience, see *Durayappah v. Fernando* [1967] 2 All ER 152.

4 See also *Barrs v. Bethell* [1981] 3 WLR 874. For the impact of the new Order 53, see the *Federation* case (below).

5 Note that s. 21 of the Crown Proceedings Act 1947 provides that no injunction lies against the Crown. See further, *R. v. IRC ex p. Rossminster* [1980] 2 WLR 1. Interim declaratory relief is not available in any circumstances: *Gouriet*'s case.

6 Locus standi in planning is discussed further in Chapter 14.

7 See *Prescott v. Birmingham Corporation* [1955] Ch. 210. However, in *Barrs v. Bethell* [1981] 3 WLR 874, Warner J denied Camden ratepayers standing when, in their own names, they sought declarations against both the Council and the controlling councillors in respect of a refusal to cut services and raise council house rents.

8 Now look at the *Federation* case (below). Why did the House of Lords refuse to extend the same protection to taxpayers?

9 For illustrative Supreme Court decisions after *Sierra Club* and *SCRAP*

(the leading cases when the English Law Commission (below) was considering reform), see *Schlesinger* v. *Reservists Committee to Stop the War* 418 US 208 (1974); *Warth* v. *Seldin* 422 US 490 (1975); *Duke Power Company* v. *Carolina Environmental Study Group, Inc.* 438 US 59 (1978); *Valley Forge Christian College* v. *Americans United for Separation of Church and State, Inc.* 102 S.Ct. 752 (1982). For an introduction to American standing tests, see Stewart (1975) and Chayes, 'Public Law Litigation and the Burger Court' 96 *Harv. LR* 4 (1982).

10   One particular difficulty derived from the method chosen for reform. Order 53 was delegated legislation initiated by the Rule Committee of the Supreme Court under the Supreme Court of Judicature (Consolidation) Act 1925. S.99(1)(a) of the Act only empowers the Committee to make rules of procedure. This raised the difficult issue of whether standing requirements are rules of procedure or substance. If the latter, then change was ultra vires the primary legislation. 'Sufficient interest' is now, however, contained in s.31(3) of the Supreme Court Act 1981.

11   So Lord Wilberforce considered that what is now s.31(3) of the Supreme Court Act 1981 does not alter the pre-existing law.

12   Lord Wilberforce was supported by Lords Fraser and Roskill. Lord Scarman, while adopting Lord Wilberforce's views concerning the procedural alterations made by Order 53, followed Lord Diplock in emphasizing the width of judicial discretion.

13   This is more clearly expressed in France: see Harding, 'Locus Standi in French Administrative Law', [1978] *PL* 144.

14   See further Collins, 'Public Participation in Bureaucratic Decision-Making: A Reappraisal' (1980) 58 *Pub. Admin.* 465. See also Gellhorn, 'Public Participation in Administrative Proceedings', 81 *Yale LJ* 359 (1972).

15   There is much American writing on the links between standing requirements and justiciability. See e.g., Albert, 'Standing to Challenge Administrative Action: An Inadequate Surrogate for Claims for Relief', 83 *Yale LJ* 425 (1974) and Brilmayer, 'The Jurisprudence of Article III: Perspectives on the "Case or Controversy" Requirement', 93 *Harv. LR* 297 (1979).

16   See also now the views of Craig, *Administrative Law* (1983), pp. 444–60.

Chapter 11: Discretionary justice?

1   But see Devlin, 'Judges as Lawmakers', (1976) 39 *MLR* 1 and 'Judges, Government and Politics', (1978) 41 *MLR* 501; Reid, 'The Judge as Lawmaker', (1972) 12 *JSPTL (NS)* 22; Greene, *The Judicial Office* (1938).

2   The quotation is from Bickel, *The Least Dangerous Branch* (1962), p. 19.

See also R. Berger, *Government by Judiciary* (1977).

3   *R.* v. *Metropolitan Police Commissioner ex p. Blackburn* [1968] 2 Q B 118 and
    R. v. *Metropolitan Police Commissioner ex p. Blackburn (No. 2)* [1968] 2 Q B
    150.

4   Particularly *Baker* v. *Carr* 369 US 186 (1962), concerning the
    inequality of electoral districts in Tennessee. For comment see
    Auerbach, 'The Reapportionment Cases: One Person, One Vote –
    One Vote, One Value', 1964 *Sup. Ct Rev.* 1.

5   The 'slot-machine' theory was demolished by Felix Cohen, 'Modern
    Ethics and the Law', reprinted in *The Legal Conscience* (1960). More
    modern discussions are H. L. A. Hart, *The Concept of Law* (1961),
    pp. 120–37; R. Dworkin, *Taking Rights Seriously* (1977), pp. 31–9; N.
    MacCormick, *H. L. A. Hart* (1981), pp. 121–3.

6   An extended analysis of the range of discretion available to the judge in
    criminal cases is Pattenden, *The Judge, Discretion and the Criminal Trial*
    (1982).

7   See further *Taking Rights Seriously*, pp. 86–105. Dworkin's ideal is the
    superhuman Hercules, but his fallible Herbert is instantly recogniz-
    able. Dworkin's theory of 'institutional morality' is criticized by
    MacCormick in 'Jurisprudence and the Constitution', (1983) 36 *CLP*
    13.

8   Twining and Meirs, *How to Do Things with Rules* (1982).

9   See also Diplock, 'Judicial Review Reviewed', [1974] *CLJ* 233.

10 R. Stevens, *Law and Politics* (1979), develops this theme. See also A.
    Paterson, *The Law Lords* (1982), pp. 170–83.

11 *The Politics of the Judiciary* (1977). See Minogue, 'The Biases of the
    Bench', *The Times Literary Supplement*, 6 January 1978; Devlin, 'Judges,
    Government and Politics', (1978) 41 *MLR* 501; Paterson, *The Law
    Lords* (1982) and 'Judges: A Political Elite', (1974) 1 *BJLS* 118, for
    alternative viewpoints.

12 See Keith-Lucas, 'Poplarism', [1962] *PL* 52 or, for a fuller account,
    Branson (1979). Bradney, 'Facade: the Poplar Case', (1983) 34 *NILQ*
    1, analyses the background of the judges involved in the case.

13 See further de Smith (1980), pp. 148–9, on the extent of a duty to give
    reasons and, on evidence, pp. 333–5. Contrasting cases are *Ashbridge
    Investments* v. *Minister of Housing and Local Government* [1965] 1 WLR
    1320 and *Cannock Chase DC* v. *Kelly* [1978] 1 WLR 1.

14 *Consolidated Edison Co.* v. *National Labor Relations Board*, 305 US 197, 229
    (1938). Further references to the American rules are to be found at
    Ch. 3, n. 3. See also Gellhorn and Byse, *Administrative Law – Cases and
    Comments*, pp. 256–7, 737. To compare the approach of an American
    court to a problem similar to the *Bromley* case, read *US Trust Co. of New*

York v. *New Jersey* 97 S. Ct 1505 (1977).

15   Judges are not supposed to refer to Hansard as an aid when interpreting statute: *Hadmor Productions Ltd* v. *Hamilton* [1982] 1 All ER 1042. Extrajudicially Scarman has said: 'They regularly look at the reports of Royal Commissions – though never, or if ever, only secretively, at Hansard'.

16   But see, for extended discussion, Dignan, 'Policy-making, Local Authorities and the Courts; the "GLC Fares" Case', (1983) 99 *LQR* 605. The Transport Act 1983 radically altered the situation by providing that the LTE should as far as practicable balance its budget. Local authority grants are by s. 4(4) made subject to ministerial guidance. In July 1983 a government White Paper, 'Public Transport in London' (Cmnd 9004), contained proposals to transfer control to the Transport Secretary from the GLC and to reconstitute the LTE as 'London Regional Transport', a quango responsible to and where necessary funded by central government. The Conservative manifesto for the 1983 election proposed the abolition of the Metropolitan Counties including the GLC. See 'Streamlining the Cities' (Cmnd 9063, 1983), which gave rise to the interesting case of *R.* v. *Environment Secretary ex p. GLC, The Times*, 2 December 1983.

17   See also Prosser, 'Towards a Critical Public Law', (1982) 9 *JLS* 1.

18   But see now the Education (Fees and Awards) Act 1983 and Education Authority (Mandatory Awards) (No. 2) Regulations 1983, which reinstate the government interpretation.

19   There is no provision in Griffith's package for a statutory delimitation of the jurisdiction of the High Court. For the reasons why this is in the authors' view a necessary preliminary, see the judgment of Lord Diplock in *Re Racal Communications* (p. 115). The Commonwealth experience is also relevant: see Evans, 'Judicial review in Ontario – recent developments in the remedies – some problems of pouring old wine into new bottles', (1977) *Can. Bar Rev.* 148; Mullan, 'The Federal Court Act – a misguided attempt at administrative law reform', (1975) 23 *Univ. of Toronto LJ* 14.

20   For example, recent English cases hint at a new principle of proportionality, i.e. that administrative sanctions should not be excessive. This idea is borrowed from European law. See further *R.* v. *Brentford JJ ex p. Catlin* [1975] QB 455. Compare and contrast the reasoning of the House of Lords in *Chief Constable of the North Wales Police* v. *Evans* [1982] 1 WLR 1155.

Chapter 12: Compensation: private rights and public interest

1   The different approaches are discussed by Ganz, *Government and Industry* (1977).

2   Two celebrated affirmations of the principle antedate the civil war: *Bate's Case* (1606) 2 St. Tr. 371; *The Case of Shipmoney (Hampden's Case)* (1637) 3 St. Tr. 825. It is still the law that administrative agencies may not levy taxes in the absence of clear statutory authorization, express or implied: *A. G.* v. *Wilts United Dairy Co.* (1932) 91 LJ KB 897. See also *Commissioners of Customs and Excise* v. *Cure and Deely* [1962] 1 QB 340.

3   Duguit, 'The Law and the State', 32 *Harv. LR* 1 (1917-18).

4   This is the principle of 'Equality before Public Charges'. See further Harlow, *Compensation and Government Torts* (1982), pp. 102-7.

5   A comparable case is *Hoffmann-LaRoche* v. *Trade Secretary* [1974] 3 WLR 104. The case concerned profits on sales of Librium and Valium to the National Health Service. The claim involved at least £8 million and a negotiated settlement was reached on the basis that the company would repay £3.75 million to the Government in respect of £12 million excess profits allegedly made over a period of two years, while the Government would make an offset of £8.25 million on the ground that prices during the dispute had slipped unduly low. (HC Deb. vol. 899, col. 1544).

6   See the Diego Garcia agreement (Cmnd 6413, 1982) and 'Diego Garcia – a Contrast to the Falklands', Minority Rights Group (1982). Further information is contained in a report by the Foreign Affairs Committee, HC 379 (1982/3), pp. 17, 24.

7   'Development and Compensation – Putting People First' (Cmnd 5124, 1972).

8   A comparable argument about the use of discretion to disguise shrinking resources is advanced by Winckler, 'The Political Economy of Administrative Discretion' in Adler and Asquith (eds), *Discretion and Welfare* (1981), p. 107.

9   Klosterman, 'A Public Interest Criterion', (1980) 46 *J. of the American Planning Assoc.* 323, argues that the public interest criterion provides a rational basis for evaluation of their work by planners.

10 The argument was based on *Metropolitan Asylum District* v. *Hill* (1881) 6 App. Cas. 193. See also *Tate & Lyle Food and Distribution Ltd* v. *GLC* [1983] 1 All ER 1159, where damages were awarded, and *Dept. of Transport* v. *NW Water Authority* [1983] 3 WLR 105.

11 Keith Davies, *Law of Compulsory Purchase and Compensation* (3rd edn 1978), p. 161. But compare *Miller* v. *Jackson* [1977] QB 966, noted Buckley, (1978) 41 *MLR* 334, with *Kennaway* v. *Thompson* [1980] 3 WLR 361, noted Buckley, (1981) 44 *MLR* 212. For another case of pollution by an oil refinery causing nuisance, see *Halsey* v. *Esso Petroleum* [1961] 2 All ER 145. See also *Page Motors Ltd* v. *Epsom and Ewell BC* (1982) 80 LGR 337, noted Cane, [1983] *PL* 202.

12 Only two English precedents, neither authoritative, were cited: *Greenwell* v. *Prison Commissioners* (1951) 101 LJ 486; *Ellis* v. *Home*

Office [1953] 2 All ER 541. For the argument that the *Dorset Yacht* decision does not go far enough, see Hamson, 'Escaping Borstal Boys and the Immunity of Office', [1969] *CLJ* 273.

13   In *Geddis* v. *Proprietors of Bann Reservoir* (1878) 3 App Cas 430, the respondents were held liable when a reservoir administered under a statutory power was negligently allowed to overflow. See further Ganz, 'Compensation for Negligent Administrative Action', [1973] *PL* 84; Craig, *Administrative Law* (1983), chapter 16, analyses the case-law in greater detail.

14   The extra-judicial views of Lord Reid on polycentricity are discussed by A. Paterson, *The Law Lords* (1982), pp. 172–3.

15   But contrast *Davy* v. *Spelthorne BC* [1983] 3 WLR 742, where indirect challenge of a planning decision by an action in negligence was allowed.

16   De Smith, *Judicial Review of Administrative Action* (1980), pp. 35–46. The leading case is *Conway* v. *Rimmer* [1968] AC 910, which allows the court to examine documents to see if the claim of privilege is justified. The principle has been used restrictively. See *R.* v. *Lewes JJ ex p. Home Secretary* [1973] AC 388; *Burmah Oil* v. *Bank of England* [1979] 2 All ER 1169; *Air Canada* v. *Trade Secretary* [1983] 2 WLR 494. On confidentiality, see *Harman* v. *Home Office* [1982] 1 All ER 532, a case which arose out of an action by a prisoner against the Home Office for damages in respect of injury suffered in the secure unit of a prison, the object of which was to expose to public scrutiny unpublished details of prison administration; and see *Defence Secretary* v. *Guardian Newspapers Ltd, The Times*, 17 December 1983. See also Jacob, 'Discovery and the Public Interest' [1976] *PL* 134; Michael, *The Politics of Secrecy* (1982), pp. 98–113.

17   *Dunlop* v. *Woolahara Municipal Council* [1981] 2 WLR 693 is discussed by Harlow, op. cit., pp. 87–101.

18   A more recent example is provided by the Falkland Islands Compensation Scheme: HC 379 (1982/3), pp. 7–8.

Chapter 13: Administrative compensation

1   See Harlow, *Compensation and Government Torts* (1982), pp. 17–33, for a brief account.

2   *Justice*, 'Administration under Law' (1971), pp. 31–2.

3   For an account of their functioning, see Micklethwait, *The National Insurance Commissioners* (1976).

4   'Report of a Committee to Review the Principles and Operation of the Criminal Injuries to Property (Compensation Act) (Northern Ireland) 1971', HMSO (Belfast) (1976), pp. 1–3.

5   The White Paper was founded on the report of a working party, 'Compensation for Victims of Crimes of Violence', Cmnd 1406 (1961).

There was also a *Justice* report, 'Compensation for Crimes of Violence' (1962). The final report was published as a White Paper: 'Compensation for Victims of Crimes of Violence', Cmnd 2323 (1964).

6 Introduced by s.3(1), Administration of Justice Act 1982, which reforms the law of damages in other ways. And see Lord Foot (HL Deb. 14 Dec. 1983, col. 292).

7 References are to the text of the 1979 scheme, which was amended and the paragraphs renumbered. The scheme and the statement are both annexed to the annual reports of the CICB.

8 See also *R.* v. *CICB ex p. Thompstone* [1983] 1 WLR 422.

8A The Government now proposes to legislate 'during the life of Parliament': see motion by Lord Allen (HL Deb. 14 December 1983, cols 283–309), where other reasons to legislate were given.

9 This difficulty was removed, though not retrospectively, by the Congenital Disabilities (Civil Liability) Act 1976. The causation problem was later investigated by the ex-PCA, Sir Alan Marre, in 'The Thalidomide Y-List Inquiry', HMSO (1978), which resulted in payments from the charitable fund to a number of children. The thalidomide story is well documented in *Suffer the Children*, a report by the *Sunday Times* Insight Team (1979). Especially relevant are pp. 183–239.

10 See also the *Hardman* case, investigated by the PCA (HC 84 (1983/4), p. 29).

10A The HSC cannot investigate action which, in his opinion, was taken solely in consequence of the exercise of clinical judgement: see Part I, Sched. 13 of the National Health Service Act 1977. The Select Committee (HC 650 (1980/1)) recommended limited extensions to his jurisdiction. No change has been made.

11 A House of Lords debate was initiated on a motion by Lord Campbell of Alloway. See HL Deb. 1 December 1982, vol. 436, cols. 1241–69.

12 In *R.* v. *Secretary of State for Social Services ex p. Loveday, The Times,* 18 February 1983, an application for review of unfavourable decisions by the Minister and a Vaccine Damage Tribunal, the tribunal's determination was quashed and remitted to a differently constituted tribunal which awarded compensation.

13 *Ex gratia payments for property damage caused by absconders in the last five years*

Financial year	Number of cases	Compensation paid
1978–9	61	£2697.92
1979–80	53	£4015.24
1980–1	59	£9360.80
1981–2	49	£4161.16
1982–3	37	£3445.27

14 *Sirros* v. *Moore* [1975] QB 135; *Sutcliffe* v. *Thackrah* [1974] AC 727. And

see Brazier, 'Judicial Immunity and the Independence of the Judiciary', [1976] *PL* 397; Rubinstein, 'Liability in Tort of Judicial Officers', [1964] 15 *Univ. of Toronto LJ* 317.

15   In the second case, because the plaintiff must prove both malice and absence of reasonable cause to prosecute, *Glinski* v. *McIver* [1962] AC 726, in the first because the damage results normally from a conviction rather than arrest.

16   See further C. Price and J. Caplan, *The Confait Confessions* (1977). The Fisher Inquiry into the *Confait* case was HC 90 (1977/8).

17   The memorandum was submitted by the Home Office to the Home Affairs Committee and is reprinted in the Report, pp. 1–5. It is too long to reprint here, but is an admirable summary of the means available for releasing from custody a defendant who has been wrongly convicted and Home Office practice in the use of the powers.

Chapter 14: Planning and participation

1   Levin, *Government and the Planning Process* (1976), a case study of the development of New Towns provides valuable insights into the decision-taking process. Hall's study of the third London airport project in *Great Planning Disasters* (1981), pp. 15–55, makes the link between spatial and economic planning.

2   See H. C. Deb. vol. 936, WA cols. 567–70. For the inquiry, see Milne, 'Belvoir: a unique inquiry or a sign of things to come?', (1980) 366 *Planning* 7.

3   You do not need a detailed knowledge of the planning process to understand what follows but familiarity with its structure is essential. The best concise account is Cullingworth, *Town and Country Planning in Britain* (8th edn 1981), pp. 1–97. See also Cherry, *The Politics of Town Planning* (1982).

4   The Report of the (Barlow) Commission on the Distribution of the Industrial Population, Cmnd 6153 (1940).

5   The Report of the (Scott) Committee on Land Utilisation in Rural Areas, Cmnd 6378 (1942).

6   The (Reith) Committee on New Towns issued interim and final reports, Cmnds 6759, 6794 (1946).

7   The Report of the (Uthwatt) Expert Committee on Compensation and Betterment, Cmnd 6386 (1942).

8   But see further, Cullingworth (1981), pp. 129–56: M. Grant, *Urban Planning Law* (1982), pp. 645–80; McAuslan, *Land, Law and Planning* (1975), pp. 602–700.

9   A simple introductory essay is Champion, 'Issues over Land', in R. Davies and P. Hall (eds.), *Issues in Urban Society* (1978).

10   P. Hall, *Urban and Regional Planning* (2nd edn, 1982), pp. 83–119; Short, 'Urban Policy and British Cities', (1982) 48 *J. of the American Planning Assocn.* 39.

11   For details of the development control system see Grant (1982), pp. 196–276; Alder, *Development Control* (1977); Purdue (n. 15 below), pp. 127–282.

12   See further Grant (1982), pp. 78–85. On p. 84 Grant publishes a table with details of delay in approval of development plans during this period.

13   For a brief explanation see Hall (1982), pp. 10–17, 274–302. See further, McLoughlin, *Urban and Regional Planning: A Systems Approach* (1969) or *Control and Urban Planning* (1973).

14   See, e.g., Eddison, 'Comprehensive Planning for Local Government', in Stewart (ed.), *The City* (1972); Wildavsky, 'The Political Economy of Efficiency' (1966) 26 *Pub. Admin.* 292; Elcock *Local Government* (1982), pp. 228–60 and the report of the Maud Committee, *The Management of Local Government* (1967).

15   Grant (1982), pp. 75–144. The relevant materials are conveniently set out in Purdue, *Cases and Materials on Planning Law* (1977). See also Telling, *Planning Law and Procedure* (6th edn 1982), for a concise account.

16   See *Planning Appeals*, an explanatory booklet issued by the DOE (1977).

17   See the *Encyclopedia of Planning Law*, Vol. 4. This loose-leaf publication is updated regularly.

18   Cullingworth (1981), pp. 66–76. See also Elcock, (1982), pp. 17–44. The changes proposed in 'Streamlining the Cities' (Cmnd 9063) would modify this position, especially in London.

19   Dobry published an interim report in 1974 and a final report in 1975 from both of which we quote.

20   The Report of the Environment Subcommittee of the Expenditure Committee of the House of Commons, 'Planning Procedures', 8th Report of the Expenditure Committee (HC 395, 1976/7). The Committee's assumptions are severely criticized by Allison and Benyon, 'Public Planning of Private Development', (1978) 56 *Pub. Admin.* 73. A recent attempt to compare the performance of different planning authorities is *Local Planning: the Development Control Function*, DOE Audit Inspectorate (1983).

21   See also Haar, *Land Use Planning* (1959); Pearce, 'Property Rights vs. Development Control', (1981) 52 *Town Pl. Rev.* 47; Sorensen, 'Planning Comes of Age' (1982) 68 *The Planner* 184; R. Jones, *Town and Country Chaos* (Adam Smith Institute 1982).

22   Bruton 'The Changing Face of Planning', 38 *H. and P. Rev.* (1983) 17, nos. 2 and 3. Loughlin, 'Local Government, Planning and Land Act: Local Government in the Welfare Corporate State', (1981) 44 *MLR* 432, 435–47; McAuslan, 'Local Government and Resource Allocation in England: Changing Ideology, Unchanging Law', 4 *Urban Law and Policy* (1981) 215, 243–57; Hall, 'Housing, Planning, Land and Local Finance: the British Experience', 6 *Urban Law and Policy* 75 (1983).

23   For a critique see Taylor, 'The Politics of Enterprise Zones', (1981) 59 *Pub. Admin.* 521.

24   See, for example, Heseltine, (1981) 37 *H and P Rev.* 5 and (1982) 68 *The Planner* 195.

25   Selznick, 'An Approach to a Theory of Bureaucracy', 8 *Am. Soc. Rev.* (1943) 47 provides a theoretical introduction. Fagence (1977), pp. 134–254 and Goldsmith (1980), pp. 68–109, deal specifically with planning.

26   See also Kiernan, 'The Fallacy of Planning Law Reform', (1982) 5 *Urban Law and Policy* 23. Forester, 'Critical Theory and Planning Practice' (1980) 46 *J. of the American Planning Assoc.* 275, provides an introduction to the seminal theories of Habermas.

27   See also Grant, 'Planning, Politics and the Judges', [1978] *JPL* 512.

28   Pateman, *Participation and Democratic Theory* (1970); D. M. Hill, *Democratic Theory and Local Government* (1974); Boaden *et al.*, *Public Participation in Local Services* (1982); Richardson, *Participation* (1983).

29   See, e.g., Crossman (ed.), *New Fabian Essays* (1952); Crosland, *The Future of Socialism* (1956) and *A Social Democratic Britain* (1971); Leonard (ed.), *Socialism Now* (1975).

30   'Advocacy planning' is planning on behalf of the competing interest groups in society. Especially influential were the views of Jane Jacobs, *The Death and Life of Great American Cities* (1961); Pahl, *Whose City?* (1970); Meyerson and Banfield, *Politics, Planning and the Public Interest* (1955); and Gans (1968).

31   See further Nevitt, 'Issues in Housing' in Davies and Hall (eds), *Issues in Urban Society* (1978).

32   See also Glass, 'Citizen Participation in Planning: The Relationship between Objectives and Techniques', (1979) 45 *J. of the American Planning Assocn* 180.

33   Garner, 'Policy Forum: Skeffington Revisited', (1979) 50 *Town Pl. Rev.* 412, collects a number of opinions.

34   Contrast this use of the word 'educative', common in planning literature, with the usage of classical authors such as Rousseau or Mill (Pateman (1970), pp. 22–44), where participation 'educates' the citizen in more responsible attitudes to his society.

35 De Smith (1980), pp. 142–6. And see *Agricultural etc. Industry Training Board* v. *Aylesbury Mushrooms Ltd* [1972] 1 WLR 190. See also the discussion in Chapter 5, pp. 155–60.

36 Boaden *et al.*, 'Public Participation in Planning within a Representative Local Democracy', 7 *Policy and Politics* (1979) 55.

·37 A partisan account is Bridges, ' "The Ministry of Internal Security": British Urban Social Policy 1968–74', 16 *Race and Class* 375 (1974–5). Higgins gives a fuller account and bibliography in J. Higgins *et al.*, *Government and Urban Poverty* (1983), pp. 12–47.

38 See also Gregory, 'The Minister's Line: or, the M4 comes to Berkshire', (1967) 45 *Pub. Admin.* 113, 269.

39 See also Brookes and Richardson, 'The Environmental Lobby in Britain', 28 *Parl. Affairs* 312 (1975). Lowe and Goyder (1983) contains valuable studies of the National Trust and Friends of the Earth in addition to more general discussion.

40 Christensen, 'Covent Garden: A struggle for Survival', (1979) 50 *Pol. Quarterly* 336; Monahan, 'Up Against the Planners in Covent Garden' in Hain (ed.), *Community Politics* (1976), p. 175. See, for another view, Milne, 'Covent Garden: A Fraught Affair', (1981) 67 *The Planner* 164. See also Anson (1981).

41 And see now paras 8.14–20 of *Development Control* (above n. 20).

Chapter 15: Planning: profit before people?

1 On balance, however, the pre-war case law went the other way: see de Smith (1980), pp. 166–71. See also *Frost* v. *Minister of Health* [1935] 1 KB 286; *Offer* v. *Minister of Health* [1936] 1 KB 40; *Re Manchester (Ringway Airport) Compulsory Purchase Order* (1935) 153 LT 219; *Johnson (B.) & Co. (Builders) Ltd* v. *Minister of Health* [1947] 2 All ER 395; *Re Trunk Roads Act 1936* [1939] 2 KB 515.

2 See further Grant (1982), Ch. 13, where Table 22 analyses planning appeals between 1968 and 1978/9 showing a steady rise (i) in inspectors' decisions, from 43 per cent in 1970 to 82 per cent in 1978/9, and (ii) in written representation procedure, from 60 per cent in 1970 to 79.7 per cent in 1978/9.

3 Celebrated decisions in the series are *Lord Luke of Pavenham* v. *Minister of Housing and Local Government* [1967] 2 All ER 1066; *Givaudan* v. *Minister of Housing and Local Government* [1966] 3 All ER 696; *Ashbridge Investments* v. *Minister of Housing and Local Government* [1965] 1 WLR 1320; *Coleen Properties* v. *Minister of Housing and Local Government* [1971] 1 WLR 433. See also McAuslan (1975), pp. 558–79.

4 This point is developed by Bruton and Nicholson, 'Non-Statutory Local Plans and Supplementary Planning Guidance' [1983] *JPL* 432.

5   See also Couper and Barker, 'Joint and Linked Inquiries: The Superstore Experience', [1981] *JPL* 631.

6   Self, ' "Nonsense on Stilts": Cost-Benefit Analysis and the Roskill Commission', (1970) 41 *Pol. Quarterly* 249. See also Kirk and Sloyan, 'Cost Benefit Study of the New Covent Garden', (1978) 56 *Pub. Admin.* 35.

7   A report of the Council on Tribunals on the Award of Costs at Statutory Inquiries (Cmnd 2471, 1964) was implemented by the DOE in a circular No. 73/65. But costs are generally awarded only to successful objectors and, at planning appeal inquiries, only exceptionally to third parties: Grant (1982), pp. 600–1.

8   *The Windscale Inquiry* (HMSO, 1978). See also Pearce, Edwards and Benet, *Decision Making for Energy Futures: A Case Study of the Windscale Inquiry* (1979).

9   McAuslan (1981), pp. 228–37, contains an excellent discussion. See also Edwards and Rowan-Robinson, 'Whatever Happened to the Planning Inquiry Commission?', [1980] *JPL* 307; Lelas, 'The Major Public Inquiry: Politics and the Rational Verdict', 6 *Urban Law and Policy* 39 (1983).

10   See also Scott, 'Select Committee recommends itself for fast breeder inquiry', (1978) 274 *Nature* 524.

11   Bridges, 'Structure Plan Examinations in Public: a Descriptive Analysis', and Vielba, 'A Survey of Those Taking Part in Two Structure Plans'. A resumé is published in Purdue (1977), pp. 55–8. See also Bridges, 'The Approval of Structure Plans – The Staffordshire Case', [1978] *JPL* 599 and 'The Structure Plan Examination in Public', (1979) 2 *Urban Law and Policy* 241.

12   See, e.g., *Edwin Bradley & Sons Ltd* v. *Environment Secretary* [1983] JPL 43, where an application to quash certain provisions of the structure plan on the grounds that the procedure used at an EIP amounted to a breach of the rules of natural justice and that the Minister had acted ultra vires by failing to give reasons and drawing unjustified conclusions from the report of the EIP failed. Glidewell J held that the EIP was an administrative procedure to which the rules of natural justice did not apply.

13   Other investigations relevant to planning procedures are C.676/78 HC 799 (1980/1), p. 15 and C.241/G HC 290 (1973/4), p. 46. For an interesting complaint concerning conduct of a PLI, see C.894/80 HC 470 (1980/1), p. 21.

14   Compare now *R.* v. *Environment Secretary ex p. Binney, The Times*, 8 October 1983, where the minister's decision not to hold an inquiry into the route of the A34 trunk road was quashed. The procedures were previously investigated by the PCA: C 886/81 (HC 40 (1983/4), p. 118).

15 A similar analysis by Lord Diplock is contained in *Town Investments Ltd* v. *Department of the Environment* [1977] 2 WLR 450. For criticism of the decision, see Brownsword and Harden, 'Rights and the Red Book', (1981) 1 *Legal Studies* 94. For background see Levin, 'A Study in Government Responsiveness', (1979) 57 *Pub. Admin.* 21.

16 See further Grant (1982), pp. 393–400; *Norfolk CC* v. *Environment Secretary* [1973] 1 WLR 1400; *Western Fish Products* v. *Penwith DC* (1978) 38 P & CR, 7, noted Crawford, (1982) 45 *MLR* 87. Craig, 'Representations by Public Bodies', (1977) 93 *LQR* 398, contains proposals for reform.

17 See, for example, notes by Evans (1971) 34 *MLR* 335, or Bradley, [1971] *CLJ* 3.

18 Bruton, 'Public Participation, Local Planning and Conflicts of Interest', 8 *Policy and Politics* (1980) 423.

19 A draft circular urging local authorities to ease restrictions on the use of green belt land was circulated for comment in August 1983. Predictably, it caused an outcry: see *Planner News*, December 1983.

20 See further Grant (1982), pp. 353–81. Purdue (1977), pp. 348–61, contains a useful selection of the cases.

21 See also Loughlin, 'Planning Gain: Law, Policy and Practice', (1981) 1 *OJLS* 61; Reade, 'Section 52 and Corporatism in Planning', [1982] *JPL* 8.

22 *Ayr Harbour Trustees* v. *Oswald* (1883) AC 623; *York Corp.* v. *Henry Leetham* [1924] 1 Ch. 557; *Ransom and Luck* v. *Surbiton BC* [1949] Ch. 180; *Stringer* v. *Minister of Housing and Local Government* [1970] 1 WLR 1281. See also Young and Rowan-Robinson, 'Section 52 Agreements and the Fettering of Powers', [1982] *JPL* 673.

23 See also Jowell and Grant, 'Guidelines for Planning Gain', [1983] *JPL* 427.

24 But see *Westminster Renslade Ltd* v. *Environment Secretary and Hounslow LBC* [1983] JPL 454, where Forbes J held a permission to allow office development subject to a condition that public car parking would be provided at the developer's expense, was ultra vires. The Minister's decision was quashed.

Chapter 16: Immigration control: a developing process

1 The previous legislation and exercise of prerogative power to exclude aliens are described by Thornberry, 'Dr. Soblen and the Alien Law of the United Kingdom', (1963) 12 *ICLQ* 414. Garrard, 'Parallels of Protest: English Reactions to Jewish and Commonwealth Immigration', (1967) 9 *Race* 47, and C. Jones, *Immigration and Social Policy in Britain* (1977) highlight the striking similarities with complaints about

'newcomers' during the periods of Irish (1800–60), Jewish and New Commonwealth immigration.

2   See Cmnd 3387, App. II, for a brief description.

3   See Castles and Kosack, *Immigrant Workers and Class Structure in Western Europe* (1973), chapter II.

4   The estimates are usefully summarized in E. Rose, *Colour and Citizenship: A Report on British Race Relations* (1969), p. 83.

5   See generally P. Foot, *Immigration and Race in British Politics* (1965). D. Steel, *No Entry* (1969) describes the background of the Commonwealth Immigrants Act 1968.

6   Radical critics use this phrase to characterize official and media emphasis on the number of immigrants entering, so presenting the 'problem' as one of 'too many blacks'. They detect a close relationship between UK immigration controls and the economy's early need for, and later surfeit of, immigrant labour. See, e.g., I. Macdonald, *The New Immigration Law* (1972); R. Moore and T. Wallace, *Slamming the Door: the Administration of Immigration Control* (1975); Sivanandan, 'Race, Class and State: the black experience in Britain' (1976) 17 *Race and Class* 347; Freeman and Spencer, 'Immigration Control, Black Workers and the Economy', (1979) 6 *BJLS* 53. For a useful (if pointed) introduction to the immigration and race relations literature, see Bourne, 'Cheerleaders and Ombudsmen; the sociology of race relations in Britain', (1980) 21 *Race and Class* 331.

7   Cited in Rose, op. cit., p. 229. 'The Hattersley formula', translated by some critics as 'a colour bar is good for race relations' (see e.g. R. Moore, *Racism and Black Resistance in Britain* (1975)), was reiterated in the Conservatives' election manifesto of 1979: 'Firm immigration control for the future is essential if we are to achieve good community relations. It will end persistent fears about levels of immigration and will remove from those settled, and in many cases born here, the label of immigrant.'

8   For detailed analysis see Rose, 'The Immigration Act 1971: A Case Study in the Work of Parliament', (1973) 26 *Parl. Affairs* 69 and 'The Politics of Immigration after the 1971 Act', (1973) 44 *Pol. Quarterly* 183.

9   In 1982, excluding EEC nationals, some 6.2m passengers were given leave to enter of whom about 70 per cent were visitors admitted for less than 12 months. 12,200 passengers were refused leave to enter. 18,000 work-permit holders and their dependants were admitted and 54,000 persons accepted for settlement. Settlement from the New Commonwealth and Pakistan (68,500 in 1972), which has fallen every year since 1976, was 30,400, the lowest annual total since 1962. Source: Control of Immigration Statistics 1982 (Cmnd 8944). For surveys see Dummett, *Immigration and Emigration* (JCWI, 1981) and the Home Affairs Committee, HC 90–i (1981/2). See also J. Evans, *Immigration Law* (2nd edn 1983), chapter 3.

10   In particular, children born in Britain will no longer be citizens by birth alone. One of their parents must also be a British Citizen or settled here.

11   See Blake, 'Citizenship, Law and the State: The British Nationality Act 1981', (1982) 45 *MLR* 179; Dummett, 'The New British Nationality Act', (1981) 8 *BJLS* 233 and generally, I. Macdonald and N. Blake, *The New Nationality Law* (1982). The Government has stated that the transformation of UKPHs into BOCs will not affect the Special Voucher scheme.

12   Evans, 'United Kingdom Immigration Policy and the European Convention of Human Rights', [1983] *PL* 91, describes the background. Draft Rules were also defeated in 1972 when backbenchers campaigned for special treatment for people from the 'old' Commonwealth: see Plender, 'The New Immigration Rules', (1972) 2 *New Community* 168; Norton, 'Intra-Party Dissent in the House of Commons: A Case Study. The Immigration Rules 1972', 29 *Parl. Affairs* 404 (1976).

13   In *R.* v. *IAT ex p. Ved*, *The Times*, 13 May 1981, the Divisional Court distinguished two types of state aid: payments, like SB, which did involve 'recourse to public funds', and facilities, like the NHS and state aided education, which did not. See further Grant and Martin (1982), App. I.

14   Control of Immigration Statistics 1982 (Cmnd 8944), Table 16. The increase may be the consequence of deliberate policy or, less directly, of more people offending because of the tighter Rules.

15   As a condition of entry, visitors are 'normally' prohibited from working and students require the Department of Employment's consent.

16   However, adjudicators and the IAT must determine appeals on the basis of the factual situation obtaining when the administrator's decision was made, so disregarding subsequent events: *R.* v. *IAT ex p. Kotecha* [1983] 1 WLR 487.

17   For further illustrations see *SSHD* v. *Moussa* [1976] Imm. AR 78 and *Memi* v. *SSHD* [1976] Imm AR 129. McNeill J applied the *Stillwagon* test in *R.* v. *IAT ex p. Naranjan Singh* [1981] Imm. AR 39.

18   For instance (AR 1976/7, p. 7): 'I think that when she has completed her course Miss Cottle will almost certainly seek to remain in the UK and if she is not given permission to do so will remain here illegally. She looks exactly like thousands of other young West Indian immigrants who can be found in London and the chances of her being detected are minimal' (Mr Housden, Adjudicator).

19   See Grant and Martin (1982); Handsworth Law Centre, *Immigration Law Handbook* (2nd edn 1980); Macdonald, *UK Immigration Law and Practice* (1983); Gray and Lowe, *The Ins and Outs of Immigration and Nationality Law* (1983); Evans, op. cit.

20   See 'Evidence', pp. 90–106 (UKIAS) and pp. 57–69 (JCWI). See also JCWI's evidence to the Select Committee on Race Relations and Immigration, HC 17–xiii (1969/70), pp. 329–79 and HC 303–II (1977/8), pp. 187–232.

21   In *Karima Bibi* (6670/74 (1282), unreported) the IAT stated that, in the subjective assessment of credibility, it devolved decision-taking to adjudicators. In *R.* v. *IAT ex p. Alam Bi* [1979–80] Imm. AR 146, the Court of Appeal stressed that the IAT could hear appeals on the facts and must intervene if it determines that an adjudicator's decision on them is wrong. However, the judges conceded that the IAT would be sparing in reviewing adjudicators' determinations on the credibility of witnesses appearing before them.

22   For a practical illustration see the explanatory statement considered in *Manmohan Singh* v. *ECO, New Delhi* [1975] Imm. AR 118.

23   With the exception of 1976, the backlog of appeals to adjudicators grew in every year between 1971 and 1979 (when it reached 16,339). But it had started to decline (12,026 in 1981) before the discussion document emerged, partly through the appointment of more part-time adjudicators and the introduction of provisions like the no-switching rule (para. 91), which made many appeals hopeless.

24   The Council on Tribunals made 'detailed comments', outlined briefly in its 1981/2 Annual Report (HC 64 (1982/3), pp. 18–19). Reiterating attachment to the Franks model, the Council opposed any reduction in oral hearings and repeated its view, expressed in the 1972/3 Annual Report, that an appeal on a point of law should lie from the IAT to the High Court. It suggested as a compromise on the reduction of rights to appeal, a preliminary sifting stage at which unmeritorious appeals would be rejected. On alleged illegal immigrants, it argued (in apologetic tones): 'if it is at all feasible, there would be a place for some form of independent adjudication in cases where the facts are genuinely disputed.'

Chapter 17: Immigration control: secondary systems

1   The police Illegal Immigration Intelligence Unit uses the Metropolitan Police C Division computer, operative since 1979. The Immigration Service Intelligence Unit has a system containing the personal particulars of some 300,000 persons who either fall within specific categories (e.g. deportees and those refused entry clearance) or are suspected of abusing immigration control. Another computer, operative since 1980, matches landing and embarkation cards and sounds the alarm if it does not receive notice of an embarkation card by the time the visitor's leave is up. The department is also testing machine-readable passports and the feasibility of checking names against a computerized (and expanded) Warning List. See Connor, 'Big Brother moves on to the immigration desk', (1983) *Computing*

(10 February) pp. 16–17; HL Deb. vol. 439, cols. 618–19 and vol. 440, cols. 821–3; Gordon, *Passport Raids and Checks* (Runnymede, 1981). See further, Chapter 19 on computers and the administrative process.

2 For illustrative PCA reports, see HC 223 (1976/7), p. 126; HC 664 (1977/8), p. 151; HC 302 (1978/9), p. 145; HC 799 (1979/80), p. 45; HC 395 (1980/1), p. 65; HC 470 (1980/1), p. 56.

3 Note that in *R. v. IAT ex p. Kassam* [1980] 1 WLR 1037 the Court of Appeal held that the Home Secretary's exercise of powers under the Immigration Act 1971 could not constitute 'unlawful discrimination' under the Sex Discrimination Act 1975. Approving *Kassam*, a majority of the House of Lords in *R. v. ECO, Bombay ex p. Amin* [1983] 3 WLR 258 held the special voucher scheme (below) similarly exempt.

4 For an insider's view of the Immigration Service, see T. Roche, *The Key in the Lock* (1969).

5 Gordon, 'Medicine, Racism and Immigration Control', [1983] *Critical Social Policy* (Summer) 6, is a useful description.

6 The Wilson Committee had seen 'no objection to the issue ... of supplementary unpublished instructions or advice on matters of administrative detail or procedure' (Cmnd 3387, para. 65).

7 The department has assured CHE, the Campaign for Homosexual Equality, that 'homosexuality in itself is not regarded as a disqualification' for entry (letter quoted in Grant and Martin (1982), p. 71). Each year over 100 people are refused entry because of 'mental disorder' and about 60 are rejected as medically 'undesirable' for other reasons (HC Deb. vol. 23, WA col. 147).

8 LAG *Bulletin* (1982), p. 105.

9 Home Office letter to JCWI, 13 December 1982.

10 The number of fiancés and husbands admitted for a probationary year fell to 2180 in 1982, compared with 2720 in 1981. Within this total there was a decrease of 790 fiancés from India and Pakistan to a figure of 890. Source: Control of Immigration Statistics 1982 (Cmnd 8944), Table 11.

11 See generally on the theme of lawful departures from legal rules, Kadish and Kadish, *Discretion to Disobey* (1973).

12 Stephen Brown J provided an alternative legal basis in *R. v. SSHD ex p. Firat*, 12 January 1983 (unreported), saying that the Minister's 'overriding discretion' derived from the prerogative. The scope and very existence of prerogative powers over aliens is controversial; see Thornberry, Ch 16, n. 1, for an historical account. The prerogative has surfaced occasionally in modern times (e.g., *R. v. Brixton Prison Governor ex p. Soblen* [1962] 3 All ER 641 and *Bhatti*'s case (below)) and is expressly preserved by s.33(5) of the Immigration Act 1971.

13   The precise scope of s. 19(2) has been a matter of dispute. In *R.* v. *IAT ex p. Prajapati* [1981] Imm. AR 199, Forbes J said that it did not apply where the Rules omitted to say what should happen. This limitation, which would extend adjudicators' discretion to intervene, appears to conflict with the Divisional Court's judgment in *R.* v. *SSHD ex p. Martin* [1972] Imm. AR 275 and was not followed by Stephen Brown J in *Firat*, whose view the IAT has preferred (*Lavs Olaf Wirdestedt* v. *SSHD* [1982] Imm. AR 186).

14   For a successful attempt, see *R.* v. *IAT ex p. Bastiampillai*, [1983] 2 All ER 844.

15   As the appeal statistics demonstrate, there has been no wholescale 'flight' from the formal structures. The liberalization of controls over foreign husbands and fiancés in the 1983 Rules and the restriction of removal powers in *Khawaja's* case (below) tend in the opposite direction.

16   Quoted in Runnymede (1981), p. 2.

17   Which Mr Raison has said is not readily available: HC Deb. vol. 989, WA cols. 237–8.

18   East African UKPHs, subjected to control by the Commonwealth Immigrants Act 1968, claimed that the refusal to admit them for settlement contravened the Convention. After attempts to secure a 'friendly settlement' failed, the Commission declared its opinion that certain complaints were well-founded (see *East African Asians* v. *UK* (1973) 3 EHRR 70). The UK Government avoided a binding precedent when the Committee of Ministers declined to declare a violation (Resolution No. 77/2 of 21 October 1977; noted (1978) 41 *MLR* 337).

19   See further R. J. Sharpe, *The Law of Habeas Corpus* (1976), esp. part IV; *Habeas Corpus Act: is it becoming less effective?* (British Institute of Human Rights, 1980) and Newdick, 'Immigrants and the Decline of Habeas Corpus', [1980] *PL* 89.

20   In Denning, *Misuse of Power* (1980 Dimbleby Lecture), p. 19.

21   Pressure groups, usually in conjunction with broader political campaigns, have made significant use of the European Convention in immigration matters. There are several advantages in turning to Strasbourg: the substance of controls can be put in issue (see, e.g., the *East African Asians* case (above)); the record of English courts might, from the immigrant's viewpoint, not inspire confidence; and determinations that the Government has infringed 'basic' human rights can be a particularly potent judicial input into the domestic political process. See further Palmer, *Rights Without Remedy – The European Convention on Human Rights and UK Immigration Law* (Runnymede, 1981); Evans, Ch. 16, n. 12; HAC Report, HC 434 (1979/80); and *X, Cabales and Balkandali* v. *UK* (1982) 5 EHRR 132, where the Commission, declaring admissible three petitions that the 1980

Rules on foreign husbands and fiancés infringed the Convention, paved the way for the more liberal 1983 Rules. The Commission referred this case to the European Court in October 1983.

22 See further Macdonald, 'Police Raids and Searches for Immigrant Offenders', (1981) 131 *NLJ* 768 and Gordon, op. cit., who highlights the role played by agencies like the police and the DHSS in internal immigration controls.

23 For the background, see *On the Road to Repatriation* (Migrants Action Group, 1981).

24 Previously (e.g., *R.* v. *SSHD ex p. Morrow* 25 July 1978 (unreported)), the courts had sometimes assumed that, to obtain leave to which they were not entitled, applicants must have practised deception. See Nicol, 'Illegal Entry After Zamir', (1982) 132 *NLJ* 935.

25 Early indications are that Mr Waddington's confidence is misplaced. In *R.* v. *SSHD ex p. Awa, The Times*, 12 March 1983 and *R.* v. *SSHD ex p. Miah, The Times*, 19 July 1983, Woolf J quashed determinations that the applicants were illegal entrants, saying that although the circumstances were suspicious the department had not discharged the burden of proof imposed in *Khawaja*. The Home Office has also allowed a Mrs Parveen Khan to stay, stating that *Khawaja* had caused it to abandon the view that she had entered illegally (The *Guardian*, 11 July 1983). By contrast, the Court of Appeal in *King* v. *SSHD* 2 March 1983 (unreported) made the assumption rejected in *Shahzan Noreen*, discounting the possibility that the immigration officer (whom the department said it could not trace) might have made a mistake. See further Macdonald, 'Illegal Entry by Deception in Immigration Law', (1983) 133 *NLJ* 475 and Newdick, 'Habeas Corpus: Zamir to Khawaja', [1983] *PL* 213.

Chapter 18: Social assistance: attacking discretion

1 See, e.g. Wedderburn (ed.), *Poverty, Inequality and Class Structure* (1974); Abel Smith and Townsend, *The Poor and the Poorest* (1965); Townsend and Bosanquet, *Labour and Inequality* (1972), *Labour and Equality* (1980).

2 See *Monthly Digest of Statistics*, March 1983, Tables 4.1–4.3. The numbers of one-parent families is understated as some families fall into other classes (e.g. widows, unemployed). But a written answer lists unemployed with unemployment benefit as 284,000 at the same period (HC Deb. 31 March 1983, WA col. 259). Further statistics are contained in the Second Report of the Social Services Advisory Committee (HMSO, 1983).

3 For an introduction to the history see O. McDonagh, *Early Victorian Government* (1977), pp. 96–120; D. Fraser, 'The Poor Law as a Political

682 Notes to pages 582–593

Institution' in D. Fraser (ed.), *The New Poor Law in the 19th Century* (1976). A more detailed study is Brandage, *The Making of the New Poor Law* (1978).

4 For the argument that the creation of vested interests or 'rights' through contributions prevents reform of the welfare system, see Kincaid, *Poverty and Equality in Britain*, (2nd edn, 1975), pp. 184–206. For the sources of social security finance, see second SSAC report (above), pp. 6–7.

5 Changes in uprating procedures are described in second SSAC report, pp. 9–10. The introduction of Housing Benefit and subsequent changes in eligibility affected many poor families unfavourably.

6 See further 'Take-up of Supplementary Benefits', SBC paper No. 7 (1978). In 1981 take-up was thought to be 85 per cent (2nd SSAC report, pp. 8–9).

7 For example, Calvert, *Social Security Law* (2nd edn, 1978); Ogus and Barendt, *Law of Social Security* (2nd edn, 1981); Lister, *Welfare Benefits* (1981); Legal Action Group, *Guide to Supplementary Benefit* (1981).

8 In March 1983, the cost of paying unemployment benefit to everyone below pension age who was unemployed, regardless of period of unemployment or contribution record, but excluding women entitled to a state pension, would be £175 million at 1982/3 rates (HC Deb. 4 March 1983, WA col. 242).

9 The SBC published five annual reports for the years 1975–9, which provide essential material for any student of the system. They are respectively: Cmnds 6615 (1976), 6910 (1977), 7392 (1978), 7725 (1979), 8033 (1980).

10 But see David Bull, 'The Anti-Discretion Movement in Britain: Fact or Phantom?', [1980] *JSWL* 65.

11 See also T. H. Marshall, 'The Role of the Social Services', (1969) 40 *Pol. Quarterly* 1; N. Furniss and Tilton; *The Case for the Welfare State: from social security to social equality* (1977); Leaper, 'Social Assistance: A Watershed?', 13 *Social Policy and Administration* 3 (1979).

12 The citation is from Boyson, 'Farewell to Paternalism' in Boyson (ed.) *Down with the Poor* (1971): Mr Boyson is now Minister of State at the DHSS.

13 See 'Payment of Benefit to Unemployed People', the second round of the Rayner scrutiny, Department of Employment and DHSS (1981), pp. 61–6: Golding and Middleton, 'Why is the press so obsessed with welfare scroungers?', (1978) 45 *New Society* 195; Moore, 'Scrounger-mania again at the DHSS', (1981) 55 *New Society* 138. Fraud, abuse and evasion of insurance contributions are the subject of a recent report from the Public Accounts Committee: HC 102 (1983/4).

14 Extracts from an internal memorandum quoted in D. Donnison,

'Supplementary Benefits: Dilemmas and Priorities', (1976) 5 *Jnl Soc. Pol.* 339.

15   Franey, *'Poor Law': the Mass Arrest of Homeless Claimants in Oxford* (1982) and Smith, 'The Oxfraud Incident', (1983) *LAG Bulletin* 13, document an incident which suggested that departmental fraud procedures merited close scrutiny. For the internal circular see Hencke, The *Guardian*, 11 July, 1983.

16   See the exchanges between Donnison and some of his critics published as 'Dear David Donnison' and 'David Donnison Replies' in (1975) 6 *Social Work Today* and 8 *Social Work Today*, 3 May 1977 and 17 May 1977.

17   For CPAG's priorities, see Coussins (ed.), 'Dear SSAC' (1980).

18   Rose, 'Who can de-label the claimant?', 4 *Social Work Today*, 20 September 1973; and *Rights, Participation and Conflict*, CPAG (1971); 'Up Against the Welfare State: the Claimant Unions', (1973) *Socialist Register* 179. See also 'Claimants Organise', (1970) 24 *Community Action* 34.

19   A more complete study of the cases in this section is Prosser, *Test Cases for the Poor* (CPAG 1983), not available to us until a late stage.

20   Ennals, 'Memories of Bygone Battles', 13 *Social Work Today*, 8 June 1982, a review of Frank Field, *Poverty and Politics: The Inside Story of the CPAG's campaigns in the 1970s* (1982).

Chapter 19: Social assistance: dysfunctional rules?

1   The changes introduced by the 1980 legislation are discussed by Lustgarten, 'Social Security: The New Legislation', (1981) 131 *NLJ* 71, 95, 119.

2   Rowell, 'Erosion of Discretion in Supplementary Benefits', (1982) 132 *NLJ* 1001.

3   See also Lynes, 'Unemployment Assistance Tribunals in the 1930s' and Bradley, 'National Assistance Appeal Tribunals and the Franks Report', in Adler and Bradley, *Justice, Discretion and Poverty* (1975), pp. 5–54.

4   See further Ganz, *Administrative Procedures* (1974), pp. 3–9; and McCrudden (Chap. 1, n. 30).

5   The main conclusions of this survey were published as 'Research Study on Supplementary Benefit Appeal Tribunals: Review of Main Findings: Conclusions: Recommendations' (HMSO, 1975). The four volumes of the research were not published on the grounds that much of the information had been obtained in confidence. For another account, see Adler, Burns and Johnson, 'The Conduct of Tribunal

Hearings' in Adler and Bradley, op. cit., p. 109. For Bell's later views, see 'Social Security Tribunals – A General Perspective', (1982) 33 *NILQ* 132.

5A   Harris, 'Solicitors and Supplementary Benefit Schemes' (1983) 34 *NILQ*, suggests reasons. Wadham and Page, 'Tribunal Duty Advocates', *LAG Bulletin*, October 1983, p. 9, describe an alternative to extension of the legal aid scheme.

6   This was changed by SI No. 1735/77, which added SBATs to the list of tribunals to which s.13 Tribunals and Inquiries Act 1971 applies.

7   See also Loosemore, 'New Supplementary Benefits Scheme: Right of Appeal to Social Security Commissioners', (1982) 132 *NLJ* 115, 143, 165, 199; R. Smith discusses later decisions in *LAG Bulletin*, October 1983, p. 123.

8   In *Bland* v. *Chief Supplementary Benefit Officer* [1983] 1 WLR 262, the Court of Appeal stated obiter that judicial review by Order 53 procedure was still available.

9   The Supplementary Benefit and Family Income Supplements (Appeals) Rules, SI No. 1605/80.

10   In *Bowles* v. *SBC*, *LAG Bulletin* September 1981, p. 202, Woolf J stresses the same point.

11   See (1982) 132 *NLJ* 380; *The Guardian*, 3 May 1982. Prosser (1983), pp. 38–42 attempts a more general assessment.

12   Fulbrook (1975), Lister (1974), Bell (1975) and Milton (1975) all interviewed claimants. See also, Frost and Howard, *Representation and Administrative Tribunals* (1977).

13   See also Bull, 'Social Workers as Advocate', 14 *Social Work Today*, 7 December 1982; 'Life Without Lawyers', (1978, LAG).

13A For comment see Harris, 'The Reform of the Supplementary Benefits Appeals System', (1983) *JSWL* 212, Mesher, 'The Merging of Social Security Tribunals', (1983) 10 *BJLS* 135.

14   *The Welfare State in Crisis*, OECD (1981); Glennerster (ed.), *The Future of the Welfare State: Remaking Social Policy* (1983).

15   Dunsire, 'Challenges to Public Administration in the 1980s', (1982) 39 *Pub. Admin. Bulletin*, discusses some priorities.

16   Sharron, 'Post and Deliver' (1982) 14 *Social Work Today* 7 December.

17   Report of the Rayner Scrutiny Team, 'Payments of Benefits to Unemployed People', Department of Employment and DHSS (1981).

18   See 'A Strategy for Social Security Operations', DHSS (1980); 'Social Security Operation Strategy: A Framework for the Future', DHSS (1982). The Report of the PAC (HC 102 (1983/4), p. vii) records,

however, that the proposed Camelot system has been abandoned at
least for the next four years.

19   See Johnston, 'Why the computer will reduce political upheavals', *The
Times*, 15 March 1983.

20   Lamb, *Computers in the Public Service* (1977).

21   Stamper, 'Computer-Aided Legal Reasoning', (1980) 5 *Poly Law
Review* 41.

22   See generally second SSAC report (above), pp. 64–73.

23   One experiment launched by the CAB in Cardiff is described by
Hencke, 'Micro-chip helps the unemployed', The *Guardian*, 2 October
1981. See also Adler and du Feu, 'Technical Solutions to Social
Problems?: Some Implications of a Computer-Based Welfare Benefits
Information System', (1977) 6 *Jnl. Soc. Pol.* 431.

Bibliography

Alder, J. (1975), 'Time Limit Clauses and Judicial Review – *Smith* v. *East Elloe* Revisited', 38 *MLR* 274.

Alder, J. (1980), 'Time Limit Clauses and Conceptualism – A Reply', 43 *MLR* 670.

Allan, C. F. (1974), 'The Inspector's Criteria', *JPL* 3.

Allen, C. K. (1965), *Law and Orders* (3rd edn).

Anson, B. (1980), *I'll Fight You For It!*

Arnstein, S. R. (1969), 'A Ladder of Citizen Participation', 35 *J. of the American Institute of Planners* 216.

Ash, J. (1979), 'Public Participation: Time to Bury Skeffington?', 65 *The Planner* 136.

Atiyah, P. S. (1978), *From Principles to Pragmatism*.

Atiyah, P. S. (1980), *Accidents, Compensation and the Law* (3rd edn).

Austin, R. C. (1975), 'Judicial Review of Subjective Discretion – At the Rubicon; Whither Now?', 28 *CLP* 150.

Austin, R. C. (1980), Book review, 96 *LQR* 297.

Baldwin, G. R. (1978), 'A British Independent Regulatory Agency and the "Skytrain" Decision', *PL* 57.

Baldwin, G. R. (1980), 'A Quango Unleashed: The Abolition of Policy Guidance in Civil Aviation Licensing', 58 *Pub. Admin.* 287.

Banting, K. G. (1979), *Poverty, Politics and Policy: Britain in the 1960s*.

Barker, A. (1979), *Public Participation in Britain: A Classified Bibliography*.

Barker, R. (1978), *Political Ideas in Modern Britain*.

Beith, A. (1981), 'Prayers Unanswered: A Jaundiced View of the Parliamentary Scrutiny of Statutory Instruments', *Parl. Affairs* 165.

Bell, K. (1975), *Research Study on Supplementary Benefit Appeal Tribunals: Review of Main Findings, Conclusions, Recommendations*.

Benn, T. (1982), *Arguments for Democracy* (paperback edn).

Beresford, P. and S. (1980), 'Public Participation and Local Politics', 49 *T and CP* 412.

Blake, C. G. (1980), 'The Death of Habeas Corpus', 130 *NLJ* 772.

Blake, C. G. (1983), 'An Analysis of Decisions of the Immigration Appeal Tribunal and of the Courts on Substantive Areas of Immigration Law' (unpublished).

Blake, C. G. and Gillespie, J. (1979), 'The Immigration Appeal Process – A

Study in Legal Ritual' (unpublished).

Blalock, I. (1981), 'Justice and Parole: The Oregon Experience', in D. Fogel and J. Hudson (eds.), *Justice as Fairness: Perspectives on the Justice Model*.

Bradley, A. W. (1976), 'Reform of Supplementary Benefit Tribunals – The Key Issues', 27 *NILQ* 96.

Bradley A. W. (1981), Book review, 1 *Legal Studies* 329.

Bradshaw, J. (1981), 'From Discretion to Rules: the Experience of the Family Fund', in M. Adler and S. Asquith (eds.), *Discretion and Welfare*.

Branson, N. (1979), *Poplarism, 1919–1925*.

Breach, I. (1978), *Windscale Fallout*.

Bridges, L. (1975), 'Legality and Immigration Control', 2 *BJLS* 221.

Brown, R. G. S. and Steel, D. R. (1971), *The Administrative Process in Britain* (2nd edn).

Bruton, M. J., Crispin, G. and Fidler, P. M. (1980), 'Local Plans: Public Local Inquiries', *JPL* 374.

Bruton, M. J., Crispin, G. and Fidler, P. M. (1982), 'Local Plans: The Role and Status of the Public Local Inquiry', *JPL* 276.

Bruton, M. J. and Nicholson, D. J. (1983) 'Non-statutory Local Plans and Supplementary Planning Guidance', *JPL* 432.

Bull, D. (1980), 'The Anti-Discretion Movement in Britain: Fact or Phantom?', *JSWL* 65.

Bull, D. (1982), 'Watchdogs Unleashed', 13 (no. 18) *Social Work Today* 14.

Butler, R. A. (1971), *The Art of the Possible*.

Cane, P. (1980), 'The Function of Standing Rules in Administrative Law', *PL* 303.

Cane, P. (1981), 'Standing, Legality and the Limits of Public Law', *PL* 322.

Carr, Sir C. (1941), *Concerning English Administrative Law*.

Central Policy Review Staff (1977), *Review of Overseas Representation*.

Centre for Environmental Studies (1973), 'Education for Planning: The Development of Knowledge and Capability for Urban Governance', 1 *Progress on Planning* 1.

Civic Trust (1976), *The Local Amenity Movement*.

Clark, D. H. (1975), 'Natural Justice: Substance and Shadow', *PL* 27.

Cohen, F. S. (1937), 'The Problems of a Functional Jurisprudence', 1 *MLR* 5.

Coleman, R. J. (1971), *Supplementary Benefits and the Administrative Review of Administrative Action*, Poverty Pamphlet 7, CPAG.

Compton, E. (1968), 'The Parliamentary Commissioner For Administration', 10 *JSPTL* 101.

Compton, E. (1970), 'My First Three Years . . .', (May) *Freedom First* 10.

Community Development Project (1977), *Limits of the Law*.

Council for Science and Society, *Justice* and Outer Circle Policy Unit (1979), *The Big Public Inquiry*.

Council for the Protection of Rural England (1981), *Planning – Friend or Foe?*

Damer, S. and Hague, C. (1971), 'Public Participation in Planning: A Review', 42 *Town Pl. Rev.* 217.

Darke, R. (1979), 'Public Participation and State Power: the Case of South Yorkshire', 7 *Policy and Politics* 337.

Davis, K. C. (1961), 'The Future of Judge-Made Public Law in England; A Problem of Practical Jurisprudence', 61 *Col. LR* 201.

Davis, K. C. (1971), *Discretionary Justice* (2nd edn).

Denning, Lord (1979), *The Discipline of Law.*

Dennis, N. (1970), *People and Planning: The Sociology of Housing in Sunderland.*

Dennis, N. (1972), *Public Participation and Planners' Blight.*

Department of Health and Social Security (1978), *Social Assistance: a Review of the Supplementary Benefits Scheme in Great Britain.*

Department of the Environment (1973), *Structure Plans: the EIP.*

De Smith, S. A. (1959), *Judicial Review of Administrative Action* (1st edn).

De Smith, S. A. (1968), *Judicial Review of Administrative Action* (2nd edn).

De Smith, S. A. (1973), *Judicial Review of Administrative Action* (3rd edn).

De Smith, S. A. (1980), *Judicial Review of Administrative Action* (4th edn Evans).

Dicey, A. V. (1885), *Law of the Constitution* (10th edn by E. C. S. Wade 1959).

Dimock, M. E. (1980), *Law and Dynamic Administration.*

Diplock, Lord (1974), 'Administrative Law: Judicial Review Reviewed', 33(2) *CLJ* 233.

Dobry, G. (1974), *Review of the Development Control System: Interim Report.*

Dobry, G. (1975), *Review of the Development Control System: Final Report.*

Donnison, D. (1976), 'Supplementary Benefits: Dilemmas and Priorities', 5 *Jnl. Soc. Pol.* 337.

Donnison, D. (1982), *The Politics of Poverty.*

Drapkin, D. B. (1974), 'Development, Electricity and Power Stations: Problems in Electricity Planning Decisions', *PL* 220.

Duguit, L. (1921), *Law in the Modern State* (trans. Laski).

Dunham, A. (1964), 'Property, City Planning, and Liberty', in C. M. Haar (ed.), *Law and Land: Anglo-American Planning Practice.*

Dworkin, G. (1979), 'Compensation and Payments for Vaccine Damage', *JSWL* 330.

Dworkin, R. M. (1977), *Taking Rights Seriously.*

Elliott, M. J. (1980a), 'Appeals, Principles and Pragmatism in Natural Justice', 43 *MLR* 66.

Elliott, M. J. (1980b), 'A.C.A.S. and Judicial Review', 43 *MLR* 580.

Ely, J. H. (1980), *Democracy and Distrust: A Theory of Judicial Review.*

Evans, H. J. (1979), 'Local Authorities and the Resolution of Grievances – Some Second Thoughts: A Comment', *Local Government Studies* 23.

Evans, J. M. (1976), *Immigration Law* (1st edn).

Ewing, K. D. and Rees, W. M. (1983), 'Closed Shop Dismissals 1974–80: A Study of the Retroactive Compensation Scheme', *ILJ* 148.

Fagence, M. (1977), *Citizen Participation in Planning.*

Farmer, J. A. (1970), 'A Model Code of Procedure for Administrative Tribunals – An Illusory Concept', 4 *New Zealand Universities LR* 105.

Farmer, J. A. (1974), *Tribunals and Government*.

Feldman, D. (1981), 'Comments on the *Justice*/All Souls Review of Administrative Law' (unpublished).

Fleming, J. G. (1982), 'Drug Injury Compensation Plans', 30 *Am. J. Comp. Law* 297.

Fraser, D. (1973), *The Evolution of the British Welfare State*.

Friedmann, W. (1964), *Law in a Changing Society* (2nd edn).

Friend, J. K., Laffkin, M. J. and Norris, M. E. (1981), 'Competition in Public Policy: The Structure Plan as Arena', *Pub. Admin.* 441.

Fulbrook, J. (1975), *The Appellant and His Case: The Appellant's View of Supplementary Benefit Appeal Tribunals*, Poverty Research Series 5, *CPAG*.

Fuller, L. (1978), 'The Forms and Limits of Adjudication', 92 *Harv. LR* 353.

Galligan, D. J. (1976), 'The Nature and Function of Policies within Discretionary Power', *PL* 332

Galligan, D. J. (1982), 'Judicial Review and the Textbook Writers', 2 *OJLS* 257.

Gans, H. J. (1968), *People and Plans: Essays on Urban Problems and Solutions*.

Ganz, G. (1972), 'Allocation of Decision-Making Functions', *PL* 215 and 299.

Ganz, G. (1974), *Administrative Procedures*.

Ganz, G. (1977), 'Public Law and the Duty of Care', *PL* 306.

Garner, J. F. (1965), 'The Council on Tribunals', *PL* 321.

Garner, J. F. (1978), 'Public and Private Law', *PL* 230.

Gellhorn, E. and Robinson, G. O. (1975), 'Perspectives on Administrative Law', 75 *Col. LR* 771.

Goldsmith, M. (1980), *Politics, Planning and the City*.

Goodhart, A. L. (1966), 'The Burmah Oil Case and the War Damage Act 1965', 82 *LQR* 97.

Gould, B. C. (1970), 'Anisminic and Jurisdictional Review', *PL* 358.

Grant, L. and Martin, I. (1982), *Immigration Law and Practice*.

Grant, M. (1982), *Urban Planning Law*.

Gravells, N. P. (1978), 'Time Limit Clauses and Judicial Review – The Relevance of Context', 41 *MLR* 383.

Gregory, R. and Hutchesson, P. (1975), *The Parliamentary Ombudsman: A Study in the Control of Administrative Action*.

Griffith, J. A. G. (1955), 'The Crichel Down Affair', 18 *MLR* 557.

Griffith, J. A. G. (1959a), 'The Law of Property (Land)', in M. Ginsberg (ed.), *Law and Opinion in England in the 20th Century*.

Griffith, J. A. G. (1959b), 'Tribunals and Inquiries', 22 *MLR* 125.

Griffith, J. A. G. (1977), *The Politics of the Judiciary* (1st edn).

Griffith, J. A. G. (1979), 'The Political Constitution', 42 *MLR* 1.

Griffith, J. A. G. (1982), 'The Law Lords and the GLC', *Marxism Today*, Feb., p. 29.

Griffith, J. A. G. (1983), 'Constitutional and Administrative Law', in P. Archer and A. Martin (eds.), *More Law Reform Now!*

Griffith, J. A. G. and Street, H. (1952), *Principles of Administrative Law* (1st edn).

Griffith, J. A. G. and Street, H. (1973), *Principles of Administrative Law* (5th edn).

Gwyn, W. B. (1971), 'The Labour Party and the Threat of Bureaucracy', 19 *Pol. Studies* 383.

Hailsham, Lord (1978), *The Dilemma of Democracy: Diagnosis and Prescription.*

Haldane Society (1983), 'Evidence submitted to the Enquiry of the Commission of Racial Equality into discrimination in the immigration service.'

Hall, P. (1981), *Great Planning Disasters* (Penguin edn).

Hall, P. (1982), *Urban and Regional Planning* (2nd edn).

Hamilton, R. W. (1972), 'Procedures for the Adoption of Rules of General Applicability: the Need for Procedural Innovation in Administrative Rulemaking', 60 *California LR* 1276.

Hammersley, R. (1980), 'The Local Ombudsman and his Impact on Planning', 66 *The Planner* 1.

Hampton, W. and Walker, R. (1976), 'The Teesside/Cleveland Examination in Public: A Report of a Survey of Participants', *Local Government Studies* 27.

Harlow, C. (1976), 'Administrative Reaction to Judicial Review', *PL* 116.

Harlow, C. (1977), 'Comment', *PL* 301.

Harlow, C. (1978), 'Ombudsmen in Search of a Role', 41 *MLR* 446.

Harman, H. and Griffith, J. A. G. (1979), *Justice Deserted: the Subversion of the Jury.*

Hartley, T. C. and Griffith, J. A. G. (1981), *Government and Law* (2nd edn).

Heap, D. and Ward, A. J. (1980), 'Planning Bargaining – The Pros and the Cons: or How Much Can the System Stand?', *JPL* 631.

Herman, M. (1972), *Administrative Justice and Supplementary Benefits.*

Hewart, Lord (1929), *The New Despotism.*

Hill, M. (1976), *The State, Administration and the Individual.*

Hodge, H. (1979), 'Test Case Strategy', in M. Partington and J. Jowell (eds.), *Welfare Law and Policy.*

Holdsworth, M. (1977), 'The Other Side of the Ombudsman', *Local Government Chronicle* 54.

Home Office (1981), *Review of Appeals under the Immigration Act 1971.*

Hood, C. (1980), 'The Politics of Quangocide', 8 *Policy and Politics* 247.

Hughes, D. J. (1983), 'Authorities Held Back on Planning Gain', 38(2) *H. and P. Rev.* 6.

Hughes, J. (1983), 'Standards of Service', 14 (no. 32) *Social Work Today* 12.

Jennings, W. I. (1932), 'The Report on Ministers' Powers', 10 *Pub. Admin.* 333.

Jennings, W. I. (1935), 'In Praise of Dicey (1885–1935)' 13 *Pub. Admin.* 123.

Jennings, W. I. (1936), 'Courts and Administrative Law', 49 *Harv. LR* 429.

Jennings, W. I. (1938), *The Law and the Constitution*.

Jennings, W. I. (1957), *Parliament* (2nd edn).

Jewell, M. (1979), 'Is There an Alternative to the Public Inquiry?', *JPL* 216.

Johnstone, D. (1975), *A Tax Shall be Charged*.

Joint Council for the Welfare of Immigrants (1981), 'Comments on the Home Office Review of Appeals under the Immigration Act 1971.'

Jowell, J. (1973), 'The Legal Control of Administrative Discretion', *PL* 178.

Jowell, J. (1977), 'The Limits of Law in Urban Planning', 30 *CLP* 63.

Jowell, J. and Noble, D. (1980), 'Planning as Social Engineering: Notes on the First English Structure Plans', 3 *Urban Law and Policy* 293.

Justice (1961), *The Citizen and the Administration: The Redress of Grievances* (director of research, Sir John Whyatt).

Justice (1971), *Administration Under Law*.

Justice (1977), *Our Fettered Ombudsman*.

Justice (1980), *The Local Ombudsmen: A Review of the First Five Years*.

Justice (1982), *Compensation for Wrongful Imprisonment*.

Justice/All Souls (1981), *Review of Administrative Law in the United Kingdom: A Discussion Paper*.

Kahn, J. (1980), 'Discretionary Power and the Administrative Judge', 29 *ICLQ* 521 (trans. Harlow).

Keeton, G. W. (1949), 'The Twilight of the Common Law', 45 *Nineteenth Century and After* 230.

Korah, V. (1976), 'Counter-Inflation Legislation: Whither Parliamentary Sovereignty?', 92 *LQR* 42.

Kramer, R. (1959), 'The Place and Function of Judicial Review in the Administrative Process', 28 *Ford. LR* 1.

Laski, H. J. (1925), *A Grammar of Politics* (5th edn 1967).

Laski, H. J. (1926), 'Judicial Review of Social Policy in England: A Study of *Roberts* v. *Hopwood et al.*', 39 *Harv. LR* 832.

Laski, H. J. (1933), 'M. Duguit's Conception of the State', in A. L. Goodhart *et al.*, *Modern Theories of Law*.

Lavers, A. (1979), 'Inquiries Without Lawyers', *JPL* 518.

Layfield, F. (1973), *Report of the Inquiry into the Greater London Development Plan*.

Leigh, L. H. (1980), 'Time Limit Clauses and Jurisdictional Error', *PL* 34.

Levin, J. (1980), 'Second Class Justice', *LAG Bulletin* 178.

Lewis, N. (1973), 'Supplementary Benefits Appeal Tribunals', *PL* 257.

Lewis, N. and Birkinshaw, P. (1979a), 'Taking Complaints Seriously: A Study in Local Government Practice', in M. Partington and J. Jowell (eds.), *Welfare Law and Policy*.

Lewis, N. and Birkinshaw, P. (1979b), 'Local Authorities and the Resolution of Grievances – Some Second Thoughts', *Local Government Studies* 7.

Lewis, R. (1981), 'Codes of Practice on Picketing and Closed Shop Agreements and Arrangements', 44 *MLR* 198.

Linden, A. (1973), 'Tort Law as Ombudsman', 51 *Can. Bar Rev.* 155.

Lister, R. (1974a), *Supplementary Benefit Rights*.

Lister, R. (1974b), *Justice for the Claimant: a Study of Supplementary Benefit Appeal Tribunals*, Poverty Research Series 4, CPAG.

Lister, R. (1975), *Council Inaction* (CPAG report).

Lloyd, D. (1972), *Introduction to Jurisprudence* (3rd edn).

Long, A. R. (1975), 'Participation and the Community', 5 *Progress on Planning* 64.

Loughlin, M. (1978) 'Procedural Fairness: A Study of the Crisis in Administrative Law Theory', 28 *Univ. of Toronto LJ* 215.

Lowe, P. and Goyder, J. (1983), *Environmental Groups in Politics*.

McAuslan, J. P. W. B. (1971), 'The Plan, the Planners and the Lawyers', *PL* 247.

McAuslan, J. P. W. B. (1974), 'Planning Law's Contribution to the Problems of an Urban Society', 37 *MLR* 134.

McAuslan, J. P. W. B. (1975), *Land, Law and Planning*.

McAuslan, J. P. W. B. (1981), *The Ideologies of Planning Law*.

McCarthy, M. (1983), 'Child Poverty Action Group: Poor and Powerless', in D. Marsh (ed.), *Pressure Politics: Interest Groups in Britain*.

MacCormick, N. (1981), *H. L. A. Hart*.

McDonagh, O. (1977), *Early Victorian Government*.

Maitland, F. W. (1908), *The Constitutional History of England*.

Marshall G. (1961), 'Justiciability', in A. G. Guest (ed.), *Oxford Essays in Jurisprudence* (First Series).

Marshall, G. (1971), *Constitutional Theory*.

Megarry, R. E. (1944), 'Administrative Quasi-Legislation', 60 *LQR* 125.

Mesher, J. (1981), 'The 1980 Social Security Legislation: The Great Welfare State Chainsaw Massacre?', 8 *BJLS* 119.

Micklethwait, R. G. (1976), *The National Insurance Commissioners*.

Milton, C. (1975), 'Appellants' Perceptions of the Tribunal Process', in M. Adler and A. Bradley (eds.), *Justice Discretion and Poverty: Supplementary Benefit Appeal Tribunals in Britain*.

Mullan, D. J. (1975), 'Fairness: the New Natural Justice?', 25 *Univ. of Toronto LJ* 281.

Nicol, A. (1981), *Illegal Entrants* (Runnymede Trust and JCWI).

Nonet, P. (1969), *Administrative Justice*.

Nonet, P. and Selznick, D. (1978), *Law and Society in Transition: Toward Responsive Law*.

Pannick, D. (1982), 'The Law Lords and the Needs of Contemporary Society', 53 *Pol. Quarterly* 318.

Parker, R. (1982), 'The Major Inquiry – Some Practical Considerations', in R. Macrory (ed.), *Commercial Nuclear Power: Legal and Constitutional Issues*.

Partington, M. (1975), 'Supplementary Benefits and the Parliamentary Commissioner', in M. Adler and A. Bradley (eds.), *Justice, Discretion and Poverty: Supplementary Benefit Appeal Tribunals in Britain*.

Partington, M. (1979), 'Comment', *PL* 1.

Partington, M. (1980a), 'Rules and Discretion in British Social Security Law', in F. Gamillscheg, J. De Givry, B. Hepple and J. M. Verdier (eds.), *In Memoriam Sir Otto Kahn-Freund.*

Partington, M. (1980b), 'Unemployment, Industrial Conflict and Social Security', *ILJ* 243.

Payne, P. (1971), 'Planning Appeals', 57 *J. of the Town Planning Institute* 114.

Perman, D. (1973), *Cublington: a Blueprint for Resistance.*

Piven, F. F. and Cloward, R. A. (1971), *Regulating the Poor: the Functions of Public Welfare.*

Planning Advisory Group (1965), *The Future of Development Plans.*

Property Advisory Group (1981), *Planning Gain.*

Prosser, T. (1977), 'Poverty, Ideology and Legality: Supplementary Benefit Appeal Tribunals and their Predecessors', 4 *BJLS* 39.

Prosser, T. (1979), 'Politics and Judicial Review: The Atkinson Case and its Aftermath', *PL* 59.

Prosser, T. (1983), *Test Cases for the Poor* (CPAG).

Pugh, I. (1978), 'The Ombudsman – Jurisdiction, Powers and Practice', 56 *Pub. Admin.* 127.

Radcliffe, Lord (1967), *The Paths of the Law.*

Reich, C. (1964), 'The New Property', 73 *Yale LJ* 733.

Reich, C. (1970), *The Greening of America.*

Reiss, A. J. (1970), Book review of K. C. Davis, *Discretionary Justice*, 68 *Michigan LR* 789.

Robson, W. A. (1928), *Justice and Administrative Law* (1st edn).

Robson, W. A. (1932), 'The Report of the Committee on Ministers' Powers', 3 *Pol. Quarterly* 346.

Robson, W. A. (1951), *Justice and Administrative Law* (3rd edn).

Robson, W. A. (1958), 'Administrative Justice and Injustice: a Commentary on the Franks Report', *PL* 12.

Robson, W. A. (1959), 'Administrative Law', in M. Ginsberg (ed.), *Law and Opinion in England in the 20th century.*

Robson, W. A. (1979), '*Justice and Administrative Law* Reconsidered', 32 *CLP* 107.

Rogers, R. (1980), 'Fighting the Cuts in the Courts', (28 November) *New Statesman* 16.

Royal Town Planning Institute (1982), *The Public and Planning: Means to Better Participation. Final Report of the Public Participation Working Party.*

Runnymede Trust (1974), *Where Do you Keep your String Beds? A Study of Entry Clearance Procedure in Pakistan.*

Runnymede Trust (1977), *Appeal Dismissed. The Final Report of the Investigation into Immigration Control Procedures in the Indian Subcontinent.*

Runnymede Trust (1981), *The Pivot of the System. A Briefing Paper on Immigration Appeals.*

Samuels, A. (1975), 'The Legal Effects of Statements by Planning Officers', 139 *Local Government Review* 428.

Scarman, Lord (1974), *English Law – The New Dimension*.

Schwartz, B. and Wade, H. W. R. (1972), *Legal Control of Government: Administrative Law in Britain and the United States*.

Scruton, R. (1980), *The Meaning of Conservatism* (Penguin edn).

Sewell, W. R. D. and Coppock, J. T. (eds.) (1977), *Public Participation in Planning*.

Shklar, J. N. (1964), *Legalism*.

Shonfield, A. (1965), *Modern Capitalism*.

Skeffington Committee Report (1969), *People and Planning*.

Stewart, R. (1975), 'The Reformation of American Administrative Law', 88 *Harv. LR* 1667.

Street, H. (1975), *Justice in the Welfare State* (2nd edn).

Stungo, A. (1976), 'The Impact of the Local Ombudsman on Planning Offices in London', *JPL* 725.

Suddards, R. W. (1979), 'Section 52 Agreements: A Case for New Legislation', *JPL* 661.

Summers, R. S. (1963), 'Justiciability', 26 *MLR* 530.

Sunkin, M. (1983), 'Judicial Review: Rights and Discretion in Public Law', 46 *MLR* 645.

Supplementary Benefits Commission (1979), *Response of the Supplementary Benefits Commission to Social Assistance: a Review of the Supplementary Benefits Scheme in Great Britain (SB Paper No. 9)*.

Thornberry, C. H. R. (1963), 'Dr. Soblen and the Alien Law of the United Kingdom', 12 *I CLQ* 414.

Titmuss, R. M. (1971), 'Welfare "Rights", Law and Discretion', 42 *Pol. Quarterly* 113.

Troup, Sir E. (1925), *The Home Office*.

Vile, M. J. C. (1967), *Constitutionalism and the Separation of Powers*.

Wade, E. C. S. (1939), Appendix in *Introduction to the Study of the Constitution* by A. V. Dicey (9th edn).

Wade, H. W. R. (1961), *Administrative Law* (1st edn).

Wade, H. W. R. (1977), *Administrative Law* (4th edn).

Wade, H. W. R. (1979), '*Anisminic* ad Infinitum', 95 *LQR* 163.

Wade, H. W. R. (1980), *Constitutional Fundamentals*.

Wade, H. W. R. (1982), *Administrative Law* (5th edn).

Ward, A. J. (1982), 'Planning Bargaining: Where Do we Stand?', *JPL* 74.

Weber, M. (1948), *From Max Weber: Essays in Sociology*, trans. and ed. H. H. Gerth and C. Wright Mills.

Whiteley P. and Winyard, S. (1983), 'Influencing Social Policy: The Effectiveness of the Poverty Lobby in Britain', 12 *Jnl. Soc. Pol.* 1.

Wilding, R. (1975), 'Discretionary Benefits', in M. Adler and A. Bradley (eds.), *Justice, Discretion and Poverty: Supplementary Benefit Appeal Tribunals in Britain*.

Winckler, J. T. (1975), 'Law, State and Economy: The Industry Act 1975 in Context', 2 *BJLS* 103.

Winetrobe, B. K. (1982), 'Assisted Passage: MPs and Immigration Cases', 132 *NLJ* 152.

Wraith, R. E. and Hutchesson, P. G. (1973), *Administrative Tribunals*.

Wraith, R. E. and Lamb, G. B. (1971), *Public Inquiries as an Instrument of Government*.

Yardley, D. C. M. (1980), 'The Functions of the Council on Tribunals', *JSWL* 265.

Yardley, D. C. M. (1981), *Principles of Administrative Law*.

INDEX

ACAS, *see* Advisory, Conciliation
    and Arbitration Service
AEGIS, *see* Aid for Elderly in
    Government Institutions
absconding prisoner, responsibility
    for damage done by, 409–11
Acts of Parliament, increasing
    complexity of, 7
adjudication
    administrative, Robson on, 21
    administrative tribunal, *see*
      tribunals
    checklist of strategic advantages
      and disadvantages, 61–7
    conflict between types of
      institution, 60–1
    distinguishing characteristic of,
      61
    flexibility of, 65
    growth of, 66
    ideal-type, 62
    impartiality of adjudicators, 66
    lacking capacity for
      accommodation and
      compromise, 62
    polycentric problems unsuitable
      for resolution through, 62–4
    procedural fairness, 79 *et seq.*
    procedural restraints placed on
      decision-maker, 61
    prevention of arbitrary
      conclusions, 64–5
    rule-making and, 146
    see also Donoughmore Committee
      on Ministers' Powers; Franks
      Committee
administrative behaviour, judicial
    reaction to, 287
administrative compensation
    absconding prisoners, 409–11
    criminal injuries, 383, 388–98
    decisions taken at operational
      level, 386
    departmental guidelines, 386
    ex gratia payments, 385

    exceptional hard cases, 386
    governmental decision more
      rational than court's, 384
    gratuitous payments, 384
    identification of general principle
      of liability, 384
    industrial injuries, 383
    legal liability, 383 *et seq.*
    lump-sum payments, 385
    misleading emphasis on political
      stratosphere, 385
    special cases, Pearson
      recommendation against, 385
    tribunals, 386–7
    victims of vaccine damage, 384,
      398–406
    wrongful conviction and
      imprisonment, 411–18
    see also unfair dismissal
administrative decision, judicial
    decision distinguished from,
      110
administrative law
    Administrative Procedure Act
      (USA), 136, 155–6, 297
    American, prevailing tradition of,
      4
    Aucoc's definition of, 14
    consensus in, 59
    constitutional law, as part of, 12
    constitutional law distinguished
      from, 1
    control,
      by courts, as centrepiece of, 48
      focus shifting from external to
        internal, 45
      theories, 42–7
    curb or control of state by, 12
    current state of, 6–11
    developed system of, 2
    Dicey on, 13 *et seq.*
    emergence as independent
      subject of study, 3
    English, prevailing tradition of, 4
    English lack of, 13–15